Ropes and Glory

The Emotional Rise of British Wrestling

by

Greg Lambert

© Greg Lambert 2017

All rights reserved, including the right to reproduce this book, or portions thereof in any form. No part of this text may be reproduced, transmitted, downloaded, decompiled, reverse engineered, or stored, in any form or introduced into any information storage and retrieval system, in any form or by any means, whether electronic or mechanical without the express written permission of the author.

ISBN: 978-1-326-92101-9

Dedicated to Kris Travis

Contents

FOREWORD by James Curtin aka Rockstar Spud

PROLOGUE - KRIS TRAVIS

CHAPTER 1 - IT'S STILL REAL IN MORECAMBE

CHAPTER 2 - THE RISE OF ROCKSTAR SPUD

CHAPTER 3 - THE FWA RETURNS

CHAPTER 4 - THE ASCENSION

CHAPTER 5 - THE HALL OF SHAME

CHAPTER 6 - FINAL FRONTIERS...AGAIN

CHAPTER 7 - BEST IN THE NORTH WEST

CHAPTER 8 - THE ORIGINS OF PCW

CHAPTER 9 - DOM TRAVIS

CHAPTER 10 - GRADO

CHAPTER 11 - PHERE THE PROMOTER

CHAPTER 12 - SPUD CONQUERS AMERICA

CHAPTER 13 - INSANE FIGHT CLUB

CHAPTER 14 - MY MATCH

CHAPTER 15 - PRESTON AND POWER SLAM

CHAPTER 16 - HEART OF A LION

CHAPTER 17 - BOOT CAMP 2

CHAPTER 18 - LUCKY MAN

CHAPTER 19 - REVOLUTION AND PROGRESS

CHAPTER 20 - ALPHA OMEGA

CHAPTER 21 - GLASGOW GLORY

EPILOGUE - THE HOLY GRAIL?

FOREWORD

by James Curtin aka Rockstar Spud

As I'm writing this it is October 12 2016, exactly four years to the day since I was travelling to Phoenix, Arizona to start the final leg of the TNA British Boot Camp reality show. I ended up winning and was offered a contract with TNA Wrestling in America where I remain to this day.

This show was the first of its kind for professional wrestling in the UK. We had all seen WWE's Tough Enough over the years and never thought that a situation like this would ever be reachable for a performer on our shores.

This was the opportunity that changed my life and now I live in Nashville, Tennessee, where I'm about to move to a high rise apartment on the main strip of Broadway.

But what of British wrestling since I left?

During my first year in the USA I was focussed on the task at hand. I kind of lost track of what was going on back home. What was going on was people were more driven and determined than ever off the back of the British Boot Camp show. There was now hope. Training schools were improving. Talent upped their game. Promoters were making changes to showcase wrestlers in the UK as some of the best performers the world has ever seen - exactly what they deserve to be.

My career has somewhat paralleled what has been going on at home since my on-screen debut for TNA in November 2013. Hopefully the rest of the world noticed through the likes of myself, Raya (Paige) and Pac (Neville) in WWE and Fergal (Finn Balor) in New Japan Pro Wrestling around the same time that you don't have to be over 6ft tall and 250lbs to be different enough to perform on the big stage. That is where I believe the changes really came.

A second season of British Boot Camp was created in 2014 with a spotlight on more talent across the UK. This series showcased 16 of the top talents in the country and made the world take even more notice. TNA British Boot Camp 2 highlighted stars such as eventual winner Mark Andrews from Wales, the charismatic chubby charm of Grado, as well as Dave Mastiff, Kris Travis, Noam Dar, Kay Lee Ray, Nikki Storm and many more.

I always said about my opportunity that it was exactly that - an 'opportunity'. It could have happened to any of us back in the UK. Right place, right time, right opportunity.

I really see one of the biggest turning points being the release from WWE of Scottish star Drew Galloway who returned to the UK in 2014 to a thunderous ovation unadvertised at an Insane Championship Wrestling (ICW) event. This man then led the charge pushing the already popular promotion to even greater heights with promoter Mark Dallas at the creative helm. ICW went on to promote a card with 4,500 people in attendance at the SECC Glasgow with the main event featuring two British stars in Grado and Drew Galloway. As we headed towards the end of 2016 they looked to eclipse that, promoting at the 10,000 seat arena The Hydro in Glasgow.

Meanwhile PROGRESS Wrestling has announced agreements with WWE and EVOLVE and has talent exchanges across the USA and Canada. Many of their amazing roster of British wrestlers are now travelling back and forth to California to compete for top US independent promotion PWG. One of the country's biggest standouts Will Ospreay has gone on to Japan to win the NJPW Best of the Super Juniors tournament.

I type this with a smile on my face. All of this was unheard of when I first began wrestling in 2001 and then still felt impossible even at the beginning of 2012. Four years later British wrestling is the place to be. It has taken a long time for the rest of the world to take note but now we are finally equal to, if not surpassing the rest of the world as premier performers in this industry.

With this smile also comes sadness. Along this journey we all lost a dear friend and one of the most beloved performers the UK ever produced. One of the men who carried the torch for the last four years to push the UK scene to even greater heights.

Kris Travis lost his battle with cancer in March 2016 when many of us Brits were in the USA either visiting, appearing or performing. The news hit everybody very hard. He was an incredible fighter and someone we all held very dear. His memory will live on in British wrestling forever.

I would like to thank Greg himself for asking me to write this foreword. Without his belief I would not be here or have had a platform to showcase what I could do.

With that I will let you all read on. Appreciate this incredible ride that British wrestling is on and will continue to be on for years to come.

We deserve this. And there are so many British men and women whose hard work has made this happen.

My hats off to everyone.

PROLOGUE

KRIS TRAVIS

The date was Friday, January 23 2015. The venue, Evoque nightclub, Preston. The time, 10pm.

Seven hundred fans were packed into a late-night venue on the main shopping street of a small city in northern England. Their attention was fixed on a wrestling ring, where in the main event of that night's charity show, 'The Masterpiece' Chris Masters had his vaunted finishing hold the Masterlock tightly applied on the crowd favourite, British wrestler Martin Kirby.

Their match was already over and Masters had won by submission. But the tall, tanned and powerful American, a former superstar with the world's largest wrestling company World Wrestling Entertainment (WWE), still had his fingers interlocked around the back of the smaller Kirby's neck. The Masterpiece was refusing to loosen his grip, hell-bent it seemed on causing his foe some permanent damage.

Referee Des Robinson couldn't convince the arrogant bad guy to let go. And the spectators, many of them wearing black T-shirts with a distinctive hot pink logo, were starting to boo and chant obscenities at the snarling Californian as he continued to crush the valiant underdog from Thirsk, North Yorkshire.

Suddenly, a figure emerged through the entranceway curtain, carrying a metal folding chair, and began running down towards the ring.

The crowd didn't seem to recognise him at first. Thin, pale and shaven-headed, wearing a hot pink DEFEND INDY WRESTLING T-shirt, skinny jeans and trainers, he looked very different to how they had come to know him over the previous three-and-a-half years of wrestling shows at this venue; a period when his electric performances made him the main man at Preston City Wrestling.

The newcomer reached his destination in a matter of seconds. He climbed through the ropes, took aim and then half swung, half hurled the chair into the bronzed wall of muscle Chris Masters calls a back. The Masterpiece finally released his prey and the bald Kirby slumped face-first to the mat. Masters spun around, moaning like a wounded lion hit with a hunter's dart, his face twisted in pain.

The fans let out a roar of delight.

Then, balancing on unusually unsteady legs, the rescuer dropped the hated Masterpiece with his trademark 'superkick' to the jaw.

As Masters toppled and hit the canvas, the audience in Evoque rose to its feet and broke into spontaneous and heartfelt applause. After checking on his fallen friend Kirby, the hero of the hour surveyed the scene of appreciation, perhaps realising that this standing ovation was not only for his actions in saving the day as part of the evening's entertainment, but for him as a performer, as a person, as a man.

He smiled, a smile mixed with joy, pride and perhaps a hint of sheepish embarrassment, as the applause went on, and on, and on. He helped Martin Kirby to his feet and the two men embraced warmly.

Richard Parker, the PCW Master of Ceremonies, then bellowed into the house microphone.

"Ladies and gentlemen, he's the reason we're all here tonight...KRIS TRAVIS!"

Then, the dressing room emptied. Wrestlers, one after the other, appeared through the curtain and walked down to ringside. They all clapped strongly, each gazing respectfully at Kris Travis who looked like he was trying hard not to cry.

This roll call of British wrestlers crossed a spectrum of generations, all coming together in an overwhelming show of support for one of their comrades in his hour of need.

They included Keith Myatt and Ricky Knight, veterans who have been active since British wrestling was on ITV every Saturday afternoon during the golden age of Big Daddy and Giant Haystacks; Mark Andrews, a young Welshman who had recently won a contract to wrestle for one of the major companies in America on an internationally-aired TV series, following in the footsteps of The

British Bulldogs and William Regal who also crossed the Atlantic to find fame and fortune more than two decades before; Marty Scurll, one of Britain's best young grapplers and host of a weekly national wrestling television chat show - its very existence symbolic of how much the UK wrestling scene had recovered from its years in the wilderness since wrestling was kicked off ITV in 1988; Adrian 'Lionheart' McCallum, himself with an inspirational story to tell, weeks away from an astonishing comeback just under a year since he lay prostrate in that very same ring with a double broken neck, wondering if he'd ever walk, let alone work again; and a who's who of today's golden generation of British wrestling stars; Dave Mastiff, Bubblegum, El Ligero, Joey Hayes, Kirby and more. All clapping in earnest.

PCW promoter Steven Fludder, the man who put this show together, was there too, beaming a smile of immense warmth and quiet satisfaction.

Even the heel (villain) Masters, from the aisleway, 'broke character' and applauded before making his way backstage. The Masterpiece had paid for his own flight from Los Angeles, so determined was he to be part of this event.

In fact, every single performer on the show appeared for free that night. No wages were asked for. None were expected. Because that night wasn't about a job of work. Everybody just wanted to be there.

And as they surrounded all four sides of the ring to form a square guard of honour, they continued to applaud, with claps that came straight from their hearts.

Meanwhile I watched, from my commentary position in a dark corner of the club, my eyes feeling misty and my heart full.

"In 12 years of covering British wrestling, that might be the most amazing thing I've seen."

After making this statement, I took off my headset. Then myself and my PCW commentary partner Matt 'Stallion' Whitfield made our way down to ringside to join our colleagues.

I climbed into the ring and saw Ricky Knight's two sons, the Norfolk tag team of The Hooligans - Roy and Zak Bevis, brothers of WWE superstar Paige - lift the man of the moment shoulder high. And as Travis was paraded around the ring to a rapturous ovation, surrounded by his peers, he looked out at the paying customers. He was thankful to each and every one of them for travelling to Preston from far and wide, to honour him and help put money in his pocket to help with what had been a torturous journey through a personal hell.

So why was there such acclaim from the British wrestling community for this one man on this particular night? Who was Kris Travis?

Kris Travis was one of the best British professional wrestlers of the past 10 years.

Kris Travis was 31 years old.

Kris Travis was battling cancer.

Kris was in the prime of his life. He was one of the best wrestlers in Europe. A good-looking, fun-loving lad who seemed indestructible. A physical and athletic specimen who was on the verge of a shot at the wrestling big-time in America.

But then on October 9 2014, he sent out this message via his Twitter account.

"So, some people don't know and a lot do. So I'm going to just clear this up here. About a month ago I was diagnosed with cancer.

"I had surgery and had most of my stomach removed and with it a tumour. I now have 18 weeks of chemo to hopefully kill the rest of this disease. I've moved into my family home with my mum and I'm being well looked after by my amazing family and friends.

"I *will* fight this and I *will* win!"

I first saw Kris Travis wrestle in November 2003, 11 years earlier.

It was at the Leigh British Legion at a show run by a fledgling North West promotion called Garage Pro Wrestling, or GPW. At the time The Shooting Star, as Kris was nicknamed, was a newcomer. He was tall, slim, with boy band good looks, and appropriately his theme tune was the cheesy ballad As Long as You Love Me by the Backstreet Boys. I don't remember much about the six-way match he was in, other than a young Rockstar Spud and El Ligero were in it too, and while the performers were full of enthusiasm, they were still very raw.

As the years went by, myself and Kris were very much on different paths in our wrestling careers. I was making my name as a manager and head booker (matchmaker) with pioneering UK promotion the Frontier Wrestling Alliance (FWA) and then as promoter with the XWA in my hometown of Morecambe, Lancashire. Meanwhile, Travis was improving all the time as a regular with 1PW, the Doncaster-based promotion which made plenty of noise in the noughties.

We finally came across each other again in late 2009, as the FWA was in the midst of a comeback after a two-year absence. Kris and his partner Martin Kirby, the team of Project Ego, were part of the FWA tag team division. I was the company's colour commentator.

Trav, as he was known to his friends, and Kirby were former 1PW Tag Team Champions. They were big darlings of the hardcore British wrestling fan base and came with a lot of fanfare. When I first saw Trav again at FWA, he definitely looked the part. In the ensuing years since his GPW debut, he'd packed muscle onto his slender frame, achieved a rock-hard slab of a stomach, and was sporting a California tan and a Beatle style haircut. He looked like a superstar.

But inside the ring, Trav didn't live up to his billing during that FWA run. At the time, I couldn't quite put my finger on why. Perhaps Kris didn't feel comfortable showing everything he was capable of during those FWA days because he wasn't enjoying himself. You will see why later in this book. But whatever the reason, his performances didn't equal his reputation.

I next saw Trav compete in June 2011. He was in the main event of a Southside Wrestling show in Preston against modern-day British great and former TNA star, Doug Williams. Doug, a former FWA colleague of mine, praised Trav's abilities after the match. This got my attention. If Doug respected Kris, then perhaps I should take him more seriously too.

So the following year in July 2012, I brought Travis to Morecambe for an XWA show for the first time, put him on with Rockstar Spud, and they had the match of the night in front of our traditional seaside family audience. Trav adapted brilliantly to his surroundings, played heel with aplomb, made every single move count, and showed he was starting to become a polished and versatile performer.

A couple of months earlier in May 2012, I received a phone call from Steven Fludder. His dynamic new company Preston City Wrestling had debuted in my home county of Lancashire the previous autumn and was already making waves. Steven asked me if I would become the lead commentator for PCW. At first, I was reluctant. I was feeling burned out with wrestling at the time. I was already planning to stop promoting the XWA. The last thing I wanted to do was take on more responsibilities. But Steven persuaded me to come on board with PCW. And I am so glad he did.

Since June 2012 I've had the pleasure of sitting at ringside month-in, month-out, while PCW became one of the hottest wrestling promotions in Britain and one of the most talked-about companies anywhere in the world. It has rejuvenated me. The star power of big international names coming to Preston like Scott Hall, Team 3D, Vader, Rob Van Dam, 'Million Dollar Man' Ted DiBiase, AJ Styles, Jeff Jarrett and Matt Hardy, combined with the vigour of an ever-increasing pool of hungry young British talent, got me excited about professional wrestling again.

And one of the UK grapplers who helped me rediscover my passion, was none other than Kris Travis.

Kris Travis was given the ball in PCW and boy, did he run with it. Fludder put faith in Trav as his go-to guy, the man he could rely on to tear down the house in a main event calibre match. This he did, time and time again, even capturing the PCW Championship along the way.

Travis had developed several attributes since his lacklustre FWA run. Two are all-important when wrestling in a main event: timing and a flair for the dramatic. He seemed to have a burning fire in that muscled belly of his, a desire to test himself against the best, that he didn't possess a few years before. He also had qualities that made him appeal to both male and female fans. Of course the girls adored the handsome son of a gun. But lads liked him too, because he was a normal bloke who enjoyed a drink and a laugh, and fought with his heart on his sleeve. So the Preston audience rallied behind him in droves.

Energised by the backing of Fludder and the Lancashire crowd, Trav also put every ounce of his being into making all of his PCW matches the best they could possibly be. He always wrestled like he had something to prove, going non-stop and at a fast pace. The results were spectacular.

In December 2012, Trav beat Chris Masters in a gripping 20-minute back-and-forth epic at PCW Festive Fury. The following month, he lost the PCW Title to T-Bone in Preston's first, and to date, only bullrope match. Next came a pair of intense duels with the relentless Canadian Kevin Steen, who just a couple of years later became NXT, WWE Intercontinental and WWE Universal Champion under the name of Kevin Owens. Then there were two more engaging bouts with Masters ending in a memorable Last Man Standing war on November 16 2013. Such was his performance level that year, I helped convince my then-boss at Power Slam magazine, Findlay Martin, to include Travis in the annual PS50 chart of the top 50 wrestlers in the world. Readers of our rival publication Fighting Spirit Magazine (FSM) also voted Trav the UK Wrestler of the Year, one half of the UK Tag Team of the Year (with Kirby) and participant in the UK Match of the Year for the second of his three PCW duels with Masters.

Continuing where he left off in 2013, Kris pushed WWE-bound Prince Devitt - the future NXT and WWE Universal Champion Finn Balor - all the way in a duo of high-octane encounters at PCW Who Dares Wins and Spring Slam in early 2014. He then engaged Mark Andrews in a phenomenal battle in May at PCW's Supershow weekend. Travis and Andrews would somehow top this display, with assistance from Bubblegum, in a stupendous three-way the following night. The fans gave the three young Brits a standing ovation at the end. It was, quite simply, one of the best matches involving UK wrestlers that I have ever seen. And a lot of the credit has to go to the affable dude in the hot pink trunks.

Trav was next due to face Austin Aries, one of America's best competitors, at PCW's third anniversary show on August 1 2014. But when the night came around, Kris wasn't there. Somebody told me he had been diagnosed with a stomach cyst. I noted this on commentary, passing on my get well wishes to the absent Shooting Star.

Still, for Trav to miss an opportunity to prove himself against a former TNA World Champion, it had to be something serious. Nobody realised just how serious.

Six days later, Trav was able to compete in the auditions for TNA British Boot Camp 2. A UK television series on Challenge TV, British Boot Camp was wrestling's answer to The X Factor. It was a chance for British wrestlers to earn a life-changing contract with TNA in the States and mass media exposure for the UK's brightest stars. Kris was handpicked for the show by its producer Jeremy Borash after he spotted Trav wrestling in PCW some months earlier. British Boot Camp 2 gave him a massive opportunity to follow in the footsteps of Rockstar Spud, who won the inaugural series in January 2013 and went on to establish himself as a worldwide TV star on TNA's weekly Impact Wrestling show.

Trav was many people's favourite to win. Having turned 30, the age many British wrestlers are told is the cut-off point for making it in America, this may have been his last shot at international superstardom.

Trav tweeted on the day of the auditions at a gym in Manchester that he wasn't feeling his best and was lacking energy. This didn't bode well for his chances.

Judging by what later aired on television, Travis certainly didn't perform at his peak at the Manchester try-outs. The judging panel, made up of veteran wrestler and trainer Al Snow, former TNA and future NXT champion Samoa Joe and multi-time TNA Knockouts Champion, Gail Kim, were not impressed and tore him to shreds. While Kris may have been a big cheese on the small-time UK circuit, the Americans didn't care about his past reputation and ruthlessly picked his faults apart. Based on the panel's critique, it looked like Trav would be ejected from the competition for sure. But he showed enough of his pure wrestling talent for them to put him through to the next round in London.

So on Saturday, August 16 2014, the remaining 16 Boot Camp contestants - Kris included - appeared on a special show at the York Hall, Bethnal Green in the next stage of the competition, where Trav faced Mark Andrews. Despite feeling nowhere near his best (he actually threw up backstage before the match) The Shooting Star still performed brilliantly. His in-ring skills, athleticism and huge heart impressed the panel so much he was offered a spot in the final six. Trav was invited to travel to America for the closing stages of the contest and a shot at the big-time.

Two weeks later, on Sunday August 31 2014, I saw Kris for the first time in months when he wrestled CJ Banks at the Winter Gardens theatre in Morecambe for a company called PAID Promotions (today re-named Alpha Omega Wrestling). I worked for AOW as a behind-the-scenes consultant and dastardly 'on-screen' manager. It was also my job to look after the wrestlers backstage in a 'stage manager' role.

About a week earlier, I'd asked Trav to do an interview with Findlay Martin for the Power Slam website to promote the show. But Kris politely declined, saying he still wasn't feeling well and wasn't up to it. Findlay ended up interviewing Martin Kirby instead and I didn't think anything more about it. That is, until I greeted Trav that afternoon at the Winter Gardens. He looked terrible. He was sporting several days' growth of beard, which struck me as unusual as he was always so well groomed, and looked tired and gaunt. He also seemed strangely lethargic in the bout with Banks. This was Trav's final match before the bombshell announcement of October 9 2014.

Trav had secretly been feeling unwell for months. He had constant hiccups and heartburn, was repeatedly sick and struggling to sleep, but doctors told him it was nothing serious. He actually went to see the doctor several times but each time he was told there was nothing wrong. Then he collapsed at his mum's house while getting out of the bath. He went to hospital, the doctors put a camera down his throat to examine him and discovered the tumour. When he was told it was cancer, his world fell apart. Kris was forced to give up his American dream with TNA and faced an agonising wait for test results to see if the cancer had spread.

When the results came back, they showed the tumour was touching his pancreas, a vital organ of the digestive system. Pancreatic cancer is one of the most lethal forms of the disease. Had the tumour remained undetected for another few weeks, Trav's young life could have been over right there and then.

The tumour was blocking the exit from Trav's stomach, leaving him too weak to face immediate chemotherapy. Instead, surgeons cut out the malignant obstruction, taking with it around 70% of Kris' stomach. Then came months of treatment.

Trav agonised about going public. The 'stomach cyst' was a cover story because he was so worried about telling the world the truth about his condition. He told his close friends at first - Ligero, Kirby and Hayes. Then eventually, he put out the public statement and told everyone.

The result was an incredible outpouring of support and affection from the British wrestling community. Everyone was in shock. This simply couldn't be happening to Trav. The guy wrestled like he was invulnerable and looked like a film star. He was about the last person you would expect to be afflicted by this creeping, crippling disease.

Social media exploded after Kris made his announcement, with nothing but good wishes and kind words from the thousands of people who work in the professional wrestling business around the United Kingdom, Europe, and across the world. Even legends like Steve Austin, William Regal and Mick Foley tweeted 'get well' messages to our Shooting Star from Sheffield. Trav was overwhelmed.

"I honestly assumed that my close friends would be shocked, maybe some other wrestlers would be a little upset, and then that most people would forget about it in two or three weeks," said Trav in an interview in Fighting Spirit magazine at the time.

"Instead, I was getting just a ridiculous number of emails from wrestlers and fans, and my phone was just text after text after text."

And then came the offers of help. Pro wrestling was Kris Travis' only job, so while he was at sitting at home, waiting and fretting about the pain and indignity of those regular trips to hospital for chemo, he was unable to earn a living. So a crowdfunding website was set up to raise money for him. Hot pink T-shirts and DVDs were put on sale to raise money for him. Promoters all over the country organised entire wrestling shows to raise money for him. Thousands upon thousands of pounds came in. Kris couldn't believe it.

On November 16 2014, Kris made his first public appearance since announcing he had cancer, at a show held in his honour in his home city of Sheffield. Affectionately named Trav Aid, this event raised thousands of pounds for Trav.

Then came the PCW event on January 23 2015. Shooting Star - The Kris Travis Charity Fund Raiser show was released in full on YouTube, with clips of interviews from wrestlers sending messages of good wishes and good humour to their mate. When combined with online fundraising, the event pulled in a massive amount of money to help Trav keep functioning throughout his ultimate fight.

For me personally, it was an emotional occasion to be involved in. With a card full of terrific bouts like Bubblegum v Marty Scurll, The Hooligans v Team Single and Stixx v Joseph Conners, it was also a superb showcase for the quality of action in British wrestling today. And it ended with Kris Travis running in to save his mate Martin Kirby from Chris Masters, with the sold-out crowd chanting his name over and over again, and with an overcome Trav taking the microphone to thank everybody for attending, and to vow that some day, somehow, he would not only beat cancer, but defy his doctors' orders and return to compete inside the PCW ring.

"Watching all the matches, it just makes me want to get back in the ring so much more," he said to the adoring crowd.

"I've got six weeks and two days of chemo left and then hopefully, fingers crossed, that will be the end of my nightmare."

When Kris was first diagnosed and 70% of his stomach was removed, his doctors told him he would never wrestle again. But on March 3 2015, Travis returned to the gym. After six months of chemo the self-confessed 'gym snob' punished himself with a rigorous workout and blogged afterwards that he was in tremendous pain "but a good pain".

Kris wrote: "It's been quite the emotional journey.

"It's so hard going from having a good body, long hair and a tan, 13.7 stone and enjoying life, to a skinny bald headed pale dude who is 10 stone odd, soaking wet, not being able to look at yourself in the mirror at times because you were ashamed of what you saw.

"But no more! Now I'm proud, proud that I have started my comeback, proud that I am getting my life back on track. And proud that I haven't let this defeat me.

"I know it's going to be a long road. I might never be in good enough shape to wrestle again. But I'm determined to give it a try.

And trust me, I won't let myself down."

Ten days later came Preston City Wrestling's annual tournament, the Road to Glory. During the first round, I watched open-mouthed from the commentary table as a young British wrestler called Will Ospreay tore the house down in a match with former WWE superstar John Morrison. Ospreay, a fearless 22-year-old daredevil from Essex with astonishing gymnastic ability, wrestled non-stop, at a fast pace, taking huge bumps in a breathless display of drama, creativity and athleticism.

I was so impressed with Will's performance, I tweeted afterwards that Ospreay and John Morrison had just had the best match in PCW history.

The first person to reply to my tweet was Kris Travis, with just one word.

"Bollocks."

Far from being offended at Kris' response, instead, I smiled.

Frustrated, envious, sitting at home in Sheffield helpless while somebody else earned the accolades and threatened to seize his spot as the perennial PCW show stealer, Kris Travis was getting back the eye of the tiger.

I knew right then, without a shadow of doubt in my mind, that Kris Travis would make a comeback.

Despite taking antibiotics, suffering from a foot infection as a by-product of the chemotherapy and continually anxious with every random ache and pain that the cancer might return, Trav soldiered on with his workouts. Then on April 16 2015, he tweeted the news the wrestling word had been hoping for.

"Scans show all normal. Phew! Thanks everyone. Appreciate it lots. So relieved."

Positive thinking, the outpouring of public support and refusing to give up despite unbearable adversity had won the day.

Kris Travis had vowed to beat cancer and it seemed he'd done just that.

On Friday, June 5 2015, Trav returned to Preston City Wrestling at PCW Showdown - the night of his great friend Lionheart's rematch with the man who broke his neck, AJ Styles. As it turned out, this was a night for emotional and unlikely returns, as Trav ventured out to the ring to make an announcement.

Sheffield's Shooting Star teased that he was going to retire from the ring, but instead ended up in a fight with the brutal East End Butcher, Sha Samuels. Completely 'in character', the unforgiving Londoner showed no respect whatsoever for what Kris had been through.

Trav saw red when Samuels insulted him and flung himself at Sha in rage, only for the villainous East Ender to pound the living daylights out of the courageous comeback kid until the dressing room emptied and a gang of his friends ran in to save him.

Afterwards, Kris was badly out of breath, understandable as this had been his first physical foray inside the squared circle for almost a year, 10 months in which his constitution had been severely weakened. But despite being exhausted and battered, Kris managed to find the fighting words to, with typical bravery, challenge Samuels to a match on Friday, August 7 2015 at the PCW fourth anniversary show.

Kris Travis was about to make the wrestling comeback he'd promised the fans he would move mountains to bring to reality. And tickets for the August 7 show began to fly out.

On commentary, I told a story of caring caution. Had Kris Travis let his heart rule his head? Was he ready to step back into the combat zone just months after getting the all-clear from cancer? And was he ready to take on the undefeated and barbaric Samuels, a merciless competitor who had no conscience?

I have to admit, these were my *real* feelings. I was concerned that Trav was biting off more than he could chew, returning to the ring too soon. Although some of his muscle tone was starting to reappear across his surgically scarred and stitched midriff, he was still well below his peak wrestling weight and hadn't seen the inside of a tanning bed in months. And for a man who prided himself on being the wrestling equivalent of the Duracell bunny, who never got tired and just kept going and going and going inside the ring, the sight of him breathing heavily after a short brawl with Samuels was extremely worrying. He had left himself just two months to prepare.

Afterwards, Trav wrote on his website.

"When I got the diagnosis, the doctor asked what I did for a living and said 'You do understand you'll never wrestle again?' At the time, I just accepted it, but now the thought of getting back in the ring has made me so much more focussed. It's a rush every time I work out and I feel more energised every time.

"Having cancer and the treatment leaves you feeling worthless, feeling useless, feeling you've got nothing to offer.

"But now I can focus on wrestling, I know I do have something to offer and I want to show it."

Wrestling was all Kris Travis ever wanted to do. It was the very thing that defined him as a human being. And I realised right then, that nobody but nobody was going to tell Kris Travis that he couldn't go back to doing what he loved most in life.

Four days before the match with Samuels, Trav updated his website.

"So this is it. It finally came around. In four days' time I get back in the squared circle and have my first wrestling match in a year. Am I ready? Should I come back at all?

"I'm going to be completely honest. I'm nervous. In fact no, I am beyond nervous. It's like starting out all over again.

"I've been watching a few of my old matches and I don't recognise that person. That Kris Travis was the old me, the person who I was before this horrible disease. I won't ever be that guy again. I *can't* ever be that guy again, I'm a totally different person. In some ways better, in some ways worse.

"I don't know how good I'm going to be. I don't have high expectations. I'm scared and nervous of letting everyone down and not being good enough to be on a PCW show. Sure the crowd will respond no matter what and will give me sympathy cheers. But I don't want that. I want to go in that ring and earn those cheers, earn an ovation and earn match of the night just like I used to every PCW show I was ever on!

"Like I have said a million times, I won't ever look like the old Travis anymore, I've come to terms with that and although it hurts I can deal with it. But I will still *fight* like the old me. It may not be pretty, it may not be athletic but *by God* it will have my heart and soul in it."

On the day of PCW The Fourth Awakens, cleverly named after

the upcoming Star Wars comeback film, I arrived at the venue to find Trav joking around in the dressing room with his mates Martin Kirby and Joey Hayes as if he'd never been away. His hair was growing back and his tan had returned. And while still a good deal lighter than his fighting peak, so had much of his muscle tone. Trav looked a great deal better than anyone who'd been through his ordeal had any right to look.

I gave him a big hug and told him "Enjoy yourself." I wanted Kris to savour this moment, one he must have thought he'd never experience again.

When the moment came, the roar from the Preston crowd was thunderous. Trav came bounding through the entranceway and soaked in the ovation. He must have been on cloud nine at the reception, which was akin to that of a conquering hero returning home from the battlefield. Stallion showed me goosepimples on his burly arm. It was a special atmosphere.

When my all-time favourite American star Shawn Michaels returned after a four-year absence following reconstructive spinal surgery to defeat Triple H at WWE Summerslam 2002, The Heartbreak Kid was a smarter wrestler. Before his injury, he used to bounce around the ring like an indestructible pinball, taking spectacular bumps for fun. After his comeback, HBK knew he had to minimise wear and tear on his back. So he cut down on the sky-high break falls and dives from the ring to the concrete floor, and instead used body language and facial expressions to convey emotions to the crowd, and made every single move contribute to whatever story he was trying to tell.

Kris Travis' comeback match against Sha Samuels reminded me of Shawn's return all those years before. Like Michaels, Trav used to wrestle like he was immortal. Like Michaels, he'd had a frightening wake-up call that he was human after all. Like Michaels, he now had to work within new-found physical limitations.

And like Michaels, Kris Travis emerged from adversity an even greater craftsman.

Trav had promised to fight, and he was true to his word, launching himself at his nemesis from the first bell with fists flying as the overwhelmingly partisan crowd willed him on. On commentary, I explained that Kris was clearly going for the quick win, perhaps worried the gruelling sessions of chemotherapy had depleted his old reserves of stamina.

As soon as Samuels landed his first blow of the bout, a vicious kick to Trav's stomach, Kris doubled over in agony, instinctively bringing his arm across his body to protect his midriff. As the mean-faced Londoner then poured on the punishment to his opponent's weak spot, Travis gave one of the finest exhibitions of 'selling' a beating I've ever seen. Feeding off the emotion of the fans, Kris made everyone feel his pain at Samuels' every blow. I suggested on commentary that the referee should take pity on Trav and stop the match to save him from himself - because Kris was never going to quit of his own accord.

But then out of nowhere, Travis hit one of his superkicks, right on Samuels' jaw. It was like a firework going off and it roused the crowd. Sha ended up outside the ring and before I knew it, Trav launched himself with a full flip over the top rope, landing perfectly to send the East End Butcher flying.

The crowd was ecstatic. Travis was euphoric. He still had it. In truth, he'd never lost it.

I was on my feet now, as I sometimes tend to do while commentating at Evoque, gripping the back of my seat with tension, as Trav continued to suffer a relentless beating, only to give the fans hope of a miracle with well-timed flurries of his trademark moves . A running knee in the corner, bulldog headlock and eventually, summoning all the strength he could muster, he hit his finisher the Tiger Bomb. As Kris went for the cover, the PCW crowd counted along...ONE...TWO...but Samuels kicked out on two-and- three-quarters, to an audible gasp of disappointment from the fans.

As lead commentator during a dramatic match, I always try to verbalise what the audience is thinking. And at that moment, our thought processes were perfectly in synch. The fans were *desperate* to see the miracle of a Kris Travis comeback win.

"I've never wanted anyone to win a match so much in my life," I blurted out breathlessly.

Then Samuels locked on his sleeper hold. You could feel the anguish in the air as Trav began to fade. Since debuting in PCW exactly 12 months before, the fearsome Butcher had used the sleeper to render all of his opponents unconscious. Mad Man Manson, Danny Hope, Charlie Garrett, Noam Dar, TNA star Mr Anderson, even the PCW Champion Dave Mastiff had gone to sleep at the brawny arms of the undefeated Samuels. This is why when the referee lifted Trav's arm up once, then twice, everybody in the building believed the match was over.

But on the third attempt, Kris' arm stayed aloft. He waved his shaking hand, to signal there was still fight left in him. The place erupted in relief.

Then Trav battled back, hitting a second superkick. Samuels was stunned. He was reeling. He was on the back foot once again against British wrestling's very own Miracle Man who still held burning belief that he could pull off an upset. Until...

Sleeper. Again. Oh no. *Oh no.*

And this time, Samuels wrapped his thick legs around Trav's middle, propelling both men down to the mat as the Butcher applied the unforgiving pressure.

This time, there would be no comebacks. There would be no hope for the partisan crowd and commentator. There would be no fairytale ending.

Trav passed out in the sleeper hold. Sha Samuels was the winner.

Everybody in Club Evoque, except Sha Samuels, was gutted.

So Sha took that feeling of disappointment and, like the exceptional villain he is, turned it into anger. The bearded brute grabbed his trademark braces and, his face twisted with complete disregard for what Trav had been through, began to whip the fallen hero with stinging, humiliating blows. The mood in the crowd was turning ugly as Samuels expertly wound them up even more with this disdainful, mocking display of post-match brutality.

Thankfully, Trav's close pal Lionheart ran in to make the save. Samuels scarpered, still jawing at the fans who greeted the London bad boy with a gauntlet of middle fingers and curses as he headed for the safety of the dressing room. Meanwhile, Lionheart helped his good friend to his feet, and locked him in a safe and comforting embrace as the fans rose to their feet in approval.

I was on my feet too, clapping heartily. Match of the night? You bet, but that would be selling it short. It was quite simply one of the most emotional wrestling matches I've ever had the privilege to witness live.

After the show, I sought out Kris Travis backstage and congratulated him on one hell of a performance.

He grinned his reply. "I'm going to feel that in the morning!"

That was the last time I ever saw Kris Travis.

Kris went on to wrestle in Ayr, Scotland, for Lionheart's Pro Wrestling Elite promotion the very next day. Then on the Sunday he actually won the Southside Wrestling tag team championships with his good pal Kirby in St Neots, Cambridgeshire. Yes, Project Ego were back! And so was Kris Travis, beaming with delight in his hot pink trunks as he posed in the ring sporting the tag belts with pride.

Over the next few weeks, it was as though Kris had never been away. He was everywhere on the British wrestling circuit, testing himself against the best the country has to offer, trying to prove to everyone that he was better than ever before. The Shooting Star was given a hero's welcome at a show in his home city of Sheffield on August 15. Then the following weekend he criss-crossed the British Isles for a trio of matches in three days; first for Harvey Dale's HOPE Wrestling in Mansfield on August 21, then Attack Pro Wrestling in Cardiff on August 22 and then he unsuccessfully challenged Drew Galloway for the ICW Title in Edinburgh on August 23. Trav was on a roll, riding a wave of emotion as his triumphant comeback went from strength to strength. His diary quickly filled up until the end of the year and his merchandise was selling like hot pink cakes.

Then on August 29 2015, Trav was due to team with former WWF Tag Team Champions Too Cool in a six-man tag as PCW debuted at the historic Empress Ballroom at the Winter Gardens theatre in Blackpool.

But when I arrived at the venue that day, I was informed that Kris had a stomach bug and had been forced to miss the show. I had a worried, almost deja vu-like nagging feeling. Remembering the events of just one year previously, I hoped Trav's absence was just due to an upset tummy and nothing more serious.

Kris recovered sufficiently to return to action. On September 6, he appeared for PROGRESS Wrestling in London. The miracle man defeated Marty Scurll, stealing the show in another emotional tour de force in front of a sold-out crowd of 700 at the Electric Ballroom in Camden Town.

Project Ego was due to be back at PROGRESS on September 13 to face an up-and-coming new team The Geezers. But shortly after the Scurll match, Trav tweeted that he was suffering from stomach cramps again. Soon he was back in hospital.

Trav's condition was such that he was forced to miss another PCW date, at the University of Central Lancashire's 53 Degrees venue on September 18. He tweeted a couple of days prior "Unfortunately I won't be attending any shows this weekend due to ill health. I shall keep everyone updated soon regarding my situation."

Ominous.

Then on Monday, September 21 2015, came the news that in the back of my mind, I was half-expecting.

"Just to clear something up. I won't be attending any bookings or shows in the foreseeable future," Kris tweeted.

"I'm basically in the hospital. Had an operation. Not going to go into much detail here.

"I'm going to put this out there right now. *I won't be wrestling ever again.*"

Kris Travis had wrestled his last ever professional wrestling match.

Within minutes, tweets and Facebook messages of love and support came flooding in from Travis' friends in the wrestling business.

Adrian McCallum posted: "This has absolutely broken me.

"Most will know that last year, Kris was diagnosed with cancer and as such was out of action for a considerable time, before he made an inspiring comeback just last month. While it appears to have been short lived, it was a special moment to witness, and one everyone will remember for a long time.

"Professional wrestling is truly the most wonderful art form on the planet, but at times it can be a very cold, cruel and lonely place. Wherever you are right now and whatever you're doing, please do take a moment to wish Kris well. If ever someone deserved success in this business for their talent and passion, it was him.

"I love you brother."

And Simon Musk, aka El Ligero.

"There's no denying what an amazing talent Trav is, but this goes far beyond wrestling.

"I've known him since we were both 16, starting out in the same wrestling school. Over the last 14 years, I've shared so many times and have so many memories with him that it'd be impossible to sum them up in a Facebook status.

"From two skinny kids wrestling each other on random tiny shows in the middle of nowhere, to having the pleasure of sharing a dressing room with him at the very upper echelon of British wrestling, we've almost grown up together.

"We've spent countless hours travelling and spending time together, and the main thing I always take away from it is laughter. Trav is one of the funniest people I've ever met, whether it's drunkenly trying to put me in Hell's Gate (The Undertaker's submission hold) outside a Sheffield nightclub or secretly ripping my plastic bag handles before I pick them up to see the contents fly all over the floor.

"Despite the length of time we've known each other, it's in the last few years that we've become especially close. He's one of the strongest and bravest people I've ever met, and the will he's shown throughout all this is nothing short of inspiring. The outpouring of support for him is incredible to see and it's no less than he deserves."

On September 25 2015, I commentated on PCW's next show, Heroes. And speaking of heroes, by rights Trav should have been there, doing what he does best, tearing the house down. Instead he was back in hospital, his life in the balance.

Just one month earlier, right in the middle of his comeback, he had a routine check-up and everything seemed fine. But just three days later, once again he was awoken in the night with terrible stomach cramps. He started losing weight again and knew something was wrong. So he pushed his doctors until they scanned him again.

The scan revealed the cancer was back.

It was on the wall of his stomach. It had spread and was blocking his bowel. And this time, doctors couldn't remove the tumour.

This time, the cancer was inoperable. And it was terminal.

Two days after PCW Heroes, Trav tweeted his thousands of followers once again.

"So weird thinking about wrestling. Knowing I won't ever have a match again. It genuinely was the only thing I have ever been good at.

"I achieved so much more than I ever imagined. Council house, not great at school. But yet became one of the best in the country. Getting to the final six of TNA Bootcamp. Wrestling so many idols. Making so so *so* many friends. Memories forever.

"I still had so much more to give. Still had so much more to achieve. I can leave with my head up high. I gave you guys everything. Each and every week. Please never doubt that.

"I abused my body for years to entertain you guys. *I would do it again in a heartbeat.*"

As Trav's health continued to deteriorate, he still showed immense dignity dealing with the disease. He found solace in the Church and in December 2015, just days before his 32nd birthday, he was baptised. He also announced his engagement to his devoted girlfriend Whitney and was able to spend Christmas at home with her and his family.

On December 31 2015, continuing to wear his heart on his sleeve just like every time he stepped into a wrestling ring, Trav sent out another hugely emotional message through Facebook.

"New Year's Eve. Hard day today. Reading everyone reflecting on their 2015s. Mine was obviously the worst of my life.

"I thought I beat cancer. Made a comeback to wrestling which lasted all of a month and then was diagnosed with terminal cancer straight after.

"I can't do anything except look back with a heavy heart. My future. My life. Over.

"Nothing to look forward to. I just pray for a pain free 2016 and to last as long as The Lord is willing.

"I hope everyone has an amazing 2016.

"Onwards and upwards."

Kris Travis knew he was dying. But his thoughts were still with others.

Trav married Whitney on January 23 2016. I saw some of the wedding photos and thought they made a lovely couple.

Kris continued to use Twitter to document his daily struggle, tweeting each day about his favourite computer games and wrestling matches, and his love of Sheffield Wednesday football team. But behind his cheerful and graceful bravery, he was desperately poorly.

In February 2016, I was thinking about Trav while writing this book. So I sent him a private message. I told him he was in my thoughts, and I had a craic with him about how he'd used a copy of my first book *Holy Grail: The True Story of British Wrestling's Revival* as a foreign object during a match with T-Bone at PCW in 2013. He replied and reminded me it was probably T-Bone who nailed *him* with the book. "He hit me with bloody everything and anything!" he joked.

Kris then asked me when the sequel was coming out, because he'd love to read it. I wrote back telling him that as soon as the book was finished, I'd make sure he received a copy.

And then he wrote something incredibly moving. It was the final message he ever sent to me. And his kind and thoughtful words meant more than I can ever possibly express.

"We never got to be close friends Greg but you were one of the good people I came across in wrestling, just so you know. Always straight up, always a nice guy and always ALWAYS professional. Thanks mate x"

I was moved beyond words.

I know now, as I kind of realised deep down at the time, that this was Trav's way of saying goodbye.

I also look back now and realise that Kris Travis was one of the reasons why I rediscovered my love for professional wrestling. I was blown away by his own passion, his own single-minded determination to return to the thing he loved most in the world despite suffering from such a serious illness.

His comeback to the ring in 2015 was an absolutely incredible, inspirational and ultimately tragic story. It hammered home to me just how much I love pro wrestling. And the support he received reinforced what an amazing privilege it is to be part of the British wrestling community.

Kris Travis also played a significant part in the emotional rise of British professional wrestling over the past decade. He was an in-ring performer par excellence. One of the best this country has ever produced, there is no doubt about that.

In short, Kris Travis was one hell of a man.

Kris Travis died, aged 32, on March 31 2016.

I am heartbroken that I'll never get to keep my promise to Trav and send him a copy of this book.

So I'm going to do the next best thing.

This book is dedicated to the memory of Kristoffer Travis.

May he never, ever, be forgotten.

CHAPTER 1

IT'S STILL REAL IN MORECAMBE

"If somebody had told me 20 years ago that one of the hotbeds for the revival of professional wrestling in Britain would have been Morecambe, I'd have thought they were having a laugh."
Doug Williams as he was inducted into the Morecambe Wrestling Hall of Fame, April 2015

When a Wrestling Hall of Fame was created in Morecambe it was easy for people to scoff. And many did.

But unlikely though it may seem, Morecambe does have its place in UK wrestling history. And in a book about my own experiences of the emotional rise of British wrestling over the past decade, my lowly seaside home town is exactly the right place to start.

Now Morecambe is hardly fashionable. Many of you might not even know where it is. So let me enlighten you.

The town is located on the North West coast of England, roughly 60 miles north of Manchester, 40 miles from our seaside cousins in Blackpool and 28 miles from Preston. With a population of 34,000, Morecambe is roughly 25 times smaller than London. It is blessed with stunning natural beauty thanks to the jaw-dropping views across Morecambe Bay from its five-mile promenade. But it also has its fair share of ramshackle buildings, drugs, crime and deprivation.

I love Morecambe, though. It is my home. The place where I was born, bred, still live today and will almost certainly remain, happy to be here until the end of my days. On a warm blue-skied day, as the orange fireball sun sets over the golden sands and the distant Lakeland Hills meet the shimmering waters in a perfect postcard panorama, you can keep Naples and Cannes. There is nowhere on earth I would rather be than Morecambe seafront, gazing out at the incredible view.

In Morecambe we enjoy the simple pleasures in life, like putting the world to rights down the pub after a hard day's graft and a chippy tea. Many Morecambrians are cynical and downtrodden by the daily grind, not to mention the soul-destroying northern weather. But they do have aspirations. Sadly the younger generation's main ambition is usually to *leave* Morecambe.

Meanwhile, the older folk long for the 1950s and 60s, the days when the town was a thriving resort, a mini-Blackpool pulling in thousands of holidaymakers to its hotels and B&Bs for a week of cheap and cheerful seaside entertainment. Today Morecambe's main tourist attraction stands on the promenade as a reminder of those good old days. The lifesize bronze effigy of Eric Morecambe, the king of British TV comedy who took his stage name from the town where he was born, waves proudly to visitors from all over the world with the stunning horizon of Morecambe Bay as his stage.

Professional wrestling has been at the heart of Morecambe entertainment since the 1930s. With a little help from wrestling historian John Lister and the Wrestling Heritage website, I discovered the first recorded match in the resort took place on August 18 1932 - British Champion Atholl Oakley battling The Black Adonis to a half-hour draw. Soon afterwards all-in wrestling, as it was known back then, became a regular attraction in Morecambe. Throughout the 1930s, the top British stars of the pre-war era grappled every Tuesday night at the Central Pier and on Thursday nights at the magnificently ornate Morecambe Winter Gardens theatre.

During Morecambe's peak years as a holiday destination, British wrestling was also enjoying a boom period thanks to weekly Saturday afternoon TV coverage. Back then, in the 1950s and 1960s, the ITV cameras visited the Winter Gardens a couple of times a year. The Native American star Billy Two Rivers was a top attraction at the 19th Century theatre during this time. While appearing in Morecambe, the Mohawk chief from Canada romanced a local girl and fathered a child. The young lad grew up to become top designer and TV personality Wayne Hemingway, who recalls as one of his earliest memories being paraded around the Winter Gardens ring on the shoulders of his famous father.

On July 24 1969, while on a UK tour, a gargantuan young Frenchman named Jean Ferre wrestled in Morecambe, beating John Cox by technical knockout. Real name Andre Rousimoff, Ferre would go onto global superstardom as Andre the Giant, the original WWE Hall of Famer.

An ITV World of Sport broadcast taped in Morecambe on August 17 1977 was an exceptional bill, with names such as Cyanide Sid Cooper, Mick McManus, Johnny Saint and the masked man Count Bartelli, a wild double disqualification between Marty Jones and Rollerball Rocco, and a match pitting future 'British Bulldog' The Dynamite Kid against Jackie Robinson, the European Lightweight Champion. Jackie loved Morecambe so much, he would in later life settle in the town to run a go-kart track on the seafront. Another British wrestling legend, Steve Logan - former tag partner of McManus - also moved to Morecambe and spent his final days living in the resort prior to his death in 2003.

The Winter Gardens closed in 1977 but bouts continued at the Pier, The Carleton nightclub, the town's Pontins holiday camp and at a brand new venue on the promenade, The Dome. TV wrestling also carried on in the resort until 1981, with names such as Tony 'Banger' Walsh, Steve Grey, Alan Kilby, Mal 'King Kong' Kirk, 'Ironfist' Clive Myers, Jimmy Breaks, and the Auf Wiedersehn Pet and Raiders of the Lost Ark star 'Bomber' Pat Roach on the bills.

The 1980s also saw the biggest household names in British wrestling, the super heavyweights Big Daddy and Giant Haystacks, pull huge crowds to the Central Pier. At this time I went to see my first wrestling matches in Morecambe. As a young man, I sat at ringside, enthralled as Daddy and Haystacks headlined bouts at the Pier then continued to do so at The Dome into the late 80s and early 90s -the years immediately after ITV cancelled pro wrestling in 1988.

In 1991 and 1992, the ageing Daddy was still the star attraction on Thursday evening summer shows at The Dome. Names such as the veteran 'Burly' Barry Douglas, 'Kindhearted' Keith Myatt and Dave 'Fit Finlay' (with Princess Paula) were regulars alongside up-

and-comers like Johnny Angel, Tony Stuart and Steve Regal, who would later earn fame and fortune as William Regal in WWE.

It was also around this time that a fledgling wrestling magazine called Superstars of Wrestling was set up at an office in Morecambe, run by Lancaster writer Findlay Martin. This magazine relaunched in 1994 under the name of Power Slam, and became Europe's best-selling and most revered wrestling publication for the next 20 years. From 2002 until the magazine closed in 2014, I was part of its writing team.

In 1994, the country's biggest ever star, The British Bulldog Davey Boy Smith, visited The Dome during a UK summer tour before returning to the WWF. Brian Dixon's All-Star Wrestling also promoted shows in Morecambe featuring ex-WWF stars The Bushwhackers and in 2000, just days before he was found dead in a Liverpool motel, the giant Yokozuna. Welsh promoter Orig Williams and The Wrestling Alliance, run by Scott Conway, also tried their hand at running events in The Dome.

Then on April 21 2003, I began my own nine-year career as a wrestling promoter. Alongside my childhood best friend Mark Kay, I ran shows for the FWA during a successful four-year stint at The Dome, when we brought a new, modern style of wrestling to Morecambe fans.

The FWA was, at the time, Britain's most pioneering wrestling promotion, as you will know if you read my first book. I apologise in advance to readers of *Holy Grail* if I am about to go over old ground but for those who haven't (yet!) read it, here is a brief potted history of the FWA, how it helped revive British wrestling, and my role in its success and eventual downfall.

Run by promoter, booker and wrestler 'The Showstealer' Alex Shane, the company shot to prominence in 2001 thanks to Shane's role on Britain's first ever mainstream radio wrestling chat show, Wrestle Talk (later re-named Talk Wrestling) on the nationally-aired TalkSport. The fast-talking Londoner and his co-host, former children's TV presenter Tommy Boyd, joined forces to promote a major show at the Crystal Palace Indoor Arena on February 9 2002, which they called Revival. Headlined by former WWE superstars Eddie Guerrero and 'Grandmaster Sexay' Brian Christopher, Revival drew 2,000 fans, a huge crowd for a British wrestling scene which had been in the doldrums since leaving ITV more than a decade earlier. As a fan, I was in the crowd that night and was spellbound by the skills of the new generation of UK wrestlers. I also met Alex Shane for the first time that day.

Revival, which later aired on Sky TV channel Bravo, is etched in my memory because it filled me with pride and kickstarted my love affair with British wrestling. I was never a major fan of the UK scene as a kid. I much preferred the American WWE, or the WWF as it was then known, because its colour, energy, OTT action and larger-than-life superheroes Hulk Hogan, Ultimate Warrior and Macho Man Randy Savage made late 80s British wrestling look ordinary and dated in comparison.

But Revival made me proud not only to be British and a wrestling fan, but to be a *British wrestling* fan. And the FWA also inspired me to get involved in the UK scene. Being at Revival and meeting Alex sparked a chain of events which completely changed my life.

In May 2002, I achieved a lifetime ambition when I qualified as a journalist. In June 2002, I succeded in another long-term goal when I became a freelance writer for Power Slam. Then in July 2002, I got a full-time job working for my local newspaper. That same month, another dream came true as I worked on my first ever British wrestling event as a commentator. Then in February 2003, I exceeded my wildest dreams by debuting for the FWA as a performer; a bombastic, loudmouth wrestling manager called Greg 'The Truth' Lambert.

Suddenly, I was sharing a dressing room with the cream of the UK's new golden generation of young grapplers like Alex, Doug Williams, Jody Fleisch, Jonny Storm, Paul Burchill, Nikita, Martin Stone and Spud, respected veterans like Stevie Knight, Flash Barker and Robbie Brookside, American superstars I'd watched on TV for years like Raven, Terry Funk and Justin Credible, and stars of the future like CM Punk, AJ Styles and Daniel Bryan, who the FWA booked in revolutionary matches with the best Brits in front of sold-out red-hot crowds at venues such as York Hall, Bethnal Green and Broxbourne Civic Hall. In 2003 I managed The Family to three FWA Tag Team Championship reigns during a storied feud with Shane and the former ECW star Ulf Herman. I was also part of the FWA roster who brought weekly British wrestling back to television in 2004/5, with a stint on Sky TV's The Wrestling Channel (TWC). And in 2005, a year when my beloved Liverpool Football Club proved that nothing in life was impossible as they came back from 3-0 down to win the Champions League against AC Milan, I shared the ring in an angle with Mick Foley. That's former WWE Champion, Hall of Famer and Hardcore Legend Mick Foley, in front of 3,400 fans at Coventry Skydome at an Alex Shane and TWC-run supershow called International Showdown, an event where the bill also included Punk, Styles, Samoa Joe and Japanese wrestling icon Mitsuharu Misawa. And I managed a team of villains in a match against Foley and ECW alumni The Sandman and Steve Corino eight months later in front of 2,400 spectators at the same venue.

For a shy kid who was bullied mercilessly at school and had entered the wrestling business green-as-grass with no prior experience, it was absolutely amazing to be part of this groundbreaking era. The sleeping giant of British wrestling was beginning to stir. And during these heady years, I also cut my teeth as a wrestling promoter.

My FWA shows in Morecambe between 2003 and 2007 featured all the emerging Brits, as well as US names Juventud Guerrera, Christopher Daniels, D'Lo Brown, Steve Corino and Colt Cabana. At the time, many of the FWA bouts from The Dome aired on TWC, putting my little seaside home on the wrestling map.

The spotlight really shone on Morecambe in 2005. The first ever War on the Shore, headlined by Alex Shane v Raven, sold out The Dome on March 26 and was screened in its entirety on TWC. Then on June 18, the first ever world tag team championship match of a Japanese promotion to be held on UK soil was held in Morecambe. Naomichi Marufuji and Minoru Suzuki dethroned 2 Cold Scorpio and Doug Williams to win the Pro Wrestling NOAH GHC Tag Team Titles - a bout that saw Morecambe, yes *Morecambe*, grace the pages of Japanese wrestling magazines.

In 2006, Alex Shane stepped away from a declining FWA and I became head booker. I was the man in charge of the most talked-about UK company of the modern era. By then, I had done almost everything there was to do in British wrestling. In less than four years, I had been a matchmaker, promoter, manager, ring announcer and commentator at the highest level of the small-time Brit circuit. Surely, this baptism of fire was unprecedented.

But then in 2007, the FWA closed down after one last glorious stand - an acclaimed Losing Company Must Close feud with rival south-east promotion IPW:UK in Orpington, Kent. My first book explains in great detail why the FWA shut. In a nutshell, it was crippled by debt, backstage infighting and generally punching above its weight. The TV show had finished. Crowds were plummeting on its shows down south. Interest was on the wane.

The FWA showed what it was possible to do with a UK wrestling company. We gave modern-day British wrestlers a platform to compete on an even keel against the best in the world. We proved that a 'new school' British wrestling organisation could produce an episodic weekly television show on a satellite channel with captivating storylines and characters. We demonstrated that British wrestlers could be featured regularly in the leading grapple magazines and mainstream press. And we broke new ground by using the internet, during its formative years, to rally Britain's hardcore legion of fans behind the British scene when previously they were only interested in watching action from the grapple hotbeds of America, Japan and Mexico.

But ultimately, the FWA stopped short of achieving its goal to return British wrestling to a free-to-air terrestrial channel with a sustainable TV show watched by millions, to turn British wrestling stars into household names who were recognised by the average man on the street, and help them make some real money without having to uproot and move to America.

This is the Holy Grail for British wrestling. I had a taste of it with the FWA. But to be honest, we weren't quite ready for the mainstream back then.

Ultimately, the Holy Grail didn't happen and the FWA bit the dust.

British wrestling was back to square one.

But the Morecambe shows carried on.

When the FWA closed in 2007, the landscape of British wrestling was very different to how it is today.

Brian Dixon's All-Star Wrestling was still ticking along as the UK's most prolific touring promotion. Established in 1970, All-Star was quietly travelling up and down the country entertaining families with a year-long diary of low budget shows in halls and holiday camps while making money to keep a basic but successful business going year after year.

Meanwhile a young rival promoter, Sanjay Bagga, was trying to build his London-based LDN organisation into a similar full-time travelling roadshow across England.

In Doncaster, 1PW was running regular shows in front of a large, loyal and vocal fan base at the Doncaster Dome, mixing the best of British such as Jonny Storm, Spud, Jody Fleisch and Darren Burridge with legendary names from overseas such as Bret 'Hitman' Hart and Ric Flair, and top talents like AJ Styles and Austin Aries. But by 2011, 1PW met the same end as the FWA and fizzled out due to overspending, internal strife and mismanagement.

As for other UK wrestling promoters, they were happy running less than a dozen shows a year and satisfied with staying on their home turf. In a nutshell, the 2007 version of British wrestling was very much like the scene in America until Vince McMahon began his aggressive nationwide expansion in the early 1980s. We had lots of different wrestling territories.

To name just a few: in East Anglia, there was Ricky Knight's longstanding World Association of Wrestling (WAW) where Ricky's teenage daughter Saraya-Jade (who later became Paige in WWE) was learning her trade. Up in Scotland, the scene was only just beginning to stir, led by PBW, BCW, SWA and a fledgling Glasgow-based outfit called Insane Championship Wrestling (ICW) who much more would be heard from in future years. The Manchester area had FutureShock Wrestling in Stockport and GPW in Wigan; both only a few years old but already with firm followings. 4FW was starting to get going down on the South West coast while NGW was about to spring into life in Hull. The Midlands and Wales also had a few small companies plying their trade.

Meanwhile in the London area, 2007 saw actor and production expert Len Davies curtail his attempts to revive regular grapple shows at the FWA's former stomping ground of the York Hall after consistently low crowds for his Real Quality Wrestling events. The genial Len instead went on to bring his considerable production talents to other UK companies. Meanwhile the capital welcomed for the first time the bizarre alternative world of Lucha Britannia - Mexican-style wrestling featuring British wrestlers in masks. And over in Kent, IPW:UK, the FWA's conquerors, was now firmly established. Like many UK promotions, it seemed to have learned from FWA and 1PW's mistakes, and rather than becoming too ambitious too soon, was happy consolidating its position running small, well-attended shows in a specific geographical area of the country.

So in 2007, British wrestling wasn't exactly setting the world on fire. And that's because most UK promotions didn't actually *want* to conquer the globe. The FWA had blazed a trail with big ideas, television, arena events and media coverage. But the company over-reached itself like Icarus and burned out. Those who were left promoting wrestling in Britain in 2007 were happy just ticking along, sending their crowds of a few hundred punters home happy, and satisfied with running events at a profit.

And with the scars of the FWA's demise still raw, I fell very much into that category. Once FWA closed, the pressure of having to follow the glory years was off and I felt a great sense of relief. The FWA had never really felt like mine, even when I took over as the boss in 2006. The company was founded by Mark Sloan and then taken to its peak by Alex Shane and his mentor Dino Scarlo. But now, after an ill-fated year in charge of the FWA where I felt hamstrung by trying to live up to its legacy, I had broken free and could finally do things my way.

So over the next few years, I tried to rediscover my passion for wrestling by running a few shows in my home town, without any of the financial stresses and behind-the-scenes chaos that dogged the FWA's final years. My plan was to simply run four, maybe five shows a year, relying on my vision, my money, my decisions, and with only my trusted best friend Mark Kay to answer to. And unlike the FWA, we would use only cheaper British talent and run the company as a profitable business.

So in March 2007 the XWA was born.

We ran our first XWA event on Easter Saturday, April 7 2007 at The Dome. The venue was completely sold out with 425 paying customers. Any worries we had that our local supporters who were used to seeing the name 'FWA' on the marquee might be put off by the name change were quickly put to rest.

Within minutes of the opening bell, our diehard band of regular fans were chanting "X-W-A! X-W-A!" like they had been doing it for years. Our gamble to change just one letter of the company's name to make it as familiar as possible to our fan base, so it felt like business as usual, paid off.

The XWA was run by myself and Mark as 50-50 partners. Our partnership worked brilliantly for four years. Mark ran the business, set up the limited company, administered the bank account, designed posters, updated the website and handled 'front-of-house' duties at shows. I was the booker who came up with most of the creative ideas and storyline direction, dealt with all the wrestlers, co-ordinated their transport and organised all our media publicity. And I also doubled as ring announcer. During the XWA years at The Dome, I also acted as the hometown 'authority figure' on shows.

By the way, I had no formal training on how to book a wrestling show. My knowledge comes from a combination of absorbing information from Alex and Dino, three decades of watching wrestling, years of poring through magazines, books and newsletters for titbits of wrestling psychology, and a general instinct for what pushes people's buttons.

Back when I was booking the XWA shows, I always planned ahead. As the XWA's money man, Mark set the wages budget, usually at a meagre £600 per show plus travel expenses. So at the start of each year, I wrote out a list of the wrestlers I wanted to use who fell within this budget. Then I wrote down a list of matches and who I wanted to win in key matchups. I also came up with possible feuds and storylines, like a TV or film scriptwriter. These best-laid plans usually changed throughout the year, because not every wrestler was available for every date. But I always tried to stick to a long-term strategy as best as possible. And the blueprint was always geared to keeping the fans interested so they kept on buying tickets and came back time and again to watch the XWA.

For those who don't know, and it's been public knowledge for many years, professional wrestling match results are pre-determined by the booker. It's the booker's job to decide what happens on a wrestling show and work out interesting scenarios to hook the audience and keep them coming back for more. I love being a booker because I love telling stories and I believe this is what pro wrestling is all about. As a journalist, telling stories is also what I do for a living, so I have plenty of practice at it.

And there is an art to booking too. In order to tell the best possible stories, I had a number of principles I tried to abide by, as follows:

1) The chase is more exciting than the capture

2) You don't always have to send the fans home happy...but *always* send them home talking

3) Babyfaces must be heroic and villains must be dastardly

4) Big personalities, not the actual wrestling, draw the casual fan

5) Real-life situations often create the best storylines

6) Put your best three matches in your opener, the match before the interval and the main event

7) Wrestling fans *love* faction warfare

8) Hide your wrestlers' weaknesses and emphasise their strengths

9) Logic and continuity are all-important

10) Wrestling is built on emotion

This last principle was the most important of all. It comes from a backstage promo by the late, great Dusty Rhodes, at WWF Summerslam 1990. When The American Dream looked intensely into the camera and said "Wrestling is built on emotion" it struck a chord with me. Dusty's words always rang in my ears whenever I booked a wrestling card. I wanted to produce shows that made the people *feel* something. Anything. Joy, love, anger, hate, apprehension, fear, sadness, regret, laughter, awe...it really didn't matter to me. My aim was to create scenarios that made fans jump out of their seats in joy or despair because they genuinely cared about the wrestlers and the result of their matches. I wanted them to keep on coming back because they desperately wanted to see the heroes win and the villains get what's coming to them.

The fans of Morecambe have incredible passion for what we do. They, more than anyone, are what make pro wrestling special in my home town. They cheer their heroes heartily. They boo the villains with gusto. Many of them believe that wrestling is real. They don't react like the hardcore fans who entertain themselves with comedic chants and applause for a big move. The Morecambe fans feel real emotion.

In Morecambe, live wrestling shows are a nod to the era before the internet and the grapple media revealed the secrets of pro wrestling, before Vince McMahon admitted in the mid-80s that wrestling was not a competitive sport but actually a highly physical form of theatre called 'sports entertainment'. They are a nod to the time when good old-fashioned 'wrassling' shows in the American southern states of Tennessee, Georgia and Texas pulled packed houses of people desperate to see their favourite star win the title and the hated bad guy get his come-uppance. The cheers (or 'pop') if the babyface (good guy) won were deafening. But if the heel came out on top, sometimes the fans ripped their seats out in anger and pelted the ring with rubbish. Done properly, wrestling incited proper full-scale *riots*.

They used to say that wrestling was real in Memphis. They say it's real in Morecambe too.

As a booker, I always tried to keep Morecambe in its own little timewarp. Other promoters book shows full of 'dream matches' where Talented Wrestler A faces Talented Wrestler B up and down the card, for no other reason than because they are bound to be great athletic contests. Fans of these promotions don't particularly care who wins or loses, as long as they see lots of fast-paced highly physical action and spectacular moves.

In bigger towns and cities, this approach often works. The ultra-physical 'Strong Style' of wrestling has become really popular, both in Britain and America, over the past few years. But in Morecambe, the crowd wants larger-than-life personalities. They want goodies versus baddies, cowboys versus Indians as Stevie Knight calls it. They want feuds. And they deeply, passionately care who wins the matches.

"British wrestling would benefit from more bookers who have a really solid story direction in mind," said Simon 'El Ligero' Musk, speaking in 2016.

"There is too much of 'here's a guy, here's another guy, let's watch them have a match'. That's fine sometimes. But there are only so many times you can see guys do their moves without any emotional investment. You can't just keep banging a couple of action figures together and expect people to care.

"It's all well and good to watch high flying Brit against high flying American now and again, but if you've got a show full of it, there's only so many times you can watch a firework display before you want to go inside and watch a film."

There are still what we call 'heel turns' in Morecambe. Once a year, or maybe every two years, a beloved fan favourite will stab one of his friends in the back and turn to the dark side like Darth Vader betraying Obi-Wan Kenobi. And the fans properly loathe him for it. They bombard him with angry messages on social media, maybe even run out of their ringside seats and physically attack the traitor. Because it's Real in Morecambe.

Here is an example. On the very first XWA show, I booked a British Inter-Federation Cup match - Team XWA v Ricky Knight's Team WAW. I knew after the overwhelming success of a collision between teams representing FWA and All-Star in 2006 that The Dome fans loved supporting their home favourites against invading interlopers. This football match-style fervour was especially strong in the one-night team competition format of the British Inter-Federation Cup. Because wrestling fans *love* faction warfare.

I also wanted to do the right thing by Ricky, who I have the utmost respect for. The Cup was his concept. It was only right that the XWA should lose this match and allow WAW to take the trophy back to its rightful home in Norwich. But we did it in such a way that set up fresh storylines for the future.

With the scores locked at 2-2, XWA lost the deciding four-on-four elimination match when erstwhile crowd favourite Stevie Knight turned heel on XWA captain 'The Pukka One' Darren Burridge by smashing him across the head with a kendo stick to enable Ricky Knight to pick up the victory for WAW. Previously, Stevie had been a hero to the Morecambe crowd. With this one simple act, he became the town's most hated heel. His actions ensured the Morecambe fans would come back next time, thirsty to see the XWA's babyfaces get revenge.

The main event of XWA War on the Shore 2007 saw 'The Wonderkid' Jonny Storm pin British wrestling legend, and future NXT coach, Robbie Brookside to win what was once the FWA World Heavyweight Title - now renamed the XWA British Heavyweight Title. After Storm took the veteran Brookside down in a 'small package' and pinned him one, two, three, and I announced the title had changed hands in my role as MC, a sea of happy fans climbed into the ring and engulfed the much-loved Storm with back slaps, handshakes and hugs, in genuine delight that the underdog hero from Essex had defeated the loathed Liverpudlian for a title he'd chased for six long years, but never managed to win before.

What they didn't realise, was the small package wasn't the planned finish. Brookside was supposed to kick out before the count of three and the match was meant to continue for a few more minutes, until Robbie would eventually lose to Jonny's finishing move, the Wonderwhirl. But due to a mix-up, referee Richard 'Youngy' Young's hand slapped the mat three times, the long-haired Wildcat did not kick out in time, the fans roared in celebration because they thought the match was over and Mark Kay, who was up in the sound booth, played Storm's music.

These things sometimes happen in wrestling where the best-laid plans go awry. But we have an old adage. If the fans don't notice the mistake, it's not a mistake. And thankfully, none of the spectators that night realised, and certainly didn't seem to care. Soon The Dome ring was absolutely crammed with delirious paying punters, many of them kids, chanting "X-W-A!" at the top of their lungs. The Dome throng were beside themselves with delight that the beloved Jonny had finally taken down the hated Scouser after a full year of build up towards their climactic Easter Saturday showdown.

It was a pure, organic, joyful reaction. Because it's Real in Morecambe.

One of the biggest ever Morecambe heroes made his debut on our second XWA show, Vendetta on June 30 2007.

The first time I became aware of Sam Slam was in late 2006,

when Ricky Knight posted on the UK Fan Forum, a notorious discussion website for British wrestling fans, heaping praise upon his new rough diamond, a graduate of Ricky's WAW training school called Sam Nayler.

Ricky posted photos of Sam which immediately got my attention. Nayler was ruggedly handsome and beefily muscular. In short, he had 'the look'. My friend Dann Read, who at the time was promoting shows in the South East under the name X-Sports Wrestling, also touted Sam to me. Dann told me Sam was raw but spectacularly explosive inside the ring, freakishly strong, and had a natural charisma and intensity.

Some fans and insiders didn't like the name Sam Slam, thinking it cheesy, cartoony and cliched. But I thought it was catchy, memorable and marketable, especially to our Morecambe family audience. As a name, Sam Slam was easy to understand, rolled off the tongue and screamed 'wrestling'. I loved it. I also know as a journalist that mainstream media are far more likely to pay attention to a wrestler with an outlandish name than somebody who calls themselves Joe Bloggs or something equally boring. It's one of the reasons why Danny Hope - who calls himself 'Delicious Danny' – was heavily publicised in the national media in the run-up to British wrestling's return to ITV in 2016.

Back to Sam Slam, and Ricky and Dann's recommendations were enough for me, so I tried to book Sam for the first XWA show in Morecambe. My plan was for him to be a member of Team WAW against Team XWA. In other words, had things worked out as originally planned, Sam would have been a bad guy on his first appearance in Morecambe. But Sam couldn't make the show. In hindsight, this was a blessing in disguise.

After Team WAW triumphed in the Inter-Federation Cup match at War on the Shore, Ricky Knight and his teenage son Zak Knight, then working under a mask as Zak Zodiac, were loathed by the Morecambe crowd. So my plan was for Ricky to main event the next show, Vendetta, in a match with Hade Vansen, former FWA Champion, who would return to The Dome as a babyface. But then Hade was signed by the WWE and couldn't make the date.

I racked my brains, trying to think of a suitable replacement.

Jonny Storm, the XWA Champion, wasn't available that night. Former FWA Champion Alex Shane was taking a break from the ring. Stevie Knight had just turned heel himself. So who on earth could main event the show against the hated Rowdy Man?

In the end, I decided to take a massive risk.

Towards the end of the night, Rowdy Ricky and the obnoxious young Zak were taunting and winding up the crowd with aplomb. Zodiac had just beaten crowd favourite Joey Hayes, with outside assistance from his dad, and the Knight duo were revelling in their dastardly victory.

"Who's going to come out here and stop me from doing exactly what I want to do, eh?" growled the elder Knight in mocking glee.

At this, Sam Slam emerged on the stage. He had already wrestled a one-against-two 'handicap match' in the first-half of the show, pulverising a hapless duo of FutureShock Wrestling graduates, former referee Lance Lenahan and his partner Jamie Flynt. So the fans knew who Sam was and were already intrigued by the newcomer.

As Ricky and Zak backed off in trepidation, Slam stood there between the red curtains on The Dome stage, as the spotlight showed off the definition in his rippling shoulders and pectorals, his eyes glaring a hole through the Rowdy Man and Zodiac. The crowd went berserk. They cheered, shrieked and screamed in excitement. Kids left their seats and ran to touch the man dubbed XWA's Secret Weapon as he strode purposefully to ringside.

It was a pop star reaction. For a guy they barely knew.

Then Sam climbed into the ring and began to pace the canvas like a caged lion, stopping only to shadow box, his thick forearms cleaving the air with forceful intent. He made eye contact with the fans, pointed directly at Ricky Knight, and looked ready to tear his prey limb from limb, his aura reminding me of world boxing champion Mike Tyson about to be unleashed on some hapless heavyweight during his mid-80s pomp.

The fans stamped their feet, clapped and chanted in anticipation.

"SAM! SAM! SAM! SAM! SAM!"

Bloody hell, we've stumbled onto something here, I thought.

The match itself only lasted a few minutes, for most of which

Ricky and Zak did a magnificent job in stalling, running away, cheating and generally making Sam look like the beast he unquestionably was. But what happened after the match ended still sticks in my mind today.

After Ricky got disqualified when Stevie Knight ran into the ring and bashed Sam across the back with a kendo stick, Zak dived at Sam with a full somersault off the top rope. Nayler not only caught the much lighter Zodiac by the legs in mid-air, he powered him up onto his shoulders in one fluid motion and slung him across the full length of the ring with a release power bomb. Then Sam himself climbed to the top turnbuckle and as the entire seated section of The Dome rose, Mexican Wave style, in awestruck disbelief, the muscleman did a full front flip to land on the prone Zodiac with a 450 splash.

The crowd reaction was deafening. Not only was Sam Slam a living, breathing superhero, he could deliver daredevil aerial moves a man of his powerful stature had no right being able to do. The fans were ecstatic. They absolutely *loved* him.

Because it's Real in Morecambe.

As ring announcer that night, I had the best seat in the house as Sam Slam became a star in one night in Morecambe. XWA had a new hero.

Sam was a regular in Morecambe for most of the next five years and eventually became XWA Champion, holding the belt from September 2008 to September 2009. While Sam was raw and sometimes didn't know his own strength in the ring, he had the 'It Factor' and this made up for his inexperience. He was also a pleasure to deal with on a personal level and he was a valued part of the XWA dressing room from 2007 to 2012. Sam is a thoroughly charming guy, who respected what we were trying to do in Morecambe and was always determined to work his backside off for the fans. He travelled the 260-mile distance from his home in Bury St Edmunds to Morecambe on XWA show days, then back again, sometimes not arriving home until breakfast time the following morning. He was so dedicated to our cause. I would go as far as to say that the popularity of Sam Slam was one of the main reasons for the success of the XWA.

Another major reason for XWA's success was 'The Psychotic Warrior' Johnny Phere.

Those of you who read the first book will know all about Jamie 'Johnny Phere' Hutchinson. You will know how highly I rate him as a performer. You will know how hard I tried to get him into the FWA during the promotion's glory days. You will know how I've always felt he was underrated on the UK scene. His film star looks, action hero physique, intensity, ring style and promo skills made him the ideal figurehead for the XWA.

While most other promoters ignored Johnny or cast him to the wayside without utilising his talents properly, I invested the entire five years of the XWA into The Psychotic Warrior and my investment paid off handsomely. Phere's character was that of a lone wolf; self-obsessed, deranged, goal-orientated and with a God complex second to none. He had to win at all costs, but when he lost, he reacted like his world had caved in. Then, bad things happened, usually to other people. When also factoring in his superstar look, his unrivalled work ethic and his unbridled passion for making an emotional connection with the Morecambe crowd, this made him a valuable asset to my company from 2007 to 2012. Johnny became XWA's number one attraction.

Phere was originally a heel when the XWA began and a very good one at that. He had already begun 2007 by vowing to go the entire calendar year undefeated, a 12 month period he christened The Year of Phere. Wins over El Ligero, Dave Mastiff, Zak Knight and Dirk Feelgood, followed by tournament victories over Simon Valour, Darren Burridge and Sam Slam, took him to the number one contender's slot and the verge of finishing the year not only still undefeated, but as the XWA Champion. But defeat to Jonny Storm at XWA Last Fight at the Prom at The Dome on November 24 2007 burst Johnny's bubble. Having failed in his quest, Phere threw the mother of all tantrums inside the Dome ring.

The storyline then took a new turn as Phere became obsessed with Jonny Storm, the man who had crushed his Year of Phere dream. JP and Jonny had terrific chemistry and their rivalry was a classic. Throughout the year, the furious Phere dogged Storm's every waking moment, interfering in his matches and brawling with him all over

The Dome as officials struggled to keep the enemies apart. Their feud culminated in a dramatic two-out-of-three falls encounter at Last Fight 2008, where the loser had to leave British wrestling for good. The Psychotic Warrior lost. And just like that, his career was over. Always brilliant at selling a setback, JP was photographed sitting backstage on the floor in a classic snap, utterly devastated by the loss of his livelihood.

In 2009, I decided that Phere should campaign to be reinstated and not take no for an answer. The result was one of the most entertaining storylines I ever produced. Through his insane determination to make a comeback, Johnny turned himself babyface for the first time in Morecambe. During his feud with Jonny Storm, the XWA fans had grown to respect JP's ability and saw him as a larger-than-life character with 'Stone Cold' Steve Austin-like qualities. Like Austin, he didn't care if the fans cheered or booed him. Like Austin, his actions were often reckless and violent. And like Austin, his attack-dog mentality was now being directed at an authority figure who was holding him down: the closest thing Morecambe had to Vince McMahon, namely, myself. As promoter of the XWA, I refused to bring him back, because rules are rules. And when you tell wrestling fans they can't have something they want, they want it all the more.

As I stood my ground, the clamour for Phere's return grew bigger and bigger. "WE WANT PHERE!" The Dome fans screamed. So JP went into maniacal overdrive on his campaign for reinstatement. He gatecrashed shows, we filmed him on a rampage at our new XWA training school beating up the students, and he even interrupted me being interviewed on a local radio show to demand I lifted his ban.

In June 2009, we shot a highly entertaining YouTube video where the cameras followed Phere around Morecambe seafront. The Psychotic Warrior ranted at the statue of Eric Morecambe that he, not Eric, was now the most famous man from the town. He bullied passers-by into supporting his cause. We even convinced a seaside fortune teller to read his palm and predict what the future held for Johnny Phere. Gypsy Sarah told the seething JP she sensed he had a nasty temper and told him he needed to calm down otherwise "it would hold him back in life". I was shaking with laughter behind the camera. It was fantastic, unscripted stuff.

A friend of mine, Steve Weatherhead, allowed us to film in his cafe on Morecambe Promenade and even agreed to appear in the video. Steve, who had no acting experience to my knowledge, proved to be a hilarious foil for the deluded Phere. When Johnny marched into the cafe, looking for me, Steve acted intimidated, then timidly offered The Psychotic Warrior a full English breakfast instead.

"DO YOU KNOW WHO I AM?" bellowed Phere, who used this as his catchphrase years before Bully Ray in TNA.

"And do I look like I need a fry-up? I'M A GOD DAMNED ATHLETE!"

Then he stormed out. It was comedy gold.

Steve's life was tragically cut short in 2012 when he died of a brain tumour, aged 54. He was the life and soul of Morecambe Promenade, an energetic and funny character who was loved by his customers, a truly great guy. I often watch back the 'Johnny Phere campaigns around Morecambe' video (still available on YouTube) to see Steve as I remember him. And I smile.

Phere's campaign ended with him defeating heel duo Damon Leigh and CJ Banks in a one-against-two handicap match at XWA Last Fight at the Prom 2009. According to the stipulation of the bout, victory earned him reinstatement as an active wrestler on the UK scene. The Dome fans were delighted. Phere had gone from most hated to most popular in the matter of 12 months.

Because it's Real in Morecambe.

To sell the significance of the storyline, Phere hadn't wrestled anywhere on the British circuit for almost a year, turning down several offers which may, long-term, have affected his chances of regular work elsewhere. That was how seriously he took the XWA and how much he wanted to repay my faith in him. He put his heart and soul into the entire concept.

This created a huge level of trust in Johnny Phere on my part. I knew if I had a creative vision, the dedicated JP would move heaven and earth to deliver it. He also lived locally, so I knew I could always count on him to be around for local media appearances to promote our events, something he was always in high demand for because of the way he looks. Seriously, I've never seen the guy take a bad photograph.

So with Sam Slam and Johnny Phere in prominent roles, the years 2007-9 were my most lucrative and creatively satisfying of my tenure as a wrestling promoter. The shows were profitable. We were doing great business. And the Morecambe crowd reacted with the desired emotional responses to virtually everything and everyone on our shows. It's a time I look back on with extreme fondness and pride.

I must mention another gentleman who was instrumental in our success.

His name is Rockstar Spud.

CHAPTER 2

THE RISE OF ROCKSTAR SPUD

I first met James 'Jay' Curtin on March 27 2004, when he debuted for the FWA at a show in Enfield near London.

I didn't realise at the time the extraordinary heights this 5ft 5in, 10 stone blond ball of energy from Birmingham would reach in his career. Spud not only became heavyweight champion of my promotion the XWA, but later won the first ever TNA British Boot Camp, twice won the TNA X Division Championship and then main evented for TNA at Wembley Arena in front of an international TV audience. Today, he is established as one of the biggest wrestling stars Britain has ever produced.

Although Spud had wrestled in Morecambe before, when it was FWA, he didn't make his first appearance for the XWA until February 2 2008. At the time, Spud was still mainly working around the country using the high-flying babyface persona he perfected in the FWA. But in a few promotions, he'd debuted a heel character. This was a radical departure from the never-say-die underdog role, and then some.

Jay's new alter-ego, *Rockstar* Spud, was like a wrestling version of Johnny Rotten from The Sex Pistols. He'd morphed into an obnoxious package of hairspray, black leather, shades, bad attitude and pure entertainment. I had seen a YouTube video of him singing (badly, on purpose) to Bon Jovi's rock anthem Living On A Prayer while he entered the ring for a small show in the Midlands, a pint-sized ego on legs strutting and preening like he owned the place. Rockstar Spud was a proper wrestling character. He was over-the-top, overblown, easy to understand, deafeningly loud and in-your-face. My kind of act. I loved it.

I wanted to bring Rockstar Spud to Morecambe. But the one thing I didn't want to do, was make the mistake of debuting the character straight away. In real life, I am not exactly known as a patient person. But when it comes to wrestling booking, I have always utilised patience as a virtue. I wouldn't just unleash the Rockstar on the Morecambe audience without warning. This would not make sense. The audience knew and loved Spud as the Pocket Dynamo, the big-hearted underdog. He couldn't just walk back into The Dome as this bad boy rocker; that would be confusing. So I wanted to build up Jay's metamorphosis into the Rockstar and create a valid reason for it to happen.

So I booked Spud in a match for the only other XWA championship I'd inherited from the FWA, the British Flyweight Title. At the time, the champion was El Ligero.

Real name Simon Musk, Ligero was rapidly developing into one of the UK's very best in-ring performers, playing the character of a masked Mexican 'luchador' from Los Sancho, Mexico, although the man behind the mask was actually from Leeds, West Yorkshire!

In the ring, Ligero was smooth, acrobatic and as reliable as they come. If I booked Simon for a show, I knew I was guaranteed a good match and more often than not, a great one. So I made El Ligero a fixture of my shows. Many UK promoters were doing the same. And to this day, they still do. The masked man gets more work on the UK circuit than just about anyone. In 2016 alone, he wrestled a whopping 288 matches and that year was employed by around 170 promotions worldwide.

"When I first started out I was quite naive to British wrestling," said Simon in 2016.

"The only shows I'd ever been to when I was younger were All-Star shows, but only a couple of them, at Leeds Town Hall. The only other exposure I had to British wrestling was through WOW Magazine, and Power Slam would do a little bit, but I didn't know how many promotions were around. All I knew is who the top promotions were. And I guess at the time the main one was the FWA.

"I saw the Revival show on Bravo (in 2002) and that was quite a big exposure to British wrestling for me. But I had no idea how the business worked. I started training in 2001 at a school in Sheffield. I was under the impression that if you trained somewhere, that was where you worked.

"Then I went to watch FWA Frontiers of Honor at the York Hall (in May 2003) and saw the difference between where I was training and the FWA, how much bigger it was, how much louder it was. I remember watching the first match, James Tighe v Paul London, and thinking this is where I want to be. Nothing could touch it in terms of scale and size. No other company had the media profile they did. It seemed like a proper wrestling company.

"Then I met Spud, about five or six shows into my career, and I gradually started to learn about the Midlands scene, breaking out into little promotions in Leicester and Northampton. I had no business being on shows at that point. I learned on the job."

And Simon learned well. The super-popular Ligero won the XWA Flyweight championship from Ross 'RJ Singh' Jones in a thrilling streetfight at Last Fight at the Prom 2007. The Hertford-based Singh was a hated villain and the feud between these two so-called 'international stars' clicked big-time with our audience, who thrived on seeing a clear-cut good guy like The Mexican Sensation battle an out-and-out rotter like The Bollywood Dream.

I have also known Ross since the FWA days. Trained by Alex Shane, Singh was originally known as Ross Jordan until he embraced the idea of a Bollywood movie star persona.

"My mum is from Trinidad but her grandparents were Indian slaves brought over to the Carribean," said Ross in 2016.

"I had never even thought about doing the gimmick but Alex recommended it to me in the early 2000s, when I started training. He said it would be cool to do a Bollywood character with a massive Bollywood entrance, with dancers. He said it would be brilliant. But I shot it down completely, thinking it would be really racist. I didn't think it would work, being naive, so I put the character aside completely.

"But then in 2007, I was in a real slump with wrestling, so I called Alex, I always turn to Alex when I don't know what to do next, and I asked his advice. He said 'do you remember when I suggested the Bollywood gimmick years ago?' And he pitched it again to me. I'd been to see the musical Bombay Dreams in London. So it suddenly popped into my head, I could be 'The Bombay Dream' Ross Jordan.

We had an RQW show coming up and Alex had got me booked on it. I went to see Len Davies and we filmed a promo officially unveiling The Bombay Dream character. I debuted in a triple threat with Jonny Storm and El Generico (Sami Zayn) which I won. So I carried on with the gimmick.

"Then they renamed Bombay back to Mumbai so Greg suggested that I use the name 'The Bollywood Dream'. I also thought the name Singh had a nice ring to it."

From a pop culture standpoint, the timing was perfect for an Indian character, because Bollywood film star Shilpa Shetty had just won Celebrity Big Brother and the hit movie Slumdog Millionaire was about to be released. Becoming RJ Singh completely revitalised Ross' career and he became one of the UK's top heels. His feud with El Ligero developed into a long-term rivalry all over the British circuit.

But Ligero v Spud was a different kettle of fish entirely. Both men were fan favourites. Traditionally, an all-babyface encounter had never really worked in Morecambe. It was a gamble, but a necessary one to kickstart the storyline.

Spud lost clean to Ligero on February 2 2008, in front of an audience who were a little confused over who to cheer for. After the match, Spud challenged the champion to a rematch. This happened on April 12 2008 at War on the Shore. This time, the fans were more engaged. At one point in the highly competitive conflict, a duelling chant broke out in The Dome.

"EL LIGERO!"
"SPUD, SPUD, SPUD-SPUD-SPUD."
"EL LIGERO!"
"SPUD, SPUD, SPUD-SPUD-SPUD."

I sat at my ring announcer's table next to the ring, soaking in the atmosphere in The Dome. It was wonderful.

"That singles match was one of my favourite matches I've ever had," said Simon Musk.

"The reaction was fantastic. In a lot of places, if you put two babyfaces on with each other, a lot of the fans will sit on their hands because they won't know who to root for, but they were invested so much, and Spud was fantastic to work with because he gets storytelling so well. I loved those matches.

"I don't want to go through the same routine all the time. My favourite thing to do in wrestling is stories. For years people have put me in cruiserweight multi-mans. I can do that style if you want me to. But I like telling stories and being given the platform to tell stories. Some promoters are more receptive to it than others. But the worst thing for me is for a promoter to say 'well, just have a good match'. That's what I intended to do anyway and there's nothing to get your teeth into.

"That's why working in Morecambe was so good. I knew I was part of a story and there is nothing more rewarding to me than key points of a story getting the reaction you have been building to."

The fans were certainly becoming emotionally invested in my Ligero-Spud story, even though they liked both men. But when the Mexican scored the pinfall for the second time, this time Spud's simmering frustration at his inability to defeat the luchador was a little more obvious. The firebrand seized the microphone and challenged Ligero to one last encounter at Vendetta on July 5 2008. This third and final match of the Ligero-Spud 'friendly rivalry' would be no-disqualification, no holds barred and fought under Last Man Standing rules where the only way to win was to beat your opponent down for the referee's count of 10.

This was the night Spud turned heel. And he did it in a way that would ensure that in one fell swoop, he would go from being adored and respected to being ostracised and despised by the fans in Morecambe.

If I came up with a good idea, like turning Spud heel, I always wanted to make it bigger. I always tried to create 'a moment'. This came from years of watching Vince McMahon's WWE. McMahon is a marketing genius, a master of creating special moments that stick in the memory and become part of folklore. Hulk Hogan slamming Andre the Giant, Randy Savage being bitten by Jake The Snake's cobra, Shawn Michaels throwing Marty Jannetty through the Barber Shop window, Steve Austin's pull-apart brawl with Mike Tyson, Mick Foley coming off the top of the Hell in a Cell. These are all 'moments'.

So it wasn't enough for Spud to just turn to the dark side. The turn had to make sense. It had to be memorable. It had to create an impact. It had to be a Morecambe moment.

Three months earlier at War on the Shore, Jonny Storm pinned Stevie Knight to retain the XWA Title and the celebration was in full swing. Then the lights went out in The Dome.

When they came back on again, Martin Stone was in the ring.

With help from fellow Londoners The Kartel - Terry Frazier and Sha Samuels - Stone gave Storm a terrible beating with his trademark cricket bat and laid similar waste to Stixx and a cavalry charge of fellow XWA babyfaces who stormed the ring in a failed bid to save the fallen champion.

After completing this barbaric assault, The Guvnor grabbed the microphone and informed the Morecambe fans that he was the man who, one year earlier, had singlehandedly closed down the FWA when he pinned Flash Barker to win the Losing Promotion Must Fold match down south. So in Stone's eyes, for Greg Lambert to come back up north as if nothing had happened and continue to run shows under the name XWA, it was an affront to everything the real-life Martin Harris had achieved. The hard-nosed bruiser then vowed that he would stop at nothing to destroy XWA just as he had the FWA.

The angle was effective and convincingly performed by everyone involved. Stone established himself as XWA's new number one heel and a threat to the very existence of the company. Once again, my tried and trusted formula of bringing in outside forces to battle the fans' favourites in a high stakes feud paid dividends. And Martin Stone was absolutely outstanding. Since the events of Final Frontiers, Martin had continued to get better and better and better. By spring 2008, he was in the best shape of his career, had developed menacing microphone skills and was now a polished in-ring performer. In later years he would go on to sign for WWE and become a regular on its developmental TV show NXT using the name Danny Burch.

The Morecambe audience was outraged by Stone's attack, but in a good way. They returned in droves on July 5 2008 to see the next instalment of the hostile takeover by Stone and his cronies, a ruthless gang of East End cut-throats known as The Firm.

Because it's Real in Morecambe.

The Vendetta show began with Spud v Ligero - Last Man Standing. As the bout progressed, Spud subtlely and masterfully told the story of a man on the edge, who'd twice been beaten by his Mexican foe, and needed to win at all costs. Then the lights went out, just as they had at War on the Shore.

By the way, in coming up with the 'lights out' gimmick I realise I was influenced by mid-90s Extreme Championship Wrestling (ECW) and how the Philadelphia arena was regularly plunged into pitch-black to allow a big surprise or sneak-attacker to enter the ECW ring under cover of darkness. Yes, I hold my hands up, I often used to recycle other people's ideas and put a modern spin on them. Take when Stevie Knight won the 2008 Goldrush by eliminating Sam Slam, even though Sam had thrown him over the top rope first but the officials didn't see it. A carbon copy of how Steve Austin ousted Bret Hart to win the 1997 WWF Royal Rumble. But in my defence, I only tended to re-hash angles that happened 10 years ago or more. That way, there was a fair chance kids wouldn't have seen the original.

Even the heel turn that night was inspired by somewhere else. I had read (and I can't recall the match or scenario but I think it was in Mexico) about a situation where a heel gang of wrestlers were beating down a babyface, only for another 'face to step between them to save the victim. But then, the rescuer's facial expression changed and he slowly turned around to join in the merciless gang attack. This sounded like the perfect way for Spud to join The Firm.

So that is exactly what happened. When the lights came back on, Stone, Frazier and Samuels were in the ring, and they immediately began to batter El Ligero helpless. When Spud suddenly joined in, the fans were furious. And then when the referee was bullied into counting Ligero out and awarded the Flyweight championship to Spud, they were apoplectic with rage.

Spud was so desperate to defeat Ligero and take his title, he sold his soul to the hated faction from down south. Now that is how you do a heel turn. That is how you create a Morecambe moment. And that was how we laid the ground work for James Curtin to become Rockstar Spud. By the next show, Last Fight at the Prom that

September, the Rockstar character was in full effect.

The Firm invasion continue to be the white-hot angle that carried us through 2008. As well as cementing Spud's heel turn, the storyline also solidified another former FWA stalwart as an unlikely babyface.

Paul 'Stixx' Grint had been a career bad guy. As one of Alex Shane's security lackeys in the FWA and later the tag team championship partner of Martin Stone, Stixx's menacing glare, shaven head and methodical, power-based style screamed 'villain'. I was the first UK booker to realise that Stixx was such a relaxed and friendly chap in real life, that he would actually make the transition to fan favourite with consummate ease.

So Stixx turned face at Goldrush 2008. By standing up to Stone, the man who Stixx teamed with to win the FWA Tag Team Titles at The Dome on our famous NOAH Limits show three years earlier, the Nottingham powerhouse became an automatic major league hero. He began the night as Stevie Knight's bodyguard until The Shining Light dispensed with his services after The Heavyweight House of Pain failed to defeat Knight's rival Sam Slam, then Stixx turned on Stevie and laid him out to booming approval from the fans.

Incidentally, the loss to Sam was Stixx's last defeat in Morecambe for eight and a half years. This run became Lancashire's answer to The Undertaker staying unbeaten for years at WrestleMania. Stixx's incredible series of victories was known as The Stixx Streak and the long undefeated stint helped him become Morecambe's biggest babyface.

Back to Vendetta 2008, where the ex-partners Stixx and Stone engaged in a pulsating 'non sanctioned brawl', a heart-stopping fight that spread all around The Dome and ended when Stone attacked Stixx with a lump hammer, laying him out. Such was the brutality of Martin's assault with a deadly weapon, we actually had a few complaints from parents and grandparents who accompanied their minors to the event. Perhaps it *was* too violent for a family show. But then again, that was the idea. I wanted to portray Stone and his gang as despicable human beings who would stop at nothing to take down the XWA. I also wanted to create a storyline reason for Stixx to miss the next show, which he was unavailable for, and for him to seek revenge on Stone next time they crossed paths.

My theory when booking top heels was always to make them look unbeatable for as long as possible. Have them win all the time through nefarious means and build the 'heat'. Make the fans believe they can't be stopped. That way, when their reign of terror was finally brought to a shuddering halt, their demise became a 'Morecambe moment' and made the babyface who conquered them into an even bigger hero. This was my plan for Martin Stone.

At Last Fight, in my role as popular authority figure, I confronted my arch-nemesis Martin in the ring and made a challenge. I would sign him to a four-match contract. If he won all four bouts, I would close down the XWA for good. But if The Guvnor lost any of these matches, he would end his violent siege and never set foot in Morecambe again.

Stone agreed with a disdainful smirk and signed the contract. But then the lights went out. When they came back on, El Ligero was perched on the top turnbuckle. The Mexican Sensation firmly turned the tables on The Firm for what they did to him at Vendetta, by surprising them with their own 'lights out' gimmick. The Los Sancho hero then flew at Stone, knocking the East End hard man hard onto his back. I immediately called for the bell and the first of my sworn enemy's four contracted matches was under way.

The heat was breathtaking as I remained at ringside, cheerleading El Ligero on and urging the crowd to get behind the underdog luchador, which they did with increasing enthusiasm. Sadly for them, Stone was able to fight back and score the pinfall with his ropes-assisted DDT, known as the London Bridge. But that match had probably one of the loudest responses from the fans we ever had in Morecambe, and that's saying something. There is a cracking photo of the aftermath of this bout, where the beaten Ligero is laying across the middle rope and I'm behind him, staring angrily at the victorious Stone.

So at this point, everything was on the line. The Morecambe fans knew that Martin Stone was just three wins away from obliterating the XWA. They were absolutely desperate to see him lose and the company saved from destruction. This angle had such incredible momentum.

But then, came a problem. And the course of UK wrestling

history was changed.

The next show was Gold Rush on February 7 2009. My plan was that Martin Stone would defeat the comebacking Stixx in a No Holds Barred match and then end the evening by winning the 15-man over-the-top rope Gold Rush rumble. This would not only notch up his second and third consecutive wins of the four match challenge series, putting himself on the brink of finishing the XWA, but every year the rumble winner earned himself a championship contest too. Had things gone to plan, the main event of War on the Shore could have had one hell of a cataclysmic stipulation. Stone would have the chance to not only finish the XWA once and for all, but add further insult by leaving Morecambe with our heavyweight title belt in his thieving hands.

Anticipating the big blow-off to the feud, Mark and I paid for a brand new XWA Heavyweight Championship belt to be manufactured in Australia, no less. With leather straps and the bright orange letters 'XWA' etched across the middle of a generously large silver plate, this title was one of the most striking on the entire British professional wrestling circuit. A thing of beauty. And a prize worth having, that would cement the importance of our British Heavyweight Title.

But then Martin revealed he'd 'double booked' himself for a show in Germany, the same night as Gold Rush. He apologised and informed me he wouldn't be able to compete in Morecambe after all. And although I'd 'signed him to a four-match contract' according to the storyline, there were in actuality no legal contracts in British wrestling. There was nothing I could do about it.

Now usually whenever a wrestler pulled out of a show, I shrugged it off, either found a replacement or rationalised that I was saving money on a wage and quickly rewrote the script. Nobody was indispensable. That was my attitude. But when Martin Stone told me he couldn't appear at Gold Rush 2009, I was crestfallen. Everything was building up towards a meticulously planned conclusion to The Firm v the XWA feud. But with Stone missing, the momentum was stopped dead. And I had no idea what to do next.

In hindsight, Stone's withdrawal was the best thing that could have happened. And it is a lesson for all wrestling bookers. No creative obstacle is insurmountable. And sometimes your back-up plan turns out to be better than what was originally intended.

For months, Dann Read had been bending my ear during our regular late-night telephone conversations that I should make Rockstar Spud my heavyweight champion. I kind of laughed it off, at first. Spud was the *Flyweight* Champion. Physically he was not a heavyweight, by any stretch of the imagination. Even though his Rockstar persona was a riot, I just didn't see him as *the guy*. Besides, my future plans for my main championship were at the time, set in Stone, if you'll excuse the pun.

But when Martin pulled out, Dann's words echoed in my ears. And I decided my back-up plan would be to book Spud in Stone's place.

It made sense. Spud was the second most hated member of The Firm and his stock had risen further since his heel turn. He had proved his worth as a main eventer on our previous show - XWA Battle of Britain at Lancaster and Morecambe College on November 1 2008. That night, he once again defeated El Ligero in a streetfight to retain the British Flyweight Title and was absolutely outstanding in a promo segment involving RJ Singh, myself and reality TV contestant Luke Marsden, a former GPW ring announcer who had been on Big Brother that year.

Spud was pure dynamite on the mic at Battle of Britain, an absolute revelation as an entertainingly irritating little sod. Since becoming Rockstar Spud, Jay had developed into an electrifying performer and was extremely reliable, humble and professional. At that point, I still didn't see him actually *winning* the championship but he was definitely a solid reserve choice as number one contender.

So that night, another sell-out at The Dome, Spud wrestled Stixx in the opening bout, losing by disqualification. Then in the main event, he ousted Joey Hayes to win the Gold Rush rumble. The crowd reaction wasn't quite what it surely would have been had Martin Stone triumphed, because the stakes weren't as high. But long-term, it definitely turned out to be the right call.

XWA Gold Rush 2009 was also the night when The Manchester Massive split up when Declan O'Connor turned on Joey Hayes.

Remember, the chase is more important than the capture - just like in romantic relationships. The longer I could keep a storyline going, the more I could hook the audience, get them to desperately want the pay-off and keep them coming back for more. So I laid out stories, like The Firm invasion and the Johnny Phere reinstatement campaign, that ran for at least a year. I generally had an idea of how these tales would start and finish. Granted, I wasn't always quite sure *how* I would get to the end. But as long as there were enough twists and turns along the way, I knew the Morecambe fans would stay emotionally invested and react the way I wanted them to when the climax finally came.

The storyline of the Manchester Massive split, feud and reunion actually lasted *four years*.

I have known both Declan and Joey (real name Damian Shovelton) since they were teenagers. Both came through the GPW training school in Wigan and were involved at the dawn of the FutureShock academy in Manchester in 2004, which Declan helped to set up. They were real-life mates, so we threw them together in the FWA in 2005 as The Manchester Massive, a pair of mischievous street chavs.

The team had a modicum of success down south. But in Morecambe, they were huge stars, like a Manchester version of The Hardy Boyz circa 2000. Not in terms of in-ring daredevil antics, they weren't anywhere near as acrobatic as Matt and Jeff. But they had a similar bond with our audience. The XWA fans absolutely loved these two cheeky chaps who bounded to the ring full of energy and enthusiasm in their Burberry baseball caps, black vests and bright yellow PVC fireman's pants.

Dec and Joey bounced off each other with their witty banter and had close-knit chemistry as a tag team. They came across like ordinary young lads out to have a laugh and so the fans easily identified with them. For me, it was the fact that O'Connor and Hayes had such different personalities that made the partnership work so well. Declan had a smart mouth and was a wind-up merchant supreme. Joey was the quieter one, the straight man, and the more skilful athlete. The XWA fans also liked them for different reasons. Declan was flashy and authentic. In the ring, he was really just being himself and didn't need to exaggerate his character - he was already over-the-top without having to turn up the volume. While Joey, with his fringey mop of brown hair and model good looks, was the heart-throb of the tandem. Teenage girls, especially, adored him.

By early 2008, Joey was progressing at a rapid rate, while Declan wasn't improving, wasn't particularly dedicated and was gaining a reputation for his inability to keep his mouth shut and stay out of trouble. Not that he really cared. He used to say to me that Morecambe was the only place he wanted to wrestle, because it was so much fun.

Over the years I cut Declan a lot of slack. He was like the naughty little schoolboy at the back of the class, desperate for attention, but he didn't really mean any harm. I knew there was a good person behind all the bravado, because of the way he treated my son Owen. On show days, Declan would always take time to talk to Owen, who was only 10 years old at the time. My eldest lad really looked up to Declan and said he was his favourite wrestler. So I always gave 'The Manchester Devil' the benefit of the doubt.

But I heard the whispers from British wrestling insiders. "Joey is better than Declan...Joey is going to be a star...Declan is holding him back." And I admit, long-term I could see that Joey had a potential as a singles wrestler. In early 2008 he was developing into Shawn Michaels to Declan's Marty Jannetty.

So I did what I always do. Because remember, real-life situations often make the best storylines.

It began on March 1 2008 at our trusty back-up venue, The Hexagon at Lancaster and Morecambe College. That night, I booked a different kind of show called Best of the North West. Thanks to the GPW and FutureShock training schools, there was a lot of up-and-coming young talent in our region at the time. So the intention for this show was to only feature wrestlers from the North West - from Manchester, Liverpool, Wigan, Warrington, Southport and anywhere else nearby. This was partly to save money on travel expenses. But also, it was a great way to put the spotlight on the North West and say to the rest of the UK wrestling scene 'hey, we've got something good going on up here'. Alongside XWA regulars like The Massive, Dirk Feelgood and Johnny Phere, we also brought in a young CJ

Banks and Danny Hope to be part of that show.

When I say it was the intention to only use North West grapplers, on the afternoon of the event came an opportunity that was too good to pass up.

Hours before first bell, Mark and I were having a snack in the McDonald's drive-through opposite the venue when my mobile phone rang and a voice came down the line.

"Hi, this is Bryan Danielson."

On the afternoon of March 1 2008, American star Bryan Danielson, the former Ring of Honor champion, a man regarded by many experts at the time as the best wrestler in the world, was in the midst of a European tour. He was supposed to catch a flight from Manchester Airport to compete on a show in Germany. But, he explained, the plane had been cancelled, leaving him marooned in the UK with no work that evening. So he asked...

"I understand you have a show tonight. Would there be a spot for me?"

I mulled this over for a minute and replied.

"No, sorry Bryan. You're too expensive and besides, this show is only for wrestlers from the North West of England."

Well, that's what I would have replied. Had I been completely stupid.

What really happened was I told Bryan that yes, of course I could offer him a last-minute place on that night's XWA show in Morecambe.

I quickly negotiated a fee (which wasn't too expensive at all), gave Bryan directions to the venue and told him to come along. And I also agreed that he could bring John 'Bad Bones' Klinger, a German wrestler he was travelling with, and they could battle each other in the opening match.

So that's what happened. Danielson, wrestling under a mask as The American Dragon, pinned Bad Bones with a small package that night at little old Lancaster and Morecambe College in front of 250 fans.

Six years later, Bryan Danielson, now known as Daniel Bryan, captured the WWE Title at WrestleMania XXX at the New Orleans Superdome as 75,000 ecstatic fans chanted his catchphrase "YES!

YES! YES!" Meanwhile a global audience of more than one million people tuned in on pay-per-view or subscribed to the WWE Network to see Bryan become the world heavyweight champion.

I think I will still be telling my grandkids the story of how Daniel Bryan called *me* and asked *me* if he could be on *my* show in Morecambe when I'm 90 years old.

Anyway, in the main event at the college that night, Joey Hayes scored a massive upset pinfall victory over the former XWA Champion Robbie Brookside to win a six-way elimination bout and lift the Best of the North West trophy. Afterwards, Declan appeared overjoyed at the biggest win of his friend's career and the two best buddies embraced in centre-ring as the crowd went wild.

But this had planted a seed. Joey held the impressive-looking large silver Best of the North West Cup, which was now established as the XWA's third singles championship alongside the Heavyweight and Flyweight titles. And he had done this on his own, by beating the great Brookside without Declan's help.

For the next year, the behind-the-scenes whispers that Declan was the 'weak link' of The Manchester Massive became part of the show. Heel opponents of The Massive rubbed Declan's face in the fact that Joey was clearly better than him. Throughout the rest of 2008, the hot-headed O'Connor desperately tried to prove that he was just as talented as Hayes, only for his overeagerness to cost The Massive numerous matches.

At Gold Rush 2009, matters came to a head. Declan apologised to Joey for letting him down, for costing him wins, and promised that he would "pay him back". But then Declan suffered a leg injury during a match with 'Dangerous' Damon Leigh. This meant he had to pull out of the 15-man rumble. In his partner's absence, Joey Hayes shone. He and Spud drew numbers one and two in the Gold Rush, and battled right the way through to the end.

At this point, Dec came limping out to ringside, seemingly to bravely offer Joey support in his quest to throw Spud over the top rope and become number one contender to the XWA Heavyweight Title. But then as Hayes and Spud were battling on the ring apron, and the Rockstar looked set to plummet to the wooden floor giving Joey the victory, Declan did the unthinkable.

O'Connor tripped Hayes, allowing Spud to eliminate Joey.

Months of simmering jealousy and frustration, of hearing from his peers that he was the weak link of The Manchester Massive, came to a head. The treacherous Declan, after showing that his 'injury' was just a ruse, then gave Joey one hell of a beating to cement the break-up of the XWA's most popular duo. And in doing so, he "paid Hayes back", just as he'd warned him earlier in the night.

The response from the sold-out crowd was rather lukewarm.

I have said many times over the years that 'everything works in Morecambe' because the fans are so responsive. But The Manchester Massive split didn't really click. Our regulars were cold on the idea of Declan and Joey fighting each other. They just didn't want to see it. They liked them as a tag team, but wouldn't buy into them as deadly enemies.

Declan and Joey tried their best to make the feud work. O'Connor turned up his natural cockiness to the max. Hayes played the role of the confused victim who didn't really want to fight his best friend. They wrestled each other twice in 2009 - at War on the Shore and Vendetta. They were really good bouts and they shared the wins. But there was a spark missing.

It was obvious we had to put The Manchester Massive back together. So in 2011, we did a big reunion angle, stretching it out over a full year. At first, Joey was reluctant to trust his best friend after the betrayal and Declan had to prove his worth. Finally they buried the hatchet to a joyful response from the fans and teamed up one final time in an emotional bout against The Blackpool Blonds at Gold Rush 2012.

I am extremely proud of The Manchester Massive's four-year tale. It didn't go exactly like I hoped, but I loved the fact that it was an episodic and logical story with a beginning, a middle and a satisying end, which played on real-life emotions of insecurity, envy, trust, friendship and betrayal.

It was fantastic to work with Dec and Joey throughout that period of time. I always looked forward to them arriving at The Dome so I could describe my vision for the next chapter in their story. They were both always excited to hear my plans and always gave 100% in an attempt to deliver what I asked for. Acting didn't come naturally to either of them, because like most young grapplers in their early 20s, they preferred to just get in the ring and wrestle. In-ring promos were a real test for them. But they were always up for the challenge.

As a result, The Manchester Massive became another massive reason why the XWA did such great business during those years.

Declan eventually drifted away from wrestling completely and I haven't seen him since 2012. I miss the cheeky sod! He was really underrated as an in-ring performer and there's no telling how good he could have been. But he has moved on with his life and in 2016, he got married. I was delighted for him.

As for Joey Hayes? Well, there's plenty more on Joey to come later...

Back to early 2009 and the Rockstar Spud/Martin Stone conundrum. I now had to decide what to do about my planned April main event. I really felt like I had to end the big angle at War on the Shore, which was traditionally our biggest show of the year. Bottom line was, I didn't feel like I could rely on Martin to see this storyline through to its most satisfying conclusion. Not that this was Stone's fault. The guy was in demand all over Europe and WWE was starting to take notice. What if he won at War on the Shore, but was then unavailable for the next show? I couldn't take the chance.

On the other hand, Sam Slam getting rid of Martin Stone in only the second bout of a possible quartet felt like a disappointingly tepid way to end a storyline that had such potential. Besides, Spud was now the number one contender. Why would I give Stone, my sworn enemy, a title shot he hadn't earned? Remember, logic and continuity are all-important. But for this show, I was forced to go against my principle. It would teach me a valuable lesson to never 'book myself into a corner' ever again.

Still, my overriding concern was that I needed to announce a main event for War on the Shore that would excite the fans and sell tickets. So I went with the original plan. Sam Slam v Martin Stone for the XWA Title. My rationale was that I was so confident that Sam was the man to rid me of the scourge of The Firm, I agreed to make it a championship match. And Spud, being subordinate to Stone, agreed to put his own title aspirations on hold to allow the Sam-Guvnor clash to happen.

The War on the Shore 2009 main event was a classic brawl and had a memorable conclusion. With Stone on the verge of victory, the lights went out. And when they came back on, Johnny Phere was in the ring. The Psychotic Warrior, then in the midst of his exile from British wrestling and his campaign to be reinstated, picked up Stone and deposited him centre-ring with his spinning spinebuster known as the Ram Slam. This allowed Sam to score the victory and retain the championship. The furious Stone was then physically ejected from the building by a posse of babyfaces and stewards, as the delighted fans serenaded him with "Na na na na, hey hey hey, goodbye!" True to the stipulation, The Guvnor of London Town was never seen in the XWA again. And Sam Slam was awarded the brand new XWA championship belt.

It was a Morecambe moment.

Storyline-wise, I'd got out of Dodge. Johnny Phere's intervention made perfect sense. "YOU'VE GOT NO CHOICE BUT TO BRING ME BACK NOW LAMBERT! I JUST SAVED THE XWA!" bellowed the tattooed crazy man, as he left The Dome after gatecrashing the main event. The downfall of The Firm had turned into a crucial plot development in what would now become our *new* biggest storyline, Johnny Phere's crusade to return to the ring.

Meanwhile, Spud was still on a roll. After scoring the winning pinfall in a six-man Firm v XWA match at Last Fight 2008 then emerging triumphant in the Gold Rush, he had also just pinned Sam Bailey at War on the Shore to retain the Flyweight belt. Bailey, a young graduate of the FutureShock training school who in later years would become part of the ITV World of Sport wrestling revival, was a talented lad who wrestled on a few shows for us from 2008 to 2010. I renamed him 'Tiger' Bailey after the world's number one golfer Tiger Woods and because we already had one Sam in the XWA, Sam Slam our heavyweight champion. In hindsight, this was a strange decision and looking back, I don't really understand what the hell I was thinking. The flyweight Bailey had an Afro like a teenage Michael Jackson and Sam Slam was built like The Incredible Hulk. No-one was ever likely to mistake them for each other.

Anyway, at Vendetta 2009, with his head growing ever bigger and his promos becoming more and more boastful and annoying with every victory, Spud engaged in an impromptu match with Stevie Knight. This would turn out to be the final bout of Stevie's long wrestling career and a 'passing of the torch' moment from one loudmouth to another.

The Shining Light retired and moved to Cyprus after losing the XWA Title to Sam Slam the previous September. He had a great run in Morecambe, particularly after turning heel in 2007. That was when we formulated a new persona based on his appearance that year on hit Channel 4 game show Deal or No Deal, hosted by Noel Edmonds, where Stevie claimed to have won "tens of thousands of pounds". Well, it was £10,000 and a penny, to be exact.

Now, Noel Edmonds has history with Morecambe. In the mid-1990s, riding high on prime time Saturday night TV show Noel's House Party, the bearded TV host and entrepreneur struck a deal with our local council to open a theme park in the seaside resort called Blobby Land. This adventure playground for kids was based on the home of Noel's telly sidekick, a gelatinous pink and yellow-spotted creature called Mr Blobby. An accident-prone buffoon who became a cult figure by embarrassing celebrity guests on Noel's House Party, Blobby was so popular at the time he even had a number one hit record, keeping Take That off the top at Christmas 1993. So our local councillors thought a Mr Blobby-themed attraction would pull record crowds to little old Morecambe. But it didn't. The theme park was a flop and closed after just a few months. Edmonds blamed the council and ended up in a legal battle which cost local taxpayers millions of pounds. Finally, the District Auditor ruled that the council was indeed culpable, having agreed to sign up to a flawed concept without investigating its chances of success more thoroughly.

Our council's reputation for bumbling later inspired me to create an XWA character called Mike Lovejoy, an over-officious health and safety freak in a yellow hard hat and hi-vis jacket who claimed to work for the local authority. Lovejoy was played brilliantly by FutureShock and NGW referee Mike Fitzgerald and was hated by fans about as much as Morecambe residents loathed the local council after the Blobby debacle.

After the Blobby episode, Noel Edmonds had 'heat' in

Morecambe too. So I again took full advantage. Stevie reinvented himself as Mr Deal or No Deal, flaunting his prize win and supposed friendship with Edmonds while wearing a dazzling all-white suit that made him look like The Man From Del Monte off the old TV ads for tinned fruit. And he was suitably offended when one night The Manchester Massive cheekily handed out Mr Blobby masks to the Morecambe fans, who then began to taunt the portly Stevie with chants of "BLOBBY! BLOBBY!"

Stevie was gloriously condescending during his 14-month run as Mr Deal or No Deal and the fans loved to hate him. The highlight was his 2008 Gold Rush rumble victory, which got so much heat the angry Dome fans began pelting him with rubbish as he revelled in his treacherous win. But by then his 17-year wrestling career had taken its toll physically. Even though he was still in his mid-30s and some grapplers carry on into their 50s or even 60s, the real-life Steve Pendle was just about ready to retire. By 2008 he was out of shape and taking way too many tablets for the constant back pain he was suffering. He struggled through his unsuccessful title challenge of Jonny Storm at War on the Shore that year, but afterwards he was utterly exhausted.

But Stevie knew the plan was for him to become champion, so he battled on manfully for two more shows. I desperately wanted him to win the title for two reasons. One, so Sam Slam could take the belt off a white-hot heel, which Stevie undoubtedly was. And two, because my old pal deserved the accolade. I wanted him to look back on his career and proudly say that he held the XWA British Heavyweight Championship, the title with direct lineage to the FWA (today the Alpha Omega Wrestling Championship has that particular honour). So on July 5 2008 at Vendetta in a four-way elimination match also including Phere and Slam, The Shining Light gave Jonny Storm a tombstone piledriver on the title belt to end The Wonderkid's 15-month reign. The fans, who had been deliriously cheering on Storm just moments before, were stunned into complete silence by the result.

Because it's Real in Morecambe.

Knight dropped the championship to Slam at XWA Last Fight as planned, then uprooted to warmer climes. But on a brief visit back home in summer 2009, he agreed to be part of one last Morecambe event.

As far as the fans at XWA Vendetta 2009 were concerned, Stevie and his good pal Richard Young were only there to sit amongst them in The Dome's tiered seating area and watch the show. That was, until Spud began goading Knight on the microphone, calling him fat and washed-up. This led to a brief brawl between Stevie, clad in his street clothes, and the self-styled Baby Jesus of British Wrestling, Spud. Knight couldn't take many bumps by that point, so he was on the attack throughout, pummeling the upstart rocker all over the building until the Rockstar eventually cheated to win by pinfall.

Despite the loss, Stevie took the opportunity to thank the Morecambe fans over the microphone. The wily old soul was then given a guard of honour by the XWA wrestlers in a respectful send-off as he waved goodbye to The Dome for the last time. I am proud that Stevie Knight chose to finish his career in Morecambe, scene of some of his greatest nights. And Spud was honoured to be the opponent in Stevie's last ever match, because he has the utmost admiration for him.

So now it was finally time for Spud to face Sam Slam for the XWA championship at Last Fight at the Prom 2009. The Rockstar was undefeated since his turn the previous summer and the string of wins, when combined with the force of his personality, gave him credibility as a contender. But still, I feared the Morecambe fans wouldn't buy little Spud as a viable challenge for the human bulldozer that was Sam Slam. Mark Kay was in agreement. He couldn't see Spud as a heavyweight champion either.

Oh God, how wrong we were.

I can't remember why or when I changed my mind. Either Dann Read's persistent badgering finally sold me on the idea, or I had become gradually impressed with Spud's displays throughout 2009, or I felt it was time for Sam to lose the title and Spud was in the right place at the right time, or because I wanted Johnny Phere to be champion long-term and he had to win the belt from a bad guy. Perhaps it was a combination of all four.

It was a late decision, that's for sure, because I only told Jay he was winning the belt on the day of the show. I called him into The

Dome ticket office and broke the news. Spud looked up at me, his face a mixture of disbelief and pride.

"No-one had really looked at me as their number one guy before and I was kind of taken aback," said Spud, when I talked to him about that moment many years later, in July 2016.

"In and out of the ring I always believe that I'm eight feet tall and I can fight anyone, because I'm not scared of anybody. But when the company says you're the top guy...it was out of nowhere. I'd just been given the Flyweight belt as well and I didn't think I'd be put in a spot where I'd be holding every belt.

"And I still looked at it as the FWA belt. So it was a big deal in that respect. Even today, the Morecambe belt has got that lineage back to the original FWA. It's sad the fans don't remember that. But at the time, because FWA had only closed down two years before, to me it was like winning the FWA World Title. And if it had been the peak of the FWA, I would have been absolutely basking in it! But ever since I'd turned heel in Morecambe, we'd created a whole different company and it was such fun, because I would go out there and those fans would f___ing hate me! I loved that whole time with the XWA."

Last Fight at the Prom 2009 was a watershed moment in the careers of three other gentlemen too because it propelled them from obscurity right into the spotlight. I'm talking about Gil 'Axl Rage' Collins, James 'James Drake' Dowell and Matt 'Stallion' Whitfield. The members of Team Rockstar.

In January 2009, Mark Kay and I opened our own wrestling training school in Morecambe. This came about after we were approached, completely out of the blue, by a contact of mine I knew from my main job as chief reporter for the town's newspaper.

Martin Shenton is a TV and film stuntman of some repute. His CV includes roles in the James Bond film Tomorrow Never Dies and as a stunt double for famous faces such as Sylvester Stallone and Coronation Street's Ken Barlow. The renowned dangerman, who routinely throws himself off buildings and down flights of stairs for a living, owns a facility in Morecambe called Regent Park Studios, where he runs training courses for budding stuntmen. Back in 2009, Regent Park Studios also housed film production classes, martial arts, trampolining, even an after school club for kiddies. It had a large matted area on the second floor and a large empty room on the top floor with loads of space for a ring. Such a unique multi-purpose venue, Martin figured, would be the perfect home for a professional wrestling school. But he needed our expert help to get it off the ground.

Martin told us he could obtain external funding to part-pay for a new wrestling ring. The rest of the money he would invest himself. All we would have to do, was run the school for him. We wouldn't make any money directly as first, as all fees would go towards paying back Martin's initial outlay. But, we realised there would be major benefits to us in the long-term. If we had our own ring based in Morecambe and could use Shenton's van to transport it, it would take away the stress and expense of hiring a ring for a show. For the past few years, we'd hired one belonging to Ashley Steel, who wrestled as the flamboyant Jules Lambrini. Ash was reliable, but he also lived in Worcester, and our worst nightmare was that his van would break down one day on the 160-mile motorway drive to Lancashire, leaving us up the creek without a ring for one of our shows. Shenton's scheme offered us peace of mind for the future.

Also at that time, aside from friends and family, and the odd volunteer, we had no crew to speak of. A new eager crop of wrestling trainees would be a ready-made team of helpers on show days who could put up the ring, take it down and assist us with any other jobs that needed doing.

And we kind of liked the idea of opening a training school, of guiding and producing a new crop of young wrestling stars. There were dozens of other schools around the country. So why not us? It would demonstrate that the XWA was a growing company.

So we agreed to Martin's deal and put him in touch with Ashley Steel, who built a brand new ring for him. Then we started to advertise the school and, after much discussion between myself and Mark, appointed 'Dangerous' Damon Leigh as our first head trainer. Our criteria was simple. We wanted somebody who was based in the North West who didn't have far to travel. We wanted someone with stature and experience who the trainees would respect. And we wanted someone reliable who could be there to host weekly training sessions on a Sunday. I have known the real life Damon Bradley, who is from Manchester, since the FWA days and he fitted the bill on all counts.

On the first day of training, a large group of around 20 excited and enthusiastic students turned up at Regent Park Studios. Among them were Kieran Engelke (more on him later), Gil Elkin and Matt Whitfield (who hates being called Matt, he prefers Stallion, so I will call him Matt.) James Dowell was there the second week. All three soon became regulars.

It was something of a surprise to see Gil there, because I already knew him. The 23-year-old from Lytham St Annes had been training for years with FutureShock Wrestling, even competed on their debut show in 2004 (I was the ring announcer for that). So I knew Gil had talent and with his flowing long blond locks and wrestler's build, he had a distinctive look. But during his FutureShock years, he'd never quite had the self-belief.

I remember one time in 2005 myself and Alex Shane offered Gil an opportunity to wrestle on an FWA event at The Dome. A nervous Elkin declined, saying he wasn't ready. Alex told him he'd just made a big mistake. Alex didn't say this in a malicious way. He wanted to make a point. At the time, many young wrestlers would have killed for a spot on an FWA card. The UK scene was highly competitive and by turning down a chance like that, Gil had just relegated himself to the bottom of the pile for further opportunities.

Gil soon fell off the radar of the North West wrestling scene. But by turning up at a brand new training school, willing to start at the bottom again, Elkin made a huge statement as far as I was concerned. He was ready to correct his mistake, work hard and if given a second chance, this time he'd make the most of it.

I didn't know James Dowell, but was aware he had a little bit of past experience. This was obvious as soon as he set foot in the ring. He was technically sound and picked up new things quickly. He was so smooth with his wrestling skills, so focussed and driven, and had such a smart mind for the business, that I was surprised to learn that he was only 15 years old.

Matt, I knew from XWA shows. A gregarious and sarcastic motormouth from South Shields, he'd been a fixture at Morecambe

Dome events for the past year or so. As a fan, you could hardly miss him. He always sat in the front row. He always wore a colourful bandana, which made him look like a Geordie version of his hero, the former WWF superstar and commentator Jesse 'The Body' Ventura. And he always heckled the wrestlers, in a loud North East accent, often mocking the bad guys with cuttingly sharp one-liners.

Stallion also used to write reviews of XWA shows for the internet in an entertaining and witty style. It was obvious he had a mind for the business. Like Dowell, he too had some past experience of wrestling training and with his burly torso and Popeye arms, he looked like a tough guy. He also had charisma to burn.

Despite the eight-year age gap, Gil and James quickly became close and, as both lived in the Blackpool area, the blond-haired pair began to travel to the weekly training sessions together. It was clear from an early stage that they were the two most talented trainees we had. With Stallion, it was a different matter. He wasn't gifted as a wrestler. But boy, did he have the gift of the gab. In terms of his larger-than-life personality, verbal skills and the way he dressed in bandana and frilly coloured shirts like a pirate in a paint factory, Whitfield was light years ahead of everybody else at the school. I knew that even if he didn't make it as an actual competitor, we had to find some kind of spot for him on the show. He was a natural fit for pro wrestling.

So here was I, racking my brains trying to come up with a plausible way for Spud to beat Sam Slam in what was a complete physical mismatch on paper. And then it hit me. We needed outside interference. And lots of it.

I thought about Elkin, Dowell and Whitfield, and how much they'd impressed me at training. And I came up with the idea for Team Rockstar.

On Saturday September 12 2009 at The Dome, the main event was progressing exactly as expected. Sam Slam was giving Spud an absolute shellacking as he threw the tiny challenger around the ring like a human ragdoll. The fans were loving it though, because they longed to see their hero shut Spud's potty mouth permanently. And it looked like they would get their wish. Surely there was absolutely no way in hell that the Rockstar could overcome the ferocious champion.

"I just wanted to make sure I was running from him the entire time," said Spud, reflecting on the match.

"For me, it was all about how to protect Sam. I look at the match now, from the experience I've gained since then, and I could have done so much more to save Sam and make him better. That just comes with years of performing. I did wonder before the match how on earth I was going to beat him and get heat on him."

But then my plan for the finish came into play. Referee Dominic Nix was standing outside the ring when Stallion, who was part of the ring crew that night and was playing the role of our 'chief of security', suddenly smashed the official in the back and knocked him out with a burly forearm. At this, Stallion frantically beckoned to the entranceway, and out came Dowell and Elkin, both dressed in torn-off heavy metal T-shirts and sporting headbands like roadies at an Aerosmith concert. They were soon joined by Anthony 'Juggernaut' Louden, a debuting 20-stone powerhouse who made his name in GPW as their champion and had been contacting me for ages, trying to attain a spot with the XWA. The trio marched to the ring with a purpose.

Spud, Stallion, Dowell, Elkin and Juggernaut soon cornered Sam Slam in the ring. And despite a valiant attempt by the champion to fight them off, the sheer weight of the five-against-one numbers proved decisive as Spud and his new army beat Slam to a pulp. Sam was soon laid out on his back by a Rockstar Spud 'Famouser' move, Team Rockstar threw the dazed Nix back into the ring and, by instinct, the referee - who hadn't seen the illegal assault - counted the decisive one, two, three.

The decision stood. Spud, after using the screwiest tactics imaginable, became the first and only man in history to hold both the XWA Heavyweight and Flyweight titles at the same time. And it was all thanks to his new backing group of Gil and James, his new tour manager Stallion and his hulking new bodyguard Juggernaut.

Then when we stuck a backstage camera on Spud and his new gang of reprobates after his victory, the Rockstar cut loose with an inspired rant which reminded me of Ric Flair's promo after he won the WWF World Title at Royal Rumble 1992. The new champ's post-title win speech was an absolute classic.

"As the Baby Jesus of British Wrestling, the Virgin Mary ain't going to be a virgin no more tonight!" cackled Spud throatily at interviewer Richard Parker. Then the new champ snogged Big Orange (as Stallion had christened the XWA title belt) and jumped up and down on the spot like an overexcited schoolboy.

"I beat the unstoppable Sam Slam! This is the best day of my life! I'm the first double champion in the XWA! I'm God here! Yeahh!"

And then he coughed out a disgusting globule of phlegm onto the floor, before he high-fived his new gaggle of adoring lackeys and continued his celebratory tirade.

"What a Rockstar wants, a Rockstar gets, and when the Rockstar wanted the XWA Heavyweight Championship, the Rockstar made damned sure he had an insurance policy. Ladies, gentlemen, marks of all ages...introducing Team Rockstar!"

So now the new XWA double champion had four men to watch his back. It made perfect sense. Given his physical limitations and sneaky outlook, Spud was always going to need back-up to help him keep hold of his newly-won championship. It was also logical that a pampered Rockstar would have an entire team of hangers-on behind him. And I was rather pleased with how the new boys had performed - although Juggernaut's appearance turned out to be a one-shot deal as he soon retired from wrestling. He was replaced as Spud's bodyguard by an agile 25-stone behemoth from the FutureShock school, a gentle giant called Alex 'Cyanide' Walmsley. The imposing Cyanide had made his name in FutureShock and GPW in a tag team called Lethal Dose with Jack Toxic, a punk rocker who later completely reinvented himself as a technical wrestling wizard. Today he is known as WWE's incomparable English Gentleman, Jack Gallagher.

Meanwhile, I gave Elkin and Dowell new names to go with their new personas. I christened them Blond Jovi and planned to use them as a tag team. Elkin was now Axl Rage - a cross between Guns 'N' Roses front man Axl Rose and Ben Rage, his old ring name from his FutureShock days. Dowell, meanwhile, became JD Sassoon - a combination of his initials and the surname of famed hair products magnate Vidal Sassoon, in tribute to James' magnificent crop of streaked blond locks. They were perfect eye-catching wrestling names for the newcomers and together, Rage and Sassoon rolled easily off the tongue.

Although Sassoon hadn't even turned 16 and was like a streaked blond rabbit in the headlights in front of the camera, I saw enough in training to realise he had limitless potential. By putting him in a stable with Spud, who was by then rapidly becoming the best performer on the UK wrestling scene, JD was bound to learn many tricks of the trade to aid his development. Stallion and Rage also slotted into Team Rockstar seamlessly.

Spud looks back on those days fondly.

"I was given camera time and two lads in James and Gil who were new and green, but I look at them now and they have taken themselves to a whole new level. Especially James.

"And Stallion, much as I rib him all the time, he was a great 'Jim Cornette'. He really was. He'd take the crappy manager bump and even though I didn't need a talker he was still able to be part of the group as a talker, which was brilliant. I loved working with those guys. I loved that whole thing."

During that glorious period of 2008/9, Spud became the star of the show in Morecambe. He rose to the occasion and proved himself a worthy heavyweight champion. He showed exactly why I made the correct decision in putting faith in him as the main man in XWA.

Yes, Dann Read, you heard me. Much as I hate to admit it, you were right all along.

And when little Jay Curtin from Birmingham went on in ensuing years to become a major international TV star with TNA Impact Wrestling in America, I was not only delighted for him, but also for me.

Because now I can proudly state that I was the first promoter to put my company's heavyweight championship around the waist of Rockstar Spud!

CHAPTER 3

THE FWA RETURNS

By 2009, the success of the XWA was helping me regain my wrestling mojo. I was having a great time running my own company and putting on live shows in my home town. We regularly pulled big crowds and we were making money. Life was good.

Meanwhile, down south, there were plans under way for the return of the FWA. It was a comeback that would shake me, and British wrestling, out of our comfort zones.

Those of you who read my first book will know all about Alex Shane, the man who gave me my big break in wrestling in 2002. A former two-time British Heavyweight Champion wrestler, the 6ft 6in Alex was also the head booker of the FWA during its glory years. An incredibly charismatic and intelligent individual, The Showstealer was a fearless promoter and persuasive salesman who put on some of the most talked-about wrestling shows of the noughties and is also the biggest supporter of British wrestling walking the planet. Nobody wanted the Holy Grail more than him. Nobody did more towards trying to achieve it.

Alex had announced his retirement as an in-ring performer in early 2007. This was shortly after neck surgery forced him to miss his scheduled IPW:UK v FWA Final Frontiers match against Martin Stone; the aforementioned Losing Company Must Fold bout where his replacement Flash Barker lost to The Guvnor, forcing FWA to shut down.

Shane then threw himself into brand new promotional projects. And true to form, Alex did nothing by halves.

On April 28 and 29 that year, entrepreneurial Shane joined forces with former FWA Champion Doug Williams to organise an ambitious two-night undertaking called the King of Europe Cup. Held at Liverpool Olympia, the show saw the best independent wrestlers in the world, each representing a different company, battle it out in an elimination tournament. Claudio Castagnoli (Cesaro in WWE), Davey Richards (one half of The Wolves in TNA), WWE superstar Rhyno and Matt Sydal (Evan Bourne in WWE) joined British stand-outs Jody Fleisch, Martin Stone, 'The Zebra Kid' Roy Knight and Pac (Neville in WWE) in the 16-man knockout contest. The shows drew 1,600 people across the two days, made money despite a £40,000 budget (huge by UK wrestling standards) because some fans paid a whopping £85 for seats, and saw USA-based Englishman Nigel McGuinness, representing Ring of Honor, defeat Doug in a terrific final. I was backstage on the second night, working as stage manager, and everything ran really smoothly in comparison to the often chaotic behind-the-curtain runnings of the FWA back in the day.

Alex and I kept in touch over the following year and in summer 2008, he asked me to help him organise TNA's first ever UK tour. Shane was previously the local promoter for Ring of Honor's first tour of Britain in 2006.

I sorted out all the work visa applications for the TNA roster - a painstaking but crucially important task - and was paid handsomely, and promptly, by the Nashville-based company in return. Then Mark Kay and I helped out with various behind-the-scenes tasks at two shows on the tour, at the Liverpool Olympia and Coventry Skydome on June 13 and 14 2008 respectively. I was impressed by how professional and well-organised TNA were as a company, compared to what I'd been used to on the often tin-pot UK wrestling scene back then.

Aside from meeting legendary referee Earl Hebner (of The Montreal Screwjob fame), former Olympic and multi-time world champion Kurt Angle, and TNA founder Jeff Jarrett, my favourite memory from working at the TNA shows came right at the end of the Coventry show. Mark and I were about to leave when tour manager Craig Jenkins collared us and asked us to go and buy Chinese food for the roster. We rushed across the road to the restaurant opposite the venue and bought as much Chinese as we could lay our hands on.

Then we raced back to the TNA tour bus and brought the hot steaming banquet on board, much to the delight of the starving Booker T, Angle, Bobby Roode and company. I don't think a group of wrestlers have ever been as happy to see me in my entire career.

Alex and I continued to chat on the phone throughout 2008, sometimes about wrestling, and sometimes the well-read Showstealer would share his theories on life, religion, the media, education, money, the government and in particular, his many conspiracy theories. He was really into conspiracies at the time.

There were also times when we discussed him maybe making a comeback as a wrestler. The Showstealer hadn't competed in Morecambe for three years and I could see value in him making a big return, especially as his rival Martin Stone was running roughshod over the XWA. They could have that big match they never had. Alex pondered over a comeback decision and eventually agreed to do a Morecambe show. But he just as quickly changed his mind.

But then on September 21 2008, right out of the blue, Alex turned up at an IPW:UK event in Bromley, London, repeatedly big booted Stone in the face, and helped an up-and-comer called Iestyn Rees win the IPW Title. It was then announced that on October 26 2008, Shane and Stone would finally have the match on IPW: UK turf that was supposed to have happened at Final Frontiers 18 months before.

Six days later, in a six-minute, expletive-filled, frighteningly intense YouTube promo, Alex cut loose on The Guvnor in a tirade where he explained that he was about to move to India to find himself spiritually, set up a wrestling school and write a book about his unusual theories on life, which he wanted to call The Unholy Babble. But before he did, he'd agreed to have one last match with Martin Stone. And one of the reasons why he decided to return was because IPW:UK promoter Dan Edler and booker Andy Quildan agreed to make him "the highest paid British wrestler outside of America".

"I don't recall how much he was getting paid but it was higher than we were paying everyone else at the time," said Andy, speaking about it in 2016.

"Alex always wants to make milestones and for a British guy to get an 'import wage' was a big thing for him."

In the promo, rounding on Stone, Alex made a damning indictment of the UK wrestling scene which he claimed, with some justification, had remained stagnant since the FWA had achieved such great things with himself at the helm.

"British wrestling is in the sh__ter!" he yelped.

"And if you're the man that's the Guvnor, at the top of the heap, as far as I'm concerned, you're responsible. You've taken everything I worked for and flushed it down the toilet."

Stone responded with an equally eye-catching YouTube promo, and another demonstration of anything-goes, nothing-off-limits real talk, where he accused Alex of being a hypocrite and a backstabber.

"I have never once said I'm in control of British wrestling," retorted Martin.

"What I have said is, that as the Guvnor, I will put on the best matches possible up and down the country.

"You're going to India, you're going to preach to everyone how wonderful you are. What are you doing for British wrestling? You're a self-centred, egotistical prick. We all know what you're like, I wouldn't trust you as far as I could throw you.

"The massive amount of money Dan and Andy are paying you, I think it's disgusting. You're going to have to f__king kill me to walk out of that place alive."

Alex's YouTube response on October 11 2008 was nine minutes long. He verbally ripped Stone to pieces and also slated British wrestlers in general, who he claimed had bad attitudes and were helping to cause the malaise affecting the UK scene, instead of trying to help move it forward.

"You're bland as f__k Martin," spat The Showstealer.

"You're a seven at best on all things. You haven't got an original bone in your body.

"If you're in something you want to change then you take responsibility. I was backstage (at IPW:UK) and all I heard was 'British wrestling is really s__t, I miss the FWA, I'm thinking of jacking it in". Well f__ing jack it in, or do something about it!

"All I heard was a bunch of whiny, pissy little girls, moaning, whinging, saying how bad it is. Well if you love wrestling so much, don't think that turning up, getting your pay cheque, walking through the curtain acting like a superstar is all you're here to do. I'm earning my money, what are you doing?"

After such a convincingly hateful build-up, the eventual Alex Shane v Martin Stone match - billed as 'the last time Alex Shane will ever wrestle in the UK' - was an understandably mega-heated 30-minute brawl. Alex put Martin over (lost) to 'pass the torch' to the Guvnor and then true to his word, went off to live in India.

Of course wrestling being wrestling, and Alex being Alex, this was far from 'the last time he would ever wrestle in the UK'. Just four months later, Shane came home and returned to IPW:UK, where he won the promotion's annual Extreme Measures tournament in Swanley, Kent. On April 18 2009, Alex knocked out Iestyn Rees in Swanley to become IPW:UK Champion, a title he would lose to Leroy Kincaide that September.

So by spring 2009, Alex was firmly ensconced back at the heart of the UK wrestling scene. But what happened next, still kind of came out of nowhere.

Alex asked me if I'd mind if the FWA came back.

He explained that a former wrestler called Tony Simpson wanted to set up a brand new wrestling company. Tony had competed for both FWA and IPW:UK as 'Superstar' Tony Sefton in around 2004/5 and had some promoting experience running shows for IPW in Swanley, Kent.

"It all started in 2008 when I decided I wanted to make a comeback to the ring, or more accurately start all over again," said Tony in 2016.

"I love performing but in the Tony Sefton days I thought I was a lot better than I actually was, so I got lazy, stopped training, saw my match quality become embarrassingly poor and became a bit of an arse. When I woke up to that fact, I decided I needed to call it a day.

"Any ex-wrestler will tell you, it's extremely hard to replace that gap in your life. So a few years later, I'd grown up a lot, realised how much I missed the squared circle and decided to start all over again from the very bottom as a trainee and work back up the ladder but with a more mature mindset to take it seriously.

"So, I started training at IPW:UK, my old home, with Dan Edler, Andy Quildan, Andy Simmonz and RJ Singh and I loved it. I felt fitter and more athletic than I did before.

"As a trainee does, I started going to the IPW shows and helping where I could. During one of the last shows at the Bromley Civic Hall, I was sitting with Alex Shane, a very good friend of mine, watching the show and talking about the state of British wrestling. I guess my feeling was that the talent had stepped up to a fantastic level but the storylines, production and overall product hadn't kept up with them.

"In the weeks following those conversations I thought a lot about my position and my comeback campaign. I came to the conclusion that maybe I could be more of an asset to British wrestling and the talent if I invested time, money and focus on helping put shows together.

"After meeting Dan and Andy a few times, we had decided that I would run a couple of IPW branded shows. I think I was seen as a bit of a 'money mark', which is fine, because that's all I really was at that point. My professional experience was in management of technology and business change delivery, financial services, running a local magazine and web design business, and property investment with a fair stint as a pro wrestler. So I had a lot to learn and had just put myself in a position where I had a very short time to learn it.

"Dan and I, who have known each other for many years, clashed on a few things in the lead up to my first show, which is understandable as it was a brand he spent years trying to build. I'd just walked in with my ideas and sort of took over for these two shows and can imagine what that was like for him. At this point I realised that implementing my longer term ideas was going to be challenging without more control.

"One day Alex and I were discussing my frustrations and I said 'We should bring FWA back'. What was originally a throwaway comment became a new vision in my mind. FWA was a key brand in British wrestling's first big step up in the mid-noughties and I thought it would be great to revive the brand again. I also felt it would add to the feeling that something big is going to happen, as it did in the original FWA.

"I ended up getting set on the idea and after weeks of going back and forth with Alex, got him to agree to bring his experience to the table and work with me on it."

So Alex phoned me. He explained that Tony wanted to revive the glory days of the FWA and use the Frontier Wrestling Alliance name. As I'd been head booker when the FWA closed its doors, Alex wanted to know if I had any objections.

If it had been really up to me, I would have said yes, I object. I am a wrestling traditionalist, and I believe that match stipulations should be adhered to as much as possible. Or at the very least, like in the Johnny Phere reinstatement situation, there should be a logical storyline reason for them to be reversed. IPW:UK beat FWA in a Losing Promotion Must Cease to Exist match. But now, just over two years later, Tony and Alex wanted to raise FWA from the ashes as if this had never happened. It didn't sit right with me. What's the point in having stipulations in the first place if they don't mean anything in the long-run?

But Alex being his usual persuasive self, he convinced me it was a good idea. Besides, I didn't have any claim on the name 'FWA'. It wasn't trademarked. I appreciated the courtesy call but they had the legal right to do whatever they wanted as far as I was concerned.

The other reason why Alex and Tony needed my co-operation was because I owned the FWA Title belt. But, as you will recall, I'd just had a new XWA Title made, so really had no further need for the FWA strap. So I sold the championship to the FWA. As part of the deal, Alex returned to Morecambe - not only to collect the belt in person - but to appear at War on the Shore 2009.

That night, the Showstealer and Martin Stone waged verbal war on the microphone in another heated segment between the two. Then, after the main event, as the victorious Sam Slam was being presented with Big Orange in the ring, our champion symbolically handed the old FWA Title back to Alex. Once again, we took a real-life situation and turned it into a storyline.

There was a real online buzz surrounding the return of the FWA. Tony and Alex released a series of cryptic and futuristic YouTube videos which simply said "It's coming." For weeks, fans speculated what 'it' was. Eventually, the FWA's resurrection was announced in the weekly Fighting Talk wrestling column in The Daily Star, to mainly positive acclaim. Most fans seemed to remember the FWA's glory days fondly and, far from scoffing at the disregard for the Final Frontiers stipulation, were excited for its return.

As matches were announced for the first show, scheduled for FWA's famed home of Broxbourne Civic Hall in Hertfordshire on Sunday, August 2 2009, two things were clear. Unlike the old FWA, this new incarnation was determined to use British talent only. And the roster would include only the best Brits around at the time. The card included Martin Stone v Doug Williams, Bubblegum v Dave Moralez (the future Dave Mastiff), a Rockstar Spud v Jonny Storm v Jody Fleisch v Mark Haskins four-way, Marty Scurll and Zack Sabre Jnr v Joey Hayes and CJ Banks, Leroy Kincaide v Pac, and appearances by El Ligero, Andy Simmonz (managed by future winner of The Apprentice, Ricky 'Hype' Martin) and RJ Singh. A mouthwatering line-up.

A series of press releases also told fans that behind-the-scenes, the new FWA would learn from the mistakes of the past.

Now this was my major bugbear with getting involved with the FWA again. I sought assurances, mainly from Tony Simpson, that the new FWA would be run as a business and would be organisationally sound. Tony impressed me during our conversations. Like Mark Kay, he'd worked in finance, so surely he would know his numbers. With him reining in Alex's more extravagant tendencies, I felt the new FWA was sure to operate on a more sensible financial footing.

The FWA also put in place a unique organisational structure, positioning itself as the moral guardians of British wrestling, and vowed to base all decisions around 10 ethical 'business principles'. They were:

1) We strive to produce the very best wrestling seen in Great Britain.

2) We go above and beyond the call of duty to show the rest of the world how talented British wrestlers are.

3) We encourage those fans with initiative who wish to break into the business, to treat the FWA as their own company and will offer help, assistance and backing to those who show us their ability to enable the British wrestling scene to grow.

4) We provide official funding, resources and help to the new

Retired Wrestlers' charitable trust fund by giving a percentage of all our profits to them.

5) We nurture the young talent on the UK scene and select several each year for subsidised training and mentoring.

6) We endeavour to work with everyone within the UK scene in order to try and create harmony amongst wrestlers and promoters alike in an attempt to create a level of co-operation and produce a British scene that our fans can be proud of.

7) We work hard to try and create a real unity between wrestling fans in the UK and work hard to offer them an actual community which they can be a part of.

8) We do all within our power to make our business model recession-proof so that British wrestlers will always have a place to perform and in turn, British fans will always have a place to come and watch them.

9) We respect the great heritage of British wrestling and will endeavour to keep this respect alive amongst the new generation of fans and wrestlers alike.

10) We will strive to be ambassadors for the sport of professional wrestling both domestically and internationally and endeavour to lead by example.

"The FWA plans to use everything at its disposal to eventually be the standard bearer for how professional wrestling should protect, police and provide for itself, its fans and those people involved in it," said a press release.

"We want to develop into a wrestling business and community that people in other countries worldwide can look to for encouragement. We want to work towards unity within the industry from all sides and present wrestling in the most positive light and produce a UK wrestling scene that fans and the general public at large can appreciate, respect and value.

"These are big dreams but ones that we will endeavour to achieve. Even if we are unsuccessful in them, we have confidence that our commitment will leave a positive shadow by making it even easier for those who should come afterwards to achieve these eventual goals, just as the FWA of old once did."

It was all very laudable and grown up. The new FWA was

representative of Shane's more mature and caring approach to life in general in 2009, compared to the carefree character he was during the original FWA days.

And the idea of an ethical wrestling company really appealed to me personally. The American wrestling scene had a dark cloud over it at the time, due to the steady stream of early deaths of wrestlers in their 30s and 40s, tales coming out constantly of steroid and prescription drug abuse, and scandals such as the horrendous tragedy in 2007 when top WWE wrestler Chris Benoit killed his wife and son, then himself. Alex was determined to lead the way for British professional wrestling to be almost angelic in comparison - an altogether safer and cleaner environment, with a clearly defined path for upward mobility.

The FWA also set up something called The Grapple Group. This was a talent agency which had signed more than 20 British wrestlers to contracts.

The idea was that this Grapple Group would act as the go-between in negotiations between top UK wrestlers and the big companies overseas, such as WWE, TNA, New Japan, Pro Wrestling NOAH and Ring of Honor. The agency would send tapes of FWA shows, filmed to a high standard, to these big organisations, hoping they would snap up UK talent. The Grapple Group would then take commission on a big-money deal that would, in theory, benefit both the wrestler and the agency.

At the time, more Brits were working for the 'big two' companies in America than ever before. Wade Barrett and Drew McIntyre, as well as former FWA grapplers Paul Burchill and Nikita (Katie Lea) were with WWE, while Doug Williams and Nick 'Magnus' Aldis had contracts with TNA. They were getting more exposure and making more money in America than they would have done wrestling in Britain. So many more Brits wanted to follow in their footsteps. The FWA, through The Grapple Group, pledged to make this a reality, as well as pay for their insurance to cover them should they suffer injuries and be unable to work, organise professional photo shoots for them and provide other opportunities to raise their profile.

The FWA also created JobsInWrestling.com - a recruitment website aiming to give fans the chance to become staff at shows.

While wrestling traditionalists rolled their eyes at the idea of the door being opened wide to outsiders, I had no problem with this if British wrestling was to grow. After all, almost everybody in wrestling started out as a fan. If the FWA was to achieve its lofty ambitions, it needed a big team of helpers to do everything from run errands backstage to write articles for its new website. It certainly seemed to be effective because during those early FWA comeback shows, there were dozens and dozens of people running around performing vital behind-the-scenes tasks. This gave the impression, to me, that the new FWA would be a well-oiled machine, organisationally, compared to the old one.

There would also be afternoon FWA Unsigned events before the main FWA shows, featuring 'non contracted' UK grapplers and youngsters from all over the country. This, Alex said, would open up opportunities for trainees from the XWA school (like Axl Rage and JD Sassoon) to develop their skills and gain vital experience in front of paying crowds.

And there was also the British Wrestling Council, or BWC. More on that later.

My job with the new FWA was as their colour commentator. I wanted this role in wrestling for years, way back before I became a heel manager during the FWA's glory days. And at FWA New Frontiers 2009, I had the chance to do it live, alongside a new partner, IPW:UK's lead announcer Dave Bradshaw.

On the weekend of the FWA's debut show, I was in Newcastle-upon-Tyne for my cousin's stag do. On the Sunday morning of the Broxbourne event, I was collected from my hotel by none other than Newcastle's very own Ben 'Pac' Satterley, the man now known as 'The King of the Cruiserweights' in WWE, Neville.

I spent a very pleasant five-hour car journey down to Hertfordshire with Ben. And although The Man Gravity Forgot was renowned for his quiet and reserved personality, and I didn't know him particularly well, the conversation between us flowed easily.

About a year earlier, Pac refused an interview with me for Power Slam. I was worried mild-mannered Ben might have been offended by me calling him 'The Man *Personality* Forgot' on a promo during an IPW:UK show in 2006. But when I asked him during our road trip, Ben laughed it off. This wasn't the reason at all. Pac said he just wasn't comfortable talking to the media as he didn't think he had anything interesting to say. I told him he was doing himself down, as he was one of the few British wrestlers working regularly in Japan at the time (for the Dragon Gate organisation) so the media was keenly interested in his story. I tried to persuade him to change his mind but he politely declined.

Bearing that in mind, it's been interesting to watch him cutting promos on worldwide TV over the past few years since he signed for WWE in 2012, became the NXT Champion as Adrian Neville and then debuted on Raw and SmackDown as just Neville. Talking is definitely not his forte but Ben has been forced to go out of his comfort zone in an environment where interviews are just as important as in-ring moves...if not more so. When he turned heel in 2016 his promos were a revelation; intense, articulate and powerful. I thought back to our car journey and couldn't believe it was the same guy who didn't want to be interviewed years before!

We eventually got to the Broxbourne Civic Hall on a hot summer's afternoon and it hadn't changed a bit in the two-and-a-half years since I'd last been there. There was a tangible feeling of happiness in the air that the FWA was back. It was great to catch up with some familiar faces from FWA days of yore like Flash Barker, Elisar Cabrera, Jody Fleisch and Phil Austin, work alongside trusted XWA colleagues like Jonny Storm, Spud, RJ Singh, Stixx and Joey Hayes, and get to know the likes of Zack Sabre Jnr, Joel Redman, Paul Malen and my new commentary partner Dave Bradshaw for the first time.

The always-friendly Len Davies was handling the production side of things and created an impressive stage and lighting layout. The twin big-screen TVs either side of the entranceway looked especially snazzy, as did the individual entrance videos for the wrestlers. Tony Simpson was running around backstage, overseeing everything, chattering away on a hands-free mobile. Everything seemed very professional and big-time by lowly British wrestling levels. I was encouraged.

Nostalgia and curiosity had ensured a big paid attendance that night and a packed house of fans chanting "F-W-A! F-W-A!" like the good old days. From the moment ring announcer Stevie Aaron emerged and voiceover man Len Davies bellowed "Tonight, the revolution returns!" there was a palpable sense of anticipation in the crowd. The fans really wanted to believe the FWA could be as good as before.

I took my seat next to Dave on the stage with a clear view of the ring. I had done a lot of research and preparation, but I was still wasn't sure how we'd gel as a duo. Remember, we had never even met, let alone worked together before.

I need not have worried. Our chemistry was instant.

Dave is such a gifted play-by-play man. He is incredibly knowledgeable, he knows how to tell a story, comes up with some killer lines (particularly when opening and closing a broadcast) and has the perfect balance of authority, seriousness, credibility, deadpan humour and raw excitement in his voice. And most importantly when working with me, he knew how to put me in my place. I absolutely loved our partnership.

As heel colour commentator, I was purposefully obnoxious and completely oblivious to my own shortcomings. But whenever I said something preposterously boastful, Dave would always come back at me. At times, we bickered like Gorilla Monsoon and Bobby Heenan during their peak years calling WWF pay-per-views. It was really important that Dave was strong enough to do this, didn't let my bombastic personality overshadow him, and instead worked with me to create an entertaining soundtrack to what was going on in the ring.

What I will say, though, is that Dave Bradshaw has the worst taste in suits of all-time. Seriously, he dressed like a grandad at a wedding.

I am really happy with the work Bradshaw and I produced that night in Broxbourne. Alex Shane was too. He told me afterwards that our commentary was the best thing on the show. And that was praise indeed, considering there were some top-notch bouts that night.

The best bout was the opener. Zack Sabre Jnr and Marty Scurll, the Leaders of the New School, defeated Joey Hayes and CJ Banks, who had been put together in a team known as Northern Xposure, in a textbook display of athleticism and tag team wrestling. With Project Ego, Stixx and Paul Malen, and Retro Pop (Dave Rayne and

Sam Bailey) also on the roster, the FWA looked set to make good on its aim to create a competitive tag team division.

Meanwhile Spud made a lasting impression with a full-on ring entrance to Living on a Prayer complete with FWA's own version of Team Rockstar. The Baby Jesus of British Wrestling was accompanied by his own personal security guard, a female bodybuilder from Australia and friend of Alex's called Lisa Carrodus, who resembled Chyna with her statuesque physique and stoic aura. And he even had a backing group, a pair of wild-haired trainees from Stixx's House of Pain training school in Nottingham, who mimed on guitars as Spud murdered the Bon Jovi classic like a drunk on Friday night karaoke, positively oozing charisma.

"He sang it like a nightingale, Dave Bradshaw! The Rockstar is in the building and the FWA will never be the same!" I crowed.

"I have blood coming out of my ears," replied deadpan Dave.

It wasn't all plain sailing on the FWA's return show though, as there were one or two baffling booking quirks. The main one was the FWA's needlessly complicated card system. The referee gave a yellow card as a first warning for breaking the rules, a red card for a second one, and then the third time a wrestler broke the rules he was disqualified. This went completely against conventional wisdom. It is ingrained in world culture that in football, a yellow card means a caution and a red card means a sending off. To have a red card not lead to a DQ was plain confusing. It happened in a match between Terry Frazier and Joel Redman that night and the fans were perplexed. I raised this issue with Alex afterwards and he was adamant he could re-educate fans to accept the new system. I felt he was trying to reinvent the wheel. But Alex's mindset was that he wanted to defy tradition and rewrite some of the accepted conventions of wrestling.

"I'd told Alex that if he wanted to do a new FWA, he needed to be different to every other UK promotion and think outside the box," said Andy Quildan, who also disagreed with Alex's version of the card system.

"I told him the main event of the first FWA show should be Zack Sabre Jnr and Marty Scurll, who were just starting to break out, against Doug Williams and Magnus, who was available at the time and they were both in TNA as the British Invasion. Alex wanted a great main event people would talk about and I thought this was it. I knew Marty and Nick were best friends and would have an amazing match with other, and Doug and Zack would do the same.

"Alex wanted to use the card system, so I suggested that he do a yellow card for a warning, and red card for a sending off, then in a tag team match if a wrestler was sent off, he'd be sent to the back. You could have Nick and Doug cheating all the time, Marty lose his rag and get disqualified and sent to the back, which leads to a two-on-one on Zack, then Nick is finally caught cheating and sent off, so you're then left with Zack and Doug who can have the blow-away match, and then in that one match you've established the new tag team rules and had a killer main event.

"But when the actual FWA red and yellow card system came in, people couldn't relate to it."

Still, the actual main event that night gave the fans everything they could have asked for and more. Martin Stone engaged Doug Williams in 20 minutes of compelling combat both inside and outside the ring. Then after a plethora of near-falls and hard-hitting moves, The Guvnor pinned The Ambassador after three London Bridge DDTs. The Broxbourne fans responded with a standing ovation as both men professed respect for the other over the microphone.

Then Bradshaw enthused: "This is a night that nobody who was here will ever forget! At New Frontiers, the FWA has been reborn!" All things considered, it had certainly been a successful comeback for Britain's most famous wrestling promotion of the noughties.

"I think the show went very well, it looked great, the boys were on board and the fans enjoyed it," said Tony Simpson.

And I got another commentary gig off the back of it. Two weeks later, I made my first appearance for FutureShock Wrestling in three years, adding my voice to their Fifth Anniversary broadcast at Stockport Guildhall alongside Chris 'G-Man' Garrett. Then Alex Shane himself turned up right at the end of the show's main event between Sam Bailey and Clinton Steele to kickstart a hostile takeover of the promotion he helped create. More on that later.

Meanwhile behind-the-scenes, there was a flurry of activity

surrounding what would turn out to be one of the most controversial aspects of the new-look FWA.

The British Wrestling Council, or BWC for short.

Alex, as well as being a wrestler and promoter, was a trainer of some repute. Over the years, he coached some of the UK's very best like former WWE superstars Hade Vansen and Nikita, and 'The Bollywood Dream' RJ Singh. And he long held an ambition to standardise how wrestling was taught. His idea was to create a 'wrestling syllabus' to be followed by training schools all over the country. Long-term, he hoped this syllabus would allow professional wrestling to be seen as a legitimate and respected discipline like martial arts, perhaps even to be taught to kids in schools.

The BWC was formed to roll out Alex's syllabus to as many of the UK's wrestling training centres as possible. This new organisation also wanted to offer help to British promoters, in an attempt to ensure all shows were run safely and professionally. The BWC hoped to make life difficult for those 'cowboys' who thought they could put on wrestling events with no experience, knowledge or regard for the health of the sports entertainers they employed (or rather, didn't employ, because wages were sometimes pathetic or non-existent). And the BWC offered medical insurance policies for UK wrestlers.

Although some inaccurately called it a governing body, the BWC was really a support group. It had no official powers delegated from any authority and no way of actually regulating the UK scene to stamp out dangerous, badly-organised and unprofessional events from taking place altogether. But it was created to bring training schools together and to offer practical help to those willing to accept it. Once again, its aims were very commendable.

What really impressed me about the BWC was that Tony and Alex recruited non-wrestling people who had experience of the 'real world of work'. A qualified solicitor was brought on board. And Helen Carr, a management graduate from the University of Manchester, was drafted in as BWC Operations Manager. When I met Helen for the first time, I was really impressed. She was bright, personable and meticulously organised. Exactly the kind of person Alex needed to bring order to his left-field thinking. Helen's administrative skills, enthusiasm and drive were the glue that held the BWC together during its first year of operation.

"Helen was an extremely hard worker who had the same mindset as me," said Tony Simpson.

"We needed the boring things implemented well to be seen as professionals to the large organisations we were looking to partner with. She was incredibly organised with this on the lead up to events and also represented the company well as front of house manager on event days.

"All these things behind the scenes are thankless tasks and roles, but I hope Helen, and all involved, know how thankful I am for their key contribution to the FWA. I hope the learnings have helped them in what they are doing now, in the same way it helped me."

To give the BWC credibility with trainees and wrestling fans alike, some of the country's biggest names were asked to endorse the project. They included Robbie Brookside, Doug Williams, Martin Stone, El Ligero, Andy Simmonz, Joel Redman, Bubblegum and the highly respected Cumbrian hard man 'The Vigilante' Johnny Moss. All were pictured on the homepage of the BWC website sporting official British Wrestling Council wristbands.

Ah yes. The wristbands.

The idea for the wristbands came from the coloured belt system used in martial arts. Alex created a grading system to be used in all BWC training schools, where trainees had to perform certain wrestling-related tasks to a required standard in order to pass a level of achievement and then received a coloured wristband as an award. In martial arts, beginners wear a white belt, then as they progress in ability they can win other coloured belts all the way up to black - the highest degree of proficiency. Alex's wristband system was very similar.

Beginners who performed a series of basic holds and manouevres to an external examiner's satisfaction received a white wristband. Lock up, wristlock, hammerlock, full nelson, waistlock, nothing more complicated than that. For Grade 2, the moves and holds were slightly more challenging and varied, and included reversals. Successful students gained a green wristband. Grade 3 (yellow) included being able to correctly deliver an armdrag, and perform numerous pinning combinations and more complex submission holds. Grades continued to increase in level of difficulty right the way up to Grade 8, the hallowed black wristband worn by the pros.

Those students who progressed to the final level had to wrestle a six-to-eight minute match, deliver a two-minute promo speech to camera and take exams in self-defence, wrestling psychology and fitness. If you earned a black wristband, you passed the BWC syllabus and were, in theory, a fully trained professional wrestler.

The wristband and grading system was perhaps the most controversial aspect of the BWC. Many dyed-in-the-wool trainers and veteran grapplers around the country laughed at the idea. They mocked the whole concept, ridiculed the trainees who wore their wristbands with pride, thinking the syllabus a rigidly inflexible way to train that didn't account for the spontaneity and hard graft that goes into creating a rounded professional who knew the job inside out.

"I don't need a bloody wristband to prove to anyone that I can wrestle," they scoffed. "So you get rated on a few moves and that makes you a pro wrestler?" they jeered.

But I absolutely loved the whole idea of the syllabus, the grading system and the wristbands. My school embraced it from day one. To be accurate, XWA trainer Damon Leigh had actually started rolling out his own similar syllabus at the Morecambe school just before the BWC was formed.

I could see the benefits of the project right away, not least of all because it brought focus and direction to our weekly training sessions. You see, your typical wrestling school usually includes a mixed bag of ages, physiques and experience levels, and the Morecambe centre was no different. We had new people joining and dropping out all the time. Some trainees picked things up quicker than others. Some missed a week and would then have to catch up. Such inconsistency makes it difficult for a trainer to devote his time to everyone in the class equally and ensure all students are progressing at the same level.

The grading system meant that all trainees had a tangible goal to aim for and allowed us to effectively monitor how everybody was developing, whatever their level of ability. It also had a positive influence on the attitude of the trainees. As soon as the XWA school joined the BWC, attendances at Sunday classes picked up. Motivation levels rose too. A core group of dedicated students were really enthused by the syllabus and saw it as an opportunity to work on their weaknesses and go over the basics time and time again until they became second nature.

We had a great bunch of trainees at Morecambe. They were super kids, so respectful and passionate about pro wrestling. Some of them had been through some real hardships in life and found escapism from their troubles and a place to belong at our school. They met like-minded people and formed close friendships with each other. It was a tight-knit group and it was a pleasure to work with them.

Alongside Axl Rage and JD Sassoon, our top student was 20-year-old Kyle Paterson. Kyle turned up the first day the school opened with his younger brother Dean.

The brothers, originally from Glasgow, Scotland, had a close bond and were terrific lads. They'd had a tough upbringing, living with an abusive mother, but this never seemed to outwardly affect them. They were well-mannered with a zest for life. And while Dean eventually gave up wrestling, Kyle kept going. His athleticism, heart and technique made him a natural inside the ring. And his placid and easy-going nature made him popular with the other students. He was a fantastic role model for the younger pupils who really looked up to him like a big brother.

Kyle also created a winning gimmick for himself, a cross between his wrestling hero Jeff Hardy and Sting. Donning white face paint to hide the pain he suffered as a child, Kyle Paterson became Jynkz - the high-flying daredevil who eventually evolved into one of the XWA's most popular stars.

Kyle, along with Axl and JD, were all in the first tranche of Morecambe trainees to pass their BWC Grade 1 on September 6 2009 and receive their white wristbands. This hard-working group was the lifeblood of the school in its first year. They included Jack Clarke, a talented 14-year-old from Chorley; Luke Vedick, also 14, who lived around the corner from my house in Morecambe; Vicky Howard, a flame-haired tomboy from Lancaster and her girlfriend Mary-Jane Johnes; Aaron Wilkinson, a mild-mannered 21-year-old with a distinctive Goth-style image from Wigan; Ross Wallis from Blackpool, the bulky loner of the group; Bryan Fulton, our talented production guru who also showed potential as a wrestler; and 'Evil' Lewis Penney from Morecambe, a radio presenter and longtime XWA fan who passed the exam with flying colours despite being partially sighted. Lewis' radio background made him a natural commentator and backstage interviewer. Seven years on, 'Evil' Lewis (who is not remotely evil, by the way) was still part of the team at Morecambe shows and in 2017, after years of diligent interviewing for DVDs and YouTube videos, graduated to a major on-screen role as the Alpha Omega Wrestling general manager.

Perhaps the biggest surprise of that first grading was that our least physically talented trainee passed the exam. This was Mikey Richardson, who I will lovingly describe as one of life's eccentrics.

The first day Mikey turned up at training, he showed very little athletic ability. Everything he did looked ungainly. I thought the guy would never make a pro wrestler if he lived to be 100.

But Mikey wouldn't take no for an answer. He kept coming back week after week. And he stood out amongst the group not only because of his dedicated efforts to improve, but also thanks to the gimmick he developed for himself - a character called Ace Ramon. Ace was a 'Pretty Fly for a White Guy' gangster type who wore fingerless gloves and American baseball shirts. Ramon thought he was as cool and edgy as Ice T, but actually had about as much street cred as a librarian. I loved the gimmick.

The main aptitude Mikey showed for pro wrestling was his promos. He gave them 100% and was a much more fiery and entertaining speaker than any of the other trainees, apart from Stallion. Having said that, I'm still to this day not sure if Mikey played Ace Ramon for laughs, or if the comedy was unintentional. Like the time he seized the microphone at one of our trainee shows at Regent Park Studios with a neckerchief entirely covering his mouth and nose. It might have been the greatest promo in the world for all the audience knew, because all they could hear was "MMMFFF...MMMFFF...MMMFFF....MMMFFFF!"

Another time at training, all the students had been asked to cut a two-minute promo to build up a fictitious match of their choice against a random opponent. The promos were pretty bad and I was getting frustrated as the trainees delivered timid and wooden speeches like 12-year-olds at school prize giving night.

"Come on guys, I need some more passion," I implored.

"I need to believe that you really hate the guy you're going to wrestle. I need to believe that you want to win this match badly. I need to believe that it's more important than life and death!"

So up to the microphone stepped Ace Ramon. And, with the utmost seriousness, he said:

"Axl Rage! I promise you, I will not only beat you in this match, but I will creep into your bedroom at night. AND I WILL F__KING STAB YOU!"

We were in hysterics for weeks.

But Mikey always took everything in such good humour and was so eager to please, that he was eventually accepted as one of the gang. And when he passed his Grade 1 and received his white wristband, nobody deserved it more.

In fact when all the trainees were presented with their first coloured bands, they were incredibly delighted and proud. We held a proper presentation ceremony at Regent Park Studios to recognise their achievements publicly, inviting families of the budding wrestlers to attend. And the feedback we got was all positive, even from protective parents who were previously sceptical of professional wrestling. One mum thanked me, saying the camaraderie of our weekly sessions and the discipline of working towards the gradings helped her son overcome shyness and stand up to school bullies. Her praise made me realise what a huge responsibility Mark and I had as the managers of the XWA training centre. We were literally changing youngsters' lives here. We were not only giving them an opportunity to live out a dream by being part of the sports entertainment they grew up watching on TV, but we were helping them to grow as people.

Of that core group from 2009, only JD, Bryan and Evil Lewis were still involved in the Morecambe shows at time of writing in 2016. One by one, the others drifted away from pro wrestling. JD has definitely been the standout of the group. Now known as James Drake and still in his early 20s, in recent years he has broken out as a singles wrestler to appear for many of the UK's top promotions. The talented young lad we first spotted in 2009 has gradually developed into a well-rounded performer and got a major career break in 2017 when he competed in the WWE's UK Championship. The sky is the limit for the artist formerly known as JD Sassoon. I still prefer that name, by the way!

Morecambe wasn't the only school to publicly back the BWC. Dave Rayne's FutureShock Wrestling in the Manchester area, New Generation Wrestling run by Richard Dunn in Hull, Stixx's House of Pain school in Nottingham, Joel Redman's DWA in Exeter, 4FW in Swindon, IPW:UK, AWW in the Midlands and Dragon Pro Wrestling in Wales were among the established training centres who came on board. Hundreds of young wrestlers all over the UK, including several who are now regulars on the UK scene, all wore BWC wristbands back in 2009/10/11. The likes of Charlie Garrett, James Davis from The London Riots, Pro-Wrestling:EVE's Rhia O'Reilly, FutureShock's Xander Cooper, Melanie Price and Zack Gibson, as well as XWA's Axl Rage, James Drake and Craig Kollins all took part in BWC grading sessions.

So while the wristband system had its critics, I felt it was something the 'outside world' could understand and take seriously. That's why Martin Shenton, himself a black belt in taekwondo, was a huge supporter of the BWC's ideals.

This was a time when pro wrestling in general was getting more respect from non-fans. The hit 2008 film The Wrestler starring Mickey Rourke had much to do with this. Directed by Darren Aronofksy, The Wrestler was about a former big-time champion who had fallen on hard times and was hustling on the indie scene to make ends meet. This film was a smash hit critically and earned Rourke a BAFTA, a Golden Globe and an Oscar nomination for his realistic performance as Randy 'The Ram' Robinson.

When I saw The Wrestler at the cinema on my 37th birthday in January 2009, I was deeply moved. I couldn't believe what an amazing job Aronofsky had done in accurately and sympathetically portraying the business I loved so much. He captured the trials and tribulations of a struggling wrestler perfectly. Randy The Ram was the larger-than-life superhero who every night pushed his body through the pain barrier just to hear the roar of the crowd and feel that rush of adrenaline. But then he had to cope with going home to his humble trailer and the harsh reality of a day job behind the meat counter at the local supermarket. The film was a triumph.

Many non-grapple enthusiasts watched and loved The Wrestler too. The film blatantly exposed the inner workings of the business for all to see - showing Robinson in the dressing room working out his match beforehand, preparing a small razor blade to hide in his wrist-tape and cut himself mid-bout to draw blood, and buying metal trays from a hardware store to smash over his opponent's head in a hardcore match. This increased 'outside world' curiosity in this strangest of professions like never before. My work colleagues at the local paper in Morecambe, who previously smirked at my involvement in wrestling, would say to me "Is it really like that?" I told them yes, it is.

Alex Shane, at the time, was obsessed with gaining respect for professional wrestling from 'the outside world' too. He saw wrestling as an art form equal to comedy, theatre, music, painting, sculpting, or any other similar genre that already had acceptance from the mainstream. Yet wrestling, he felt, had always been treated as what he called "the bastard child of entertainment". It was seen as lowest common denominator working class family fun, dismissed by non-fans as "that fake wrestling crap". Alex put it on a higher pedestal than that. To him, professional wrestling was a highly skilled, complex form of physical theatre performed by improvisational actors and stuntmen who had enormous reserves of fitness and conditioning. Wrestling's answer to Che Guevara was determined to open eyes and make everybody involved in his new FWA and BWC community feel proud, and not ashamed, to be involved in the British scene.

On September 22 2009, the debut episode of the new FWA TV show was aired. Not on Sky Digital's The Wrestling Channel, as the original FWA series had in 2004/5. No, TWC ceased transmission in the UK the year before. So without a 'proper' television station willing to broadcast British pro wrestling at the time, Alex and Tony used the easiest mass media tool at their disposal in the 21st Century to spread their product and its message - YouTube.

This was a groundbreaking episode. It was more than an hour long and contained no actual wrestling action or traditional promo segments. Instead, it was Dave Bradshaw, Flash Barker, Alex Shane and FWA referee Chris Roberts sitting around a table, completely casting kayfabe aside as they chatted about the rules of pro wrestling and openly discussed the psychology of why and how certain moves were performed. It was like an interview panel show on Sky Sports. It was radically different. It was real behind the curtain stuff. Some wrestling fans loved it. Others hated it. The new FWA was once again polarising opinion. But it always got people talking.

FWA ran a show four days later in Bridport, Dorset, which I couldn't make as it was my wedding anniversary weekend. But a week later on October 3 2009, I was back behind the commentary table for our return to Broxbourne for FWA Carpe Diem. I travelled down in a coach laid on by Dave Rayne with some of the Morecambe and FutureShock trainees, including Blond Jovi and Jack Gallagher.

Alex and Tony's idea to boost crowd numbers at FWA shows was to encourage these student coach trips. The deal was that I charged a fee to each trainee, which covered their ticket to the show and a contribution towards the coach hire and fuel, then took a cut as my own wage, before paying the balance to the FWA. But despite XWA and FutureShock bringing 15 trainees between us, the overall attendance was definitely less than New Frontiers two months earlier. A worrying sign.

Three of the main FWA roster stood out to me on the show. The monstrously muscular Johnny Moss, Cumbria's answer to Brock Lesnar, marmalised Dave Rayne with some of the most brutal suplexes I have ever seen. Andy Simmonz, playing a new egomaniacal heel role as the self-professed 'All Time Great', drew great heat defeating Jonny Storm (with help from Spud) using a Boston Crab.

As for the incomparable Rockstar, once again he was different class. The blond braggart tone-deafed his way through a caterwauling rendition of Bon Jovi's Keep The Faith until his nemesis The Wonderkid gatecrashed the 'Rock Concert' and smashed up the backing group's instruments. At the time, Jay seemed to be on a mission to shine in every single match or interview segment he was placed in. Spud was red-hot on promos, positively burst through the camera and had unmistakable fire in his eyes. He was the undisputed star of the new FWA.

"I remember Paul Heyman once said in a documentary that if people have an axe to grind these days, they go on social media and moan on Facebook," said Spud.

"But nobody picks up a camera any more. That's what Stone Cold Steve Austin used to do. When he was fired from WCW he was angry and so did a promo about how he would become the star he always knew he could be. So I thought, that's what I'm going to do, because no-one else is doing it. I was doing it to hone my craft and I thought f__k it, if any (promoter) sees one of my promos they'll realise I'm a good promo, that I can talk solidly for three to five minutes, keep people's attention and sell the town. That's all that was in my mind right then. Sell tickets, get people in the building, keep them interested."

Three newcomers also caught my eye that day in Broxbourne. I got my first sighting of a youngster from Hull named Nathan Cruz, who appeared in a rumble on the FWA Unsigned afternoon show and showed confidence and swagger beyond his years. Cruz would soon develop into one of Britain's very best performers. Carpe Diem also saw the debut of a pretty backstage interviewer called Katie Webb, who used the stage name Francesca Wood. Katie would go on, a few years later, to become host of WrestleTalk TV.

At Carpe Diem, I also met a young grappler from Wolverhampton called Nik Bali.

Nik, who was 25 years old at the time, struck me as a likeable lad with great passion for pro wrestling. His role that night was to sprinkle rose petals on the stage as RJ Singh made his entrance and carry the flag of India as he accompanied The Bollywood Dream to the ring for his match with young Essex high-flyer Paul Robinson. Nik had a great look and attitude, and seemed set for a regular FWA spot as one of Singh's entourage The Bhangra Knights which also included Adil Khan, Darrell 'Anwar' Allen and megaphone-wielding manager 'The Director' Tebraiz Shahzad.

But then fate intervened in the most tragic of circumstances.

On November 27 2009, Nik Bali stepped in at the last minute to compete in a tag team match for a small promotion called Celtic Wrestling at Canton Community Hall in Cardiff, Wales. Nik wasn't even supposed to be wrestling at all that night. But during the bout, Bali was on the receiving end of a complicated double team move similar to AJ Styles' finisher the Styles Clash.

The manoeuvre went terribly wrong.

Nik landed badly and suffered a devastating spinal injury. He was rushed to hospital where he went under the surgeon's knife. But the operation was unsuccessful.

Nik Bali was paralysed.

Two days later, I arrived at Sports Nottingham at Notts County Football Ground for the next FWA event, Hotwired 2009. Nik's injury was the talk of the dressing room. There were a lot of sad faces and sombre moods that day. Ross 'RJ Singh' Jones and James 'Spud' Curtin were hit particularly hard. Nik is a close friend of theirs.

"Nik and I had just started tagging up in Birmingham and LDN, and he'd been at my wedding in summer 2009," said Ross, speaking in April 2016.

"He was meant to be part of the Nottingham show. But I woke up that day and saw an online message from Dann Read, who put it out there that Nik'd had an accident.

"I rang Nik over and over again. But his phone just kept ringing out. I left a message asking him to call me. Then details started emerging of what had actually happened. I went to Sports Nottingham that day and it was awful. I had to tell people and others kept asking me what was happening.

"A few days later my phone went off and it was Nik's number. I thought, oh my God, maybe he's OK. But it was actually his brother. He told me Nik was going into surgery and they didn't know what the outcome would be. Then there were long periods of waiting to hear, until his brother got back in touch and told me that Nik might never walk again.

"It was about a year later when I was doing an LDN show, we were driving down and Nik called me. He actually apologised to me for not speaking to me for all that time. He said it had taken him so long to get to that point. The weekend when the accident happened he didn't even want to be alive.

"He told me he was still in Wales. So the following weekend my wife Laura and I drove to see him in the hospital he was in. It was really surreal. He was in a wheelchair, he was charming all the nurses, they all loved him. And we spent a good couple of hours just chatting away. He asked about wrestling, how it was going.

"Then when we left and said goodbye, we walked round the corner and just broke down in tears. It was awful.

"We were back in regular contact after that. He moved to a care home in Birmingham and we went to visit him there. The love of wrestling has never died with him. I go to see him now and he's always putting wrestling on. Myself and Chris Roberts, if we go to see him, we'll take an autograph from a wrestler Nik likes. Chris got Jushin Liger's autograph for him. I wrestled Tatanka once and got his autograph for Nik.

"I'd like to say he's in a happy place because he seems to have accepted how his life is now. He loves seeing us whenever we go up there. It's good that he's found happiness despite what happened. He can move his neck and shoulders, and his wrists. But he has no fine motor skills in his fingers. He can't grip anything. And nothing from the waist down, he's still in a wheelchair. It's a degree of life, as it were. But he's happy.

"One of the best days we had with Nik was in 2014. We did a show for Kamikaze Pro Wrestling in Birmingham, myself and Darrell Allen. We took Steve Corino to the show and we told Steve 'I hope you don't mind but we've planned to go and see a friend of ours, because he lives half an hour from the venue'. Steve said 'Sure, no problem'. So we had this wonderful moment where we walked in and said to Nik 'Hey, you remember former ECW Champion Steve Corino?' And then Steve Corino walks in! Nik was like 'Oh my God!' We spent a couple of hours watching old WCW videos with Steve Corino telling us stories. It was a lovely afternoon."

Spud became even closer to Nik after his injury and like Ross, speaks with great respect and fondness for his courageous mate.

"We were good friends and afterwards, we became even better friends. I talk to him most weeks. He's such a good human being and it's horrible that something like that happened to such a good human being.

"Nik is the one who helped me with promos in the years that followed (his injury). He's the reason why I have a job with TNA. I wouldn't be the performer I am today but for the hours sitting with Nik in his room in Sutton Coldfield doing wrestling promos and watching wrestling.

"The first time he went out, after the injury, was to my 30th birthday party in 2013. He had the best time because the wrestlers were there, who he loved, and nobody treated him any different. It was good for him. He's been out since, he comes to the TNA shows when we're in the UK.

"I don't know how he still cares so much about wrestling because for the first three months after the injury, he wanted to die. He really did. I don't know how he's smiling. He's more of a man than me, because I don't know how I'd be able to cope."

On the night of the FWA show at Sports Nottingham, Spud himself was at the centre of an eerie and scary moment echoing what happened to Nik Bali.

Spud went out to the ring for the opening tag team match, where he joined forces with CJ Banks to face Marty Scurll and Jonny Storm. Towards the end of the contest, Storm picked Jay up and hung him upside-down as Scurll delivered a drop kick to the RockStar's back. In one fluid motion, Jonny then dropped down to drive Spud head-first to the canvas, in a version of the See You Later double-team finisher Scurll regularly performed with his usual tag team partner Zack Sabre Jnr.

For some reason, the combination move went wrong. Spud's head hit the mat full-force, jarring his neck badly. Storm then followed up with his Wonderwhirl slam and scored the pin.

But as The Wonderkid celebrated finally getting one over his nemesis, Spud remained flat on his back in the ring, clutching his neck. Referee Steve Lynskey was clearly concerned. Other referees and stewards entered the ring to help check on the fallen Rockstar. This wasn't part of the show. Spud was hurt, for real.

"I landed on my forehead and that's not how you're supposed to land, it was brutal," said Spud.

"I knew nothing was broken because I managed to turn myself over, but I knew there was something wrong."

Thankfully, after a few nervous minutes, Jay was able to haul himself upright and, on rubber legs, was assisted to the backstage area where he slumped, in severe pain, before eventually going to hospital. He had suffered a neck injury that would keep him out of the ring for months.

"I had two weeks off work afterwards, I was moving like Robocop, it was horrible.

"I had to self-medicate too because when I went to the hospital they told me they couldn't do anything about it. They didn't tell me what was wrong. Then a long time down the road I had an MRI, 45 minutes in a tube coughing and spluttering, and they still couldn't tell what was wrong.

"But I'm glad it happened. It got me to think more about the performance side of things instead of taking bumps. It's why you don't see me taking many bumps to this day. The bumps don't matter. I started to remember all the things Stevie Knight used to say. 'You get the biggest reactions for doing nothing. Less is more. You only learn how to work when you get injured.' So that's when I started picking up a camera and talking and making people care about my matches before they even got to the building."

Spud would eventually return to action and suffered no permanent damage. Unlike his good mate Nik Bali, Jay was very very lucky. But the irony that he almost suffered a similar fate as his friend was not lost on James Curtin.

With the injuries to Spud and especially Bali, the BWC's mission to make British wrestling a safer place had just been completely validated. Shortly after the events of that weekend, Dave Bradshaw wrote an article on the BWC website.

He said: "I don't know all of the facts about Nik's tragic accident so it would be wrong to make too many judgements about it but suffice to say that having listened to the opinions of various people in the industry whom I trust, I am sure there are at least some serious questions about the whole episode that need to be addressed.

"In the short 18-month period since I started working in British wrestling I have heard of some truly ridiculous incidents that not only damage the industry's reputation among fans but place unnecessary safety risks to both the wrestlers and the audience: trainees being put on shows after just a few weeks of training; entire shows being run without qualified First Aiders in the building; outdoor fireworks being used on an indoor show; the list goes on and on.

"Add everything together and you are left with a very fragile-looking industry. The bottom line is this: without some unified effort to self-regulate, British wrestling is a powder keg waiting to explode.

"Given how much untapped potential we have in this country, it is absolutely criminal that British wrestling is in its current state. There are brilliant performers who deserve to be household names but are currently unlikely to draw 100 fans to see them wrestle.

"The industry needs to band together and ensure that every show that takes place on our shores reaches minimum standards of quality and safety. In this decade, the BWC could be the catalyst that returns British wrestling to the mainstream of our national life. Or it could be dead by the end of the year, leaving the industry to continue its decline into obscurity.

"For everyone who has an interest in the success of British wrestling, 2010 is a moment to stand up and be counted."

2010 was set to be one of the most, let's say, *interesting* years of my pro wrestling career.

CHAPTER 4

THE ASCENSION

As 2009 drew to a close, the FWA comeback was definitely showing promise.

Hotwired was a memorable show. Highlights included a gripping main event between Martin Stone and the formidable Johnny Moss, a slick technical tussle between Joey Hayes and Zack Sabre Jnr, and an angle where RJ Singh viciously snipped the horns off El Ligero's mask to embarrass The Mexican Sensation. The footage of The Bollywood Dream desecrating Ligero's precious mask was shown many times over the ensuing years in various video packages on WrestleTalk TV. It was arguably the most iconic moment of the new FWA.

Well, apart from the Patrick Lennon video. More on that later.

Stone's hard-fought victory over Moss and Andy Simmonz' defeat of Bubblegum the same night ensured that The Guvnor and the All-Time Great would meet in the climax of the tournament to crown a new FWA Champion. As Stone and Simmonz had been IPW:UK's two main men for the previous few years, the company's top face and biggest heel, it was no surprise to see them square off for the championship of another South East-based promotion. Their match would main event FWA's first show of 2010, British Uproar at Broxbourne Civic Hall on February 13.

As for me, I was just happy to get out of 2009 unscathed. It was a difficult year for me for a number of reasons, both personal and professional. That summer, I had a minor health scare which thankfully, didn't turn out to be what I feared. I also had a short real-life feud with a rival wrestling promoter who, in August 2009, organised a terrible show at a venue close to The Dome. Weeks of bitterness between us left me feeling drained.

And then there was the uncertainty over the future of the XWA.

The previous couple of years had been good ones for myself and Mark Kay, but we had also lived with the threat of The Dome's closure hanging over our heads since 2008. We were never quite sure which show would be our last at The Dome. The cash-strapped local council was always talking about shutting it. Although our XWA shows always did well, the venue was losing money hand over fist. Its regular programme of music concerts and dance festivals wasn't pulling crowds big enough to cover astronomical overheads in a tiny seaside town. Plus the council had one eye on a land deal with developers. It was no surprise when, at the end of 2009, they announced it would finally close for good in March 2010.

And I was devastated.

It may sound sappy and overly romantic, but The Dome meant everything to me. I watched wrestling there since the early 1990s, then created so many of my own amazing memories there in the noughties with the FWA and then the XWA. That funny breast-shaped building beside the sea was so much more to me than bricks, mortar and glass. It was the heart and soul of our operation, a classic venue with a unique atmosphere, and was held on a pedestal not just by us, but by wrestling fans all over the country, and many of the wrestlers too.

Our last ever show at The Dome took place on Saturday, January 30 2010, the week after my 38th birthday. XWA Gold Rush 2010. It was an emotional night.

And given my turmoiled state of mind at the time, I decided it would be the perfect time to channel my inner dark side...and turn heel.

It made sense. XWA storylines had been building up to it. As authority figure, I was slowly becoming irritated by two men in particular. I was annoyed at how they were rallying the Morecambe fans to support causes I couldn't agree with and, in my mind, challenging my authority as owner of the company.

For the past year, Johnny Phere had been forcefully lobbying to come back to British wrestling. But I resisted until Last Fight at The Prom when he won his reinstatement match. At the same time, I'd developed a new XWA character, my 'cousin' Tom Lambert. Played to perfection by London wrestler Tom Chamberlain, Cousin Tom caught on massively with the Morecambe fans. Tom was a loveable dreamer who wanted to become a pro wrestler. Having his best interests at heart, I refused to let him put himself in danger. So Tom started a campaign to change my mind. And the fans got behind it.

At Last Fight at the Prom 2009, we gave out dozens of cardboard signs to the spectators during the interval. LET TOM WRESTLE they said. When I came back out to ring announce after the break, I was greeted with this mass of signs and deafening "LET TOM WRESTLE!" chants. As I entered the ring, Tom was there to greet me. With innocent charm, he managed to finally persuade me to allow him to compete in a match.

The wannabe's debut would be at Gold Rush against his real-life friend RJ Singh, who viciously attacked Tom in 2009 as revenge for my relative costing him a match against Sam Bailey. But first, we released a music video of Tom training with Johnny Phere. It was hilarious to see Tom try and fail to keep up with The Psychotic Warrior's rigorous boot camp-style workouts - especially as Mark Kay had picked the cheesy 80s pop tune So Macho by Sinitta as the backing music. Cousin Tom? Macho? Hardly. He looked like he couldn't fight his way out of a paper bag. But this made him a sympathetic figure. By the time Gold Rush came around, the fans couldn't wait to see him stand up to Singh.

The match only lasted about eight minutes. It wasn't what you'd call a five-star classic. It didn't even have a conclusive pinfall or submission finish. But it didn't matter. In terms of emotion and storytelling, RJ Singh v Tom Lambert remains one of the top five matches of my wrestling career. Ask Ross Jones and Tom Chamberlain, and they will tell you the same. Their performances that night were exceptional.

Tom emerged through The Dome curtain to a booming response. Clad in an I LOVE MORECAMBE T-Shirt and skimpy wrestling trunks, the floppy-haired underdog was beaming ear to ear as he bounded out like an excited schoolboy. He even signed an autograph on the way to the ring. Such was his giddy enthusiasm, anyone would think it really was his debut match. In reality, Tom was an experienced wrestler. He appeared regularly as Sir Thomas Chamberlain, a snooty blue blood, for IPW:UK and other UK promotions. My fake cousin wouldn't have been able to play the character with such depth and believability if he hadn't been such a polished professional.

Clad in a dark suit with black tie, I was sitting at my regular spot behind the ring announcer's table as Tom came face to face with RJ Singh. And I watched as The Bollywood Dream cut an absolutely outstanding promo to set the scene.

"You think you can stick on a gawdy pair of tights and kickpads and that makes you some kind of star?" spat Singh.

"You are an insult to everything I stand for, to everything I am! You have no idea how ridiculous you look in your 'I love Morecambe' T-shirt."

At this, the crowd booed. Tom's expression changed. He looked sad. And then, worried.

"You see kid," continued RJ. "I'm not interested in pinning you, I'm going to punish you.

"I will destroy you. And Greg Lambert, there will be only one way out for your cousin, the only way you can get me to stop is to throw in this white towel."

At this, Singh produced a towel and threw it to me. I acted surprised as the manipulative RJ issued a chilling warning.

"When you think your boy has had enough Greg, throw that towel into the middle of the ring and maybe, just maybe, I will stop."

The match began. The atmosphere in The Dome was one of tension...and hope that somehow Tom could pull off the upset. Or at the very least, survive without getting badly hurt.

As I paced up and down at ringside, clutching the towel as if considering RJ's ultimatum, Singh locked up with Tom in the ring and easily took him down, first with an armdrag, then a hiptoss and a body slam. The Bollywood Dream expertly paused to soak up the derision of the crowd as he toyed with his overmatched foe.

But then the Indian superstar got overconfident. Out of nowhere, Tom delivered his own armdrag, hiptoss and slam, the fans were cock-a-hoop, Singh slid out of the ring in disbelief, and Tom fell to his backside as if he himself was stunned that he was able to pull off a series of actual wrestling moves!

I sat back down at my table. My facial expression was a combination of shock and fake pride.

The embarrassment of being dumped on his rear by a 'clueless rookie' fired up RJ Singh. When he returned to the ring, he began to batter Tom with eye rakes and knees.

Meanwhile commentators Evil Lewis and Stallion were themselves telling a great story.

"How is your dream going Tom?" cackled the heel Stallion.

"Is it everything you thought it would be? I don't want to see Greg Lambert throw the towel in. I want to see Tom have his backside handed to him!"

But then Tom got a two count out of nowhere with a roll-up. The fans were temporarily out of their seats. Surely...*surely* their unlikely hero couldn't pull this off.

But Singh was soon back on top. A quick snap suplex later, and Tom was locked in a camel clutch. But he wouldn't quit. Singh flashed the crowd a sadistic grin as he released the hold, then stood on Tom's back to add insult to injury. This sparked "LET'S GO TOM!" chants as I once again stood up and inched closer to the ring, as if to get a closer look at Tom's plight, towel poised ready to save him from the beating.

But suddenly, Tom blocked a Singh superkick and then executed the trademark moves of his favourite wrestling heroes. He blasted RJ with a Stone Cold Stunner. He did the John Cena 'You can't see me!' wave and hit a Five Knuckle Shuffle. He even dropped his rival with a deliberately awkward version of Johnny Phere's finisher the Ram Slam. Or was it the *Lamb* Slam? It didn't matter. The fans were going out of their minds with delight.

Getting carried away, Tom then made the familiar throat-slitting gesture of The Undertaker, and lifted Singh up into position for a tombstone piledriver. But referee Dominic Nix quickly informed Tom the piledriver was an illegal move in the XWA. If he dropped RJ on his head with the dangerous manoeuvre, he would be disqualified. Tom was frustrated. He put Singh down and turned his back in disappointment. But when he swivelled back around, RJ booted him full in the mush with a terrific superkick. Tom was knocked down and out.

Then Singh hooked Cousin Tom's arms and dropped him face-first with his finisher, a modified version of Triple H's Pedigree known as Sweet Bollywood Dreams. I put my hands to my head in horror. The match looked over as RJ went for the cover, but he pulled my 'flesh and blood' up at the two count. Singh clearly had no intention of winning via a simple pinfall. Remember, he'd vowed to continue the punishment until Tom was a physical mess. So The Bollywood Dream shook his head, glared straight into my eyes, and demanded I throw in the towel.

By this point, I was standing right next to the front row of The Dome's tiered seating area opposite the stage. In their regular seats, a group of our most passionate fans, a quartet of young women who have come to every single show for years and years, were looking concerned for Tom's well-being.

Ruth Dobson, Natalie Vranjes, Kyrie Walker and Sarah McDermott, who Stallion affectionately christened 'The Morecambe Divas', are proper wrestling fans. They always cheer their heroes with gusto and boo the rulebreakers with fervour. When one of their favourites is defeated, they are genuinely upset. When one of the villains cheats to win, they are genuinely angry. And whenever a hero of theirs wins a big main event match, they leap to their feet and hug each other in genuine ecstasy.

They believe wrestling is real. Because It's Real in Morecambe.

Ruth, Sarah, Kyrie and Natalie were my booking barometer when it came to writing storylines for wrestling in Morecambe. If they cared about someone, or something, then I knew my stories were working...or 'getting over' as we call it in the business.

That night, they absolutely loved Tom Lambert and desperately wanted him to win. And they absolutely despised the heartless RJ Singh for brutalising their beloved Tom and desperately wanted him to lose. So I knew the storyline I'd planned would be a winner.

They also liked and respected me. In the past, they'd even worn T-Shirts with my face and the words 'Greg's Gang' on them, I kid you not. And they really believed that Tom was a true Lambert, my own flesh and blood.

So I realised for my heel turn to be effective, I had to do it right in front of the Morecambe Divas. I had to make sure they could see my facial expressions and body language slowly change. I had to break their hearts.

After Singh landed his first Sweet Bollywood Dreams, the fans still believed I wasn't throwing the towel in because I still thought Tom could make a miraculous comeback. My facial expression was conflicted. Evil Lewis, on commentary, picked up on this immediately.

"Obviously Greg's got his cousin's best interests at heart," he said, keeping me babyface until the moment was exactly right. Then when Singh drove Tom down with a second Sweet Bollywood Dreams and got right in my face through the ropes and screamed "THROW THE TOWEL IN!" I still looked upset. My arms were folded, but this could easily have been in angry defiance at Singh's orders.

Then RJ hit a *third* Sweet Bollywood Dreams. Tom now lay prone on the canvas, not moving. I realised when planning the angle that there would come a point in this massacre when the fans would stop hoping Tom would fight back and instead would start feeling uncomfortable. I reckoned that after Ross executed his finisher three times, the spectators would switch from wanting Tom to win, to hoping the slaughter would be stopped. Over my shoulder, I sensed the mood changing. The Morecambe Divas were no longer cheering for Tom. They went eerily quiet.

And the soap opera played out, almost in slow motion. I unfolded my arms and covered my face in horror as Tom's face hit the canvas for the third time. He was out cold. He was badly hurt. There was no coming back from this. So I looked set to finally surrender on my courageous cousin's behalf.

But I stopped short. I looked down at the towel. I looked at Singh. Then I looked at Tom.

At this point, for the first time, Evil Lewis said that perhaps I should throw the towel in. At this point, for the first time, I heard fans - including The Morecambe Divas - yell at me to throw the towel in. Just about everybody in The Dome began willing, pleading, *begging* me to throw the towel in.

This was the moment. This was the perfect moment to turn heel.

As the fans continued to call for me to show mercy on my cousin, I began to shake my head slowly. Then more vociferously. And as Singh hooked the dead-weight Tom and delivered a *fourth* Sweet Bollywood Dreams, I turned my back on the ring and faced the crowd. The towel was at my side. My expression had changed to one of blank, emotionless detachment. "No...way!" I mouthed at the startled Morecambe Divas.

In order to add to the believability factor, I managed to persuade my wife Sharon (who took some persuading because she hates wrestling) to get involved in the angle. Showing just the right level of concern and anger that I was refusing to save her 'cousin-in-law', the wonderful Mrs Lambert - who was working on the ticket office that night - approached me, flanked by trainees from our wrestling school. I immediately whirled around and screamed at her.

"NOBODY TELLS ME WHAT TO DO! KEEP AWAY FROM THE RING!"

Sharon backed off, shooting me a marvellous glare of horror and disappointment at my actions. It's a look she has perfected during 20 years of marriage.

At this point, the feeling in the crowd was turning ugly. It got even more heated when RJ Singh physically attacked Dominic Nix as he tried to stop the match, then hit a fifth Sweet Bollywood Dreams on the limp carcass of Tom Lambert. So the crowd noise when Johnny Phere suddenly raced to the ring with a Psychotic one-man cavalry charge was absolutely ear-splitting. "PHERE! PHERE! PHERE!" bellowed the fans as Singh fled, Sharon and the trainees finally managed to enter the ring to surround and protect the fallen Tom, and Johnny stood over his fallen protege's battered body, staring a hole right through me with a menacing scowl.

My face was impassive and cold.

Then, and only then, did I finally throw in the towel. It sailed into the ring and landed at Johnny's feet. Phere picked it up and eyed me with disgust.

Then with carnage raging all around, I calmly picked up the microphone and announced, with an ever-so-slight smirk.

"Here is your winner...RJ Singh."

Then, ignoring the boos and looks of hatred from the Morecambe Divas and the rest of the 350-strong crowd, I walked slowly around the ring, up the stairs and onto the stage, where I paused in the entranceway, and looked back at the chaotic scene in the ring as Phere, Sharon, Dominic and the trainees attended to the injured

Cousin Tom.

With a look of cold-hearted disdain, I gave the crowd one last sarcastic wave goodbye. Then I exited through the curtain, leaving The Dome arena for the very last time.

When Ross, Tom and I were finally together backstage afterwards, I grabbed them both in a tight embrace. I could not have been happier with how the angle had played out. I was now a bad guy once again, in a heel turn that nobody who witnessed it would ever forget.

The three of us told one hell of a story.

The match is still one of RJ Singh's all-time favourites, because he and Tom Chamberlain were real-life close friends. In fact, they both started in the wrestling business around the same time as trainees of Alex Shane.

"We have wrestled each other a lot but that was our best match because of the way we played off Tom's character," said Ross.

"That whole match took them up and down, but it was like a horror ride atmosphere because at the end it went down and down and *down*. The place went cold. It was great. We were so proud of how it went and the reactions we got.

"I had some of my favourite matches in The Dome. I absolutely loved my debut match there, against Stixx in 2004, my match with Ligs (El Ligero) in 2007, and my tag with Andy Simmonz against The Manchester Massive that year where Declan and Joey won for the first time and the place went bonkers. That was the thing with The Dome. When you got a big reaction at The Dome, it was *huge*. You just felt it.

"I think the match with Tom was one of those. The slow build of his character leading up to that was just brilliant. Tiny things, like when XWA unveiled a new belt and Tom came onto stage and started walking towards the belt because he just wanted to touch it. And Greg told him off saying 'Get away from the belt!' I think Tom did such a good job playing that character. The audience just bought it."

Later that night, the final wrestling action ever seen at The Morecambe Dome saw Johnny Phere gain a measure of revenge on RJ Singh, eliminating him to win the 15-man Gold Rush rumble. The ring soon filled with fans and wrestlers alike, all wanting to savour the moment as stand-in ring announcer Richard Parker brought the curtain down on 30 years of grappling history.

My final act at The Dome was to film a backstage interview to cement my heel turn and explain my actions.

Richard Parker set the scene perfectly.

"Tom Lambert has been rushed to hospital!" he gasped, before cornering me for an interview.

"Greg, why did you not help your cousin? Why did you not throw the towel in?"

My reply was measured, sinister and completely lacking in compassion.

"Tonight I did what was right for the XWA, what was right for the wrestling business and I did what was right for you Cousin Tom...my dear Cousin Tom. Because I always told you Tom. You're not a wrestler. You have no business being a wrestler. I had to protect you Tom. I did it for your own good. I had to teach you a lesson.

"And XWA fans, I warned you what would happen if you told me what to do. 'Let Tom wrestle!' you said. Well I let Tom wrestle and look what happened. I said Tom, don't come crying to me if it went horribly wrong. Well, you've got plenty of time to cry now, Tom, in your hospital bed.

"XWA fans, you crossed the line. You stuck your nose in family business. HOW DARE YOU! HOW DARE YOU! And as for you Johnny Phere, you're the worst of all, encouraging my cousin to follow his preposterous dream by training him, by helping him.

"I am Greg 'The Truth' Lambert and the truth is, XWA fans and Johnny Phere, it is you who has Tom Lambert's blood on *your* hands. You're to blame. You're all to blame..."

As I walked away from Richard, he looked into the camera and puffed out his cheeks with a sigh of disbelief at my behaviour. It was the perfect reaction to my promo. Parker debuted for the XWA on our previous show and he was already doing a tremendous job. Smartly dressed, enthusiastic and with smooth delivery on the microphone, the Mancunian became the ideal choice to take over from me as Master of Ceremonies for future shows. Today, as the host of Preston City Wrestling, Rich Parker has evolved into one of the best ring announcers in the country.

The Dome closed six weeks later. It was demolished in January 2011. The venue has never been replaced. Five years on, there is still nothing there but flat land.

What a waste.

Today I often jog along the gorgeous Morecambe seafront and stop at the site to look around, trying to visualise the many great wrestling nights of the past. It will always be hallowed ground, to me.

We had already found a replacement venue, The Carleton nightclub just along the promenade. The manager, Stewart Aimson, was a big grapple fan and keen to have us. But we had concerns. Unlike The Dome, The Carleton had no public car park. Unlike The Dome, The Carleton was in a rough area of town. Unlike The Dome, The Carleton was a dingy nightclub. XWA was family friendly. Almost half of our audience was children under 14. We feared that the new home of the XWA would not be palatable for parents to bring their kids for a night of safe and entertaining fun.

And we were right. Ticket sales for XWA War on the Shore 2010, our debut Carleton event, were way down on what we were used to. And they never really picked up. We were right in the grip of recession at the time. This may have been a contributory factor as hard working people had less money to spend on entertainment. But I firmly believe that had The Dome remained open, we would have continued to regularly draw more than 300. Carleton attendances never broke the 200 mark. So, even allowing for the fact the new venue was about £250 cheaper to hire than The Dome, our income was still reduced by around £1,000 per show.

Changes, regrettably, had to be made. Costs had to be cut. The biggest hit came to the wage and wrestler travel expenses bill. For Dome shows, I would bring two, sometimes three, car-fuls of wrestlers the 250-plus miles from the South East. For Carleton events, this would be slashed to just one car, to keep petrol bills down. This meant established Morecambe favourites like Sam Slam and Jonny Storm were told that, at least for now, their services wouldn't be required. The only southern-based wrestlers to feature on

XWA events in that first year at The Carleton were RJ Singh and Tom Lambert, the participants in our hottest storyline.

Oh, and a gentleman by the name of Alex Shane.

At the start of 2010, Alex was ready for a full-time comeback as a professional wrestler. He'd tested the waters with his run as champion in IPW:UK. The new FWA had started promisingly. The British Wrestling Council was gaining momentum. So The Showstealer finally agreed that he would return to compete in Morecambe for the first time in five years at War on the Shore on April 3 2010.

Our plan that night was that a babyface Alex, as the returning former champion, would team with the local hero Jynkz against the fledgling duo of Blond Jovi. Kyle, Gil and the future James Drake all debuted at the Gold Rush and performed creditably. This, however, would be their first proper match in the XWA. Alex, having seen all three first-hand at BWC gradings, was enthused about the idea of working with the newcomers. Gil, especially, had turned his young career around so much he'd just been awarded the first BWC Scarlo Scholarship - named after Alex's mentor Dino Scarlo - which entitled him to free training for a year and other perks.

But Alex's big triumphant return to Morecambe would also be a storyline smokescreen for his real agenda. Shane wanted to turn heel. He wanted me to be his manager. And he wanted to debut a new persona, the likes of which had never been seen before.

The Ascension.

But before that, we had two more FWA events to contend with.

On February 13 2010, Martin Stone pinned Andy Simmonz to win the vacant FWA Title at British Uproar in Broxbourne. I really loved the story of this match. Simmonz, who was becoming more and more egotistical with every win, claimed he'd had a pre-bout premonition that he would make The Guvnor tap out with his Boston Crab finisher. So during their main event, I wove a tale on commentary that The All-Time Great believed winning the title was his destiny. "What are you, a TV evangelist?" scoffed the brilliant Dave Bradshaw in quick-witted riposte.

Simmonz did indeed make Stone give up, but referee Steve Lynskey was down after a 'ref bump' and didn't see it. Andy was beside himself. His premonition had come true but he hadn't won the match. With no Plan B, Simmonz was taken down into a crossface and as Lynskey recovered, he himself tapped out to give Stone the win and the championship. The loss to Stone signalled the end of Simmonz' FWA run. This was a shame, because he is one of the most underrated performers on the UK scene of the past 10 years. Andy went on to become a commentator for Revolution Pro Wrestling alongside Ollie Bennett, doing a fine job.

After the bout, Martin Stone laid the groundwork for a big storyline which would carry FWA through the next year. Seizing the microphone, he shockingly turned heel with a promo where he summed up the status of British wrestling as merely a training ground. Stone claimed that the FWA was just a showcase for him to perfect his skills and be seen by international talent scouts. His eye was on the real prize of a lucrative contract with the multi-million pound World Wrestling Entertainment in America.

"Now I'm champion, I'm going to use the FWA, so I can go across the Pond, make some money, and not have to perform for you sacks of s__t!" spat Stone at the fans with venom.

"I am going to rape, punder and pillage everything I can...for me!"

At this, all of the FWA roster, who had come out onto the stage to applaud the new champion, looked on with disgust at Stone's words. Although deep down, Martin knew that most if not all of them would surely take the same opportunity for riches if it was offered. After all, a good heel always has to believe he's right and there must be a vein of truth behind his rhetoric.

And every good devil needs an angel too. In this case, FWA's saviour was Leroy Kincaide. Leroy, a former All-England Champion from the FWA's first run, came through the crowd of his fellow grapplers that night to take up the mantle as the defender of British wrestling. The well-built and streetwise Kincaide volunteered himself as leader of The Resistance, a team of grapplers who believed that the UK scene could stand on its own two feet and become more than just the USA's poor cousin. As Stone and Kincaide had their first confrontation, Dave Bradshaw summed the situation up perfectly.

"Martin Stone has declared war on British wrestling and everyone in it!" he announced.

"He just spat in the face of everyone whose blood, sweat and tears built the British wrestling industry!

"War has been declared...and a fight for the soul of British wrestling is on!"

At first, I loved the concept of this storyline because it was real. Despite the fact that our style of wrestling is admired all over the world, we really are small-fry in comparison to the big-budget, internationally televised WWE in the States. Alex's idea was to play off this inferiority complex to position Kincaide and The Resistance as the ultimate babyfaces.

Just like the new FWA itself, The Resistance members were the moral guardians of British wrestling, the underdogs raging against the machine. In contrast, Stone's group was the mega-heels, mercenaries marking time before being snapped up for lucrative contracts overseas. The story seemed really simple to me. It was a fight between clearly defined good guys and bad guys, doing battle for a reason the fans could emotionally invest and believe in.

At this time, Alex and I were having regular long conversations on the telephone, the kind of intense one-hour chats we used to have when we were booking the original FWA. He excitedly laid out his plans for the feud and bounced ideas off me. But he needed a name for Martin Stone's group. I suggested The Agenda, because that's exactly what Stone had - an agenda to get to America. Shane loved the name. And The Agenda was born.

Meanwhile, the regular FWA YouTube TV shows had evolved into a weekly series called FWA Front Line. Hosted by Len Davies with assistance from Francesca Wood and sometimes Dave Bradshaw, Front Line was groundbreaking in its presentation. Len, as link man, hosted from in front of a BBC-style spinning globe backdrop, almost like he was a TV newsreader, as he introduced clips from matches and updates on FWA storylines.

Once again, the style of Front Line divided opinion with fans. Some liked its polished Newsnight-style seriousness. Others found it stuffy and pedestrian.

At this point, the first grumbles about the new FWA began

behind-the-scenes too. These were sparked by the contracts many of the roster signed with The Grapple Group. As part of the deal, the contracted stars agreed to wrestle a stipulated number of FWA dates for no money. By March 2010, for some of them, the novelty of the FWA's return had already worn off. They didn't see the bigger picture and were under pressure from some of their non-contracted peers who saw any wrestler who 'worked for free' as lacking in self-respect or a 'mark for the business', as it's sometimes called. So a few of them wanted out and were vocal about it.

FWA wrestler Dave Rayne wasn't on a Grapple Group contract. But he'd warned Alex this might happen.

"I said at the time to Alex, the promise of something that might happen won't motivate people when they've heard promises so many times - it will alienate people," he said.

"The moment one of them decided they're not getting what they were promised, they will grumble to other people, and everyone will go 'Nah'.

"The FWA was another booking to them. It wasn't their passion. Bringing back the FWA was Alex's passion. If you want people to put your promotion ahead of somebody else's, you have to give them something. You have to pay them. And there was no downside to not being involved. The guys who weren't on a contract were still getting work elsewhere. They weren't making less money. The carrot with FWA was, I'll make you look like a star. But the guys weren't getting money from the DVD sales."

Simon Musk, who *was* on a contract, was one of those becoming disillusioned.

"If I was offered the exact same thing now, six or seven years later, I would have immediately said no," he said.

"We were given a contract and certain things were promised to us in lieu of getting paid. Merchandise we could make money off. Supplements and discounts on them. Every few months two British wrestlers would get sent to America because Alex had ties to ROH and TNA at the time. None of that happened.

"Alex's greatest asset is his ability to talk. He's a very convincing salesman when he wants to be, and he's an especially convincing salesman when you're not wise to it. When you start to get wise to it, you start taking it with a pinch of salt. At the time, Alex had a great reputation because of the first incarnation of the FWA. His goal then was to get British wrestling back on TV and everyone looked at Alex and thought if anyone's going to do it, it's going to be him, because of the FWA and the supershows and everything else. So at the time, there was no reason not to believe him.

"I only ever worked for the original FWA a couple of times. I never did Broxbourne, I only did Morecambe and Blackpool, right at the very end of the initial hot run. So I had no real experience of Alex. And in 2005/6, Alex was, backstage at shows, a very intimidating person. Especially to me who was quite new to the job and I used to be a quiet person who'd just hang around with my mates. He was an imposing figure because of what he'd built himself up to be. So when he started pitching these ideas...he's very good at making people feel good about themselves. I think he uses that to persuade them into his way of thinking. So all this contract business happened. But the long and short of it was, anything that was promised, we didn't get.

"It was more infuriating at the time because we were told, at the time, that *nobody* would be getting paid. For the first show, the impression I got was that *everyone* was on a contract. Then I remember Kirby texting me to say Alex had asked him and Trav to do the second show, and that he wanted them under the contracts. So I thought, well, now they're on board. There was me, Joey Hayes, CJ Banks, our group of mates, we just presumed everybody was under contract. But then we started to hear that a certain group of people *were* getting paid. This immediately caused us, the ones not getting paid, to become disillusioned with the company.

"At the time, wrestling wasn't my full-time job, I had a part-time job as well, so it wasn't the be-all and end-all as far as paying my bills go. Nowadays it is. So if it was in today's climate and the FWA was coming back and they offered the contract, I would say flat-out no, unless you were getting guaranteed money. I think also a few of the wrestlers knew people in certain legal stations who had a look at the contract, who said they're not worth the paper they're written on."

Ligero's friend, the late Kris Travis, was also becoming unimpressed with the new FWA. Trav pulled no punches with his feelings in a tweet he sent out in 2015.

"I remember it being rotten," he said.

"Rotten storylines and a sense of everyone not wanting to be there."

Alex made his own feelings clear at FWA Battle Lines, held at Wulfrun Hall in Wolverhampton on March 21 2010. In another pioneering moment, he allowed his pre-show pep talk to the roster - a speech traditionally held behind closed doors - to be broadcast to the world on YouTube. This was a startlingly transparent move, even for a man who believed exposing the business was necessary in a modern era when most fans know full well that pro wrestling is pre-determined.

Sitting next to Tony on the edge of the ring, Alex addressed the entire crew of FWA wrestlers, referees, officials, backstage crew and commentators.

"We promised you when we started, we will make a British wrestling company that shows you in the best possible light, we will use the best possible production. We will show you a way of working that means you don't have to break your necks to get stuff over.

"We've got a 24 month plan. The first six months was to make the FWA look like a credible company that's watched around the world. This is something you can show your family and friends and be proud. If you don't watch Uproar and say that's the best British wrestling has ever looked in 10 years, then seriously, you're in the wrong country, man.

"This is not a hobby. The amount of effort you guys put in, it's more than a hobby. Some of you view it as a job, but in all fairness if it was a job, you'd make a lot more money from it. Some people, like me, see it more like a religion. All of you risk your life for this, more than you would for a religion.

"What we need from you guys to understand is that some of your brothers in this room are weak. They will sit in front of the others in a changing room and go 'FWA this, FWA that, I work for free' and this stuff comes back to me. Some of those guys aren't on this show tonight.

"Guys, if you're slagging the effort we're putting in, let me tell you right now, if you're willing to risk your bodies and your lives, you've got to be proud of this. But when Nik Bali gets dropped on his head and breaks his neck, he was rolled around the ring, kicked and stomped for five minutes and nobody stopped, even when he was screaming 'I can't feel my legs', every single person (in here) including me is responsible for that happening.

"I'll tell you the difference between the people who make it and the people who don't. The people who become world champion are the guys who stand up and be an individual. The ones who sit in the back and be one of the boys and say nothing, they're the ones who get released.

"I don't want boys any more. I want men. Tony moved back in with his parents so he can fund this to make you look like stars. I turned down running TNA Europe. If I wanted a boss, I'd get a job. What I want to do is see the industry that I love rise to levels it's never gone to before. If you can't see what we're doing is something special, you have to look in the mirror and ask, what am I giving back?"

After Alex finished, there was a huge round of applause. But, there was also an uncomfortable feeling in the room. Alex's passionate, powerful speaking always inspired and motivated me. There was so much truth in what he said. He was right. What kind of a business is this where a young man can end up paralysed, his life ruined, when he was probably only paid a few quid...if at all? He was also right about many of the wrestlers acting like 'boys' with their playground quibbling on social media and internet forums, a lack of professionalism that always drove me up the wall.

Although Alex's critics always accuse him of being out for himself, I can tell you first-hand that Shane was completely genuine. He really saw himself as the leader of a crusade to right his small corner of the world and get British wrestling the respect it deserved instead of always being the butt of the joke. But he felt some of the wrestlers were holding back the revival of the UK scene through negative attitudes. He wanted them to see the bigger picture and not get hung up on FWA's failure to pay them a few quid.

On the other hand, some of the wrestlers felt like a bunch of naughty schoolkids being told off by the teacher. For them, wrestling *was* a paid hobby. It was fun. But they felt Alex was sucking the fun out of it.

So not everybody was taking the new FWA as seriously as the likes of Leroy Kincaide, Spud and RJ Singh, who all raised their games because they realised the weekly YouTube show gave them a platform to be seen all over the globe. To this day, RJ Singh maintains that most of the FWA 'boys' had the wrong attitude.

"I think it's a shame, the whole atmosphere that came with the return of the FWA," said the real-life Ross Jones.

"Everyone felt like the FWA comeback was a chore, it was hard work for most people. Spud and I were two of the only ones who grasped the opportunities that came up. We embraced what was happening and wanted to help push the product further. So Spud got to do (BBC3 TV show) Snog, Marry, Avoid and I got to do a BBC Asian documentary and a TNA Gutcheck try-out through the FWA.

"I remember one of the TNA fan parties we were invited to because we were with the FWA. I was sitting in the VIP area with all this free food, being treated like a star, thinking 'this is how it should be'. None of that would have happened but for the new FWA.

"But I think most people couldn't see further than 'I need a pay cheque, I don't have £40 in my pocket at the end of the show, so I don't see the point in it'. People didn't want to promote it or push it. And I thought that was a real shame. People didn't give it the time. People just wanted the money now.

"I don't know if people will look back in time and think we missed a bit of an opportunity there. It seemed to me that FWA was readying British wrestling for TV. Everything they did was to try to build a TV show. Spud and I felt we were ready-made TV characters so we jumped on it. When I look back at the FWA footage, Spud and I appear on the YouTube TV shows all the time. The Flyweights were given a lot of prominence.

"I'm not saying the FWA was perfect. They could have done things a lot better. But it did open doors and I don't think people let those doors open wide enough before they packed it in."

Another contracted FWA grappler, James 'Rockstar Spud' Curtin, agrees.

"We weren't getting paid great but we were getting constant

attention in front of TV cameras, learning how to work the 'hard-cam'.

"I felt like, give me the ball and I'll run with it. If you don't want to run with it and just want to phone it in, then cool. But what are those people doing now? You've got to be able to run with an opportunity.

"What was around at the time that was as good as the FWA? Nothing. If you want to work for WWE or TNA or ROH or anybody who's got television, then FWA was teaching you how to work for television, how to nurture your own character. I used it to hone my craft, to become a commodity, and that's how it should be. SAS Wrestling, the second run of the FWA and OVW are the places where I picked up the most, got to watch my stuff back and learned how to develop my act. But I think it was too mature for a lot of the lads who were there at the time. People didn't get it."

Tony Simpson says the contracts were part of a definitive plan to give the FWA and British wrestling more of a big-time, professional feel.

"The whole point of the first handful of shows was to create marketing material so we could sell FWA differently. One key thing I learned many years ago is that promoting, as in selling tickets to fill a venue, is difficult, expensive and time draining. With the efforts of our small team being focused on building a high quality product and professional business, promoting in the medium term was not sustainable.

"The plan was to get to the point where we could sell out FWA events by selling one high value ticket or partner with other organisations - MCM Comic Con, Memorabilia, Thorpe Park. This allowed the team to focus on the product and give us a setup that would lend itself well to a TV contract or online show. New Frontiers played a key part in that marketing pack, so I was happy with that.

"We'd also implemented the things behind the scenes that we'd all need to get used to if this was to run like a true production and entertainment business. Contracts, expense budgeting and reports, busy days backstage with promos, photoshoots, agent and booking meetings, and promo scripting.

"I also wanted to ensure the guys got experience of having interaction with people who had no appreciation or experience with the wrestling business, as they would need to get used to this if we were to partner with larger organisations. So I brought in people from with other business and event management backgrounds and collected feedback on everyone's interactions to ensure we were moving toward a professional backstage image.

"We needed to move towards event days being business and product focused. I know that sounds boring but it's what I felt would be required to take British wrestling to the next level.

"I guess it took a lot of the 'fan' out of it for the talent, which was a horrible byproduct of my intentions."

From my point of view though, in early 2010 the new FWA seemed to be developing nicely. Battle Lines was another strong show which ended when Dave Moralez, Joel Redman and Iestyn Rees joined forces with Martin Stone in The Agenda. At the time, Martin was teasing that he'd signed for WWE. Nobody was sure if this was part of the story, or if he'd really been recruited for a spot in America. I found the whole situation intriguing.

On the undercard, there was also an absorbing feud emerging between Johnny Moss and fellow hard man Jon Ryan. Moss had been mightily impressive in his FWA appearances to date. But then Ryan, The Bad Boy of British Wrestling, started getting in his face. Ryan's interference cost The Vigilante his FWA Title tournament semi-final bout with Martin Stone at Hotwired 2009. Then the bald-headed submission expert destroyed my lads Axl Rage and JD Sassoon in a one-versus-two handicap match at Wolverhampton. Anticipation was high for a clash between Moss and Ryan, who had trained together at the Hammerlock gym in Kent. It was on the books to happen sometime in 2010. Although sadly, for one reason or another, it never did.

The Resistance v The Agenda and Moss v Ryan were getting over because they were simple, easy to understand rivalries. But if the new FWA had a creative weakness, it was in Alex's tendency to take good ideas and make them convoluted. The red and yellow card system being a prime example.

Take the FWA Flyweight Title tournament. El Ligero, Spud,

Bubblegum and RJ Singh had qualified for a Round Robin to determine the new champion. Four of Britain's best. It seemed a can't miss situation to have this quartet wrestle each other in a series of singles bouts. But the tournament went on forever. The points system was confusing. The series lasted for far too many shows. And the fans quickly lost interest, no longer caring who ended up as champion.

Attendances still weren't great either. The Midlands is always a traditionally tough place to draw big crowds and with local marketing never an FWA strong suit, so it proved at Battle Lines. A large amount of free tickets were given out for the debut Wolverhampton show and once again, many seats were taken by BWC trainees shipped in on coach trips.

So the new FWA was far from perfect. But its next outing in May 2010 gave the company the kind of exposure Tony and Alex were looking for. They wanted British wrestling to reach new markets, so struck a deal to run a series of FWA shows as an 'exhibit' at the MCM Expo, a science fiction, gaming, comic, TV and film memorabilia weekend at the London ExCel Centre attended by celebrities and 40,000 autograph hunters, movie buffs and computer geeks. The footage from the FWA matches looked great, as the ring was surrounded by huge throngs of people, who loudly appreciated the action even though many of them weren't actually wrestling fans.

RJ Singh absolutely loved the whole experience.

"I enjoyed getting the chance to do new things, like wrestle at sci-fi conventions.

"It was new and exciting stuff. At one of the Comic-Cons (TNA ring announcer) Jeremy Borash was there and ring announced a match I had with Max Angelus. Alex came up to me and said 'I know we've finished for the day but Jeremy Borash is here and we need to put a match on'. And most of the guys said 'ohh, we can't be bothered now'. And I said 'I'll go wrestle, he works for TNA, I'll do the match!'

"Once I'd done that, Jeremy knew who I was. So when TNA British Boot Camp 2 came up in 2014, he spoke to Spud and asked him to throw some British names out, Spud threw my name out and Jeremy said 'Oh, I know him'. So I would never have got onto TNA British Boot Camp 2 but for the FWA."

Rockstar Spud again turned out to be the weekend's MVP, thanks to a hilarious YouTube skit where he wandered around being fabulously egotistical while trying to convince Expo guests to attend an audience with him. After an homage to Spinal Tap where he got lost in a maze of ExCel Centre corridors trying to find his own Q&A, the segment ended with him arriving to find there were only three sci-fi fans dressed as aliens in the audience.

"I told literally everyone in the ExCel Centre and nobody wanted to come," Dave Bradshaw informed the vainglorious rocker during the skit.

Spud's face was a picture.

I couldn't make the Expo and after watching the footage, I felt like I missed out on a sublime weekend. Despite the little cracks starting to appear, I was still enjoying myself, at the time, in my FWA commentary role and very much excited about plans for Alex's return to Morecambe and our new, dark, heel XWA alliance. I even came up with a name for it.

The Authority.

The debut XWA show at The Carleton on April 3 2010 was an interesting day. Alex arrived after everybody else and insisted on his own dressing room, where he could burn incense sticks and create a relaxed atmosphere with positive energy, he said. As Shane prepared for his match in solitude, there were murmurings among some of the other wrestlers in the main changing area. They thought the spiritual Shane was losing his marbles.

"I understand in some ways he was method acting and trying to get into the gimmick, trying to blur the lines between reality and fiction," said Simon Musk, who was backstage that day.

"But to the more level-headed of us, he became a bit of a joke."

The tag match passed off as planned, with Alex and Jynkz defeating Blond Jovi. Then came the main event, Rockstar Spud v Johnny Phere for the title. The Psychotic Warrior ended Spud's six-month reign with a clean Ram Slam-inspired pinfall to thunderous acclaim from the crowd.

"That was my favourite moment of my whole title run with the XWA," said James Curtin in 2016.

"When I dropped the belt to Phere, I adored it, because I'd never seen a building react like that before. But I was upset that we did the angle taking it off him straight away. My title run built to getting the top babyface over, which was Phere, and if we'd have given the audience that moment there and then to party down the beach at Morecambe it would have been great."

But instead, Alex came out to be first to congratulate Johnny. Then I emerged on the stage and announced that Phere's first defence would happen right there and then. As The Psychotic Warrior and the fans glared at me in confusion, Shane turned on the new champion, booting him in the head. I called for the bell, Alex hit his One Night Stand finisher, and the XWA Title had changed hands twice in a matter of minutes. Cackling at the infuriated crowd, Alex and I stood over the fallen Phere and then raised our hands above our heads, before bringing our thumbs and first fingers together to form an 'A' sign.

A for Alex. A for Agenda. A for Authority. A for Ascension.

The origins of The Ascension character came from Alex's real-life interests. Shane believed that the world's major institutions, including governments and the media, were controlled by an unseen force, a secret Freemason-like society called The Illuminati. By 2010, Alex was reading all kinds of books on philosophy, politics, religion, sociology and psychology. Naturally a deep thinker, his new-found knowledge led him to question all of society's norms. He would often talk about his 'third eye Chakra', a spiritual technique from Hinduism, and how it was helping him to realise how we are conditioned from an early age to think in a certain way. But he wanted to rebel.

Many of Alex's intense beliefs at the time rubbed off on me. It was impossible not to be influenced by him. I listened as he preached his off-the-wall ideas on the telephone several times a week, and then listened as he lectured the Morecambe trainees when he visited for BWC gradings. He spoke to these impressionable kids not only about wrestling, but gave his opinions on life, the universe and everything. His view of the world at the time was heavy, heavy stuff. His speeches were lengthy and confusing although there were nuggets of genius to be found. Often his opinions were so 'out there' they left me bewildered and a little scared.

Having said that, I admired Alex's individuality and marvelled at his strong-willed refusal to work a 9 to 5 job so he could commit himself completely to furthering British wrestling. He was a man of principle, determined not to be pigeon-holed by society. People like that inspire me.

Alex also looked very different to when I first met him in 2002. Having stopped eating meat, his build was much slimmer. His training methods altered and his 6ft6in frame was in tip-top condition. He shaved his head, donned eye-liner to darken his glare, and completely changed his mannerisms, gestures and movements. He kind of resembled a human serpent.

The Ascension was more than just a guru or a cult leader. He was wrestling's answer to the deranged preacher transfixing his throng on a street corner or at a rally. He hinted he was a representative of dark forces, perhaps even a disciple of the Devil himself. And he was utterly convincing in the role, to the point that many people believed Alex had gone nuts and really thought he was the Antichrist.

Alex's new alter-ego reminded me very much of Kendo Nagasaki. The masked Kendo was one of British wrestling's biggest stars of the 70s and 80s who protected his character to the point that he was rarely seen in public without his full Samurai clobber. Like The Ascension, the Nagasaki character was a multi-layered, spiritual persona played by a man of principle who didn't care if the other wrestlers viewed him as a fruitcake. And Kendo always insisted on his own dressing room too.

Shane's promo style also did a complete turnaround, from chirpy North London patter to deeply philosophical rhetoric. His 'coming out' speech as The Ascension explained why Johnny Phere had been targeted, and introduced his new persona to the world. We released the video, deliberately, on Ascension Day. May 13 2010.

The video began as the All-Seeing Eye of Providence, a famous religious symbol of an eye surrounded by rays of light and enclosed by a triangle, appeared on screen. Then the picture faded to show Alex Shane sitting in his incense-filled lair at The Carleton with Big Orange, his hands clasped together as if praying.

What followed was a breathtaking monologue. Cerebral. Chilling. And compelling.

"Johnny Phere, I will use you as a martyr, to get across a message for the people I am in union with," hissed The Ascension.

"You see, in this life, there is love and there is fear, and everything else in the middle is an illusion and a misconception. Every single solitary decision ever made in this putrid disgusting excuse for a world comes down to love or fear.

"Now there is one almighty being who champions the quality of love and another who utilises the unstoppable tool of fear. And when you give and you give and you give, and the Father gives nothing back, you start to question your actions, and you realise that everything you fought for is in a state of despair, anarchy and chaos, and that chaos needs order. So a man will sell his soul to the devil to bring about that order, and Johnny Phere, the sad fact is that you are just a mere pawn in the game of the immortals.

"Greg Lambert employed me to take that belt because, my friend, you are going down, not in a blaze of glory, but in a fiery cannon of destruction and despair!

"Tonight was the first step in taking whatever legacy you believed you had by standing over your broken, crippled disgusting body and using it as a human sacrifice to give to the gods above and below...and bask in the dawn of a new era and age.

"It is an age that you will respect. An age of authority. And you *will* respect The Authority."

I had never seen anything like it. It was different, edgy and thought-provoking. As with anything involving Alex, it polarised opinion on the forums and social media, with some fans finding the Ascension character too highbrow for pro wrestling and some mocking Alex's portrayal of it. But by 2010, I no longer cared what the internet critics thought. My sole barometer for success and failure was the reaction of the live crowds at venues. And I was personally invigorated by The Ascension gimmick. I felt privileged to be chosen as my mentor's sidekick. Besides, Shane believed British wrestling needed something this radical to shake it out of its stupor. "Desperate times call for desperate measures," he often said.

As Ligero alluded to, Alex described playing The Ascension as like 'method acting', often comparing his edgy portrayal of the character to that of Heath Ledger playing The Joker in the latest

Batman film. Inspired by this, I too went through an image change.

I started training harder in the gym, especially on cardio, and lost about a stone in weight in an attempt to look skinnier and slimier. Gone was the full-length Harry Potter coat I wore during my previous stint as a manager from 2003-7. Gone were the staid suits I wore as mild-mannered law-abiding XWA boss for the past three years. In their place, came a headmasterly grey jacket and trousers, black tie patterned with white crosses in a nod to the Church, tiny brown sunglasses and, in the most important touch of all, a pair of sinister black leather gloves I bought off Morecambe market. My promo style altered too. I spoke more slowly with gravel in my voice and made proclamations demanding that people listen to the message of The Ascension. I slowly rubbed my gloved hands together, a sick grin etched across my face, and my movements at ringside became more deliberate and staccato. While Alex was the religious oddball, I was the power-crazed political figurehead. I saw my new character as a bizarre hybrid of a Nazi Gestapo agent, The Emperor from Star Wars and Richard Hillman, the murderous insurance salesman from Coronation Street.

Alex had unleashed The Ascension on Morecambe and YouTube but he hadn't yet appeared as a wrestler in the FWA. This was intentional, as he didn't want to be accused of using his position as booker to put the spotlight on himself. But after launching The Ascension so successfully, his aim was to bring the character into the FWA by the end of the year.

First, though, he decided to rid himself of his Showstealer nickname once and for all. He did so after a pivotal feud with Nathan Cruz in New Generation Wrestling, where Alex was still a babyface. Like myself, Alex had recognised Cruz's untapped talent and handpicked him as his successor as the Showstealer. So they had a match, where if Alex lost, Nathan would take on his name.

Their Last Man Standing bout on June 6 2010 in Hull was really special. After outstanding performances from both men in an engrossing arena-wide brawl, it ended amidst disturbing scenes. The arrogant heel Cruz spread a bleeding Alex's arms out wide in a crucifix position and taped his wrists to the top rope. Then he began to whip him hard across the back with a leather belt, while screaming at Alex to "SAY I'M THE SHOWSTEALER!" Shane was defiant, so Cruz kept on whipping him like a man possessed, each sadistic thwack drawing lines of blood across Shane's exposed back. After around a dozen agonising lashes, Alex passed out, but after the NGW roster raced out to buy him some time, he managed to regain consciousness and stagger to his feet. The crowd at the Eastmount Centre was firmly behind Alex as he came alive, but he turned around into a full-force Cruz chair shot which caromed off Shane's shaven head like a gunshot. Alex was done for. Referee Mike Fitzgerald completed the formality of counting him out. And 'The Showstealer' Nathan Cruz was born.

This awesome match is available in full on YouTube. And it's a typical example of how much thought, effort and intensity Alex put into his performances back in 2010. Nathan also performed brilliantly and in the ensuing years, the Hull man has gone on to become one of Britain's very best as the first ever PROGRESS champion and the franchise of his hometown promotion, NGW.

"At that time, I don't think that match did as much for me as it would now, just because British wrestling was still fighting its way up to get noticed again," said Nathan, reflecting in 2016 on the bout with Shane.

"It certainly didn't help me with All-Star, because Brian has never wanted me to use The Showstealer name on his shows. But it did definitely help with me getting booked for XWA and other promotions, and definitely put a lot of eyes on me from people within the job, from those who knew Alex and knew his reputation, and knew how big it was (for him to drop the Showstealer name). People started taking notice of this 19 year-old from Hull.

"(NGW booker) Rich Dunn has a good brain for wrestling. He saw something in me and wanted to put me in that spot, Alex saw something in me and wanted to give me that rub, and as a result I became the next NGW Champion. Seeing NGW grow in the time I was the champion and putting on main event matches, every single month we got more people into the Eastmount Centre. By the time I dropped the title to Matt Myers, we were turning people away at the door."

Two weeks after the NGW match with Cruz, Alex made his

return to the FWA as an in-ring competitor at Art of War, held at Sport Nottingham. The angle to set it up and the ensuing main event match, I believe, was the undisputed highlight of the FWA's comeback years.

It was an eight-man tag team bout pitting The Agenda (Stone, Rees, Redman and Moralez) against The Resistance (Kincaide, Sha Samuels, Terry Frazier and TNA star Nick 'Magnus' Aldis). Interestingly, The Agenda's logo - and that of the Art of War show itself - both made use of the same All-Seeing Eye used by The Ascension in the XWA. Hmmm.

The match began, in front of a responsive crowd in the Nottingham sports centre, with Magnus attempting to lock up with Stone. But instead, the muscular Norfolk native stopped before physical contact was made, flashed a big disingenous smile at the crowd and shook The Guvnor leader by the hand.

Magnus was actually part of The Agenda. It made perfect sense. After all, he was already a Brit plying his trade in America.

"Guys like me, guys like us, we make friends with the right people in the right places," the smug Magnus explained cryptically on the microphone.

"And when you make friends with those people, you become the right people in the right places!"

With Magnus having defected and refusing to fight, The Resistance was now a man down. Kincaide, realising his team was outnumbered, took the mic and sent out a rallying call to anyone who wanted to step up and fight for the cause.

"To all my brothers in the back, this is The Resistance and we need your help," he begged.

At this, the entire roster of FWA babyfaces emerged, all wanting to stand up to The Agenda. At the forefront, was Robbie Brookside.

With his background as one of the few remaining active British wrestlers who competed on ITV during the World of Sport era, the respected veteran was the ideal figurehead to speak with passion on behalf of The Resistance.

"If you want a fight!" he told Stone..."I will pick up the banner and lead the proper, 100% wholehearted British, who believe in the spirit of British wrestling, of Kent Walton, Mick McManus and

Rollerball Rocco!"

Martin sneered at the sight of the ageing Brookside and cut an absolutely amazing promo in response. It was the best of his career.

"Robbie Brookside. That is a name that is uttered on the lips and hearts of all proud British wrestling fans. But you are the biggest hypocrite going. You've had a career of 30 plus years and where was that time spent? Yeah, it was spent in Britain and in England, but where else was it spent? WCW! And Germany. You can't look me in the eye and say you don't care about America, you don't care about making money.

"I am 100% British but I have to go to America to make some money and make a name for myself. If you want to stand here and say how great Britain is, if British wrestling was that good, you wouldn't have gone! Tonight ain't about a wrestling match, tonight is about ending (Kincaide, Samuels and Frazier's) careers. If you want to be a part of that, I will wipe the floor with whatever career you think you had.

"British wrestling is dead. It's a fossil, like you, like your career, and like everything you've ever represented. Liverpool Lads? Where's Doc Dean now? Gone, forgotten, buried, these fans don't even know who Doc Dean is."

Brookside was actually reduced to tears by Stone's verbal decimation of his credentials and that of his former tag team partner, the long-retired Ian 'Doc' Dean. Without a word of riposte, the proud Scouser turned and left. Kincaide and his squad were bereft.

But this brought out Alex Shane. In his wrestling gear. And boy, was he fired up, and ready to renew his rivalry with Martin Stone.

"What you just said to Robbie Brookside is the single most disgusting thing I've ever heard in my life!" he howled.

"I believe in British wrestling! Martin Stone, you are an arsehole! I will answer the call for The Resistance and we are going to war!"

So Shane took Magnus' place. And the elimination match was a classic, full of drama and suspense. After Alex Shane was counted out following interference from Nathan Cruz, it came down to Leroy against Martin and Dave. But the heroic Kincaide fought back to eliminate both against the odds, lastly pinning the startled Stone with a small package to a rousing cheer and enthusiastic "F-W-A!" chants.

"Just calling it a match does not do it justice," I enthused on commentary.

"That was a *happening*."

But the 'WWE-bound' Stone still had the last word.

"You may have won the battle...but this is a war you cannot and won't win!" he warned Kincaide, The Resistance and the happy members of the FWA dressing room who joined in the mid-ring celebration.

The Guvnor claimed that "Resistance is futile" and that "This Agenda goes much higher than anyone can possibly imagine". But what did he mean by that? The fans had their feel-good finish but were still left with plenty of questions unanswered. It was smart booking.

Alex was delighted with how Art of War panned out. In a sit-down interview with Dave Bradshaw for Front Line a few weeks afterwards, he was in buoyant mood about the direction the FWA was heading in.

"Art of War was the single best wrestling show I've ever seen," he said.

"You can sit in the pub with a friend and watch it and they will not fall off their bar stool laughing."

He also had overwhelming praise for Leroy Kincaide and Martin Stone.

"Leroy Kincaide is better than John Cena. He can rap, he's popular with the ladies, he can work main event style, and he can wrestle.

"Martin Stone is our most improved professional in the past six months. He is the best wrestler in the world right now. His promo against Brookside was off the charts. I think he will be the Steve Austin of this country."

Alex also railed against his critics - the hardcore fans, veterans and rival promoters who loathed his out-of-the-box methods.

"I piss people off because I'm opinionated and I'm passionate.

"Look in the mirror and ask yourself, do you disagree with what we're doing because you completely disagree with it and you're doing everything within your power to make British wrestling better or are you saying it because you're petty, insecure in your own achievements and jealous of people who really will go the extra mile to manifest the stuff needed to take British wrestling to the next level?

"Contact us, work with us. Let's debate it and discuss it. I'll even pay your fare. There's serious serious stuff going on. I don't have time for this petty s__t. You and your ilk are embarrassing, you're a f__king disgrace. Shame on you.

"We've got 17 schools in the BWC chain and 400 students. The industry is awakening. My inspiration is to get to the point where the FWA guys can be on full-time salaries.

"The Agenda storyline is part fact, part fiction. For British wrestling to move forward, we need to answer some of the questions. Can it return to the glory days? Can it ever be more than a stepping stone? What better way than to build your entire promotion around that storyline.

"Books will be written about this."

He was certainly right about that.

I too, believed Art of War marked a positive turning point. By now, I was convinced that Simpson and Shane's unorthodox blueprint was working. The Agenda v Resistance storyline had clicked and appeared to have limitless potential. The BWC training syllabus was having a hugely positive effect on the XWA training school, with several students on the verge of joining Jynkz, Stallion, Rage and Sassoon in breaking out onto main shows. The school was turning a profit for the first time, too.

I was also galvanised by my XWA pairing with The Ascension and our feud with Johnny Phere. Particularly because the upcoming Shane v Phere match at Vendetta, scheduled for July 17 2010 at The Carleton, would be the realisation of a long-standing ambition of mine. It was a matchup I had always wanted to book.

When Alex was in charge of the original FWA, I touted Johnny to him for years. Alex didn't rate The Psychotic Warrior at all back then. But after working with him in Morecambe, Shane changed his mind. I believe Alex realised that he and Johnny were kindred spirits. They both had all-consuming passion for professional wrestling. They both poured every ounce of their souls into their characters. And they were both strong-willed outsiders on the UK scene who weren't interested in being one of the boys. I respected both Alex and Johnny as people and performers, and hoped they would bring out the best in each other in the squared circle.

So with all that in mind, I decided to be more hands-on and offered my help to run FWA behind-the-scenes. Alex and Tony were pleased to accept my assistance. To show my faith in the FWA brand, I agreed to lend the XWA name to FWA's Unsigned afternoon shows, which were renamed the Adrenaline division. Prior to The Art of War show, I made an in-ring speech to the Adrenaline roster, which included hot prospects like Jack Gallagher, Zack Gibson, Nathan Cruz and James Drake. My words reflected my real-life feelings at the time.

"The new FWA has organisation and structure, it's got things it didn't have before," I said.

"Now is the time where guys like you can come into the British wrestling industry safe in the knowledge that you have a career path and that you have a future, and this is your time to shine.

"I am so impressed with what the new FWA has to offer that it's time to put the X back into the FWA. The XWA and the FWA are going to create a coalition and take British wrestling to heights it hasn't seen in 20 years."

Next on the...ahem...agenda was the full debut of The Authority. The new gimmick received its premiere on two shows over the weekend of July 17 and 18 2010; Morecambe first on the Saturday and then on to Stockport on the Sunday for FutureShock Wrestling where Alex was also the champion.

When Alex arrived at The Carleton that day, his main priority wasn't to go over his match with Johnny, but instead he spent a good half-an-hour choreographing our ring entrance. He was very precise in his instructions, he had an entire vision for the presentation of our new gimmick laid out in his head. We were also joined by trainees Aaron Wilkinson and Vicky Howard, who would be making their debuts as our two brainwashed helpers Aaron Inferno and Faith Tanner - The Minions.

The show wasn't one of our best. RJ Singh and El Ligero engaged in an untypically bad ladder match for the XWA Flyweight Title. It wasn't their fault. The metal ladder I bought from the local DIY shop wasn't sturdy enough. It bent and almost gave way every time they tried to climb it. I blame our budget restrictions because it really was a cheapo set of steps.

At least the bout ended memorably enough, as Tom Lambert made a triumphant return for revenge on The Bollywood Dream disguised in a Ligero mask. The distraction allowed the Mexican Sensation to tentatively scale the rickety ladder and grab the title to become a three-time Flyweight champion.

But when the main event rolled around, the time spent perfecting our ring entrance paid off. By British wrestling standards, it was a mesmerising spectacle.

I chose a rousing piece of satanic goth-metal march music as The Authority's theme, which fit the gimmick like a black leather glove. It began with a soft guitar lick, as the revolving All-Seeing Eye appeared on The Carleton big screen. When the deliberate rhythm of the drums kicked in, I power-walked through the curtain in time to the beat to a heated reception, grinning maniacally, and stood just off to the side of the stage, my head bowed. The Minions followed close behind, before stopping either side of the entranceway. They too bowed their heads and waited for their leader.

As the strings section ebbed soothingly over a heavy guitar riff, The Ascension appeared, slithering through the curtain almost like an apparition. He eyed the nervous crowd with the detached gaze of a serial killer, then dropped to his haunches and began to move his hands in time to the music as he slowly pulled himself back upright. On cue, The Minions thrust out their arms to the side and their heads began to jerk and twitch, like they were stringless puppets and Alex was the puppet master. Then all of us made the 'A' sign of The Authority above our heads. Tanner then followed The Ascension as he paced like a panther around one side of the ring, Inferno following me as I virtually goose-stepped around the other, making sure each slam of the sole of my shoes landed with the beat of the drum. And we took our time as we walked.

Almost everybody in British wrestling was in such a rush to get to the ring. Not The Authority. We had all the time in the world, as Louis Armstrong once said.

Finally, we met at the far side of the room, where I placed Big

Orange on the floor, and all four of us paused in front of the ring, standing in a line to soak up the uneasy atmosphere in the building. Then Alex climbed, ever so slowly, into the ring and once again conducted The Minions. Then we all made The Authority sign again before The Ascension placed himself calmly on the middle turnbuckle, his hands clasping together in prayer at the exact time the music ended, as his guy-linered eyes gazed a burning hole right through the bemused Johnny Phere.

Hardly anybody else in British wrestling had a set ring entrance ritual at the time. And some of our peers actually scoffed at us for creating such an OTT routine with its dark theatrics and attention to detail. Yet in the WWE, the world's largest wrestling company, everybody has an elaborate ring entrance routine. If a trademark entrance was good enough for Hall of Famers like The Undertaker and Triple H, then it was good enough for us. Alex and I wanted our performance to be at that big-time level. We presented ourselves like larger-than-life stars and set an example hoping our professionalism would rub off on others in Britain.

The ensuing Shane-Phere bout was an exciting enough brawl and the two men had the in-ring chemistry I'd hoped for. But the finish spoiled it. The match ended in an inconclusive no-contest decision and a post-fight angle which was mainly Alex's idea. After Shane rendered Johnny unconscious with a 'towel soaked in chemicals', we tried to turn our nemesis into a human sacrifice, quite literally. As I read creepily from a mysterious book, chanting in tongues, Alex revealed a sharp implement and threatened to carve out Phere's eye in the middle of the ring. Cousin Tom ran in to make the save and he too almost became a victim of The Ascension's quest for "an eye for an eye" until Stixx, Joey Hayes, Jynkz and El Ligero led the XWA roster to the rescue.

Although my son Owen still says it was the most believable angle he has ever seen in Morecambe, I didn't like it. I felt it was too dark for the Morecambe audience and went too far. The XWA was a PG company and that night we dabbled in the occult while vowing to gouge out a human eye. There is a fine line between being intimidating heels and scaring the youngsters in the audience to the point that their parents never bring them again. I feel we crossed that line, that night.

But what we got wrong in Morecambe, we corrected the following night at Stockport Guildhall. In FutureShock, The Authority gimmick really clicked. A lot of credit for this must go to Dave Rayne, the promoter and head trainer of the FutureShock Wrestling school, who had also recently replaced Damon Leigh as the trainer in Morecambe after DDL decided to focus on his developing career in the police force.

Stockport born and bred, Dave started training as a wrestler with GPW in 2003. Then in 2004, he became involved at the inception of FutureShock Wrestling. During its formative years, FutureShock was a North West off-shoot of the FWA, run by Alex Shane.

"I was heading up to Wigan every Sunday to train. I had a Sunday job and no matter how hard I tried, I was always missing the first hour of training every week," said Dave, talking about the orgins of FutureShock.

"A load of lads who were also travelling from Manchester - including Declan O'Connor and a lad called John, who wrestled as Decoy - had a sense of frustration about a lot of things with GPW, and came up with the idea of getting a ring, opening a school in Manchester and getting Alex Shane to come and teach.

"Alex was involved at the outset of GPW, he was on some of the initial shows. (GPW promoter) Lee Butler was rubbing a lot of people the wrong way. So these Manchester lads approached Alex, he came on board to teach classes, and they set FutureShock up.

"Now I didn't have any personal problems with anyone in GPW. I did my best to do Saturdays in Manchester and then Sundays in GPW, to get the best of both worlds and extra ring time. That continued for a while until Lee Butler told me he'd stop putting me on his shows unless I trained exclusively with him. I wanted to be a wrestler and wanted to perform. Then this guy told me I had to do things his way, and I said no.

"About six months after FutureShock started at Salah's gym in Manchester, they ran their first show at Stockport Guildhall. There was about 50 people there. 35 of them I sold tickets to, because I was at the college across the street and grabbed all my friends from the Students' Union to watch me.

"Declan and John weren't really making any money out of FutureShock and were going to stop, so Alex offered to buy it off them. He was the biggest outgoing anyway, for his training fee. So FutureShock Wrestling became Alex's. The shows themselves were being promoted by Paul Gardiner, who wrestled as Paul Zantar, who was in the very first match of the very first show with Dom Travis. I was in a tag with Joey Hayes against Ben 'Axl' Rage and Marco di Fiore.

"At that point in my life, I lived for training and wrestling. I was at every class. I'd do postering and flyering. I'm a big believer in being helpful. I think I've lost a lot of money-making opportunities by just wanting to help out, to make sure things are running smoothly.

"In 2006/7, two years after Alex took over, he had just done the Ring of Honor tour, was looking into the TNA tour and wanted to put his energy elsewhere. Being tied to coming to Manchester was affecting this, so he wasn't coming up as often. Declan was teaching the classes but after a while, it was *me* teaching the classes. FutureShock ended up owing a lot of money to the facility we were training in. Alex and Declan had a bit of a falling out over it. Alex said he would shut it down. FutureShock was everything to me, so I said 'don't do that'. There was a core group of us, myself, Dom, Si Valour, Jack Domino, a lad called Mean Mark. We were a group of about eight who were coming along nicely, they were my friends, and then an undergroup of guys who were developing like Sam Bailey and Jack Gallagher. Zack Gibson came a little bit later.

"I was offered the opportunity to take over but I didn't want to inherit a debt that wasn't mine. So I didn't want to do it in Salah's. The wrestler Ruffneck, who was well known around the gym scene in Manchester, knew a fella who had a room in a gym going spare. I went and had a look, it was perfect size, I moved everything over, bought a new ring off Mark Sloan. I had a van, picked the ring up, and there was no canvas or ropes, so I had to meet Greg and Mark Kay at some motorway services at ridiculous o'clock at night as they were coming back up from London from a show, to get the ropes and canvas. It was all very clandestine. And when we eventually got the full ring, I have a distinct memory of Jack Gallagher setting it up in the new facility. This unassuming kid, who went on to become phenomenal.

"So I took over the training and the shows, inherited a couple of dates at the Guildhall, and with very little money and budget, I had to rebuild everything. As with a lot of things with Alex, everything had been done on promises and handshakes, but these people hadn't made promises and handshakes with me, so I had to start again."

So Dave became the creative force behind FutureShock and by 2009/10 booked a storyline where Alex established himself as the top heel, leading a stable called The Hierarchy. This laid the groundwork for the rise of The Authority. So by the time I returned to Stockport at Alex's side, the fans were already incensed by Shane's antics and baying for blood.

Our entrance again got great heat, as did Alex's successful title defence against Ray 'Raynaldo' Mellon, an immensely popular FutureShock trainee. Raynaldo was the ideal opponent for The Ascension. Their styles meshed well and as the working class, no-frills underdog, Mellon's personality was the antithesis of the overblown, controlling and power-crazed Ascension. We kept things simple, with no convoluted extras or attempted human sacrifices, and were really happy with the match. We debuted one signature Ascension-Truth 'spot' which I particularly loved. Alex distracted the referee while I swept his opponent's leg with my hand from outside the ring. Raynaldo took a hard back bump on the ring apron and as he writhed in pain I slowly walked around ringside, gloved hands behind my back, head bowed, in mock guilt about my interference. I called this 'The Walk of Shame'.

Afterwards in his private incense-filled dressing room, Alex even started talking about taking The Authority gimmick on the road, with me as his manager. He wondered aloud if All-Star Wrestling would be interested.

I smiled politely and tried to imagine how good old Brian Dixon, the ultimate bastion of family-friendly wrestling fun, would react to The Ascension.

British wrestling's top ringside photographer, Tony Knox, then snapped some photos of Alex, myself, Faith and Aaron together making The Authority sign. These photos made us look the business.

For the first time in my wrestling career, in my life, I felt like a star.

An old rival of ours, Welsh Wrestling promoter Alan Ravenhill, wasn't as impressed when the pictures of Alex and myself in our full Authority garb were made public on the UKFF.

"What a pair of idiots," he wrote.

But despite the usual criticism from Shane's enemies, things were going rather well for us in the late summer of 2010. Off the back of The Art of War, tickets were selling well for FWA's next show Hope and Glory in Wolverhampton. Twelve months on from New Frontiers, Hope and Glory on August 28 2010 would be the second highest paid attendance of the FWA's second coming - with 300 fans. Power Slam even agreed to review the show. As Findlay Martin hardly ever covered British wrestling, this was a coup.

I had hope, therefore, that the FWA was heading back to the glory days.

But instead, Hope and Glory would be the night when the FWA began to self-destruct. Again.

CHAPTER 5

THE HALL OF SHAME

In the summer of 2010, I started to worry about Alex. He was becoming increasingly paranoid about how The Ascension might be viewed by 'the outside world' and believed that people were out to harm him. Some of our conversations at the time left me feeling extremely concerned for his well-being.

Alex also thought WWE was ripping off FWA storylines. He went public with this accusation - that somebody within the world's largest wrestling company was watching FWA on YouTube and passing on ideas to Vince McMahon. His first piece of evidence was the June 2010 debut of a new WWE stable called The Nexus. Fronted by British grappler Wade Barrett and including a South African called Justin Gabriel who trained in the FWA Academy years before (when he was known as PJ Black) The Nexus was a group whose mannerisms and aura bore a passing resemblance to The Agenda. They also wore wristbands a little bit like the BWC's. Alex was adamant. He felt his ideas were being plagiarised. Even if this was true, it didn't really matter. In pro wrestling, storylines are often copied and recycled. But Alex made a big thing of it. He was really anti-WWE at the time, mainly because he was frustrated that they toured the UK every year, made a lot of money, signed our best talent but he felt they gave nothing to the struggling British circuit in return.

Alex's agitated state of mind was on full view the day of Hope and Glory. In his pre-show speech to the talent (and thankfully this one wasn't aired on YouTube) he went on a rant again about FWA wrestlers who he felt were letting the side down. He was angry that not enough of the team were sharing FWA match announcements and promo videos through social media to help spread the word. And he was infuriated that certain members of the roster were working for other companies that day instead of the FWA; that they hadn't checked the date of his show and had instead accepted an alternative booking. It was an uncomfortable scene.

"He sat everyone down and basically bollocked everyone, and said I've got all you c-words under contract, under lock and key," recalled El Ligero.

"It turns out he didn't. It was no different to any other promotion but he made out that it was. And at the time, we probably should have been smarter to it than we were. But it wasn't long until the cracks started to show and people saw through it, to the point that when you look back now at the FWA second incarnation, we regard it as a bit of a joke."

Was the pressure of bringing back the FWA getting to Alex? Was performing such a dark alter-ego as The Ascension warping his mind? Or was his super-inquisitive brain overloading because he was questioning absolutely everything going on in the world at the time and he didn't like the answers? Whatever the reason for his behaviour, it was worrying to see.

Alex seemed off-kilter during his promo segment on the show that night too. Confronting Martin Stone (who was on crutches after knee surgery), Shane began to vent his real-life feelings about Vince McMahon.

"I risk breaking my neck and my brothers and sisters risk breaking their necks for this business," he informed the bewildered Wulfrun Hall crowd.

"But Vince distances himself from this business when he refuses to call it *wrestling*."

He was referring to the WWE chairman's insistence on describing professional wrestling as 'sports entertainment', which Alex found distasteful. But his verbal attack on the most powerful figure in pro wrestling, on a small hall show in the Black Country, went over the heads of most of the family audience that night.

Incidentally, the following year Alex took his accusations of WWE plagiarism to new levels when he claimed that CM Punk's famous 'pipe-bomb' promo of June 27 2011 attacking the WWE's behind-the-scenes business practices was influenced by Shane's own public criticism of Vince McMahon's methods in 2010, and that

Punk's guru-like persona as leader of The Nexus was similar to his own character The Ascension.

The rest of the first-half of Hope and Glory passed off with little incident. But then, straight after the interval, came a segment which has passed into the annals of notoriety.

And I believe it's the segment that began the downward spiral of the new FWA.

Patrick Lennon is the writer of The Daily Star's weekly wrestling column and a devoted supporter of the UK scene. Alex had convinced the affable reporter to shoot a video speech to play on the big screen during Hope and Glory. Alex had told me beforehand that this promo would take The Agenda v The Resistance storyline to new heights. He believed it would get people talking and seize the attention of everybody in the wrestling world.

Reading a prepared statement purported to be from Doug Williams, Lennon began to speak. It didn't help that Pat's voice is rather deep and monotone, and he isn't a natural performer. Nor did it help that his speech was a tedious seven minutes and 16 seconds long. And nor did it help that its content went over just about everybody in attendance's head, including mine.

I will try to summarise it for you.

Patrick claimed that Doug had been approached by a small group of international businessmen, who own most of the world's corporations. He was hinting, although he didn't actually come out and say it, that they represented The Illuminati. Lennon said this group was trying to infiltrate the wrestling industry to brainwash young people for their own agenda, and therefore, they aimed to take over the WWE (not named, but referred to as 'the world's largest wrestling company'). He said this group would engineer events to put the WWE under massive political pressure and to highlight the 'moral plight' of the UK scene, by firing British wrestlers who were under contract to the company. This would lead to WWE losing its lucrative British market. Eventually Vince McMahon (again, not named but strongly alluded to) would lose his position as chairman and a plant within the company representing this mysterious group (insinuated to be his son-in-law HHH) would then take over.

Got that?

As Lennon spoke, the fans quickly became bored. They stopped listening to the video. Instead, they began to boo and chant "WE WANT WRESTLING!"

They absolutely hated it.

I have never heard such an overwhelmingly negative response for anything in my entire wrestling career.

After an excruciatingly awkward few minutes, the video mercifully ended. And now it was my job, on commentary, to try to make sense of it.

I did my best, even though I didn't fully understand it myself. During the next match, a six-man featuring the cream of the BWC trainees, I discussed with Dave Bradshaw what Doug's message - delivered through Patrick - was all about. I felt bad for the six youngsters in the match, because we barely mentioned their hard work and athletic prowess, as we were too busy debating the bloody video. But it was what we were employed to do, to put across the storyline that Martin Stone and The Agenda were part of this international, cross-promotional conspiracy that went much higher than anyone could possibly fathom - just as The Guvnor had said.

At least the show ended strongly, as Doug turned up in person and teamed with Leroy Kincaide to defeat Dave Moralez and Joel Redman. But The Agenda still had the final word, as Scottish veteran Drew McDonald came out and stood by Stone's side to reiterate that "this Agenda goes much higher than you can possibly imagine". As McDonald was WWE's chief scout in Europe at the time, his coalition with the bad guys added credibility to the Lennon claims that there were 'plants' in the world's largest wrestling company.

Power Slam described Kincade/Williams v Moralez/Redman as a "worthy main event". But the rest of their review damned the FWA with faint praise.

"On the night, the matches were well-received," they wrote.

"However, the long, convoluted promos, particularly the one supplied via video by Patrick Lennon, did not meet with audience approval. In the case of the Lennon video, spectators didn't have the faintest idea what he was talking about.

"Hopefully (at the next show) FWA will provide some answers to the allegations in a simplified format its audience can understand and enjoy."

Power Slam never reviewed an FWA show again.

Exactly what I'd feared had happened. It wasn't Lennon's fault. I like Pat and no national newspaper journalist has done more to publicise British wrestling over the past 10 years. He was just the messenger and didn't deserve the shooting he got from fans and critics alike. The problem was, a promising storyline was ruined by overcomplication. Alex's real-life interests and beliefs, about The Illuminati and conspiracies, infected the Agenda v Resistance plot and weakened its effectiveness. And his mission to make pro wrestling a more intellectual art form utterly bombed in front of a live audience.

At the end of the day, wrestling fans have simple tastes. They want to watch wrestling. They want to be entertained. And they want to suspend their disbelief. The Patrick Lennon video delivered the exact opposite.

Still, Alex being Alex, he managed to justify the entire angle.

Shane explained his reasoning a few weeks after Hope and Glory, during a YouTube Round Table discussion with Tony Simpson, Dave Bradshaw, female wrestler Jetta and veteran former FWA Champion Justin Richards.

Bradshaw set the scene by openly admitting the Patrick Lennon video was hated by the live crowd.

"Is there any place for a storyline this complex in a professional wrestling show?" he asked.

Alex replied, with a straight face.

"Yes. It's the biggest storyline in wrestling history.

"Every day on the street, people are reading The Da Vinci Code, and Angels and Demons. Blurring the line between what's really going on in the world of wrestling and an FWA storyline...that's what I thought we needed to do.

"The video was placed after the interval. It was done to bring people down. Next match was an Adrenaline six-man tag. It was the most heat those guys had ever had in their life. And it set out our main storyline for the rest of the year. The biggest pop of the night came at the end of the show when Leroy scored the pin.

"This is not a product for the people in the hall. This is about reaching a bigger market. Their memory is temporary. That footage is for life. We are doing television recordings. Online TV *is* TV. It's as relevant as being on ITV 20 years ago.

"It is the most watched video in the history of the FWA since it returned and it was the cheapest we ever produced. I have restrictions on our wage bill. Even rival promoters watched it to see 'what are these idiots doing now'."

When quizzed by Bradshaw for his thoughts on the video, Tony Simpson called it "the most uncomfortable minutes of my life".

"I trust Alex's judgement 100%," said Tony.

"The storylines we are going with, I give Alex full control. But I'm also trying to give those fans a product they enjoy, that entertains them. I think that went slightly too far.

"I was sitting there thinking, do I stop the video? I made the decision to leave it rolling. But it turned ugly."

Justin Richards made his feelings clear. He thought the video was terrible and let Alex know it.

"I once said Alex Shane was either the best thing for British wrestling or the worst," said the traditionalist Richards.

"You took great offence to that, Alex. This is one of those moments. The audience weren't booing for the right reason. They didn't approve of what you were presenting to them. I believe you have turned people away from your product."

As always, Alex had an answer.

"We *may* have turned people away. But in a recession, the businesses that thrive hit a niche. We're not looking to compete with Brian Dixon. He has a niche, the family market, covered. He has funds to do newspaper advertising. We haven't got that. We need to draw people to our YouTube channel. We're drawing 1,000 people to our YouTube channel every week. We're drawing the same number of people without having to pay for a show. And it's not costing us. It was cutting edge. The Attitude Era turned a lot of people off but it drew a lot more."

And then Alex, after saying he was being "persecuted" for trying to push British wrestling forward, began to elaborate on the words behind Lennon's message, which he claimed were based on real-life fact.

"The reason Patrick Lennon put this storyline forward is because he knows it needs to be outed. WWE know they're under attack because they're asking for support. By chance, we are starting a moral war against them because they have it coming.

"This corporation (WWE) has enemies in very high places. People are being put in wrestling companies to make sure they do not succeed. Plants. Look at (TNA). That company was turning a profit, until Vince Russo and Hulk Hogan, and that company is not turning a profit any more. They are the same two people who turned a multi-million dollar profit making company, WCW, into being sold for $2.5m to the very person they were at war with.

"If I had the biggest wrestling company in the world, how would I make sure I had no competition? I'd set up a rival, sign up everyone who could be draws, make it look completely independent, and make sure it doesn't turn a profit."

What was Alex getting at? Well, at the time, Vince McMahon's wife Linda was running for a place on the US Senate (although she failed in this endeavour, twice, she went on to become head of America's Small Business Administration in 2016, appointed by new President Donald Trump). Linda's political career made her fair game for a rigorous examination by the American media (the enemies in high places, perhaps?) And as she was the former CEO of WWE, this meant her husband's company was fair game too.

At the time, US newspapers and TV interviewers were having a field day examining WWE's record on drug testing, questioning the high number of steroid-related deaths among former WWE superstars, and highlighting WWE's policy of referring to its roster as 'independent contractors' meaning they weren't entitled to medical insurance. In October 2010, under fire from the media, Vince 'asked for support' by launching the Stand Up for WWE Campaign, a public relations exercise where he urged loyal WWE fans to write to newspaper editors to defend the company's honour. Alex was suggesting this was because he knew he was 'under attack'.

Meanwhile former WWE head writer Vince Russo and ex-WWE Champion Hulk Hogan were both working for TNA, the company regarded as WWE's biggest competition. Hogan's arrival in October 2009 was expected to be a game-changer for the Nashville-based firm. But it wasn't. Reports are that the company turned a profit from 2007 to 2009 but has not been profitable in any year since then. In America, their weekly TV ratings remained well short of WWE numbers even with Hogan on the show. But to suggest that Vince McMahon 'planted' the Hulkster and Russo in TNA as sabotage? This was simply conjecture.

Alex went on to insinuate that other US wrestling companies had plants in them too and revealed he wasn't actually getting paid to work for the FWA.

"But, a moral and just war is never life in the fast lane, financially," he said.

"As Gandhi and John Lennon knew."

Tony had the final word, which seemed to sum things up.

"Sometimes, I don't know if what Alex is telling me is the truth. Or part of the storyline."

So was the Round Table video real, or part of the storyline? Well, I was talking to Alex constantly during that period of time. And let me tell you, he really did believe the claims he was making.

But, there were occasions when even I wasn't quite sure if what Alex said was real or was being said to embellish his Ascension character and the FWA's main plot. There were times when Shane definitely used his real-life beliefs to add layers to his story of David v Goliath, the underdogs of British wrestling v the megabucks American machine. He really did want to take the storyline 'much higher than you can possibly imagine' by transforming it from The Resistance v The Agenda into FWA v WWE. In doing so, he was blurring the lines of fact and fiction to a head-spinning level in an attempt to grab worldwide attention for us Brits, while also exposing how WWE was run in comparison to his squeaky-clean utopian vision for British wrestling.

But while I found the entire debate intriguing and different, intriguing and different doesn't always appeal to the masses. And after the clumsy way the plot development was executed at Hope and Glory, the FWA and British wrestling felt more niche than ever - and still as far away from the Holy Grail as we were 12 months earlier.

We didn't know it at the time, but Hope and Glory would turn out to be the last FWA show run the traditional way - by generating income from ticket sales. There were no more FWA events at Sports Nottingham, Wulfrun Hall or the expensive Broxbourne Civic Hall. Tony simply didn't have the cash flow to hire venues any more. So while the FWA was trying to boost YouTube hits and DVD sales, this clearly wasn't making them enough money. So Simpson had to find more creative ways of running shows.

"Having spoken to Alex and drank the Kool Aid more than a few times, I understand where he was coming from with the new FWA," said Dave Rayne.

"He wanted an actual business. But he didn't have the one thing a business needs. Money. Everything was done on promises."

These flaws in the financial set-up of the company had been obvious for months, what with the controversy over contracted wrestlers working for free and my own payment agreement where I took a percentage from organising trainee coach trips to shows, instead of receiving a direct wage. So how much longer could Tony Simpson go on funding the FWA? How long *would* he go on?

I started to get some answers in the week of the FWA's next show, European Uprising.

Six years before, the original FWA ran its biggest ever event, British Uprising 3 at Coventry Skydome in front of 1,500 fans, starring legends Terry Funk and Jimmy Hart, and modern-day names AJ Styles, D'Lo Brown and Colt Cabana. The cost of running this show in a 3,500-capacity arena crippled the company and quickened its decline.

Ironically, six years later another show called Uprising was about to have a similar effect. In rather different circumstances.

European Uprising was held at the National Exhibition Centre in Birmingham, the UK's top venue for trade and consumer shows, on the weekend of November 20 and 21 2010. In a similar deal to the MCM Expo appearance in London six months earlier, FWA arranged for a set-up at the venue's annual Memorabilia and Sci-Fi fair. Huge names from the world of TV, films and sport would be there to meet their fans and sign autographs. We are talking the likes of world champion boxers Thomas 'Hit Man' Hearns and Barry McGuigan, motorcycle ace and I'm A Celebrity...Get Me Out of Here winner Carl Fogarty, virtually the entire 1977 Liverpool European Cup winning football side, John Challis who played Boycie in Only Fools and Horses, even the bloke who played Greedo in Star Wars. Around 80,000 people were expected to attend over the two days and they could come and watch the wrestling for free.

Exciting stuff. Great exposure for the FWA, I thought.

Alex had long pinpointed European Uprising as the day he would finally turn heel in the FWA and debut The Ascension character he had been perfecting in FutureShock and XWA. And he definitely *was* starting to perfect it. On September 26 2010 he dropped the FutureShock Title to Raynaldo in a thrilling, interference-filled roller coaster of a brawl where the fans were out of their seats screaming from beginning to end. We were *despised* in Stockport that night. So the crowd noise was ear-splitting when special guest referee Johnny Phere counted three and Alex lost the title.

Such was the heat, one fan turned up wearing a large wooden crucifix strapped to his back. There were no crowd control barriers in the Stockport Guildhall, so this guy was free to approach Alex at ringside during our patented Authority entrance. I thought for one second this nutty fan was going to attack my man. Instead, still wearing the home-made crucifix like Jesus confronting the Devil, the bloke kissed Alex full on the lips. Far from being spooked by this bizarre piece of crowd interaction, The Ascension stayed typically calm, stared a hole through the guy, and carried on walking to the ring.

That night, we debuted another new aspect to our Authority gimmick, the pre-show press conference. As a real-life journalist, I thought this was an ideal way to add an extra dimension to our characters, show how we could control the media like our paymasters The Illuminati allegedly do, and hype up that night's big match into the bargain. We tried it again at XWA's next show, Last Fight at the Prom on October 2 2010, before The Ascension teamed with RJ Singh against Phere and El Ligero. We let the fans in early and did a unique Q&A in The Carleton bar area, hosted by Richard Parker, where we all remained completely in character. It helped crank up the tension between the rival teams and increased anticipation for that evening's main event, which saw my guys Alex and The Bollywood Dream emerge victorious in an overly-long and rather tedious encounter.

According to the stipulation of the bout, Alex now got five minutes in the ring with a terrified Tom Lambert. The Ascension toyed with my overmatched cousin and looked like he was going to finish him for good. But Tom managed to lay his hands on the same 'towel soaked with chemicals' used by Shane to render Phere unconscious at Vendetta. Tom turned the tables, smothered The Ascension with the cloth, and after Shane passed out, was declared an unlikely winner.

The crowd reaction to Tom's triumph against the odds was a lot milder than I hoped for. It was my fake relative's final appearance in Morecambe and although on paper, it was a fitting way for the character to bow out, having finally achieved his dream of winning a wrestling match, I look back now and feel that we missed an opportunity. Storyline-wise, I didn't get the climax to the Tom Lambert angle quite right. It was too dark.

"Nobody was more gutted about that than Tom," said Ross Jones.

"He felt that Tom Lambert deserved a win over RJ Singh at some point after the match we had at The Dome. Then again, if that match with Alex had been at The Dome, it might have been completely different."

It's a shame, because when we kept things simple, The Ascension and The Truth proved to be an effective heel combination. It didn't matter if we won or lost. What mattered was the fans cared deeply about the outcome of our matches. So I was very much looking forward to European Uprising and the chance to test our on-screen partnership on a new audience.

But then in the run-up to European Uprising, Alex gave me an off-screen task. He wanted me to organise an important part of the weekend's festivities. He wanted me to invite some of the UK's most respected veteran wrestlers to the FWA's first ever British Wrestling Hall of Fame ceremony.

This was another laudable FWA idea. Alex and Tony wanted to honour the veteran UK wrestlers who paved the way for the youngsters of today by inducting some of them into a brand new Hall of Fame. They were hoping 'The Man of 1,000 Holds' Johnny Saint, Steve Grey, Robbie Brookside, Skull Murphy and Darren Walsh would be available to come along. Five-time WWE Champion Bret 'The Hitman' Hart, who wrestled on the UK circuit during the World of Sport days, was also scheduled to be at the Memorabilia fair, so Alex and Tony hoped to surprise the Canadian legend with his own Hall of Fame award.

But here is where things began to go badly wrong. The Hall of Fame turned out to be a monumental cock-up, blighted by the kind of poor organisation, miscommunication and lack of cash which brought down the first incarnation of the FWA.

FWA announced the Hall of Fame before anyone had agreed to appear. This was the first mistake. Then, instead of contacting the veterans directly, I was told to speak to Robbie Brookside and ask him to persuade his buddies Saint, Grey, Murphy and Walsh to attend. But there was one catch. Unless a sponsor could be found, which was not guaranteed, there was no budget to pay these guys. Remember, there would be no income from ticket sales as European Uprising was a free show.

This created a ludicrous situation. In essence, Robbie and I were both middle men. And I have always got on famously with Brookside. I like and respect him immensely. Aside from Alex, Dann Read, Findlay Martin and maybe one or two others, Robbie was the only wrestling person I could have an hour-long telephone conversation with back then. We used to talk about the business but also music, the history of Morecambe and our friendly rivalry on opposite sides of the football divide where Rob was an Evertonian and I was a devout Red. Great chats, they were. I valued our friendship and didn't like being put in this awkward position of asking Brookside to ask his mates to do something they clearly wouldn't want to do.

But, I dutifully called Robbie and told him the score. As I expected, the exasperated Scouser told me straight - there was no way the 'old schoolers' would appear at the Hall of Fame without getting paid.

I reported back to Alex, who was incredulous.

"But it's an awards ceremony!" he cried.

Shane believed the veterans should turn up for nothing to help British wrestling, to be part of his crusade. But to the previous generation, the FWA and this new Hall of Fame were nothing special. It was just another booking. And they wouldn't come along to Birmingham that weekend without guaranteed money.

I was told to call Brookside back and tell him about the possible sponsor. We got to the point where Robbie said both himself and Johnny Saint might be able to do it. But the day before the show, we were at an impasse. The sponsor hadn't come through. I was going back and forth with Robbie on the telephone, trying to reach an agreement. We were both getting frustrated.

At this stage, I wanted to make sure my own wage would be covered for the weekend. I was spending hours of my time trying to sort out this farce and I wanted fairly compensating. There was no trainee coach trip planned for his show. The novelty of the FWA's return was starting to wear off with the students, too, and I hadn't been able to persuade enough of them to travel to make the coach trip viable. So I texted Tony and informed him of my fee.

The next thing, Alex telephoned me in a rage. He ranted at me that Tony was stressed about the upcoming weekend, he was worried he might shut down the FWA and the last thing he needed was me asking him for money.

I couldn't believe it. What the hell was going on here? We ended up having a massive row, just because I had committed the heinous crime of wanting payment for doing a job.

Shane and I eventually talked things through, as we always did whenever we fell out. But the whole episode left a sour taste in my mouth, especially when Brookside called me again as I was travelling down to Birmingham with Stallion on the morning of European Uprising. I had never heard Rob so angry. He told me that he'd heard from Alex, who tried one last time to persuade him to appear for free, and he felt insulted. Robbie said he had no time for Alex's 'mumbo-jumbo' and had a message for me to pass on - that neither himself nor Johnny Saint would be there.

Then he hung up.

I felt sick. Not that the Hall of Fame was off, but that Robbie was annoyed. I felt so bad that Brookside wasted his time that I paid him to host a class at the XWA training school two months later, so at least he got some kind of recompense. Everything was smoothed over between us and I was pleased about that. Robbie's *the man* as far as I'm concerned, and I am delighted for his current success as a trainer in NXT. His daughter Xia is now wrestling on the British circuit and shows a lot of promise. She was due to debut in Morecambe in 2017. Given her dad's rich legacy in the town as a former FWA and XWA Champion, I can't wait to see Xia follow in Robbie's footsteps.

So while the British part of the Hall of Fame had fallen through, Bret Hart *did* actually get his award that weekend. Although to call it a Hall of Fame ceremony would be a gross exaggeration. Instead Alex and Axl Rage, a big fan of The Hitman's, turned up as Hart was finishing off a Q&A with fans at the NEC on the Sunday afternoon and presented him with a framed certificate to honour his classic Wembley Stadium WWF Summerslam bout with Davey Boy Smith in 1992. It was certainly a great moment for the beaming Gil as he shook hands with his hero.

As for me, I was infuriated and embarrassed by the whole Hall of Fame saga. To think, I had put my faith in the new FWA, thinking things would be different. Thinking the mismanagement was in the past. How wrong I was.

The Uprising show itself was a bit of a disaster too. Partly due to the booking and partly due to the lack of atmosphere generated by a transient crowd. You see, most of the audience weren't at the NEC to watch the wrestling. They were there to see any number of attractions - the celebrities, the comic and action figure stalls, the computer gaming sections, or the dozens of costumed sci-fi and superhero characters walking around. So once they had seen a bit of wrestling, they lost interest and moved on to another exhibit. But European Uprising was a two-hour show.

When the first bell rang, there were 300 people watching. By the time the final match ended, this number had halved.

The infernal red and yellow card system ruined the opening match between The Leaders and Stixx and Malen. The umpteenth bout between El Ligero and RJ Singh ended in a cheap countout. And due to injury, Spud was unable to compete as advertised in a three-way ladder match, deflating those few wrestling fans who were in attendance because he was the performer they most wanted to see.

Instead, the Rockstar temporarily took my place on commentary as his long-term rival Jonny Storm downed Axl Rage and Nathan Cruz to little reaction.

The main event was Martin Stone v Leroy Kincaide for the FWA Title with Alex as special referee. Shane's swerve turn, when it came, was entirely predictable but well executed, as he booted Leroy in the head and cost him the match. After months of touting The Resistance, Alex revealed that he was the head of The Agenda all along.

This angle received a tepid response from a tiring, confused, depleted audience.

But on video, the Shane turn came across much better. Alex's big boot nailed Leroy perfectly as he charged in attempting to finish Stone with a spear. Replacement referee Chris Roberts made the count under duress and then I left the commentary table to join Alex, Martin and the rest of The Agenda in the ring to bask in our duplicity.

"What you have just seen is the great work of the ages in its final stages!" proclaimed the triumphant antagonist.

"Alex Shane is no more and The Ascension is the head of this faction! Call it The Agenda, call it The Authority, but right here tonight in the NEC, it will reveal itself for what it truly is, and that is the infiltration of professional wrestling by The Illuminati!"

Then as we headed for the backstage area, The Ascension stopped to spit right in poor Dave Bradshaw's face. The way Dave sold this, totally bewildered, removing his headset, wiping away the spit, his face a picture of shock, was beautiful.

Alex was immensely proud of the angle. He said it was the ideal way to end 'Season 1' of the FWA. The company would eventually release a box set DVD with highlights from the revived company's first 15 months.

But I felt rather deflated. Afterwards, a few of us made our way into nearby Walsall for a post-Uprising Saturday night out. I drowned my sorrows over a few drinks with Francesca Wood, Tony Knox, Tony Simpson and his girlfriend, and enjoyed a good reminiscing session about the glory years of the Morecambe Dome with Spud. Then I burst out laughing when Jay came back from the toilet just as Living on a Prayer came thumping over the pub jukebox. Out of character, the Rockstar was not amused as we all mocked him by uproariously singing along to his theme tune.

My experience on the Sunday afternoon cheered me up a little too. I amused myself by marching around through the crowds of punters in the sprawling hangar of the NEC, in my full Authority gear, Big Orange on my shoulder, flanked by the ideal pair of bodyguards in Joel Redman and Iestyn Rees, who are two absolute physical specimens. We got plenty of attention, posed for photos with Stormtroopers and had a rare old time. I even got to interview a Dalek. Not many journalists have that on their CV.

The weekend's wrestling action closed with an inconsequential Adrenaline show which did, admittedly, have a stunning conclusion when a young grappler from the South West called Nick Riley actually pinned Alex to win the XWA Title.

Why have you never heard about this before, dear reader? Well, that's because we struck the result of this bout from the record books.

So unless you were one of the few in attendance at the NEC Birmingham on November 21 2010, the Riley-Shane title change never actually happened. Such was the power of The Authority.

That weekend saw another major nail in the coffin of the new FWA. Or more accurately, the BWC. Helen Carr departed. This was a hammer blow for the British Wrestling Council. Without Helen to organise the gradings, send out the wristbands, do all the admin, arrange Alex's diary and basically keep the whole concept running smoothly, everything ground to a halt.

In 2011, the gradings stopped. At the time, a large number of trainees were on the verge of finishing the syllabus and graduating, including my dedicated team in Morecambe, where seven had passed the Blue stage seven and only had the final Black wristband to earn.

I maintain that the BWC syllabus was a great idea. The problem was, nobody ever completed it, through no fault of their own. Later there were efforts to relaunch the BWC as the British Wrestling Coalition. But it never really got off the ground.

The wheels were coming off. By this time, a tiny minority of hardcore fans were ripping into the FWA on the forums every chance they got.

One longtime wrestling fan whose opinion I respect is Ben Corrigan, who has travelled all over the British Isles watching shows for years and knows his stuff. A few weeks after European Uprising, Ben wrote an online piece which for me, summed up what was wrong with the new FWA.

"I think the new FWA is essentially a 'demo tape' for British wrestling," he said.

"They recognise there are a number of decent, international-standard wrestlers on these shores and are giving them a platform to actually get noticed.

"They get their matches down on decent quality footage, with good all-around production and in front of decent-sized crowds, hence the bus trips to fill up the studio audience.

"I don't think the issue of people working for free is essentially a bad one, since the concept is to give them decent footage, promotional materials, supplements, sponsorship and media opportunities which will then allow them to potentially get more paid bookings than before in other companies.

"Problem is, however, still the same as it was when FWA first relaunched. Although they have many benefits to the wrestlers and visions of benefits to the British industry as a whole, there simply isn't much for the actual fans themelves to be interested in that you can't get elsewhere.

"While I admire FWA for actually trying to do something to raise awareness, there isn't much of substance to actually draw fans in, keep their attention and make them come back for more. Although the future of television is over the internet, it's almost impossible to follow the storylines in the promotion and, even if you do, it's even harder trying to take in everything and understand it since there is simply too much going on at once.

"The problem is, however, that I think that while more people have become aware of FWA and what they are doing, they are only making more people turn off and give up on it. Essentially, more people are becoming aware, but deciding it isn't something that they want to see."

Steven Fludder, future promoter of PCW, also gave his assessment of the FWA when he posted on the UKFF forum that

December.

"The problem is, they're trying too hard," he said.

Well, I'd given up trying. After European Uprising, I went home to Morecambe, turned off my phone, and spent two days in seclusion. I did a lot of soul-searching. And I decided to pull XWA's name from the Adrenaline project and withdraw from FWA's management team.

There was no way on this earth I was going to re-live the stress of the dying days of the original FWA. My hair was already thinning. It was time to recognise the warning signs from past experience and jump off the ship before it sank.

I appeared at one more FWA show, a return visit to the NEC in March 2011. And that was that. I never worked for the promotion again.

CHAPTER 6

FINAL FRONTIERS...AGAIN

The FWA limped on for another year or so until the promotion finally stuttered to a halt, for the second and hopefully final time.
But along the way, it did have a few success stories.
The inaugural BritWresFest event, held over two days on February 21 and 22 2011 from historic venue The Old Vic Tunnels at London Bridge, received some good reviews.
The following month, Alex struck a deal with the actors' union Equity to allow pro wrestlers to hold equity cards - which he felt was a major step towards acceptance for wrestling in 'the real world'.
And there were returns to the London ExCel in May and October 2011, then another show at the NEC Birmingham in November where Jonny Storm pinned Spud to *finally* end their feud and *finally* end the FWA Flyweight Title tournament, more than two years after it began.
Meanwhile in August 2011, Episode 1 of Season 2 of FWA Front Line aired. The programme did little to further any traditional wrestling storylines or promote matches or feuds, and instead spent 27 minutes rabbiting on about the Patrick Lennon video from 12 months before and continued to claim that WWE was stealing FWA ideas.
Overall, some of this episode was quite clever. But the storyline had become so convoluted and contrived that I struggled to get my head around the whole thing. And if someone with a university degree and postgraduate diploma couldn't fully understand it, you can bet the average wrestling fan was utterly perplexed.
Having said that, my ears did prick up when in ensuing years, the WWE actually introduced characters called The Authority and The Ascension. So who knows? Maybe somebody within WWE *was* watching the FWA in 2010/11. Although I should point out that

Triple H and Stephanie McMahon of The Authority, and the Road Warrior lookalike tag team Konnor and Viktor from The Ascension, bear little physical resemblance to myself or Alex.

Episode 1 of Season 2 turned out to be the final episode of Front Line. And after live events in Birmingham in late March/early April 2012, a follow-up weekend of shows scheduled for May 2012 was cancelled. The FWA never promoted again.

Meanwhile, Alex carried on his Ascension character for much of 2011 in XWA and the FWA, albeit mainly in angles and running interference in his Authority and Agenda cohorts' matches. His performances as the omnipotent guru were as engrossingly powerful as ever. But he was a frustrated man for most of that year. Suffering with nagging injuries, he either couldn't or wouldn't physically wrestle any more. He was still irritated by the WWE's policies, the constant online criticism of his methods and the small-minded attitude of most other British wrestlers. He also remained extremely paranoid and demanding, lashing out whenever he felt his displays as the Ascension weren't being filmed properly or he wasn't being paid enough for the effort he was putting in.

Meanwhile, it turned out that the FWA Champion Martin Stone *had* indeed signed for WWE (back in April 2010, in fact) but his knee surgery had delayed his move to America. But in 2011, with his knee now fixed, The Guvnor was finally on his way to the world's largest wrestling company.

Sadly Martin's career has never really caught fire in America. WWE released him in 2014. Stone returned in 2015 and 2016 as a non-contracted regular on the weekly NXT TV show, but hardly ever won a match. It seems the world's largest wrestling company sees "the best wrestler in the world", as Alex once called him, as little more than enhancement talent. And that's a shame, because I believe Martin is better than that.

Back to 2011, and with the FWA and the XWA Champion both out of commission, we tried a gimmick where anyone from The Authority or The Agenda could defend either belt on any show. This gave an opportunity to a newcomer, a protege of Alex's called David Deville, who also happened to work at Buckingham Palace as a footman for Her Majesty the Queen. Deville is a nice guy and a good wrestler, and his royal day job attracted national media attention for himself and Alex. But storyline-wise, having the unknown Deville defend belts he didn't actually win just didn't feel right to me.

At the end of 2011, I needed Alex to drop the XWA Championship to Johnny Phere. I wanted him to compete in a six-man tag at that year's Last Fight at the Prom, captaining a squad against Phere's team, which would set up their final battle for the XWA Title at Gold Rush 2012. But in the days leading up to the show, Shane informed me he was still injured, didn't feel he was being paid well enough for the long trips to Morecambe ("I know my own worth" he'd often tell me) and felt exhausted from playing the mentally taxing Ascension role.

Alex hadn't defended the title in a proper bout for over a year. He suggested he take a six month sabbatical and then return in 2012 to do the honours for Johnny. But I'd run out of patience. So I told him I'd be crowning a new champion in his absence. And he accepted my decision.

So I drafted in Dave Rayne to replace him. It kind of made sense. I'd been managing Rayne in FutureShock throughout 2011, after Dave pinned Raynaldo to win the FutureShock Title and joined The Authority, turning heel for the very first time.

"I was actually first scheduled to be a heel on the first FutureShock show in 2004," explained Dave in 2016.

"Alex said I had great heel features but I told him it's not going to work because I had 30-odd people coming who would refuse to boo me. And I was right, the place went nuts when the hometown boy came out. But from then on, I ended up being booked as a babyface everywhere and I was generic, bland and middle of the road. I later tried to do a party boy gimmick and had an entrance that was quite popular, but it was average.

"Then when Alex was working shows for us as a heel (in 2009/10) I'd been written out for a while to do backstage stuff, and it was time for my return. Alex was to drop the belt to Raynaldo, who again wasn't the most spectacular wrestler but was super-popular with that crowd. The original idea was that I would come back as a hero to help Raynaldo, clean house and Ray would hit his finish and get the win. Johnny Phere was special referee and I liked it because although The Authority and Phere were feuding in both promotions, the two XWA and FutureShock stories stood alone, so people who went to one could follow it and so could people who went to both.

"So the original idea was that I'd go on to wrestle and beat Alex, then turn heel. I came back, not for the fans, but because he attacked me and took me out of FutureShock because he didn't respect me, but then I'd take a lesson from his book and become the big heel. But then Alex decided he didn't want to come to the shows any more. I'm not sure what his mindset was. There was never any intention for me to become FutureShock Champion. I didn't want to be the guy who puts himself over but I needed to be top heel. We had guys like Cyanide who were almost there but not quite. And we had a new top babyface-in-waiting in Jack Gallagher (who had a breakout performance in Stockport that summer against Davey Richards). Again, not quite there yet. We needed an instant foil for Raynaldo, that night.

"So we had Alex film a video where he challenged somebody to step up and take the opportunity to join The Authority, and I did it, hit Raynaldo with the belt, wrestled the match as a heel, won, and I was the champion. The crowd went quiet, Greg got in the ring with the belt, his character was trying to hitch his cart to me with Alex gone and people in the crowd wanted me to hit Greg. They didn't want to believe that I'd turned heel.

"It was a big time for me. I had a lot of changes in my life for the better. I got in better shape. I'd rehabbed recurring injuries to my hip. I changed my gear, new music, and I got to talk and cut heel promos, be a character, which I'd never done."

I thoroughly enjoyed being in Rayne's corner for two entertaining FutureShock Title defences at Stockport Guildhall in summer 2011 against Phere and the American star Colt Cabana. Dave was really improving and we get on really well. So I trusted him with a very difficult spot as The Authority's handpicked caretaker XWA Champion.

Rayne took Alex's place as captain of The Authority team at XWA Last Fight at the Prom on October 8 2011, alongside Nathan Cruz and a giant Yorkshireman called Colossus Kennedy. Dave did a tremendous job as the smug replacement who could hardly believe his luck that he was carrying Big Orange around. My trio lost to Phere, Stixx and Sam Slam (who had returned to the XWA earlier that year) in an absorbing contest full of excitement. But that wasn't the end of it. As Johnny was the man to score the pinfall, he earned himself an immediate title match, and he quickly Ram Slammed poor Dave in 30 seconds to win the belt. Then he gave me a Ram Slam too.

Booking-wise, it wasn't an ideal scenario for Dave Rayne to lose a championship he never actually won. But the Morecambe fans didn't care, because their hero The Psychotic Warrior had the belt back around his waist and The Truth finally got his come-uppance. I retired the black leather gloves and the rest of my sinister apparel soon afterwards. Playing such a twisted character over the previous 18 months took a lot out of me, too.

Meanwhile, Alex put out this message on Facebook.

"I'm feeling truly blessed today for all the amazing people I have the honour of knowing. I've been even more hard work to deal with than normal for the past two years, doing far more things than one person can handle.

"I've made a choice to pull back and appreciate those around me more. All of you are awesome, even the people who I've 'had words' with and I'm really grateful to know you all!"

It was a dignified exit from a man who'd given so much he'd burned himself out.

So the FWA was finished, again. Without achieving the Holy Grail, again.

Tony Simpson explained why he believes things went wrong and why he decided to close the FWA down.

"We had pockets of issues along the journey but I think the talent and crew lost confidence in us when I was working to close a huge partnership deal that would have been the game changer for the industry," he said.

"The partnership negotiations and planning took a lot of effort and time but I was 99% sure it was a done deal. As such I decided to temporarily cut the budget on our events to free up funds to be focused on nationally marketing the launch of the new partnership.

"The negotiations and planning went on longer than anticipated and rather than increase event budgets again to keep the product strong, I kept them static, which in retrospect was the wrong thing to do. I forced us to book on budget rather than our true values. I was looking to the strategy rather than the current delivery.

"When the partnership deal fell apart, morale was at an all-time low and I felt that confidence in my ability to deliver something special had dropped. I also had a host of personal and health problems. Between FWA and my day job, I was regularly working 12 to 16 hour days and weekends, which doesn't do your health or personal and family life any good at all.

"As such, I decided it would be better if I stepped back and allowed someone else to take the reins with my support. Unfortunately I didn't manage to mobilise the right team for this, so decided to close down and focus on getting back into a normal life routine again."

Today, people say to me that the FWA should never have been resurrected. Like when Vince McMahon brought back ECW in the mid-noughties, they say the FWA comeback tarnished the memories of the original. Some of Alex's 'wacky' ideas during those years are regarded with scorn by many within British wrestling circles. I myself didn't always agree with how he went about things. And ultimately, the FWA comeback left me feeling disappointed and drained.

"I believe the new FWA could have worked," says Andy Quildan.

"But it needed to do what the original FWA did and that's innovate. It had to provide something different to what everyone else in the industry was doing at the time. But I believed what it turned out to be was almost an inbetween, between RQW and IPW. They had the production, but after the second and third show, I saw the writing on the wall."

But at least Alex was willing to have a go. He regularly told me during those days, that he knew it wouldn't be him who would lead British wrestling to the promised land. He knew it would be somebody else, one day, who would pick up the baton and run with it - and it wasn't long before the likes of PCW, ICW, Revolution Pro and PROGRESS did just that. But at the time, nobody else was prepared to stick their head above the parapet and shout from the rooftops that modern-day British wrestling could be something special.

Nobody was taking risks on the UK scene at the time. It was boring. At least Alex tried to shake things up. His approach was controversial but it was *interesting*.

And I believe that the FWA's return *does* have its own legacy, of sorts.

The new FWA gave British wrestlers an opportunity to learn their craft in front of TV cameras and set new standards for production in British wrestling. It was a revolution some embraced, particularly RockStar Spud and RJ Singh.

"The FWA was blueprinting some of the stuff that goes on today," said RJ Singh.

"They had a really good go at upping production values with smarter video packages and trying to get content online. I don't believe many companies had YouTube content up at that time, to the same extent. But you look now, in those five years since, look at where we've gone. Wrestling companies in Britain now use HD cameras, good lighting, entrance videos, and now they're using On Demand services. ICW, PROGRESS, Rev Pro are all doing it. That might not have happened had FWA not made such a big push.

"Alex used to say that online and mobile is the new TV. That's how we consume TV now, we consume it on our tablets and mobile phones. He saw that coming, ahead of its time, and jumped on it. That is a big part of the legacy there."

Tony Simpson certainly looks back with pride on what his FWA tried to do.

"I'd love to think that the FWA set a benchmark that other organisations have pushed to surpass today," he said.

"I've seen some great stuff coming out of British wrestling since the FWA's closure. I mostly hope that the talent took a lot from the FWA experience and learnings and I'm happy to see many making waves on the global stage.

"I thank them all for their contribution to what was something special and wish them and the whole industry all the success they deserve."

Tony is no longer involved in wrestling. Today he works as a freelance management consultant. In 2016 he married his wife Stephanie and in 2017 they hope to travel the world then start a family. But Tony still believes he may return to wrestling one day, if the timing, project and product is right.

As for Alex Shane, he learned a lot from making those YouTube episodes of FWA Front Line, many of which he edited himself. His new-found TV production knowledge stood him in good stead. One month after Front Line finished, in September 2011, he began producing a new YouTube programme called WrestleTalk TV - a television version of his old TalkSport radio chat show - hosted by Patrick Lennon and the former Radio 1 DJ, wrestling fan and top bloke Joel Ross.

WrestleTalk TV later made the transition to national television in August 2012, with a regular Sunday night slot on Challenge TV after TNA Impact Wrestling. WrestleTalk TV defied critics and remained on Challenge for the next three-and-a-half years.

"The problem with Alex is he has the big dream, and amazing amazing visions for things, but so many of them and he never followed through on the stuff he put out there," said Dave Rayne.

"I think WrestleTalk was the first one where he did follow through on his vision. And that's because he was mainly out of the wrestling bubble."

So Alex stuck at this particular project, which even I didn't believe he'd be able to do. After a few early teething problems, WrestleTalk TV gradually evolved into a polished half-hour weekly programme, featuring intelligent discussion about WWE, TNA, ROH, New Japan and also British wrestling, and interviews with special guests. Some of the biggest names on the worldwide wrestling scene appeared on WrestleTalk TV, like Hulk Hogan, Kurt Angle, Bret Hart, Rey Mysterio and Sting.

The online Shane haters loathed the programme, of course. But to me, the show had a simple and digestible format for all wrestling fans to enjoy. There was nothing complex or confusing or overly intellectual. And that's why it worked. Alex learned his lesson from The Ascension years. It was a shame when Challenge cancelled WrestleTalk TV at the end of 2015 because it was just hitting its stride.

As the FWA wound down, Shane continued his moral crusade on behalf of British wrestling by setting up a project called 'Wrestling With Ethics' (note the initials?) Alex and RJ Singh launched this during an interview on BBC Radio London in September 2011. This was another example of Alex opening doors for Ross. This is one of the reasons why RJ has always been extremely loyal to his mentor and to this day, defends him to the hilt.

"Alex has got a magnetic side to his personality and you can't help being drawn in by him," said Ross.

"He could probably sit there and in a calm voice tell you he'd just bombed a building and you would listen! You can get lost for hours talking to him.

"And if it wasn't for Alex, I would never have been a wrestler. He trained me. And every time Alex started something new he would always bring me in. He gave me the opportunities in the FWA. When I needed something new, he was the one who was there to suggest I started the Bollywood character. He got me into RQW, Boot Camp, Gut Check. And then when he first started WrestleTalk, I was the first (guest) on it. When he did a club night with X-Pac he rang me up and invited me. So every time he does a new venture he asks me to get involved.

"He always used to say to me 'I like bringing you to stuff because you're normal, you're well-spoken, you're down to earth and you act like a human being'! He used to say how he was sick of working with boys and wanted to work with men. So he knew if he brought me to a TV station that I wouldn't embarrass him. And I know a lot of those things benefited him too, but there was always something for me as well. People have their reasons why they don't like Alex and I'm not denying some of the things he's done in the past. But actually, he has always, wholeheartedly, done right by me. He's never screwed me over or done anything that will affect me in a negative way. I owe the fact that I'm a wrestler to him."

Under the Wrestling With Ethics banner, Alex organised the second annual BritWresFest at The Coronet Theatre in London's Elephant and Castle on April 1 2012, with proceeds going to Great Ormond Street children's hospital. As it was a charity show, it was free admission. Therefore many families were in the crowd that

Sunday afternoon. BritWresFest was also attended by EastEnders TV soap stars Jacqueline Jossa (Lauren Branning) and Tony Discipline (Tyler Moon) who in real life is Dino Scarlo's son.

The concept of BritWresFest 2012 was that it would showcase one match from several of the top UK promotions. I was back as colour commentator, alongside a new play-by-play colleague called Ollie Bennett. Ollie was knowledgeable and showed promise. I enjoyed working with him. He went on to become lead commentator for Andy Quildan's new promotion, Revolution Pro Wrestling.

It was an enjoyable show all round, in fact. The opener saw El Ligero, Nathan Cruz and Rampage Brown, a talented brawler from Leeds who had recently returned home after a short stint in WWE developmental, represent New Generation Wrestling in a fast-paced battle for the NGW Title.

By this point, Ligero was widely regarded as one of the best wrestlers in the country, versatile, consistent and able to have a good match with just about anybody. The following year, he joined Kris Travis in the Power Slam top 50.

"I don't think I became what I would call 'good' until 2010," said Simon.

"I had shoulder surgery in 2009 and was off for seven months. But I kept myself involved in wrestling and went to a lot of shows as a ring announcer and commentator. I sat at ringside for matches and that helped me learn what parts of my act I was still missing. When I came back in late 2009 I felt like I'd improved a lot by taking a step back and watching more.

"Until I got injured, I started to break out and make a name for myself with 1PW and I'd get big matches with imports, and I think a lot of it went to my head because I never expected to be anything in wrestling, because of my size. I was always told by bigger heavyweights that I would never achieve anything. I always wanted to prove those nay-sayers wrong by showcasing myself. But the injury knocked me back a peg and when I came back, I was more humble, I learned about showcasing not just myself but everyone in the match, and I became a better all-round worker.

"And I had a lot of help from people like Spud, Dave Mastiff, Kirby, Trav and CJ Banks. There's a group of us who help each other when we can and give each other advice. Our group were kind of self-taught from travelling together, wrestling each other all the time and giving each other feedback."

Nathan was becoming an outstanding all-rounder by this point. But in storyline, he had recently lost the NGW title to his childhood friend Matt Myers.

"At primary school Matt arrived one day and had a WCW poster with him, and that was it, we hit it off straightaway," said Nathan.

"Wrestling bonded us and now Matty is the closest thing I've got to a brother. I couldn't imagine my life without him. What's been awesome is that we started training together. We debuted in the same week. And we've main evented Hull City Hall against each other, in a place where we used to watch wrestling together. I've been very fortunate to have a friend so close to me for so long and be able to share so many amazing moments with him, within wrestling."

Myers lost the NGW Title to Rampage just a few weeks before the Coronet Theatre show. Real name Oliver Biney, Rampage's name always comes up in discussions about the best British grapplers of the modern era. A true man's man and a no-nonsense performer, Brown is one of the few UK wrestlers who has made a full-time living from the business, pretty much right from the get-go of his 16-year career.

Rampage began his career in Stoke-on-Trent in September 2000 with Chris Curtis and GBH Wrestling, whose training school also spawned Dean Allmark, Mikey Whiplash, Johnny Phere, Bubblegum, Robbie Dynamite and Dirk Feelgood. The Yorkshireman very quickly gained work with All-Star, then through his mentor Drew McDonald branched out to also appear for longtime UK promoters Orig Williams and Ian McGregor. By wrestling all the time, the Leeds bruiser gained a wealth of experience and skills, competing in up to 200 matches a year while still in his early 20s.

Brown soon caught the eye of WWE and signed a contract to go over to their then-developmental group, Florida Championship Wrestling, in 2010. But Ollie's experience in America proves that the grass is not always greener in the States.

"It was a strange experience, frustrating but a good learning experience in life," said the 33-year-old Biney in 2016, reflecting on his time with WWE.

"It was fun and I get what they were trying to do there. I did get taught a lot, especially from Ricky Steamboat who took a lot of time out with me because I knew his son Richie from when he came over here to work for All-Star. William Regal helped me out a lot too. I made a lot of friends there as well. Roman Reigns and Seth Rollins were there. We'd train together every day and it's nice to see them doing well now because at one point, we were all struggling together. The moment I met Roman Reigns I knew he'd be a star, it was like they'd put him together in a factory!

"But I wasn't perceived as much more than just 'a body'. I don't mean just in terms of putting people over (losing all the time), this wasn't my gripe. It was the fact that I was little more than a training dummy during the week and then at the weekends, I wasn't on the shows. I was standing around watching shows and doing odd jobs. There were times when I thought 'I'm under contract to the WWE but it certainly doesn't feel like it' because I was digging ditches at the side of a motorway, putting up signs, going to hardware stores, making frames out of wood. And there were other things going on at the time, situations I fell into that I didn't like.

"I got signed by John Laurinaitis who made his money in All-Japan where everything was very aggressive, rough and physical. So he liked my style in the ring because I'm quite aggressive too. But then they sent me to FCW where Dusty Rhodes wrote the shows and led on people's characters. He was into razzle-dazzle so he looked at me and didn't see anything for me. At the time I was 6ft1, 230lbs, I could take everybody's finish and I could wrestle, but that was about it.

"So I saw the writing on the wall. I was getting hurt a lot in training, just from taking moves off guys. But every time I complained and said I was hurt, it went down in a file and went to the office. I thought, I can't win. It wasn't my fault I was getting hurt. So I thought, I'm not getting on TV, I wasn't getting much encouragement, I'd try to talk to the trainers and they'd kind of brush me off. So I thought I could either go back to what I was doing before, doing the schedule in Britain, travelling to France, Germany and Denmark, doing my own thing, being happy and making some decent money. Or I could see it out in America.

"A lot of guys stayed because they didn't have anything else. And they're on TV now. So it could have worked for me. I could have stayed and gone on to bigger and better things. But I might not have done. So I'm more than happy with the decision I made at the time."

Rampage left the WWE, of his own accord, in 2011 and returned to the UK circuit where he quickly won both the All-Star and NGW Heavyweight Titles, and made a name for himself in PCW, PROGRESS and other top British companies.

Five years on, now the WWE developmental system has been overhauled, and the state-of-the-art Performance Centre in Florida and NXT is giving huge opportunities to so many, would Rampage consider going back?

"I've asked myself that question," said Ollie.

"I've got a two-and-a-half year old daughter now and she's more important to me than anything. But on the flip side of that, the way I'm going now, I've probably only got another three years in the ring if I'm lucky, assuming the business in Britain stays as good as it is. Then I can walk away, still healthy, carry on teaching wrestling and help anyone who wants to listen, but do other things. The travelling all the time, living out of a suitcase, the lack of sleep, it bothers me now. So if I went back to WWE, I could make the big money now while I can, for my daughter.

"I've done wrestling for 15 years and it's always either shafted me or broken my heart. I used to think I've put all this work in and never got anything out. I have in a way, because I've travelled the world. But I've never felt like for all the pain, I've got enough back."

So at BritWresFest 2012, Rampage was determined to impress. Certainly his performance in the three-way with Ligero and Cruz that day in London showed why he'd been picked for WWE in the first place. Brown won to retain the NGW Title.

The Ligero-Brown-Cruz three-way was followed by The Leaders of the New School retaining their IPW:UK Tag Team Titles over Jonny Storm and Dean Allmark. Swedish grappler Jenny Sjodin lost her Pro-Wrestling:EVE Title to a tall and powerful Brigitte Neilsen lookalike from Germany called Alpha Female, who Alex had taken under his wing hoping to get her noticed in America. Jack Gallagher beat Zack Gibson in a technical wrestling bout to retain his FutureShock Title. I got my first look at Mark Andrews, who delivered some impressive high-flying moves in winning a ladder match against Sam Bailey, 'Wild Boar' Mike Hitchman and Xander Cooper.

The XWA was represented, of course, in the best way possible too. Our match was between two of my favourite characters and people, Rockstar Spud and RJ Singh. And the main event saw the last stand of The Resistance v Agenda feud, as Doug Williams, Nick Riley and Sha Samuels beat Joel Redman, Colossus and David Deville in a match where Johnny Phere, who appeared on some of the final FWA shows too, was ringside enforcer.

My personal highlight of the day was commentating on the Lucha Britannia guest match. This was my first taste of the bizarre world of Lucha Britannia and its cast of colourful characters, who were some of UK wrestling's most recognisable names playing masked alter-egos to emulate the crazy superheroes and villains-inspired world of Mexican Lucha Libre-style wrestling.

For example, 'The Cockney Crusader' Greg Burridge reinvented himself as Metallico, complete with metal-plated mask and body armour. Metallico hilariously had a tendency to 'rust' and grind to a halt whenever his opponents threw water in his direction. Meanwhile IPW:UK cruiserweight Paul Robinson became the heroic Leon Britannico who was locked in a perennial rivalry with his villainous alter-ego Dark Britannico played by Will Ospreay.

I loved the pageantry, acrobatics and unusual rules of Lucha Britannia, and had a ball working alongside the promotion's regular Master of Ceremonies Benjamin Louche, a flamboyantly camp and creepy Burlesque and cabaret host who joined me on commentary for a Lucha bout pitting Metallico and Leon Britannico against Dark Britannico and the giant Santeria (Sam 'Berry' Gardiner).

"Lucha Britannia shows aren't really wrestling shows, they are a night-out experience in London," said Ross Jones, who worked for Garry Vanderhorne's unique promotion under a mask as The Bengal Tiger.

"When I first started, every member of the roster was a well-known British wrestler as a different character. Nowadays it's very different, it's all guys who have come through their training school, trained by Greg Burridge. I was on a couple of shows when (TV personality) Jonathan Ross was there. He's a big fan of Lucha Britannia.

"It was such a good laugh. Lucha Britannia opened doors for me. I got to do some fun nightclub stuff and Comic-Cons. We were the first to do the Download Festival, which NXT went to this year. It was also nice to see guys like Will Ospreay, who got his start as Dark Britannico. BritWresFest was one of his first big shows."

BritWresFest was a worthwhile experience for me too, not least of all because it meant my commentary later appeared on national television. When Alex secured a second TV show on Challenge in April 2013, the monthly British Wrestling Round-Up, he aired matches from the BritWresFest show. Alex could now rightfully claim he'd brought British wrestling action back to a mainstream TV channel.

Once all the BritWresFest 2012 matches were screened, Alex struck a deal with Richard Dunn, promoter of New Generation Wrestling. This resulted in regular bouts from the Hull-based company airing on Challenge TV on both British Wrestling Round-Up (until its run ended in December 2014) and WrestleTalk TV, including matches from a follow-up BritWresFest show at Liverpool Olympia in June 2015. For a time, NGW carried the banner for British wrestling on national television. After their Challenge run ended, Alex and NGW continued to produce a 45-minute TV show for YouTube called British Wrestling Weekly.

These days many UK promotions have a free 'TV show' on YouTube or upload footage to a paid-for Video On-Demand channel. For me, British Wrestling Weekly is the blueprint for how modern-day British wrestling should be presented on mainstream TV. It is family-friendly, the roster includes some of the best Brits such as Ligero, Bubblegum, Mark Haskins, Doug Williams, Zack Gibson, Rampage Brown and Nathan Cruz, and the show is easy to follow with just the right mix of matches, video packages and interviews.

Nathan agrees.

"The production in the latest series has skyrocketed," said Cruz.

"I watched the debut episode of Series 3 and it looked like it belonged on Saturday night prime time TV. It took me back to when

I used to watch Gladiators as a kid. It had the same kind of feel but with a modern tint.

"My favourite match (on British Wrestling Weekly) was a time limit draw I had with Zack Gibson. We'd both just come out of a WWE try-out and we were both so hungry, we have a like-mindedness about how wrestling should be done, and we managed to combine the independent style of wrestling with the British style of wrestling and still tell a story. Every time I watch it back I'm so pleased with what we achieved. It was quality. Zack is a supremely hard working, dedicated talent."

Dave Rayne is also impressed with what NGW are trying to do.

"It's good they call their TV show 'British Wrestling' because if you're scrolling through your On-Demand service or your Sky TV planner, nobody is going to stop if it says 'NGW'," said Dave.

"And I agree that all that effort to push NGW as a brand is a good idea because they have excelled. I didn't agree with British Wrestling Round-Up having lots of promotions on it because it was lots of little bits of different brands, and people can't follow all these products. There should be one British wrestling product on TV that people can get behind."

Alex Shane, now fully retired as an active wrestler, added another string to his bow as NGW's main commentator. Ironically, Alex has slotted into a role Richard Dunn originally offered to me.

I was offered the NGW commentary job after I made a guest appearance as ring announcer and commentator for NGW's Destiny show in March 2013. I enjoyed the experience, and was particularly impressed with the production values and branding. Destiny was a good show too in front of a packed house, ending when Mark Haskins ousted El Ligero to win the main event 30-man rumble and become NGW Champion.

Rich later asked me to return as a regular NGW commentator, starting with a two-day weekender of shows in November 2013. Sadly I wasn't available that particular weekend. But even if I had been, in all honesty committing myself to a monthly trip to Hull and back didn't really appeal at the time, mainly due to some personal stuff I was going through. Perhaps this was an opportunity missed, for myself. NGW's vision of how pro wrestling should be done is very similar to my own and I think we'd be a great fit.

Shortly afterwards, Alex became the voice of NGW. Then in 2016, Dave Bradshaw returned to the microphone as NGW's main commentator with Alex slotting into the colour role.

As well as being a commentator and producer, Alex also got involved in the creative side of NGW. Simon Musk wasn't happy about this, at first.

"When he first got involved in NGW, I was very very very against it because I've been with NGW since 2010, since the start of their second year and the promotion used to be very homegrown," said Simon, speaking in February 2016.

"Rich Dunn was lead booker, Luke Ingamells was the owner, and there was a bunch of us who would see each other all the time, at training and such, and all the angles weren't just one person's vision, there was a bunch of us all discussing stuff, working out what would work and what wouldn't, and pitching ideas for different characters.

"But when Alex came in, my first impression was that it would just be Alex's vision now and he'd take over the shows. I know how domineering he can be.

"For a while, it wasn't like we butted heads as such, but there are certain things he pitched that I flat out didn't agree with. I've now had more matches than Alex ever had and in my opinion, I'm better than he ever was.

"He's got a good mind, there's no denying how intelligent he is, but even now to this day, there are some things on the shows that I don't particularly agree with. I've had to argue my case quite a lot with my own stuff, not to get my own way, but for it to make sense with where we're going.

"The positive aspect of him being there is that people now view him more as a producer rather than an on-screen character. It has erased partly, the impression people had of him from five or six years ago. So that's a positive."

As for my own relationship with Alex, well, at time of writing I haven't worked with him since BritWresFest 2012 and haven't seen him for nearly four years. The last time was at a Royal Rumble fan party at a bar in Shepherds Bush in January 2013.

We still stay in touch with the odd message and phone call now and then. We even had chats about me working with him on WrestleTalk and NGW, although nothing came to fruition. But not having Alex in my life has been weird, because there was a time when we were very close.

We hadn't spoken in well over a year when I telephoned him on April 21 2016 to interview him for this book. A conversation followed which, in classic Shane style, lasted two-and-a-half hours, and at times went off on a tangent or three.

Alex, now 36, told me he was settled in a long-term relationship. He doesn't wrestle any more, nor does he run training sessions other than his online mentoring service the School of Wrestling Knowledge. Most of his time was spent running his own TV production business, Trident Vision Media, which he said was in talks with "a major UK broadcaster" about bringing WrestleTalk back to television. He also revealed that Challenge only cancelled the show due to TNA losing its TV deal in the US ("The theory was that WrestleTalk had less value as a UK TV property because TNA lost its contract in America. It was actually really very little to do with what we did. We needed to keep a certain percentage of the TNA audience after Impact finished, 30-35%, and we were doing that. Sadly by the time we were halfway through series seven, the TNA audience in January 2016 was about a third of what it was when we signed to Challenge in 2012...") He also told me Trident was financed out of his own pocket with help from a business partner. He even had an office in Dagenham and four full-time staff working for him.

"I was waiting so long for a TV production company to come along to produce a British wrestling show, I thought I might as well do my own," he said.

"We are now officially recognised as a production company who can pitch to the BBC. We make AAA's weekly show dubbed in English, NGW British Wrestling Weekly, Challenge quiz show Beat The Beast with Mark Labbett and have even begun making a medical show for Discovery called Ask Dr Nandi (NOTE – they later added What Culture Pro Wrestling Loaded to their CV). Not to mention the amazing online growth of WrestleTalk as a YouTube channel. It now does around 10 million views a month and growing, actually making it more of a financial asset now than at any point during its time on television, with much smaller overheads. Oh and we kept the WrestleTalk studio, which is still ready and waiting, some fans will be happy to know."

Alex also informed me that his company recently bought out New Generation Wrestling.

"Rich Dunn and I pretty much book it together now," he said.

"Things are going really well. In Hull, NGW has moved from a community centre to Hull City Hall and drew 1,000 on December 22 2015 on a Tuesday, which is pretty awesome. We will do the same in 2016 too.

"British Wrestling Weekly is now on local TV. If you're on Freeview we're on Channel 7 at 4pm on a Saturday afternoon in Liverpool, Birmingham, Grimsby, Cardiff, Hull, Leeds, Tyne and Wear, Brighton, Bristol and we're adding five more stations in the next few months.

"It's a really positive step. This is opening the door to other broadcasters who suddenly have an interest in British wrestling. We've been trying for a family show instead of an adult orientated brand, which the UK is full of. Ideally NGW is something that appeals to smart fans too but importantly won't offend parents. Our model is different to pretty much all of British wrestling but we've got some really exciting deals on the table now."

Alex seemed happy and was doing well for himself, still working full-time in the business he loves. Alex also seemed to have conquered some of his demons from the FWA days, something he admitted he rarely talked about. As he opened up about 'The Second Coming', he found it a tough subject to tackle. It was clearly painful for him to revisit such a dark and stressful time in his life.

"It all began when Tony Simpson called me while I was in India.

"Martin Stone had told him the only thing that's going to work would be to bring back the FWA. I wasn't really enjoying sitting on the India-Pakistan border in Punjab waiting for TNA to get their s__t together so I said to Tony, let's do it, I'm coming home.

"The main problem was that we tried to do too many things at once, and without the right money to do it all. We tried to set up an agency, run a wrestling company, implement a national training syllabus, raise the production values and profile of British wrestling and get a TV deal. All on an investment of just £10,000! It was too much for anyone to do, all at once. Especially as there was no big money backer.

"I have chosen to believe that one of the main reasons it didn't work was because I personally wasn't capable of doing all the things I had to do, as a man. I was 29 at the time and just wasn't the person I needed to be as a professional at that point. I'd had over 15 years of living in the wrestling bubble from a teenager and that doesn't always make you well-adjusted in the larger business world. I was basically still a wrestler, with aspirations of being more but without the self-awareness to see my limitations at the time. Working for a giant corporation like Sky for four years sped up my evolution dramatically, but sadly FWA Volume 2 was prior to that experience and it paid the price.

"What I've learned is that success in anything, particularly wrestling, follows this rule. It's not about how you deal with the successes themselves, it's about how you manage with the failures. Success will usually come if you persevere and do the right thing for long enough. Yet it won't last unless you're exceptionally good at dealing with the more challenging things that come along with it. In wrestling fans' and wrestlers eyes, you're only as good as your last show.

"There were times in British wrestling when FWA seemed unstoppable or 1PW for example seemed invincible. Yet this was often due more to momentum than solid business substance. I'm sure there are companies in the UK now that feel the same way. Yet lasting success as I see it now is a marathon and no longer a sprint. When you get to the point where you're not just as good as your last show or even your last 10 shows, then you have a solid business and not just a momentum-driven, show to show project. I wish I'd have understood this during the FWA.

"I realised I had to have a big life change. I've spent six years since the second FWA rebuilding as a professional and dare I say it, a grown up. Now I'm in a six year plus relationship with someone not connected to the wrestling business - which has given me a real sense of distance and clarity for the first time since I broke in at age

13. I like to view it like this now. What happened was no-one's fault but my own. I had bouts ranging from mild annoyance to anger over various elements of the FWA for years. However, I lay the blame at my own feet now by choice, as that's the only way you can ever really grow, right?"

But while willing to admit his own mistakes, and he conceded that some of the storylines *were* too complex, Alex still rightly feels that the FWA's return never got the credit it deserved.

"I think the second FWA did far more than the first one in helping British wrestling as an industry get ready for television, but you've got to look for it. The first FWA inspired more British fans to become wrestlers and promoters. Yet the second FWA really upped the overall quality of production on the scene, how to present British wrestling storylines on camera and how UK talent were expected to perform on screen."

I asked him about the contracts. I told him there are people who remain disgruntled to this day, who believe they never got what they were promised. Alex responded with a combination of understanding and defiance.

"I appreciate all the stuff the guys did in FWA. I wrongly thought we were all in it together. But I should have accepted that we weren't meant to be. That's just not how capitalist business works. I wasn't one of the wrestlers in reality, but my brain had not fully taken on board that I was now 'management'.

"They were promised insurance. They all got it. They were promised a great platform with really good quality content so they could say, this is me. I think many of them got that too. Particularly as we did get on TV in the end with WrestleTalk and British Wrestling Round-Up. But sadly the only two original FWA members who really stuck around to see it were Francesca Wood and Lisa Carrodus. Guess what? They became national TV regulars as a result. I felt I had something to prove to those people who said 'Alex will NEVER get British wrestling on TV'. Believe me, there were a lot of those both in front of and behind the curtain.

"Spud went on a nationally televised documentary and heavily credited the FWA for the ability to learn the things that he is now doing in TNA. That meant a lot to me. Often in life, the people who succeed, see things as opportunities. While the ones who don't, look for things to become obstacles so that they have an excuse. It's often about not owning your own part in a failure, which I've come to find is pretty unproductive."

Alex also had a few words for El Ligero. He believes that Simon should be grateful for the exposure Shane has given him.

"I felt for a while that Ligs was a bit funny with me. Yet when British Wrestling Round-Up had a list of the Top 10 UK wrestlers, he was number one for three months above everyone else. I put that list on national TV and it was a fairly major nod to him. And when we aired BritWresFest as the first nationally televised British wrestling in over 25 years, he was in the first match. I'd like to think his TV profile has done well out of me since FWA.

"We've likely spoken over 100 times in the last few years and he never said anything about there being an issue. I even brought him into a room at a show recently and I asked if things were cool. He said yes and we shook hands as men. That's good enough for me. The way I see it, anything else said elsewhere really isn't my issue now and is often par for the course with the wrestling business. You've just got to let people get on with it.

"Look, nobody wanted the FWA to work more than me. Nobody paid more of a price for it than me either I believe. I was really all right financially at the start of the FWA, but by the end... not so much. You see the first FWA show went really well, but after the second one we realised that nostalgia alone wouldn't sell tickets long-term.

"FWA almost sent me under. I had one day where I was so hungry because I hadn't eaten. I found an out of date, gone-off packet of cous cous at the back of the kitchen cupboard. That's the day I found out that my kettle was broken, so I ate it cold. The worst thing was that it tasted brilliant because I was that starving. Yet at the same time, all I was hearing was 'Oh Alex has got us wrestling for free'. It was one bloody day a month! They didn't appreciated that I edited over 120 videos in just 12 months, ran the shows, appeared as talent and I never got paid either. I was often doing 15 hours a day working on FWA stuff.

"A few idiots tried to call me a con-artist. Some seemed happy to see me burn. But I genuinely wanted to do all the things I set out to and I think history has proved that now. At the time though, it nearly f__king killed me. In the long run, I think it was well worth the effort."

Alex went on to talk about the inspirations behind The Ascension and The Agenda-Resistance storyline.

"I think I was watching too many conspiracy videos and had a partner at the time who smoked a lot of weed. You can do the maths. I believed for a while that it was an amazing artist's tool. I felt so creative at that point, but it was a potential road to disaster.

"The Patrick Lennon thing...we wanted FWA to be a YouTube sensation. I knew the Illuminati was going to be a big thing based on the number of YouTube views videos about it. Was it too complicated for fans? Definitely. 100%. But Hope and Glory was a good show apart from that one thing. I was always pissed off at the Power Slam review that buried the whole show based on just 10 minutes out of over three hours of awesome wrestling. I was annoyed at Findlay Martin after that for ages. Now it's water under the bridge. He actually regrets not getting more behind British wrestling after about a decade of me begging him to do so.

"Maybe it *was* all a crazy concept. The basic Agenda versus Resistance idea was actually pretty good but it got way too overcomplicated.

"The inspiration behind the creation of the Ascension character was really Brian Pillman. I wanted to create a character that was so genuinely feared, multi-dimensional and believable that like Brian Pillman, you'd look at him and wonder how much was actually real. You would think 'if that guy stopped, stared at me and gave me a look like he was going to kill me, or putting a spell on me, I'd believe it'. Yet it was so that when The Ascension got beat, the fans would want to cheer their f__king lungs out. And when Raynaldo beat me in FutureShock for example it was super over! Man was it over!

"I didn't want to be a success financially back then. I just wanted to revolutionise British wrestling as a character and narrative hub. Tony rightfully wanted to have a successful business, but I wanted to go through my Paul Heyman years with a mixture of Kendo Nagasaki meets Sabu. But the more I got into that character, the more that character took over. I think it nearly killed me and many of my friends say 'we thought we'd lost you back then'.

"I'd go to the gym in Romford where I lived at the time, a tough area, with my Egyptian-style eye-liner on. All these guys who were jacked up and massive, some probably drug dealers, would avoid making eye contact. I was told later that a fair few were pretty terrified of the black magic-looking psycho. I turned vegetarian, did yoga for 90 minutes a day and lost so much weight. I think I went all Russell Brand before Brand did himself. I could see my eight pack for a while.

"I had serious character tunnel vision. I wanted to be Darth Vader and The Emperor all as one character. For all those narrative structure and movie geeks out there, I was both the chess master and the dragon. Like Goldfinger and Odd Job all at once. I'm not a Christian but I do believe in God or a greater force as you might call it. So I never wanted to out and out say The Ascension is the Anti-Christ or the Devil, yet it was implied. There was clear Paganism and Egyptian symbolism all in there. And it was the most popular I'd ever been with women on nights out. It was all getting too alluring for me in the end and a recipe for disaster. I was trying to revolutionise what it was to be a heel and felt success was actually being attacked by the fans.

"I studied all sorts of stuff to understand the character more. Quantum mechanics, mysticism, religious texts. Yet there is one theory I still believe over all others, and that is you pretty much create your own reality through a mixture of focus of will and the way your brain receives the information you're allowing it to filter. And let me tell you that some crazy stuff happened during that Ascension period that I try not to think about any more, because I can't 100% say it was real. I know what happened and so do a few other people who were around. Suffice to say, when you decide with that much focus to go as deep down the rabbit hole as you can, don't be surprised if you find some monsters at the bottom too.

"I haven't spoken about this stuff in wrestling circles much before. No wonder I f_king cracked. In the end, I had a massive meltdown and deleted all The Ascension stuff off YouTube."

He's right. With a few exceptions, you will find very little trace of

The Ascension on the internet today.

"The irony was, that the person I am outside of the ring now 'ascended' to a far better way of being. In many ways I think that entire character was one giant ritual for my own personal evolution. Either that or I just really wanted an excuse to wear eyeliner!"

Alex told me that when FWA ended, he bought all the production equipment and cameras off Tony Simpson, and used them to film WrestleTalk. And at the time, he believed that his subsequent experiences in the world of television made him the most qualified and likely person to eventually bring an episodic British wrestling programme to one of the really big channels.

"When you have a provable track record of delivering programming to a major TV network every week for three and a half years, it's an experience that can't be taken away. So many people in British wrestling want to make a TV show, but what they don't realise is when a TV station manager comes to you and says 'can you make me a TV show?' what they are really saying is 'I want to exchange an amount of money for you to fill a gap in my schedule'. Ultimately it must be delivered without excuses, it must be OFCOM compliant and it shouldn't get any viewer complaints. Essentially it's there to buffer the most important thing on the station and that's advertising. If any of the previous things I mentioned don't happen then there are serious legal ramifications and that's why they often only take programming from people with a track record of delivering. Looking back now it's amazing that The Wrestling Channel took anything off me back in 2004.

"There are a few people who for some reason or another won't work with me. I've now got so much experience in how to approach and deal with a TV network, how to deliver to TV play out centres all over the world and how to make serialised content. You would think I would be inundated with messages from UK promoters seeing as so many want to get on television. But a lot want to try and do it all themselves and think that sharing the load means sharing the credit. The biggest breakthrough I had in business was when I realised that some people are smarter than me at certain things and the smartest thing I could do was to employ those people. Taking credit from people I don't really know or listening to criticism from self-appointed pundits who often don't have all the facts, becomes pretty low down on your priority list when you really begin to feel secure in what you do.

"And many of the promoters dislike each other too. They often won't work with one another. It's all a bit silly really."

Alex sighed. Even after all these years, he remains incredulous that so few of his peers and UK wrestling fans will give him his due. But unlike in his youth, he won't feed the trolls any more. The criticism rankles with him privately, but publicly he rises above it. He told me he hasn't been on the UK Fan Forum in five years.

But even after all this time, I still believe there is nobody as committed to British wrestling and the Holy Grail as Alex Shane. And there are still few who can top him when it comes to salesmanship. As our conversation came to an end, he teased me with a mention of his latest project. Top secret, he said. But when it was eventually made public, he claimed it would blow the roof off British wrestling.

"I can't say publicly what it is yet," said the promoter supreme, with a laugh.

"But I will tell you this, Greg. If television was the Holy Grail, then this is the Ark of the Covenant!"

CHAPTER 7

BEST IN THE NORTH WEST

"Thanks to everybody who came last night and to everybody's support during my last nine-and-a-bit years of being a wrestling promoter. Despite defeat, in a strange way I will always remember last night as my crowning achievement. Dusty Rhodes once said 'wrestling is built on emotion' and his words always struck a chord with me. Anyone who was there last night will know that XWA vs GPW was built on emotion. Never seen anything like it. What a show. What a crowd. But that's it for now. I need a break."
Greg Lambert, July 29 2012

The night before I posted this on Facebook, I ran my last ever wrestling show as a promoter. Emotionally, creatively and financially, I went out on the highest of highs, even if the show was booked to leave the character Greg 'The Truth' Lambert having sunk to the lowest of lows.

In a nutshell, XWA v GPW Vendetta on Saturday, July 28 2012 at The Hexagon, Lancaster and Morecambe College, was my crowning glory as a wrestling booker and promoter. What a way to go out.

To explain how this show came about, it's important to go back in time to put the North West wrestling scene into its historical context.

The North West of England has been a hotbed of professional wrestling since the early part of the 20th century. Not only has the region spawned some of the greats of the British ring, names such as William Regal, The British Bulldogs, Marty Jones, Giant Haystacks and Rollerball Rocco, and hosted countless live wrestling events in front of passionate crowds from Morecambe to Manchester and all points in between, the North West is also famed as the home of Billy Riley's infamous Snake Pit gym in Wigan.

The Snake Pit is legendary as the back-to-basics home of an uncompromising style of wrestling which placed the emphasis on taking your opponent down to the mat to stretch him with agonising submission holds. From its origins in the 1940s, the Snake Pit would go on to develop talent such as British champions Bert Assirati and Billy Robinson, cousin of Jackie. Billy took his ground-based catch style all over the world and helped lay the foundations for the success of Mixed Martial Arts and the Ultimate Fighting Championship today.

As a mining town, Wigan had its roots firmly in the working class, and British professional wrestling was mainly a working class form of entertainment. So the connection between the town and the grapple game has always been a strong one. It seems poetic that when I first became involved in wrestling in the early part of the 21st century, it coincided with the rise of a new wrestling promotion in Wigan just 45 miles down the road from my home in Morecambe.

GPW was originally known as Garage Pro Wrestling because its founder Lee Butler set up his first training gym, complete with wrestling ring, inside a Wigan garage. The company was later taken over by one of Butler's trainees, Johnnie Brannigan, and later changed its name to *Grand* Pro Wrestling.

My first experience of a GPW show came on November 2 2003 when myself and Mark Kay went to watch Nemesis, the company's second event. In terms of the quality of the wrestling and the wrestlers involved, the show was a level below what the FWA was doing in Morecambe and Broxbourne at the time.

Held at the unfashionable venue of Leigh British Legion just outside Manchester, the show was dominated by Butler's trainees, a gaggle of young, skinny, athletic and eager rookies from the Wigan and Manchester area. At four hours in length, there was far too much going on. But it was still packed with action and entertaining in its own way. It was also the first time I'd seen proper production values, such as pyrotechnics and a large plasma screen showing entrance videos, at a British wrestling show outside of the FWA.

We had already become friendly with Butler's lieutenants at GPW, 'Dangerous' Damon Leigh and Mike Bishop, through our link to the FWA. GPW Nemesis was also our first glimpse of the likes of

Joey Hayes, El Ligero, Dave Rayne, Kris Travis and Spud, who were all very new to the pro ranks and just starting out on their journey to greater things.

"GPW was where I first made my name," said El Ligero in 2016.

"My feud with JC Thunder is what put me on the map. Myself, Cameron Knite, JC Thunder and Jack Hazard used to go down and train in Wigan when it was called Garage Pro Wrestling. Cameron got booked on the first GPW show, then myself and JC got booked on the second one and wrestled each other. That was the first time that I worked in front of a crowd that was a little bit smarter to wrestling. I did the Nemesis show, which was the first time I read an internet review, which was Greg's review of the show.

"Back in 2003/2004 at GPW, there were storylines, but they weren't well written. We were left to our own devices quite a lot."

Brannigan himself also caught my attention at GPW Nemesis. He wrestled under the name of Heresy, a gruff, outspoken and unscrupulous preacher man, whose strength was his mic work. Brannigan was one hell of a talker and he captivated me with his fierce verbal delivery and religious rhetoric.

"I started out with a company in Wigan, a glorified back yard fed called NPWA, in 2000 and I was with them for a couple of years," said Johnnie in 2016.

"Damon and I were meant to do a ladder match in a main event. We had about 100 people there that night, which was good for NPWA. But NPWA management forgot the ladder! At this point I got so frustrated, I walked out of the promotion mid-show. I grabbed my girlfriend and stormed out, leaving the show without a main event and Damon without an opponent. It was unprofessional of me. But I was 20-21, hot-headed, and it had been a brewing problem for a while.

"Then Lee Butler started helping out with NPWA training. He was a bit of an established name at the time. Damon and I were on the phone all the time and he was trying to persuade me to come back, but I was stubborn. Then Lee tried to take over NPWA but when he couldn't, he decided to set up his own company. This is how GPW was born. Lee then phoned me and asked me to come back. That's how my involvement started in the early stages of 2003.

"Lee got affiliated with Alex Shane who started to come up and take seminars. It was never going to be run as a 'show promotion' just as a training school, but it didn't take long before Lee changed his mind and ran his first show on July 2003, with a mix of FWA and GPW guys. Alex, Paul Travell, Ian DaSciple and Stevie Knight were there. That was a weird show. We didn't have a ring announcer so Lee announced the show from the balcony. I can only imagine what the crowd was thinking. It was at the Monaco Ballroom and we drew about 120."

On April 21 2004 Mark and I went to see another GPW show, Hostile Takeover, at Darwen Leisure Centre near Blackburn. Alex Shane and Drew McDonald were both part of the line-up. But the highlight was a main event between American indie star Chris Hero and a tall Swiss grappler who wrestled in a shirt and tie, who is today better known as WWE superstar Cesaro. Their match was impressive, even though it went on for an hour and dragged the show into the wee small hours of the morning. Of the GPW contingent, DDL, Joey and Heresy once again impressed me the most.

It wasn't long before GPW brought me in as a heel manager. By then, the company was being run by Brannigan and settled at the Monaco Ballroom (now The Rose Club) in Hindley, Wigan, which would go on to become their permanent home.

"My first show in charge was GPW Wanted (on March 18 2015)," said Johnnie.

"Lee had done maybe five or six shows in nearly two years and made a mess of things. He started off well but created bad feeling amongst everybody. He left in late 2004 and I haven't seen him since. I stepped up when Lee left. Damon and I were running the training school together and Damon ran a couple of shows, including the last ever show at the Leigh British Legion (on January 16 2005) before it got converted into flats. That was the night he dropped the GPW British Title to Alex Shane in a 'Montreal Screwjob' angle.

"There was real tension in the air that night. A lot of our guys were legitimately angry that Damon (as booker) had given our title to an FWA guy. After that, Damon didn't want to do it any more so I thought I'd better do something. When I was at school I'd done fantasy booking with made-up wrestlers with my mates in the playground, I'd run small businesses before, so I started to run the shows. And Damon won the title back (at Back With A Bang 2006) in front of 400 fans. I wanted to get the title off Alex as soon as possible. I'll always have good things to say about Alex, he taught me a lot, but he was asking for a lot of money per show, way above what everyone else was getting."

I worked a handful of shows in 2004/5 in the corner of a tag team called Damage Control, 'The Dragon' Sean McClane and Flood. Nice guys, but not the greatest wrestlers in the world. Not that I was the greatest manager at the time either. I still had a lot to learn.

My stint with Damage Control didn't exactly set the world on fire, although I did manage them in one memorable encounter with a tag team of young GPW trainees called WKD - D'Lyrium and C-Juice - today better known as Alpha Omega Wrestling ring announcer Matt Taylor Richards and CJ Banks, who is now one of the country's very best in-ring performers. This match happened at Wanted on Johnnie's first show in charge. Future WWE superstar TJ Wilson (Tyson Kidd) also wrestled that night.

One of my clearest memories of my stint with GPW is the night I was ring announcer for a dramatic and controversial No Holds Barred match between El Ligero and JC Thunder.

"JC and I used to travel together a lot," said Ligero.

"I got hurt on a weekender for GPW and dislocated my collar bone. JC was wrestling Gangrel in the main event on the second night and off the cuff, I became JC's sidekick. I had no idea what I was doing, flying on the seat of my pants. The sidekick thing seemed to take off in Leigh a little bit.

"Then one night there was an 'incident' (backstage fight) between Alex Shane and Lee Butler, and Alex was meant to wrestle Cameron Knite but didn't wrestle because of said incident. I was drafted in to wrestle Cameron. Damon was in charge of booking at the time and we decided to do an angle where I turned on JC, which got a good reaction, we had a match on the next show which ended in a disqualification, then we did the No Holds Barred."

This blood-soaked brawl on Saturday, July 23 2005 at the Monaco could so easily have marked the end for GPW just as it was starting to gather momentum. The incident that sticks in my mind came just yards from my ringside position, when the cocky blond heel Thunder chucked a steel chair at his masked opponent, but it slipped out of his hands, missed Ligero and instead smacked into a fan who was sitting in the front row.

"JC threw the chair, I was against the ring post, I was meant to duck it and he was meant to hit the post with the chair, but it went flying out of his hands," said Ligero.

"We didn't have guard rails back then.

"Pretty much everything we got told in advance of the match, that we couldn't do, we did. JC wasn't allowed to get colour (bleed). I wasn't allowed to jump off a ledge. We can't do this, we can't do that. JC was determined to get colour, he wanted to make the match memorable. He led the match, a lot of the ideas were his, in a good way.

"Heresy was booking at the time but he was in America and left Damon in charge. As soon as we came backstage from the match, both of us got bollocked by Damon and rightly so. If I was running a show and people went against what we said, I'd be fuming as well. For a while they lost the venue. It was a strange situation because we were in loads of trouble, but we knew we'd done something memorable that people would talk about. And here we are talking about it, 11 years on. That was the first match that put me on the map. I still wasn't very good though."

Thankfully for GPW, the fan wasn't seriously injured.

My tenure with GPW ended in early 2006. I was struggling to get to their regular Friday night events at the Monaco Ballroom, due to work commitments. I also missed a show when, just as I was setting off for Wigan, my youngest son Dale split his head open on a swinging car door in our driveway, and was rushed to casualty to have a nasty cut glued shut. That was the last time I was ever booked for GPW, but I didn't particularly mind at the time. I'm not sure if Johnnie had any future plans for me anyway and besides, 2006 was the year when I tried - and failed - to expand the FWA nationwide and I had enough on my plate.

No longer part of the show, I popped down to GPW now and again over the ensuing years whenever time allowed. Mark and I usually arrived unannounced, paid our £5 admission fee on the door and scooted up to the spectator balcony overlooking the ring to hang out with other North West wrestling people who weren't part of the night's performance. Then after the show ended, we would say hello to Johnnie and our friends on his roster.

I've always liked Johnnie. He is straight talking and has an excellent mind for booking and creating strong storylines and fresh characters. His blueprint for success was very similar to ours and indeed that of our mutual neighbours FutureShock Wrestling in Stockport, run by Dave Rayne. All three companies, XWA, GPW and FutureShock, ran regular family-orientated events at an established venue centred around big personalities, with stories the spectators could follow show-to-show, enticing them back time and again to see what happened next. This approach had allowed all three promotions to create a loyal, passionate and distinct fan base.

It was an exciting time for North West wrestling because we were right at the forefront of the UK scene. North West talent such as Bubblegum, CJ Banks and Joey Hayes were regarded as among the very best in the country, while the likes of Jack Gallagher, Cyanide and Zack Gibson were just starting to emerge behind them. And in the mid-to-late noughties, XWA, GPW and FutureShock were riding high. All three companies were doing great business.

"The advent of PCW and their big budget, bringing people over from abroad, put a focus on the North West," said Dave 'Rayne' Pownall.

"But that roster is held together by a core group of guys, all of whom to some extent cut their teeth and became stars in their own right by working for FutureShock, GPW and XWA. PCW has been great but a major cog in the machine are the stars we built."

Now I'd be lying if I said there wasn't an element of competitive, but friendly, rivalry between the three companies at the time, especially between XWA and GPW. I always felt that, although at face value things were cordial enough between us, there was an underlying current of professional tension between the Morecambe and the Wigan crews. And I would be proved right about that.

"It was a different world back then," said Johnnie.

"It was the same with GPW and FutureShock. Anyone who left GPW to go to train at FutureShock was hated. *Hated.* Even now, some of the old school GPW wrestlers who remember that time will scoff 'Oh, that FutureShock lot' or 'Oh, that XWA lot'."

Mark and I watched GPW shows with a critical eye, mainly to scout for new talent, but we also picked holes where appropriate. We also told ourselves that XWA was a superior product. Our rationale was simple. In our opinion, The Dome was a better venue than the Monaco Ballroom. We drew more fans to our shows, in a rundown seaside town with less than half the population of Wigan. And while GPW was built around DDL, Hayes, Banks and Ligero as well as our old mates Dirk Feelgood and Bubblegum as its main stars, these guys were mid-card at best in Morecambe. At the time, XWA's top names such as Robbie Brookside, Jonny Storm, Stevie Knight, Ricky Knight, Sam Slam, Stixx, Spud, Martin Stone and RJ Singh were competing on a national, sometimes international level. Our top wrestlers had a much higher profile than the core roster of both GPW and FutureShock, at the time. These were also our peak years creatively and our shows were gaining rave reviews.

So between 2007 and 2010 I really do believe XWA was the best pro wrestling company in the North West of England.

Of course, both Johnnie Brannigan and Dave Rayne would beg to differ. And I respect them for that. I wouldn't expect anything else.

Things began to change once we lost The Dome. As I already mentioned, the XWA crowd numbers, roster and product dipped once we moved across Morecambe prom to The Carleton. Between 2010 and 2012, my real-life opinion is that both GPW and FutureShock overtook us. They raised their games, while we were going backwards.

We were no longer the Best in the North West.

There you go. I've admitted it!

But 2010 was also a year when the new XWA wrestling school in Morecambe was flourishing and our best trainees were knocking on the door of a spot on the main shows. Before XWA's school opened in January 2009, both GPW and FutureShock already had established training centres and therefore a supply line of hungry new young talent, all eager for a chance to shine in front of a paying audience. It seemed like a good time for all three companies to work together and share talent, thus increasing the opportunities for all of our top trainees to learn their craft.

At the time, the North West triad had settled into a pattern where, at least three times a year, our events fell on the same weekend - GPW on a Friday in Wigan, XWA on a Saturday in Morecambe, FutureShock on a Sunday in Stockport. It seemed like a good idea for the three companies to promote our events as one big weekend of North West wrestling, to hammer home what a mecca we had become, and to attract fans from outside the region to stay over and watch all three promotions in three days, therefore increasing all of our audience figures. Thus, the concept of the North West Weekender was born.

In late 2010, Johnnie, Dave, myself and Mark met up to discuss ideas for a working agreement. We decided to try to use each other's trainees on shows wherever possible, and push each other's shows and the North West Weekender as a whole through our own websites and fledgling social media pages - this at the dawn of Facebook and Twitter. Not long afterwards, Dave Rayne became head trainer at the XWA school, cementing the relationship between ourselves and FutureShock all the more. Meanwhile GPW came up with an idea called the North West Rookie League, allowing XWA trainees Jynkz, Axl Rage, JD Sassoon and Action Jackson (Jack Clarke) spots on GPW events as part of a year-long series.

In return, I gave matches on XWA events to two of GPW's brightest prospects, Ricky J McKenzie (Sam Gradwell) and Ste 'Bin' Mann, and planned to bring more GPW and FutureShock youngsters to Morecambe when the time was right. Myself and Mark attended the first North West Rookie League match at GPW Back With A Bang on February 3 2011, and were proud as Punch at seeing Axl, JD and Jack perform on a show outside of Morecambe.

So at first, all was going swimmingly with the North West Axis. Or so I thought.

The next North West Weekender fell on the weekend of June 3-5 2011, when GPW, XWA and FutureShock held their events on consecutive days. By this point, Mark had decided to quit as XWA co-owner, and so a lot of my time running up to the XWA show was preoccupied with paperwork to transfer the company into my sole directorship. As the upcoming War on the Shore was my first ever show as lone promoter, I admit I did focus most of my attention on marketing the Morecambe event. But I also managed to do some advance promotion online for the whole North West weekend as agreed. I even got it a mention in Power Slam, to keep up my end of the bargain.

Then on June 3, the night of GPW's show Heroes and Villains, I was booked to appear on a Southside Wrestling event at Preston College, where I managed Dave Rayne in a match with a muscular black wrestler with a gangster-rap look called Val Kabious. I decided to take the booking and not attend the GPW event, not that I made any assurances to Johnnie that I'd be there anyway. My main motivation was because Stixx, who was wrestling in the main event of War on the Shore the following day, was also at the Preston show and needed a lift to Morecambe, where he would stay overnight at my house.

That Friday night in Preston I was also feeling wound up by a heated phone conversation I'd had with a wrestler about transport arrangements for XWA that weekend. So I was already stressed when on Saturday afternoon, the day of my show, I received a call from Johnnie Brannigan.

Johnnie asked if he could have two complimentary tickets to watch XWA War on the Shore that night. I was taken aback. This wasn't part of our agreement. And it wasn't something I would usually do - call up another wrestling promoter at the last minute and ask for free tickets, unless I was covering their event as a member of the media. I thought it was a bit cheeky, particularly as I had always paid to get into GPW shows unless I was an invited guest, as I had been for Back With A Bang a few months' earlier.

As promoters, we worked hard to put bums on seats, to convince the punters to part with their money. Out of respect for these efforts, on the rare occasions when I went to see another UK promotion, I always wanted to pay. I expected Johnnie to do the same.

War on the Shore VII was my first show flying solo, the advance ticket sale was only 150, lower than hoped, and I was worried I might not break even. So I have to admit, I was a little irked by Johnnie's request to be allowed in for nowt. Declan O'Connor once said to me "You're too soft with people, Greg." These words have usually rung in my ears ever since, whenever I feel people are trying to swing the lead.

Back then, I had a rule about free admission to XWA shows. If any wrestlers working for me wanted complimentary tickets for friends and family I usually allowed them two, but no more. After all, it was a business I was running, not a charity. I was a wrestling promoter, spending a few thousand pounds of my own money each time I ran a show, usually making a profit, but there was always the chance of making a loss. While the wrestlers risked their bodies to entertain the fans, I was taking a risk of my own - a financial one. If I wanted to stipulate no free tickets to wrestlers from another company, that was my right.

With hindsight, perhaps I should have shown North West solidarity and let Johnnie in for free. But at the time, different thoughts were whirling through my mind. So I told Johnnie he could get in for half-price. He didn't seem happy at that. The conversation ended amicably enough, but the miffed Brannigan didn't turn up to the show after all.

Anyway, XWA War and the Shore VII at The Carleton on Saturday, June 4, 2011 turned out to be a perfectly acceptable show and in the end, I did manage to entice enough fans through the door to make a decent profit. It ended up being a full weekend's work though, as the following day, I supervised as Alex Shane and Joel Redman hosted an afternoon training seminar at our school. When I eventually managed to get home on Sunday night, I was exhausted after 48 hours of non-stop wrestling, training, related shenanigans and manual labour.

You see, one of the most draining aspects of running shows during that particular era was manouevring our ring from its home at the training school to The Carleton and back. We only had one wrestling ring and used the same one for training and for shows. So on a show day, myself and Mark would meet the willing team of XWA trainees at noon, take the ring apart, and then carry the four heavy ringposts, 16 long metal support beams, eight wooden boards, four sets of ropes and associated equipment from the top floor of the centre down a narrow winding metal staircase to the van in an alleyway below. Then we drove the fairly short distance to The

Carleton and the team would again shift each piece of the ring up another steep flight of stairs into the nightclub's main auditorium, before setting it back up for the show. At night, the team took the ring down after the main event, down the staircase, and back into the van for storage overnight. Then the following morning came the real killer, as we again unloaded the van and lugged everything back up that horrible staircase into the training room to build the ring again in time for Sunday's session. Little wonder that the number of trainees helping us on a Sunday was always less than the number who turned up, bright-eyed and bushy-tailed, on the Saturday.

So I was knackered, tetchy and short of patience when I got home on the evening of June 5 2011 and logged onto Facebook, where I saw a comment posted by GPW wrestler and co-booker, Gary 'Jiggy Walker' Mason.

I had known Jiggy for a few years, even booked him once for a Morecambe show in 2008, when he was one half of an unusual GPW tag team with Danny Hope. Danny and Jiggy called themselves The Mil-Anfield Connection because stylish Danny was billed as being from the Catwalks of Milan (when in reality he was from Hertfordshire and lived just outside Preston) while Jiggy was a loudmouth Scouser and, like me, a fervent Liverpool FC supporter.

As Milan and Liverpool were inextricably linked at the time due to their classic pair of Champions League Final tussles in 2005 and 2007, The Mil-Anfield Connection proved a surprise odd couple hit with GPW fans. They were a typical out-of-the-box act for a company that later unleashed similarly wacky gimmicks such as Australian surfer dude Bruce Sheila, mad scientist Professor Mike Holmes and his masked sidekick Voodoo, ninja warrior Ben Zen, UK wrestling's resident refuse collector Ste 'Bin' Mann and an equally puntastic trio of athletics stars called Mike Track, Ian Field and Jim Nastic.

Gary was one of the endless line of acquaintances you meet and work with on wrestling shows with whom you exchange a few cordial words and then don't see again for a few months, or maybe even years. We had always been pleasant to each other and never had any problems before. So it was a massive shock to read his words - which were posted on Johnnie Brannigan's public Facebook page for all to see. They amounted to quite a diatribe against the XWA and what appeared to be a personal attack on me.

"How was XWA lad? I know you planned on going to support the North West scene, especially with all those roster members we helped polish as performers. Was it a banging show that featured no convoluted booking and absolutely no characters that you would define as off-putting 'noncey' if pressed? I hope so…"

Then, later, he wrote:

"I asked my mate to buy me a drink last night as he owed me a few. He told me he couldn't, but he'd go halves with me if I really wanted one. I was aghast."

Aghast? He wasn't the only one.

If you have a problem with me, email me privately, call me up, say it to my face. Air it on a public forum and you're guaranteed to rile me no end.

I hardly ever criticise anyone on social media. If you can't say anything nice, keep quiet, is my motto. There is enough nastiness in this world without Facebook bile adding to it. Unless you are in character to push a wrestling storyline. Which Walker most definitely was not.

Convoluted booking? Off-putting 'noncey' characters? Even if that was true, how would Jiggy Walker know? He hadn't been to an XWA show in three years.

So yes, I was furious.

The following day, I telephoned Johnnie and asked him what the hell Jiggy was playing at. He apologised and said Mason had a habit of posting angry rants on social media. After hearing each other out over 'ticket-gate', we smoothed things over in an awkward but positive conversation.

I was still seething over Walker's comments though. He really pushed my buttons.

But once I calmed down, I began to analyse the situation. Clearly there *was* real-life tension between the two promotions. What if we put this animosity in front of the fans and created a storyline out of it? As you know, I had long seen the value in inter-promotional rivalries.

So why not find out, once and for all, who really was the Best in the North West!

And with that, the XWA v GPW feud was born. I called Johnnie back and he loved the idea.

At the time, Brannigan was writing a regular blog for the GPW website under the alias 'Richard Noble'. This gave fans a fascinating insight into his thought processes as booker and some of the real-life trials and tribulations that go into preparing for and running a wrestling show. It was a good read and a valuable source of information for GPW fans and trainees alike. The fans believed every word in this blog was real, or a 'shoot' as it's known in the wrestling game. So I suggested to Johnnie that he use his online memoirs to vent his frustrations with myself and XWA over ticket-gate.

Brannigan and Walker were also irked for other reasons, at the time. They felt I wasn't doing enough to push the North West Weekenders and that I had shunned the GPW show in June 2011 show by attending the Southside event. Although I totally disagreed with their opinion, it no longer mattered by that point. The lines between reality and fantasy were about to be blurred for our companies' mutual benefit. The misguided real-life beliefs of Johnnie and Jiggy provided enough ammunition to fire the first shots in a North West wrestling war.

Johnnie's next GPW blog contained exactly the kind of strong words required to plant a seed in fans' minds that there was a real-life issue between the two promotions. In fact, he really went for the jugular with his feelings towards me, as follows. He wrote...

"In every update and tweet leading up to the show, both Dave Rayne and myself mentioned the (North West Weekender) but there was nothing from Greg. Not even a single tweet. Without Greg pulling his weight, it certainly didn't feel like we were in it together and there was a sour feeling coming over. So much for North West solidarity.

"I was mad. And I wasn't the only one who'd noticed.

"It had caught the attention of Jiggy Walker. He was as pissed off as I was, and that spelt T.R.O.U.B.L.E. I've never met anyone, other than myself, more fiercely passionate about GPW . He would gladly march into the bowels of fiery hell to fight the GPW cause.

"He said 'When are we f__king the XWA off? Dave wants to help, but Lambert isn't interested one bit. He's missed the entire point of this North West Weekender and we're making mugs of ourselves. As long as 'his boys' are getting bookings, he's not interested. He's not even got the good f__king manners to come to our show and he's going to Preston instead.'"

"As usual, he was right and I couldn't argue Greg's case for him, even though there was surely a side to his story. I wanted to hear Greg's side of things on it.

"I rang Greg Saturday lunchtime, told him I was thinking of coming to his show and asked if he could put me on the comp'd guest list. But me asking to be comp'd was clearly an ask too far for Greg 'The Truth' Lambert...

"Let me get this in right at the start – I have no problem paying for tickets for anything, I don't have a Hollywood complex whatsoever – it wasn't the money, it was the ask. The times that Greg and his entourage have graced us with their presence at a GPW show, they've never been charged. I often go and watch FutureShock and Dave never expects any money from me and vice versa. It's called working together.

"I was shocked and taken aback. I put the phone down, walked around for a minute or two, trying to think about it from Greg's perspective but I couldn't. The smoke started coming out of my ears. I was ready to bury this, bring it up in polite conversation and move on. But this latest disrespect was really, really the last, and final straw. I picked my phone back up and made a call I knew would do nothing to help the situation. I called Jiggy Walker.

"Jiggy said 'You f__king what? He said what? How many times have we charged him? Does he not get this Triple Header working together thing? I hope you told him to do one.'

"Needless to say, I didn't go to XWA and I planned on not working with Greg ever again.

"I wasn't even going to waste my time telling him why, I didn't think he deserved to know. But, he'd seen Jiggy's posts before I did and got in touch with his tail between his legs. We spoke on the phone but his defence was flimsy to say the least and he knew it. There was no defence. He accepted he'd not done enough and vowed to make a difference in the future.

"I was happy with his apology, but can't trust him until I see more action from his corner. Can we repair the damaged GPW/XWA relationship and get back to the North West promotions working together for a common goal? Between a hot headed Jiggy Walker, a willing to work for it Dave Rayne, only interested in himself Greg Lambert and myself – time will tell…"

Wow.

If those were indeed their real-life feelings, that was quite the insular over-reaction from the GPW contingent. But again, it didn't matter. Jiggy's rant didn't bother me. It didn't even matter that there were some outright inaccuracies in the blog, such as the claim that I never paid to get into GPW and that I apologised to Johnnie on the phone with a 'flimsy defence'.

None of it mattered, because this piece of writing was perfect. This was exactly what was needed. People would really believe the two sides didn't like each other one bit. And I quite liked the idea of being portrayed as the heel of the situation to the GPW audience. I wanted them to blame me and hate me.

When deciding to suggest this online approach to promoting the fight between XWA and GPW, my main aim was to sell tickets. As a form of marketing, the website blog was targeted at the die-hard GPW regulars who never came to watch XWA. I wanted them to be hooked by the rivalry and enticed to buy tickets for XWA shows, because they wanted to root for GPW. I knew that our regular Morecambe fans would come along anyway so the online jibes were designed solely to bring new spectators in from outside the town.

Then on October 5 2011, I made my response to GPW's blog with a YouTube video. Whilst sitting at my computer wearing an XWA: The Future is Now T-Shirt, I defended myself calmly to camera against Brannigan's allegations. I stated my real-life beliefs that GPW should not have "aired dirty laundry in public" and said I did not appreciate them "casting aspersions about my professionalism". I firmly denied the accusations of not pulling my weight and gave my side of the story on ticket-gate. Then, with just enough of a patronising tone to rile up any GPW sympathisers watching, I said that I had always been a GPW fan myself and didn't hold any grudges.

"We're going to put the issue behind us," I said, with a tad of condescending superiority.

"And I've made it clear that anybody from GPW is welcome to come to our shows at any time, *as long as they pay for a ticket*."

This last line was deliberately chosen to annoy GPW fans and plant another seed.

Some of GPW's most vocal and passionate supporters picked up on the video and came down firmly on the Grand Pro side of the argument with posts on Facebook and Twitter. One diehard Grand Pro fan in particular, a notorious keyboard warrior called Kristian 'Hitman' Bennett, took great delight in having a pop at both myself and the XWA on forums any chance he got. Great, I thought. It's getting us attention. Bennett was a fixture at GPW but never came to XWA. I made it my mission for that to change.

By this time, I got in touch privately with Jiggy Walker in an attempt to bury the hatchet. I felt that if Walker could rile me up with his cutting Scouse spiel, he could do the same to the XWA fans and would be an ideal figurehead for a GPW invasion of XWA events. We had a polite exchange of messages and by the end of them, Jiggy said he was on board.

Now it was all well and good creating an online buzz for the feud. But for it to work in the live arena we needed to establish GPW as invading outsiders for our fans to hate. After all, the majority of the Morecambe crowd would never have even heard of Grand Pro Wrestling. So my plan was to debut the GPW-XWA angle at Last Fight at the Prom on October 8 2011 at The Carleton with something a bit different. My idea was to have three GPW wrestlers 'buy tickets' to the show, mingle visibly with the crowd during the first-half, then cause a scene and be very publicly thrown out. I talked to Johnnie and we agreed the three GPW invaders would be Walker, Ste 'Bin' Mann and Dylan Roberts.

The perfect time to execute the angle would be during a three-way bout that night between El Ligero, CJ Banks and GPW's very own Ricky J McKenzie, to determine the next challenger to the Best of the North West Title now held by Jynkz. Young RJM, with his ripped physique and strong ring presence, was already establishing himself as a heel in Morecambe.

I saw Sam 'RJM' Gradwell as the most promising of all the talent coming out of the GPW school and planned to push his developing rivalry with Jynkz as a centrepiece of the XWA v Grand Pro feud. The Flying Scot had defeated McKenzie on numerous occasions leading in to Last Fight and, in the storyline, the bald-headed Ricky was becoming more and more frustrated and jealous of Jynkz's success and popularity.

Although Kyle was unable to wrestle that night having just come through nasal surgery, we kept the rivalry going by having him sit at ringside to watch the three-way. The hometown hero got a great reaction. Our fans loved Jynkz and already, they despised RJM. Anyone who associated themselves with McKenzie, I figured, would get the same heat.

By the way, the day before XWA Last Fight at the Prom, GPW held its own event Friday Night Thriller at the Monaco. But it didn't go well. Johnnie and his crew experienced one of the worst things that can happen to any wrestling promotion. Their ring broke during the show and couldn't be repaired. Friday Night Thriller had to be called off after just three matches. In real life, I felt bad for Johnnie and his team. In storyline, Greg 'The Truth' Lambert felt smug at his rivals' misfortune.

Back to Last Fight 2011, where I carefully set everything up for our angle with attention to detail. I even left tickets on the door for the GPW trio to add to the realism and told them to queue outside the venue in their green and yellow GPW T-Shirts like they really were fans attending our show. But there was just one problem.

Jiggy Walker no-showed.

Johnnie had the task of apologetically informing me by telephone that Walker wasn't coming. He decided last-minute that he didn't want to do the angle. And he didn't even have the decency to tell me himself that he was pulling out.

"Jiggy always had this 'them and us' attitude," said Johnnie, speaking in 2016.

"He's all or nothing in a lot of respects. I'd always thought I could work with Greg because I respected him and I always felt we could do the invasion angle and do it right. I knew he was passionate about getting it right and so was I. My only reservations at the time were about how GPW might look coming out of it and I was concerned about giving time to XWA storylines on our own shows. And Jiggy, who was co-booker, didn't want to give XWA any air time on GPW shows *at all*.

"I got a message off Jiggy that day saying he was about to set off but then decided he wasn't going to go. I can't remember what his reasons were. And he'll never say that he regrets it but I hope he does, because he knows how much I loved the XWA-GPW feud, and it's something he could have enjoyed and would have fit perfectly into. But I think sometimes his confidence beats him. I'm not saying that's why he didn't show that night. But I remember before he had a big main event match with Danny Hope in GPW one time he was extremely nervous and afterwards, he said he didn't want to do a main event again."

Well, whatever Jiggy's reasons were for no-showing, it was his loss.

By the way, I don't hold any grudges about Walker's behaviour. I saw him again a few years later when he attended a PCW show. We said hello and shook hands. It's water under the bridge as far as I'm concerned.

As for Ste Mann and Dylan Roberts, they were professionalism personified and the angle worked like a dream. Although there were now only two of them, once inside The Carleton, Mann and Roberts made enough noise for an entire GPW gang. During the first-half they drank beer, heckled XWA fan favourites and broke into spontaneous "G-P-W!" chants. By the time the interval came around, our regular fans were already getting annoyed by the rowdy pair.

Then during half-time, I instructed Mann and Roberts to start giving out flyers to our fans promoting the next GPW show. This brought out XWA production manager Bryan Fulton, flanked by a couple of XWA stewards. Making sure our fans could see the kerfuffle unfold, Bryan confronted Ste and Dylan, and confiscated the flyers. Clearly furious at having their attempts to promote GPW cut short, Mann and Roberts were escorted back to their seats for the second-half.

Next up was the three-way match and it was a great one. Ste and

Dylan cranked up the volume of their "G-P-W!" chants whenever RJM gained the advantage. But when McKenzie was eventually pinned by Ligero, they were furious. As Jynkz entered the ring with his Best of the North West trophy and eyed the Mexican's British Flyweight Championship, perfectly setting up their Champion v Champion match for all the marbles on the next show, the bearded Roberts stood on his chair, pint in hand, cursing and shouting in anger. This was the final straw for the XWA security team.

Led by Carleton manager Stewart Aimson - who was always up for involving himself in angles - the venue security staff and Bryan Fulton politely asked the GPW duo to leave. After an uneasy stand-off where the protesting Mann and Roberts were backed up by McKenzie who had now left the ring to support his fellow GPW brothers, the interlopers were eventually escorted out of the venue, Mann complaining to the camera every step of the way that "You can't do this, I bought a ticket!"

And from backstage, I was delighted to hear our fans chanting "THROW THEM OUT!" and "NA NA NA NA, HEY HEY HEY, GOODBYE!" as they went.

The angle worked like a dream.

We made sure we got good pictures and 'fan cam' footage of the incident and leaked them out onto the internet afterwards. Then GPW put out their side of the story, claiming I had given permission for Mann and Roberts to give out flyers but changed my mind because I was jealous of Grand Pro. I put out my own statement saying Ste and Dylan went too far with their behaviour and had to be ejected because they were intimidating nearby fans and spoiling their enjoyment of Last Fight.

Meanwhile I encouraged the XWA trainees to defend us on Facebook and get into arguments with GPW students wherever possible, to add to the realism. It also turned out the Searle family, John and Mary Searle and their children who have been front row regulars at North West shows for years, overheard XWA crew members poking fun at GPW during our show for the unfortunate ring-breaking incident the night before. John Searle was outraged and vented his disgust at the XWA on the internet. I rubbed my hands in glee when I saw this. This was bound to fan the flames of tension between the two companies. Fans were beginning to react exactly how I'd hoped...picking sides, pointing fingers, getting hot under the collar.

In short, they *cared*.

With a four-month gap until the next XWA event, we did a few little things to keep the momentum going from the Last Fight angle. First of all, I put out a statement firing Ricky J McKenzie from the XWA. This really angered the GPW online crowd, especially the obnoxious Bennett who by now thought I was the devil incarnate. Then the two companies got into a battle to see who could get the most Twitter followers. This got us a lot of attention. It was really impressing me just how much Johnnie and his team (well, most of them) threw themselves into the storyline. They were doing everything possible to make people believe XWA and GPW really couldn't stand each other.

In January 2012, RJM put out a video from the GPW training school, flanked by some of the trainees. Scowling at the camera in disdain, McKenzie hinted that I had never allowed him to win any XWA matches because he was GPW through and through.

"I never really was an XWA guy, was I Greg?" he sneered, blurring those lines between fantasy and reality.

"You tried to embarrass me."

Then RJM absolutely buried the XWA training academy, calling it a "big joke" while his mates egged him on in the background (trivia point- they included future FutureShock promoter Chris Brooker and future North West star 'Sexy' Kev Lloyd). Then McKenzie threatened to show up at the next XWA event before delivering the 'money' line of his promo, proclaiming that "GPW is the Best in the North West".

I responded with my own YouTube promo, flanked by Jynkz and the XWA trainees. I dared McKenzie, Mann and Roberts to turn up at Gold Rush 2012 where there would be an "XWA welcoming committee" waiting for them. I ended my fiery speech by saying "XWA, not GPW, is the Best in the North West...and don't you forget it!"

So who really was the Best in the North West? Already, the fans and trainees were debating this question on Facebook, Twitter and website forums. There was a real buzz surrounding this feud, the likes of which I hadn't seen in a long time. Why? Because it was *real*.

The next episode in the XWA-GPW rivalry played out on Saturday February 4 2012 at Gold Rush. It was a cracking storyline development and worked better than I could ever have visualised.

First of all, Jynkz and El Ligero had their match for the Flyweight and Best of the North West titles. Ligs showed what a great in-ring professional he is that night, bumping around for the Morecambe-based Glaswegian like a heel, even though he was equally popular with the XWA faithful. They had a tremendous back-and-forth battle which ended with Jynkz pulling off the upset. It was without doubt, the biggest moment and victory of Kyle Paterson's short wrestling career. And Ligero did a magnificent job of selling it as such. The masked man officially endorsed the young Scotsman with a hearty handshake, before sportingly leaving the ring to allow Jynkz to bask in the limelight.

Earlier that evening, I well and truly put the Authority era to bed by apologising to the XWA crowd for my evil actions of the previous two years and begged for their forgiveness. My speech was so heartfelt, I got a round of applause. This enabled me to slot back in to my previous role as Master of Ceremonies and respected XWA leader. Just like that.

So as Jynkz celebrated in centre-ring with his two championships, I was right there at ringside to congratulate him. Knowing everything Kyle had been through in his personal life, how hard he worked to follow his dream of becoming a professional wrestler, and what a lovely genuine guy he is, I couldn't help but burst with pride for him. As his music pumped and the XWA fans applauded him with gusto, I shook his hand through the ropes with a grin and a "well done". This was one of those moments in pro wrestling that was as real as real can be.

And it's at exactly those kind of moments, when booking magic can happen.

Just as I finished shaking Jynkz's hand, Dylan Roberts and the Bin Mann charged into the ring out of nowhere. As the fans shrieked in horror and I uttered a rare expletive (which you can clearly pick up on the YouTube clip of the angle), Roberts chucked his pint of beer in Jynkz's eyes. Mann then viciously speared the new double champion and both of the GPW invaders began to pummel him aggressively with fists and feet, until the XWA trainees stormed the ring to restrain them.

There was uproar in the building. Jynkz was lying winded on the canvas. Bin Mann was being held at bay. And Dylan Roberts' GPW shirt was torn from the melee as two Carleton security staff dragged the tattooed Welshman from the violent scene, a beautifully graphic image which photographer Tony Knox managed to capture for posterity.

Meanwhile, Kyle's brother Dean Paterson came rushing out of the crowd and approached the ring to check on his fallen sibling. Even though Dean gave up wrestling two years before, he always came to XWA shows to show family solidarity. The fans knew this, because I made a point of giving Dean and his dad James a special mention on the microphone earlier in the night.

Then just when the situation appeared under control, another hooded figure came through the crowd, pushed past me and climbed into the ring to himself assault the helpless Jynkz. It was Ricky J McKenzie!

As RJM hammered away on his foe with a flurry of blows, Bin Mann and Roberts broke free of security and returned to aim punches and kicks at anyone who got in their way. "IT'S YOUR FAULT!" screamed McKenzie in my direction, as the GPW thugs cleared the ring of the XWA trainees while RJM continued to bash the semi-conscious Jynkz's brains in. The heat in The Carleton was off-the-charts as this gang mugging played out. It was absolute pandemonium.

Then, Dean Paterson rushed into the ring. As far as the fans knew, he was not a trained wrestler. Jynkz's brother tried his best to interject, throwing a desperate salvo of weak punches at RJM's back. "DEAN! NO! NO!" I screamed from ringside, to sell the fact that the younger Paterson was out of his depth and could get badly hurt. Sure enough, the sneering McKenzie turned around and then, as if swatting an annoying insect, decked Dean with one solitary right hand punch to a huge 'Ooooh!' of horror from the XWA fans.

Gradwell was brilliant here. His face changed to an expression of shock, as if he himself realised he had gone too far. After all he had just knocked out somebody who was, as far as the storyline was concerned, a paying customer.

I slapped the canvas, barely able to contain my rage.

"THAT'S HIS BROTHER!" I yelled. "THAT'S HIS BROTHER! YOU ANIMALS! THAT'S HIS BROTHER! THAT WAS THE BIGGEST MATCH OF HIS LIFE! WHAT ARE YOU DOING?"

Unrepentant, the GPW 'animals' stood in the ring in their green and yellow T-shirts, the boos raining down on them.

"G-P-W!" they yelled with defiance.

"X-W-A! X-W-A!" countered our fans, with what was probably the loudest XWA chant I had ever heard.

Then the three GPW thugs left through the front door, their dirty work done. There was carnage in the ring as XWA staff surrounded the prone Patersons. I called for an early interval on the microphone to sell the seriousness of the situation. As Kyle and Dean were carefully helped to the back, the fans responded with generous applause followed by a murmur of excited disbelief at what they had just seen.

This was the best angle I ever booked.

XWA and GPW were now at fully-fledged war.

Everything was going swimmingly, but we still had two setbacks to overcome before the next show. First of all, RJM suffered a serious knee injury. He tore his anterior cruciate ligament (ACL) during a match at GPW Northern Soul on March 2 2012. This meant I needed to change plans for McKenzie to be at the forefront of the GPW invasion. It was a severe blow for RJM who was really enthusiastic about the feud. It said a lot about his professionalism that, even though he now faced months of rehabilitation, he still wanted to be involved in some way.

Then The Carleton closed down, pretty much out of the blue. The club was struggling financially. At short notice, we were forced to switch War on the Shore 2012 to our trusty back-up venue, The Hexagon at Lancaster and Morecambe College.

At the next trainee show at Regent Park Studios, I filmed a promo calling for a public face-to-face apology from GPW for their actions at Gold Rush. Dylan, Bin Mann and RJM quickly responded with their own perfect video riposte.

"Lambert, you idiot," spat the hobbling but still defiant McKenzie.

"We are GPW. We are highly motivated individuals. I'm sorry I knocked Dean out, I'm sorry I bust his jaw but in a way, I'm glad I did, because it made it clearer that if you cross us, you're going to go down."

Bin Mann, a mega-popular cult figure with GPW fans who was really starting to come into his own as a heel in XWA, then added: "I'm sorry...I'm sorry we didn't do this sooner! You want an apology? Maybe *we* want an apology! You Greg, are a selfish man."

All of this led to Johnnie Brannigan's arrival in XWA at War on the Shore on April 12 2012.

Oh, and Kristian Bennett was there too. He bought a ticket for the show and was at ringside cheering GPW on.

Mission accomplished.

The story that night was that Brannigan, as GPW leader, was coming to Morecambe to defuse the situation. He would meet me face-to-face in the ring, he would issue the desired public apology, we would shake hands and move on.

But this being wrestling, things didn't go exactly to plan.

Brannigan, clad in leather jacket, T-shirt and jeans, entered the Hexagon ring that night and, after a few awkward pleasantries between us, offered his apology for the gang attack on the Patersons at Gold Rush to a disingenuous cheer from the audience - many of whom were actually chanting for us to hug it out. That would have been a step too far. So instead, we both shook hands.

After the handshake, I made to leave the ring, as if satisfied by the outcome. But then the grinning Heresy hit me with a real zinger.

"Gregory, I've apologised, but I will NEVER apologise for GPW being better than XWA!"

At this, I stopped, slowly turned around.

Nobody, not even my mother, calls me *Gregory*.

As Brannigan tried to get Bennett and a tiny pocket of Wigan fans to start a GPW chant, I walked back to the ring and confronted my nemesis, miffed beyond belief. Now the gloves were off!

In a heated verbal exchange, we both cut loose on each other with a series of vicious insults. We both proclaimed our own companies to be the Best in the North West. We both held nothing back as we ranted at each other like petulant schoolkids. The Morecambe fans were right behind me as I absolutely buried GPW and its roster in a maniacal tirade and Brannigan did exactly the same to XWA. It was an aggressive confrontation, we were really shouting at each other...sometimes *over* each other. It looked like a real argument, for sure.

Later, Spud told me that he really didn't like this angle. Jay felt the confrontation would have been more effective if we both acknowledged the strengths of XWA and GPW instead of focussing on each other's weaknesses. He thought Johnnie and I should have done more to build each other up, instead of taking great delight in knocking each other down. The old wrestling adage is that if you tell the audience that your opponent is a loser and then you beat him, then you've only beaten a loser. So what does that make you?

Jay has a point and I always take on board his comments because he is a student of the game. But looking back, I feel my confrontation with Brannigan was an exception to the rule. My aim was for the fans to really believe the two sides hated each other. I wanted there to be nothing but vitriol between XWA and GPW. No grudging respect or admiration. Just spiteful nastiness. This, I believed, would draw money. And I was proven right in the end.

The angle ended in fine style. First, Brannigan booted me in the balls, crumpling me over in agony. Then, as I lay writhing on the canvas, he poured a carton of potted shrimps all over me. Why shrimps? Well, Morecambe is famous the world over for them. The Queen herself is a fan of Morecambe Bay potted shrimps. So I felt that by covering me in the town's most beloved delicacy, this would be the perfect way for GPW to add insult to injury, the ideal method to mock myself, the XWA and Morecambe. And Brannigan had a rare old time doing it, whooping and cackling and skipping around the ring like a demented hyena as I lay in a pool of stinky shellfish, my best suit ruined. Johnnie was a *great* heel.

"The XWA-GPW feud was the first time I'd had the chance to be me, Johnnie Brannigan, and not Heresy," said Johnnie in 2016.

"I was looking to break out and do something different and this gave me the opportunity, to come out from the shadows as the GPW owner which had previously never been revealed."

War on the Shore ended with an XWA Title match between Johnny Phere and Stixx. The Psychotic Warrior was suffering with a rib injury that night and wrestled all strapped up, in intense pain, but still got through the bout and managed to deliver a Ram Slam to The Heavyweight House of Pain. At this, ring announcer Richard Parker rang the bell, calling the match off for no apparent reason. The motivation for his actions soon became clear.

Brannigan led his GPW thugs in a cavalry charge to the ring and then Heresy, Bin Mann, Roberts, RJM and burly GPW trainee Jason Logan battered XWA's two biggest heroes Phere and Stixx in another gang mugging. This brought out the XWA contingent, led by Jynkz, Spud and The Manchester Massive. A wild XWA v GPW brawl ensued all over the Hexagon, where perhaps some people involved got a little carried away with the intensity of it all. One or two 'potato' punches were certainly thrown, as we say in the business. But it all ended with the desired response from our fans. There were ear-splitting chants of "X-W-A! X-W-A!" as the challenge was made for an XWA v GPW match on the next show Vendetta on July 28, to settle things once and for all.

I was really impressed with the post-show promo by Brannigan and Richard Parker. The ring announcer, as it turned out, had defected to the GPW cause and was revealed as the 'insider' who had allowed the invaders into our venues to carry out their dastardly attacks. Parker, who was fantastic in the role of conniving little weasel, came up with a killer line too.

"You talk about your Authority and your Agenda? Well I have an agenda and it has three letters...G-P-W."

Then Johnnie, the talker supreme, grabbed Jason Logan and pushed him right into the camera. Logan's nose was busted from the brawl and he looked in a right state, with blood running down his chin.

"Look at this!" screamed the GPW head honcho.

"Well, on July 28 the streets of Morecambe will run RED WITH BLOOD!

"You mark my words. The Best in the North West is GPW!"

So the match was set in stone. And tickets for Vendetta began to fly out. Not just to XWA fans, either. But a large number were sold to GPW regulars, just as I hoped. My plan had always been to make big money from this show. I make no apologies for that. That's why they call it the wrestling *business*.

And I succeeded. Not just on ticket revenue, but also on sales of DVDs of the show afterwards. XWA v GPW Vendetta was a record-breaking show for me, financially.

The plan for Vendetta was to revisit the successful format of the British Inter-Federation Cup days. There would be four matches and then a decisive four-on-four 'Survivor Series' match. A pinfall or submission win in a singles bout would earn two points for the victorious team; with one point for a countout or disqualification win. The winners of the elimination match would gain two points per surviving team member.

The matches would be Spud (XWA) v Kris Travis (GPW), Stixx (XWA) v Damon Leigh (GPW), Jynkz, Axl Rage and JD Sassoon (XWA) v Dylan Roberts, Bin Mann and Jason Logan (GPW) and a mouthwatering clash between Johnny Phere (XWA) and Johnnie 'Heresy' Brannigan (GPW).

The Phere-Brannigan bout had an interesting back story. When JP was in GPW, he was a member of Heresy's heel faction SIN. So in the old GPW storyline, Phere was subordinate to Heresy. When Johnnie cut promos on JP in the lead-up to Vendetta, he played off their past. His speeches were really close to the bone.

"You've always tried so hard to climb the ladder, you've tried hard to be a better person and a better wrestler," said Brannigan, talking about JP during one particularly venomous YouTube promo.

"But what's happened every time you tried? You've fallen down. You've failed. You've lost."

Brannigan went even further in his final pre-Vendetta speech as he told the true story about how he first met Jamie, backstage at an FWA show in 2005.

"You were a man who'd always tried for the best in life. I gave you a break. The first chance I had, I brought you into GPW into my faction and I surrounded you with the best wrestlers in the UK. You even made it to the main event. But you were never a champion.

You're a born loser."

Then, Johnnie took things to a whole new level of spite. He brought up JP's young daughter. Now, Jamie loves his daughter more than anything. But due to personal circumstances, he rarely got to see her. So Brannigan twisted a real-life scenario and hit JP where it hurts most.

"Johnny Phere failed at being a father. Ha ha ha haaaa! What happened, Johnny? You packed your bags and you left town. You may be able to hide from your duties as a father but you will never hide from me. You don't scare me. You don't intimidate me. I built you!"

Christ, this was personal. But "personal issues draw money" as Jerry Lawler says in his book It's Good to be the King...Sometimes. I knew that Brannigan had crossed the line by bringing JP's family life into it. But that excited me. I knew our fans would want to see Johnny Phere destroy him.

By the way, Johnnie did get permission off Jamie before doing this promo. I would have never allowed it otherwise.

While the tensions simmered between the two promotions ahead of Vendetta, GPW showed its lighter side too. Not least of all the regular YouTube comedy show Science Fiction. Created by GPW grapplers Professor Mike Holmes and his brother Greg 'Voodoo' Tasker, Science Fiction poked fun at GPW wrestlers and storylines with a series of comedic sketches parodying everything from Monty Python to Star Wars. When the XWA became the target of their surreal and cutting humour, the result was comedy gold. I particularly liked how they compared me to that ultimate heel Adolf Hitler with a parody of the theme from the old sitcom Dad's Army ("Who do you think you are kidding Mr Lambert...if you think old Grand Pro's done?") and a spoof rap video taking the mick out of me screaming "THAT'S HIS BROTHER!" after RJM punched Dean Paterson at Gold Rush. I was in stitches.

Saturday, July 28 2012 dawned and it was a warm summer's day. Backstage at The Hexagon, there was great camaraderie between the GPW and XWA crews. If there was real-life tension a few months earlier, it was now forgotten. Everyone was excited and determined to savour this moment. We knew the build-up had gone well. We knew the building was going to be full, or close to it. We could relax and have fun. Johnnie Brannigan particularly, was in a great mood. He was really psyched up for this. He later told me the XWA v GPW feud was the best experience of his pro wrestling career.

And it's right up there with my favourites, too.

Once the doors opened and the fans began to file in to The Hexagon, it quickly became clear that this wasn't just an ordinary show. We were sold out and the atmosphere was electric. Virtually one side of the venue was filled with green and yellow GPW T-shirts. It was like a group of away football fans entering hostile territory but determined to outshout the hundreds of home supporters.

Led by the rowdy Bennett, another GPW die-hard called Phil Robertson and the still-injured Ricky J McKenzie - who we planted in the crowd - the "G-P-W!" chants were incredible. And this was before the show even started. Soon, the XWA fans began to stir, led by Greg's Gang of Ruth, Sarah, Kyrie and Natalie from their usual front row spot. And an uproariously partisan chant battle began as the two sides tried to drown each other out.

"G-P-DUB!"

"X-W-A!"

I listened backstage as this passionate wall of sound grew louder, and louder, and *louder*.

"G-P-DUB!"
"X-W-A!"

"There has never been an atmosphere like this in British wrestling," said our commentator, the former FutureShock ring announcer 'The Vocal Terrorist' Jesse Ellis.

And he was right. The reaction when Richard Parker and myself emerged for the start of the show was absolutely unreal. The place became unglued. And we were just the ring announcers.

Spud got an even bigger welcome when he emerged for the opening match. The Rockstar gimmick was so entertaining, he'd turned back babyface on XWA shows a few months earlier. At Vendetta 2012, The Baby Jesus of British Wrestling was greeted with sheer adulation from the Morecambe regulars and he milked every single moment.

The Spud-Travis match was a quality battle, as you would expect from two of Britain's best. It also set the tone for the entire evening because the crowd was making noise from start to finish. First, the sneaky Parker introduced the cocky Travis. Three-quarters of the venue booed and the other quarter cheered. Then I introduced Spud. Three-quarters of the venue cheered and the other quarter booed. The fans were going *bonkers*!

"It was the only time I got to wrestle Trav which meant a lot to me," said Spud, reflecting on the events of that incredible night.

"It was so much fun. It was a good swansong for XWA, one of the best shows I've ever been involved with, because everybody worked together."

It kind of reminded me of the split FWA v IPW:UK Final Frontiers crowd response from 2007, only turned up several notches. That day in Kent, the support for the FWA was out of nostalgia and very few people believed the Frontier squad was likely to win. But at Vendetta, the result was in plenty of doubt. Nobody was quite sure who was going to emerge triumphant at the end. As a result, both sets of spectators got behind their favourites with a rabid passion. And they had completely bought into the build-up to the point that even the two sets of fans despised each other. Spud played off this with aplomb, taunting the portly Bennett every chance he got!

By the way, there is a fantastic photo, snapped by Tony Knox, of the Rockstar goading an angry Hitman while our security man Colin Wild tries to keep them apart. Tony Knox really is a superb photographer. Few have done more than him over the years to chronicle British wrestling and make us all look like stars.

The Spud-Travis match got more and more exciting down the stretch, with loads of false finishes and big moves. Eventually the Rockstar finished off the Shooting Star with a beautiful top rope elbow to a massive pop from the Morecambe faithful. Then Jay jumped into the XWA audience to celebrate, while giving the finger to the outraged GPW contigent.

What a start.

Bryan Fulton had created a big screen scoreboard for the night's proceedings. And after match one, it now read XWA 2 GPW 0.

Stixx kept the momentum, and his undefeated streak, going with victory over DDL in match two in another gripping encounter. But the win came at a cost. The storyline called for Damon Leigh to injure The Heavyweight House of Pain's knee with his own chain in a super-heated post-match attack, writing him out of the rest of the show. So although XWA led 4-0, our talisman was now 'en route to hospital'. We would be without Stixx for the climactic elimination main event.

With the Hexagon still in utter bedlam, GPW finally got a win on the board in match three, thanks to dissention between Jynkz and the ex-Blond Jovi, who I'd renamed The Blackpool Blonds in a nod to their seaside roots after a suggestion from Robbie Brookside that Rage and Sassoon should ditch the rocker roadie gimmick and embrace their Blackpool heritage. Dylan Roberts, Ste Mann and Jason Logan took full advantage of the arguments between Jynkz and The Blonds to make it 4-2, much to the delight of the unruly Grand Pro ringside mob.

The interplay between myself and Parker at the ring announcers' desk was, by now, becoming a highlight of the show. We both lived and breathed every single match and every single move. Whenever XWA gained the advantage, I punched the air like a bespectacled cheerleader, while Parker sat quietly in his chair. But whenever GPW was on top, Richard grinned smugly and taunted me, while I looked subdued and disgusted.

When Johnnie Brannigan and Johnny Phere emerged for match four, the heat went up another level, if that was even possible. There was a crackling sense of anticipation and the people believed they might even see a proper fight. Brannigan smirked as he led the beer-swilling Grand Pro fans in unpleasant chants of "FAILURE! FAILURE!" as the bellowing Phere stalked around the ring, snorting like a bull and working himself up into a state of explosively violent intent. Brannigan then retreated to the stage with the microphone and continued to wind up JP, pushing his buttons, calling him a failure, then challenged Phere to actually put the XWA Title on the line. At this point, the XWA chants were so loud they momentarily drowned Johnnie out. The fans were *indestructible* that night.

The fight got under way and it was, as expected, a no-frills, take-no-prisoners brawl. The action was clunky at times and it was by no means a classic. But it didn't matter. The personalities were so over, the fans so captivated by the issue between the two men, that the quality of the bout was secondary to the overall result.

By the end of the match, Phere was so angered by Brannigan's misdeeds that he was a man possessed. The champ kicked out of an illegal piledriver when the referee was distracted, then took Heresy down into his painful War-Lock crossface submission hold. The villainous preacher had no choice but to tap out. At this, I began dancing around the ringside area, getting in the GPW fans' faces, conducting my own one-man celebration party. It seemed that XWA was home and dry.

But Phere hadn't finished. Incensed by Brannigan's pre-match words, the victorious JP reapplied the War-Lock and wouldn't let it go. As he wrenched and tore at the helpless Heresy, referee Russell Smith had no choice but to show the crazed Johnny the red card and reverse his decision. Brannigan was announced as the winner by disqualification. Instead of being up 6-2, XWA's lead was now only 4-3. The GPW fans were ecstatic. Despite almost having his shoulder torn from its socket, Johnnie had enough energy left to stagger out of the ring where he celebrated with a sick smile of satisfaction.

This finish was influenced heavily by Jerry Lawler v Bret Hart at Summerslam 1993. I thought it would be the perfect story. Just as The Hitman (that's Bret, not Bennett) showed when he pulverised The King all those years ago, Phere proved he was better than Brannigan. But then he blew it because he lost the plot, riled by the mind games of the GPW promoter. Delighted that Johnny had snatched defeat from certain victory, the Grand Pro fans began their "FAILURE!" chants again in earnest. Distraught at the turn of events, I was forced to give an impassioned pep-talk to Phere to try to get his mind on the game ahead of the decisive main event.

The way I booked the first four matches meant that whoever won the elimination match would take overall victory. Whoever won this main event could also claim to be the Best in the North West.

"This is it," said Stallion on commentary. "It all comes down to this."

The XWA team was positioned as the total underdogs. We had

the loose cannon Johnny Phere and the under-sized Spud and Jynkz taking on the much bigger Mann, Roberts, Logan and Travis. As for Stixx's replacement, we drafted in inexperienced XWA trainee Action Jackson. So we looked to be in serious trouble.

Sure enough, young Jack took an absolute beating early on. But then, out of the blue, he surprised Roberts with a sneaky roll-up for an unlikely three count.

"He's been pinned by the rookie, I don't believe it!" exclaimed Stallion, as the eliminated Roberts threw an angry tantrum. Still, Team XWA didn't have long to enjoy their early advantage. Jason Logan quickly grabbed Jackson and destroyed him with a power bomb to even matters up at three against three.

The match took another twist as Spud hit a Stunner, Phere delivered a Ram Slam and Jynkz landed a top rope splash to eliminate Logan. But then Bin Mann speared The Flying Scot into the middle of next week, before spearing Rockstar Spud for the three count too. GPW's resident rubbish collector was on fire. He had pinned both Jynkz and Spud in double-quick time. Now Johnny Phere had to battle both Kris Travis and the Bin Mann all by himself.

Phere was able to execute his Ram Slam and eliminate Trav, though, and now the fans were on their feet as it all came down to The Psychotic Warrior v Ste Mann. The duelling chants were deafening again as the two final survivors stared holes through each other, realising what was at stake.

In the closing moments of this epic show, Johnny appeared to have matters well under control, as he applied the War-Lock to Bin Mann, but then Richard Parker climbed onto the ring apron to distract the referee. But I pulled RP down, then shoved the treacherous MC so he fell over, right on his tailored suit!

At this, Bin Mann charged but JP sidestepped and his Grand Pro foe speared the ref. This brought out both sets of wrestlers and another tumultuous brawl broke out between XWA and GPW factions. Bin Mann took advantage to sneak in with his trademark large metal rubbish bin, which he aimed at Johnny's head, only for Phere to spear him hard before he could deliver the knockout blow.

Bin Mann was winded. Johnny was setting up for the Ram Slam. The XWA fans were going berserk. Surely XWA was about to win.

Redemption for all the sneak-attacks, all the taunts, all the lies, everything, was just around the corner...

Until Joey Hayes...XWA's Joey Hayes...slid into the ring and dropped a charging Johnny Phere on his head with the JKO with sudden, perfect, shocking timing.

The Hexagon was stunned.

The GPW throng then threw Russell Smith back into the ring as Bin Mann slid over and made the cover. Smith's hand slapped the mat three times and Team GPW was proclaimed the winners.

Joey Hayes, the beloved, squeaky-clean teen heart-throb, a career babyface in Morecambe up until that point, but crucially a *GPW original*, had turned heel on Johnny Phere. And he cost XWA the match against our hated rivals. It came completely out of nowhere.

Our fans were open-mouthed.

"Damn you Joey Hayes!" yelled The Vocal Terrorist from the commentary table.

"For the first time in my career, I'm lost for words. I never want to see that man again in my life."

The post-match scenes were storytelling perfection. Joey stood in the ring above the fallen Phere, with a detached look on his face, and lifted the XWA Title belt over his head. The GPW faction celebrated raucously with their fans like they had won the World Cup, the Ashes and the Olympics combined. The XWA fans were devastated. For real. The members of Greg's Gang were literally in tears of anguish at the result, collapsing into each other's arms. Meanwhile Johnny Phere lay in the ring, his face etched with pain, disbelief and vengeful anger.

Everyone in the Hexagon that night had been through the emotional wringer for the past three hours. They had experienced intense joy, anger, shock, awe, worry, fear, laughter and tears. Everything. It was exactly how a pro wrestling show should be.

Built on emotion.

Because It's Real in Morecambe.

Ste 'Bin' Mann pinned three XWA stars in one match. He was the undisputed star of the night for GPW, which was all by design. I was impressed by the young Mancunian's contribution to the entire feud and wanted to repay him by giving the trash talking trash man his big moment. He seized it, and then some. To be fair to the GPW roster, they all did. To a man, they were fantastic that night. And so were their fans.

"We are GPW and we are the Best in the North West!" yelled Ste 'Bin' Mann into a camera. And at this, Mann, Brannigan, Roberts, DDL, Logan, RJM, even their fans led by the triumphant Bennett began chanting "G-P-DUB!" long into the night.

Meanwhile, I entered the ring, looking absolutely bereft at Joey's betrayal and the loss to our worst of enemies. I picked up the microphone and surveyed the scenes of carnage. A solitary tear glistened on my cheek.

Then I spoke.

"Normally, I'd come out here at the end of an XWA show and say see you next time," I said.

"But after what's happened here tonight, I'm not sure there's going to be a next time."

I placed the microphone in the middle of the ring and walked out of The Hexagon.

Then I went home.

And I never promoted a wrestling show again.

CHAPTER 8

THE ORIGINS OF PCW

While XWA and GPW were spatting over who was the Best in the North West, it wasn't long before Preston City Wrestling blew us both, and FutureShock, out of the water.

PCW became not just the Best in the North West, but one of the best in the entire country.

I first met Steven Fludder at Southside in June 2011, on the show that caused so much controversy with GPW. Steven, who also worked as a pub and club doorman, was running the event in partnership with Southside promoter Ben Auld. Soon afterwards, Fludder broke out to run shows on his own, in his home town of Preston.

Now Preston means a great deal to me. Preston North End was my late grandad's favourite football club and its legendary winger 'The Preston Plumber' Sir Tom Finney was his favourite player. And Preston was where I studied to become a journalist at the University of Central Lancashire in 2001/2. I spent one of the best years of my life there, meeting some fantastic people who are still close friends today.

So whenever I get off the bus or the train in Preston after the short journey from Morecambe, I feel very much at home. The streets and the buildings are comfortingly familiar. And so is the Lancashire weather!

Fludder ran the first PCW show in rainy Preston on August 26 2011. While PCW later gained a reputation for using high class overseas talent, the debut show A New Beginning had just Colt Cabana and the best of British, in front of a small crowd of around 200 people.

"I was on the very first Preston show and the draw was nowhere near what it built up to," said El Ligero in 2016.

"When we did that first show we couldn't tell it was going to take off. The atmosphere was OK, but on those first few shows a few of us didn't enjoy it that much because the fans didn't appear to care about many of the characters at that point because they hadn't got to know them yet. It seemed like PCW was just somewhere to go before a night out."

The second show on September 23 2011, when Tyson T-Bone was crowned the first PCW Champion, also had no foreigners at all. The third event in November was built around inter-promotional matches between PCW and Premier British Wrestling from Scotland. Again, no imports. And this British-only pattern continued right the way through until I made my PCW debut in June 2012. By then, the shows were already close to selling out. PCW built its following slowly, gradually, using UK talent.

"The Christmas show in 2011, that was the first time I wrestled for PCW and I thought 'this is something special'," said Ligero.

"The fans started to care about the characters, and rather than talk amongst themselves during the action, they started to get invested in what they were seeing. It has skyrocketed since then."

At Guild Wars on June 2 2012, Fludder brought in the dynamic Japanese grappler Akira Tozawa to wrestle Ligero in the main event. Tozawa, a standout from Dragon Gate who appeared in WWE's Cruiserweight Classic in 2016, is regarded as one of the best independent stars in the world. I was lucky enough to sit at ringside and commentate on the Ligero-Tozawa bout on my very first PCW show, alongside Chris 'G-Man' Garrett. It was a scorching bout too, one of Ligero's greatest ever performances in my book (and this *is* my book!)

I enjoyed working with G-Man because he is a lot of fun. He has an irreverent style and came out with some bizarre comments on-air to keep me on my toes. For example, on every show we did together he mentioned that Kris Travis loved eating cat biscuits and also talked about how Dave Mastiff enjoyed sadistically tying dogs to radiators (I have no idea if either of these claims were true!) And, he constantly insisted that Irish wrestler Mad Man Manson had passed away. "I thought he was dead, Greg!" bleated Garrett, every time Manson came out to the ring looking very much alive. Half the time,

I had no idea what G-Man was on about. But I played along with his wackiness and I felt we were just hitting our stride as a double act when he was suddenly removed from PCW in 2013.

As for the Ligero-Tozawa match, the buzz from it gained PCW plenty of positive publicity with the wrestling magazines and internet sites. But Fludder didn't run before he could walk. Appearances by overseas stars were minimal on the next few shows too until Steven really pushed the boat out with his first Supershow, PCW Festive Fury on December 9 2012, headlined by John Morrison, Eugene and Chris Masters. By then, PCW was 12 shows old.

I had a great time at Festive Fury. This was my first experience of a full day of PCW shows and I was impressed with Steven's business acumen. He ran a show on the Friday night, then the Saturday afternoon, and then Saturday evening, and sold all-weekend passes - at a discount - as well as individual tickets. And as part of the deal, fans got to meet their favourite wrestlers and got a T-shirt or signed photo thrown in. And the meet-and-greet was organised with military precision, such a far cry from when FWA used to make a pig's ear of them back during its first incarnation.

Festive Fury 2012 ended with an awesome main event of John Morrison v Noam Dar. Morrison was fresh out of WWE, a former Intercontinental and tag team champion, The Shaman of Sexy, all washboard abs and flowing locks, a worldwide star. At the time, Noam was this relatively unknown teenager from Scotland, who had moved to Ayr from his native Israel as a young boy and then burst onto the emerging Scottish wrestling scene just a couple of years after starting training at just 13 years old.

"I remember going to my first training class, I went along with an older friend who was very serious about being a professional wrestler," said Noam in 2016, reflecting on his early days in the business.

"I didn't even realise you could *be* a professional wrestler. I thought that was something for Americans, not a young lad from a small town in Scotland. But I was a huge wrestling fan so I tagged along, because I wanted to see what was involved in wrestling training.

"For the first six or seven months I didn't even get in the ring. I trained on mats. That has really helped me to respect the ring and respect this business.

"The first day was a whirlwind. I feel like I might have almost cried after a few bumps. Actually, I still cry now when I bump! That's been the only constant in my wrestling career, I always cry when I bump. Sometimes I watch other people's matches and I catch myself cringing, but I've done those things myself. It's mad, but when you're in that element you switch off to any sensibility, I guess."

Despite his reaction to taking back-first falls on mats, Noam was clearly a natural. And he would soon cross paths with a man who would become his friend, mentor and fellow PCW star, Adrian 'Lionheart' McCallum.

"I met Adrian at one of my first training classes," said Dar.

"I was doing flip bumps and rolls. This was the time when he was in 1PW and Lionheart was at his most Lionheart-est, for lack of a better term!

"I remember doing a flip and my foot caught his shoe. He gave me this look, like, who is this kid? He was so angry and I remember feeling petrified at the time. But to be fair to him, from that day he always helped me with my training. He stayed and watched my training match that night and gave me advice. Then when I started getting on shows and got to know him, I liked his personality. Then he began to help me get into England and got me my first English booking in Leeds.

"From there it steamrolled. We lived close to each other, we travelled together, we trained together. He's just a genuine kind hearted human being. We're very close friends."

Noam was only 19 at the time of his match with Morrison, but was already the Fighting Spirit Magazine Wrestler of the Year and earlier that year, had engaged in a much-praised battle with AJ Styles for Pro Wrestling Elite. But I hadn't seen much of young Dar and knew little about the mop-topped Oasis fan with the penchant for putting his hands behind his back, Liam Gallagher-style. I honestly didn't realise what he was capable of.

Dar was sensational against Morrison. His pacing, positioning, precision and coolness in the ring was incredible for one so young.

He was so smooth, quick as a cat, technically proficient and never seemed to get tired. His performance was so confident and mature, you would never have known how much the youngster had soul-searched about whether he belonged in such a marquee bout against a megastar opponent.

"That was the first time when I was in a match environment where I couldn't actually picture myself in that situation," said Noam.

"I'd had big matches before where I could visualise myself in the ring with these guys, being in the same bracket, that was how I could keep myself calm and content. But with John Morrison I could not see myself in there, I didn't know how it was going to work. Then it turned out he was one of the nicest guys you could meet and once I got in the ring with him, I felt comfortable. That's a testimony to how good a worker he is.

"After that match I thought 'I might be OK at this professional wrestling stuff'. I'm a very pessimistic person towards myself. But that match gave me a lot of confidence going forward."

Although Noam lost the match, he went on to win the Road to Glory tournament at PCW's next big weekend of shows in February 2013, defeating Joey Hayes in a stunning final after a trademark merciless assault on Joey's leg and a leglock finishing hold named, in a nod to his favourite Manchester indie group's song Champagne Supernova, the Champagne *Super Kneebar*.

Afterwards as Dar was receiving congratulations from the rest of the dressing room, I too offered a handshake and told him "Don't peak too soon!" The kid wasn't even 20 years old and he stole the show in a tournament that also included Brian Kendrick, Paul London, Super Crazy and a line-up of far more experienced British grapplers than him.

"At that time, PCW was bringing in a lot of imports and big stars, first-time names who had never been before," said Noam.

"The attention on Preston was massive. For me and Joey to main event the Road to Glory tournament in a match that is still one of my favourites, that made me feel very proud. When you're with a company that you believe in and you want to be a part of, you want to represent it well. I felt like Joey and I represented it well in that tournament final."

After the runaway success of Festive Fury 2012 and Road to Glory 2013, I realised I was part of something special with PCW. It felt different to any other wrestling company I had ever worked for. It just felt *big-time* by British wrestling standards. Organisationally, PCW was a different world to the FWA days.

For years, the best thing about my career with PCW was that I could just turn up and go to work. I rarely had to concern myself with behind-the-scenes organisation, because PCW's extremely professional and capable backroom staff always made sure the shows ran smoothly. I rarely had to think about whether or not there was going to be a big crowd - because they were usually queuing right down the road outside Evoque on show days. I hardly ever had to worry about anything. Everything organisationally was taken care of by Fludder and his team. I just put on my headset, watched some of the best wrestling action anywhere around the globe, talked about it for three hours, and got paid for it. What an amazing job to have.

It is December 2016 as I write, and although there have been some changes in backstage personnel over the years, PCW can still count on a large group of people behind-the-scenes who are all pulling in the same direction - a team of unsung heroes who are crucial to the success of the promotion.

On a show day I usually walk into PCW's home - the nightclub on Fishergate in Preston formerly known as Tokyo Joe's, later Lava & Ignite and now Evoque - about two hours before bell time. The ring, supplied by Tyson T-Bone, is already set up. A gang of PCW trainees are working feverishly to assemble the gigantic entranceway. Steven Fludder's wife Liz and the 'merch girls' are presiding over the meticulously arranged merchandise section, which is more like a mini-shop filled with a treasure trove of custom-made PCW and wrestler T-shirts, DVDs and action figures. Longtime PCW camerawoman Tracy Hendley and the rest of the production team are setting up HD video cameras to ensure the event is filmed to the highest possible standard. The sound crew of Christopher and Andrew Leary are sound-checking the entrance music. Backstage, photographer Gordon Harris is setting up his green screen. And in the midst of it all, Steven Fludder, who is always dressed in a suit jacket and trousers at shows, is directing operations and making sure preparations run like clockwork.

Referee Des Robinson started with PCW on their first show on August 26 2011. The Liverpudlian met Steven at a 1PW card in Ellesmere Port that year and then a few months later, got a message asking if he wanted a job. At time of writing the well-liked Des was still there, one of two regular PCW referees alongside Joel Allen.

"I didn't realise how big PCW would be at that time," said Des.

"But right from the outset it had a great following.

"1PW promised a lot of talent and sometimes they didn't turn up. This was a letdown for the fans and they didn't get their money back. This tarnishes wrestling in general. Some people don't separate one promotion from another. If one promotion is bad people assume all wrestling is bad. But Steven always delivers what he advertises. If certain things don't happen he's quick to tell people and he's straight up. He doesn't pull the wool over the eyes.

"Backstage, talking to the guys, there's a good atmosphere, no egos, everybody is good to talk to. We all get along. Nothing has changed, even today. We all enjoy what we do and we support each other. In wrestling sometimes, that's not always the case. Some guys are stepping over others to get to where they need to be.

"There's never been anyone used on PCW where I've thought, why is this guy in here? Everybody has something to bring. PCW is to the UK what WWE is to America. If you're going to make it somewhere in the UK, it's got to be PCW, for me. It's the promotion that's brought in the most imports, but they help to build up the guys they are in with. It's a good place to be."

I too take working for PCW extremely seriously. In the days leading up to a PCW show, I do an extensive amount of research about the wrestlers and matches I will be commentating on. I am always armed with two note books filled with scribblings, facts, figures, phrases and comments I am planning to make. This is because I know that PCW has a worldwide following. Video On-Demand screenings of PCW shows are viewed across the world, in America, Australia, even Russia. I need to be super-prepared. If I make an error, usually they will edit it out in post-production. But even so, I *hate* making mistakes in the first place.

I have found Steven to be a great person to work for. You know where you stand with Fludder. He is a straight talker, a typical gritty Northerner. He says what he means and he means what he says. There is no flannel or skirting around the subject. He is all business. And in four-and-a-half years of working for him, he has always treated me well and never let me down. I have a lot of respect for him.

Fludder was a massive wrestling fan, travelling the UK for years before he became a promoter. He watched shows up and down the country, including the FWA and my own events in Morecambe, analysing and learning. A shrewd operator, he never strays from his ultimate goal which is to run Preston City Wrestling as a profitable business.

For years, whenever I talked to Steven at PCW shows, the conversation was usually more about business than storylines. He'd tell me about his latest fan ticket package, or a deal he struck with the local media, or the next piece of production kit he was looking for, or his future plans to expand to an even bigger venue or another town. His economic focus is a rarity among promoters in the UK wrestling business.

Steven is a real character and he has many sides to him. He is ruthless in business for sure and will not stand for being messed around. But he will always be honest with the fans and bend over backwards to give them value for money.

He is also quite the socialiser. Fludder likes to go out partying after shows, sometimes even holidaying abroad with the wrestlers. He struck up firm friendships with overseas grapplers like Chris Masters and Uhaa Nation (now Apollo Crews). He works hard and he plays hard. And he really *cares* about the talent. He will go the extra mile to look after them if they suffer an injury or have a problem. This creates a very positive backstage atmosphere at PCW shows.

I also must mention Steven's wife Elizabeth. Liz too is a huge wrestling fan and has been an invaluable support to her hubby over the years, selling tickets or merchandise at shows, picking up wrestlers from airports and making them welcome in her home. Mrs Fludder is another underrated reason for PCW's success.

PCW has an overseas following because, as already mentioned,

Fludder books names who are recognisable to wrestling fans all over the world. He brings in legends of WWE, the latest hot independent talent from the US, Japan and Europe, and existing TNA stars who appeared every week on UK television. These names hook fans to buy tickets to PCW shows and attract interest from people sitting at computers or smart TVs around the globe who have never been to PCW in person.

"Fludder and I are friends, we have a friendly rivalry, but we have a totally different approach to running shows," said PCW wrestler and former FutureShock promoter Dave Rayne.

"The point of FutureShock is to create stars out of trainees. The point of PCW is big shows, sell tickets, make money."

Big shows. Sell tickets. Make money. That is exactly what Preston City Wrestling has done, consistently, for the past four years. It makes me very proud that a world class wrestling promotion has sprung up just a one hour door-to-door bus ride from my house. And it's an honour and a privilege to be part of Preston City Wrestling.

The success of PCW, and my role within the company, was one of many reasons why I gave up promoting with the XWA. I saw that in PCW, the North West wrestling scene was in great hands.

I also knew I couldn't compete with Steven. But to be honest, by then I had no desire to. And here's why.

CHAPTER 9

DOM TRAVIS

Being a wrestling promoter is really difficult. And it's not for everyone.

Dann Read once joked with me that if we wrote down the pros and cons of being a wrestling promoter, the pros list would be tiny and the cons list would be off the page. It is definitely a thankless task.

As I write, it is four-and-a-half years since I promoted my last wrestling show with the XWA. And I don't miss it.

I don't miss the thought of having to go out for hours, tramp the streets and ask shopkeepers if they would pop a poster in their windows. I don't miss my phone or my Facebook inbox going off every five minutes with wrestlers looking for work. I don't miss trawling round to find one of the few companies willing to take the risk of underwriting public liability insurance for wrestling. I don't miss telling disappointed wrestlers that they're not booked for the next show. I don't miss my wrestling ring breaking down every five minutes and arduous trips to DIY shops to find new parts when I am about the least practical person you'll ever meet. And I don't miss how I became an absolute pain in the backside for my family to live with as, in the week prior to a show, I obsessed over every little detail and worried if I would sell enough tickets to break even.

When we started running shows at the The Carleton in 2010, it just wasn't the same. It didn't have the ambience or gravitas The Dome had. I considered stopping right then, I really did. At the end of 2010, after my bad experience at FWA European Uprising, I told Mark Kay my heart wasn't in it any more. But I felt a responsibility to carry on - particularly to the trainees at my wrestling school in Morecambe, some of whom were just starting to show real promise, and to the XWA fans who followed our product with such passion.

So I continued as a promoter for another year-and-a-half.

Don't get me wrong. I love wrestling. I love watching, reading, writing and talking about wrestling. I think about it constantly. But being a promoter was slowly killing my enjoyment of wrestling.

And being a promoter was also affecting my personal relationships. My wife Sharon felt I was immersed in sports entertainment to the point that I wasn't offering any emotional support for her. For years I spent too much time dealing with wrestling issues for not much financial reward and not enough time with Sharon and my two boys Owen and Dale.

Dave Rayne had a similar issue in his own personal life. His own experience kind of summed up how things were at home for me at that time.

"I spent a decade building FutureShock from the ground up and I lost a lot of my personal life doing it," he told me in February 2016.

"I was engaged to a girl I was madly in love with. I've just started a teaching degree at college. The catalyst for doing that was because she wanted a real life. She'd finished uni and got a job, and she realised that if I carried on in wrestling, she'd be working Monday to Friday 9 to 5 and I'd be swanning off on Friday evenings, and there would be no life together. So I was looking to grow us a life away from wrestling but I feel it was too little too late. Doing a degree is three years more for her to wait.

"She had a lot of hang-ups about the nature of wrestling and how my high, my drug, is to go out and get that applause and attention from strangers, and then I would come back home. I loved my life with her, but I think she felt very strongly that if I wasn't wrestling, I wasn't myself, and what she was getting Monday to Friday was a shadow. What people in Preston and those I was teaching at FutureShock were getting was the real me. The energy I put into wrestling was so much more than what I did during the week.

"She was the absolute love of my life. I don't think I'll ever find anyone else like her. Unique and amazing woman. And wrestling took her away from me. I don't blame anything. These are my decisions. I'm going to have to live with it."

I relate to this, 100 per cent. My own obsession with wrestling put a strain on my marriage. My alternative world was certainly becoming harder to justify to Sharon and the kids, year after year. By early 2012, I basically had six jobs; newspaper reporter, radio host, boxing Master of Ceremonies, wrestling promoter, wrestling magazine writer and wrestling training school manager. This didn't leave enough time to be a husband and a dad.

Life was non-stop back in 2012. I worked at the newspaper 9 to 5, five days a week, including a late shift until 9pm on a Monday. I hosted a local community radio show on Tuesday nights. I played pool for a pub team on Wednesday evenings. I spent other nights researching, interviewing or writing up my next article as a freelancer for Power Slam magazine. And at weekends I would either go out drinking to unwind, take a booking as a boxing show compere somewhere around the country or work on a wrestling show. And every Sunday, I was at the training school for most of the day, coaching the students, dealing with admin and planning trainee events. On XWA show weekends, I was hardly home at all.

Things have changed since then. I still love keeping busy but these days I spend a lot more time at home too. I found a better balance between my two great loves - my family and the wrestling business.

There were other factors for my decision to close the XWA. I needed to finish and publish my first book and while I devoted all my spare hours to my crazy working and social life, this was never going to happen. Also, the Morecambe venue jinx struck again just after Vendetta 2012, for the second time that year! The Hexagon closed for 12 months due to refurbishment, just six months after The Carleton shut down. So I was becoming disheartened with the process of finding new places to run my shows.

I was also thoroughly fed up with the egos that surround the wrestling business. I don't have a particularly thick skin, I took far too many things to heart over the years and it wore me out emotionally. I just wanted to ease the pressure. It wasn't doing me any good, making me stressed-out, egocentric and a pain to live with.

I knew I was quitting way before XWA Vendetta. I knew for months that I wanted GPW to win despite the fact that I knew July 28 2012 would be my final show and my wrestlers would never get the chance for proper revenge. But that was the right thing to do.

GPW was carrying on. XWA wasn't. So what would have been the point in an XWA victory?

My hope was that GPW would take the bragging rights associated with having 'forced XWA to close' and use it to help boost the status of Grand Pro Wrestling. I am not sure if they really capitalised on the opportunity. They did try, though. Johnnie Brannigan wanted to book Johnny Phere for a GPW feud with the turncoat Joey Hayes in the autumn of 2012. But Johnny's day job, at the time, meant he worked Friday nights and he couldn't make the dates. So that was that. The XWA v GPW feud was still red-hot after the events of Vendetta. But there was never any proper follow-up. It was like a great unfinished work.

"From GPW's point of view, Vendetta was a great way to finish," said Johnnie, reflecting on the feud.

"Greg hadn't told us he was finishing, I didn't have a clue. I would have loved to have continued the feud because it was such a good storyline. It was an abrupt ending but if we'd continued it we wouldn't have looked back on it as fondly as we have done. There are things in life where you leave them wanting more and this was one of them."

He's right. The show got so many fantastic reviews.

"The atmosphere and emotion were amazing," wrote Rob Butcher, former Power Slam writer.

"It was a tremendous spectacle," was the view of Ben Corrigan.

"The best wrestling show I've seen," wrote GPW fan, Jimi Calves Bailey.

I don't think it was possible for me to top what happened that night. It was everything I ever wanted to create in a wrestling show. So I have always felt I got out of promoting at exactly the right time.

The wrestlers were generally supportive of my decision to shut down the XWA. While disappointed, James 'Spud' Curtin and Paul 'Stixx' Grint were particularly understanding. That was important to me. They are two gentlemen who put their bodies on the line for me and for the Morecambe fans for years. They have achieved so much elsewhere in their respective careers, yet wrestling in my tiny seaside hometown still has a special place in their hearts. Spud and Stixx are two of the best professionals to come out of this country in the modern era and I am proud to be associated with them.

But our die-hard fans were not happy. The Morecambe Divas started up a 'Bring Back the XWA' Facebook page and bombarded me with messages begging me to reconsider. They were used to having a regular fix of good quality wrestling shows in the town. For some of them, XWA Wrestling was what they most looked forward to in their lives. Because it's Real in Morecambe. So I did feel bad for them. And a little guilty.

Some of our staff were also a little put out too. Bryan Fulton said to me "But you've got to carry on, it's your 10th anniversary as a promoter next year." But it's only a date. It doesn't really mean anything. This was my life. And this was my choice. Walking away was simply something I had to do.

Another reason why I quit promoting was because it just wasn't fun anymore. And the main reason for that was because Mark Kay, my best friend of 35 years, and business partner and co-promoter since 2003, was no longer running shows with me.

Mark told me his decision at the end of 2010. He'd been promoted in his real life job as a bank manager and didn't have time to co-run a wrestling company in his spare time any more. Without my partner-in-crime to share the highs and the lows with, being a wrestling promoter just wasn't the same.

I missed working with Mark. Still do. I miss how he always used to provide the relaxed voice of reason to counterbalance my excitable energy. I miss how he used to amble backstage during the interval to casually tell me how many fans were in attendance. I miss his wise little sayings like "doing nothing is always an option" and his surprising knack for designing superb posters and websites. I miss our long road trips to shows when we would come up with storylines for the wrestlers, put the world to rights and sing along at the top of our voices to 1980s rock classics on the radio. And I miss our after-show visits to Gizmos takeaway near Morecambe prom, where we ordered giant pizzas then drove back to my place for a post-mortem about the evening's event, share in the satisfaction of a job well done, and start to plan the next show.

But Mark got out and stayed out. We are still best mates but he's not involved in wrestling at all now.

So there were many factors behind my decision. I don't regret it. I have perspective on it. There is no point in carrying on with something if you're not happy. Enjoy yourself, as Prince Buster once said. It's later than you think.

In spring 2012, at around the time I was making my decision, a terrible tragedy occurred. And it showed me once again how short and precious life can be.

Dom Travis, a popular young wrestler from Bolton, took his own life in April 2012, aged 31, leaving the North West grapple community in a state of shock. A quiet, unassuming guy, no relation to Kris Travis (Dom's real surname was Treavis), he was a regular for GPW and FutureShock for years and a former FutureShock Champion.

I shared a dressing room with him many times on FutureShock shows in Stockport and on FWA events in Morecambe and further afield during the mid-noughties. In fact Dom was in the opening match of the very first ever FutureShock event in August 2004, and as Master of Ceremonies that night, I had the pleasure of announcing him to the ring.

But being perfectly honest, short of shaking his hand and exchanging pleasantries at shows, I didn't know Dom very well. And I hadn't seen him for some years when he died. However a lot of people on the scene I am close with, like Dave Rayne and Johnnie Brannigan, were hugely affected by the tragedy.

"Dom was a wonderful guy," said Dave.

"When we started FutureShock and had a core group of guys, if any of us was going to make it and be a star, it was going to be Dom. He had the look and the attitude. He had intensity and he knew what it took to get over. He was selfless as a wrestler and genuinely a really nice guy.

"We didn't talk much in the year before he passed away. Dom was a few years older than everyone else. That's one of the reasons why I got on with him so well, we were the grown ups, in our mid-20s. Si Valour and Jack Domino were university age. Jack Gallagher and Sam Bailey were high school age.

"When I found out he had passed away and the manner in which he passed away, I was absolutely devastated. I was at training and I got a phone call from Johnnie Brannigan. He'd found out, told Damon and then told me. To be that high up in the list of people who needed to know, I was touched and honoured.

"I'd felt excited for training that day. Dom had messaged me on the Thursday and asked what time was training on Sunday. He wanted to get back involved. I was so excited to have Dom Travis back. We had a lot of new trainees who hadn't see him at all and people who hadn't seen him for years.

"Then it got to about 12.30pm on Sunday and I inboxed him on Facebook, asking him 'Are you coming?'

"I got the phone call two hours later.

"*He wasn't coming.*

"I went cold. It was horrible. I told the guys what had happened. I talked about Dom. Then I went and sat outside for a bit. Then I went to GPW training. I got there, Johnnie was there, everyone had drifted towards there. There were GPW and FutureShock guys together and I spent the day there. I didn't want to go home and mull things over."

Johnnie Brannigan had known Dom since 2003 when he started training at GPW before moving to FutureShock.

"I sum Dom up with one word. *Calm.*

"He was always very calm. Always in control and capable. I always used to get het-up and angsty backstage but Dom was never nervous and he gave great advice. We had some good bouts against each other in GPW. He hit hard and so did I.

"We used to have this joke that in 30 years' time it would be me, Dom and Damon backstage, still wrestling, giving the youngsters advice. We always used to talk about that. It won't happen now.

"Then in 2009 I wanted to do a tag team and I wanted my tag team partner to be a bit zany or crazy. We thought about Johnny Phere but we decided on a new character. Jiggy Walker showed me a picture of a gimmick Johnny Stamboli was doing, a masked monster gimmick called Relik. Bingo. Dom was available, we brought him back into GPW under the mask as Kastor Levay and we formed a team called Paradise Lost. We did that gimmick for a couple of years and had some really good matches and some really terrible ones as well!

"Every wrestler has 'the wrestling dream' where their music plays and they're not changed ready for the match. Well, it actually happened to us. One night I'd changed the running order but hadn't told the ring announcer. So our music started playing for a match against The Eastern Bloc and we hadn't changed into our wrestling gear. Dom just looked at me and said 'It will be fine.' But it wasn't! It was awful!

"When we came to the end of our run as a team, we were always going to bring Dom back as himself. We never got the opportunity. Dom will always have a close place in my heart. I think about him often. I'm surprised about what happened."

The manner of Dom's death shocked Dave Rayne too.

"I don't think I'll ever understand why he decided to do that," said Dave.

"I try not to think about the end. In that frame of mind, that's not who Dom was. He's a guy who always smiled when he saw you. His favourite word was 'delighted'. He used that word all the time. And he was delighted about everything. He'd always be delighted to see you, and delighted at news.

"I thought he was the one who'd go the distance. He went to train at Lance Storm's academy and kicked arse. People who knew him loved him. Colt Cabana inboxed me a few days after his death. He'd met Dom years before and been on a few nights out and he said he was really sorry and upset and concerned. And Colt's the kind of guy who travels a lot of places and meets a lot of people. This guy lives halfway around the world and he was gutted. That's the effect Dom had on people."

The passing of Dom Travis actually inspired his own younger brother, Nate, to become a professional wrestler. Dedicating his career to Dom, Nate debuted two years later, ironically in a match against Dave Rayne on GPW's annual Dom Travis Memorial Show.

"I was honoured," said Dave.

"Nate came out to Dom's music, he had Dom's entrance jacket on, they have similar features, and he did Dom's entrance move for move. I had goosebumps. It was insane. It was like wrestling Dom.

"Nate did really well. I am really proud of that match. Very emotional. Not the prettiest wrestling but a big story and people were desperate for Nate to win. It was great. Nate didn't win. But it was magic.

"I sat in the dressing room afterwards for 45 minutes. Everyone came in and was slapping my back, telling me how good it was. I didn't even look up. I was taking it all in.

"I love wrestling but I see it very much as a job. I don't normally get excited that 'I'm wrestling this guy'. But this was an occasion when it meant something. I have a lot of affection for Nate."

I had my own chance to honour Dom Travis just a few days after his passing. I was humbled to be asked to share my memories of him on a backstage sit-down panel interview segment for DVD release, hosted by G-Man, at FutureShock's own Dom Travis Memorial Show on April 22 2012. I listened intently as my fellow panellists, Dom's close friends and training partners Jack Gallagher, Matt Taylor Richards and Simon Valour, told stories about him.

Later, at the end of that night's show at Stockport Guildhall, the entire FutureShock roster gathered around as a large framed portrait of Dom was brought into the ring in tribute to him. I stood alongside a weeping crowd of wrestlers, staff and fans; united as we applauded with respect for the man known affectionately in FutureShock as 'The Champ'. It was an emotional scene.

"Today, we still honour Dom as much as we can," said Dave.

"When Dom passed, we did a lot of events for (mental health charity) MIND. Johnnie was in contact with Dom's family a lot. GPW do a Dom Travis show every year and we still do a lot for MIND. Dom was our first Trophy Tournament winner and FutureShock Champion and we talk about that a lot. He set the standard for that belt. I wish there had been 250-500 people at shows back then because he was a phenomenal champion.

"We have a big framed photo of Dom on the wall of the gym. Occasionally people come in, like The Wolves, and ask 'who's that guy' and we tell them."

Over the years many of my American wrestling heroes, like Owen Hart, Eddie Guerrero and Brian Pillman, died unexpectedly in their 30s. I watched on television as their colleagues and peers stood in tearful tribute on the next episode of Monday Night Raw, then shared their memories of their fallen comrades with the TV audience.

I never expected to experience anything like this personally. It had a profound effect on me.

Dom's death showed me that life is fragile. You have to seize every moment and never take it for granted.

I am proud of what I achieved as a wrestling promoter. But it was no longer making me happy. And you only get one life.

Being a wrestling promoter had also made me narrow-minded. I lived in my own little bubble and believed that my promotion, my vision of pro wrestling, was the best. And I looked down on some of my rivals. I experienced this first-hand with my attitude towards GPW. The real-life strains of our feud made me realise that I needed to get out of the bubble, take a step back and survey the landscape. I wanted to see what else was happening on the British wrestling scene with the biased blinkers taken off.

The time was right to move on.

British wrestling was stirring. I had already become part of the exciting new dawn in PCW. But I wanted other new experiences, to take in new environments and meet new people in this crazy business I love so much.

And there was no better place to start, than in Scotland.

CHAPTER 10

GRADO

"One of our biggest problems is that today, we don't have a British grappler who is as recognisable to the average man in the street as Daddy and Haystacks were in the 80s or even the British Bulldog was in the 90s. I don't believe there is a single British-based wrestler capable of drawing game-changing crowds on name value alone. Until that situation changes, until we have our very own Hogan, Rock or Austin, even the decent houses will remain in the hundreds, and the thousands will continue to be a rarity."

Greg Lambert, Holy Grail: The True Story of British Wrestling's Revival, November 2012

When I wrote these words four years ago, if somebody had told me that our version of Hogan, Rock or Austin might turn out to be a flabby Scotsman wearing a baseball cap back-to-front and a bum bag around his waist, who comes out dancing to Like A Prayer by Madonna, I would have thought they were high.

But then along came Grado.

I first clapped eyes on Grado in early 2013. I was watching a YouTube video, and there he was, working out with weights while bouncing on a trampoline in nothing but blue swimming trunks that were unflatteringly way too tight for him. As his man-boobs and beer belly wobbled to the rhythm, I burst out laughing and was immediately taken with the self-styled "chubby wee chancer from the tap end of Stevenston".

Dubbed 'The Trials and Tribulations of Pro Wrestler Grado', this was no ordinary wrestling promo clip. The cameras followed the hapless underdog, real name Graeme Stevely, on his mission to get booked for Glasgow-based Insane Championship Wrestling. This gritty 16-minute mini-movie was filmed on the mean streets of the

Scottish city and starred a cast of foul-mouthed working class Scots who I would soon come to know and love as the roster of ICW.

Grado was a wide-eyed super-fan who wanted to wrestle for ICW. But ICW didn't want to know. Why? Because Grado was an out-of-shape buffoon, the butt of everyone's jokes.

"But I packed out Clydebank with 75 people!" he protested after being rejected, with flawless deadpan comic timing, then sobbed in his car.

His acting ability was incredible, a level above any other British wrestler I had ever seen. I empathised completely with the character, his frustration, his passion and his misery. Grado drew the viewer in, he got you on his side, and made you want to know more about him. He had bum bagfuls of charisma, could laugh at himself and most of all, was riotously entertaining.

For more information on Grado, I looked up another YouTube video. This was a documentary called The British Wrestler made by VICE, who specialise in hard-hitting behind-the-scenes exposes of little-known subcultures.

The blurb said: "VICE looks at the UK's underground wrestling scene, from the community centres of Plymouth to the streets of Glasgow. A far cry from the now faded memories of terrestrial TV's World Of Sport and even further from the glitz and glamour of the stateside WWE, Brits across the country have been escaping the banality of their everyday lives by moonlighting as pro wrestlers in the largely unheard of scene of today."

Once again, Grado took centre-stage in this 45-minute epic and I began to find out more about his background. He told how he had been a wrestling fan since he was 12 years old watching Raw and SmackDown on Sky TV, when he became obsessed with The Rock and wanted to be just like him because "he was the coolest guy on the planet". Then he revealed how he got started as a wrestler, and it was through the Wrestle Talk radio show hosted by Alex Shane, eerily echoing how I myself broke into the wrestling business in 2002. The young Grado used to phone in to the TalkSPORT studios every Saturday night, either to ask a question, or do an impression of a wrestler, or just talk about wrestling. Through Wrestle Talk, he found out about Scottish company BCW (British Championship

Wrestling) and eventually began to train with them.

As the documentary progressed, Grado's antics became even more endearing. He got his mum Maureen to film him cutting promos in the hallway of their humble terraced house in Stevenston, Ayrshire, while worrying about how his double-chin looked on camera. He had wrestling posters plastered all over his bedroom wall, including one where he had superimposed his own head onto Triple H's muscular body. Sitting on his bed, he kissed his precious replica WWE Championship belt and could remember the exact year he was given it as a Christmas present. This manchild, this self-confessed loser, was actually a working class hero. Regular people identified with him because he was an everyman with insecurities and foibles, just a normal bloke chasing a dream.

The British Wrestler also first introduced me to the man responsible for catapulting Grado into the limelight, Mark Dallas.

Mark Dallas is no ordinary wrestling promoter. He is a force of nature and very much a product of his own environment. In 2006, while in his early 20s, Dallas founded ICW when he and his pregnant girlfriend Helen were living in Glasgow's notorious Red Rose flats with junkies for neighbours. Depressed, broke and fearing for the upbringing of his unborn son, grapple fan Dallas decided to set up his own wrestling promotion. Only ICW would be no ordinary wrestling promotion.

ICW was bloody, violent, shocking, uncensored adult entertainment. It was hardcore wrestling, Scottish style. And it was nothing like the cuddly Grado. Not at all.

His eyes burning a hole through the VICE camera, Dallas seized my attention as he raged at the falseness of reality-TV obsessed, social media-driven 21st century culture, in a bitter and foul-mouthed rant.

"How is it the world became so f__king plastic?" he seethed.

"People are celebrities for being f__king celebrities. What the f__k is the deal with that? Jordan is on every f__king front page when there are people dying in the world. And that was fine when there was s__t for me to watch (on TV). But now there's not. There's f__k all for me. I'm not meant to have an option.

"So I created my own f__king option. It's called Insane

Championship Wrestling."

Then, this compelling figure sucked on his cigarette, leered into the camera as the rain blurred half the lens, and with his grey hoodie surrounding his head like a shroud, he spat one final line of defiance to the outside world he had come to despise.

"And I f__king promise you. You will *die*."

Jesus, this was heavy stuff.

Mark Dallas' edgy, wild-eyed angst in squalid surroundings made this one of the most effective wrestling promos I had ever heard, because it made me desperate to find out more about ICW. Dallas was real and he meant every single world. This visionary, this alchemist from the wrong side of the Glasgow tracks, was out to tap into the same feelings of disenfranchised youth that Paul Heyman had targeted so effectively when creating Extreme Championship Wrestling in Philadelphia some 20 years before. Dallas was hell-bent on rallying both fans and wrestlers behind a cause; a cause that represented society's desperate and frustrated misfits who needed a place to belong.

Graeme Stevely needed a place to belong. And Dallas welcomed him with open arms.

Under the name of Grant Dunbar, Stevely spent years floundering on the Scottish wrestling circuit. That is, until Dallas hatched a plan to put out a series of YouTube videos showing the loveable lug's crusade to get booked for ICW. The vids caught on and fans fell in love with the character, beginning their own Facebook and Twitter campaigns to 'Get Grado Booked'. Realising he was onto something, Dallas came up with a storyline that would not only see Grado earn a permanent spot on the ICW roster, but propel him towards British and international wrestling superstardom.

On July 1 2012 at an ICW event in Glasgow city centre called Insane in the Membrane, the late Scottish wrestling legend Drew McDonald and crowd favourite Wolfgang were under attack from The Official Community, or OffCom for short. In a storyline clearly ripped off from Attitude Era WWF, but brought right up to date and given a Scottish makeover, OffCom were the tartan equivalent of Right to Censor, a group of buzzkillers out to bring PG family entertainment to the 18-rated ICW, which automatically made them the biggest heels in Glasgow.

You see, ICW had already had a run-in with the real OFCOM, the regulators of television in the UK. Earlier in 2012, Insane Championship Wrestling had its own TV show on obscure satellite channel My TV. But then ICW was thrown off the air in May 2012 when an episode was found to be in violation of OFCOM rules. Instead of being disheartened by the setback, Mark Dallas used this real-life situation to his advantage and created a storyline out of it.

A man after my own heart.

As OFFCom members pounded on the faces, Grado hopped over the guard rail, having come through the raucous crowd at The Garage nightclub, ready for a fight. Although this was Grado's first appearance in person, the fans knew exactly who he was, and responded with a roar of appreciation, followed by deafening chants of "GRADO! GRADO! GRADO!" As ringside security held the unlikely hero at bay, Mark Dallas took the microphone, and announced that there would be a six-man tag team match: OFFCOM members Damian O'Connor, Jamie Feerick and Scott Maverick versus Drew McDonald, Wolfang and...Grado! The fans roared with delight as Grado was finally booked, an unbelievably positive reaction for a guy who had never wrestled a match for ICW.

The next month at ICW Super Smoking Thunderbowl, the unthinkable happened. Grado got a shot at the ICW Title and pinned Red Lightning to become champion. Once again, The Garage went nuts with joy. Fans invaded the ring. They carried Grado shoulder high in celebration. They screamed at the top of their lungs in sheer ecstasy that their man, the star they had created by supporting a grass roots movement to get him booked, had become the champ.

Never mind that video footage later showed that Lightning's foot was under the bottom rope. Never mind that the pin was illegal, the match was restarted later that evening and Red quickly scored the win to regain his belt. Never mind about all that.

Even if it was for a matter of minutes, Grado was the ICW champion. He was in the main event. He had arrived.

From there, Grado's momentum knew no bounds. Already the biggest star in ICW after just two shows, by early 2013, he was starting to attract interest from promotions in England. He was being covered in FSM. He was all over the internet.

So it was time to see for myself what all the fuss was about. I had to go and see the man in action.

So I contacted Mark Dallas and asked him if I could make ICW one of the stops on my national tour in early 2013 to promote my first book. Mark agreed to let me sell copies of *Holy Grail* at his next event in Glasgow, even though he had never spoken to me before and there was nothing in it for him. I immediately thought he was a class act.

So on the afternoon of Sunday, March 3 2013, I packed a load of copies of *Holy Grail* into a holdall and set off for Glasgow with two friends - Colin Wild, an affable fellow who helped out behind-the-scenes at Morecambe wrestling shows, and trainee wrestler Ross 'Rossion' Wallis.

Now Rossion was a little different. On the first day he turned up at the Morecambe wrestling school, he hardly spoke a word to anyone. Instead he stood in the corner arms folded in defiance, eyes burning a hole through anyone foolish enough to catch his glare. I christened him 'The Loner' and encouraged his anti-social ways as part of his wrestling persona. With his long straggly hair, unkempt beard, deep voice and intimidating stare, I felt Rossion was the perfect companion for a bespectacled geek in a suit about to venture into the lion's den of Insane Championship Wrestling.

Before going to see ICW, we were invited to an afternoon show run by Scottish grappler Ross 'Kid Fite' Watson and his company Premier British Wrestling. PBW was one of a number of successful promotions in what was slowly becoming a thriving scene north of the border. When my pro wrestling career began in 2002, the only Scottish wrestler with any kind of national profile was Drew McDonald. But then in the mid-noughties, a raft of talented Scots began to make names for themselves, like Drew Galloway, Lionheart, Kid Fite, Wolfgang and James 'Darkside' Scott, while promotions like ICW, PBW, BCW, SWA and Lionheart's Pro Wrestling Elite all started doing well. Slowly, gradually, Scottish wrestling began to grow until by 2013, it was on the verge of exploding.

The PBW matinee show followed a similar family-friendly

formula to the one used by All-Star Wrestling. It was two-and-a-half hours of good guys, bad guys, booing, cheering, and lots of over-excited kids waving foam hands in the air. Harmless, knockabout, wholesome fun, held before a big crowd inside the friendly old Pavilion Theatre in central Glasgow.

Two hours later, I found myself in the dark, sweaty Garage nightclub just half-a-mile down the road, fearing for my very life. I was surrounded by hundreds of crammed-in, beered-up Scots, all screaming "I-C-DUB! I-C-DUB!" at the top of their lungs, as I was swept away on an insane rollercoaster ride of extreme violence, explicit content and pure unadulterated chaos.

What an atmosphere. It was like being at the world's most dangerous rock concert.

Harmless knockabout wholesome family fun, this most definitely was not. This was ICW. This was Get To Da Choppa! - one of the most breathtaking wrestling events I have ever had the pleasure to witness. And it was one hell of a culture shock.

Perhaps I should have known my first experience of an ICW live event was going to be somewhat different when I popped to the grimy Garage toilet before the first bell even rang. At the sink, I was confronted by a wrestling fan who was dressed from head to paws in a furry animal onesie - complete with tail. He leered at me drunkenly.

"Can ye zip me up, big man?"

Thankfully, he didn't mean his flies.

Fearing for my health, I zipped up the back of his animal suit, smiled politely, and fled.

Back at ringside, the benevolent Mark Dallas allowed me to sell my books from a table next to the commentary desk. This was manned by the voices of ICW's weekly online TV show ICW Worldwide - commentators Sean David and Billy Kirkwood. Billy, a wild-haired standup comedian and the most outrageous talker in the whole of British wrestling, had welcomed me with a big smile and hearty handshake earlier in the evening. Flanked by Colin and Rossion, who were dressed in dark suits and revelling in their roles as my 'security team', I had the best possible view of the ring.

The name Get to Da Choppa! paid tribute to a famous Arnold

Schwarzenegger quote in the film Predator. But even The Terminator himself would surely have had his hands full with the first competitor to pace maniacally through the curtain that night, Chris Renfrew. Behind-the-scenes, Renfrew was Mark Dallas' writing partner, an intelligent creative mind who helped script the anarchic plotlines of ICW. But 'on screen', Renfrew was utterly convincing as a menacing, bloodthirsty, borderline-psychotic danger man who simply liked to hurt people.

Now, back in Morecambe, I used to like to begin my shows with a 10-minute, high-flying, fast paced opening match, usually with the good guy winning to make the crowd cheer and warm them up nicely for the evening's entertainment ahead.

But ICW's idea of warming up the crowd was for Renfrew to cut a promo using the F-word five times and the C-word once, piledrive a hapless referee, then try to stab his bitter rival BT Gunn in the face with a pair of scissors. As security hit the ring to save Gunn from a certain trip to Glasgow A&E, the baying crowd of ICW lunatics implored the crazed anti-hero to "F__K HIM UP RENFREW, F__K HIM UP!" as I looked on, utterly bewildered but completely transfixed by the scene.

Next, things got even more Parental Advisory, as Project Ego battled Fight Club (Kid Fite and Liam Thomson) in tag team action. Halfway through the match, Kris Travis and Fite simultaneously knocked Thomson and Kirby to the canvas. Nothing sinister there, you might think, and you would be right. But then Travis and Fite both decided to pull out their manhoods in the middle of the ring, grinned at each other and dropped their exposed balls (or 'baws', because we were in Glasgow after all) across the faces of Thomson and Martin Kirby in one of the most unique...well...wrestling moves I have ever seen, as the crowd cheered loudly to egg them on.

I have watched pro wrestling for 30 years and I thought I had seen it all. Clearly not.

I was open-mouthed (no, not like that) at what I had just seen, not to mention caught completely off guard, and slightly repulsed. A helpful ICW fan later explained to me that I'd just had my first experience of the noble Glaswegian art of 'teabagging'.

Soon, The Garage came completely unglued as a 1990s techno

track came thumping over the loudspeakers. "HERE WE...HERE WE...HERE WE F__KING GO!" yelled the fans in time to the music, as out came a tracksuited pair of louts accompanied by a petite blonde wearing a low-cut top and the miniest of mini-skirts, and a wiry little fella in a Burberry cap and white vest with matching shellsuit bottoms, who swaggered about the ringside area to the pounding bassline as he swigged from a bottle of Buckfast - the drink of choice for many a Saturday night reveller in Glasgow city centre.

The latter, Neil Bratchpiece, better known as The Wee Man, was already a cult figure in Scotland even before he hooked up with ICW some years before; a rapper and comedian known for his hilariously unsavoury YouTube videos. The Wee Man grabbed the microphone and, in a hilarious speech which had the fans roaring with laughter and appreciation, introduced his three cohorts.

"This is the lassie that's so hot she recently had to lop her shoe off the groin of Harry Styles, the Storm in a D-Cup, Lambrini!" and "the man who is responsible for more teenage pregnancies than the cheap Jager Bombs at the bar, Tyrannosaurus Sex himself, ma cousin, Davey Boy!" and finally "the man who is half as legless as Oscar Pistorius but twice as homicidal, his cousin, Stevie Boy!"

This was a phenomenally lairy piece of mic work from The Wee Man, which had the fans chanting along with all his catchphrases like he was a miniature Glasgow chav version of The Rock.

This was my first experience of The Bucky Boys - Davey Blaze and Stevie Xavier - two NEDs (Non-Educated Delinquents) who, in Davey's words, "represented going out, getting drunk, having a laugh and smashing people's heads in". The Bucky (short for Buckfast) Boys were typical Glasgow lads and massive fan favourites in ICW who, when combined with the sex appeal of the tarty Lambrini and the patter of The Wee Man, had developed one hell of an entertaining act.

The Bucky Boys could really get it done inside the ring too, as they proved by proceeding to put their bodies at risk in a raucous stuntfest of an ICW Tag Team Title ladder match against their opponents and reigning champions, The STI (William Grange and Dickie Divers). The closing moments of this thrillingly reckless encounter were stark staring bonkers. First, Stevie Boy drove Divers head first to the canvas off the top of a ladder wedged between the top and middle turnbuckles, with a jaw-dropping version of Petey Williams' Canadian Destroyer somersault piledriver. Then, Xavier jumped off the top rope, 15 feet across the ring, and drop kicked a ladder into Grange's ribs as he slumped in the corner...a move so spectacularly dangerous it led to a classic line by Sean David on commentary that "the stuff Rob Van Dam thinks about when he's high, is the stuff Stevie Boy actually goes out and does!"

Finally, Blaze and Xavier both scaled ladders at the same time, unhooked the ICW Tag Team Title belts from the ceiling, and the ICW faithful let out the most bloodcurdling, spine-tingling, eardrum-splitting scream of celebration I think I have ever heard at any sporting event, let alone a wrestling show. It was just fricking amazing to be there, right in the middle of the sweating, bouncing, party atmosphere that ensued as The Bucky Boys became the Insane Championship Wrestling tag team champions.

And the show went on, like a runaway train, only with surprisingly normal, solid and relatively sane matches like El Ligero v Mark Coffey and James Scott v Jimmy Havoc thrown in every now and again, just to remind me that this was actually a wrestling show, and not a breathlessly cathartic religious experience with a cast of nutty larger-than-life characters like Mikey Whiplash, who wrestled Noam Dar while wearing a full basque and suspenders...and Jack Jester, a jet-black bearded 'zombie pirate' hardcore match specialist and fetishist in Undertaker-style contact lenses carrying a sharp metal corkscrew...and the arrogant Jackie Polo, blond hair tied back in a Lex Luger ponytail, who entered the ring wielding a polo mallet as he sang his own theme tune of the 1960s Scott Walker easy listening hit 'Jackie'...and the Save Pro Wrestling Movement stable of the satanically scary Joe Coffey, the self-absorbed 'Best in the Galaxy' Nikki Storm and its leader, the ICW Heavyweight Champion Red Lightning, a loudmouthed egotist who consistently managed to loophole his way into keeping hold of the title despite having far less pure wrestling talent than almost everybody else on the roster - a fact which made him the most hated man in the promotion and the perfect 'old school' heel champion.

And what of Grado? What of the man who had drawn me to this

hellpit of wrestling debauchery in the first place? Well, when his theme music Like A Prayer hit halfway through the show, to interrupt a planned live mid-ring performance of the new single by Justin Bieber wannabe 'The Teen Sensation' Christopher, it was like Hulk Hogan himself had entered The Garage. The place was in uproar as this wee fat lad from Ayrshire came dancing, strutting and...erm...*eating* his way down to ringside.

As the fans clapped, stomped and sang along, I had never heard anything like it.

"LIFE IS A MYSTERY! EVERYONE MUST STAND ALONE! I HEAR YOU CALL MY NAME! AND IT FEELS LIKE HOOOOOOOOOOOOOME!"

It was mass hysteria.

As Grado climbed onto the turnbuckles, held his bumbag aloft and sniffed the rarified Glasgow air like The Rock entering to fight Stone Cold at WrestleMania, the crowd noise was absolutely unreal. It was a genuine superstar reaction to ICW's version of The People's Champion.

"IT'S YERSEL! IT'S YERSEL! IT'S YERSEL!"

I once again turned to a nearby ICW steward and asked him what on earth the crowd was chanting now. He explained that "It's yersel!" (It's yourself) was a greeting Grado used on the streets of Stevenston, an Ayrshire version of "How are you?" which caught on big-time as his catchphrase to the point that "IT'S YERSEL" T-shirts were selling faster than Tunnock's tea cakes.

Grado proceeded to confront the obnoxious Teen Sensation and his talented manager, agent-to-the-stars and George Michael lookalike James R Kennedy, until Jamie Feerick ran in to attack him. But then the familiar riff of Hungry Like The Wolf by Duran Duran kicked in, and the reigning ICW Zero-G Champion and future WWE UK Championship semi-finalist Wolfgang charged out to the rescue, which of course led to an impromptu tag team match.

So now came the acid test. Grado could definitely entertain, but could he actually wrestle? Turns out, it didn't matter. Grado wrestled like a chubby wee chancer from Stevenston is supposed to wrestle, appearing to make it up as he went along.

As the match began, he ran the ropes back and forth for no

apparent reason, before pulling up to catch his breath. He went for the trademark moves of the wrestling heroes he had seen on TV, the Dusty Rhodes 'flip flop and fly', The Rock's famous People's Elbow, even his own version of a Brock Lesnar F5. He tottered up to the top rope but needed the burly Wolfgang's help to steady his balance, then suddenly got vertigo and thought better of jumping off. And with everything Grado did, he had a huge smile of childlike joy on his chubby-cheeked face. His personality oozed from every part of his being, he constantly made eye contact with the audience, drawing them in, and was so likeable, they couldn't help root for him. And when he pinned Feerick to win the match, The Garage once again erupted and began singing and dancing along to Like A Prayer to share in their hero's victory celebration.

It was quite clear to me right there and then, that Grado was something special.

He is also a special human being. After the show was over, I discovered that in real life, Graeme Stevely is just as fun-loving, down-to-earth and loveable as the character he plays in the wrestling ring.

In our first ever meeting, he came marching over to my table, shook me warmly by the hand, and bought a copy of *Holy Grail*. Graeme even asked me to sign it for him, which I did, scrawling "To Grado, It's Yersel!" on an inside blank page. I couldn't believe it. Me? Sign for him? The star of the show? I felt truly humbled. And I had a feeling that it wouldn't be long before it would be Grado signing autographs for me.

I have to admit, I fell in love with Glasgow that night. And ever since my ICW initiation, I have had a soft spot for the Scottish wrestling scene and its people. In stark contrast to their anti-social actions inside the ring, backstage Mark Dallas and his crew could not have been more welcoming. Everybody was so nice and there was such a sense of camaraderie and purpose, like they were building ICW into something amazing, with everybody pulling in the same direction. Sheer professionalism. It was an absolute privilege to be there; one of my favourite all-time experiences in wrestling.

Once my mind had cleared from the intensity of that day and I had time to reflect, it was easy to see why the Scottish wrestling scene was becoming red-hot, white-hot, hell, *tartan*-hot in 2013. I'd seen two entirely separate and different British wrestling promotions each put on a show, on the same day, on virtually the same street in Glasgow city centre, and draw a combined total of 1,400 fans with not a single big-name American on either bill. Instead, PBW and ICW were headlined by a never-ending production line of Scottish wrestling talent who the fans treated like gods.

Later, I wrote about my encounter with Insane Championship Wrestling in my column for the Wrestle Talk TV website.

"ICW is more than just a wrestling show, it's an experience. It's a brand. It's a self-contained, brilliantly-conceived alternative world of weapon shots, busty babes, risqué and energetic promos, unpredictable angles, strong characters who the crowd respond to like genuine superstars, and solid wrestling thrown in to the overall package. In short, ICW is the British version of ECW at its peak. And I absolutely loved it."

I also remained struck by the unlikely superstardom of Grado, a man who, when you think about it, didn't fit the ICW mould at all. He was totally different to the other violent renegades in the promotion, indeed, completely unlike anyone else in the wrestling world. But that is why the character worked. Grado stood out.

Alex Shane used to call it the 'out of context principle'. Alex said that Hulk Hogan became the biggest star in wrestling because he came along in an era of plain old trunks-and-boots wrestlers, but unlike them he had a superhero physique, funky catchphrases and a jackhammer theme tune; he was a cartoon character. But then more than decade later when just about everybody in wrestling was a larger-than-life muscleman and a walking gimmick like Hogan, along came Steve Austin, who became the biggest star in the business as a trunks-and-boots wrestler and ushered in a boom period by playing not a living cartoon, but an exaggerated version of his real personality, a hard-living, foul-mouthed brawler. More than a decade later, when pretty much everybody in ICW was a hard-living, foul-mouthed brawler, along came Grado.

On The British Wrestler, Dallas revealed that the Grado character was actually a humanisation of ICW itself. You see, when Mark ran his first show in October 2006, only 80 people turned up to watch.

"I was seen as a joke, my company was seen as a joke. But nobody's laughing now."

He wasn't kidding. In 2013, ICW was already drawing regular crowds of 1,000 people to its monthly shows in Glasgow. Then on August 25 2013, they conquered the Scottish capital of Edinburgh too, drawing 1,000 to the Picture House for a show headlined by Jack Jester v ECW legend Sabu, and Grado v former WWE superstar and CM Punk's best mate, Colt Cabana. Their rib-tickling bout ended with the comic pair toasting each other mid-ring in a parody of Steve Austin's post-match beer bash celebration, only Grado and Colt used cans of that quintessential Scottish fizzy drink, Irn Bru.

By the end of 2013, Insane Championship Wrestling was riding a wave of unstoppable momentum and the phenomenal popularity of Grado. But in 2014, ICW was about to get even bigger.

Mark Dallas and company were about to get their own TV programme on BBC1.

The late, great Kris Travis is lifted up by his friends and colleagues at PCW's Shooting Star Fund Raising show in January 2015.

Nikki Storm (Nikki Cross) and Viper, seen here at a show at Morecambe Winter Gardens, have helped put UK women's wrestling on the map.

Mad Man Manson and El Ligero clowning around before an XWA show in Morecambe in 2008.

Johnny Phere stares at the PAID Promotions banner at Vendetta 2015 at Morecambe Winter Gardens.

Rampage Brown clobbers Bubba Dudley during a PCW match in 2014.

The sheer intensity of the XWA v GPW feud is captured by this photo of Dylan Roberts being dragged from The Carleton after the 2011 invasion angle.

Big Damo (with the author in his corner) takes on Mikey Whiplash and Johnny Phere in a triple threat match at Morecambe Winter Gardens in March 2016.

The author celebrates with Grado moments after he won the ICW Title at the SECC Glasgow on November 15 2015. Note Mick Foley's flannel shirt!

Kenny Williams, The Wee Man, Davey Blaze, Noam Dar and Grado at an ICW event in 2015.

Lionheart battles AJ Styles in one of their emotional bouts for Preston City Wrestling.

Marty Scurll ties up The Lion Kid during a Morecambe Winter Gardens bout in 2014.

Spud goads GPW fan 'Hitman' at the amazing XWA v GPW Vendetta showdown on July 28 2012.

CHAPTER 11

PHERE THE PROMOTER

After I made the decision to close down the XWA in 2012, the first wrestler I told was Johnny Phere.

When I decided to stop promoting, Jamie Hutchinson was reigning XWA Champion. He was the top guy in our territory, a local celebrity in Morecambe, and had also taken over from Dave Rayne as head trainer of my wrestling school. Aside from his brief run with GPW a few years earlier and the odd show for FutureShock and the FWA, JP also rarely performed for anyone else. So I knew XWA closing down was going to affect him more than most. The XWA, particularly the training school, was an important source of income for him.

Since we first met in 2002, I have always got on well with Jamie. He can be a troubled soul, so I've always felt protective towards him. I understand his real-life frustrations. I share his passion for professional wrestling and respect his desire to always throw his entire being into his performances with no stone unturned in preparation. I see him as the talented, hard-working underdog who never got the break he deserved. But others in the UK wrestling business don't view JP as I do. I've tried many times to explain my opinions on Jamie to various British wrestlers, promoters and staffers. But a lot of them either don't see his talent or have found it hard to work with him in the past.

"The reason why Jamie has never fulfilled his potential...is Jamie himself," said Johnnie Brannigan, giving his views on JP in 2016.

"I've always liked Jamie and felt a kinship with him. I always wanted him around in GPW and he had opportunities. But he was sometimes difficult to deal with and didn't always see the long-term goal in things."

I never had this problem during the XWA era. Quite the opposite, in fact. An example of Jamie's professionalism came on October 8 2011 at The Carleton. That night Johnny hit me with his vaunted finishing move, the Ram Slam spinning spinebuster, to signify a definitive end to our XWA feud. Being an untrained, gangly, unathletic non-wrestler, I hardly ever take bumps, and I wouldn't have taken just anybody's finisher. But I trusted Jamie implicitly. My trust was well-placed. As the new champion whirled me around like a human spin dryer and dropped me hard on my back to a massive whoop from the crowd, he might as well have been lightly placing a bag of feathers on the canvas. Although I laid there for the best part of 10 minutes to sell the devastating move, in reality I never felt a thing. This is the art of pro wrestling, to make it look like you've destroyed your opponent without hurting them at all.

So I have a lot of time for Jamie, and 12 months later in October 2012, I handed over the running of the Morecambe school to him. I didn't ask for any money. We were only getting an average of six students attending classes each week by that time anyway, and I was only making a pittance because most of the income was being used to pay Jamie's wage.

You see, as expected, the closure of the XWA disheartened many of the trainees. They had nothing to motivate them anymore, no goal to shoot for. My thinking was that at least if Jamie took over, he could focus all his efforts on building the school back up again to re-energise the students. And because he did all the coaching himself so wouldn't have to pay a trainer, he could reap greater financial benefits than I ever could.

At first, Jamie thrived on the greater responsibility. He outlined plans to start running student shows at the school again and numbers increased at the Sunday classes as a result. The trainees began responding to his highly disciplined but effective style of training, based around physical conditioning and getting the basics right. The school was booming again and Jamie was making a decent living. I was happy to have left my legacy in capable hands.

Around this time, I suggested to Jamie that if he was going to start running small trainee shows now XWA was finished, maybe he should do so under a new name. So I came up with the name 'PAID Promotions'. The character of Johnny Phere had always talked about the PAID principles by which he lives his lone wolf lifestyle. PAID, by the way, stands for Passion, Ambition, Intensity and Dedication, four qualities Johnny Phere had in abundance. So if Jamie was now going to promote his own wrestling shows, I suggested he should name his company after his own PAID principles. The name PAID Promotions rolled off the tongue. It was the perfect fit for a company run by Johnny Phere. He loved the idea.

The first PAID Promotions show was held at Regent Park Studios on November 25 2012. In the main event, Johnny Phere pinned Ste 'Bin' Mann clean in the middle of the ring. It certainly wasn't the blow-off it could have been, but at least JP gained small revenge for the loss at Vendetta and drew a line under the XWA v GPW feud.

By this time, everything seemed to be going well for Jamie. After living much of his life as a nomad, moving from place to place, he had now been settled by the seaside for about four years. He had a regular job, working for Martin Shenton at Regent Park Studios. Jamie also had a steady girlfriend, a local girl called Helen Louis. They lived together in a flat in Morecambe having met at the training school, where Helen had enrolled as an unlikely student some years earlier.

When Helen first started training to be a wrestler, she was quiet, slight of build, and wore braces on her teeth. She looked about as much like a professional fighter as I look like The Rock. But as she grew older, an astonishing transformation occurred. Helen blossomed into a beautiful young woman. Sharing in Jamie's rigorous training regimen, she developed the body of an athlete. Some of his in-ring aggression and performance skills rubbed off on her too. And she eventually developed an alter-ego called Serenity, an enigmatic, slightly unhinged femme fatale whose trademark was to put her finger to her lips and tell wrestling fans to 'SSSHHHH!'

By early 2012, I realised Serenity could be a fantastic asset to our main shows. We didn't have a regular female character, and Serenity was intriguing and different to any other woman on the UK circuit at the time. Although she wasn't yet seasoned enough to wrestle, I felt Serenity had just the right combination of deviousness and sex appeal to be a highly effective valet or manager. Much to Helen's surprise, I told her just hours before XWA Gold Rush on February 4

2012, that she would be making her debut that night, accompanying Dave Rayne to the ring for the 15-man rumble main event. She repaid my faith, making a solid debut as a ringside antagonist. Over the next few months, she trained hard, listened to advice and strove to improve. When Jamie started running monthly student shows in late 2012/early 2013, Serenity became a regular character and her performances impressed me more and more.

So at face value, Jamie seemed to have it all. But he always had his issues; in particular his own sense of self-worth. I remember shortly after Rockstar Spud won TNA British Boot Camp in January 2013 and I was on cloud nine for my old mate's success, Jamie told me he too was pleased for Spud. But seeing a man he had beaten for the XWA Title just three years earlier achieve a life-changing contract in America made him reflect on his own career and how he had never reached his potential. He was also disillusioned that he felt 'blackballed' on the UK scene, as despite his tremendous back catalogue of work in Morecambe, he still couldn't gain many opportunities elsewhere. And, approaching his 30s, he wasn't getting any younger.

"When the time comes to call it a day as a wrestler, I really want there to be something to show for it," he sighed.

That same month, I received a phone call from a blast from my past. On the other end of the line was Sanjay Bagga, promoter with LDN Wrestling.

I have known Sanjay since my early days in the wrestling business, when he was basically a young hustler, trying to get noticed at FWA shows by selling programmes to make a few bob, while also writing for my website. In 2004 he set up his own promotion. The London-based LDN was low budget, family friendly wrestling built around low-profile British-based talent and veterans of the World of Sport era. LDN was never going to capture the imagination of the 'smart' UK wrestling fans who prefer the high-octane, anything-goes, cooler brands of PCW, ICW, Revolution Pro and PROGRESS.

But Bagga didn't care. By keeping costs low, and by making the job of wrestling promoter his full-time career, Sanjay made enough money to run a busy schedule of shows, particularly in the south of

England. In terms of quantity, LDN's calendar of events per year rivalled that of All-Star Wrestling. Bagga also prided himself on his marketing skills and often said that his back-to-basics promotional tactics, focussed around a large quantity of posters in shop windows and local advertising, was the secret of his success.

Bagga and I had always got on well up to that point. In my first book, I praised his vision for LDN. Remembering his younger days as a brash teenager with ambition and energy, I admired how successful he'd become.

But while I always defended Sanjay, others on the UK circuit loathed him. He brought much of this on himself, thanks to an unashamedly ruthless attitude to promoting. If another promoter is running a show in the same area at the same time as an LDN event, Sanjay has been known to try everything in his power to cause problems for his rival.

An interviewer called Hari Ramakrishnan directly asked Bagga about his tactics during a chat for an internet site called The Only Way is Suplex in November 2014.

"When a wrestling show comes to town, and then there are two wrestling shows, then as a businessman I'm going to make sure that they go to my show," said Sanjay.

"There's only one wrestling place and that's LDN. That's business. If Tesco come to town, they want to be the only giant company in the area. I care about my business and that's the way life is."

Anyway, back to January 14 2013 and Bagga's phone call. He was ringing to ask if I was definitely retired from the promoting game because he wanted to bring LDN to Morecambe. I told him I definitely had no plans to promote wrestling shows any more, which was the truth. I also told him the only wrestling taking place in my home town was Johnny Phere's small trainee events, in a venue with barely room for 50 spectators. These tiny shows wouldn't affect any plans Bagga had because JP only sold tickets to friends and family of the trainees and hardly did any marketing in the town.

On hearing this, Bagga told me he was planning to run an LDN show on Saturday, July 13 2013 at The Platform venue in Morecambe. The Platform, by the way, is a former railway station turned arts venue, located on the promenade opposite where The Dome used to be.

I thought it was rather decent of Sanjay to telephone me personally and check if I minded him promoting in the town where I'd had the virtual monopoly on wrestling for the previous 10 years. During the conversation, Sanjay also offered me a job on his show as a manager and we negotiated a fee. He was also interested in booking Johnny Phere but balked when JP told him his wage demand which was more than Bagga was willing to pay. Talks quickly broke down. Jamie had overpriced himself out of a job but in truth, he wasn't really bothered. At that point, he wanted to try to make some real money out of wrestling. If Bagga wouldn't pay Jamie what he believed he was worth, then he wasn't going to lose any sleep over it.

The following month, I was shocked to learn that Dann Read's wife Emily had been rushed to hospital. Emily suffered a brain seizure, due to medication she was taking at the time, and was seriously ill. It happened the day before the Reads' company, Pro-Wrestling:EVE, was due to run a show at their home in Sudbury, Suffolk. Immediately and understandably, Dann was forced to cancel the event.

Thankfully, Emily made a full recovery. With his wife out of the woods, Dann rescheduled the EVE show for The Delphi Club in Sudbury on April 27 2013. But just five days after his wife was hospitalised, Dann sent me a text. He told me Bagga had booked an LDN show at The Delphi one week before the new EVE date. Dann said this was because he'd hired Bagga to supply the ring for the original date which had to be cancelled – but Sanjay still wanted the agreed fee. Dann said he offered to pay LDN's expenses as a compromise instead of the full agreed fee, but Bagga refused and decided to book his own show to make money from Sudbury himself.

An LDN event at The Delphi just a week before Dann's was bound to affect EVE's ticket sales. Many EVE wrestlers, who themselves missed out on a wage due to the cancellation, were terrific with Dann and understood he'd only postponed his show due to a family emergency. But Sanjay wanted the cash he had been promised.

At this point, I really wish I'd stuck up for my friend and told Bagga where to stick his LDN booking. But at that point, I hadn't heard Sanjay's side of the story. So I stayed out of it and, at least in public, I stayed neutral.

Bagga ended up switching his Sudbury show to April 13 2013, two weeks before Dann's date. But when the day came, he cancelled the LDN event just hours before first bell.

The Sudbury Free Press newspaper ran the story.

"Sudbury Town Council has defended itself after a wrestling promoter claimed the authority's incompetence resulted in him cancelling a show.

"LDN Wrestling was due to hold an event at the Delphi Centre on Saturday but the show was called off at the last minute. Promoter Sanjay Bagga said this was due to organisers being locked out of the venue, which was hired from the council, as staff arrived 40 minutes late.

"Sue Brotherwood, town council clerk, admitted a 'minor error' had been made which led to the doors being locked but said it was unnecessary to cancel the event.

"'For some reason, the bowls club locked the doors when they left and this caused a problem.'" she said.

"'However, there are emergency numbers that are on a board outside the centre and Sanjay could have rang them. When the bar staff arrived and offered to help, he said it was too late and cancelled.'"

"Mr Bagga, 27, said he had arrived at the venue at 5.30pm to get everything ready for a 7.30pm start.

"'We needed to set up the ring, steps and music system but we could not get in,'" he said."

Fans who bought tickets for the LDN show were understandably furious that it was cancelled just 30 minutes before doors were due to open. It was certainly a bizarre incident. Had it been me, I certainly wouldn't have cancelled the show even if I'd only gained access to the building an hour before bell time. It doesn't take *that* long to set up a ring.

Two weeks later on April 27 2013, Pro-Wrestling:EVE's show *did* go ahead at the Delphi and went off without a hitch, although crowd numbers were down. And Dann believes the LDN debacle definitely affected his sales.

Back in Morecambe, at around the same time, I started bandying a few figures around, wondering how much it would cost to quit my day job and return to promoting, full-time. I wasn't really serious about it. I confided in Jamie, then just as quickly changed my mind and abandoned the whole concept.

But it seems that the discussion had been a light bulb moment for Phere. A few weeks later, he revealed he wanted to expand PAID Promotions, so he himself could try to make a full-time living as a wrestling promoter.

Remember his comment of just a few months earlier?

"When the time comes to call it a day as a wrestler, I really want there to be something to show for it."

Jamie was serious about it. Numbers were declining at the training school and he had left his full-time job with Martin Shenton. So he needed a new livelihood and wrestling was all he knew. So he'd struck a deal with Helen's parents to come in with him as financial backers. They would buy a ring and a van to transport it to shows. He was already looking at venues in Morecambe, his home town of Warrington and Fleetwood near Blackpool. And he wanted me to work with him, to help him work out storylines and more importantly, give him the benefit of my experience as a promoter.

Now this put me in a quandary. I knew Bagga's show was coming up in July and I had already promised to work for him. Jamie wanted to run an event at the end of August 2013, in the 300-capacity function room at the Globe Arena in Morecambe, a brand new stadium and home of the town's League Two football team. This would be just six weeks after Bagga's event and only half a mile down the road.

But the deal JP was offering was too good to pass up. It would mean none of the stress of being the main promoter, with a chance to have creative influence on the matchmaking and storylines. In addition, Jamie planned to build the shows around the Morecambe trainees. It would be a chance for them to work in front of much bigger crowds than they were used to at Regent Park Studios. I also knew Jamie would throw himself into the project and be faithful to my vision of professional wrestling, because we shared many of the same views on how things should be done.

So I agreed - on one condition, that I wouldn't help Jamie promote his first show until *after* LDN's event. I still wanted to be fair to Bagga. Even so, knowing Sanjay like I do, I warned Jamie, he'd better watch out. If the LDN leader found out about the PAID show, he surely wouldn't be happy. But Jamie wasn't worried. He researched LDN's product and believed he could provide a better one for the wrestling fans of Morecambe.

JP threw himself into his expansion plans. He spent hours in his flat designing posters and a website. We spoke on the phone almost daily that summer, going over storyline ideas and business plans.

Then on June 25 2013, I got a message from Bagga. He was in Morecambe and said he had spent the entire day plastering the town with hundreds of posters. He wanted to meet up. Out of curiosity, I agreed to meet him.

We spent about an hour catching up at a pub next door to The Platform. Bagga was exactly as I remembered him. Friendly enough, but with an edge. It was a strangely un-nerving conversation. For starters, he began talking about how much he hates Alex Shane. I listened, incredulously, wondering what on earth Alex had done to make Bagga despise him so.

Then I asked him about the recent incident with Dann Read in Sudbury. Bagga explained that Dann still owed money to LDN and had no remorse whatsoever. In fact, he seemed to find the whole thing amusing. His demeanour was like a mischievous little boy who had played a practical joke. "I'm terrible," he giggled. He just didn't care. I felt so sad. Bagga and Dann used to get on so well. I remember the day of FWA British Uprising 2 about a decade earlier, when Sanjay, Dann and Mark Kay had gone off sight-seeing in London together. Those days were clearly long gone.

Bagga also pumped me for more information about Johnny Phere and his trainee shows. At this point, JP was still running his tiny events every month at Regent Park Studios. So I answered honestly. I had nothing to hide. Sanjay didn't ask me if JP was planning to run any bigger shows. If he had, I wouldn't have lied. But I certainly wasn't going to bring up the subject of Jamie's Globe Arena date voluntarily. It wasn't worth the hassle.

Our chat ended amicably enough and Sanjay gave me a lift home. I have to admit, I felt a little guilty when I got through my front door that night and reflected on my conversation with Bagga. I felt like I was betraying Dann and Jamie by working for their rival, even though I had made the agreement before either of them started having trouble with him. I really couldn't wait to get July 13 out of the way.

Saturday July 13. Ironically it was that very same date in 2002 when I made my debut in the UK wrestling business, on a show promoted by Dann Read, starring Johnny Phere in the match of the night. Funny how things work out.

When I arrived at The Platform that night, I was on my guard. I had this notion in my head that Bagga would surely know about the PAID show in August. I was paranoid that Sanjay would think it was my event, not Jamie's, and that I had lied to him back in January, which of course, I hadn't. So I had this worry in the back of my mind that Bagga might try something. I didn't know what, but I just didn't trust him. It was also bizarre to work on a wrestling show in Morecambe and not be in charge.

But, I was there to do business, hold up the end of my bargain, and be a professional.

Backstage at The Platform, I met some of the LDN crew. What a mixed bag they were. Familiar faces like Martin Kirby and Paul Malen, solid and reputable pros. A polite young lad from New Zealand called TK Cooper, later a regular with PROGRESS Wrestling but at the time an unknown who was eager to learn. Alan Travis, Bagga's dependable right-hand man and LDN Champion, a nice bloke. And there was veteran 'monster heel' Karl Krammer, a blond behemoth of a man known as The Barbarian, but with a wicked sense of humour and full of sage advice. I really liked Karl and we spent a lot of time chatting backstage that night.

Despite Bagga's pride in his mastery of postering and despite an article previewing LDN's show in my newspaper, the draw in The Platform that night can't have been much more than 120. This was poor by Morecambe standards. And as wrestling shows go, it was as simple as it gets. While XWA used to have video screens, an entranceway, lights and smoke, LDN was just a ring in the middle of a room. Five matches, good guy versus bad guy, no storylines and a main event rumble. A spit and sawdust, by-the-book holiday camp-style grapple show. And a step backwards compared to what the Morecambe fans had been used to for the past decade.

When I came out, to manage Alan Travis (who was playing a masked heel character known as The Dark Lord) for a match with TK Cooper, I surveyed the crowd and couldn't have seen more than a dozen of the old XWA faces. It seemed my decision to close my company almost exactly 12 months earlier had killed many of my old followers' enthusiasm. The town had gone almost exactly a year without its fix of live professional wrestling, save for Johnny Phere's trainee showcases. And it would take much more than an average show by a travelling company from London to regain momentum.

That night, I turned heel on the Morecambe audience, ranting on the microphone that the fans had betrayed me by welcoming LDN to my hometown with open arms. I then slotted comfortably back into my old role as ringside manager, riling up the spectators, interfering behind the referee's back, and doing everything possible to break the rules so The Dark Lord could win against the eager young high-flyer Cooper...which he did. We celebrated our ill-gotten victory and the boos rained down in The Platform.

Everything up to that point had gone exactly as planned. But then, came something that was totally unscripted, that hadn't been discussed with me beforehand, and that I didn't know was going to happen.

Bagga was ring announcer. He took the microphone and announced that as punishment for my behaviour, he was putting me in the 10-man, over-the-top-rope Battle Royal, later that night.

The crowd loved this announcement. I reacted with a combination of anger and fear in front of the delighted fans, complaining with gusto that I wasn't a wrestler, that I didn't belong in the ring, that this was a conspiracy.

I returned backstage. My adrenaline was flowing and I acted excited at how the match had gone. I didn't want any of the wrestlers to realise what I was really feeling. Because I was feeling put out. I was feeling concerned. I was feeling that Sanjay had put me in an awkward position on purpose.

I am not a trained wrestler. And if you're not proficient at it, being thrown over the top rope to a hard wooden floor can be extremely dangerous.

But I was determined to be professional. To complain about my treatment would have been a sign of weakness.

I immediately sought out Kirby and Malen, two men I knew and trusted. If I had to enter the Battle Royal, I was determined to get in and out as quickly and safely as possible. So I asked Martin and Paul to make sure they broke my fall when I went over the top rope. They agreed.

The time came for the Battle Royal. My music played (some cheesy tune Bagga chose to humiliate me further) but I didn't emerge. It played again. Still, I didn't come out. Finally, I burst through the entrance door, as if pushed by some unseen force backstage, and reluctantly made my way to ringside, moaning every step of the way at the unfairness of it all. When I finally reached my unwanted destination, I turned my back and tried to flee, but Kirby scooted out of the ring and bundled me under the bottom rope and into the lions' den. I sprang to my feet and looked around in fear.

Out of the corner of my eye I saw the dominant Karl Krammer, who was sending bodies flying left, right and centre. It flashed through my mind that I had to avoid any kind of physical contact with the beastly Barbarian in order to leave that ring in one piece. Thankfully, I was quickly confronted by Cooper, my nemesis from earlier in the evening. He booted me in the stomach (safe as houses), grabbed my hair, hauled me over towards the top rope and strained to wrench me over it.

Now, bear in mind, there is a technique to going over the top rope. And despite watching the trainees practice it time and again at the Morecambe wrestling school, I am about as athletic as a dried pea. So my elimination was probably the most untidy, sloppy and awkwardly clumsy in the history of Battle Royals. With a little help from my designated crash mats Kirby and Malen, poor TK eventually managed to haul my dead-weight, gangly frame up, over and out. I landed on the Platform floor with all the grace of a constipated warthog.

As I lay there, trying to protect my specs and thinking how bad that must have looked, all I could hear was Bagga on the microphone, mocking my plight. "What the hell was that?" he sneered derisively.

So there you have it. My first ever wrestling match. It lasted about 15 seconds.

When I returned to the dressing room, Bagga shook my hand and apologised for putting me in that situation, but justified it by saying he thought it would be entertaining for the fans. He told me that despite the disappointing crowd numbers, he was pressing ahead with plans to run a follow-up event in February 2014. Then he paid me the agreed amount. Everything was cordial between us and Karl Krammer gave me a hug, which was nice of him, even though the big man had just come out of the shower and was dripping wet through.

I left the building, having completed my one and only appearance for LDN. Unscathed.

What do I think about the whole LDN experience? Well, I enjoyed working with Kirby, Malen, Travis, Cooper and Krammer. I could now say I'd competed in a Battle Royal. But I can't help feeling that Bagga was irresponsible pitching me into that match without asking me first.

Still, what doesn't kill you, and all that.

The show itself? It was all right. Nothing to write home about, certainly not a patch on the XWA. But it was passable.

I texted Jamie as soon as I got home to tell him how it went.

He replied that some of the trainees had been at the show, filmed part of it on a mobile phone and showed it to him. And he wasn't impressed with LDN at all. He was now extremely worried fans would be put off from watching any future wrestling in Morecambe and that included PAID Promotions.

I texted back to reassure my old friend.

"Having competition is not a bad thing in any business. But you have all the advantages over Bagga to do better than him. A better product, you're local, a better venue and better promotion."

But Jamie was starting to feel the pressure. He was struggling for cash and thinking about closing down the school because attendance was declining and he felt not enough of the trainees were putting in the required effort.

I told him to be patient. It had been the same every year since the school first opened. Numbers and motivation levels always dropped during the summer months when the trainees' thoughts turned to holidays in the sun. Jamie expected all of his students to have the same passion, ambition, intensity and dedication as him. But this wasn't possible because Johnny Phere is one of a kind when it comes to his obsession with physical conditioning. Some might say he was pushing them too hard. The enjoyment was going out of it for many of them. But I don't blame Jamie for his 'drill sergeant' approach to training. Pro wrestling is no picnic and his methods sorted out the men from the boys. But now he had to realise, he was also running a business. The more trainees who fell by the wayside, the less money he was earning.

So Jamie's frustration was building. He wasn't getting booked to wrestle anywhere. The training school wasn't making enough for him to pay his bills. And his first show was still six weeks away.

Those six weeks turned out to be really stressful for both of us. And here was me hoping for an easier life now I was no longer in charge.

Jamie had all kinds of problems to deal with. He tried to buy a ring. But the manufacturer failed to deliver it on the pre-arranged date, just days before the show. Furious, Jamie cancelled the order and never got all his money back. Thankfully he was able to buy the old XWA ring off Martin Shenton at short notice but the whole episode left him raging and feeling paranoid that the world was out to get him.

Meanwhile three of his top trainees, Aaron Inferno, Action Jackson and Jynkz all decided to quit wrestling at the same time. Jamie was relying on them all to be part of his new roster. But they all lost their passion for being wrestlers and wanted to do other things in their lives. It was disappointing, particularly in the case of Jynkz, who had such great success in the XWA. But I was philosophical about it. Their bodies. Their choice. For Jamie though, their decision only added to his seething inner tension, which was building by the week.

Eventually, we ended up having the first proper argument we'd ever had. Jamie was already peeved that Bagga was planning another show and irritated when I openly told him I thought there was no reason why the two companies couldn't co-exist in Morecambe. I believed they should leave each other alone and both concentrate on putting on the best show they possibly could without trying to kybosh the other - and may the best man win. With a level playing field, I firmly believed this would be Jamie.

But JP didn't have the same confidence. Bagga really got under his skin and he was worried that his Globe show would flop. He felt that because I was his business partner, I should be 100% loyal to him. And I was. He just didn't see it that way. Especially when I conducted what I felt was some unfinished business by messaging Bagga to tell him about the Globe Arena show. As expected, Sanjay already knew, but it was important to me that I informed him. "I'm still going to run Morecambe, just got to be a bit more creative," was the ominous reply. I warned Jamie about this and he started to become even more paranoid.

I guess at this point I was just trying to show integrity with both of them. Trying to please everybody, but in actual fact I was just digging myself a hole.

Then two days later Bagga announced plans to run a show at the Marine Hall in Fleetwood, the same town where Phere had announced a PAID event would take place that September. He also publicly tweeted that he was doing it "to teach a northern wrestler a lesson". JP went mental. He accused me of being far more on board with Sanjay than I was with him. This wasn't true. And as Johnny Phere's biggest and most public supporter over the past 10 years, I was really rather hurt by the accusation. My sole motivation was to be honest and fair with Bagga, just like I try to be with everyone. After clear-the-air talks, I assured Jamie I would now focus completely on PAID's debut event on Sunday, August 25 2013.

We needed to sell tickets fast and we came up with the perfect publicity stunt. The show was taking place at Morecambe Football Club, so Jamie went to see team manager Jim Bentley and offered to give his footballers some wrestling-style fitness training. It just so happened that in the same week as the show, Morecambe had a big televised League Cup match with the Premier League's Newcastle United, and Bentley was looking for something unusual to give his side an edge. All the stars aligned. I used my press contacts to persuade the BBC, Granada TV and Sky Sports to come along to film the session. Suddenly Johnny Phere training the Morecambe football team was all over regional and national television. JP was in high demand. He was interviewed on BBC Radio 5 Live and made the national newspapers. The media lapped up the story of the crazy wrestler preparing the lower league underdogs for their Sky Sports battle with the giants of the Toon Army.

By complete coincidence, a few days before the show, Jamie was asked by Martin Shenton to film a skit for a new ITV travel programme called Weekend Escapes, hosted by popular TV personality Warwick Davis, the tiny star of Life's Too Short and Celebrity Squares. The footage was shot at Regent Park Studios, where Shenton trained the presenter in how to be a stuntman. The diminutive celebrity then put what he had learned into practice in a James Bond-style fight sequence with the mean Psychotic Warrior.

The photos of Warwick Davis and Phere together showed such a physical contrast between them, they were an absolute dream for a PR man looking for another can't-miss piece of publicity. My editor at the newspaper absolutely loved the photos and splashed them all over the front page.

Johnny Phere's action hero look, aggression and unique personality were once again major assets to wrestling in Morecambe. He attracted national mainstream media attention. I believe all the publicity helped shift tickets for Battle of the Brits and proved Johnny Phere was a bankable attraction. But other British wrestling promoters didn't seem to care. The Psychotic Warrior had been filmed for TV news bulletins and a highly-publicised prime time show with a famous celebrity, all in the same week. I plastered the stories all over the internet to raise awareness of JP's television stardom. But it hardly raised a stir inside the UK wrestling fraternity. As usual, I was mystified.

And as usual, I tried to turn a negative into a positive, by using our resentment at JP's stagnating career to fuel a wrestling storyline.

Johnny had already turned heel on the trainee shows because he was always far more comfortable playing the baddie. So now, for the first time ever, we decided to join forces on-screen. I would become Johnny Phere's manager. It made sense. After all, I was his most passionate advocate in real life.

We called ourselves Phere The Truth. And anyone who opposed us, we would brand 'liars'. Quite literally, we would brand them. Ripping a page straight out of the New World Order manual, I came up with the idea of writing the word LIAR on the back of Johnny's beaten opponents. But instead of using spray paint like the NWO, I would use a black marker pen. After all, for a journalist, the pen is always mightier than the sword.

We started coming up with other ideas to get attention. The best one was Phere's. He wanted to start calling himself The Best in Europe. CM Punk had just enjoyed a long WWE World Title reign using the moniker The Best in the World. By making an equally arrogant claim to be the greatest wrestler on the continent, Phere hoped to incur the wrath of fans all over the country.

Our motivation as heels was simple and it was real. We were angry that Johnny Phere didn't get respect. We both believed JP deserved to be the biggest star in UK wrestling. Anyone who disagreed was a liar and would suffer the consequences.

We even had Phere The Truth T-shirts made, with Johnny's face on them. And they sold pretty well.

Weeks prior to the Globe Arena show, we began putting our plan into operation. The last ever trainee show at Regent Park Studios, and Jynkz's last ever match, was on July 7 2013, the day that Andy Murray became Britain's first Wimbledon tennis champion in 77 years. But Murray's fellow Scotsman bowed out in defeat, as I turned heel during his main event match against Phere, costing the facepainted Glaswegian the bout. Due to the stipulation, and Kyle's real-life desire to finish, the loss meant Jynkz's career was over. Afterwards, Phere and I branded Jynkz, writing LIAR on his back with the marker pen, to debut the gimmick. In another twist, I snapped a photo of the fallen Jynkz on my smart-phone and shared it across my social media channels to put everyone in British wrestling on notice that Phere The Truth had been formed and nobody was safe.

Incidentally, during that same angle we also attacked a teenage trainee called Phil Tomkinson. The promising Phil later went on to train at the PCW Academy and in 2016, debuted at PCW events under the name Philip Michael, where the Accrington lad performed creditably in matches with Noam Dar, Ashton Smith and Charlie Garrett.

Now in recent years, Paul Heyman has earned deserved plaudits for his work as the advocate for Brock Lesnar. Heyman's approach has been simple. Every time he picks up a microphone, or shoots a video, or tweets on social media, his job is to talk up the abilities of his client, to put all the attention possible on Brock Lesnar. I decided to take the same approach as the manager of Johnny Phere. So every chance I got, during podcast interviews, in website columns and particularly on Twitter, I proclaimed Johnny 'the Best in Europe' and tore into all the liars in British wrestling who were holding him down. I challenged all the top names in the UK to face Johnny in the ring so he could prove he was the best and all the leading promoters to book Phere so he could show his worth. I was doing my job as his manager, and doing it rather well, I thought.

Sunday August 25 2013 soon dawned and Battle of the Brits turned out to be a positive start for PAID Promotions. The afternoon event ran smoothly and there were plenty of plus points. The hall was packed and the show made a wholesome profit. And the venue itself was superb; modern and clean, a far cry from some of the pokey leisure centres and dingy halls I have worked in over the years. The changing facilities for the wrestlers were among the best I have ever experienced. We got changed in the same modern, airy, spacious dressing room where the Newcastle United players prepared for their big match with Morecambe just days afterwards.

Newcastle won 2-0 by the way. I guess Phere's training didn't work!

The original plan was to hold a tournament on the show to crown the first ever PAID Promotions champion. But I convinced Jamie to change the storyline. Recalling how much heat Triple H got with a similar angle in 2002, I suggested Johnny Phere - as owner of the company - should award himself the PAID championship. This was the ultimate tyrannical heel act. What a way to abuse power, to seize the title without actually winning it in combat. The best heels always have to feel justified in their actions. And as the man who never lost the XWA championship, the Psychotic Warrior believed nobody deserved that title more than him. We did the angle right at the start of the show and when I handed the new PAID championship belt over to my man, the fans were absolutely disgusted.

The tournament instead turned out to be for the number one contender's spot. Craig Kollins, a standout trainee from the Morecambe school, made it to the final where he faced Stixx - the one other established wrestler Phere had booked for the show. Before the main event could begin, Johnny and I came strutting out to ringside. Such was our arrogance, we actually plonked ourselves in the front row, sitting next to the fans, to observe the bout. We thought we owned the place. Well, we kind of did.

Kollins is a real talent. A rugged hard man from Barrow-in-Furness, he had been training at the school since late 2010. Craig grasped the fundamentals and the psychology of wrestling quickly and responded well to Phere's punishing tutelage because in many ways, they were cut from the same cloth. Kollins was fearless and aggressive, and knew exactly what kind of persona he wanted to portray - a no-nonsense street thug. The One Man Riot also had exquisite timing in the ring and looked much older than his 21 years.

Stixx still had his undefeated streak going on. After a powerful tussle, and despite us yelling support for Craig from our ringside seats, he pinned Kollins with a cradle. But Phere had the last laugh. He rushed into the ring, blindsided The Heavyweight House of Pain, locked him in the War-Lock submission hold then laid him flat out with a piledriver. Then Phere signalled to me to pass him the marker pen, so he could brand Stixx a liar as we had planned.

Buggar! I'd left it in the dressing room!

So instead, we shot a video after the show. Phere jumped the injured Stixx again as he was being helped into the dressing room and wrote LIAR on his back right in front of the cameras. It was a powerful piece of film which firmly established us as a devillish pair of egomaniacs.

The Phere The Truth alliance was a smash hit in the live arena, in terms of how well we performed and gelled as a duo, and the heated reaction we got from our audience. Johnny and I were at our peak as performers and we knew exactly what to do to push the buttons of the spectators. We bounced off each other perfectly. In fact, I would go as far as to say our run as Phere The Truth saw both myself and Johnny produce some of the greatest work of our wrestling careers. But despite that, the reaction to Phere The Truth from wrestling fans, insiders and performers was rather negative, verging on the bizarre.

The concept of Phere awarding himself the belt raised the ire of hardcore fans, as expected, with some dismissing PAID Promotions as a "vanity project". They said the only way Johnny Phere could get booked was to form his own company and build it around himself. Well, yes. That was the gimmick. We were heels. We did it on purpose because we knew it would infuriate and get attention.

It was the response of some of the UK wrestlers that really confused me though. One veteran tweeted me publicly to express his outrage that Johnny Phere would dare to proclaim himself the Best in Europe when there were so many better wrestlers across the continent than him. And he was being serious. He wasn't working. This guy had never appeared for me in Morecambe, never worked a programme with either myself or Phere. He wasn't doing this to build heat for a feud. He was offended, for real, by our temerity. And he has been in the wrestling business for more than 20 years. But it's a gimmick! We were working! We were being heels! We were meant to make outlandish claims! That was the whole point!

Other British wrestlers mocked the gimmick too. Some tweeted to poke fun at us. Again, it was people who had no business reason. They were just being spiteful or having a laugh at our expense. It was disappointing.

I didn't get it. I just didn't get it. We were staying in character, being totally professional, creating a unique and forceful gimmick, and getting ridiculed by our peers for doing it. Wrestling can't half be a strange business sometimes.

One top British pro who did understand what we were trying to do, though, was Kris Travis. Kris publicly challenged Johnny to a match, using Twitter to demand Phere put his money where his mouth was over his 'Best in Europe' claim. He was trying to do business and I could see the value in a Phere v Travis feud. Kris even mentioned it to me backstage at a PCW show. As he was using his ever-present hair straighteners one night preparing for a match at Evoque he asked me: "When are you bringing me in to PAID to wrestle Phere?" Trav was really up for it. But it was ultimately Jamie's decision and sadly, the match never happened. There were a few ideas I pushed for at the time which he simply didn't want to do, usually for financial reasons.

But in general, there was a backlash towards Phere The Truth, for sure. But all this did was motivate me. It made me determined to hit the bullseye with this angle every time Phere and I set foot in an arena during our brief but highly-charged six month association. And we did. Some of my promos as Johnny's manager were among the best of my career, because I really and truly believed in my heart what I was saying.

Despite the promising start at Battle of the Brits, Johnny Phere's PAID Promotions failed to set the world on fire over the next few months. Crowd numbers for PAID shows were generally poor. Jamie ran three events in late 2013/early 2014 at a dingy venue called The Loft in Fleetwood, and there can't have been any more than 70 people in the crowd each time. It became a struggle for him to get more than 100 people to his Morecambe shows too.

Granted, most of these events made a profit. But that was only because Jamie's business model was to keep wage costs incredibly low by building the shows around trainees like Kollins, Rossion, Shaun Vasey, Ryan Grayson and Serenity, as well as Phere The Truth and a handful of established names like Bubblegum, RJM, The Blackpool Blonds and Stixx. So it was virtually impossible not to make money. Having said that, most of the profit was being used to pay back the initial outlay on the ring and van. So Jamie wasn't making much from the shows to live on. Without any other source of income to fall back on, he barely had two pennies to rub together.

It was a bittersweet time for me. I loved managing Johnny, he had some tremendous matches during that run as heel PAID Promotions Champion full of great drama and WWE-style psychology, and we got great heat with our post-match LIAR branding of beaten opponents. We were *proper* heels, hated by everyone.

On October 13 2013 at The Globe Arena, JP put in an outstanding display in the main event against Bubblegum despite suffering from a serious rib injury which rendered the right side of his body totally useless. Once we were back behind the curtain after the match, I gave Jamie a huge hug because I knew how much pain he was in, yet he still managed to perform at an exceptional level alongside the supremely talented Pip 'Bubblegum' Cartner. Then in Fleetwood on January 11 2014, JP had an excellent no-DQ main event with the towering rookie 'Mr Big' Shaun Vasey. Phere The Truth was on fire that night and the fans absolutely despised us. Our heel chemistry as champion and manager was bang on the money.

But behind-the-scenes, I was miserable. I was so frustrated with how things were going. I personally didn't feel Jamie was doing enough to promote his events. But the problem was, Jamie wasn't exactly a people person. His natural instinct was to keep himself to himself. Not the best characteristic for a wrestling promoter.

There was a crowd of 97 at a Globe Arena show on December 1 2013, a terrible turnout for a Morecambe event. And there were more injuries to contend with. Nottingham wrestler Joseph Conners, a promising talent who would go on to compete in the 2017 WWE UK Championship, suffered a dislocated shoulder during his match with Vasey, who was doubling up on shows as scary wrestling 'zombie' The Creeper as well as Mr Big. Then in the main event six-man tag pitting Johnny's squad against Stixx's team, The Heavyweight House of Pain got a concussion. Stixx was so out of it he actually cut his planned post-match promo twice, repeating what he was supposed to say because he couldn't recall saying it the first time. Afterwards, Paul couldn't remember the match either and ended up being checked over at the local hospital. It is never pleasant to see your colleagues get hurt. Suffice to say, I wasn't in a great mood that night.

The crowd was dead too. Usually our local fans were so responsive. Why was this happening? From past experience, I felt that it was overkill to run three shows in Morecambe in as many months. I also didn't think the shows were good enough. We had some promising youngsters but they were still learning the trade. We needed more experienced talent. And there wasn't enough creative depth. Phere The Truth was carrying the card and there weren't any other compelling storylines.

I told Jamie my concerns. I desperately wanted him to succeed. But all I could do was advise him and hope things would turn around. It wasn't my baby any longer. I had to keep telling myself that. But it was so hard not to care. Wrestling in Morecambe had been my life. I didn't like what was happening to it.

It didn't feel like it was Real in Morecambe any more.

Meanwhile, the shadow of Bagga was still looming. He cancelled plans for his own Fleetwood shows almost as soon as announcing them, but was still going ahead with his February 2014 event in Morecambe. Tensions between PAID and LDN blew up again when somebody removed PAID flyers from the local shopping centre. Jamie thought Bagga had done it. One of the Morecambe trainees actually messaged Sanjay and accused him. But it turned out Bagga was innocent. The manager of The Platform had taken the flyers by mistake. I tried to smooth things over, play the middle man. I didn't want to take sides. But this rankled with JP. Once again, he thought I should be 100% behind PAID Promotions. I hated the fact that we kept falling out. This had never happened before in the 12 years we had known each other.

Things were going badly. We needed a boost. And fast.

Re-enter Rockstar Spud.

CHAPTER 12

SPUD CONQUERS AMERICA

"And the winner of TNA British Boot Camp is...Rockstar Spud!"
TNA President Dixie Carter, TNA British Boot Camp, January 22 2013

When I watched Hulk Hogan and TNA President Dixie Carter announce Rockstar Spud as the winner of TNA British Boot Camp on my 41st birthday, it was the best present I could have wished for.

I can't recall ever being as excited about anything in British wrestling before. I knew how much it meant to Jay. And I knew how much he deserved it. But I also knew how big this was, for British wrestling as a whole.

My old mate had won TNA's groundbreaking and critically acclaimed reality TV series to uncover the next British wrestling star. In victory, he earned himself a life-changing contract with the number two company in America. He massively raised his own profile. And he was the main star of a television show that put an unprecedented amount of positive attention on the modern-day UK wrestling scene.

The timing of British Boot Camp really couldn't have been much better. At the start of 2013, British wrestling was really starting to stir into life again - thanks in the main to a quartet of promotions who, at time of writing, have become established as the UK's 'Big Four'.

As you have already read, ICW was creating a buzz over the border and Preston City Wrestling was starting to make waves up north. And in London, PROGRESS Wrestling and Revolution Pro Wrestling ran their first shows in 2012 and were already pulling big crowds and earning rave reviews.

In early 2013, TNA was pulling a weekly audience of between

200,000 and 300,000 viewers for its flagship show, Impact Wrestling on UK digital channel Challenge TV. In fact, TNA Impact was regularly the channel's highest rated programme. On home soil in America, TNA was struggling to compete with the undisputed industry leader, World Wrestling Entertainment. But in the UK, TNA had a much bigger market share of the wrestling audience. This is because unlike WWE, which broadcasted on subscription channel Sky Sports, the company was free for viewers to watch on Challenge. This is why Impact, with stars such as Jeff Hardy, Kurt Angle and Hulk Hogan on the programme at the time, rated favourably alongside popular quiz shows like The Chase and Bullseye.

Now when taking into account repeats, pay-per-views and the additional WWE programmes on Sky Sports such as SmackDown, there is no doubt that many more Brits watched WWE in a week than they did TNA. But TNA Impact was clearly the most-watched weekly episodic wrestling programme in the British Isles.

This is one of the reasons why Dixie Carter and her team realised the value of signing up a new British wrestler and making him a star.

And there was suddenly a huge amount of British wrestling talent to pick from; much more depth than we have arguably ever had in terms of young, world class grapplers. It felt like there were quality workers around every corner who were still only in their late teens, 20s or early 30s. Most of them had grown up wanting to wrestle after watching WWE on Sky during its peak years and now they were all maturing at the same time.

We had great technical wrestlers like Zack Sabre Jnr, Jack Gallagher, Noam Dar, Zack Gibson, Kris Travis, Martin Kirby, CJ Banks, Joey Hayes, Mark Haskins, Mikey Whiplash, The Coffey Brothers, Robbie Dynamite and Noam Dar. We had spectacular high-flyers like El Ligero, Kay Lee Ray, Will Ospreay, Dean Allmark, Jonny Storm and Mark Andrews. We had big personalities like Grado, Mad Man Manson, Lionheart, Nathan Cruz, RJ Singh, Johnny Phere, Bubblegum, Nikki Storm, Dave Rayne and Danny Hope. We had agile big men like Cyanide, Stixx, Wolfgang and Dave Mastiff. We had rock-hard brawlers like Rampage Brown, Jack Jester, Jimmy Havoc, Johnny Moss, BT Gunn, Sha Samuels, Chris

Renfrew and T-Bone. And we had top-notch tag teams like Roy and Zak Knight, Fight Club, The Bucky Boys, The Blackpool Blonds and The Owens Twins. And there are bound to be some I have forgotten. Such was the blossoming talent pool in the UK in late 2012/early 2013.

TNA must have had a real headache trying to choose just four Brits for their new reality show. In the end, they picked The Blossom Twins, Marty Scurll and Rockstar Spud.

The Blossoms, Hannah and Holly, were 24 years old at the time. Real names Lucy and Kelly Knott, they grew up in Stockport and began wrestling when they were 16 years old. They established themselves as regulars with Dann Read's ChickFight and Pro-Wrestling:EVE all-female promotions, and also with their home company FutureShock. And they already had experience in America for TNA feeder group Ohio Valley Wrestling. Their wholesome, sweetness-and-light image was no act. The Blossoms really are lovely girls in real life. And as good looking identical twins, who worked as primary school teaching assistants and loved baking cupcakes, but by night beat people up in the wrestling ring, they were a marketing dream. Little wonder Hannah and Holly attracted the bulk of the pre-Boot Camp UK media attention. I felt they were Spud's biggest competition because TNA didn't have any twins on their roster, let alone two English roses like Hannah and Holly. The Blossoms could potentially fill a niche spot in the company.

'Party' Marty Scurll worked for me in XWA on several occasions from 2008 to 2010, as well as for the FWA, so I know him pretty well, and he has a lot of attributes. Then 24, Marty was a good all-rounder with wrestling and high-flying skills, a strong personality and could work heel or face with aplomb. Scurll had also gained mainstream media attention already, after appearing on ITV dating show Take Me Out in January 2012.

Around the same time as his TV appearance, Marty's picture appeared on the front page of The Sun newspaper in a story about the contestants taking part in a wild sex and booze party at a £4.5m mansion. Scurll used this notoriety to boost his wrestling character as 'Party' Marty - a ladies' man and party animal. The Cambridge man was the best technical wrestler of the four and was great mates with

Nick 'Magnus' Aldis, so already had a friend backing him for a spot in TNA. And Scurll was already feuding with Spud on the UK circuit, thanks to Spud ripping into him for his Take Me Out stint in a series of brilliant YouTube promos. So TNA British Boot Camp had a ready-made rivalry. I know from talking to TV documentary-makers over the years how much they love on-screen conflict.

Then there was Spud, the eldest of the four at nearly 30. After more than a decade honing his skills around the small halls and holiday camps of Britain, this was probably the former XWA Double Champion's last shot at international stardom. But this also meant he had the experience advantage. And despite being small in stature, the sheer force of his personality gave him a fighting chance.

Spud also has an intelligence, an understanding of how to promote himself and a degree of professionalism, that set him apart. In November 2012, I interviewed him for Power Slam magazine. We talked about how he used social media to upload smartphone videos of himself cutting promos and a dedicated Facebook fan page to market his character. Not many British wrestlers were doing that, at the time. So much of what he said during our chat, I strongly agreed with.

"I see a lot of British wrestlers who are just their real-life selves on social media," said Jay. "But I believe you've got to carry yourself as a star at all times, because people are interested in you as a performer. You've got to make people want to pay money to see you. That's my job."

Amen to that. It drives me up the wall when British wrestlers post on Facebook or Twitter after a match with a hated rival about how much they respect their opponent in real-life and enjoyed working with them. Or even worse, I hate it when British wrestlers, promoters or personalities use social media to criticise other people involved in the business. This makes them look small-time and petty in the eyes of the fans who pay to see them. I have seen promoters posting about how much they hate a bitter rival, or veterans reacting to criticism with angry diatribes, various wrestling people sharing mocking videos of bad British wrestlers or matches, even top British professionals slagging off a young grappler on Facebook for making a mistake when they could have just pulled him to one side at training and had a private word. How is any of this stuff helping?

As a journalist, I often expose the business. I am doing it in this book, after all. But never with malice. Everything I ever do in my wrestling career is with the intention of making the UK scene a better place.

I believe British wrestlers and promoters should be using social media as a positive force for the good of the business. They should treat a Facebook or Twitter post like it's a television camera pointing at them, as an opportunity to sell themselves to the public. Stay in character, entertain, sell tickets for their next match. Instead, in the social media age, too many UK wrestling people use it to spread negativity or revel in the fact that this is all a work. What good is this doing the business? More to the point, what good is it doing *them*? If you're involved in professional wrestling or indeed any form of entertainment, you should always act larger than life, and above all of the pettiness that sometimes makes social media a cesspit.

"Too many British wrestlers think too much about wrestling," continued Spud.

"They are obsessed with 'Oh I must have a good match.' They need to start thinking they are in the entertainment business. There's about 80 different TV channels to choose from these days, so what's going to make people want to watch your channel? It's not going to be the wrestling, it will be someone who is entertaining."

Absolutely right. Remember, big personalities, not wrestling, draw the casual fan.

Jay also didn't believe his short stature would be a detriment to him winning British Boot Camp. Quite the opposite.

"What everyone sees as my biggest weakness is actually my biggest asset. It's the one thing that makes me stand out. Look at Floyd Mayweather in boxing. He's not big but he's a draw. Yes I am one of the smallest guys in professional wrestling but I am a phenomenal entertainer."

At the time, Spud had cut right down on his UK bookings. I asked him why.

"I don't want to overexpose myself and I want to rest up. If I'm going round the country, working everywhere, then by the time I appear on TV that won't make me special. I want to be a special attraction. Overexposure ruins people. I understand that British wrestlers want to do three shows a day for the money, but why not develop your character so you can work one show a day and earn as much money as you would working three times?"

After reading the transcript of our chat, Findlay Martin said it was the best interview in Power Slam by a Brit in more than a decade. So Spud was clearly savvy when it came to the media. This gave him a huge advantage.

Filming of British Boot Camp began in September 2012. TV cameras followed Spud, Marty and The Blossoms everywhere, shooting footage for a six-part series to air in January 2013 on Challenge. This came during a rich time for television documentaries about British Wrestling. In July 2012, Channel 4 aired the acclaimed The Wrestlers: Fighting with My Family, a fly-on-the-wall peek into the life of the Knights of Norfolk - Ricky Knight, Sweet Saraya, Roy, Zak and Paige. A filmmaker and wrestling fan called Adam Gill was about to start filming a superb documentary on the history of the UK circuit called Two Falls to a Finish. Starring a 'talking heads' cast of British wrestling names including Danny Boy Collins, Marty Jones, Robbie Brookside, Alex Shane, Jonny Storm, Doug Williams, Brian Dixon, Zack Sabre Jnr, Rampage Brown and little old me, this stellar review of the rise, fall and revival of UK grappling would eventually air on Challenge TV, to huge acclaim, in August 2015.

And in December 2012, BBC4 screened a historical look back at World of Sport era British wrestling called Wrestling: Grapples, Grunts and Grannies. It featured interviews with legends such as Max Crabtree and Adrian Street, and was a fine slice of nostalgia. But I really hated the ending of the show, because it made out that modern-day British wrestling was dead and buried, and couldn't hold a candle to the 'good old days', when nothing was further from the truth.

I hoped against hope that TNA British Boot Camp would put a more positive spin on 21st century British wrestling and the four young Brits gunning for superstardom. But I feared TNA might screw it up and make the quartet look like chumps, inferior to their American counterparts.

I need not have worried. With TNA ring announcer Jeremy Borash at the helm, the show was in great hands. JB, as he's known, once very kindly referred to me as a "champion of British wrestling". But in actual fact, Mr Borash has done far more for British wrestling than I ever have. His creative input and editing skills as executive producer of both series of British Boot Camp made British wrestling, and its wrestlers, look like the world-beaters we undoubtedly are.

TNA British Boot Camp shot out of the blocks with episode 1 on New Year's Day 2013. Right from the start, we found out about the contestants, their personalities, their goals, their background, their families and what drives them as individuals. Spud, Marty and The Blossoms were all given plenty of TV time to get across why the viewers should care about them. It was brilliantly done.

Marty talked about how he started training at 14 to "stay out of trouble". Then it showed him outside Wembley Arena, where TNA was due to appear as part of their upcoming Road to Lockdown UK tour. Scurll spoke about how he'd always wanted to perform there, have his name alongside Hogan, Hardy and Sting on the marquee. 'Party' Marty certainly came across well on camera.

But Spud came across much better. As soon as he appeared, the Rockstar was dynamite. He oozed charisma and self-belief. He was that irritating and entertaining little so-and-so I'd come to know and love in Morecambe over the previous four years. But his sincerity was such, he still managed to make you root for him. The little guy, who worked in a bank in Birmingham, who everybody always said was too small to be a professional wrestler, made it clear this was the biggest moment of his life.

"I'm always trying to prove people wrong," he said.

"When I first told my mum and dad I wanted to be a professional wrestler, they kind of laughed. Trying to get your own family to believe in what you are doing was kind of soul-destroying but motivating at the same time.

"Professional wrestling is what I love and nobody's going to stop me doing this. I want to stand in front of those people who ever said to me I'm just not big enough and tell them that I'm going to be the biggest star in Impact Wrestling, and you're still at your job being a plumber or an electrician. Your words, you're going to eat every single one of them."

Jay then spoke about how Hulk Hogan was his idol, how he'd been "mesmerised" by The Hulkster as a kid. Then Hogan himself appeared on camera and said: "Rockstar Spud said his prayers and took his vitamins, now he may be the next TNA Wrestling superstar."

To see Hulk Hogan...yes, HULK HOGAN...putting over Rockstar Spud on national television, well, it was just surreal.

Meanwhile the Blossoms were as wholesome, likeable and marketable as I'd expected. To boost their family image still further, their dad Graham and mum Louisa were interviewed, and talked about how proud they were of the girls. Then the cameras followed Hannah and Holly into the classroom and their pupils clearly adored them too. The Blossoms came across as absolute sweethearts.

The highlight of episode 1 was when the quartet went out on the town after the launch party and storylines for the series were established (because while British Boot Camp was marketed as a fly-on-the-wall reality show, a lot of it was actually pre-planned). There was a touch of romance, as Marty confided to camera that he fancied Hannah Blossom. Spud stayed true to his Rockstar character by knocking back his favourite tipple Jagermeister and got roaringly drunk. Then he and Scurll had a petty row in the limousine over who had the most Twitter followers (it was Marty at the time) and the lairy Rockstar slapped his rival across the face while the goody two-shoes Blossoms tried to defuse the situation. It was great TV.

Around 113,000 people watched the debut episode of TNA British Boot Camp on Challenge TV on New Year's Day 2013. These were encouraging numbers for a show built around a quartet of British wrestlers who essentially, were complete unknowns. It also exposed the UK wrestling scene to a brand new audience of regular TNA watchers who may not have even been aware that British wrestling existed.

British Boot Camp also attracted a fabulous amount of mainstream media attention. There were articles about the show in The Daily Mirror, The Sun, The Star, The Daily Express, The Daily Mail, The Guardian and Cosmopolitan magazine. Hulk Hogan was even on ITV daytime chat show This Morning and BBC Radio 5

Live talking about it. The concept of the programme and the characters involved captured the imagination of the mainstream British press like nothing in British wrestling for decades. And of course it did no harm that Hogan, the biggest name in sports entertainment history, was the front man.

Episode 2 was built around the first in a series of 'challenges' where the Boot Camp cast needed to prove their worth. TNA drafted in UK wrestling legend Mark 'Rollerball' Rocco to put the foursome through their paces in the ring. This was a real coup, as Rocco rarely appears in public. One of the greats of the ITV era of pro wrestling, Rocco had to retire in 1991, aged 40, after he collapsed in the dressing room following a match with Dave 'Fit' Finlay and was diagnosed with a heart condition. He now lived in Tenerife.

Spud really got the chance to shine here and get his character across to the viewers. Nursing a stinking hangover from his night on the tiles, the blond-haired braggart was sick outside the gym and earned the wrath of Rocco. Clearly under the weather, Spud was then easily bested by Scurll in an in-ring exchange of holds. Furious with the Rockstar's tardiness, Rocco then entered the ring himself to teach Spud a lesson. Rollerball rolled back the years and showed glimpses of the super talent who had such stellar matches with Marty Jones and the Dynamite Kid in the 1980s, beating Spud to a pulp. But the story was, the Rockstar would not quit. He earned Rocco's respect.

The rest of the episode saw the Boot Campers interviewed by Patrick Lennon for The Daily Star. Then they made an in-ring appearance at PROGRESS Wrestling at The Garage in Islington. This was fantastic exposure for PROGRESS, at the time still a fledgling company.

Episode 3 saw the crew fly out to America. Phoenix, Arizona to be exact, where they were guests at TNA Bound for Glory and Sting's TNA Hall of Fame induction. Here they met Dixie Carter for the first time, were introduced to Hulk Hogan and The Stinger, and sat at a table for the Hall of Fame ceremony with Kurt Angle. Once again, TNA did everything possible to make our boys and girls look great. Spud still owned the show, though. Particularly inspired were his complaints when TNA fans only wanted photos with the twins, and how he embarrassed Marty in front of TNA ring announcer

Christy Hemme by claiming Scurll had a picture of her on his bedroom wall.

At the start of episode 4, the hopefuls were at the TNA office in Nashville. Here they met with Dixie, who gave them feedback on their debut appearance at Bound for Glory, when the camera had panned onto them sitting in the crowd for just a few seconds. Marty got the brunt of Ms Carter's criticism for chewing gum on camera. "That's not a star," she told him, as Scurll hung his head. I can relate to this, for I am also a prodigious gum chewer. But I have always spat it out before promos ever since that day.

Later, the gang went out and got drunk with TNA star 'Cowboy' James Storm. Once again Spud couldn't hold his liquor and ended up stripped to his undies in a Tennessee bar. It was the most memorable scene of the episode. Spud was doing everything possible to put all of the attention on himself and succeeding, despite Marty copping off with Hannah Blossom a few minutes before.

The penultimate episode saw Spud, Marty and The Blossoms visit Ohio Valley Wrestling, where they did a work out in the ring with trainers Al Snow and fellow Brit Doug Williams. Then they competed on an OVW show, where the Rockstar and Scurll teamed up but failed to get along. Al Snow gave them a convincing dressing down afterwards, while Doug was clearly trying hard not to laugh!

But as it turned out, Williams wasn't long for the job anyway. Ironically as TNA was on the verge of finding its new British superstar, the former British Invasion member wanted out. On May 31 2013, Doug's five-year TNA career ended after he told bosses that he wanted to leave if they had no plans to use him as a wrestler and not a trainer. The Ambassador returned to the British circuit and remains one of the very best around to this day.

The best part of the episode was when TNA stars gave their opinions on who was going to win. This made the series, and the contestants, look important. Jeff Hardy, Taz and Tarryn Terrell backed 'Party' Marty, saying he was the most proficient in the ring. Mickie James singled out The Blossoms. But Bully Ray gave the most ringing endorsement, cutting a typically rousing promo to extoll the virtues of The Baby Jesus of British wrestling.

"Any guy with the balls to call himself Rockstar and Spud in the same name, I want to see win," said the former and future Dudley Boy.

"The guy is a piece of fricking dynamite."

Kurt Angle put Spud over too.

"There's something special about him, size doesn't matter any more," said the multi-time world champion and Olympic gold medallist.

I can't possibly put into words how fantastic it was to hear these major stars speaking so highly of Rockstar Spud.

So on January 22 2013, I watched the final episode on my birthday, grinning from ear to ear for virtually the full half-hour.

First of all, Hulk Hogan gave the stakes the full typical Hulkster hype job.

"This is your future!" The Immortal One told the wannabes and the viewing audience. "Somebody is going to get picked to be a TNA superstar from here to eternity! And what'cha gonna do when TNA Impact Wrestling picks you?"

The grand finale saw all four Brits get the chance to compete in the Impact Zone, while Hogan and Dixie watched and critiqued them on monitors backstage. The Blossoms lost their match to Gail Kim and Madison Rayne, but definitely held their own. But the biggest praise was reserved for Spud and Scurll, who finally got to settle their differences in a scorching one-on-one battle.

As Spud emerged to Living on a Prayer and gave Orlando, Florida the full cocky Rockstar entrance, the Hulkster gushed: "The kid looks like a movie star!" Then as Party Marty and Spud went at it, Hogan was wide-eyed in amazement.

"Some of our guys could use some tips from these kids," gushed Hulk.

"They get it. The characters are so well-developed."

After Marty won an impressive match with a Death Valley Driver, Hogan could barely contain how impressed he was with all four competitors.

"I think all of them would be a great addition to the company. I was blown away."

He even described the Blossoms as "a new version of the Spice Girls". Seriously, Hulk could not have done any more to hammer home to the viewing public that Rockstar Spud, Marty Scurll and The Blossom Twins were the real deal.

The only drawback in the whole process was they announced who was getting the TNA contract in a bloody trailer. Surely they could have picked somewhere a little more posh?

When Dixie told Spud he was the winner, Jay dropped to his knees, head in his hands. He hadn't been told beforehand that he'd won. The emotion was real. And it was Real in Morecambe too, where I raced around the house like an excited lunatic, before grabbing my phone to text my friend with congratulations.

Just before the credits rolled on a memorable series, Spud's voice cracked with emotion as he gave his acceptance speech.

"I wasn't born ready, I worked hard and now I feel I'm ready. I love this and I was born to do this.

"Maybe I can look my parents in the eye now and say I'm not a failure any more. Wrestling is my job. I'm so happy.

"I've got this far, people didn't believe me, but believe me when I say this...*I will be a champion with Impact Wrestling.*"

Spud had done it. He'd beaten Marty Scurll, a former colleague from the FWA days and largely felt to be the most talented in-ring worker of the quartet, and The Blossoms who were many people's favourites to win, to earn a job with one of the biggest wrestling companies in the world. And he'd done it by using the skills he'd honed during the comeback of the FWA. It wasn't about being the best wrestler. It was about talking, working the camera, being a character, being *remembered.*

"I found out afterwards that TNA originally wanted The Blossoms to win," said Spud, reflecting on the experience in 2016.

"Marty and I were just meant to be fodder for them. But they didn't capture the audience as much as I did.

"I got the job because Jeremy Borash went to bat for me. He edited the whole series and said that out of the footage that they'd filmed, they couldn't not give me a job. That's really nice to hear from him, because he's grown into a close friend of mine. Not just because of that, but because he's a good dude.

"The moment it all changed was when we went for the meal with Dixie. That's when she made the decision of who she wanted to win, after she met us all as people. Then I had to go in the ring and back it up.

"Boot Camp was also the first time my dad was really proud of me in wrestling, because Hulk Hogan was in it!"

The final episode of TNA British Boot Camp drew 130,000 viewers, having gained 17,000 viewers during the series.

Four days later, I sat in the crowd at Wembley Arena and watched Rockstar Spud pin Robbie E in his official TNA Impact Wrestling TV debut in front of a crowd of 8,000 people. Stevie Knight, RJ Singh and Stallion were with me. We had all gone to see Spud's moment of glory and we were proud as Punch to see our mate hit the big-time.

Marty Scurll and The Blossoms also wrestled on the Wembley show and other dates on the Road to LockDown tour. But the tour would be the final chapter of their TNA careers to date.

Marty did a great job on Boot Camp and was unfortunate that he came up against a Rockstar Spud who would not be denied. Since then, though, Scurll has developed even more as a wrestler and performer. The catalyst for this improvement came in 2014 when he dropped the Party Marty persona and reinvented himself as The Villain, a fur coat-wearing and umbrella-toting baddie. He also had a stint presenting WrestleTalk TV giving him exposure on Challenge every week. Then in January 2016, Scurll had a breathtaking match with Will Ospreay for Revolution Pro Wrestling at the York Hall. The bout was so incredibly good, it earned unprecedented plaudits for British wrestling from industry-leading US newsletter the Wrestling Observer. Later that month, Marty captured the PROGRESS Championship in another cracking encounter with Ospreay. Scurll also became a globetrotter thanks to bookings with top American indie feds PWG and EVOLVE. And in a first for a UK promotion, Rev Pro even made an action figure of him. Momentum is growing for The Villain and surely, another shot at the big-time is just around the corner for him.

"For years I've been behind Marty and been his biggest supporter and every time he's been given an opportunity he's taken it and made the most out of it," said Andy Quildan in 2016.

"And he continues to evolve, in every single aspect of pro

wrestling. The way he has worked on his body, the way he has changed his move set. Every time he steps in the ring with someone of a higher level, he ups his game, then next time he wrestles he brings that level to that match. We're so lucky to have young veterans like Marty who is only 28 but has been around a long time and is so in-tune with who he is. That's why he's flourishing, because he's found himself."

Spud feels losing on British Boot Camp was "the best thing to happen to Marty".

"Now he's got that fuel to go 'I'll show them'," said Jay.

"He wasn't a character then. He was Marty from the Leaders. There was no depth. It was the same with The Blossoms. They were twins but where could they go with it? Adaptability is key. If you're one-dimensional you can't be in the pro wrestling business."

As for The Blossoms, they took a break from wrestling in early 2014. Both Hannah and Holly got married, to OVW wrestler Chris Silvio and referee Chris Sharpe respectively (Hannah's dalliance with Marty turned out to be just a fling for the Boot Camp cameras). They blogged about making cupcakes and began their own YouTube show called Life is Sweet. Ahhhh.

As for Spud, he flew out to the promised land of the USA in late February 2013. But not before popping in to the Morecambe training school for a brief visit. That Sunday, he gave the trainees the benefit of his Boot Camp experience. Then, before he left, Jay handed me a photo of himself in his full Rockstar regalia. He signed it as follows.

"To Greg, thank you for helping make me a star."

This photo is one of my most treasured possessions.

Now, those of you who read the first Holy Grail may recall how Steve Lynskey, British wrestling referee, agent and a colleague of mine and Spud's from the FWA days, predicted that Jay would win British Boot Camp. And his prediction came true.

But, Lynskey's crystal ball also came with these words of warning about Spud's chances of having a successful career in TNA.

"Spud in his street clothes is just another guy. There will be interest but as soon as the series ends...then what?"

Steve's scepticism was fairly typical of the views of most wrestling fans, journalists and insiders at the time. Very few really thought little Spud could make it in America's land of the giants. And indeed, as soon as he arrived in the States, there were fears that winning British Boot Camp would turn out to be the peak of his career.

Jay spent months in Ohio Valley Wrestling when he first got there. Many critics wondered if he would ever get called up to become an Impact Wrestling regular. Some wondered if the winner of British Boot Camp would be soon be on the next plane home, his dream in tatters.

But then on the November 28 2013 episode of Impact, Rockstar Spud appeared. But this was as we had never seen him before. And nobody could have predicted the change he'd gone through.

Gone were the gawdy shades, leathers and rocker attitude. Gone, in fact, was the entire Rockstar gimmick, apart from the name. Spud instead sported a bow tie, a suit and a cheesy grin. As Dixie Carter's new Chief of Staff, his new persona was that of an annoying corporate lackey.

It suited him down to the ground.

"Two days before I was being brought to TV, (TNA talent relations head) John Gaburick called and said 'we want you to be Dixie's Chief of Staff, kind of like her secretary, so get yourself a nice suit. Do you reckon you can do this?' I said 'John, not only can I do this, I will knock it out of the f__king park.'"

Spud then phoned his original trainer, Barry Charalambous, for advice.

"He told me to think about obnoxious things about suits. I said 'Well, whenever somebody walks into a bar with a dickie bow on, I think they're an absolute t__t.' So he said 'Get one!' And he said 'That belt you wear when you wrestle, it doesn't match anything else you wear. So wear that too. And make sure you're overly-tanned as well.'

"As the weeks went by the suits got even sh__tier. Even sh__tier than Al Snow's suits, and he's got some sh__ty suits! Now people think of the suits as Rockstar Spud suits. I loved being that character. I think it's my favourite character I've portrayed so far. I think if I went to another company that's what they would want me to be, which I'm fine with."

On his very first episode as Chief of Staff, Spud was given

microphone time to preside over a Thanksgiving dinner held in tribute to the heel Carter family of the boss Dixie - who he affectionally referred to as 'Madam' - and her nephew, the undefeated Ethan Carter III, or EC3 for short.

"My lords, ladies and gentlemen!" announced the beaming Spud, his chest puffed with pride as the Impact Zone booed him heartily. "Here is the Winner Winner, Turkey Dinner!"

The Rockstar then invited all the winners of that night's bouts to enjoy a slap-up meal in the ring. Of course, this being a wrestling TV show, the banquet ended in a huge brawl. As the food fight raged all around him, the furious Spud's face was an absolute picture.

It was clear from the very start of his TNA TV career, that Spud was going to run with his new character, play it for laughs, and do his damndest to make it a success.

Two weeks later, Spud was an absolute riot in a series of skits where he was sent by Madam Dixie to Gainsville, Georgia, home of TNA Champion AJ Styles. The Rockstar's mission was to retrieve the championship belt from Styles, who had fallen out of favour with TNA management and was about to finish with the company (in both reality and storyline). The segments were priceless as Spud, the fish out of water Brummie in the American Deep South, got completely lost, ended up in a backwater bar, ordered a Ladyboy Chaser from the confused barmaid in hilarious homage to Alan Partridge, then got thrown out while singing a deliberately appalling version of God Save the Queen on karaoke. Later, Spud broke into AJ's house and got his hands on the belt, only for Styles to catch him in the act. The terrified Chief of Staff then fled! It was comedy gold.

The following week, Spud's stock rose even further as his colourful suits got even more outrageous. As Magnus battled Jeff Hardy for the vacant TNA Title, the Rockstar's interference directly helped the pride of King's Lynn become TNA champ. This was a big moment for British wrestling. Nick Aldis, one of our very own, was now on top of the second biggest company in the States, billed as the first world heavyweight champion from Britain in 108 years. And alongside Magnus, EC3 and Madam Dixie, Spud was now a key part of the top heel stable in TNA.

I watched from the crowd, again, on January 31 2014 at the

Manchester Arena as Jay wrestled MVP on the annual TNA UK tour and although Spud, competing in his trademark bow tie, was squashed by the former WWE United States Champion in two minutes flat, he later returned to help Magnus retain the title in the main event against Gunner. Although his size meant he wasn't yet being portrayed as a serious threat in the ring, Spud was still being given TV time in a high profile spot and got a heated reaction off the crowd. The TNA fans hated this cowardly little arse-kisser who hid behind Magnus and EC3 while treating the power-crazed Dixie like she was royalty.

As Spud confidently predicted during his Power Slam interview, he was making his lack of size work for him.

After the Maximum Impact tour ended, Spud was at a loose end for a few days before he was due to return to America. We got talking on Facebook and I discovered that he was free on the date of the next PAID Promotions show. We struck a deal, I convinced Jamie to come up with the cash, and the next thing I knew, international television star Rockstar Spud was coming back to appear in Morecambe...one more time!

Tickets flew out as soon as Spud was announced. And on Sunday, February 16 2014, it was just like the old days. The Globe Arena was packed out. The atmosphere was electric. And despite playing a heel on TV, Spud received a hero's welcome as he power-walked to the ring like Peter Kay in the Amarillo pop video.

To show what kind of guy he is, Jay insisted that night on putting over one of our most promising trainees, an extremely bright young grappler from Edinburgh called Ryan Gordon. Known as 'The Edinburgh Elite' Ryan Grayson, the young Scot was getting over strongly playing the gimmick of a loudmouthed patriot - with Serenity as his valet. In almost an exact reversal of the match he had with Stevie Knight five years earlier, Spud battered Grayson for their entire five-minute bout, only for Ryan to cheat and beat the Chief of Staff right at the end. Then Jay went backstage, watched every other match on the monitor, and gave feedback to help the younger wrestlers improve their performances in future. What a pro.

The main event that night was meant to be the culmination of Johnny Phere's feud with Stixx. But Paul couldn't make it, for understandable reasons, because his wife had just given birth to a baby daughter. We racked our brains to decide on a replacement. And I saw the perfect opportunity to capitalise on a storyline we began, but abandoned unfinished, around 18 months earlier.

Instead of defending the PAID Championship against Stixx, Johnny Phere would have to face a blast from his past. None other than Joey Hayes!

Joey emerged at the start of the show as a big surprise. Some of the Morecambe fans weren't sure how to react. Even though his treacherous actions at XWA v GPW Vendetta were in the dim and distant past, our faithful supporters have long memories. I half-expected this, and I instructed Joey to use the microphone to explain his actions of 18 months earlier. Hayes was never the most comfortable at cutting promos but he did the job as required.

"Last time I was here in Morecambe, I did something I'm not proud of," said Joey.

"But I only did it because I can't stand Johnny Phere!"

The fans cheered. They couldn't stand Johnny Phere any more either. In one fell swoop, Joey was a babyface again. Because it's Real in Morecambe.

In typical heel fashion, Phere The Truth forced Joey to earn his title shot by putting him in an unscheduled match with Craig Kollins. But Hayes won. Then in that night's main event, Joey and Johnny had a memorable bout for the title, full of heat and drama. Phere dominated, but the courageous Joey kept on kicking out. I was getting more and more frustrated at ringside, and Phere was also losing his cool as the fans got more and more excited at the prospect of a title change.

Finally, JP set Joey up for a piledriver on a metal chain. But then Phere's younger brother Simon (who he'd renamed Triston) ran in and superkicked the champion. On a recent Fleetwood show, Johnny had attacked his brother, who is also a pro wrestler but had been inactive for many years before making his comeback for PAID. The superkick was Triston's receipt. The dazed Phere staggered from the kick, right into an instinctive JKO from Joey Hayes. My man landed badly, face-first into the metal chain, Joey collapsed on top of him, and referee Charles Nelson Riley counted one, two, three!

The Morecambe fans were on their feet, hugging each other, cheering the place down like we were back at The Dome. It was complete redemption for the Phere The Truth angle. A sold-out crowd was going absolutely bonkers in delight at our demise. After months of dominance from our dictatorship, the tables had been well and truly turned.

There was only one way to put an exclamation point on the end of the Phere The Truth reign of terror. As I tried to sneak away from ringside, I was confronted by Rockstar Spud. And he wasn't alone. Ricky J McKenzie, Dangerous Damon Leigh and Mr Big Shaun Vasey were with him. They were all previous victims of the Phere The Truth marker pen. We'd branded each one of them liars. It was only fitting as they joined Joey Hayes, dragged me into the ring, kicking and screaming, stripped off my shirt, and wrote LIAR on my back in the most appropriate revenge imaginable. The fans absolutely lapped it up! And there is an absolutely classic photo of Spud, Joey, Gradwell, DDL and Vasey, standing over my half-naked face-down body, as they mocked the fallen heel manager with gusto!

That night was the undisputed highlight of Johnny Phere's tenure in charge of PAID Promotions. We made a healthy profit and the feel good factor returned, at least temporarily. And in my opinion, the success of this show was mainly thanks to Spud sprinkling a little magic back into Morecambe.

Incidentally, Sanjay Bagga went ahead with his second Morecambe LDN show at The Platform six days later but again didn't draw particularly well. LDN hasn't promoted in Morecambe since. Going head-to-head with Bagga, running shows in the same town in the same week, Johnny Phere's PAID Promotions had won the turf war just as I hoped.

Not long afterwards, Bagga and I had a heated exchange on Facebook. He'd clashed with Dann again and this time I stuck up for my friend. Bagga didn't react well. Suffice to say, I don't speak to Sanjay any more.

Anyhow, back to more positive matters, namely Spud, who continued to appear on Impact Wrestling week-in, week-out in 2014, continuing as the toadying sidekick of the entitled Ethan Carter III and his good old Aunt D. As the mega-talented EC3 began an undefeated streak and a steady rise towards main event status, the pesky little Spud was at the side of the man he lovingly called his 'best friend', running interference, abusing his power and generally being a pain in the backside as he helped Ethan rack up the wins. The pair had terrific chemistry and were entertaining as hell. Spud even got to wrestle Kurt Angle on TV that April, although he got destroyed. Even so, my mate Spud was in the ring with Kurt Angle, yes, KURT ANGLE. His career was going from strength to strength.

The Dixie Carter reign of terror built to a big angle at the Hammerstein Ballroom in New York in August 2014. For weeks TNA's anti-hero Bully Ray had vowed to put the President through a table. Spud, clad in his most outrageous rainbow-coloured suit yet, was determined it would never happen. "SHE'S MY QUEEN!" he hilariously yelled, as he tried to protect his beloved Madam Dixie. But then out came a gang of TNA babyfaces. Spud fainted, and could do little to stop his boss and meal ticket from being power bombed through a table by the Bully in a memorable pay-off to the storyline.

Matters then took a twist as Ethan Carter blamed Spud for his aunt's demise. Over the autumn months, the fans began to warm to the Rockstar as the smug EC3 belittled him at every turn. The result was a classic feud, one of the best in TNA history. It worked because it was based on a simple premise everyone could understand. The little guy was bullied by a man he respected and ultimately had to fight back to preserve his own self-respect. And it was performed superbly by Spud and EC3, every step of the way. Their acting, their intensity, their commitment to each and every segment was so strong, they raised each other up a level. By the end of their episodic, beautifully-built five-month rivalry, both men had elevated their profiles considerably.

The story really kicked into gear on the October 1 2014 episode of Impact Wrestling, when smarmy Ethan told Spud that he had never really been his best friend and was a mere employee to him.

"My friends have trust funds and join yacht clubs, Spud you just don't fit in," grinned EC3 with the kind of smug face anyone would want to slap. But instead, it was Spud who got a slapping. The distraught Rockstar looked like a little boy lost as he was first rejected and then assaulted by the man he'd looked up to. This rallied the TNA fans right behind him for the first time.

The next week, Spud was forced to apologise to Carter for failing to save his Aunt D. This wasn't enough for the suited megalomaniac. Ethan took great delight in calling Spud a loser. But for the first time, the Chief of Staff stood up for himself.

"I'm not a loser, sir, I'm Rockstar Spud!" said the defiant little man, getting more and more fired up as the TNA fans began to get more and more behind him. Spud's bravery just amused the super-arrogant One Per Center, who pie-faced him, then slapped him over and over again, repeatedly mocking him, calling him a loser with the dismissive air of a playground bully. When the Rockstar could finally take the abuse no longer and cracked EC3 across the chops with a huge slap of his own, the Impact Zone became unglued. Firing up, Spud ripped off his bright purple jacket and got right in Ethan's face. So Carter fired him.

After this pair of tremendous angles, Spud turned fully-fledged babyface. He was soon reinstated, only not as the Chief of Staff any more, but as a full-time wrestler. Meanwhile, EC3 hired a new bodyguard, the hulking Tyrus, who was known as Brodus Clay during a recent WWE stint. But gone was the fun-loving dance machine that was WWE's Funkasaurus. Tyrus was near 400lbs of mohicaned bad attitude and a devastating heart punch that laid poor Spud out on many occasions as the plucky underdog tried his best to get revenge on EC3.

The two men continued to cut great promos on each other throughout November 2014. Now wearing an I'm with Spud T-shirt and badge - an image masterstroke to make TNA fans think they were part of Spud's club if they bought his merchandise - the Rockstar was gaining support week after week. Then on November 19, Carter dared the gutsy underdog to fight him, Spud indeed launched himself at EC3 with fists and feet, but ended up taking a right kicking from both Carter and Tyrus in a heated beatdown which left both the Rockstar and his silver-spooned nemesis bloody. Then the evil Ethan cut off part of Spud's hair to humiliate him still further. The feud had turned extremely personal. It was compelling to watch. I couldn't wait to tune in each week to see what happened next.

This was all building to Spud v EC3 in a climactic Hair v Hair Match. This happened, fittingly, at Wembley Arena as part of the 2015 TNA UK tour on January 31, and aired as the main event on TNA Impact on March 13.

Rockstar Spud. In the main event. On an international television show.

Spud got an incredible reaction from his countrymen as he emerged in an England tracksuit and Three Lions tights. Then he led Wembley in a blood-pumping rendition of our national anthem. It was a goosepimples moment.

The match was brilliant. Simply brilliant. I know Jay was really proud of it. He describes it as "the match I'll be most remembered for". A simple story, beautifully told, exquisitely executed.

Spud started fast, his face twisted in fury, taking the fight to the bigger Ethan, stunning him with fists and chops with a surprising assault. A top rope somersault plancha to the outside from The Ultimate Underdog had the undefeated EC3 reeling. But then Tyrus ran out and power bombed Spud on the concrete floor. This allowed the cocksure Carter to take over and dominate with a brutal beating. And the Rockstar began to bleed from his forehead. Badly. Blood is rarely spilled so graphically on TV wrestling in these PG days. It really added to the drama.

Thanks to his ally Mr Anderson coming out to neutralise Tyrus with his Mic Check finisher, Spud was able to stay alive despite a merciless pounding. As Carter poured on the punishment, the bloody Rockstar sold like a good 'un, reaching for help like Ricky Morton or Ricky Steamboat, those great babyfaces of the past, as if reaching out for support from the thousands upon thousands of his fellow Brits in the crowd. Their noise grew louder and reached fever pitch as Jeremy Borash, Spud's great friend who had also been bullied by Carter during the feud, ran into the ring and delivered a low blow to the tyrant...which Spud followed up with a Stunner for a heart-stopping near fall.

At this point, Josh Matthews and Taz were doing an awesome job on commentary, telling the story to perfection.

"Can the biggest underdog in the history of Impact Wrestling end the streak of EC3?" asked Josh, as Spud miraculously continued to fight back, despite Carter screaming at him to stay down.

"You've got to admire and respect the heart and determination of Rockstar Spud!"

The British fans were beside themselves with anticipation as Spud called on immense reserves to land a flurry of fists to Carter's jaw. His face the proverbial crimson mask, my little pal dropped Ethan with a Pele kick and then went for his new finishing move, a version of Brian Kendrick's Sliced Bread Number 2 he called The Underdog. But EC3 slipped out, turned around and walloped Spud across the forehead with the brace protecting his supposedly-injured forearm. Carter made the cover...and Spud still kicked out at two! EC3's face was a combination of shock and fear for his undefeated streak. He couldn't believe it.

The fans were on their feet as Spud desperately tried to stand on rubber legs. Maybe he could still pull off the supreme upset?

But then the performance of his life came to a sudden, crushing end. Our courageous hero was finally put down by Ethan's finisher The One Per Center for the one...two...three.

After the match, Carter cut an exceptional promo, in which the real-life Michael Hutter expressed his real-life feelings about James Michael Curtin.

"Without a shadow of a doubt, you have the most heart and determination I've ever seen in professional wrestling," said Carter to the bloodied, battered Brummie warrior.

"I've done some heinous things to you, but there was a time when we were best friends and I ruined that. Spud, in front of your home people, your mom and your dad, you proved you belong in Impact Wrestling. Hell, you proved that despite your size, your heart weighs more and there is a chance that one day, you could be a world champion!

"I'm not going to shave your head tonight. You don't deserve it. You proved you're a fighter, a lion, a tiger, a gazelle, and DAMN IT, YOU PROVED YOU'RE A MAN! I'll shake your hand right now."

Then they shook hands. And all seemed right with the world. Until EC3 decked Spud with a big right hand and shaved him bald in front of his home crowd. What a heel!

EC3 went on to become TNA World Champion later that year.

Well deserved, too.

As for Spud, later at the Wembley tapings he defeated Low Ki to lift the TNA X Division Title.

The Rockstar had made good on his British Boot Camp vow. He *did* become a champion in Impact Wrestling.

He held that title twice that year, before giving it up to fight Kurt Angle for the TNA World Title at Destination X in the summer of 2015. Although the Rockstar lost, he was infinitely more competitive than in his match with the Olympic Hero the year before. There were times, in fact, when the audience thought The Ultimate Underdog might spring the upset as he put on another stellar display before tapping to the vaunted ankle lock.

At the end, Kurt Angle, one of the greatest wrestlers of all-time, lifted Rockstar Spud's arm in the air in a show of respect. And Josh Matthews, on commentary, summed things up poetically.

"Rockstar Spud never thought he would be a professional wrestler at this level. Rockstar Spud never dreamed he would be in the ring with someone like Kurt Angle. And Rockstar Spud almost became world champion.

"How can you not believe in miracles? Dreams do come true."

So that's the story of how Rockstar Spud conquered America against all the odds. Little Jay Curtin, the banker from Brum, proved everybody wrong by becoming one of the hottest new young stars in professional wrestling anywhere in the world. First as the heel Chief of Staff, then as the babyface Ultimate Underdog, he excelled at every role he was given. And he achieved his goals, quite simply, by being a consummate performer and professional, by using his brain, and by having more passion and heart for pro wrestling than just about anybody I know.

He's a credit to Great Britain. I could not be happier for him.

CHAPTER 13

INSANE FIGHT CLUB

"For years, I wished that TV executives would take a chance on actually making a programme about the lives of modern-day British wrestlers, like the BBC did so successfully with Robbie Brookside's Video Diaries way back in 1993. We have so many talented characters with interesting life stories to tell, who are ready-made to come out of the shadows and become TV stars."
Greg Lambert, Holy Grail: The True Story of British Wrestling's Revival, November 2012

Eleven years after Video Diaries, BBC1 TV executives actually did take a chance on British wrestling...or more specifically, *Scottish* wrestling.

Insane Fight Club - the behind-the-scenes story of Insane Championship Wrestling - debuted on BBC1, Britain's most watched television channel, at 10.35pm on Tuesday, March 11 2014. And it was brilliant. As a piece of filmmaking, Insane Fight Club was an artistic triumph. It could not have been any better.

The strength of Insane Fight Club was that while its late-night slot, swearing, violence and blood made it firmly for over 18s, the programme had mass appeal. I know this, because I know many non-wrestling fans who watched it and loved it.

Insane Fight Club worked because there wasn't that much actual *wrestling* in it. Yes, there were a few clips from ICW shows, of weapons, wild brawls and blood, but they were used primarily to set the scene, to position ICW as modern-day, adults-only entertainment, an altogether darker beast than the Daddy and Haystacks 'glory days'. The director, double BAFTA-award winner Adrian McDowall, clearly recognised that wrestling fans would watch the programme anyway and so, to attract casual viewers, Insane Fight Club needed more depth. It needed to explore real-life issues like family, poverty, insecurity and aspiration. It needed to tap into thoughts, worries and emotions we all experience on a daily basis.

McDowall did this by introducing the viewer to three men - Mark Dallas, Grado and Jack Jester. But not by having them play their professional wrestling alter-egos, not by showing them cutting promos like you might see them do on a regular wrestling show, but by visiting their homes, meeting their families, uncovering their real-life hopes and dreams.

In short, Insane Fight Club did everything possible to hook the viewers' interest not just in Mark Dallas, the wrestling promoter, Grado, the clown prince of Scottish wrestling, and Jack Jester, the hardcore heavyweight, but in Mark Dallas, Graeme Stevely and Lee Greig as human beings.

Insane Fight Club also had inspirational messages for the youth of today. Namely, that it's good to be different, the underdog can prevail, and anything is achievable if you really put your mind to it.

"When I was at school I wanted to be a tattoo artist, a wrestler, and a clown...so far I've been able to do all three," said Jack Jester.

"Always be yourself, don't go with the flow and do whatever everybody else is doing."

It was admirable stuff.

Anyone who watched Insane Fight Club would have found something, or somebody, they could identify with. For me, it was Mark Dallas. As a former wrestling promoter who chased the Holy Grail with the FWA, I empathised completely with his lofty goals for Insane Championship Wrestling. I shared his joy and pride when he saw a long queue outside his venue, his excitement at coming up with a great idea for an angle, his delight when the fans cheered wildly at the culmination of a meticulously-planned main event match, his genuine admiration for his wrestlers and the physical pain they endure to help put food on his table, and his overall passion for his product and for professional wrestling as a whole.

Because I have been there. I have experienced those feelings.

Dallas had unconditional support from his family and all of his friends for his wrestling dream, support he was determined to repay. He repeatedly stated how he wanted a better life not only for his partner Helen and son Danny, but for his ICW wrestlers - his mates - who laid their bodies on the line for him on a monthly basis. He aimed to grow ICW to a level where the roster could earn a full-time living from professional wrestling.

The first step towards Dallas' own personal Holy Grail was to sell out their biggest ever show - Fear and Loathing at the 1,100-capacity Glasgow ABC on Sunday, October 13 2013.

"Can they reach a new audience and put their Insane Fight Club on the map?" asked the narrator, as Dallas was shown gazing around the gaping venue, wondering how on earth he was going to pack it out.

"Everything is riding on this, my rent, my wee'un's Christmas....1,100 tickets is no laughing matter," said Dallas.

As Dallas chased his goal, he came across superbly as a spokesman for British wrestling, as he explained eloquently the immense skill and extensive preparation that goes into what we love to do.

"It's a drama, a comedy, a soap opera, it's a performance art, it's a stunt show...it's theatre for a new generation," he said, his eyes dancing with enthusiasm.

As the cameras showed Dallas and Chris Renfrew poring over a script, and Mark talking openly about how Jack Jester was going to win the ICW Title at a show which hadn't even happened yet, there were no attempts to 'keep kayfabe' or portray wrestling as anything other than pre-determined entertainment.

There was also defiance towards those who scoff at pro wrestling and call it fake.

"I think a lot of people are afraid of things they don't understand," he said.

"In life, a lot of people think you're meant to get a 9 to 5 and a house and a mortgage and you're not meant to do things you want to do. But you can. A lot of people don't have the courage to pursue those career paths."

Alex Shane, who has been saying much the same thing for years, would surely have approved.

The canny Dallas also displayed a flair for marketing which put other grapple promoters to shame. His razor-sharp mind came up with some genius out-of-the-box ideas to promote ICW - such as risking arrest by putting a traffic cone emblazoned with the ICW logo on the head of Glasgow's Duke of Wellington statue, and by organising a flash mob pillow fight between Davey Blaze and Wolfgang in George's Square.

But Mark also showed his sensitive and vulnerable side, laying bare the rawest, most personal of feelings about his son Danny.

He explained that when he first discovered that Danny was autistic, he shut himself off, didn't talk to anyone, bottled it up inside and hit the booze hard. He eventually realised that Danny would be able to live a normal life, and was able to comfort his son when he himself struggled to cope with his condition, and didn't want to go to nursery because he felt different to the other kids.

"I walked into another room, put on an ICW video, and put Danny on my knee," explained Mark, his eyes filling up at the memory.

"I said, 'Look, your Daddy is different. You don't want to be the same as everyone else. Because that's boring'."

Christ, I felt for him. And when Insane Fight Club ended with ICW indeed selling out the Glasgow ABC, with Jester winning the ICW Title and breaking down in tears as his proud dad watched from the audience, and with Dallas feeling vindicated after all the hours of thought, worry and preparation came off big-style, I again felt exactly what I was supposed to feel. Sheer delight for Mark Dallas. The ICW promoter had achieved his mini-goal and Insane Fight Club had well and truly hit the mark in its aim to show the triumph of the human spirit against adversity.

"This has lit a fire under me even more," said Dallas, summing up.

"Maybe this *can* work? Maybe we *can* make a full-time living off this business. The only way we can do that is branch out. New cities. Bigger, badder, better...see how far we can go with it.

"Shoot for the moon and if you miss, you're still amongst the stars. That's what we'll do and if we miss...f__k it."

Then Insane Fight Club ended as Moving On Up by Primal Scream played over the credits.

The programme drew 1.05m viewers, 10.9% of that evening's

overall TV audience, which was a pretty fair result for such a niche piece of programming. And the UK wrestling community went wild for it. Social media went into overdrive with plaudits and virtual backslapping for Dallas and his team. Far from being envious of ICW's success, British wrestlers and promoters recognised Insane Fight Club for what it was - a fantastic showcase of what we do - and shared proudly in ICW's moment in the sun.

The irony for ICW, who had positioned themselves as the ultimate outsiders, was that the national exposure generated by Insane Fight Club gave them a foot into the door of mainstream culture. National newspapers - and not just the trashy tabloids, but the thinking man's broadsheets - reviewed the programme.

The Daily Telegraph gave it four out of five stars, saying it "grabbed you in a headlock and didn't let go until you stumbled off the sofa an hour later", while the Guardian called it "hugely entertaining, with real moments of pathos, as ICW founder Mark Dallas risks bankruptcy to chase his boyhood dream". The Metro was less glowing, saying it "talked up a good fight but didn't deliver the killer punch".

But the media and viewers were united in agreement over one thing. The star of the show was Grado.

From the moment Insane Fight Club began with Grado re-enacting his ring entrance to Like A Prayer in his bedroom, it was clear this documentary would be the making of him. Not just in wrestling but outside wrestling, as a UK wrestler known to the average man in the street. Grado just had that crossover appeal in abundance.

As the narrator told the story of how his online videos transformed him from ultimate fan to super popular wrestler, Grado laid his insecurities bare for the camera, talking openly about his battles with his weight, worrying that he'd dyed his hair blond but wanted it brown again for an upcoming show in London. But he always managed to turn everything into comedy, as he ended up dialling 118 to ask for advice on hair dye, before eventually arriving at celebrity hairdresser Nicky Clarke's salon in London, dressed in full wrestling gear, where he told a bemused stylist "I normally get my hair cut in Cheryl's in Stevenston, next to Fisher Fine Foods in

New Street, have you heard of it?" then managed to convince Nicky himself to say "It's yersel!" He turned up at Edinburgh Airport to collect his friend and upcoming opponent Colt Cabana, bellowing "COLT CABANA! IT'S YERSEL!" through a megaphone in the arrival lounge, having sprayed 'WELCOME COLT!' in silly string all over his car. Meanwhile his long-suffering mum scolded him for getting hit with a steel chair during a recent match. "There was blood everywhere...I was raging!" said Maureen Stevely, whose love for her son was obvious behind the scolding.

As a piece of television to establish exactly who Grado is and why we should all fall in love with him, it was just about perfect. And after Insane Fight Club aired, Grado was in high demand, and not just for wrestling bookings. He was in The Daily Mirror, The Daily Record and The Scottish Sun. He gained acting roles on BBC Scotland police drama series River City and sitcom Scot Squad. He was invited to the Great Scots Awards where he rubbed shoulders with celebrities like Sharleen Spiteri from pop band Texas and impressionist Rory Bremner. He even made friends with Pop Idol winner Michelle McManus, who turned up at an ICW show and sang Like A Prayer live as he danced to the ring.

Thanks to Insane Fight Club, Grado became a household name in Scotland and was en route to becoming the most famous UK-based wrestler we've had in years. Further TV shows, maybe a commercial or two were surely on the horizon for the pride of Stevenston. All he needed was a stint in panto. Then he'd really cross over into the mainstream.

A few weeks after Insane Fight Club, on Sunday April 27 2014, I took the train up to Glasgow with Dann Read. As part of his stag weekend, Dann, his mate James 'Yully' Yull and myself had decided to go to see ICW Show Me Your Lizard at The Garage. This was also the day when Steven Gerrard had his infamous slip against Chelsea which ultimately cost Liverpool FC a chance to win their first Premiership title in 24 years. But the Reds' 2-0 defeat was not the only disappointment that day. Grado was on holiday so wasn't at the show. Seriously, I was gutted. I really wanted to see the cheeky chappie perform again in Glasgow so I could get to sing along drunkenly to Like A Prayer.

And I don't care if you think I'm a 'mark' for saying that. It's a ridiculous term and anyone who uses it as an insult needs to take a long hard look at themselves. I was a wrestling fan before I got involved in the business and I am still a wrestling fan today. And I am damned proud of it.

Anyhow, off my soapbox and back to Show Me Your Lizard, where I noticed that one or two things weren't too different to my last visit to The Garage 13 months earlier. The Bucky Boys, with Davey Blaze fresh off following Marty Scurll onto the dating show Take Me Out, were still as popular as ever. Reigning ICW Champion Jack Jester (who came to the ring holding a huge green lizard, hence the show name) was getting his usual great reaction. But there had also been quite a few changes on the ICW landscape. Fight Club - the long standing team of Kid Fite and Liam Thomson - were on the verge of splitting up for a feud. Red Lightning was no longer leader of the Save Pro Wrestling Movement and was instead now the self-styled 'People's W__ker- still a conniving cheat but one who directed his machinations at the ICW heels, making him a babyface by default. His former stablemate Joe Coffey was also hearing cheers, after reinventing himself as the 'ICW Iron Man' who specialised in long, hard hitting 30-minute bouts. And taking the Save Pro Wrestling Movement's place as ICW's top evil gang was the New Age Kliq (or NAK for short) headed by the amoral Chris Renfrew, who was now aligned with James 'Darkside' Scott, Dickie Divers and even his former enemy BT Gunn, despite trying to gouge his eyes out with scissors last time I saw him.

I also got to see a newcomer to ICW. Someone who'd grabbed my attention a few months earlier, like Grado, with a YouTube video.

Joe Hendry, Local Hero.

On Christmas Day 2013, I was perusing social media when I stumbled across a link called 'the new and improved ICW theme song'. Intrigued, I clicked the URL and ended up watching what is, in my opinion, the single greatest introductory vignette for a new British wrestler I have ever seen.

"Joe Hendry presents I C Double Me and You...financed and paid in full by James R Kennedy."

Filmed on location in Edinburgh, with fake snow falling across the screen just in case we weren't aware it was Christmas, I C Double Me And You was a parody music video of a song written and performed by Scottish wrestler and real-life musician Joe Hendry, and his band Lost In Audio. This cheesy ballad was basically an easy listening rip-off of the heavy metal track used by ICW as its theme song, with lyrics designed to introduce Joe Hendry - nicknamed The Local Hero - and establish him as the company's hot new heel.

"Joe Hendry makes things better...but there's still so much to do
"Joe Hendry makes things better...for I C Double Me and You!"

As Hendry began to sing, while standing on a hill overlooking his home of Edinburgh and wearing a suave suit, flanked by his manager and agent James R Kennedy, it immediately became obvious to me that the kid had something incredibly special. Not only was he a great singer and had a wrestler's physique, but his confidence, verbal delivery, presence, facial expressions and mannerisms were better than most British wrestlers who'd been doing the job for a decade. He also had fabulous smarmy smugness. This was a guy who believed he was a somebody. And when you believe you're a somebody, then quite often, you soon actually *become* a somebody.

"I'm going to take both of the titles...the Heavyweight and the Zero-G
"Because I know your lives are all boring...but you can live your goals through me!
"'Cos baby I'm the star of the heavyweight division
"I'm gonna take out all of the swear words and violence 'cos I can get us back on television!"

It was funny, original and most of all, brilliant. Especially when, on a couple of occasions during the video, he sang his own name.

"JOE HENDRY! LOCAL HERO!"

Anyone with the self-absorbed gumption to sing their own name, had to be a heel star in the making.

I loved the video. I watched it over and over again. I found myself walking around the house on Christmas Day singing "JOE HENDRY!" which irritated my wife no end. And I began to tweet, share and promote Joe's video through as many outlets as I could, even mentioning the rookie in my regular Home Front British wrestling news round-up in Power Slam.

After doing some research into the brash Local Hero, I discovered Joe Hendry had only been training as a wrestler at the SWA Source Wrestling School in Glasgow for less than a year - which made his outstanding performance in the video even more astonishing. He'd only made his in-ring debut in October 2013, for crying out loud, and debuted for ICW just a few weeks later at Fear and Lothian in Edinburgh on November 3, where he cut an obnoxious promo lecturing the fans for their liberal use of the F word, before being battered by his real-life trainer, the 23 stone 'Beast of Belfast' Damian O'Connor. The ICW faithful booed Hendry out of the building and roared with approval when Big Damo splattered the loudmouthed upstart.

Undeterred, the deluded Hendry put out another YouTube promo - this time while sitting in a conservatory wearing a fantastically uncool wooly cardigan - where he forgave the fans for their insolence and promised to return to ICW. Then he appeared again at ICW 100% Shenanigans on December 1, this time at The Garage, for An Evening With Joe Hendry, where he gave a super-conceited live performance of I C Double Me and You while sitting in the middle of the ring playing acoustic guitar. Again, Big Damo interrupted and destroyed The Local Hero. Again, the fans lapped it up. Again, Joe Hendry had been put in a major ICW angle and done unbelievably well for someone with such little experience.

Conventional wrestling wisdom says that trainee wrestlers should learn their craft for two to three years minimum before being let loose anywhere near a paying audience, and then they are usually broken in slowly and carefully. But Mark Dallas, as you have probably realised, wipes his backside with conventional wisdom. He believed in Joe Hendry. He knew he was capable of delivering on the big stage. So he gave him a chance and The Local Hero seized it with both hands.

Hendry was doing so well, that when legendary American wrestling manager Jim Cornette visited Glasgow in February 2014 as part of a national tour put together by Alex Shane and Wrestle Talk TV, Dallas pitted his new prodigy against The Louisville Lip, as well as Grado and Wolfgang, in a burger eating contest at a local restaurant as one of his typically inspirational promotional stunts.

Now Cornette, Wolfgang and especially Grado - as we know - are well known for their large appetites. But guess who won? You've guessed it. Cornette gave up, Wolfgang couldn't finish, and Grado was sick. The last man standing was Joe Hendry.

So there seemed no end to Joe Hendry's talents. The guy could sing, play guitar, cut a fantastic promo, and eat monster burgers until the cows came home. Turns out he was a skilled national level amateur wrestler and a first dan in judo too. As a pro wrestler, though, he was still green. At Show Me Your Lizard, Hendry teamed with the high-flying Kenny Williams against the brutal Dutch duo of Michael Dante and future NXT star Tommy End - the Sumerian Death Squad. It was clear from the match that Joe was not yet quite as polished as a wrestler as he was on the microphone. But it didn't matter, because the guy was still super-over with the ICW crowd. As soon as his theme music hit, the fans began singing along, just like they did for Grado. They waved their arms in the air in time to the music and gave Hendry a...well...Local Hero's welcome. Six months after debuting, Joe's act had been so entertaining that he was already in the process of turning face. This was fast-track development, and then some.

After the show, I went backstage and shook Joe's hand. Classily, Hendry thanked me for all the kind words I said about him online, saying "You're the first person in England who has really touted me." He told me it was his burning ambition to make it to the WWE. I looked in his eyes and saw fiery determination, and believed he could achieve his aim.

I believed even more when I saw him a few weeks later in Preston at a PCW training camp and realised that, unlike many other young wrestlers who get a whiff of success early in their careers, he didn't believe it was beneath him to travel the country to training schools, continuing to learn and develop. He also ventured down from Scotland to work out at Robbie Brookside's school in Leicester. That showed dedication and also intelligence, because as Brookside is now a trainer of hopefuls at the WWE Performance Centre in Orlando, Florida, the veteran Scouser is exactly the kind of guy Joe Hendry should have been trying to impress.

Just a few months later, on November 10 2014, Joe Hendry stood in the ring on WWE Monday Night RAW, live from the Echo Arena in Liverpool, alongside WWE superstars Rusev and Lana, playing the role of Rusev's Russian spokesman. He was even allowed to cut a promo, and did so, with typical confidence, clarity and even a flawless Russian accent. This was 13 months after his professional wrestling debut, and was actually Hendry's second appearance as a WWE 'extra' that year, as he'd already appeared as one of Adam Rose's entourage The Rosebuds on Smackdown in May.

I am not aware of anyone in British wrestling who has achieved as much in as short a period of time as Joe Hendry. By 2016 he had become one of ICW's biggest stars, broke out to make appearances for numerous English wrestling companies including PCW and Alpha Omega in Morecambe (where I actually managed him for a match against Stixx), was getting better in the ring all the time, developed his already impressive promo skills to become one of the best talkers on the UK circuit and debuted for Ring of Honor. This driven, articulate and extremely talented young man has everything required to be a real player in the wrestling business - the build, the exceptional speaking skills, an understanding of how to market himself, and the right attitude.

Show Me Your Lizard was another sell-out at The Garage for ICW and afterwards, Dann and myself were made typically welcome by Dallas and the ICW roster for after-show drinks. And some of those boys and girls can't half drink! I awoke the following morning in a Glasgow hotel room with an extremely sore head vowing 'never again', as you do.

One week later on May 4 2014, ICW ran its first show in England, at the 800-capacity O2 Academy in Islington, London. There were plenty of question marks about whether the overtly Scottish nature of the ICW product would translate quite as well to English audiences and whether ICW could pull the same level of crowds on the other side of Hadrian's Wall. ICW provided the answers that night. The venue was as packed and rowdy as The Garage, the ICW regulars like Grado, Jack Jester and The Bucky Boys were treated like touring rock stars and the only thing that seemed to have changed was the accent in the chants of "HERE WE...HERE WE...HERE WE FACKING GO!"

The timing of ICW's breakout into England was perfect. Insane Fight Club was still fresh in people's minds and clearly the programme had raised awareness of ICW enough to make a full tour of English cities a viable proposition for Dallas and his team. So after a successful return to the Islington venue on July 13 2014, they announced a Magical Mystery Tour of O2 Academy venues in October 2014, starting in Newcastle on October 5, then Liverpool on October 11, Leeds on October 12 and Birmingham on October 19.

Viewers got an intimate behind-the-scenes look at ICW's first ever UK tour when Insane Fight Club 2 (This Time It's Personal) hit the TV screens in 2015. The sequel to Insane Fight Club aired on BBC1 Scotland on January 21 2015, before premiering on BBC3 in June 2015. This was a slight downgrade from the nationwide BBC1 coverage of Insane Fight Club and meant the TV ratings wouldn't be as high as for the original. But as BBC1 Scotland and BBC3 are available on many digital and satellite platforms throughout the UK, the audience reach of Insane Fight Club 2 was still significant. It was also impressive that the narrator for Insane Fight Club 2 was renowned Scottish actress Ashley Jensen, famed for her role alongside Ricky Gervais in the hit comedy Extras. This gave ICW another rub of mainstream credibility.

The storyline hook for Insane Fight Club 2 was whether ICW could branch out successfully into England and then sell out the iconic 1,600 capacity Barrowlands Ballroom in Glasgow for Fear and Loathing VII on November 2 2014.

"We're reaching a point where we can't get much bigger in Glasgow...we announce a show, it sells out," explained Dallas.

But at first, tickets for the UK tour weren't shifting.

"Everything hinges on this tour," said a worried Dallas.

"If this tour screws up, there ain't gonna be any more tours."

So the cameras followed Dallas, Grado and Jester as they piled into a camper van, stocked with copious amounts of canned lager, and set off around the country to spread the news that ICW was coming to a city near you, pulling their trademark wacky promotional stunts along the way. They put the ICW traffic cone on the famous bull statue outside the Bull Ring shopping centre in Birmingham city centre in the dead of night. In Liverpool, they joined forces with former Brookside actor and pop culture icon Dean Sullivan, aka Jimmy Corkhill, and in Newcastle, recruited members of the cast of reality show Geordie Shore to boost their marketing onslaught and grab attention from locals.

Street buskers were brought in to play Like A Prayer as Grado danced around in Leeds city centre, barking "IT'S YERSEL!" through a megaphone to turn heads of passers-by. Best of all, they drafted in Chris Toal, a dwarf wrestling personality who makes regular appearances on ICW shows. In a hilarious stunt, Jack Jester was shown pushing a baby's pram around a packed Leeds city centre when out of the pram jumped the tiny bald-headed Toal, who began giving out flyers to startled shoppers.

Of course, the UK tour ended up being a smash hit with 2,000 tickets sold for four shows. The highlight came at Liverpool when ICW's new mate Dean Sullivan actually came down to the ring and knocked out the hated Jackie Polo with one punch, as the fans serenaded him with chants of "JIMMY F___KING CORKHILL! JIMMY F___KING CORKHILL! NA NA NA NA, HEY!"

Insane Fight Club 2 continued in the same vein as the original and followed many of the same themes. It updated the audience on Grado's comedic battle with his weight, as he resorted to a gastric band and even hypnosis to control his chronic urges to overeat, telling the hypnotist what he ate in an average day ("Two rolls of bacon, mince, pasta, tomato soup, a Cumberland fish pie from Marks and Spencers which serves four, a packet of Sport Mixtures, Nibbles, packet of Minstrels, crisps, a chocolate orange and two slices of bread with mayo..."). It also expanded on Dallas' desire for a better life for his family.

And it also introduced the viewers to a new 'cast member', Drew Galloway.

Drew is someone whose career I have monitored very closely for the past decade, as the Ayr native actually received some of his early training as a teenager at the FWA Academy in Portsmouth run by my old FWA cohort Mark Sloan. By his early 20s, Drew's 6ft 5in height, well-proportioned physique, long hair and heartthrob good looks helped him stand out from the crowd on the UK scene. As 'Thee' Drew Galloway, he was thee top star in Scotland, becoming the first ever ICW Champion in 2006. I also got to work with him on a few occasions, including when he visited FutureShock Wrestling in Stockport in 2005 with his diminutive bald-headed companion Graham McKay - aka Charles Boddington, one of the best wrestling managers Britain has produced. Drew and I have always got on really well and I have a lot of time for him. I always found him friendly, humble and eager to learn - a true professional. It was clear he had all the attributes to go far.

And go far, he did. In 2007, Drew signed for World Wrestling Entertainment and enjoyed a rapid rise to the top as Drew McIntyre, The Sinister Scotsman. WWE chairman Vince McMahon, in a famous promo on the TV show SmackDown in September 2009, even referred to Drew as a "future World Champion". After such backing from the most powerful man in wrestling, Drew was christened The Chosen One and on December 13 of that year, he captured the Intercontinental Title from John Morrison at the WWE pay-per-view Tables Ladders and Chairs in San Antonio, Texas. It was a watershed night for Britain and Ireland because at the very same show, Sheamus defeated John Cena to become the first Irishman ever to win the WWE World Heavyweight Championship.

Drew and Sheamus had been contemporaries learning their trade on the UK scene just two years before. Now they simultaneously held two of the biggest titles in the world. It was a ringing endorsement for the modern-day British wrestling circuit that it was capable of producing the Heavyweight and Intercontinental Champion for the world's largest wrestling company.

But perhaps it was a case of too much too soon for Drew, who was still only 24 years old when he became I-C Champ. Or maybe The Chosen One tag weighed too heavily around his neck. But for whatever reason, Drew struggled to show his personality playing a cold, calculating and measured villain, and the character didn't seem to click with the WWE audience. The Scotsman lost the championship in May 2010 and over the next few years, he suffered a gradual spiral down the WWE pecking order. He ended up in a trio with fellow strugglers Heath Slater and Jinder Mahal - the Three Man Band. 3MB was an entertaining act with a cult following but it was strictly lower card comedy and never really went anywhere.

Then on June 12 2014, Drew was released from his WWE contract. WWE had no future plans for him. Galloway hadn't become the World Champion and hadn't lived up to the lofty touting of Vincent Kennedy McMahon. It had to be a gutting experience for him.

But Drew Galloway's WWE rejection lit a fire under him. He returned to Britain with something to prove.

On July 27 2014, during the closing moments of ICW Shug's Hoose Party at Glasgow ABC, Jack Jester had just defended the ICW Title against Martin Stone, when he was attacked and beaten down by Darkside, Dickie Divers and BT Gunn from the NAK. Their assault was a set-up so the New Age Kliq's leader, the manipulative Chris Renfrew, could attempt to cash in a guaranteed title shot he'd earned by winning ICW's annual Square Go rumble earlier in the year. But then the lights went out, and when they came back on, a hooded figure was standing in the ring to confront the NAK. The interloper removed his hood to reveal a bearded Drew Galloway. The ICW fans lost their minds in delight. The prodigal son, the first ever ICW Champion, the Scotsman who had made it big in America but then lost it all, was back home and determined to make an impact.

His eyes burning with intensity, Drew took out the NAK single-handedly in explosive fashion and stood alone in the centre of the ring as the ICW crazies serenaded him with fervent chants of "I-C-DUB!" and "WELCOME HOME!" Jester then grabbed Drew in a tight embrace of gratitude and the two men lifted each other's arms in the air in celebration of Galloway's homecoming. That seemed to be the end of it - a standard wrestling angle where the returning hero saves the good guy champion from the heel gang. But then as the smiling Galloway and Jester prepared to leave, and turned from the entranceway stage one last time to soak up the cheers of the crowd, Drew's expression of joy changed to one of bitter recrimination. He glared at Jester, who returned his glance with a frown of confusion. The next second, Galloway booted Jack in the face and knocked him out!

Drew then seized the microphone and cut one of the greatest promos I have ever heard in a British venue. It was a dynamic, reality-based and unshackled speech, typical of the life-affirming freedom of the ICW environment, in which he vented the frustrations of the previous few years in WWE and described himself as the best wrestler in the world and ICW as the best promotion the world, the hot ticket, the place to be. And it was a complete revelation coming from a man who'd never shown, or perhaps been *allowed* to show, the ability to cut a 'money promo' during his time in the stringent WWE, where a team of scriptwriters provided him with his lines each week for soulless, dead-eyed, blandly-delivered monologues - light years away from the ferociously fierce rallying cry he was about to deliver.

"My name is Drew Galloway, I'm the former British Champion, the former Irish Champion, the former WWE Tag Team Champion, the former WWE Intercontinental Champion, I was the first Insane Championship Wrestling champion...and HELL, I'm from SCOTLAND!" roared the prodigal son.

Then, mid-promo, Drew stomped on the fallen Jack Jester, while imploring him stay down as the ICW Champion tried to struggle upright.

"Please...I don't want to have to do this!" he pleaded, then picked up his groggy ally and body slammed him off the stage through a table to a Neanderthal bellow of approval from the ICW faithful who realised something incredible was unfolding.

Then, his face etched with a mixture of regret and ferocity, the returning anti-hero walked with purpose back to the ring and climbed back in, all the time calmly continuing his impassioned speech.

"All I've ever wanted to do is be a professional wrestler, I wanted to entertain the fans, give my family and friends something to be proud of, give Scotland something to be proud of. But I was at a crossroads in my life recently, I looked in the mirror once I stopped with WWE and I asked myself, do you want to do this anymore? You've been doing this 13 years, you had a good seven-year run with WWE, maybe you should give it up? You're 29 years old, you've got years left, you could get a regular job, live the regular life for the first time in your life.

"Then one morning I woke up and I looked in the mirror and I reared back and I bitch-slapped myself right in the face! And I said 'Screw you, Drew! Not only are you going to keep going, you're going to become the biggest and best wrestler on this planet!' I don't need the WWE Machine behind me, I'm going to come home to the craziest people, you crazy b__tards!

"Let's talk about what's 'best for business'. What makes a professional wrestler? How tall they are, how they look, their body, their in-ring work, their talking ability on the microphone, charisma, yes, all these things make a marketable character and that's what you need to be a real superstar. Once upon a time, Vince McMahon, the most ruthless man in the world, named me The Chosen One for a reason. Trust me, I'm bringing those attributes here. What's best for business? When used to the best of my ability, I AM THE F__KING BUSINESS!

"So let the business cash you a reality check. Let's talk about what I just did tonight. I took out the NAK, the bad guys, I sent them packing. I also took out one of my best friends Jack Jester. When I was in America rising the ranks of the WWE, he was here rising the ranks of Scotland, and I'm not sorry whatsoever. I want what he's got, I need what he's got, when I get my hands on the ICW Title, I can take ICW to the next level.

"I'm not a good guy, I'm not a bad guy, Drew Galloway is an entity and if I'm willing to do that to one of my best friends, what the hell will I do to everybody else? I see people texting, I hope they're videoing and tweeting. You're part of a moment. This is a moment for professional wrestling. Not just Scotland. This is going to go across the world and I want you tell everybody, tell someone in the street, tell your sister, tell them to tell their dog, their cat and their cousin, I don't care, put it out there! Right now, we're making a stand for professional wrestling! It doesn't have to be The Machine! You started a movement and I plan to get it to the next level! I'm Drew Galloway! Tell them I'm coming! Tell them ICW's coming and tell them hell is coming with us!

"World, look into my eyes! When you see me on a show and when you see these fans, you're seeing the best in the damned world. This is ICW and you're going to know our name!"

In just a few minutes of verbal perfection, Drew Galloway positioned himself as the saviour who would lead ICW to the promised land. It was spine-tingling stuff. And his words struck deep into my heart and psyche, because they felt so familiar and real.

Although Galloway's speech was watched by thousands on ICW Worldwide on YouTube, when Drew said "I will get us back on television" his aim was for ICW to have a weekly, episodic wrestling show on a prominent TV channel, a British equivalent of WWE Raw or TNA Impact, with matches, promos and week-to-week storylines. In other words, Drew Galloway verbally encapsulated the struggle, the fight, the campaign, the desire for British wrestling to once again have a slot in the consciousness of mainstream culture, the dream myself and so many others have been working towards for so long.

The Holy Grail, people! The Holy Grail!

Of course ICW already had TV, in a manner of speaking, thanks to the second one-off documentary that was Insane Fight Club 2, during which the relationship between Andrew Galloway and Lee Greig, the man behind the Jack Jester persona, took centre-stage. The two of them came up the ranks in Scotland at the same time, had been close friends for years, training partners, been there for each other through good times and bad. Jester had even comforted his pal after Drew's mum died in 2013 while he was in America, and the-then WWE superstar was wracked with feelings of remorse that he hadn't been home in Scotland for her final hours.

Now, the two comrades were going to headline the Barrowlands against each other - Drew Galloway v Jack Jester for the ICW Title at Fear and Loathing - in a battle for more than just the championship.

Galloway v Jester was also a fight to determine the ICW figurehead for the future, a fight both men passionately believed in. It was an emotional match for both - Jester because he'd bled bucketfuls for the ICW cause during a year as champion and felt he deserved to remain on top, especially ahead of a guy who had just waltzed back into the country after being away for years. Meanwhile, Galloway had a sense not of entitlement, but of righteous belief he was the best. He returned from America rejuvenated, saw how much the little company he left behind had grown with Jester leading the way and believed he was the man with the experience, talent and name value to propel ICW to even greater heights - even if it meant taking down his best friend to do it.

The best wrestling storylines are the ones based on real life and personal issues draw money, remember? And Galloway v Jester was as real and as personal as it could get.

The build-up to the November 2014 showdown was phenomenally intense, showing how thin the line between love and hate can be, and Galloway-Jester became 2014's UK feud of the year as a result. Back at The Garage at ICW 1.21 Gigawatts on August 31 2014, Drew became number one contender after beating Darkside and was then confronted by Jester. Infuriated when Drew informed him "you're not the guy" to take ICW forward, the champion became unhinged, flattened his friend with the title belt, tied him to the corner turnbuckles with a rope around his neck, then set his trademark corkscrew alight and began to douse Galloway with petrol. The demented Jester stopped short of turning Galloway into a human barbecue, instead allowing his actions to serve as a threat about how far he was prepared to go to keep the ICW Title. As Drew untied himself, he was apoplectic with rage.

Three days later, the rivals brawled violently after Jester gatecrashed a Q&A session with Galloway at a Glasgow bar, with Drew going as far as to attack Jack with a glass bottle and threaten: "I'LL F__KING KILL YOU!" Then in October, Galloway did a sit-down interview with Billy Kirkwood where he said he'd told his own family not to come to Fear and Loathing, and warned Jester to "kiss his little nephew goodbye".

The build-up was as close to the bone as it could possibly get. But in terms of shifting tickets, as a method of turning Galloway v Jester into a must-see grudge match, it could not have been better. The Barrowlands sold out. 1,600 tickets. Galloway v Jester was a bloody classic. with both men pulling out all the stops. Jester elbow dropped Drew through a table. Galloway tried to gouge off Jack's face with a barbed wire baseball bat. Jester retaliated by smashing a chair into Drew's skull before planting him with a tombstone piledriver. Finally, an epic war ended when Galloway struck with his finishing move, the FutureShock double-arm DDT, for a second time. Jack Jester's title reign was over. The two men hugged. Drew Galloway was still The Chosen One. Jack Jester still had his self-respect. And the pair emerged from the most gruelling of battles, still best friends. What a story.

Insane Fight Club 2 told this story perfectly. And it ended with a triumphant Mark Dallas vowing that ICW would continue to move mountains.

"We will sell out the f__king world," said the Insane alchemist.

"That's how good we can be. We'll either capsize or sail off into the sunset but either way, it's going to be one hell of a f__king journey."

The journey continued throughout 2015, with Galloway becoming a dominant ICW Champion who battled all-comers all over the British Isles. Drew even defended the title in other parts of Europe and America, where he still lives, meaning the belt was rechristened the ICW World Heavyweight Championship. With Drew defending his belt in exciting bouts as company figurehead, ICW continued to build its fan base by touring all over Scotland and England in 2015 with shows in Sheffield, Nottingham, Newcastle, Dundee, Southampton, Norwich, Liverpool, Manchester, Birmingham, four nights as part of the world famous Edinburgh Fringe Festival in August 2015 and a night at the KOKO nightclub in Camden - one of the most high-profile live music venues in London.

Then came ICW's biggest event to date at one of the most famous entertainment venues in Scotland - Fear and Loathing at the Scottish Exhibition and Conference Centre on November 15 2015 - with the two biggest stars in the country on the marquee as Drew Galloway defended the championship against Grado. On that night, Drew Galloway really *did* take ICW to the next level.

The Insane train showed no signs of derailing. ICW became the UK's only 'cool' nationally touring wrestling promotion that catered solely to adults. And they did it by using hardly any overseas talent.

Sure, there was the odd appearance by the likes of Colt Cabana, Sabu and Rhyno, and the Hardcore Legend himself Mick Foley was guest commissioner for the night at the SECC. But British wrestlers were front and centre of the ICW revolution - Scots like Galloway, Grado and Jester, but also some of England's top grapplers like Danny Hope, Sha Samuels and Martin Kirby became ICW regulars as the company expanded. British wrestlers were the marketable stars of the show, the reason why the fans paid their money to see ICW, and it was fantastic to see.

But the ICW, and indeed the Scottish wrestling revolution wasn't just confined to these shores. America also grabbed a taste of exactly what the new dynamic generation of Scots can do.

More on that later.

CHAPTER 14

MY MATCH

I have said it many times during my wrestling career. I am a writer, not a fighter.
When I was a kid, creative writing was my passion. From the age of four, I was producing my own little books at home. In primary school, it was always my stories being read out in class. This may have been when years of bullying started. The school swot, they called me. And I dealt with it badly.
My mum is from Liverpool, my granny was Irish, my great granny was a Scot, and I have always felt the potent blend of Scouse and Celtic blood created an emotional powderkeg inside me. So I was a crier. When schoolkids called me names, or punched me on the arm, or gave me a wedgie in PE, the tears always came. The more I sobbed, the worse it got. I was bullied mercilessly throughout primary and secondary school, and at university, because I couldn't take abuse, or even teasing banter, on the chin.
Too sensitive. Not a thick enough skin. Not hard enough.
My head of sixth form told me as much during my careers interview in 1990. I told him my dream job and he replied with six words that part-haunted and part-drove me in future years.
"You will never make a journalist."
Hmmm. He messed up there, didn't he?
But he was right in one respect. I *was* soft. I love wrestling and I am a massive boxing fan. I have always been attracted to combat sports. But when it comes to actually having a fight myself, I would rather hide in the toilets.
So why on earth did I decide to have a professional wrestling match?
As a wrestling manager, Greg 'The Truth' Lambert is a gutless sneak. He cheats, manipulates and acts like a demigod. But he can't

fight. He *definitely* can't fight. That's why he hires the best pro wrestlers in the world to make him money, by doing the fighting for him. That's why he runs from their opponents after interfering in their matches. That's why he gallops around ringside in fear with legs long and gangly like John Cleese goose-stepping around Fawlty Towers. He doesn't want to get hit. And he definitely doesn't want to get Ram Slammed, Stixx Bombed or JKOd. Simply put, just like Shaggy and Scooby Doo, The Truth is a card-carrying member of The Cowards Association.

So why on earth did I decide to have a wrestling match?

At school, despite my love of sport, I was terrible at PE and games. I was rubbish at rugby and football. I always came last in school sports day races. And as an adult, my disastrous attempt to go over the top rope at the LDN rumble proved that I have all the athletic co-ordination of a rancid goat.

So I repeat the question. Why, oh why, oh why did I decide to have a wrestling match?

And it *was* my idea. I can blame nobody else but myself.

After Jamie Hutchinson's best ever show as a promoter in February 2014, I was worried the momentum might quickly be lost. PAID Promotions Golden Chance Rumble did decent numbers at the box office but JP still owed money to the Louises, had no other income and was unable to afford another Rockstar Spud-level name for the follow-up shows. The Morecambe training school was on its last legs too. It closed down later that year.

I looked at Jamie's line-up for the next few PAID events and didn't feel inspired. I felt we needed something unusual to grab attention and sell tickets. And after my LIAR humiliation at the hands of Joey Hayes and his gang at Golden Chance Rumble, and after Joey had embarrassed the XWA by siding with GPW two years before, it seemed only natural and logical that I would seek revenge.

So I suggested to Jamie that we promote a match between Joey Hayes and Greg 'The Truth' Lambert.

As soon as the words left my mouth, I regretted them.

I am not a trained wrestler. I have only ever taken part physically in one wrestling training class. That was at the Camp of Pain in 2004. I decided to find out, first-hand, what it takes to become a professional wrestler so I could write about the experience for my website. So Chris Curtis invited the 32-year-old me along to his gym in Stoke. And after three hours of constant back bumps, being stretched on the mat by Bubblegum and snap suplexed by Johnny Phere, I staggered out, aching all over. I could barely move for a week afterwards. And I told myself, never again.

This is why I have so much respect for professional wrestlers. I have no idea how they manage to cope with the constant pain they must endure. Because believe me, wrestling bloody hurts.

But I stuck to my suggestion and Jamie went for it. He liked my idea for a storyline. After being publicly embarrassed at Golden Chance Rumble, The Truth would go into a downward spiral. I would grow a beard for the first time ever, dress dishevelled, and act like I had lost my mind. Then I would challenge Hayes to face me in the ring. In theory, my first ever wrestling bout was bound to attract the punters. Surely the Morecambe crowd would flock to the Globe Arena to see the hated heel manager get well and truly pasted by the PAID Promotions Champion.

Now, I wouldn't have agreed to get in the ring and trust the well-being of my lanky, pasty, hairy body with just anyone. I wanted to wrestle Joey Hayes.

I have known Joey since he was 17. I've seen him grow as a performer. I like him and I trust him. And at that point, Joey was one of the very best in the country. As I already mentioned, he has been one of Morecambe's top stars for a decade as a babyface, aside from that brief turn to the dark side at XWA v GPW Vendetta. But I had also seen him excel in the other North West promotions and prove what a versatile entertainer he can be. In FutureShock, he became 'Hot Stuff' Hayes and formed a highly effective partnership called The Models with 'Delicious' Danny Hope and their valet, the Victoria Beckham of British wrestling, Melanie Price. Meanwhile in GPW, Joey had a run as Heresy's heel sidekick *Joseph* Hayes in the SIN stable alongside Johnny Phere, among others.

"Joey and I go back to about 2001 and we've done lots of stuff together," said Johnnie Brannigan.

"We've travelled to Holland together to wrestle over there. We set up a wrestling school in Germany and had some really good times.

"When he was younger, he did lack a bit of confidence at times. There were times when he had to be be physically forced to do just about anything. We had to pick him up and take him to shows to make sure he got there! Even when I managed to get him a WWE try-out and rang him and told him, he didn't believe me and he had to be coerced to go. We had arguments about him cutting promos and I had to write them down for him to help him do them. But he's much better these days!

"Some of my best matches have been with Joey. He's a brilliant natural. At one point he had a body that would rival Bruce Lee. He looked amazing. I saw a heel in him and I thought it would be a great step forward for Joey's career and it was. It helped him hone his craft. We're so lucky to have him in the North West. I value the time I've spent with him and he's such a great guy."

On March 28 2014, Joey reached his career peak when he became the PCW Champion. A longtime cocky heel in Preston, Hayes cashed in the Money in the Bank briefcase on his mate Danny Hope just moments after the underdog Danny brought the house down by winning the Who Dares Wins Rumble. Joey's opportunism in attacking, then defeating Danny during his title celebration ruined one of PCW's greatest ever feel good moments. The Manchester reprobate's unwanted victory led to a major feud with 'Delicious' Danny, whose tasseled ring wear, penchant for catwalking in the ring and awesomely catchy theme music has made him a huge favourite on the UK scene in recent years. He's a great guy too.

So in the spring and summer months of 2014, Joey Hayes was right at the top of his game. He was the perfect opponent.

On April 13 2014 at PAID Promotions Aftermath, we pulled the trigger on Hayes v Lambert. It was a funny old Sunday afternoon. My beloved Liverpool FC were right in the midst of their unlikely Premier League title charge and I spent the hours before the show in the pub watching their thrilling 3-2 win over close rivals Manchester City. So when I arrived at the Globe Arena, unusually dressed in a hooded jacket, black baseball cap and with several days' growth of stubble to put across my character's deranged state of mind, I was actually in a great mood.

It didn't take long for the positive feelings to evaporate. Crowd numbers at the Globe were down again, Jamie was stressed to high heaven, and after his match against Triston, he threw a backstage wobbler at Bryan Fulton. The PAID promoter was furious with our technical wizard over a missed music cue. He was ranting and raving. I had never seen Jamie so angry behind-the-scenes. Helen had to calm him down. Bryan was miffed at being blamed. I tried to convince Jamie to apologise to Fulton, but JP was never one for apologies.

The row between JP and Bryan put a dampener on the whole day. Despite the tension behind the curtain, the show must go on. So I went out as planned after the main event between Joey Hayes and big Alex Cyanide, and made my challenge. The angle went well. But afterwards when I told Jamie how things had panned out, he didn't seem to care. He sat in the Globe Arena weight room, brooding, silent, and deep in thought.

It soon became clear to me that Jamie was fed up of being a promoter and wanted out. My match with Joey was set for Sunday, June 1 2014 at the Globe, at a show Jamie aptly named Truth or Consequences. But aside from creating a basic poster, JP didn't seem interested in doing much to publicise the event. He began to talk of quitting, of handing the company over to someone else. I did feel frustrated that he was losing interest, especially as I was willing to risk my health for the cause.

Still, I did all I could to promote my match. I got us some local newspaper coverage, an interview on local radio station The Bay (thanks to a friend, radio presenter Darren Milby) and plugged it like crazy on social media. And I also came up with the idea of shooting a three-part series of mock training videos for YouTube.

My knowledge and love of boxing played a major influence here. I have been a fan of the fight game since my teenage years, when I regularly stayed up into the wee small hours to watch big title bouts featuring Mike Tyson, Marvelous Marvin Hagler, Sugar Ray Leonard and Thomas Hearns live from America on free ITV. I was captivated by big-time boxing's combination of primitive violence, technical skill and Las Vegas razzmatazz.

Being such a huge boxing and wrestling enthusiast, I have always found it strange that I can't stand Mixed Martial Arts. I find UFC really dull with far too much rolling around on the canvas and not enough action. I call it the Ultimate Cuddling Championship. I can't get into it at all.

But boxing always fascinated me. And during my adult years, I have been lucky enough to do some freelance work as a ring announcer for semi-professional and amateur boxing companies. In the process, I have met and MC'd for former world champions 'Terrible' Tim Witherspoon, 'The Dark Destroyer' Nigel Benn and 'The Celtic Warrior' Steve Collins. It was also a huge thrill when an acquaintance of mine who lives in Morecambe, Tyson Fury, became Undisputed World Heavyweight Champion in November 2015. Yes, for a short time until highly publicised personal issues saw the 6ft 9in 'Gypsy Warrior' vacate the titles in 2016, my humble seaside town was the home of the Heavyweight Champ - owner of 'the richest prize in sport'.

So in spring 2014, boxing played a major part in my strategy for promoting my match with Joey. Fight fans out there will know about the fly-on-the-wall 24/7 programmes in the build-up to world championship fights, following the boxers on their journey towards the big night. In recent years we've had Mayweather-Hatton 24/7, Calzaghe-Jones 24/7 and Mayweather-Pacquiao 24/7, to name but a few.

So I created a trio of videos called Lambert-Hayes 24/7. Although admittedly, there wasn't much Hayes in them. They were all about Lambert.

The idea for Lambert-Hayes 24/7 was that the cameras would follow me during my preparation for the match. In this spoof documentary, I claimed to be training hard, in the best shape of my life and issued threats of physical violence towards my hated enemy. And while my demeanour was deadly serious, it was painfully obvious that I was well and truly out of my depth. I think they are the best and funniest vignettes I have ever filmed.

The first episode, called At Home with the Lamberts, took viewers inside my semi-detached suburban Morecambe home and 'training camp'. Now sporting a full beard in an attempt to channel Daniel Bryan, wearing a Phere The Truth T-shirt and a stripey dressing gown while slumped on my living room couch, I aggressively told the viewers that I was ready for the fight of my life. "I'm going to prepare like a WARRIOR!" I vowed.

"I am going to stand toe-to-toe with him! I'm going to throw punches, kicks and knees! I'm going to gnaw on his forehead! I am going to spit down his throat!"

I made all these bold claims with intensity in my eyes. Then I slurped sedately from a mug of tea, tackled nothing more strenuous than a pile of ironing and went off to mow the lawn.

I also spoofed Grado by training on a trampoline. "IT'S YOURSELF!" I cried as I bounced around like a deranged 42-year-old man (which I was). Then I fell awkwardly and bashed my elbow. On purpose, of course.

Meanwhile Owen, my teenage son the budding thespian, also appeared in the clip and pretty much stole the show with his sarcastic wit. The star of such Morecambe High School musicals as Oliver, Chicago and Little Shop of Horrors eloquently explained why he thought I had no chance of victory whatsoever, as he sat on the kitchen worktop munching his way through a bag of crisps.

Episode 2 was filmed on location in Glasgow during Dann Read's stag weekend. The story was that I'd decided to go to an ICW show to help with my preparation, as watching Britain's most insane promotion would help me "channel my inner beast" and turn me into a tough guy. Instead, the usually straight-laced Truth got pathetically drunk on two pints of lager and a JD and coke. Then, while swigging from bottled lager in a hotel lobby, I slurred at Dann that I was bound to beat Joey Hayes because I had Johnny Phere as my trainer and informed him that in my case, the PAID Principles didn't stand for Passion, Ambition, Intensity and Dedication after all, but instead stood for "Peroni...Arseholed...Inebriated...and Dann Read!" Then I kissed my good mate on the forehead, told him I loved him, and began drunkenly singing He's Got the Whole World in His Hands because in my intoxicated state, I thought Dann looked a bit like Bray Wyatt.

Later, still off my face, I gatecrashed the massive queue outside The Garage for ICW Show Me Your Lizard, roped in the queueing Insane die-hards to join me in a horrible rendition of Like A Prayer, asked them to teach me some Glaswegian lingo so I could act hard, convinced a few bewildered Scottish fans to say "Greg Lambert is going to beat Joey Hayes" to camera, bought an ICW T-Shirt, announced that I was now a "hardcore extreme wrestler", then eventually passed out in my hotel room. Meanwhile, a worried Dann told the viewing audience that the pressure of having to fight Joey Hayes was causing me to lose my marbles. It was comedy gold.

Episode 3 saw a who's who of British wrestling give their predictions on 'the fight everyone is talking about'. Billy Kirkwood, Chris Brooker, Bubblegum, Triston, Charles Nelson Riley, Dave Rayne, The Blackpool Blonds, Ryan Grayson, Dave Mastiff (who brilliantly called me a "four-eyed t__t") and my fellow wrestling managers Gilligan Gordon and Alan Alan Alan Tasker all picked a side.

The closing moments of Lambert 24/7 saw both gladiators sum up ahead of the big fight.

"I vow Joey Hayes, that I will take the PAID Promotions Championship from you, and that's The Truth!" said the bearded, wild-eyed, hoodie-wearing challenger, still sitting on his living room sofa.

Then, right at the end of the final episode, Joey finally made an appearance. The easy-going Hayes' remarks were rather chilling, for him.

"Greg Lambert? I'm going to kill you."

Whoops. Maybe I'd provoked Joey a little too much.

We filmed the final episode of Lambert-Hayes 24/7 on May 13 2014, the day of the next PAID Promotions show at a new location, The Layton in Blackpool. Shooting the vignettes were the only enjoyable part of the day. The venue was inadequate - just a room at the back of a pub, it was painfully obvious no proper marketing had been done and to make matters worse, it was the last day of the football season and Liverpool blew their best chance in 24 years of winning the league title.

So all things considered, I was in a dark mood that Sunday in Blackpool. And so was Jamie. As was Bryan Fulton. Still seething from his treatment at Aftermath, Bryan turned up under duress and only stayed for a short time. JP had to set the entranceway up himself and find a trainee to operate the sound system. About 40 people turned up to watch, I shot an angle where I stacked the odds against Joey by forcing him to wrestle - and lose - a four-on-one handicap match against The Blonds, Grayson and Shaun Vasey. And that was that, really. A day best forgotten.

Four days later, Helen messaged me and asked if I'd be willing to take over the booking of PAID Promotions. She said her parents were now in charge.

Jamie had indeed decided to quit as PAID Promotions promoter.

I told the Louis family that I wasn't interested. I didn't want the responsibility. Nor did I have any intention of being caught up in the crossfire between them and Jamie. Relations there were tense at the time.

A few days later, I learned that Helen's mum and dad had decided to sell the wrestling ring and van, and all the PAID Promotions branding and championship belt, to our referee Charles Nelson Riley and his brother Liam. Without the support of either Jamie or myself, the Louises realised they didn't know enough about wrestling to run the company. So they made the sensible decision to cut their losses.

So the day of Sunday, June 1 2014 dawned. And with all the behind-the-scenes machinations and uncertainty over who was actually in charge of PAID Promotions now, I was hardly in the best frame of mind to have a wrestling match.

Having said that, I was physically as ready as I would ever be. For all the mucking about on Lambert 24/7, I had actually done quite a bit more training than normal. Especially on cardio. I went out jogging three times a week on Morecambe Promenade and put in the miles on the treadmill. I certainly needed to be fit, because I planned to do a lot of running during the match.

Running, that is, away from Joey Hayes.

They say image is everything in wrestling, so I also spent a great deal of time thinking about what to wear to the ring. The most important thing was to cover up my unappealing physique. I also thought, in keeping with the bullish theme of my promos in Lambert-Hayes 24/7, that I should at least look like I was intending to have a proper scrap. So I bought an army camouflage jacket and a hooded Everlast training top bearing the logo 'Fight to Win', and borrowed a pair of khaki pants off Johnny Phere. I also cobbled together a matching baseball cap, fingerless gloves, kneepads and sweatbands.

Once I was dressed up in my full combat gear, I looked like a prize idiot. Which was the intention.

I also thought long and hard about how the match should go. I remembered something legendary WWE manager Bobby 'The Brain' Heenan wrote in his autobiography. "A great manager should manage like a wrestler and wrestle like a manager." In other words, a manager should act and talk tough. But once a wrestler actually gets his hands on him, he should prove that he's anything *but* tough and be completely out of his depth. My main concern though, was that I didn't want the physical interaction between Joey and myself to look *too* aesthetically horrible. Hayes is used to wrestling against premier athletes. So I needed to carefully choose a few moves he could hit me with, which were low-risk in terms of my safety, but that would also look like he was believably beating me up.

My overall aim was firstly to survive in one piece, and secondly to do everything I could to make the fans believe they were watching an entertaining match, when I had absolutely no intention of delivering one. Dann Read was of major assistance here. We actually laid out the whole 10-minute scenario for Hayes v Lambert in a Glasgow cafe on Sauchiehall Street the day after ICW Show Me Your Lizard.

There was a bizarre atmosphere backstage when I arrived at the Globe Arena that day. Bryan was still in a huff. Jamie himself seemed more relaxed than in months, as if a great weight had been lifted from his shoulders. As for Liam and Kieran Engelke (Charles Nelson Riley's real name), they were great with me. I got positive vibes off both of them. If they were indeed taking over PAID Promotions, perhaps the future would be a little brighter.

Johnny Phere wrestled The Creeper that night in a Last Man Standing match, and lost. He then grabbed the microphone and told the fans "I QUIT!"

For that moment, at least, once again it was Real in Morecambe.

Joey Hayes v Greg 'The Truth' Lambert was the main event of Truth or Consequences. The attendance, I have to say, was once again below expectations. Despite all my efforts, my match wasn't quite the draw I hoped for. But at least the people in the crowd that night were hyped up and ready to see Joey tear me limb from limb. They included two of my bosses from the newspaper, who are not wrestling fans. In fact, this was the first and only time they had been to see a wrestling match. They later told me they felt cheated, because they expected me to actually stand and fight toe-to-toe with the champion like I promised.

They obviously don't know The Truth very well, do they?

I came out to John Cena's theme music. The reason for this was twofold. I thought that as soon as the first bars of Cena's song struck up, the gullible kids in the Morecambe crowd might actually believe the 15-time WWE World Heavyweight Champion was about to come out. Then when I emerged instead, they would be even more likely to boo. I also thought that because Cena is such a polarising character with wrestling fans, using his signature tune was bound to get me some extra heat anyway. I also thought parodying his ring entrance would be fun to do. So I greeted the crowd with the trademark Cena salute and You Can't See Me hand signal, then stalked to the ring with my hands aloft like Mr Hustle, Loyalty, Respect entering the hostile Hammerstein Ballroom to face Rob Van Dam at ECW One Night Stand 2006.

When Joey arrived, he looked almost amused. It was clear he wanted to hurt me, but was also not taking me seriously. And let's face it, why should he? Still wearing my specs, I was shadow boxing in the corner, doing the famous Ali Shuffle and repeatedly touching my toes, long dark socks tucked into my army pants below ill-fitting kneepads. I looked ridiculous.

Charles Nelson Riley showed off the PAID Promotions Title belt, as is traditional, to the fans. I grabbed it off him and thrust it above my head, eyes bulging and yelling "YEESSSSS!" at the audience just to get some more heat. CNR scolded me as he seized it back, handed the belt to the timekeeper, a young Morecambe trainee called Ethan Berry, then called Joey and I to centre-ring for his final pre-match instructions. I came forward to listen and felt brave enough to spit some choice insults in Joey's direction. At this, Hayes took a threatening step forward, and I backed off like a wuss, covered up and ducked out between the top and middle turnbuckles to protect myself, yelling at the ref to keep the champion back.

As a smirking Hayes retreated back to his own corner, I slowly recoiled back into my own, and CNR asked me if I was ready for him to ring the bell. I nodded yes, took a ginger step forward, then changed my mind and instead informed Riley, Hayes and the fans that I needed to say a post-match prayer. "What can I say? I'm a deeply religious man!" I explained, even though I haven't been to a Sunday church service in 30 years.

At this, the crowd began to get restless. They could sense that I was stalling for time and booed with frustration. "YOU'RE ALL GOING TO HELL!" I bellowed, as if exasperated that the fans wouldn't allow me to pray. I kneeled, recited the Lord's Prayer as the audience continued to heckle, then crossed myself about a half-dozen times - a move inspired by Frank Bruno's ring walk for his rematch with Mike Tyson in 1996, when Big Frank nervously crossed himself over and over again like a condemned man before being flattened by Iron Mike in three rounds.

Once again, Riley asked if I was ready. I braced myself, put up my dukes in the orthodox stance, shuffled a couple of steps towards centre-ring, and nodded with false determination. Joey, looking supremely fit, toned and dangerous, nodded too, with a knowing smile. Charles stood between us, arms apart, keeping us separate, and was just about to call for the opening bell when I suddenly turned tail and slid out of the ring. Years of watching Jim Cornette stalling with The Midnight Express during WCW matches really paid dividends here.

By now, the fans were in uproar. I pranced around at ringside, explaining to Riley, Hayes and anyone who would listen that I hadn't done my proper warm-up. Without the correct stretching exercises, I could easily pull a muscle. So I began to do some deep, exaggerated knee bends and squat thrusts. By now, Joey was starting to look angry. He beckoned at me to get back into the ring and fight like a man. Instead, I called for a bottle of water. Ethan Berry brought one over, I took a swig, gargled for a few seconds, then spat a jet of liquid right in the poor lad's face. As Ethan wiped the water from his eyes, I laughed hysterically. At this point, I think the crowd actually wanted to lynch me. My two bosses *certainly* did.

Looking stern, Joey now seized a microphone and warned me that he would count to 10, and if I didn't enter the ring and start the match, he would come out after me. He started to count, but as he reached six, he was blindsided by Ryan Grayson. The Edinburgh Elite was my first line of defence and his assault wasn't against the rules, because the match hadn't actually started. But the champ was too much for him, and he recovered to send Grayson flying.

With the Scot out of the way, Joey decided enough was enough, and he came after me. The foot race was well and truly on as Hayes chased me around the ringside area. But just as he seemed likely to finally get his hands on the slippery Truth, Danny Hope - my second line of defence - came running in out of nowhere and sent his Models partner flying into the steel post.

Danny now battered Joey down at ringside and, as my devious plot began to unfold, I felt brave enough to re-enter the ring. Hope then rolled the prone body of the champ back under the bottom rope and I demanded CNR start the match. As the bell finally sounded to officially kick things off after about seven minutes of delaying tactics, I laid down and covered Joey, but he kicked out on two! Furious and worried, I ordered Danny Hope to bring a chair into the ring, but his attempted swing missed and he ended up flat on his face from a Joey Hayes JKO.

Hayes was still weak from the sneak-attack, though, so in desperation I grabbed the steel chair myself, looking to use it on Joey as a weapon. But I had reckoned without the referee doing his job. Charles Nelson Riley snatched the chair from my hands, I angrily asked him what he was playing at, and this gave Joey the recovery time he needed. When I turned my attention away from Charles, Hayes was standing right in front of me. I gulped and looked around for help, but Hope and Grayson were both nowhere to be seen.

There was no escape.

I think Joey really enjoyed the next few minutes. Gleefully, he picked me up and gave me a hard body slam. I sold it kicking and thrashing like the dying fly in 70s kids' TV show Tiswas. Gasping for breath - legitimately knackered already because all that stalling was deceptively tiring - I pulled myself upright using the ropes for help, only for Hayes to grab both my legs, lift me horizontal, look to the delighted crowd for approval, then boot me right in the stomach,

Hardcore Holly-style. I clutched my guts and spun right around into a reverse atomic drop, which Joey delivered perfectly. I tried my best to sell the devastating knee to my groin like Rick Rude against The Ultimate Warrior at Summerslam 1989. I am not entirely sure I achieved the top class facials and body language of The Ravishing One in agonised pain, but my bouncing around like a human pogo stick certainly got the desired reaction from the crowd who were now baying for my blood.

"Finish him, Joey!" they implored. Thankfully for me, and them, the torture was nearly over.

I didn't think it was a good idea for me to take a JKO, so instead we went for a simple sleeper to 'take it home' (finish the match). I say simple, but being clamped in a sleeperhold is actually not very pleasant at all. The champion really hooked it on tight. Already 'blown up' (exhausted) from my earlier exertions, my arms flailed and my legs turned to jelly, and to be honest, I was legitimately struggling to breathe.

How on earth Joey and his peers manage to exchange holds at a fast pace for 20 or 30 minutes is beyond me. I was exhausted and I'd hardly done anything.

"Take some pictures if you like!" laughed Joey to the fans, as I faded rapidly, my tongue ululating in my mouth like Jabba the Hutt being choked out by Princess Leia. As Charles checked in, lifted and dropped my limp arm once, and then twice, I was counting down the seconds until the cavalry arrived, with just one thought racing through my mind as Joey applied the unforgiving pressure.

"Please Craig, hurry up and save me."

My third line of defence was Craig Kollins. Just as my arm was about to drop for the third and final time, The One Man Riot raced into the ring and chop-blocked Hayes' knee out from under him. Joey crumpled to the canvas, I slumped into the corner, pretending to be semi-conscious, and Riley called off the match due to the outside interference. CNR then tried to restrain Kollins, but the crazed Barrovian instead continued his brutal attack on Hayes, before producing a metal crowbar to pulverise the champion's knee even more.

Then Craig, who had won the Golden Chance Rumble a few

months earlier to earn himself a shot at the PAID Promotions Championship at a time of his choosing, informed everyone that he was cashing in his title opportunity right there and then. The bell rang and Kollins duly beat the incapacitated Joey Hayes, becoming at 22 years old, the youngest ever heavyweight champion of the Morecambe wrestling era.

With his crowbar in one hand, and the belt in the other, the bearded thug Kollins then helped me stagger back down the aisle as the boos rained down in the Globe Arena.

The official result of my match? Joey Hayes beat me by disqualification. But my defeat didn't matter. It was all part of a carefully concocted masterplan. It emerged that I had lured Hayes into a trap by tempting him into a match with me. Then I sacrificed my own body so Joey would let his guard down long enough for Craig Kollins to spring a nasty surprise on the Morecambe fans. This gave The One Man Riot the PAID Promotions Championship, and earned me my revenge on Joey Hayes.

I'd told Joey I would take the PAID Promotions Title from him. And I had. Because now, I was the new manager of the new champion.

Afterwards, Joey and I hugged backstage and had a photo taken together. I thanked him for the match and told him I was happy with how things had gone. Looking back on it now, I am so proud of what we achieved together. I was delighted not only to survive in one piece but also with how we executed the scenario and delivered on the ultimate aim of the match, which was for me to get heat and transfer it to my wrestler. This should be the aim of all professional wrestling managers. And by doing this, we established Craig Kollins as the new major force in PAID Promotions.

My only regret, is that the issues between Bryan and Jamie meant that the only solo wrestling match I've ever had, and am ever likely to have, was not filmed properly. The only footage I have was shot on a cameraphone by a work colleague. Not exactly ideal. Remember how Alex Shane used to get frustrated whenever his performances weren't captured for posterity? Now I know how he felt.

I went home afterwards, ran a hot bath, cracked open a beer, and had my first proper shave in three months. Which was a relief. While some thought my beard suited me, I hated it. It itched like hell.

I look back on my match now and think I probably conquered a few demons from my childhood by going through with it. It was also another notch on my grappling CV. There can't be too many people in British wrestling who have been a referee, booker, promoter, both play-by-play *and* colour commentator, ring announcer, manager, leading journalist for Europe's top wrestling magazine for 12 years, author, run a wrestling school, and been a wrestler too.

In fact, there isn't anyone else. Just me.

A few days after Joey Hayes beat Greg 'The Truth' Lambert by disqualification, Liam and Kieran officially bought PAID Promotions. And Johnny Phere walked away from wrestling, disillusioned by life as a full-time promoter after less than a year. He wouldn't return to the ring for eight more months.

Like I said earlier, being a wrestling promoter is difficult. And it's not for everyone, as Jamie discovered.

Shortly afterwards, I met up with Liam and Kieran. They wanted me to stay on as assistant booker. Then they got down to the business of turning Morecambe wrestling back around. It quickly became obvious that the brothers would bring back the glory days. Their new regime reinvigorated the trainees and created a real sense of teamwork and community that PAID Promotions hadn't had before. They coaxed Bryan out of his mood and got him back on board as production manager. They had more cash behind them than JP, so could invest in bringing in more of British wrestling's star names like Marty Scurll, Dave Mastiff, El Ligero and Grado. And they focussed on marketing and a proper, workable business plan.

Kieran soon became the main front man of PAID Promotions and was a breath of fresh air at the helm. He is a charismatic and caring character, deeply passionate about wrestling, enthusiastic, positive, cheerful, a people person and was willing to put in hours and hours of promotional graft, tramping the streets, putting up posters, giving out flyers, meeting and charming potential customers, in order to put bums on seats. And hard work pays off.

His first show in charge on July 20 2014, headlined by Craig Kollins' first title defence against Bubblegum and an appearance by Grado, drew a packed house to the Globe Arena. The second show on August 16 2014, and the first wrestling event at Morecambe Winter Gardens since 1977, also pulled in a large crowd. When babyface Ricky J McKenzie pinned CJ Banks to win the main event that night, the fans erupted in joy. The Morecambe Divas were hugging each other in the front row, just like the old days.

Morecambe wrestling was about to get its mojo back.

And gradually, I got mine back too.

CHAPTER 15

PRESTON AND POWER SLAM

So much has happened during my four-and-a-half year tenure with PCW it's hard to know where to start. Here are some of the many highlights, in no particular order.

In mid-2013, Evoque temporarily closed for refurbishment and Preston City Wrestling moved for two shows to a smaller club down the road called Rumes. This coincided with a change in my commentary partner as Steven Fludder decided to replace G-Man with my old friend Stallion.

A walking, talking gimmick, one of British wrestling's most underrated characters, and one of my favourite people in the business. That's Stallion. It is a pleasure to work with him. Don't tell him I said that, though.

Stallion is outrageous. You only have to look at his clothes to see that. And on-air, he comes out with some hilarious one-liners. But don't let the funnies fool you. He is also very knowledgeable and knows when to get serious, especially during main events when we need to kick things into top gear and bring the 'big fight feel' to our commentary.

We first worked together at the PCW second anniversary show at Rumes on August 2 2013. The main event was one hell of a commentary challenge for our first night together - a one-hour Iron Man match between Doug Williams (then PCW Champion) and El Ligero. I was in a really dark mood at the time due to the stresses of PAID Promotions and other things going on in my personal life. I really wasn't having fun at all. But the Williams-Ligero match was an absolute classic and Stallion helped get me through it. By the end, I was screaming myself hoarse. One trait of my commentary is that I really throw myself emotionally into the main events, my voice getting louder and more excited as they build to their conclusion.

This definitely happened that night. To grab the audience for a full hour, especially in these days where short attention spans rule, takes a load of skill. Full credit to Doug and Ligs for their performance and to Stallion for keeping me focussed.

Stallion and I have developed a solid partnership. We are an odd couple for sure, but opposites usually make for an entertaining commentary duo - just look at Jim Ross and Jerry Lawler, and Gorilla Monsoon and Bobby Heenan. There's me in my suit and specs, straight-laced, easily offended, favouring the babyfaces and calling the action. And then there's Stallion, in his dazzling shirts and matching bandana, Geordie accent, all sexual innuendo and macho posturing, backing the heels and adding colourful analysis. It just works.

I feel very proud that the bloke I plucked from the Morecambe front row seven years ago is now by my side as my commentary partner for one of Britain's top wrestling companies. He shares my passion for British wrestling and PCW, and we have a great rapport.

Having said all that, anyone not knowing any better would think Stallion and I don't get along. "Hello, s__thead!" is his typical greeting whenever I arrive at a PCW event. The Geordie Gob is constantly trying to wind me up and embarrass me with little digs, both on-air and off. But it's all good-natured. In reality, we have a hate-love relationship. Stallion pretends to hate me but he actually loves me. He admitted it once on Facebook and I saved his post for posterity, so there's no backing out. And we usually have a beer together after shows. Sometimes, I even pay!

One last word on Stallion. Don't *ever* get in a car with him if he hasn't eaten properly. He suffers from a sugar imbalance which turns him into a monster when he is hungry, as I once discovered to my cost when we got stuck in traffic near the Albert Dock on the way back from an Infinite Promotions show in Liverpool and it was like the Geordie Gizmo had turned into a bandana-wearing, ranting, raving Gremlin. You *really* wouldn't like him when he's angry.

But as long as you feed him, stick a Bowling For Soup song on the radio, and can cope with listening to an endless stream of filthy double entendres, then Stallion is the best driving buddy in the world.

As Richard Parker was on a break, Rumes also saw the debut of a new ring announcer. Joanna Rose was very tense ahead of her first outing in PCW. I remember chatting to her backstage to try to ease her nerves. But Joanna did a terrific job.

She went on to not only be an excellent ring announcer but a marvellous heel manager in PCW. When Joanna took over the stable Friends With Benefits in 2015, managing Chris Masters, Team Single, Iestyn Rees and Bubblegum, she was a revelation as a bad girl, playing the role with just the right combination of deviousness, sex appeal and aloof superiority.

As anyone who has seen Jo in in the flesh will know, she is a very pretty girl. The English Rose was the centrefold in Fighting Spirit Magazine in February 2016 and was very proud of how the photos turned out. She is also very driven and eager to progress her wrestling career. Jo travels regularly to America to ring announce for Gabe Sapolsky's EVOLVE promotion and even appeared on WWE pay-per-view during the 2015 Royal Rumble - ironically as an Adam Rose Rosebud! Backstage at PCW, she always listened when I gave her heel manager tips and took feedback on board. And she is a great singer too. The blonde bombshell has a great future in the wrestling business.

At time of writing, Joanna has just been replaced as PCW General Manager by Dave Rayne. Working with Dave is always a lot of fun. In fact, he might be the most improved British grappler of the past decade. The former FutureShock promoter always had a great mind for the business. But in his younger days, as mentioned earlier, he never stood out as a performer. In his early years as a pro, Dave could take great bumps and was a willing workhorse. But at the time, he was an average wrestler with an ordinary look and physique.

Then his heel turn galvanised him. After his stint with The Authority in 2010 and 2011, Rayne further developed his gimmick and turned into a wannabe playboy hailing from a swish apartment in Deansgate, Manchester, who believed he was God's gift to women and was obsessed with collecting championship belts. He grew facial hair, wore better wrestling gear, found catchy theme music and carried himself like a star. As he cranked up the self-absorbed, delusional side of his character, Rayne's confidence on the microphone grew. The Stockport sleazeball became a master of delivering a stream of wicked one-liners to insult opponents and fans alike. These inspired rants usually culminated with a yell of "HASHTAG BOOM!" and crowds would chant along.

I'm guessing the 'Hashtag Boom' catchphrase came from Dave's real-life habit of saying the word 'Boom!' - particularly while teaching at the FutureShock and XWA training schools. After demonstrating a particular move or hold to a wrestling trainee, Dave often shouted 'Boom!' as a way of emphasising his point. With the rise of Twitter, he put a hashtag in front of 'Boom' and it became one of his trademarks. It's amazing how some of the most obscure catchphrases often become the most popular. But that's professional wrestling. If you say or do anything often enough, it usually gets over.

Dave established his heel character in FutureShock, GPW and XWA, but really picked up steam in PCW where he became a cult favourite. Although still a villain, the fans cheered him. You see, part of Dave's charm is that he isn't larger than life. He looks like an everyday bloke off the street. So the PCW fans identified with him, no matter how much he insulted them and broke the rules. In fact, they found him so entertaining, they all wanted to be like him! The more Dave got annoyed at their cheers, the more they chanted "WE'RE ALL DAVE RAYNE!" and rallied to his side.

Rayne worked like a heel in PCW for years. The slimy Stopfordian opportunistically cashed in his Money in the Bank briefcase on Noam Dar to win the PCW Cruiserweight Title at Road to Glory 2013, but only after the Scot had been first battered senseless by CJ Banks. He sneak-attacked female wrestler April Davids at Final Fight 2013 by smashing her from behind with a broomstick then screamed "HASHTAG *BROOM*!" He tried to cheat his way to victory in a Masterlock Challenge with Chris Masters by dousing his body in slippery baby oil. And best of all, he awarded himself his own made-up title, which he called the Hashtag Boom Championship. The tricky Rayne then defended his own belt for months against all-comers in matches he invariably lost, only to produce a rulebook and convince the referee to reverse the decision due to some ridiculous loophole such as 'the Hashtag Boom Title can't change hands on the last Friday in the month when the referee has an Afro'. And of course, PCW referee Joel Allen does indeed have an Afro.

But no matter what shenanigans Rayne got up to, the PCW fans still supported him because he was so damn funny.

"I've done everything in PCW," said Dave.

"In FutureShock I was the conniving bad guy champion who gets away with everything but who you want to see get punched. In PCW I was the hapless idiot who tried so hard but never quite got it. PCW had a lot of too-cool-for-school heels nobody wanted to boo. They weren't really heels. But I was getting booed.

"Until, it got to the point that when my music hit, the fans realised the entertaining stuff was about to start, so they would get excited and start cheering. They started loving my put-downs.

"No matter what I did as a heel, I was cheered. At one point I even held a toddler from the front row in front of me to protect myself against the babyface, dropped the kid at his feet and punched the babyface, and the PCW fans still cheered it and thought it was the greatest thing they'd ever seen.

"So I embraced it, and PCW embraced it. I was a dick, but I was the PCW fans' dick. I never won, everyone was mean to me, but the PCW fans enjoyed it because if I could succeed, so could everyone.

"When I won the Money in the Bank match at Festive Fury 2012, everyone went nuts. Later when I came out to try to cash in on Trav, when he was doing the mutual respect thing after his first match with Chris Masters, I got a big pop too. This started all my stuff with Masters, our team The Legion of Boom and I eventually beat Chris in a blindfold match."

So Dave became a fully-fledged 'face and he was brilliant in the role of cheeky underdog. While still mainly used as comic relief, The One and Only also proved his worth further up the card in his marquee bouts with Chris Masters, Goldust and Jeff Jarrett. In 2016 Rayne became a heel again, proving his versatility as a solid all-round grappler who after years of struggling to stand out from the crowd, worked on his weaknesses, hid his limitations and made the most of himself by finding a niche role that connected with the audience magnificently.

Dave is also really good company. I like and respect him a lot and

I'm delighted he has done so well in PCW. He is one of my favourite people in wrestling, even though he is the only person in wrestling I ever had to sack. Legitimately.

In late 2011, I fired Dave Rayne as trainer of the Morecambe wrestling school. Even though it was the right decision, I absolutely hated doing it. By then, Dave had run the training classes at Regent Park Studios for about a year. He was a good coach with a lot of creative ideas. But although he put in maximum effort whenever he took training, I soon realised that it was only natural that Dave would always make FutureShock Wrestling his priority. At the time I had Johnny Phere waiting in the wings. Jamie lived in Morecambe, he lived and breathed the XWA, so I felt he was a better option than Dave. But I felt absolutely terrible as I sat Rayne down in the Regent Park Studios kitchen and delivered the news that his services would no longer be required. Far from being angry or disappointed, Dave took his axing in good spirits and actually thanked me, saying I was probably doing him a favour as he was spreading himself too thin by running two training schools. Now he'd have time to reprioritise his life. I hope he meant it, because I still feel guilty to this day.

Backstage at PCW shows, I speak to Dave a lot. It's because we have history, we have similar views on wrestling, he is a clever bloke and a good conversationalist, and we both understand the mindset of the performer *and* the promoter. We will spend a good half-hour before every single PCW show catching up with each other, putting the UK wrestling scene to rights and having a right good chinwag. I value our chats and I admire how Dave turned FutureShock Wrestling, which started in 2004 as a series of tiny trainee shows, into one of the big players on the British scene. I was delighted in August 2014 when the company reached its 10th anniversary show and Dave invited me to appear once again in front of the FutureShock crowd, managing the promising newcomer Big T Justice.

Now, the North West of England has long been a hotbed for comedy, spawning the likes of Peter Kay, Les Dawson, Bernard Manning and of course my hometown's own Eric Morecambe. So humour is a major part of PCW shows, perhaps more than in any other major UK promotion. Steven Fludder contributes a lot of his own funny ideas but he's also given wrestlers like Dave Rayne and Mad Man Manson free rein to be creative and come up with their own.

The PCW fans, too, love to have a laugh. They are creative and have come up with some fantastic sing-a-long chants over the years. Perhaps my favourite example of the Preston audience's enthusiastic wit is how they took Uhaa Nation to their hearts.

From the moment the Dragon Gate favourite debuted in PCW in November 2013, the Preston faithful took a shine to him. I will never forget the look of sheer bemusement on Uhaa's face as he entered the ring and was serenaded by fans singing famous pop songs while substituting the word 'Uhaa' into the lyrics. So we had 'Knowing me, knowing you...UHAA!" and "UHAA just a little bit, UHAA a little bit more!" 'Heyyyyy, hey baby! U-HAA! I wanna knooooooww will you be my girl?" and perhaps the best, the PCW fans' cover version of cult 1998 track 'Witch Doctor' by Cartoons.

"U-HEE UHAA-HA! Ting tang wolla wolla bing-bang!"

Uhaa is a warm-hearted guy with a smile that lights up a room. So once initial confusion had lapsed, the genial American embraced the Uhaa Karaoke Nation with gusto, conducting the fans during their singing like it was a wrestling ring Last Night of the Proms. It got to the point where none of his PCW matches could actually start until the crowd exhausted its singalong repertoire. This interaction created an unbreakable bond between Uhaa and the Preston audience. This, not to mention his unparallelled combination of muscularity and athleticism, carried the powerhouse from Stone Mountain, Georgia all the way to the PCW Championship when he defeated Chris Masters and Dave Mastiff in a triple threat at the PCW/ROH Supershow on November 29 2014.

The popular Uhaa had an emotional send-off from Preston four months later after dropping the belt back to The Masterpiece in a Loser Leaves PCW match. Now he is in WWE, I am delighted a worldwide audience is getting to see what I had the pleasure of seeing first-hand on commentary over the past couple of years...that Uhaa...sorry, *Apollo Crews* is a major-league talent.

Uhaa is just one of the worldwide stars I had the pleasure of working with in PCW. Goldust, The Pope, Tommy Dreamer, Kevin

Owens, Ultimo Dragon, Lance Storm, Road Warrior Animal, Awesome Kong, Bob 'Hardcore' Holly, Scott Hall, Sean 'X-Pac' Waltman, Mickie James, Austin Aries, Too Cool, Sabu and So Cal Val were just some of the big names to come to Preston City Wrestling over the years.

"You have to remember there are lot of loyal fans who come to the shows even if there are no big overseas names," said Dave Rayne.

"But if Fludder runs a show without big overseas names, he gets 400 people. Then he announces Rob Van Dam and gets 700 people. There are 300 people who want to see Van Dam and hopefully they will become fans of the British guys."

One of the biggest overseas names was Jushin 'Thunder' Liger. It was a privilege to commentate on the Japanese legend's matches with Martin Kirby and Dean Allmark at the PCW Supershow weekend on November 15 and 16 2013, and to shake hands backstage with the real-life Keiichi Yamada.

Facing Jushin Liger inside the squared circle was a big deal to Dean Allmark. Dean is a lovely guy. I call him 'Style with a Smile' because he is so smooth in the ring and always has a big grin on his face. Dean has more than 15 years' experience with All-Star Wrestling, run by his father-in-law Brian Dixon, but his stint with PCW has enabled the die-hard British fan base to appreciate the Stokie's skills. Allmark loves what he does and he's such a genuine bloke who is great to talk to. He is also a true family man. Never was this more obvious than the night he faced Liger. His wife Letitia, young son Joseph, mother-in-law the former wrestler Mitzi Mueller and Brian himself were all in attendance at Evoque that night. This showed how important the match was to the Dixon and Allmark families. Brian was the first British promoter to bring a young Liger - then known as 'Flying' Fuji Yamada - over to the UK in the late '80s before he was repackaged as a masked daredevil superhero and became a worldwide star with New Japan Pro WrestlIng and WCW. When Dean pinned Liger in a huge upset, the emotion was etched all over his face. Allmark shook Liger's hand and bowed with respect, then hugged his family at ringside. I nearly broke down myself. It was touching to see how much it meant to him.

My all-time favourite experience in PCW wasn't anything to do with commentary or a wrestling match. It was the night I went head-to-head with Mark 'The Beast' Labbett.

Mark Labbett is a star of award-winning TV quiz show The Chase. He is 6ft 7in tall, weighs 27 stone, and is a trivia mastermind. With his dark suit, menacing glare, cerebral one-liners and mammoth frame, The Beast has become a huge name all over the world. Television has never seen anyone that big, that clever, with that much charisma. The man is a megastar.

And he is also a huge wrestling fan.

So never one to miss a trick, Steven Fludder booked The Beast to appear at Supershow III on November 16 2013. Being something of a general knowledge buff myself, I saw an opportunity. So I publicly tweeted Mark and challenged him to a wrestling trivia contest. The Beast accepted.

I hoped Fludder might allow our quiz confrontation to take place in front of the PCW crowd. Instead, Steve asked us to film it backstage for YouTube. This was fine with me. So I gave Stallion the role of quizmaster and asked him to come up with 30 questions on the history of wrestling, half for me and half for The Beast. Then I walked through the PCW dressing room doors, wondering why it appeared so dark behind their windows. I soon realised it was because Labbett was already there, his back to the door, holding court regaling a group of PCW wrestlers and staff with tales of The Chase's success in America. He was so tall and his shoulders so wide, he was virtually blocking out the light. TV doesn't do this guy justice. The Beast is *massive*.

Thankfully, he is also a really nice guy. Labbett was respectful of the wrestling business and appreciative to be there. He has no ego at all. So he was more than enthusiastic about filming our little trivia tete-a-tete and played right along in full Beastly character.

I was really happy with the finished video. It is the kind of clip I can show to non-wrestling fans and they will be impressed. My mum and dad certainly were. When I told them in 2005 that I'd performed in front of 3,400 people at Coventry Skydome in an angle with Mick Foley, they barely batted an eyelid. But when I told them I had taken on Mark 'The Beast' Labbett in a quiz, they were the proudest parents on earth.

PCW Wrestling's version of The Chase began with me, in full-on heel mode, boasting about my credentials as I sat side-by-side with my genius nemesis.

"You might know the capital of Burkina Faso and can probably recite the periodic table backwards, but I know wrestling, sunshine!" I warned Labbett.

His tree trunk arms folded, The Beast sneered and reeled off his own list of achievements. Captain of the Welsh National quiz team, represented Wales in the world quiz championships for nine straight years, finished four times in the British quiz top 10, and now regarded as one of the greatest super heavyweight quizzers the world has ever seen.

"Good luck," sniffed The Chaser supreme, derisively.

My confident expression changed and I turned even paler than normal.

"Do I get multiple choice or a Smartphone, or maybe Phone a Friend?" I asked Stallion, nervously.

"You don't know how to use a Smartphone and you don't have any friends," laughed my broadcast colleague.

"No problem, I'm still going to best the Beast!" I grinned, rocking back in my chair and wringing my hands in mock confidence.

"I can smell your fear from here," was Mark's calm retort.

"No, he's back in Morecambe."

Johnny Phere loved that quip.

Then the quiz began and Stallion played the role of quizmaster with aplomb. But if I have one criticism, it is that his chosen questions were really easy. Any wrestling fan with half a brain would surely have known that Hulk Hogan and Andre the Giant main evented WrestleMania III, and that The Road Warriors consisted of Hawk and Animal. So I fared extremely well. The only answer I didn't know was that the theme tune Imagine What I Could Do To You belonged to effeminate 1970s UK wrestler Adrian Street.

As I correctly answered the final question, scoring 14 out 15, I punched the air in delight. Even The Beast, who had been smirking throughout my round, gave me a sporting round of applause.

I sat back in my chair, relaxed and smug.

But then came Beasty Boy's questions. They were actually slightly harder than mine. But as Labbett answered each one correctly, I became increasingly agitated. I stared at the quiz legend with a combination of wonder and angry shock, feeling like most of the contestants on The Chase whenever the big man with the big brain gets on a roll. When The Beast got the 10th question right, my head was in my hands.

"Are you sweating?" inquired Mark of my well-being, before correctly telling Stallion that The Warlord was The Barbarian's partner in The Powers of Pain. He also knew that Dustin Rhodes was also known as Goldust and that Paul Bearer was the host of The Funeral Parlour. Labbett tied me with 14 correct answers and it all came down to the wire.

Stallion peered at his clipboard and asked his final question.

"Who is known as the Texas Rattlesnake?"

"OH THAT'S RIDICULOUS!" I shrieked, eyes popping out of my head, knowing full well this was the easiest wrestling-related question known to man.

"YOU CAN'T GIVE HIM THAT! EVERYBODY KNOWS THAT!"

"WHAT?" taunted The Beast, to show that he knew the answer even before he delivered it. Then The Chaser put his hand - which is more like a coal shovel - on my shoulder. Labbett stared right at me, with a knowing grin, and answered.

"Stone Cold Steve Austin."

The Beast had won, 15 points to 14.

I reacted to defeat like I'd just been told I'd won the Lottery but lost the ticket.

"That's a fix, Stallion!" I protested.

"You must have given him the answers!"

Well, dear reader, now it's time to reveal a little secret of pro wrestling. The Beast actually *had* been given the answers.

This is what you didn't see on camera.

We actually filmed a first take of Lambert v Labbett, which we didn't release. In this version, neither of us was given the questions and answers beforehand. It was a complete shoot. And in a legitimate, fair, wrestling trivia head-to-head, I won comfortably by

14 points to eight.

You see, while The Beast was a big grapple enthuasist for sure, wrestling isn't his speciality subject. But it *is* mine. In a real contest, I knew too much for him.

But I wasn't happy with the result. So afterwards, I called for a second take. I just didn't think a Greg 'The Truth' Lambert victory was what the audience would want to see. It wasn't entertaining enough. People love to see The Truth act all cocky but get his come-uppance because pride comes before a fall. So we re-did it and this time it was fixed so The Beast got every question right, to pip me by a single point. This is the version we put out to the world. And I think this was the right decision.

Afterwards, Mark shook my hand and thanked me for 'putting him over'. What a gentleman. For the record, there is no way on earth I would beat him in a proper general knowledge battle on The Chase. And in an actual fight, the mammoth mastermind would probably squash me.

I entered The Beast's world and lived to tell the tale. And later that night, he entered mine. Labbett managed the team of Martin Kirby and El Ligero in a tag title match against Team Single. Then he turned on them, helping the heels to win. The Beast proved to be a dab hand as a wrestling manager too. It would be great to have him back in PCW someday.

And now I will be able to tell my grandkids of the day I *almost* beat The Beast...even though I *did* beat him really!

The next month, Vader came to PCW. I was really looking forward to this. I got to know Leon White, The Man They Call Vader, in a series of phone conversations leading up to his arrival in Preston. Fludder put us in touch because I wanted to interview Vader for Power Slam.

Getting the interview was hard work. Leon was a gentleman but a tough negotiator and as hard to pin down in real life as he was during his storied career as one of wrestling's best ever super heavyweights. And he wanted payment. I was surprised but happy when Findlay Martin agreed. Apparently Vader was only the second wrestler he'd agreed to pay for an interview in 20 years as editor of Power Slam, so he must have felt the big man was worth it. The money changed hands and, after a few scheduling pitfalls and many telephone conversations, I eventually contacted Leon at his Colorado home for an enjoyable hour-long Skype chat. It was a great interview.

When I met Vader in person at PCW Festive Fury on December 6 2013, the former WCW Champion shook my hand politely and said: "Mr Lambert, how are you sir?" He was there to wrestle Dave Mastiff. This was something of a dream match to UK fans and seemed the obvious bout to me too. Mastiff is arguably Britain's best big man, a 22-stone agile bully from The Black Country who can deliver a standing drop kick just as effortlessly as he can maul an opponent with a German suplex.

In his prime, Vader was a hard hitting beast who combined brute force and surprising speed for a 360lb behemoth in memorable matches with Sting, Stan Hansen and Mick 'Cactus Jack' Foley. Had Vader been 20 years younger, this could have been a classic. But 2013 was a good 20 years past Vader's prime. The bout with Mastiff ended in a disappointing disqualification after three awkward minutes.

Vader returned to PCW on April 25 2014. This time, not wanting to take any chances, Fludder made him a ringside lumberjack alongside fellow veterans Rikishi and Terry Funk for a PCW Championship main event between Joey Hayes and Danny Hope. Vader didn't seem comfortable for the majority of his time in PCW but at least he went out having fun, doing the 'Too Cool' dance in the ring with Rikishi, The Funker and Chris Masters. But in doing so, this was one time when two of PCW's British stars *were* completely marginalised.

"At the end, there was me and Danny in the ring with Masters, Rikishi and Terry, and they were going to do the Rikishi dance," said Dave Rayne.

"It was Danny's match and I was the local super-over babyface. Vader was being the ring general and marshalling the troops. He said: 'Chris, you stand here, Rikishi you here, Terry, you stand here' then he looked at me and Danny and said 'not you guys'. So me and Danny had to sit in the corner and wait for them to do the dance.

"Earlier during the match, there was a wonderful moment. I was a babyface lumberjack, there was a big brawl going on, and Terry

Funk spins me round and punches me, and I scream 'I'm on your side!' and run away. He didn't know who I was!"

Charles Wright, who came over for the Road to Glory weekend in February 2014, had a ball in PCW. Best known as The Godfather, The Pimp Daddy of the WWE Attitude era was coaxed by Fludder into reprising his old early 1990s voodoo persona Papa Shango. Charles and I sat down on the Saturday afternoon for a Power Slam interview in which the jovial Las Vegas strip club boss told me he hadn't wrestled as Shango in years. But he had been so impressed with Steven Fludder as a businessman, he'd been persuaded to bring the black hat, smoking skull and Baron Samedi facepaint out of retirement for one night only.

Wright had a blast in PCW and had obvious fun in the ring that weekend against PCW's resident Rascal, Pip 'Bubblegum' Cartner. On the Friday, it was Bubblegum v The Godfather. Then on Saturday, Bubblegum v Shango. This was a real exclusive for PCW and another example of how surreal and unpredictable our shows can be.

"You do sometimes get a clash of egos when the Americans come over, but I think that's because they don't know anyone for toffee, they're thousands of miles away from home, and if they get hurt who's going to look after them?" explained Dave Rayne.

"They don't want to get hurt so they don't want to do anything. So they're hesitant. And that's fine. But a lot of the British guys get worked up over it. It's because they think the guys have been brought in because they're better. And some of them are. You can't argue that Jeff Jarrett and Goldust aren't better. But some of the Americans are guys who just happen to have a lot of Twitter followers. So the Brits get frustrated.

"You see, with the amount of work there is in the UK right now, a lot of the British guys do more wrestling. A lot of the British guys get more work in a week than the Ring of Honor guys get in two months.

"I had a match with Goldust in 2013. A veteran, done everything in WWE, a second generation superstar who lives in wrestling. Very cool, easy to chat to. I said to him 'what do you want to do for the match?' He said 'you tell me, it's your crowd.' He made me plan the match. Once or twice he said 'let's do this instead'. That's quite a rarity. He wanted to see what I could do. And his suggestions didn't really change things much, he wasn't blocking anything.

"I had a great match with Shane Helms in 2014. It was more of a move-heavy match. And one of my big moves is a backcracker off the ropes. He asked 'how do I take that?' I told him. He said OK, he thinks about it, and he says ' I was in a car crash recently, I have metal pins in my ankles, I don't feel comfortable taking that.' He asked me to do it as a Codebreaker, he met me in the middle. The higher up guys are, the more relaxed they are about things.

"Jeff Jarrett and I planned this big emotional babyface underdog match at Fright Night 2015. Then we watched the show, and during it Jeff leaned over and said 'this crowd doesn't want to see wrestling, they just want to laugh and cheer'. So he came up with a new plan, this comedy match where because it was Hallowe'en I'd be The Rock and hit all The Rock's moves, so people could get cheap pops. It was the main event but I don't think anyone felt short changed. Guys like Jeff come wanting to work.

"Chris Masters, I think was a bit hesitant when he first met me, then I broke him (made him laugh) during the first Masterlock Challenge, then he had a great match with Trav, and he relaxed and became part of the roster."

Our foreign friends really showed what good sports they were in PCW's regular 'PC Fiction' skits. The GPW Science Fiction film crew members were regulars backstage at PCW shows in 2013 and 2014, where they somehow managed to convince some of the biggest names in wrestling to film the most surreal stuff for their wacky YouTube show. If you check out PC Fiction on-line, you will find everything from Terry Funk and Rikishi re-enacting the opening scene from Raiders of the Lost Ark, Kevin Owens and Jushin Liger pretending to be Power Rangers, and my personal favourite, me hosting The Jeremy Kyle Show with special guests 'The Miracle' Mike Bennett and Maria Kanellis, who then failed a lie detector test for, of all things, 'having sex with Danny Hope's tassels'.

I have no idea what the Tasker boys, and their cohorts Ash Preston and Kris 'From The Lab' Forster were smoking when they came up with the PC Fiction scripts but the segments were always great fun to do. I was sad when they ended.

Another era came to an end in summer 2014 when Power Slam closed down, bringing to an end my 12-year freelance tenure with the magazine. Findlay texted me to say 'prepare for the worst' and then phoned to let me know the magazine was no longer financially viable. Twenty years after its debut issue, Britain's most influential grapple mag was no more.

I was gutted but not entirely surprised. I had felt for some time, from my regular conversations with Findlay, that the writing was on the wall and that he would get out while PS was still making a profit. He had recently recovered from a battle with skin cancer and after two decades of working his backside off to produce the hard-hitting monthly publication, it was the right time for him to move on and do something less stressful with his life.

I have so much respect for Findlay Martin and the way he ran his business for more than 20 years. He turned Power Slam into a wrestling institution and he did so with principled professionalism. It was an education to work for him. Findlay always demanded excellence and his exacting standards improved me as a writer, interviewer and all-round journalist.

I first met Findlay at a wrestling convention in Croydon in 1993. But during my time working for him, although we regularly spoke on the telephone for more than a decade, I can count on two hands the number of times I was actually face-to-face with him, despite living only five miles away. Over the years, he worked every hour God sends perfecting each issue of Power Slam in his tiny office in Lancaster - an office, incidentally, I never visited. I have certainly seen Fin a lot more since PS ended. Recently we've been out for a drink in Lancaster and sometimes he attends PCW shows too.

But back in the PS era, Findlay deliberately kept his distance from the wrestling business so he could report with objectivity. Findlay's reclusive nature ensured complete unbias in his coverage. It was a sensible approach.

Although Findlay's attitude to pro wrestling differs greatly from my own, I was hugely influenced by his writing style. His Power Slam articles were informative, meticulously researched and entertainingly cutting. And he was brutally honest with his assessments of wrestlers and matches. In an industry where egos are often fragile, some of his more scathing reviews didn't always go down too well with the subject matter. A number of British wrestlers and promoters, over the years, reacted badly to articles about them in Power Slam. This is part of the reason why Findlay used to steer clear of covering British wrestling, especially during its lean years. It was far too much hassle for too little reward. Because until recent years, British wrestling simply didn't sell magazines.

Findlay wanted his team of writers to compete for space in Power Slam in order to produce the best possible product. So my monthly phone calls to Fin were a bit like standing in front of the terrifying panel on TV show Dragons' Den. I used to call him up every month and pitch an idea for an article. Sometimes the tough taskmaster Mr Martin turned it down and it was back to the drawing board. Often I had to prepare three or four different concepts before he approved one. The incentive was always there, because the money was so good. If Findlay didn't like my ideas, I didn't get a job that month, and so I didn't get paid. The trick was to come up with such a strong idea that he spread the article over four to six pages. The higher the word count, you see, the bigger the wage.

Findlay was an editor in the truest sense of the word. It wouldn't be uncommon for him to edit great chunks of my copy, sometimes even most of the article! But I never felt precious about this. Power Slam was his magazine and livelihood and he had every right to present my work however he wanted. It did mean, though, that I used to spend days, weeks even, researching, writing and rewriting my Power Slam stories, mainly out of professional pride in a usually vain attempt to have my words pass the strict Findlay Martin litmus test! It was hard work but such a buzz to see my byline in the magazine I used to read as a young man.

In later years I was glad to settle into a pattern of mainly doing Q&A style interviews for Power Slam because they were much easier to write up than feature articles, and less stressful and time-consuming. Unless, of course, the interview subject either refused the interview altogether, or agreed the interview and then changed their mind, or became difficult to pin down by phone or Skype because they were never at home at the agreed time. And whenever an interview fell through it drove me round the bend, because it hit me in the pocket.

I always wanted to interview Shawn Michaels for Power Slam. I tried several times over the years but was his management team always sent a polite message saying he wasn't interested. Others who did not want to be interviewed included Val Venis (who agreed at first but then never answered my calls), Jake Roberts (who agreed at first but then his agent never replied to follow-up messages) and Goldust (who politely declined).

But many *did* agree. I said my wrestling contacts were a double-edged sword and certainly, my roles with the FWA and PCW ensured easy access to many interview subjects over the years. My final interview for PS was backstage at the PCW Supershow Weekend on May 30 2014 with Gregory Shane 'The Hurricane' Helms. It appeared in the last ever issue of PS, Issue 237, released on July 14 2014. Ironically my first interview for Power Slam was also conducted in a wrestling dressing room, at an FWA event with Christopher Daniels for Issue 110 in August 2003. I am extremely grateful to The Hurricane, Vader, The Godfather, Daniels and the many other top overseas and British wrestlers and personalities who allowed me the chance to interview them for PS over the years - especially Daniel Bryan and Colt Cabana, the only two people I managed to interview on two separate occasions.

Some of my favourite Power Slam interviews were with Jim Ross (2013), Diamond Dallas Page (2013), Bret Hart (2008), Raven (2005), Balls Mahoney (2008), Bully Ray (2013), D'Lo Brown (2004) and CM Punk (2004).

JR was fantastic to talk to. I think my chat with the legendary WWE and WCW commentator was probably my longest phone interview for Power Slam, clocking in at a whopping two hours. Page was a fun guy, although he did chastise me for referring to his revolutionary exercise plan as just 'Yoga' and not 'DDP Yoga'! And the Raven and Punk interviews were memorable due to the random locations where they took place - the Station pub in Morecambe (Raven) and Southbury Leisure Centre in Enfield (Punk).

The Balls Mahoney interview came about thanks to Dann Read, who hooked me up with the ECW 'Chair Swinging Freak' after meeting him on a tour of Portugal. Balls held nothing back and was an engaging character, even if it's the only interview that took me three attempts to finish. I called him up, he answered a few questions, then cut the conversation short because he was busy. This happened twice in the space of a week, then on the third time I finally managed to complete the interview while he was driving to a rock concert, Aerosmith, I think it was. Balls struck me as a free spirit and I was sad when he passed away in 2016.

My friend the TNA press officer Simon Rothstein arranged the interview with Bully Ray while he was TNA Champion. At one point I asked Bully about his longtime tag team partner D-Von. Bully insisted that D-Von was his actual brother, even though most fans by that time realised The Dudley Boyz were not siblings in real-life. I respected Bully for protecting the business but I insisted that he and D'Von were not blood relatives and pressed him on the issue. Bully stuck to his guns too. It led to an awkward moment.

But Findlay always encouraged me to explore the difficult subjects other interviewers shied away from. This is why I quizzed Bret Hart about his revelations of infidelity in his book Hitman: My Real Life in the Cartoon World of Wrestling and asked D'Lo Brown about the horrendous injury suffered by Darren Drozdov in 1999 when a Brown running power bomb went wrong during a WWE match, 'Droz' landed on his head and was rendered a quadriplegic. It wasn't always easy to ask these tough questions. But it was my job and it led to some of the best work of my journalism career.

If I had to pick my best ever PS interview, it would be the one I did with Paul London for Issue 198 in December 2010.

I first worked with Paul in 2003 for the FWA. London was with Ring of Honor at the time and part of the crack ROH squad, alongside Samoa Joe, Christopher Daniels and AJ Styles, who'd come over to compete against the FWA's finest in an inter-promotional event called Frontiers of Honor at the York Hall, Bethnal Green. Many years later in 2010, after London's tenure with WWE saw him capture tag team championships and the cruiserweight title, he returned to the independent circuit. As WWE contracted wrestlers rarely gave interviews to Power Slam, Paul's release offered up the opportunity to phone him for a chat.

A free spirit who hated the corporate restrictions of the world's largest wrestling company, London really cut loose during that interview and held nothing back with his opinions of WWE.

He also told a memorable tale about the time when, fed up at his treatment in WWE, he decided to repackage himself as a King Neptune-style character, walked up to Triple H backstage at RAW wielding a trident and challenged the future Chief Operating Officer to a fight. It was a peach of an interview thanks to Paul's outspoken bravado, the kind journalists dream of.

In 2013 and 2014, Paul came over to the UK and appeared for PCW. It was great to get reacquainted with The Intrepid Traveller. The zany Texan told me our Power Slam conversation was his favourite ever interview and we had a right good laugh. I also loved commentating on his ring entrances because they were the longest in the history of wrestling. Dressed in a space suit, the Astro-Nut appeared at the top of the Evoque stairs, then pretended to get lost on the way to the ring, shook hands with just about every fan, went to the bar, wandered over to the commentary table to offer sweets (at least, I think they were sweets) to myself and Stallion, checked out the merchandise stand, disappeared into the street (his ring music still playing), then returned, did a full lap of the nightclub and eventually clambered into the ring to face his exasperated opponent after taking around 15 minutes to reach his destination. Paul's epic entrances made such an impact that Fludder even named a PCW show in September 2014 after him, calling it 'Just Get in the Bloody Ring'!

The annual Fright Night is always one of my favourite PCW shows. Traditionally, the PCW wrestlers and staff don fancy dress costumes for the Hallowe'en show to celebrate the spooky time of year. Fright Night is where you get unusual situations like Martin Kirby competing as a smaller version of Kane, Uhaa Nation confronting Joey Hayes dressed as the Grim Reaper, and Dave Rayne and Mad Man Manson bumbling around the ring trying to wrestle in a pantomime horse costume. It is completely bonkers but entertaining as hell, and typical of the anarchic humour often on display at PCW where it is not just about great wrestling.

After weeks of racking our brains, myself and Stallion decided our contribution to 2014's Fright Night would be to swap clothes. So The Ultimate Male donned a dodgy wig, specs, a crooked nose and a grandad suit, hunched his shoulders and clutched a copy of *Holy Grail: The True Story of British Wrestling's Revival* like his life depended on it. Meanwhile, I dressed in a classic Stallion crimson frilly shirt, bandana and leopard skin boots, with a drawn-on beard, big smile and fake Geordie accent. Then we both went to the ring before the show, where I cut a promo as Stallion. Way-ay man!

I had so much fun that night and got far more female attention than I normally do. In character, of course, as I am a happily married man.

I don't think Stallion did quite so well with the ladies while dressed as me, though.

The first PCW v Ring of Honor Supershow Weekend took place in November 2014. This was poetic, for me, seeing as though it was 11 years since I worked on the first ever ROH inter-promotional show in Britain. Working for PCW has given me many similar deja vu experiences. I've had chance to catch up with many overseas stars I worked with during the FWA days and had hardly seen in years; like Paul London, D'Lo Brown, Terry Funk, Christopher Daniels, AJ Styles, Samoa Joe, Low Ki (who was on the first ever show I ever worked on, for Dann Read's New Era Wrestling in July 2002 at Ipswich Corn Exchange) and Juventud Guerrera, who main evented the first show I ever promoted, FWA British Breakout at the Morecambe Dome in April 2003.

Brodus Clay was at the first ROH Supershow Weekend in 2014 and seemed a fish out of water. Like Vader, a hulking monster of a man, Brodus was quiet, headphones on, and kept himself to himself. He also gave the Leary brothers the fright of their lives when they dared to play his WWE entrance music for his match with Michael Elgin on the Friday night. Having just left for TNA, the man now known as Tyrus was furious the PCW sound crew would remind him of his days as the dancing Funkasaurus, and didn't he let poor Chris and Andrew know it.

Tyrus did cheer up though, when Booker T arrived on the Saturday night. As the legendary Five-Time WCW Champion received a hero's welcome, Clay joined him in the ring, apologised to the fans for being moody the night before and joined in the fun as Booker treated Preston to its very own Spinerooni. "I didn't know Booker was going to be here!" explained the big man.

It was a pleasure to work with the Ring of Honor stars at those weekenders. Adam Cole, the ReDragon team of Kyle O'Reilly and Bobby Fish, Roderick Strong, The Briscoe Brothers, Mike Bennett and Maria Kanellis, Tomasso Ciampa, Cedric Alexander, Dalton Castle, ACH, Michael Elgin, Silas Young, Jay Lethal and booker Hunter 'Delirious' Johnson fit right in to our dressing room environment. The ROH crew understood what the PCW crowd wanted to see and worked their socks off to produce the combination of quality in-ring action and tongue-in-cheek tomfoolery that always goes down a storm in Preston. After the first Supershow Weekend in 2014, Hunter Johnson gave both rosters a rousing pep talk backstage, telling us how much he'd enjoyed himself. He put PCW and its talent over so strongly, it made us all feel about 10 feet tall. It was a great moment.

So it was a real shame when two years later, the ROH-PCW agreement ended after the American company booked a show in Liverpool head-to-head with a PCW event in the same city on the same day. Once again Fludder put his business first and told ROH where to go. Then he ran his November 2016 weekender with indie talent from CZW, WXW and Beyond Wrestling instead, making the best of a difficult situation as always.

Mad Man Manson's name has come up a few times in this chapter. No story about PCW is complete without mentioning the real-life Darren O'Byrne, the bare footed wrestling lunatic from Ireland who wrestled his last ever match at the November 2014 ROH weekender. A truly unforgettable performer and a hell of a guy.

I first met Manson when I worked for Len Davies' Real Quality Wrestling at Bethnal Green in 2007. Back then Darren was just establishing himself on the UK scene playing his gimmick of a crazy man with a big toothy grin and ridiculous hair who rolled down the aisle to the ring in a straitjacket. But Manson was not your typical wrestling psycho. He scrawled weird messages all over his body with marker pen, including the result of his match on the sole of his foot. He lost his bouts by placing himself in submission holds before tapping out. He cut promos revealing the secrets of pro wrestling and got away with it because he was so damn funny. Nobody had ever seen Manson's like before. The guy was completely off his trolley and totally hilarious.

Manson worked in Morecambe a few times over the years. In 2008, we did a spot at XWA Gold Rush where he got the rumble and the raffle confused. The Mad Man came out during the raffle and tried to throw me over the top rope. Then he came out during the rumble and tried to sell raffle tickets to his bemused opponents. Then in 2014, he was supposed to wrestle Grado at the Globe Arena, home of Morecambe Football Club, as you may recall. But instead they started booting a ball around and ended up having a one-a-side kickabout in the middle of the ring. Manson was such a character and he would do anything...*anything* to entertain the fans. The weirder the better.

Prior to his arrival in Morecambe for XWA Gold Rush 2012, Manson did a promotional YouTube video where he cut one of the funniest promos I've ever heard. He mused on what the letters 'X-W-A' stood for. While sitting in front of a fish tank. For no apparent reason.

It's perhaps the only promo by a British-based wrestler I can recite verbatim.

"It was bound to happen, it was always going to happen. Mad Man Manson is back in the XWA. The A, for Association, the W for Wrestling, which I won't be doing very much of, and the X...the X...the X?

"What does it stand for, Lambert? Is it Xylophone? Oh yes, very clever. Internet.

"Is it Xanax Wrestling? Naming your promotion after a prescription drug, Lambert? Oh yeah, you and your Wellness Policy.

"Is it...Xenophobe Wrestling? Are you serious? You racist Lambert! Well how about this, Lambert. I'm entering myself into your Gold Rush rumble and me, a foreigner, a black man...or at least, a man who wears black wrestling gear, is coming to Morecambe to win your rumble. And not just that, I'm also going to win the raffle.

"February 4. At some venue. XWA. Manson returns! And also sorry Greg, but I am going to ruin your show. Sorry in advance.

Thanks."

And true to his word, he did indeed ruin my show. Manson's job in PCW was as comic relief. He didn't do much wrestling at all. He just clowned around in his own inimitable style. In between all the great matches and big famous names at PCW, you could always rely on Manson to bring something different, to have everybody crying with laughter at his shenanigans.

There was the time he and Danny Hope did an entire dance routine to Beyonce's Single Ladies in the middle of a match. There was his god-awful bout with a terrible wrestler called Freight Train, the Five Dollar Wrestling Champion and 'internet sensation' from America, which was so bad, it was almost good. There were the bouts when he deliberately wrestled in super slow-motion. And check out the YouTube video where Ted DiBiase teaches Manson how to apply the Million Dollar Dream by choking out interviewer 'Magic' Mark Adams. It is absolute gold.

Manson was always playing jokes or 'ribs' on El Ligero. Travelling the road together, the two were great friends. But at PCW shows, Darren always found a way to humiliate Ligs because he knew the 'masked Mexican' 'spoke no English' and couldn't verbally fight back without completely breaking character. So Manson made little digs at Ligero during promos. The Irish nutter even got the ring announcer to introduce him as Simon Musk - Ligero's real name.

Then one night Manson was being interviewed by Richard Parker backstage and began telling an emotional story about his first ever wrestling match 10 years before in Ireland.

"My opponent was injured during the match, quite badly," said Manson, in what appeared to be a rare moment of seriousness.

"He went to hospital and about a week or so later, he passed away due to complications with a blood clot."

As Parker looked at him, concerned and genuinely surprised, Manson continued, his voice cracking with emotion.

"I remember when he went to hospital, he was in an induced coma," said the tearful Darren.

"I went to see him. I asked if he was all right, and he only said two words to me, and I'll always remember them.

"He had tears in his eyes as he looked at me.

"And he said...F__K LIGERO!"

As the Mad Man grinned evilly in triumph at his ruse, having made the whole story up so he could belittle El Ligero on camera, Parker had to abandon ship, walking off shot howling with laughter.

You can see this interview, in all its glory, on YouTube.

The only problem with Manson was that I found it nearly impossible to commentate on his matches because he never did any moves. Having said that, one of the biggest crowd reactions in PCW history came when one night, out of nowhere, Manson delivered a Canadian Destroyer somersault piledriver to Bubblegum. The Evoque crowd collectively lost its mind. For Manson, supposedly the most unathletic grappler on the roster, to deliver one of wrestling's most spectacular manoeuvres...well, it blew the roof off the club. It showed what a smart performer he could be. He rarely did anything dangerous in the ring but when he did, he made it count.

Manson really came into his own on the PCW Saturday afternoon shows. We called them 'Hangover Shows' because a lot of the wrestlers, staff and fans went out drinking after the Friday night show. While I don't think any of the performers were *actually* hung over (with the possible exception of Stallion) the wrestling was usually at a gentle pace on Hangover Shows with lots of stalling and comedy. For example, in November 2014 at the PCW/Ring of Honor Supershow Weekend, we even had a 'No Loud Noises' match between American stars ACH and Cedric Alexander, where the wrestlers chopped each other softly and the crowd chanted in whispers so not to give ACH and Cedric an even bigger headache after their night on the tiles!

During that weekend, Manson came to the ring for a Hangover Show six-man tag team match with Dave Rayne and Dave Mastiff against T-Bone, Rampage Brown and Bubblegum, dressed for no apparent reason as a gangster rapper. As the gurning and very white-skinned Irishman pretended to be The Same Old G from the West Side, hard man Rampage Brown was standing on the ring apron, covering his face in an attempt not to burst out laughing.

Later the...ahem...*unique* finish of this match saw the Insane One tie his own tag partner Rayne's hands behind his back, gag him, produce a sex toy and tease an unspeakable act of violation upon poor Dave. I am not kidding. Thankfully, Bubblegum rolled Manson up and pinned the Mad Man to save Rayne from becoming PCW's answer to the Pulp Fiction Gimp.

I literally had no words to describe this repulsive scene of depravity. It did cross my mind, however, that it was exactly the kind of thing tradition-loving British wrestling veterans would hate and completely contrary to anything you'd ever allow on a family wrestling show. But in Preston, Manson got away with it. Why? Because he's Manson.

Later that evening, after teaming with Dave Rayne to defeat Delirious and Paul London in a typically bonkers encounter, Mad Man Manson grabbed the microphone and matter-of-factly announced that he had just wrestled his last ever match. He thanked the fans and left the PCW ring for the final time. He meant it, too. Manson retired from pro wrestling in much the same way as he'd tackled his career. By going completely against the grain.

Just over a year later, Manson returned for an after-show Q&A with the PCW fans and was asked why he had retired. I wasn't there that night but Dave Rayne later told me what Manson had said. He said there were three reasons. He was now in a well-paid job running a warehouse, he now had time to go to the theatre at weekends, but the main reason was he could not mentally cope with wrestling. He liked to perform, and how people reacted to him. He enjoyed being the centre of attention and getting the rush. But then he would have to drive home to his real life. And while he was wrestling, his real life felt inferior.

At time of writing, Manson has stuck to his retirement. This is a rarity in pro wrestling where 'retired' grapplers usually come back within a few months. And he's left a huge comedy-sized hole on PCW shows that's difficult to fill.

Mad Man Manson the character was politically incorrect and off his rocker. But Darren O'Byrne the man is a highly intelligent fella who is culturally aware. He also became a big fan of Morecambe after his trips here and has revisited the town with his wife Sammy since his retirement. He particularly raves about the humble Old Pier Bookshop on the Promenade and the annual outdoor theatre show at Williamson Park in nearby Lancaster. When I gave him advice on what to do and see in my hometown, he even christened me 'Mr Morecambe'. I then started using that nickname to get heat on Morecambe shows.

It may be a mistake to admit that in print, in case Manson asks for royalties. And believe me, he will.

In 2015, I ended up taking part in another battle royal, in rather unusual circumstances. You see, on commentary, I constantly used to criticise Joanna Rose's manipulative actions as PCW General Manager. This led to a rather unique punishment. At the annual Who Dares Wins show on March 29 2015, Joanna forced me to compete in the 30-man rumble!

PCW rumbles are always a hoot and typical of the outside-the-box lunacy that gives Preston shows a life of their own. There have been some nutty moments over the years. Like in 2013, when referees Des Robinson and Daz Bateman both entered the rumble leading to a bizarre referee catfight and duelling crowd chants of "DES!" and "DAZ!" as they rolled around the ring in their striped shirts; like when Professor Mike Holmes hypnotised the chubby fitness guru Gym Powers, giant Viking powerhouse The Nordic Warrior and heel manager Gilligan Gordon into halting the rumble to perform cult dance craze The Harlem Shake; and like when WWE legend The Million Dollar Man Ted DiBiase inexplicably became Mad Man Manson's manager and paid off several participants to eliminate themselves!

And in 2014, when Danny Hope climbed on the back of Cyanide during the rumble and rode the mammoth Toxic Terror while the Miley Cyrus song Wrecking Ball played over the PA, then Cyanide sent a string of opponents flying over the top rope by bumping into them like...erm...a wrecking ball; and when my good mate the veteran Keith Myatt entered the rumble dressed as Coronation Street's Deirdre Barlow in full blonde wig, glasses and...well, greying beard.

In 2015, it was my turn to immerse myself into this surreal hilarity. And why? Because the show was on a Sunday night and the last train back to Morecambe was after Who Dares Wins was scheduled to finish. So being the lateral thinker he is, Fludder suggested I should be pitched into the rumble as a cover story so I could leave early! Unlike Sanjay Bagga, Steven had the good grace to give me a week's notice to psyche myself up.

About halfway through the rumble, Joanna Rose interrupted me on commentary and ordered me down to the ring. I was in my full suit and a new shiny silver scarf I had bought for £30 from Salford Quays shopping centre. Of course, I vehemently protested because remember, I am a writer, not a fighter.

But then a strange thing happened. The PCW fans began to chant my name. "GREG! GREG! GREG!" This had never happened before. The Preston lot usually boo the very mention of Greg 'The Truth' Lambert, despite my role as babyface commentator. With the fans behind me, I handed my specs to a ringside steward and climbed onto the apron, feeling 10 feet tall, my chest puffed out with pride. Although I couldn't see anything without my glasses (thanks Velma) I was ready for anything.

Well, anything except a Keith Myatt Stone Cold Stunner. I really like and respect Keith, who I've known since my early years in the business, and it was a strange pleasure to have my jaw jacked by the 50something Deirdre lookalike. The move sent me flying into the corner where Dave Rayne had handcuffed himself to avoid being eliminated, while dressed completely in protective bubble wrap (you couldn't make this up, could you?) As I lay against the bubble-wrapped Dave, dazed from the Myatt Stunner, the Scottish female wrestler Viper pressed her generous buttocks into my mush and gave me a Rikishi-style Stinkface.

This, I have to admit, was not entirely unpleasant.

You may remember from my LDN experience that going over the top rope is not my speciality. So I insisted that this time, I would eliminate myself. After wiping my face with mock disgust from the Viper Stinkface, I hauled myself upright and awkwardly clambered over Dave Rayne and the turnbuckle, touched down on the floor, stormed back to the commentary position, ranted at Stallion who was splitting his sides with laughter, grabbed my bag and stomped out of Evoque. As the rumble continued I then sprinted down Fishergate and made my train with seconds to spare. I was halfway back to Morecambe by the time Dave Mastiff won the damn thing.

Some of the biggest names in wrestling kept on coming to Preston throughout 2015. One of my favourite weekenders was PCW Supershow V on April 24 and 25 2015, starring Rob Van Dam, Eric Bischoff and the Jarretts.

Van Dam was as chilled out in real life as his 4:20 persona and was even relaxed when he discovered he couldn't hit his trademark 5 Star Frog Splash due to the notoriously low Evoque ceiling. Like many high flyers who competed at the venue before him, RVD quickly realised he was likely to knock himself out if he went for such a spectacular leap off the top rope. So The Whole F'N Show instead nonchaltantly rolled his opponent Bubblegum outside the ring, hit a frog splash from the apron, then threw him back in for the pinfall.

Eric Bischoff's appearance was a great moment. He wasn't backstage immediately before the Friday night show. I wondered if he was going to show up at all. But then, just before the scheduled main event between Lionheart and Jeff Jarrett, his familiar "I'M BAAACK!" theme struck up, and the former Executive Producer of WCW poked his head through the entrance curtain, grinning maniacally like Jack Nicholson's 'HEEERE'S JOHNNY!' in One Flew Over The Cuckoo's Nest. The arrival of The Bisch was one of those times when I was virtually jumping off my commentary stool, the veins bulging in my neck and the decibel levels rising as I bellowed that Easy E, the man who inspired WCW to beat Vince McMahon in the ratings for 84 consecutive weeks during the Monday Night Wars, was here in little old Preston.

By the way, as I mentioned before, I do get very excited on commentary when the time is right. But I would rather be over-the-top than sound bored. I have heard some UK commentators whose voice level never changes during a show. Whether they are describing an opening match wristlock or a huge main event bump off the top of a ladder through three tables, they sound like they are voicing the Shipping Forecast on Radio 4. I have heard other commentators who yell and scream constantly. Neither is the right way to do it. You have got to vary your volume to convey the emotional ebbs and flows of a professional wrestling event. So during technical bouts like Noam Dar v Johnny Kidd, my voice is usually calm and steady. But when Team Single and The Hooligans are hurling tables and chairs at each other in an arena-wide brawl, or a main event between Lionheart and AJ Styles is reaching its dramatic climax, I will crank my throat up to fever pitch.

I have worked with Jeff and Karen Jarrett a couple of times in PCW. The Jarretts are true professionals and are really nice behind the scenes. But once they get in front of the people, Jeff's old school Southern 'wrasslin' background really comes to the fore. The King of the Mountain sure knows how to work heel the right way and so does his sassy wife. It is hard for villains to get heat from a 'smart' crowd these days. Not for the Jarretts. They know exactly how to push buttons. I watched the aftermath of a dramatic 10-man main event tag on April 25 2015 in which Lionheart, Dave Mastiff, Dave Rayne and The Hooligans beat Chris Masters, Bubblegum, Team Single and Jeff Jarrett. As Mrs Jarrett screeched some extremely personal insults at Mastiff, then hurled her high-heeled shoe at him, leading to a tense staredown between Dave and Double J, there was crackling tension in the air at Evoque. I wasn't quite sure if the hatred between Mastiff and the Jarretts was real or not. That's proper working.

The Dudley Boyz also had a whale of a time in PCW. When Bubba and D-Von made the first of two outings in Preston at Just Get in the Bloody Ring on September 26 2014, they had such a good craic with the fans that the grinning Bully Ray, who was coming to the end of a tenure with TNA, grabbed the mic and told our spectators: "I've been here five minutes and I'm having more fun than I've had in the past five years!"

The former Team 3D beat Team Single by DQ that night then returned to face T-Bone and Rampage in a non-title tables match at the second annual PCW Tribute to the Troops on July 11 2015. Now Tribute to the Troops is the kind of event that makes Preston City Wrestling stand out. It is typical of Steven Fludder's business acumen and shows how far British wrestling as a whole has come in the past few years. In 2014 and 2015 it was held outdoors in the Preston Flag Market, a square in the city centre with capacity for 5,000 people to watch in the shadow of some of Preston's most historic municipal buildings.

Although the shows were free so no money was generated from ticket sales, it didn't matter because the local council helped to fund it. Imagine that! A council paying for a British wrestling show!

Why? Because the councillors know PCW events bring money into the Preston economy. PCW fans travel to the shows from all over and during their weekends in the city, they stay in hotels and B&Bs, and spend in pubs, shops and restaurants. PCW has become a big part of Preston's social scene and a money-spinner for the city coffers. Credit must also go to Councillor Drew Gale, a regular at PCW events and a big supporter of what we do. In summer 2016 Fludder held the show indoors at the 2,500 capacity Preston Guild Hall, another step up for PCW in its home city.

Tribute to the Troops is also great publicity for PCW because it is held on Armed Forces Day. The army, navy and air force were represented at the event and money was raised for forces charities. So on the afternoon of Saturday July 11 2015, there just happened to be a giant military tank parked near the ring in the Flag Market. After The Dudleys defeated Team Single, the 23-time world tag team champions climbed up to celebrate on top of the tank! That was quite a sight and an iconic moment in PCW history.

Later that afternoon, Dave Mastiff captured the PCW Championship from Chris Masters in the main event. To illustrate this momentous title change, I actually called the new champion by his proper nickname on commentary (I usually refer to him as the B-Word). So this was the first and only time you will ever hear the profanity-hating Truth refer to Dave by his true moniker of 'The Bastard'. Well, apart from just then.

Tribute to the Troops also saw Martin Kirby capture the Money in the Bank briefcase. Martin is a really good guy and another intelligent and versatile in-ring performer. Before he became a wrestler, the North Yorkshireman used to sit in the front row as a fan at FWA shows and take everything in as if doing research for his upcoming career. I first saw him actually compete on a Triple Team Promotions event in Carlisle in 2007, run by Cumbria brothers The Nattrass Boys. In the role of a snivelling heel, it struck me how much Martin resembled a young Stevie Knight. This was the time when the pride of Thirsk was establishing his Project Ego team with Kris Travis as one of the best around. Fast forward to the PCW years and Kirby was now a likeable babyface, a silky smooth technician highly respected by fans and peers alike. Fludder could always rely on The

Engine Room of PCW, as I call him, to have a solid mid-card match with everyone from Tomasso Ciampa to Lance Storm. But by early 2015 Kirby was kind of treading water in Preston.

Meanwhile Joey Hayes' PCW Title reign ended at the hands of Chris Masters at the third anniversary show on August 1 2014. For a few months afterwards, Joey was kind of lost in the shuffle. Then, out of the blue, Joey was thrown together with Kirby.

Suddenly, at the Who Dares Wins Rumble in 2015, Joey and Martin found themselves in the ring together. And the bossy Hayes somehow cajoled the affable Kirby into joining forces with him. Over the ensuing months, they formed an odd couple tag team. Joey still broke the rules and arrogantly claimed to be the team captain, while Kirby remained a law-abiding good guy who reluctantly went along with his partner's scheming. The duo had chemistry and the dynamic worked a treat.

On April 25 2015 at Supershow V, an unlikely catchphrase was born. Before a scheduled bout between Maria Kanellis and April Davids could get under way, Joey turned up carrying a Poundland carrier bag, produced chocolates and a big lollipop, and declared undying love for the gorgeous Maria. But The First Lady of Wrestling's husband Mike Bennett and his partner Matt Taven did not take kindly to the Leigh lothario and challenged him and April to a six-person tag team match. At this, Hayes looked to the entranceway and screeched "MAAARTIN!" in an over-the-top, high-pitched, Monty Python-style voice, and out came a puzzled Kirby on command. Of course, the PCW fans immediately picked up on the "MAAARTIN!" and began shrieking it themselves, over and over again. The constant cries of "MAAARTIN!" provided a surreal backdrop to a side-splitting bout pitting Hayes, Kirby and Davids against Bennett, Taven and Kanellis, one of my favourite ever PCW matches to commentate on.

Later, Joey presented Kirby with a gift of a new pair of wrestling trunks, with "MAAARTIN!" written on them. He also organised new theme music for his partner, a peace song popular in American schools called Sing About Martin. When Kirby first heard it, he shook his head in resigned disbelief. The song was about Martin Luther King, not Martin Kirby! But PCW fans loved the tune immediately and began waving their hands in the air rythmically whenever the music played. Another example of the strange world of PCW!

After Kirby won the Money in the Bank briefcase, Hayes immediately seized it off him and started acting like *he* owned the contract for a title match of his choosing. This selfishness backfired at the Ring of Honor weekend in 2015 when Joey and Kirby ran out after PCW tag team champions Team Single were weakened by a ferocious streetfight with ReDragon, Hayes handed the briefcase to the referee, called for the cash-in, the odd couple quickly hit a double-team move, scored the pinfall and appeared to have become tag team champions, only for Joanna Rose to reverse the decision because only Kirby was allowed to cash in the briefcase.

Although Hayes and Kirby failed to win the tag team titles on that occasion, the duo now known as 'Two Mates Pissing About' eventually became the champs in September 2016, ending the astonishing reign of Team Single. Joey is having the time of his life playing an obnoxious funny guy. It is also pleasing to see him cutting in-ring promos. Joey always used to shy away from the microphone. It was a confidence issue. I have always tried to encourage him, because the lad knows how to talk. He just needed practice and self-belief. Now he looks entirely comfortable when speaking. It is great to see.

I mentioned Team Single, another duo to have flourished in Preston City Wrestling. Tyson T-Bone and Rampage Brown won the PCW Tag Team Titles on June 1 2013 in a three-way match against Fight Club and the legendary Steiner Brothers. Their subsequent three-and-a-half year reign became the stuff of legend. In that time the heavily tattooed T-Bone from Malvern, real name Tom Clifford, and Rampage faced a who's who of tag teams including The Hooligans, ReDragon, Brian Kendrick and Paul London, The Briscoes, War Machine and The Dudleys. On commentary, Stallion and myself described Team Single as the best tag team in the world. They are so believable. T-Bone and Rampage look like tough guys, carry themselves like tough guys, *are* tough guys, and can wrestle or brawl with the best of them.

"Bone and I have been friends for a long time outside of the ring," said Rampage when I spoke to him about his bond with Tom.

"When the opportunity came up for us to team, we already had that friendship and understanding. It wasn't like two guys who had just been thrown together. He looks out for me and I look out for him.

"We've had a few matches during our PCW run which I've enjoyed the most. The one with London and Kendrick felt like a real fight, that was good. A few weeks earlier I was reading Hardcore Holly's book and he was talking about how tough they were, and when I got in the ring and felt some of the kicks and punches I thought woah! I know what he's talking about now! Working with ReDragon was also very enjoyable. Kyle O'Reilly is one of the best workers I've ever been in the ring with. I could sit and watch his matches, he's like silk. The Briscoes as well. I've always felt they are what a tag team should be. I thoroughly enjoyed that match too."

I also loved T-Bone and Rampage's matches with The Hooligans in 2015 and 2016. Team Single had some choice brawls with Roy and Zak Knight, crammed with non-stop and breathtakingly violent action. Until their PCW debut at the Kris Travis charity show, I hadn't seen Zak, now 26, since his XWA days as the skinny masked teenager Zak Zodiac. He hasn't half grown. Zak is now much bigger than not only Roy, but their legendary dad Ricky too!

The Hooligans have a pure joy in their eyes whenever they are in the ring. You can tell they are from a wrestling family. Paige's older brothers were born to wrestle and it's obvious how much they love what they do. They are so easy to commentate on because their matches feel like real fights. The Knights go full-pelt with their hearts on their sleeves and never take a backward step. I always find myself getting swept away on commentary by their carefree violence inside the squared circle. The Hooligans quickly became big fan favourites in Preston and I was surprised they weren't the ones to end Team Single's reign. Instead Roy and Zak lost a pulsating Tables, Ladders and Chairs match to Tyson and Brown at Showdown on June 5 2015, and also came up short in an even better TLC rematch on September 24 2016.

Perhaps Team Single's most notorious match during their title run came at the fourth anniversary show on August 7 2015. The night of

Kris Travis' emotional comeback against Sha Samuels would also be remembered for Bone and Rampage 'shooting' on an upstart team who had won an internet fan vote to face them. The champions' opponents that night were South Coast duo The Brolievers - Josh Bodom and his brother Ryan Hendricks.

I recall Rampage being agitated backstage before the match. This was unusual, as Ollie is usually so relaxed and friendly, a bit of a joker in fact, in contrast to his mean and moody persona. It turns out that Brown had been riled by the attitude of the cocky Josh Bodom, for real.

The match was scheduled to go 10 minutes and be competitive. Instead, a one-sided beating ended after about two minutes when Rampage clamped on a forceful chokehold and Bodom tapped out. This wasn't part of the plan. Brown decided to teach Josh a lesson. The fans were confused. They realised something wasn't quite right. A bloody Bodom was livid and threw a paddy at ringside. But Team Single was unrepentant. The incident only added to their image as men not to be messed with, inside or outside the ring.

"What happened was out of character, for me, because I am usually easy to work with both in and out of the ring," said Ollie.

"Drew McDonald always told me if you can put people over, you'll always have a job. So my mindset has always been not to go in there and put myself over, but be easy to deal with and keep everybody happy. It's hard to do, especially in this job.

"So it wasn't a work, like a lot of the fans said online."

After Bone and Rampage turned face in early 2016, the PCW fans got right behind them and the duo continued to dominate the promotion. Rampage even won the Road to Glory tournament in 2016 after defeating Drew Galloway in a thrilling final.

Team Single's 'little brother' Bubblegum turned babyface at the same time. The Rascal is another Brit who has shone in the PCW wrestling ring.

I have known Pip 'Bubblegum' Cartner for more than a decade. Pip was originally trained by AIWF-GB promoter Chris Curtis at the Camp of Pain in Stoke-on-Trent which also spawned Johnny Phere, Dirk Feelgood, Mikey Whiplash, Dean Allmark, Five Star Flash and Robbie Dynamite. I used to go to watch AIWF-GB shows at Bidds nightclub near Stoke and in 2003, this is where I first clapped eyes on the teenage Pip. Then using the name Symon Phoenix, Pip was small, with a mop of hair, funny facial features and no physique to speak of, but it was obvious he had talent. Sweet guy, too. After he changed his ring name to Bubblegum, we brought Pip into the original FWA during its dying days. Young Cartner was starting to turn heads as a likeable underdog and as his skills improved, he became one of the UK scene's very best as a high-flying fan favourite.

It seemed unthinkable that cute little Bubblegum, the kids' hero from Hubba Bubba Ville, could ever become a villain. Johnnie Brannigan and GPW were the first to turn Bubblegum heel in 2010. He was surprisingly great in the role of cowardly cruiserweight crybaby. Like Rockstar Spud before him, Pip proved to be a versatile performer who was equally at home being good or bad.

"Pip came to GPW with a recommendation from Dirk Feelgood and at the time he wore bright green pleathers with bleached hair and looked like a little boy, but I watched the audience and I could see the reactions he was getting," said Johnnie Brannigan.

"His first feud with GPW was with me in 2006 and he was so good in the ring, doing things nobody had ever done with me before. He was fighting back like a proper babyface, firing up and I'd never been tested like that before.

"We created our Crazy Cruiser 8 tournament for him in November 2006 and put him over. He wrestled three times that night and what a pop when he won. He's grown up with the fans ever since then. We turned him heel and had him join Dirk's faction, The Masterplan. And he was great. I had reservations to be honest. But Pip convinced me. And it really worked. He's still heavily involved in GPW now. He's the first name on the team sheet and keeps getting better and better."

By the time PCW was formed, Bubblegum added further layers to his heel character. He became The Rascal, a dirty little street chav who would stoop to any depths to win a match.

Bubblegum was in the first PCW match I ever commentated on, ironically against his future ally T-Bone. The opening bout of PCW Guild Wars in June 2012 saw a fan favourite T-Bone, then the PCW

Champion, pulverise The Rascal who had stolen his championship belt and sold it to high street pawn shop Cash Converters. In reality, this was a cover story so Fludder could unveil a brand new belt! Over the ensuing months, T-Bone actually joined forces with Bubblegum and when Rampage Brown was added to the alliance, the Team Single trio became PCW's leading triumverate of trouble-causers. When Bubblegum captured the PCW Cruiserweight Title, the vile threesome held almost all the gold in Preston City Wrestling between them.

Bubblegum's Cruiserweight Title reign lasted 18 months. The Rascal won the belt at Who Dares Wins on April 28 2014 and held it until Fright Night on October 31 2015. During his run as heel cruiser champ, the conniving chav had a string of entertaining matches with everyone from Al Snow to Ashton Smith. He also main evented Just Get in the Bloody Ring, beating his childhood hero Brian Kendrick, a match that meant a lot to him. His three-way defences against Kris Travis and Mark Andrews at Supershow IV, then with Mandrews and Austin Aries at the third anniversary show, were particularly outstanding. He won the Road to Glory tournament in 2015, turned face and then regained the Cruiserweight Championship in 2016.

I personally believe Bubblegum is PCW's premier performer because he can do absolutely everything. He has become the perfect mix of reliable wrestler who never has a bad match, and outrageous entertainer you can't take your eyes off. Whether he is tearing the house down in a main event, clowning around on a comedic afternoon show, or playing the fall guy for an overseas star, Bubblegum always rises to whatever the occasion demands. As a heel, he was a master of getting heat, whether it was by wearing a Manchester City top and beanie hat to the ring (although in reality, Pip supports Everton!) or by threatening foes with his version of the Crane kick from The Karate Kid film, or by giving fans the V-sign, or worst of all, by sticking his hands down his trunks before disgustingly rubbing his smelly fingers into his opponent's eyes. As a face, he is so easy to like and has unbelievable emotionally-charged matches. Pip is one hell of a talent and these days his physique ripples with muscle too. He is unrecognisable from the Symon Phoenix era.

His success has come despite a real-life fight that's been much much tougher than any match he's had inside the squared circle. Pip has been very open about his ongoing battle with depression. Other British wrestlers, including Pip's great friend Chris Ridgeway, have also talked openly about similar struggles. As mentioned earlier, many wrestlers find it difficult to balance the rush of performing in front of live crowds and going back to their everyday lives. Wrestling itself is also an extremely tough discipline not just on the body, but the mind too.

In recent years we have lost so many pro wrestlers all over the world, far too young, for numerous reasons. In 2012, the UK scene mourned the tragically early passing of Dom Travis. Then in 2014, the British circuit rallied behind Kris Travis when he was diagnosed with cancer and grieved as one when he passed away two years later. When one of our own dies or suffers serious adversity, we are all affected. This is because British wrestling scene is one big brother and sisterhood.

There are so many of us involved on the UK wrestling scene of all ages, from all over the country, from different backgrounds, with different day jobs. We may not see each other from one week, or month, to the next, as we return to our daily lives after a weekend living out our childhood dreams. We might not even talk much about what's been happening in each other's lives outside wrestling, about our families or even just what's going on inside our heads. But when push comes to shove, we are all there for each other.

It's because we all have one thing in common. We all love professional wrestling.

When Pip opened up about his issues, he received an outpouring of love and respect from the UK scene. What I like best about him is that he will always give positive and supportive advice to the younger wrestlers backstage. They look up to him and value his tips and feedback. And he loves giving something back to the up-and-comers by passing on his knowledge, most recently as one of the trainers at the PCW Academy. He is a wonderful, positive influence to have around the dressing rooms in both PCW and also Morecambe, where he has competed many times over the years for FWA, XWA, PAID and Alpha Omega.

Pip was feeling much better personally in 2016 and professionally, he continued to excel. When PCW debuted in Liverpool city centre on May 21 2016, he had one of the best matches in company history. A racucous, sold-out crowd at Fusion nightclub was treated to an epic encounter between Bubblegum and Dean Allmark, full of crisp sequences, near falls and heart-stopping drama. When Pip finally beat Deano with a top rope shooting star press, the fans were on their feet roaring with appreciation. Afterwards, Pip and Dean took the plaudits of the dressing room with typical humility. But I could tell how much the respect of their peers meant to both of them. Bubblegum v Allmark is up there with Travis v Samuels, Travis v Andrews v Bubblegum, Morrison v Ospreay, Dar v Hayes and Ligero v Tozawa among my favourite PCW matches.

The Liverpool debut meant a lot to me, because of my family background. It also came just weeks after PCW ran its second sold-out show of the year at Club Domain in Blackpool. And with more events planned in Blackpool and Liverpool, as well as debuts in Manchester, Bradford, Hanley and Wrexham later in 2016, PCW began to explore new stomping grounds and spread its brand further than just Preston. As a result, in 2016 I worked more dates than I had in years, loving every minute of being part of a great company with a top-notch roster of tremendous wrestlers and good people. And I'm booked for plenty more dates in 2017 too.

I won't take it for granted. I know from past experience, with the FWA and Power Slam, that nothing lasts forever.

But as I write this book, Preston City Wrestling is riding high. And I feel as proud as Preston itself to be part of it.

CHAPTER 16

HEART OF A LION

"In approximately 24 hours, it happens. The greatest comeback story in modern British wrestling comes full circle, as one year on from not only a career threatening, but life threatening injury, I make my return to the ring as an active wrestler. I make no claims or promises but this. In those breathtaking minutes, as a crowd of over 1000 fans await in anticipation for a moment 12 months in the making, when that music hits, and I walk through the curtain, my heart beating almost out my chest, and I circle that ring, and every one of those 1000+ fans stands chanting for the 'holy s__t' moment they are witnessing, know this. There is no man alive who can be prepared for the intensity and vengeance of this uncaged lion. Feel that moment, for the rest of your life. Because I will..."
Adrian 'Lionheart' McCallum, March 12 2015

When his head first hit the canvas, I didn't see what had happened.

It's the only bugbear I have with working in Evoque. The commentary desk is next to the wrestlers' entranceway, a good distance away from the ring. At times, my view of the action is obstructed. And because of the angle of impact, one of the corner posts was in my direct line of vision.

But while I may not have seen, I definitely heard.

Usually when a wrestler hits a spectacular move, the audience reacts with a loud "WHOAH!" followed by loud applause or a chant of appreciation. But on the night of Saturday, March 1 2014, when AJ Styles delivered the Styles Clash to Adrian 'Lionheart' McCallum, the "WHOAH!" was followed by shocked, eerie, disbelieving silence.

When AJ jumped and fell forward, holding Lionheart around the waist upside down in front of him, Adrian was supposed to keep his head back, free, and safe from harm.

Instead, he tucked his chin.

So when AJ landed, Adrian's head was trapped underneath his own body, sandwiched between the canvas-covered wooden boards of the ring and the weight of a 15 stone man falling on top of him. His neck took the full force of a sickening collision.

McCallum would later say that as his head hit the mat, he heard a crunch.

As Adrian lay face down, not moving, I looked to my right and locked eyes with the American wrestler Chris Hero, who had been greeting fans at the nearby merchandise table just seconds before. His mouth hung open, his expression etched with horror. He'd seen what happened clearly and his wrestler's instinct told him instantly, something had gone terribly wrong.

"He landed on his head," said Chris.

I still wasn't sure. I had seen the match referee Des Robinson put his hands to his head in dismay as AJ delivered the move. But this could have been the normal reaction of a referee trained for years to 'sell' or react to the action in the ring as if it was a real fight.

And professional wrestling is not a real fight. Wrestling is two individuals, co-operating, trusting each other with their bodies, telling a story through a series of blows, holds and manoeuvres which, while at times physically punishing, are not intended to cause serious or permanent injury. But at its most skilful, the combat inside the wrestling ring can look incredibly believable. And that is the ultimate goal of the professional wrestler. To make the audience believe that the fight they are seeing is real.

Was Lionheart really hurt? Or was he being a skilful professional wrestler, making it look like his opponent's devastating finishing move had incapacitated him? I honestly didn't know at first.

Now I can't actually remember what I said on commentary in the moments following the Styles Clash, and I haven't gone back to check. But I'm 100% certain that my intention would have been to say that Lionheart, the PCW Champion and the company's top heel at the time, who had earlier cheated to defeat Styles in the main event of the two-day Road to Glory weekend, had received his just desserts, and that the crowd favourite AJ had gained a measure of revenge on the conniving Scot.

That's what I do. My role is to assist the illusion being played out in the ring, to interpret whatever story the wrestlers are trying to tell, and get it across verbally to the viewers as simply and believably as I possibly can while putting over all the participants. When a PCW show begins, I could be John Motson at the Cup Final, Murray Walker at the Grand Prix or Ian Darke at a big heavyweight championship boxing match. As far as I am concerned, I am commentating on a real sporting occasion. So while the jobs of Lionheart and AJ Styles that night were to convince the paying audience that they were bitter rivals and, in their desperation to be the PCW Champion, they were really trying to hurt each other, it was my job to play along.

Wrestlers and bookers blur the lines between reality and acting all the time. I have lost count of the number of times I have booked an angle which called for a wrestler to pretend to be injured. One particular time that springs to mind, and which is relevant in this case, was in 2011 at a trainee show in Morecambe.

In the closing moments of the event, the giant Alex Cyanide picked up the underdog babyface Dave Rayne across his meaty shoulder, then dropped him head first onto the ring apron. Dave collapsed and lay on the ground, not moving, for a good few minutes. The referee, ring announcer, stewards and fellow wrestlers gathered around, showing concern for Rayne's well-being. Then an announcement was made that all the fans should leave the venue, the show was over, and we needed to get the unconscious Rayne to a hospital. The spectators duly left, shocked and worried for Dave's welfare. But as soon as the building was evacuated, and everyone had gone, Dave sprang to his feet, perfectly fine. He'd only been 'selling', following to the letter the instructions given by myself backstage before the event. He feigned serious injury to rally the fans behind him and create interest in a future 'revenge match' against Cyanide. It was all part of the show, but performed so skilfully by Dave that the audience believed he was badly hurt.

Even then, bearing my Dave Rayne analogy in mind, can the few people who believed the Lionheart injury was all 'a work' (part of the show) really be blamed? Unless they had a clear view, I don't believe so. Emotions were running high in the days following the incident, and some fans were ridiculed and accused of insensitivity for suggesting as much. But in my opinion, when we participate in a form of entertainment that, in its very essence, is built on a lie, we can't become precious when people don't believe the truth.

And as Lionheart lay motionless on his face, I couldn't be 100% certain what had happened. Not at first. But referee Des Robinson knew straight away. The third man in the ring that night had the closest view of the stomach-churning impact of the Styles Clash.

"When AJ set up Lionheart for the move, I could see that for some reason, Adrian's arms weren't (locked in) properly," said Des, reflecting on the incident one year later.

"I could sense something was going to go wrong. It just didn't look right. The next thing I saw was his head being tucked and him coming down on it.

"As soon as it happened, I went straight to the floor to ask if he was OK. He said no, I can't move.

"I told him to stay there, we'll get some help, and then just kept talking to him the whole time. He couldn't move his arms or legs. I kept on reassuring him that everything would be fine."

As the referee, ring announcer, stewards, staff, the venue medical officer and Steven Fludder gathered around the stricken star showing concern for his well-being, and as an announcement was made for all fans to leave the venue so Adrian could be taken to hospital, I began to slowly realise that Lionheart *was* seriously injured. I saw the reactions of his close friends Noam Dar and Kris Travis, who were almost in tears. Then I saw Mad Man Manson, who normally takes absolutely nothing seriously. His face was ashen with worry. I saw PCW staff members clinging to each other, crying. I saw Steven and his wife Elizabeth, looking absolutely devastated. I saw others wandering about the arena, like lost souls, powerless to help as Lionheart lay face down, still not moving.

As minute by gut-wrenching minute passed by, I watched, from a respectful distance, as the venue medic spoke softly to Adrian, trying to keep him calm, trying to determine if he had any feeling in his limbs. I felt like a wretched voyeur, like an observer of a motorway car crash, as I looked on, hoping and praying that he was going to be all right. Then I heard that an ambulance had been called. For real.

It seemed to take an eternity to arrive. When it did, the paramedics carefully rolled Adrian over to get him onto a stretcher, and the wounded warrior let out a deep moan of agonised pain that echoed through the near-empty club and sent a shiver of sorrow through my entire being.

I will never forget that sound. That sound was a sobering reminder of the dangers professional wrestlers face every time they step into the ring. Mere written words cannot do justice to the respect I feel for Adrian 'Lionheart' McCallum and my other friends, colleagues and comrades on the UK wrestling scene for the risks they take to entertain the paying public.

Fludder and the medic both told me Adrian was slowly starting to regain some feeling in his hands and legs. They were hoping it was a trapped nerve or a muscle spasm and not something more serious.

But Adrian McCallum's neck was broken in two places. He was rushed to Royal Preston Hospital. Steven Fludder, Noam Dar and Kris Travis went with him.

"We all stayed until we were thrown out and were in constant contact throughout the night," said Kris in a website blog in March 2015.

"Genuinely every last second of that night will stay with me forever."

The next day Kris was scheduled in a match in St Neots, Cambridgeshire for Southside Wrestling. But climbing into the ring that Sunday was the last thing Trav wanted to do.

"All that day I was convinced I wouldn't wrestle again.

"I was 100% serious about getting out of the business. All I could envision was my friend laid motionless from a fairly simple move. Here I was expected to tear the house down with risky move after move and for the first time in my career all I could imagine was every move going wrong. What if I landed on my head on a dive? What if I hurt my opponent?

"I *had* to have that match and I am glad I did. It was fairly average in all truth partly because I just couldn't stop thinking about the risk and second guessing my movements."

It is little wonder Kris felt the way he did. As Adrian lay in his hospital bed that Saturday night in Preston, waiting for results of an X-ray, he was told by doctors they didn't know if he would walk, let alone wrestle, ever again.

"It was the first time I'd been exposed to a really dangerous situation in professional wrestling," said Noam, reflecting in 2016 on what happened that night.

"I've been lucky, I've worked in environments where things like that don't happen often. Freak accidents can happen. But to see that live, and see it happen to one of your closest friends, and then go to the hospital...as a wrestler you always have that 'shake it off' mentality, we never think it's as bad as it could be. But this was the opposite. It was much worse.

"When we got to the hospital and went through the whole process of him hearing the news from the doctor, and having to tell his loved ones, it was a very sobering experience to have...with *anyone*, but the fact it was one of my closest friends..."

What had happened to Nik Bali in Cardiff five years before, was now happening to Adrian 'Lionheart' McCallum. The PCW Champion broke down in tears at the news and spent most of the night lying wide awake, his mind racing, frantically worrying about his future quality of life.

It was a living nightmare for a man who ate, slept and breathed professional wrestling.

The 31-year-old Scot had turned pro 12 years earlier, learned his trade in Scotland and then gained national notoriety in 1PW as the promotion's last ever Heavyweight Champion. Lionheart soon became regarded as one of Britain's best, a solid all-round wrestler and entertainer; good at just about every facet of the game. He was equally comfortable as a heart-on-the-sleeve babyface or an entitled heel you loved to see get smashed; great on the microphone, slick on the mat, graceful in the air, with a cerebral mind and an ability to create controversy and stir up interest amongst wrestling fans. Lionheart could do it all.

In 2011, McCallum got his big career break. First, he faced Jeff Jarrett in a high-profile bout on a TNA house show at Glasgow's Braehead Arena. Lionheart lost but performed well. Later that year, he had a try-out for WWE too. His taste of the big-time raised hopes that he might be offered a contract by one of The Big Two to seek fame and fortune overseas.

But when the TNA British Boot Camp quartet were selected the following year, Lionheart's name was not among them. The fiery Scot was not happy.

"Not being selected was, to me, complete bulls_t," said McCallum in an interview with Fighting Spirit Magazine in December 2013.

"It's a 'British' Bootcamp, so make it British. The last time I checked, that included Scotland. At this point, I think it's fair to say I'm still, arguably, considered the top all-round worker in Scotland, and I have mainstream history with TNA and one of their biggest stars (Jeff Jarrett). So it begs the question, was a lack of talent the reason I didn't make it? Or did I just not know the right people?

"TNA lacks a mainstream Scottish star and that should have been me. It will always be my loss, not theirs, but they dropped the ball, in my opinion."

In December 2012, just before British Boot Camp aired on television, Lionheart announced his retirement from the ring.

"I'd always been of the mindset that if I hadn't made it to one of the Big Two - either WWE or TNA - by the time I was 30, I'd walk away," he told FSM.

"The nail in the coffin for me was when I wasn't selected for the British Boot Camp."

Adrian intended to focus on promoting his Pro Wrestling Elite company in Ayr. But the lure of the ring proved too much. Just four months after wrestling his final match before retiring against Joey Hayes at Evoque, the PCW original returned to Preston in April 2013 as a shock entrant and ultimately, the victor, of the annual Rumble. Four months later Lionheart was PCW Champion, for the second time, when he beat Doug Williams while turning heel at the second anniversary show.

Meanwhile, AJ Styles was coming to the end of a near 12-year tenure with TNA. For all of that time, The Phenomenal One had been rated as one of the very best in-ring performers on the planet and Styles certainly went out with a bang too. In October 2013, the

Gainsville, Georgia native captured the TNA Title before doing an angle where he refused a new contract and walked out of the company still holding the belt. TNA declared the championship vacant, but the high-flyer defended it anyway in Mexico and Japan. With Styles' contract with TNA due to expire for real a matter of months later, fans were speculating constantly. Was AJ still with TNA or not? It created a real buzz around him.

Meanwhile, Lionheart told the audience at PCW Supershow III in November 2013 that on December 6 at Festive Fury he would be facing somebody "phenomenal". Days later, the Scot issued a challenge to Styles on Twitter and posted an image of himself saying "this is what a real champion looks like" and AJ replied saying "Let's go!" to seemingly accept the challenge.

PCW immediately announced that AJ would face Lionheart at Festive Fury on December 6. But this was amidst a backdrop of confusion over Styles' status with TNA. In the end, AJ was required to return to TNA on December 5 - the day before Festive Fury - to lose his version of the title to Dixie Carter's newly-crowned champ Magnus in a unification match. The bout with Lionheart was postponed and instead, McCallum beat El Ligero at Festive Fury. To add further spice to his rivalry with the American, Lionheart polished the challenger off with his own version of the Styles Clash. Meanwhile, contract talks broke down for real between AJ Styles and TNA, and he departed the company, becoming the hottest free agent in the wrestling world.

A master of pushing buttons, McCallum then cut an awesome promo for YouTube, calling Styles a "hypocrite" for not turning up at Festive Fury.

"AJ Styles, you knew you were going to get your arse kicked," said a seething Lionheart. "This belt I'm holding over my shoulder right now says I am the best. Not you, not anyone else is ever going to take this away from me."

The night before the rearranged Lionheart-Styles bout, the two men were thrown together as a tag team against Team Single on the first night of the PCW Road to Glory weekend. The match ended with McCallum abandoning Styles, causing him to lose the fall, cranking up the tension.

"AJ Styles, fans can chant and argue all night long over who is better, but there will never be an argument for who is smarter," Lionheart told 'Magic' Mark Adams afterwards.

"That was phenomenal. Did *he* look phenomenal? No he didn't. This is not TNA, this is my house, bitch! Where's your championship? You don't have one any more. PCW is the house Lionheart built and you just broke into the wrong God-damned one."

So it is somewhat forgotten, overshadowed by the tragic events of March 1 2014, just how much anticipation surrounded the Lionheart-Styles match before it happened. It has also kind of been erased from history that McCallum actually won that night, pinning AJ with a roll-up using his tights for leverage.

The next morning, the result didn't matter. Nothing mattered to Adrian McCallum apart from the results of a crucial MRI scan.

Thankfully, this revealed the damage wasn't as bad as first feared. Adrian would not require surgery. And, miraculously, he was slowly able to get up and walk a few tentative, painful steps. Eventually, he was discharged and went home to begin the slow and agonising road to recovery.

Meanwhile, messages of support for Lionheart flooded in from fans, and his friends and colleagues on the UK circuit.

"After it happened and he got taken away by the paramedics, I messaged him as soon as I got home, wishing him all the best," said Des Robinson.

"I was genuinely concerned for him. I tend to keep myself to myself but I have a lot of respect for the guys, so when something like that happens you want them to be safe. He messaged me back a few days later and gave me an update."

Meanwhile Kris Travis conquered his own fears for the future, inspired by his friend's struggle.

"Speaking to Lionheart the next few days was the only thing that stopped me from quitting," he wrote in his March 2015 website blog.

"His attitude of wanting to get back in the ring, his attitude of wanting to once again be the star of the show made me forget my own concerns and reaslise that we all know the risks.

"The doubt is always there but as wrestlers we ignore it. It's why 90% of the wrestlers you see entertain you week in and week out have been struggling all week with an injury, hitting the gym when they should be in a doctor's surgery."

In the immediate aftermath of his injury, Adrian was housebound, unable to walk more than a few steps without getting out of breath, and at first he couldn't go back to work in his day job as a call centre manager.

But unbelievably, just 27 days after suffering a double broken neck, the man with the Heart of a Lion returned to the scene of the tragedy - that very same PCW ring.

On March 28 2014, walking stiffly and not moving his neck, Lionheart struggled down the aisle at the start of PCW Who Dares Wins to a rapturous ovation. After a short speech thanking everyone for their support, he vacated the PCW Championship. But he told everyone, that his ambition was to return to wrestling somehow, some way, some day.

In an interview filmed backstage during the evening, Adrian told 'Magic' Mark Adams that he did not blame AJ Styles.

"Things like this happen. It's an accident. But the fault was mine. I tucked my head in the wrong direction. Whether it was fatigue from the match or pure instinct, I don't know. But I heard a crunch, and from there I couldn't feel anything.

"I'm angry at myself and the situation. I walked away from British wrestling before, angry and bitter, and not making a good example of myself, and I wasn't prepared to do that again. It's really s__t but I can either sit and be bitter and angry, but I'm not going to get healthy any quicker by bitching about it on Facebook and Twitter. For me to be negative would be a big slap in the face to everyone who has supported me."

While Lionheart was magnanimous over AJ's part in his injury, others wondered if perhaps the Styles Clash itself was to blame.

This wasn't the first time the move had hurt an opponent. Frankie Kazarian in 2003, Sterling James Keenan (WWE commentator Corey Graves) in 2006 and Stevie Richards in 2010 had all fallen on their heads when taking the Styles Clash and narrowly avoided serious injury. Then on January 4 2014, Roderick Strong landed directly on his head during an ROH match with Styles. Strong's neck injury was less serious than Lionheart's but still forced him out of the ring for a month. And of course, there was the Nik Bali tragedy, which was caused by a double-team version of the Clash - albeit not involving AJ Styles.

In early 2014, after two high profile casualties of the Styles Clash in as many months, there was debate about whether AJ should stop using the move altogether. Wrestlers have it drilled into them from the first day at training - when taking 99% of wrestling moves, they should always tuck their chin to protect their neck. But with the Styles Clash, it was the exact opposite.

"RJ Singh called me moments after (Lionheart's injury) happened and it brought me instantly back to the moment in 2009 when he called me to say Nik Bali had broken his neck after taking a Styles Clash, and Nik is in a wheelchair for the rest of his life," said Alex Shane, speaking on WrestleTalk TV in April 2014.

"The question is, are there certain moves that need to be banned? There aren't many moves where you have to arch back, it's not natural to do that. I think certain moves should be used sparingly because of the trajectory, angle, and what you have to do, the margin for error is greatly increased over, say, a suplex. Something like a Styles Clash, if you're not used to it to taking it all the time...some of the best wrestlers in the world have gone the wrong way."

I appeared on Stevie Knight's podcast that month and he asked me my opinion. I sat on the fence in my usual diplomatic style but as a former wrestler, The Shining Light was more forthright.

"To me it's simple, if I was doing a move that had injured a lot of people over a period of time, I'd stop doing it," said Steve.

"I would hate to think that he'd rather have a move he was synonymous with, than break someone's neck."

On April 9 2014, I spoke to Adrian over the telephone for Power Slam, and I asked him his view on the future of the Styles Clash. He remained philosophical about it.

"Every move in pro wrestling can be dangerous if not done right.

"Is it more dangerous than your average finishing move? Probably, because it goes very much against the grain of what is instilled in us as pro wrestlers.

"I wouldn't take the move again. But it's not mine or anyone's place to tell AJ that he should stop doing that move. That decision would have to come from him."

By May 2014, Lionheart was well on the road to recovery. He had started physio, returned to the gym, and regained motion in his neck. His drive and determination to get back in the ring, better than ever, was almost superhuman.

That month, he returned to PCW and was unveiled in a new non-wrestling role as the promotion's General Manager. This kept him in the PCW spotlight and allowed him to use his speaking skills without getting physically involved while his neck healed. Revelling in his authority figure role, he dressed suavely in a suit jacket and showed the swagger of old. The PCW fans were right behind him with every decision he made, even affectionately chanting "SEXY B__TARD!" whenever he entered the ring. This always made Adrian smile! It was good to see him enjoying himself again.

That same month, AJ Styles turned up in New Japan Pro Wrestling and became its IWGP champion on his first night, joining top heel stable The Bullet Club. The Phenomenal One had never been hotter.

Then in June 2014, Styles broke his silence on the Lionheart incident during a chat with Chris Jericho on his Talk Is Jericho podcast. His comments caused uproar.

"Some indy guys aren't what they think they are," scoffed Styles.

"I put Lionheart over because he was the top heel. We gave the people what they wanted - we gave them the Styles Clash so they would go home happy. Previously, in the locker room, I told him, listen man, the one thing you can't do in the Styles Clash is tuck your head. Do nothing and you'll be fine. But this guy was nervous about taking it. I don't know why. It's so safe. He didn't say anything because of pride, or what-not.

"When I gave him the Styles Clash, I didn't know (the injury) had happened. But I saw a picture, and he tucked his head harder than anyone had ever tucked their head for anything. It's a terrible thing, I wish he had never got hurt. But the first time I did this move, on a trampoline, I did it to my brother and *he* didn't tuck his head.

"What I'm saying may sound inconsiderate and that I don't care about the well-being of the guys. That's not it at all. But this is an easy bump to take. I can't hurt you on this move. You have to hurt yourself. Who tucks their head on a face bump?"

Shortly afterwards, Lionheart gave his response on Facebook.

"I have never once spoken ill of AJ or even the situation. I have remained humble, respectful, thankful, and above all, professional.

"Since the incident, I have had no communication from AJ (other than) a reply to one tweet, something which I again do not hold against him in any way.

"Now the thing that now in hindsight stands out for me is his statement on the same podcast. 'I didn't know it had happened'.

"Now, I've watched (the footage of my injury) several times now. Trust me when I say, he knows. To the point he makes a very obvious and very mocking gesture of me tucking my chin, followed by him shaking his head in disbelief at the moron lying in the ring.

"So while he is in no way at fault for the injury, his claim of 'I didn't know' is one I am publicly calling bulls__t on right now. He knew I tucked, he knew I landed on my neck.

"After he left the ring, on his way to the back he is heard clearly on camera saying 'Cashing cheques and breaking necks...that's how it works'. Now I'm more than aware the argument here is, he's in character etc, and this doesn't bother me all that much. I'll let you judge this one.

"So, there are the facts. Never once blamed him and remained respectful and professional throughout. Now having both seen and heard his reaction, I'm annoyed..."

Now, having met AJ Styles a few times myself over the years, he strikes me as a businessman first and foremost. He's a pleasant enough guy, but he's not in wrestling to make friends, his priority is to pay the bills. So his manner can sometimes come across as abrupt and clinical. The Jericho interview was one of those times. When Styles talked about how "some indy guys aren't what they think they are" no wonder Adrian took offence, because he has a lot of belief in his own ability. And with good reason, because McCallum is a good wrestler. One terribly unfortunate mistake did not make him a bad worker.

But I do know that Styles did have compassion for Lionheart's plight. On the night of the injury, once the fans had left the building, I noticed AJ come back out of the dressing room to check on his stricken opponent. He did seem concerned for McCallum's well-being.

Even so, the Jericho podcast had reignited the war between the two men. Meanwhile, Adrian was now recovering at a steady rate, enough to actually get physically involved as special referee of the Chris Masters-Joey Hayes PCW Title match in August 2014 at the third anniversary show and even take a blow to his vulnerable neck. Lionheart sold it expertly as though he had been shot, but in reality he was right as rain. He had passed an important physical test with flying colours.

Then on November 8 2014, it happened again. Yoshi Tatsu tucked his head during a match with AJ in New Japan and the Styles Clash claimed another victim. An MRI revealed two breaks of his cervical vertebrae. Tatsu was finally fit to return to action in 2016, more than a year later.

Shortly after the Tatsu incident, McCallum wrote a heartfelt online plea to AJ Styles.

"There can be no move in wrestling history that carries more (documented) serious and potentially career threatening injuries than this," wrote Adrian.

"The question I want to put to you honestly is, what does it take? What will it actually take for you to stop using this move? How will you feel the day you receive the news that the man you just wrestled has a broken neck and will never walk again? Statistically, that day is coming. It is a mathematical certainty.

"I take this opportunity now, to openly and publicly beg you. Please, stop using the Styles Clash. You are unquestionably one of the greatest in ring performers of our time, I truly believe that. But the time is now, to put all pride, ego, blame aside, and acknowledge that irrelevant of fault, circumstance or anything else, the move is a direct risk and a danger to the safety and well-being of your fellow wrestler."

Styles did not respond. But on November 29 2014, he had Japanese wrestling legend Satoshi Kojima up in the Styles Clash position during a match, only to accidentally fall backwards instead of forwards. Kojima's neck was jarred by the impact but he walked away unscathed. Still, it was another near-miss.

That same night at the first PCW v ROH Supershow Weekend, Lionheart quit as General Manager during an in-ring confrontation with his long-term nemesis Joey Hayes. He then dropped Hayes with a Uranage slam and announced his comeback as an active wrestler in the Road to Glory tournament. Evoque was ecstatic.

Anticipation for Lionheart's return began to build. At the Kris Travis charity show in January 2015, while Joey Hayes was being his usual irritating self inside the PCW ring, a clever video package appeared on the screen showing Lionheart training in the gym, putting him across almost as a Bionic Man with a tagline of 'We can rebuild him' as he worked out like a demon to prepare for his date with destiny. Then he strode to the ring to rock Joey with a series of right hands, before flattening his tormentor with another Uranage. He looked in tremendous shape and the fans went wild.

"Is this a preview, is this what we can expect at Road to Glory when Lionheart makes his big return?" I yelled on commentary.

For Lionheart's part, he took the microphone and had just one thing to say.

"I'm back."

But while the Scot appeared to have made an incredible physical recovery, experts still wondered how the trauma of his injury might affect him psychologically.

Wrestler Greg Burridge, speaking on WrestleTalk TV, said: "The worst fear any wrestler has is breaking his neck.

"Once you get that fear, it's hard to wrestle at a certain level, because you don't want to get hurt.

"But Lionheart is a fighter. I think he'll come back like it was nothing, a broken nail. But if you've broken your neck in two places, taking bumps is risky.

"I know I wouldn't do it."

But Lionheart did. Defying all known logic, on March 14 2015, just over a year since he was nearly paralysed, Adrian McCallum returned to in-ring action against Joey Hayes at the Road to Glory tournament.

As Lionheart prepared quietly in a corner of the PCW dressing room that night, Richard Parker cornered me for a YouTube interview, to give my thoughts.

"You've got guys here tonight like Matt Hardy, John Morrison, Carlito, lots of top international wrestlers coming to PCW as always," I said.

"But not taking anything away from those guys, the thing I'm most looking forward to is seeing the inspirational Adrian 'Lionheart' McCallum, back in the ring.

"I spoke to him earlier today and I think he's understandably a little nervous. I think anybody would be after what he's been through. Not only with the injury but the rehabilitation and the mental side of that, as well as the physical. But you don't forget how to be a professional wrestler. You don't forget how to be a champion. And when he gets in that ring tonight, I think we're going to see something special."

Des Robinson was the official, as he had been 12 months earlier.

"As I was waiting for him to come through the curtain, I was nervous," said Des afterwards.

"I was hoping everything was going to be all right. And it was."

A superlative video played on the Evoque screen telling the story of Lionheart's PCW career. The disheartenment of his retirement in December 2012. The reinvigoration of his comeback and PCW Title win in August 2013. The tragedy of the injury in March 2014. And now, the redemption of March 2015.

As the video ended, and as Joey and Des waited inside the ring, a hush descended over the PCW crowd. Lionheart's mum and dad were among them. Expectant. And no doubt, worried.

Then Lionheart's music hit and the noise of the crowd was like a rocket going off as the returning superman emerged to a hero's welcome.

Once inside the ring, he never missed a beat. He took bumps, some on his neck. All his trademark moves were delivered as crisply as ever. The snappy superkick, the well-timed Uranage, and a picture-perfect Torture Rack into a cutter that eventually finished off Joey Hayes for a crowd-pleasing one, two, three.

On the Saturday, Lionheart actually wrestled three times. He beat Martin Kirby in the afternoon and edged his way past T-Bone in the evening. The finish of this match, though, saw the Team Single bruiser angrily pick up McCallum and drop him head-first with a devastating Tombstone Piledriver, much to the shock of the PCW audience.

As Adrian lay prone in the ring, in a chilling deja vu moment, I sold this on commentary like it was the most heinous act in the history of professional wrestling. I told the audience that I couldn't believe T-Bone would target Lionheart's weakened neck so remorselessly. As officials surrounded the fallen hero, checking on him as he lay groaning in pain, I couldn't help having flashbacks to the year before. I watched with half-worry and half-admiration that Lionheart would agree to take a move that carried such risk of re-injuring his neck on his comeback weekend.

Thankfully, the Tombstone was executed safely. This time, as Adrian was helped slowly to his feet, clutching the back of his neck, he was just selling. But you see what I mean. Sometimes, the acting from professional wrestlers is so convincing, that it is hard to tell if they are really hurt or not.

Had Lionheart managed to complete his Road to Glory and win the tournament final against Bubblegum, it would have been the perfect comeback fairytale. But the combination of being softened up by T-Bone, Pip's sneaky skills and the presence of The Rascal's cohorts in Friends With Benefits proved too much for the braveheart from Scotland. The match ended with a Bubblegum pinfall victory. Still, it was an astonishing performance from McCallum and one that was rewarded with a deserved standing ovation from the packed house in Evoque.

Four matches in two days, 12 months after a double broken neck.

No wonder they call him Lionheart.

"Some people may have had the wrong impression of him years ago but after everything he went through in Preston, to go through that and come back to doing what he loves, you've got to have a lot of respect for him," said Noam Dar in 2016.

"I was with him a lot during his healing process, at his house when he would struggle to even get up and make a cup of tea. But he worked hard at his rehab, he got all the support of the independent fans and his family and friends, and he got international support, people who reached out to him and helped him.

"I really believe that's what helped him get back to where he is today. Now he's back I don't think he's ever going to let it go again."

The day after his comeback, Adrian wrote a message on

Facebook.

"A very special thank you to those who took care of me this weekend.

"They know who they are. My 100% trust in them was rewarded by them keeping me safe and allowing me the opportunity to do this again.

"Professionally, I'm feeling very proud. 12 months on the shelf with a devastating injury, put behind me with not one but four matches in a just over a 24 hour period. Win, lose, love, hate, it doesn't matter. I went out there and gave my all when every one of my inner fears told me not to.

"Thanks to everyone who welcomed me back in spectacular fashion, I love you all."

Just over a month later, on April 24 2015, PCW announced that Lionheart and AJ Styles would face each other in a rematch.

Nobody saw it coming. It was the match nobody thought would ever happen.

Days before he stepped back into the ring with Styles, Adrian spoke to my ex-Power Slam colleague and Daily Mirror journalist Neil Docking. His comments reopened the old wounds with The Phenomenal One. But this time, he had a match to sell.

"Truth is, I'm nothing to AJ Styles. He's one of the best wrestlers in the world and in the grand scheme I'm a nobody.

"His behaviour bothered me, yes. When he said he didn't know (he'd injured me) he out and out lied. He clearly did, and no doubt can be cast in that when you watch the footage.

"It's simply about me standing in that ring face to face with him again. Whatever he says, whatever he does, and whatever he tries to do... I'm ready...that's about all I can say."

Lionheart also vowed that he would not, under any circumstances, take the Styles Clash again.

On the day of Saturday, June 5 2015, I felt incredibly chilled and focussed on the show ahead, more so than usual. I knew how important this occasion was. I was more ready than ever to commentate on the biggest match in PCW history.

Lionheart-Styles II. I knew it was going to be a special night.

The show was already under way when Lionheart and AJ arrived at the building. Steven Fludder had told them both to turn up late, to reduce the chances of the fans seeing either of them before the match. There was an unprecedented buzz in the air.

As I came backstage during the interval, I saw them there, standing together, working out what they were about to do. Bearing in mind everything that had gone before, this was a surreal sight.

When Lionheart emerged to a massive pop, there was also a noticeable smattering of boos. Adrian was always going to stay a huge babyface while the PCW crowd felt sympathy because of his injury. But once his comeback began, there was always the chance they would start to turn on him because he is such a great heel. This process was already under way.

Still, this tiny pocket of anti-Lionheart feeling was nothing compared to the wall of vitriolic sound that greeted the arrival of the hooded AJ Styles. As Adrian paced around the ring, the IWGP Champion strolled through the curtain, chewing gum, arms outstretched, soaking in the "gauntlet of hate", as I described it on commentary.

Boos, catcalls, crude gestures, "F__K YOU AJ!" chants and even "F__K YOU AJ!" T-shirts. That night, the Preston faithful absolutely despised AJ Styles.

The reaction was genuine. It was organic. The majority of those fans desperately wanted AJ Styles to be beaten. And it was rare for Preston City Wrestling, where the crowd usually doesn't mind who wins or loses, as long as they get a show full of great wrestling and entertainment.

"PCW fans are normally known for their good humour," I noted on commentary.

"Even for the people they don't like, sometimes the chants they come up with are quite creative and even light-hearted. But there is nothing humorous about the reaction AJ Styles just got."

Playing the heel role with aplomb, Styles just smirked, basking in the hateful reaction of the Preston supporters. Lionheart, meanwhile, fixed an icy glare in the direction of the man who had haunted his thoughts for more than a year.

"What is going through the mind of Adrian 'Lionheart' McCallum right now?" I asked.

His career, the highs, the lows, the retirement, the return, the injury, its aftermath, his brave recovery, the war of words between the two, the debate over the Styles Clash, everything in the run-up to this match. I reckon that's what was going through Lionheart's mind.

Everything in the run-up to this match had been completely real. That night, it was Real in Preston.

The match was a masterclass. The atmosphere was a cauldron. And the emotion was palpable. It was the kind of match I love to commentate on, because the story was so easy to tell. It was a tale of a man bravely conquering his mental demons, climbing back into the ring with his bitter rival who could have put him in a wheelchair for the rest of his life, proving something to himself, maybe even having thoughts of revenge.

Or as Stallion perfectly described it many times that night, maybe Adrian 'Lionheart' McCallum just wanted *closure*.

As the thrilling minutes ticked by and the drama built and built, AJ went for the Styles Clash. Every time, Lionheart escaped it in heart-stopping fashion. Then several times, it looked like McCallum was going to win. Every time, the IWGP Champion was able to survive. As the action ebbed and flowed, Stallion and myself were on top verbal form. It wasn't difficult. It was that good a match. We produced what was, in my opinion, our best piece of commentary ever. And it was an absolute pleasure to do so.

In the end, Lionheart tapped out to AJ Styles' submission hold the Calf Killer - or Calf Crusher as they now call it in WWE. This finish was always on the cards. True to his word, Adrian would not take the Styles Clash again.

At first, fans were angry at the result as Des Robinson, the referee once again, raised AJ's hand in victory. But then, Styles took the microphone. And he turned the mood of the crowd around.

The real-life Allen Jones told Adrian McCallum that for coming back against all the odds, he'd earned nothing but his respect.

The two men shook hands. And I summed up the scene for the viewing audience.

"This is what closure looks like."

In the end, it didn't actually matter who won or lost this wrestling match. The main thing was that Adrian McCallum cleared a personal, professional and most importantly, a psychological hurdle by facing AJ Styles across the ring, one more time.

Afterwards I hugged Adrian backstage and told him: "I felt the emotion of every single thing you did out there.

"You should be very proud of yourself."

Dusty Rhodes, the man who said "wrestling is built on emotion", certainly would have been proud of Adrian 'Lionheart' McCallum that night.

Like many others, I was deeply saddened when Dusty passed away later that same week.

Later on that year, Lionheart turned heel again when he superkicked PCW trainee Lauren Codling in the middle of the Evoque ring after she drew the raffle at Fright Night. His rehabilitation was complete.

Three months later, AJ Styles debuted in the WWE at the Royal Rumble. On April 4 2016, the day after WrestleMania 32, on a live edition of Monday Night RAW in Dallas, Texas, Styles won a four-way match to become number one contender to the WWE Title.

And how did he win?

He pinned Chris Jericho with a Styles Clash.

Meanwhile, that very same weekend at the Barrowlands in Glasgow, Lionheart captured the ICW Zero-G Championship in a six-way scramble match.

And how did *he* win?

How do you think.

He pinned Davey Blaze with a Styles Clash.

Closure.

CHAPTER 17

BOOT CAMP 2

On January 29 2015, I was sitting 10 rows from the front at the Glasgow Hydro Arena, one of a crowd of some 4,000 wrestling fans, mainly Scots, who had turned out on a chilly Thursday night to watch the Scottish leg of TNA's annual UK tour.

Some of the biggest names in American wrestling were there. Former world champions like Bobby Roode and Austin Aries, former WWE superstars like MVP, Mr Anderson and Matt Hardy, Olympic gold medallist and bona fide wrestling icon Kurt Angle, and the-then TNA World Champ Bobby Lashley, whose participation in the main event of WrestleMania 23 helped set the highest worldwide pay-per-view buy rate in World Wrestling Entertainment history at 1.2million people.

And what was the crowd bellowing at the top of their lungs?

"I-C-DUB! I-C-DUB! I-C-DUB!"

And who had I, and indeed most of the Glasgow crowd, come to see? Was it Angle? Hardy? Lashley?

No. None of the above.

It was Grado.

Grado was the main draw that night. Grado was the main event. Grado, the chubby wee chancer from the tap end of Stevenston, the self-confessed loser who was never supposed to be a professional wrestler, the cheeky lad who still lived with his mum and who three years earlier was a complete unknown, was the name on everyone's lips on a show promoted by America's second biggest wrestling company to be aired on television around the world.

How the hell did this happen? Let's rewind a few months.

Grado was picked to appear on the second series of TNA British Boot Camp and basically stole the show through the force of his personality, his developed wrestling character and a thorough understanding of his role as the wide-eyed underdog super fan with an unlikely dream.

When Episode 1 aired on Challenge TV on October 19 2014, a mainstream pro wrestling audience got to see the level of talent on the Scottish scene - as Kay Lee Ray, Viper, Noam Dar and Nikki Storm all shone at the try-outs in front of Al Snow, Gail Kim, Samoa Joe and the TV cameras. But the episode was clearly built around Grado, with a story all planned out to get the viewers right behind him.

Grado was shown strutting and dancing outside the egg-shaped Hydro, "the biggest arena in Scotland", saying it was his dream to wrestle there. "I'm gonna sell that place oot!" he grinned, while posing with a group of confused Japanese tourists. Then he emerged at the top of the stairs at the Source Wrestling School gym, yelled "IT'S YERSEL" and began to act starstruck in front of the judging panel, even convincing Samoa Joe to sign some DVDs before taking a cameraphone 'It's Yersel-fie' of the bemused Samoan Submission Machine.

"Tell us what Grado is all about," asked Snow, as the try-out finally began.

"Well, I'm one of the best professional wrestlers in the world," replied our hero, with deadpan irony. The usually stoic tough guy Joe almost cracked up from behind his judging table.

Then Grado - who described himself as "like Big Daddy, only I'm more Medium Daddy" - began to perform a series of jumping jacks in the ring, his belly hanging out like a British tourist on the sands of Marbella. Snow's eyes bulged in disbelief as he looked on, completely aghast. It was comedy gold.

After deliberation, and much reluctance particularly from Al, the panel put Grado through to the next round. Stevenston's finest immediately began to run around the ring, whooping in celebration, before he dropped to his knees, Kurt Angle-style, his arms thrust out in delight. The panel were laughing their heads off. It was immediately obvious that Grado was capable of making anybody chuckle and connecting with any kind of audience. His unique humour and charisma wasn't just appealing to Brits.

The story moved forward as Grado was late for the second stage of the try-out - wrestling practice. Snow went absolutely ballistic, refused to accept any of Grado's apologies and excuses that "I'd been for something to eat and lost track of time" and turned the air blue with anger.

"I tolerated your fun and games earlier but this is not a joke!" said the stern Snow, in a drill sergeant-style reprimand.

"I don't appreciate people disrespecting what I do, and disrepecting me, by thinking you can waltz in here any time you f___ing well want to!"

Then the grizzled veteran got right in the meek Grado's face and ordered him to leave.

"GET OUT OF HERE NOW...OR I'LL PUT YOU OUT!" yelled the American. That was it. Grado's shot at the big time was over. Being late had cost him his dream. Head bowed, bottom lip quivering, his duffel bag slung over his shoulder and ever-present baseball cap clutched in hand, Grado sadly departed, realising he'd blown his opportunity.

The altercation between the grizzled veteran trainer Snow, with his rules and rigidity, and the ill-disciplined upstart Grado was a carefully-calculated wrestling angle to set the scene for a match between the two somewhere down the line. The rivalry was easy to identify with. Grado was like the kid who'd forgotten his football kit for a big inter-schools cup final, while Snow was the bullying sports teacher who forced him to do a cross country run in his undies as punishment. The whole scenario was designed to make the viewers feel sorry for the 'Rab C Nesbitt of Wrestling' and tune in next time, hoping he'd get a second chance.

Grado did indeed turn up for the try-outs in Manchester screened in Episode 2, where he begged Snow for another shot in a tense confrontation outside the FutureShock wrestling gym. Thankfully Grado had an ally in Gail Kim, who promised to try to talk Al around, but only if the Scot was deeply apologetic and could convince TNA how badly he wanted it. So the plucky trier drove 10 hours to gatecrash the London auditions on Episode 3 and pleaded again with Gail's better nature. Finally the Knockout relented and managed to convince Snow to readmit Grado into the competition.

Grado then joined the likes of Dave Mastiff, RJ Singh, Martin

Stone and Sha Samuels in the York Hall, Bethnal Green ring while Gail, Al and Joe evaluated their wrestling skills. And after Grado suffered a beating from the vicious Samuels but managed to survive and even hold his own, the panel was convinced. Our boy showed he had heart to compliment his undoubted personality. He redeemed himself and was sent through to the next round.

Episode 4 was a joy to watch because the cream of the UK wrestling scene made it through to a big stage. Nikki Storm, The Owens Twins, Joel Redman, Richard Parliament, RJ Singh, Dave Mastiff, Kris Travis, El Ligero, Sha Samuels, Rampage Brown, Kay Lee Ray, Noam Dar, Mark Andrews, Grado, Martin Stone - every single one of the 16 finalists had the ability to become a worldwide TV star. This was how far British wrestling had come.

It turns out, though, that the auditions had all been a work. TNA already knew who they wanted to put through.

"We pretty much knew the 16 for the London show coming into the auditions, except for Richard Parliament," said RJ Singh.

"They added him because they liked him. Originally it was going to be Tiger Ali from 4FW but he pulled out due to injury so they genuinely picked Richard during the day because they really liked his (politician) character.

"But even though the last 16 was a given, Jeremy still told us to make a big effort during the auditions because they might change their minds.

"We genuinely didn't know who was getting through from the last 16 though. But I knew I was going to struggle. I had a new deputy head teacher job starting in the September and I told them it wasn't likely I'd be able to go. They told me I should still do the show though. If I had got picked, it would have been a huge decision for me to make."

Spud, winner of Boot Camp 1, was given a behind-the-scenes role on the second series as talent liaison between the British wrestlers and TNA management.

"I had to talk to everybody because TNA felt it would be better for them to have a face who knew them," he said. "It was another feather in my cap but also a way of the Brits feeling comfortable. But it was still a legitimate competition. People say TNA knew who was going to win from day one. But no-one f__king did. Early on, I think Dave Mastiff was the hot favourite."

A series of matches taped at the York Hall - Dar v Ligero, Travis v Andrews, Kasey and Leah Owens v Kay Lee and Nikki, Samuels v Grado, Parliament and Singh v Redman and Stone, and Mastiff v Rampage, entertained a raucous crowd in Bethnal Green as the judging panel scrutinised their every move. But in the end, only the top six performers would go through to the final stages in America. It was always going to be a tough choice and I wouldn't have liked to have made it. But in the end, Joe, Kim and Snow announced the chosen few were Travis, Andrews, Kay Lee, Rampage, Mastiff and Grado.

As an aside, I have to be honest, I was shocked Nikki Storm and Sha Samuels weren't picked by TNA for the final six. And this isn't taking anything away from anybody else, because any of the 16 would have been worthy finalists. But to me, throughout the whole British Boot Camp 2 process, Sha and Nikki stood out.

I believe the winner of the show needed to bring something new to TNA - something the promotion didn't already have. Either Samuels or Storm could have given TNA a fresh act for their roster. Both are great people in real life and have the understanding of how to play a television character, the polished in-ring skills, the right look and the single-minded determination to be a success for a major company.

Sha is so intense and in your face, he bursts through the television screen, and his East End bad boy persona would be easy for American audiences to understand. He was a revelation, subsequently, as PCW Champion in 2016. And Nikki is just so over-the-top, self-assured and incredibly entertaining. Even after being told she'd been eliminated, The Best in the Galaxy remained in character and tossed her hair with indignation as she told the viewing audience the decision was "TNA's loss and everybody else's gain". Brilliant!

Spud was also surprised Nikki wasn't picked.

"Although TNA didn't have any idea who they wanted and the favourite kept changing throughout Boot Camp 2, ideally they wanted a girl.

"We all said Nikki Storm was the one. But Al, Gail and Joe chose different and chose Kay Lee."

Incidentally, Spud actually wrestled that day at the York Hall against none other than my old PCW nemesis, Mark 'The Beast' Labbett. It was a dark match where Spud lost to the massive mastermind in a typically entertaining squash. The footage has never aired.

"It was Mark Labbett's only ever wrestling match," said Jay.

"He came out with me, I called all the Boot Camp 2 contestants 'Johnny come latelys' and said that I'd brought my guy, The Beast, who was going to win the series. But then I started insulting him. 'He may be fat, he may be out of shape...' and he said 'What did you say little boy?' and we ended up having a match. He picked me up, press slammed me, gave me a big splash and covered me for the three, and then Joe gave me the Muscle Buster! There is photo evidence but for some reason they didn't air it on YouTube."

RJ Singh didn't make it through, as he expected. For my old friend and FWA/XWA colleague The Bollywood Dream, at 33 years of age this was his final shot at the big-time. He told me more than a year earlier, when I stayed at his house in Hertford, that he was going to give everything to make it to TNA and if it didn't work out, he would quit wrestling altogether and concentrate on his career as a teacher. On British Boot Camp 2, the real life Ross Jones gave everything and then some. His exceptional talking, character and wrestling skills shone through and he came so close only to fall at the final hurdle.

Spud feels Ross had the potential to become a TNA star but needed to make sacrifices and understands perfectly why he didn't.

"Ross loves wrestling but I don't know if he loved it enough to go to that plateau," he said.

"He met his wife young, he had a great teaching career young. He has the woman he loves, a career he loves, so why would you give that up if you also get to do what you love at weekends? I just wonder how big Ross could have been because he's so talented. But I'm happy for him because he's my friend and he's got it all."

And Ross didn't particularly mind being knocked out of the process, because he had a whale of a time anyway.

"Before British Boot Camp 2, the nay-sayers were rippling through British wrestling again, saying TNA was going to make us all look silly," he said.

"But I am the eternal optimist. If I ever start talking negatively about anything you should all be worried about me. I always try to see the strengths and good points in every situation."

Another man after my own heart.

"So when people were saying 'Ahhh, Boot Camp is going to be s__t', I was saying 'Give it a chance, let's see what comes out of it'.

"And I had the best time at Boot Camp. The audition was great fun. I got to be insulted by Spud for a couple of hours of my day! I got to get in the ring with Joel Redman and Dave Mastiff who I'd never wrestled before. I did a match at York Hall in front of a massive crowd who were really up for it. Loads of friends and family came to watch. The pop I got when my music hit was phenomenal. And I got to hang out with some of the best guys in British wrestling. We had great camaraderie and wanted to put on a really great show. Nobody was trying to screw anyone over. We all thought whoever the six who got picked, we would be happy for them.

"I was talking to Gail Kim on the way out and I was beaming about the whole thing. She said 'But you just got eliminated' and I said 'I don't care, I had a brilliant time!' It was a really great experience. And I can say I was on TV and nobody can take that away from me."

True to his word, RJ fought his last match some months later, losing a Loser Must Retire showdown to his great pal 'The Heavyweight House of Pain' Stixx. Held at a PROGRESS Wrestling show on November 30 2014, the same weekend that Mad Man Manson retired, this emotional bout was a fitting way to bring down the curtain on the career of the man who quite rightly claims that Singh is King. If you get chance, load up YouTube and check out RJ's ring entrance that night, an elaborate, joyous five-minute dance routine where the self-styled 'Indian superstar' was surrounded by an entire troupe of Bollywood dancers in an explosion of noise and colour more befitting of a WrestleMania ring entrance than the Electric Ballroom in Camden Town.

"It's funny because when PROGRESS first started I nearly turned them down, I didn't know who they were," said Ross.

"They pitched it wrong, they emailed me and said 'we're going for a mixture between Dragon Gate and Ring of Honor' and I emailed back saying 'Are you sure you want me, that's not really what I do - I wrestle more like a mid-80s WWF guy!' But they really did want me. Ligs had said they should book me. So they did, and I was going to wrestle Colt Cabana, which was amazing. But I couldn't do the show.

"Then they brought me onto the second show and I started doing a series of RJ Singh Open Challenges. The last one I did was against Darrell Allen, who beat me, and the whole PROGRESS crowd knew Darrell and I were tagging up elsewhere as The Bhangra Knights. I really wanted to do the Bhangra Knights in PROGRESS so we went on to do that as well. I knew it was the right place to do my retirement. They gave me a good position in the company and I knew the crowds were behind me.

"So I said to (PROGRESS promoter) Jon Briley 'I'd like to do a retirement match' and he said 'Who with?' It came down to three choices, Stixx, Ligs and Spud. Those were the three guys I'd known the longest in wrestling and wrestled the most. Spud was in America, Ligs was mixed up with other things in PROGRESS so it came down to Stixx.

"I knew when it came down to the last match it needed to be against Paul. It just felt right. I first met him at the FWA Academy. Paul used to throw pay-per-view parties at this house and everyone would go round and watch the WWF. We built our friendship from there. Mark Sloan really liked Stixx and wanted to use Paul on his academy shows but Paul couldn't drive, and I was the closest London guy. I could drive, so I got on the shows as well and we started driving together. Then another promoter from the Midlands met us at Mark's shows and decided he'd like to use us too. That's when we met Ligs and Trav and all those guys. So we then made a conscious effort to get booked together. We ended up on holiday camp shows and spent extended time together wrestling every day, learning our craft. It started out as a wrestling partnership but we became best friends and we were best men at each other's weddings.

"The big Bollywood entrance - we pulled it off. I got Tebraiz 'The Director' and Adil Khan back, and Darrell had some Asian friends he got involved, and Jon got the dancers, and literally we did the entrance Alex Shane had pitched all those years before. It was stunning. Nothing had been done in British wrestling on that scale before. It was such a fantastic way to bow out."

Please bear in mind, though, that RJ made a comeback in February 2016. Those pesky wrestling retirements!

So with RJ Singh and others now out of the Boot Camp 2 process, Grado was off to America, where he was joined by Mastiff, Kay Lee, Rampage, Andrews and Noam Dar, who replaced the unfortunate Kris Travis. There, the six hopefuls met up for dinner with TNA President Dixie Carter and Boot Camp series 1 winner, Rockstar Spud.

"Personality is everything," the Texas belle-turned-businesswoman told the finalists. Then she gestured towards Spud.

"This young man is testament to that. I can't have the British Boot Camp 2 winner not surpass this guy. And who has it in them to do that?"

As these words left Dixie's mouth, I honestly thought Grado was going to win. Everything was geared towards him coming out on top because he was the only one of the finalists with a TV personality capable of outshining even the ultra-charismatic Spud. The other five were there mainly for their in-ring skills.

But as Episode 5 developed, Dave Mastiff began to shine. The big bad B-Word began to show aspects of his own quirky real-life personality. In real life, Dave is an intelligent fellow - football fan, musician and straight talking conversationalist, and he started to come out from behind his intimidating front to show he had hidden depth to his character. The bearded Black Country bruiser deliberately gave Grado bad advice in an attempt to sabotage his chances, he surprisingly sang along to camp pop tune Smalltown Boy by Bronski Beat on the radio to pass the time as the finalists criss-crossed the country in a bus, and put Spud firmly in his place during a tour of Washington's famous landmarks as the Rockstar - who was dressed in a magnificent Stars and Stripes suit - boasted about his knowledge of the Presidents of the United States, but got every single fact about them wrong.

"I've known Dave for 15 years and I think he's a wonderful,

wonderful bloke," said Spud.

"I just wish he'd open that out a bit more because when he lets you see that personality, he's entertaining as hell. But Dave's a man's man. He's very big on how you should get your rewards out of respect and hard work, and not the schmoozing that sometimes goes on in the industry. Dave is Dave, and he'll never change, and I don't want him to because he's one of my best friends and I love him. But he deserves something out of wrestling. He's that good. Mad Man Manson says he's the best wrestler he's ever been in the ring with and Manson doesn't put anyone over. Dave has helped build PCW along with Trav, Joey, Lionheart and others. And he's also a great trainer."

He certainly is. One of Dave's proteges was Tyler Bate, who in 2017 became the first ever WWE UK Champion at the tender age of 19.

Back to Boot Camp 2, where Episode 6 was still The Grado Show, as now TNA thrust its hottest rising star - Ethan Carter III - into his path. The privileged EC3 was shown shaking hands with all the finalists but when he came to Grado, he ignored him like footballer Luis Suarez refusing to acknowledge Patrice Evra before an infamous Liverpool vs Manchester United match. But eventually, the obnoxious Carter did lock eyeballs with Grado and shook his hand, only to then call him a "Scottish piece of Haggis" and promise to slap him in the face. Later, when Grado showed off his unorthodox in-ring style during a mat session with Noam Dar, the watching EC3 said "I would rather see my mother make out than watch you compete." Grado snapped, fed up of Carter's teasing, and demanded EC3 get into the ring and say it to his face. It showed another side to the comedic Scottish superstar, that he could display real aggression when provoked.

Episode 7 was judgement day, as the six finalists got to compete in an eight-person match in front of the TNA Impact Wrestling audience, to determine who would make the final three. Before the bout, The Hardy Boyz - arguably the most popular tag team of the past 20 years - entered the hopefuls' dressing room to give them a pep-talk, only to be pounced on by an overexcited Grado, who seized Matt in a hug and declared himself to be the Hardys' biggest fan. The disgusted look on Mastiff's face as Grado 'marked out' for Matt and

Jeff was absolutely priceless.

The match saw Grado, Kay Lee and Mark Andrews team with Al Snow against Mastiff, Rampage, Noam and their partner, TNA Knockout Angelina Love. All the Brits performed well, but Kay Lee's daredevil style and fiery aggression stood out for me. At this point, I could definitely make an argument for the flame-haired Glasgow girl winning the show. Again, going by the principle that the winner should offer something different to TNA, the company simply didn't have a female wrestler on its books who was British, with long red hair, and who possessed the kind of high-flying arsenal Kay Lee had in her locker.

Sure enough, when push came to shove, Kay Lee Ray was picked for the final three. A surprise to me was that Mastiff didn't make the cut.

And then in the biggest shock of all, Al Snow announced that Grado was also eliminated.

"You don't have what it takes," said the gruff trainer.

At this, the Clown Prince got serious, and challenged Snow to a match at the Glasgow Hydro on TNA's upcoming UK tour, to prove he had made the wrong decision. Amused, the WWE and ECW legend accepted.

It was obvious to those of us in the know, that Grado didn't need to make the final. He had already impressed TNA. They already had big plans for him. And it was a better story for him to be ousted at the last by an unimpressed Al Snow, to add fuel to their feud and sell some tickets for their big clash at the Glasgow Hydro.

Instead, Rampage Brown was chosen for the final trio alongside Mandrews and Kay Lee, a testimony to his talent but not his desire to actually win. It's fair to say that Ollie didn't enjoy the Boot Camp process anywhere near as much as RJ Singh did.

"I didn't want to do it from day one, to be honest with you, because I don't like the concept of 'The X Factor of Wrestling', I despise it," he said, speaking in 2016.

"But when they asked me to do it, they explained to me it would be different to Boot Camp 1. I still wasn't convinced. I spoke to some guys, like Samoa Joe, who I wrestled that year in PROGRESS. I told him, man to man, I didn't want to be made to look like some wannabe wrestler. I'd wrestled for 15 years, been all over Europe and to the States, I didn't want to prostitute myself. I was exploring doing some work in Japan at the time, too, so I didn't want to look like a chump. Joe said 'don't worry about it, it will be fine'.

"So I thought about it more, but I decided I didn't want to do it, so I pulled out. They talked me around. And my girlfriend said 'the money you can make for one day of auditions, one show in England and two weeks in the States, you could make enough for us to all go to Disneyworld in September - think about it like that'. So that was my mindset going in. I was thinking about getting the money.

"Then there was the whole promo bulls__t. Promos make me cringe in general because they can be unnatural. They can be like watching a bad school play most of the time, even some of the WWE guys. I'm not saying I'm any better but it seems so hokey a lot of the time. Some guys are really good, don't get me wrong, but it's not my style to go in there ranting and raving, and trying to put myself over. So I get to the auditions. Borash says 'don't worry, everything's fine, you're on to get through to the next round'. But then I get in front of the panel and they start asking me questions about the WWE. I told them I wasn't happy, and that's why I decided to leave. Then Al Snow came back with 'Well why should we invest in you if you quit WWE?' I talked my way out of it but the pressure was on, at that point. And I was thinking, woah, I've just walked into the firing line here. Then they brought my daughter up, saying that if I got this contract, I'd have to leave her behind. Would I do that? So now what am I supposed to say? Because if I say yes, I'll look like an even bigger t__t. I felt they really set me up with those two big questions, there.

"So I was getting mad and then they said 'Right, cut a promo on Joe.' So I've got this 300lb Samoan staring a hole through me and I've just been asked these two questions to trip me up. I thought, f__k this man, I didn't even want to be here in the first place. My head was all over the place."

So Rampage struggled on his promo but excelled where he feels it mattered most, once the auditionees actually got to wrestle. His in-ring skills, combined with his believable image as a hard man, got him through the process to the final stages. But when the winner was announced, Brown admits he was actually praying it wouldn't be him.

"Dixie Carter didn't like me, she didn't like any of us, I don't think. Borash told us that we didn't make a good impression on her. We didn't stand out. I still don't know what that means. In the first British Boot Camp there was a lot of tears and emotion, a lot of 'I'm a real human being' and all that bulls__t. But they weren't getting that from us. At one point they even told me to use my daughter as an angle and I thought f__k you! That's my kid! I'm here because you came to me, not because I need a job because people feel sorry for me because I've got a kid to feed!

"I know what they were trying to do. They were trying to get us all against each other. Trying to make a TV show. But it got to the stage where it was the three of us left, and I was praying it wasn't me. I wasn't going to America without my kid or my missus. They knew this. They would have to either pay to bring them over too or pay me really well to fly me back and forth. I think that's the way they saw it at the time too so that's why they cut me. And if you watch it back, when they announced the winner, I have the biggest smile on my face. I was thinking, get me out of here!

"And yeah, we did enjoy Disneyworld that year!"

So Mark Andrews ended up winning Series 2 of TNA British Boot Camp, after all three finalists entered strong in-ring showings during their final matches in the Impact Zone - Andrews against DJ Zema Ion, Kay Lee versus Gail Kim, and Rampage in a hard hitting duel with fellow Brit Tom 'Bram' Latimer. I was pleased for Mandrews. The Welshman is a top bloke and a phenomenal aerialist, and showed previously unseen microphone skills during TNA British Boot Camp 2. But I was shocked. I felt sure Kay Lee Ray would win from the final three.

"I was surprised Mark won too," said Spud in 2016.

"Dixie liked Rampage but he wasn't a good promo. She liked Kay Lee but didn't think she was a fit for the Knockouts division. Mark she really liked but was worried he was like me. I said to her 'Mark's nothing like me'. I wanted it to be Rampage from the final three, personally, but it was Mark and since he's been on air I've tried to help him as much as I can. He's a really nice kid and it's nice for someone to have that opportunity. He's like me in that he was always told by people he was s__t, what he's doing is wrong, he shouldn't be making music videos of himself...but now there's fat Grado, little James and skinny little Mark, the three of us on television every week. We were told it wouldn't happen by pretty much everybody and look what happened. It's a cool thing to see."

All in all, I personally enjoyed the level of exposure British Boot Camp 2 gave to some of our top UK talent. Having said that, the sequel was not a ratings hit compared to the original. British Boot Camp 2 peaked at 104,000 viewers for the November 30 2014 episode, compared to a season's best of 130,000 for Boot Camp 1.

Andy Quildan was certainly no fan of the second series.

"Season 1 was great but Season 2 was terrible," he said.

"The show was crap and they used York Hall, the venue for Revolution Pro. I got an email from someone in TNA who said 'One of our partners from over here has booked York Hall, I hope this is OK for you, all the tickets are free and we'd like you to be a guest'. Then I got a call from York Hall saying 'Thank you so much for putting us in touch with TNA, they said you recommended them!' And I thought, whatever. Typical wrestling.

"And I'm not going to lie, it pissed me off seeing guys like Martin Stone, Joel Redman and Sha Samuels, superstars who deserve a lot better than a lot of the TNA roster at the time, seeing them having to beg for a job. We've reached a point where we don't need to do that.

"We should appreciate what our true value is and it's beyond begging for a job with a secondary company. You don't have established singers going on The X Factor. I was a little bit offended for the guys. I don't think it benefited anybody involved and I genuinely mean that. All that happened was there were a lot of UK promoters who were now able to say 'As Seen On TNA British Boot Camp' next to wrestlers on their posters."

Rampage, who just slotted straight back into his full-time work on the UK circuit after his Boot Camp stint, believes the TV exposure had little long-term benefit to his career.

"Maybe afterwards I got paid £30-£40 more (for UK shows) which helps. But the top UK guys are still making a quarter of what the top American independent guys get when they come over here.

So it didn't really help me.

"One or two people noticed me (from being on TNA TV) but people notice me in the street from watching PROGRESS On-Demand, PCW or What Culture Pro Wrestling too. I'm getting recognised a lot, which never used to happen, but it's not down to one thing. It's down to the fact that the UK scene is so good now and a lot of the top promotions I work for have On Demand, so we're getting exposure through that."

But back in January 2015, British Boot Camp 2 was at least benefiting Grado, who was on his way to the Hydro. And so was I. On a chilly January afternoon, myself and my travelling companions from Morecambe, Kieran Engelke and Matt White, ventured up to Glasgow to share in the biggest moment in the life of Scotland's unlikeliest wrestling superstar. And, thanks to a chance encounter, I also got to share the biggest day of Grado's life with his family and friends.

On the afternoon of the Maximum Impact show, I had just finished a delicious burrito in a Wetherspoon pub in Glasgow city centre when I noticed a fella coming back from the toilet. He was wearing a T-shirt with the logo 'It's Yersel!' My first thought was, how nice to see a Grado fan, even though he didn't look like a typical wrestling enthusiast. But then I saw the back of the shirt read 'I'm Grado's Dad'. I craned my neck over to where he was sitting and instantly recognised one of his companions from the Insane Fight Club documentary.

It was Grado's mum! It was Grado's parents! In Wetherspoon's, hours before their boy's big moment, enjoying a pre-show dram with a large group of family and friends!

Of course me being me, I had to go over and introduce myself, and it wasn't very long before I myself felt like part of the Stevely family. Maureen and her husband John were warm and welcoming people, as you would expect having raised such a down-to-earth son. Within minutes Maureen, who was wearing an 'I'm Grado's Maw' shirt, and Grado's Auntie Jackie, in a white 'It's Yersel!' shirt, were excitedly chattering away to me like old friends, posing for photos, and offering me family snaps of Grado as a "wee boy" for my book.

They proudly told me how Grado had been wrestling daft since he was knee-high and how many beds he'd broken by crash-landing on them imitating the flying elbow drops and splashes he'd seen the wrestlers perform on TV. And John was telling me all about how in 2002, he drove the teenage Graeme the seven hours and 420 miles to FWA British Uprising in London. But they got lost and were slapped with a speeding ticket, and never actually made it to the show.

Then Grado's best mate 'Patty' started telling me the story of how Grado got his name. They were on holiday in Magaluf aged 17, got steaming drunk and ended up in a tattoo parlour where Graeme revealed he used to be called Grado at primary school and had the name etched on his arm. The next day when he sobered up, he couldn't remember a thing and frantically tried to remove the tattoo. He couldn't and from then on the name, quite literally, stuck. The weird thing was, according to Patty, he couldn't recall Graeme ever being called Grado at primary school. At this, brassy blonde Auntie Jackie chipped in, saying she actually used the name Grado back then, when she used to call him in for tea. The pair then began to good-naturedly argue over which of them was the first to use the name Grado. It was hilarious to see.

Maureen then revealed the family would be sitting front row at the Hydro and would actually have some involvement in the show. "But don't tell anyone".

I put my finger to my lips in the international sign of kayfabe and promised I wouldn't. Well, at least until *now*.

Hours later in the Hydro arena foyer, fans assembled for a pre-show meet and greet with the stars of British Boot Camp 2. And it was packed. Not for Kurt Angle, Matt Hardy, Bobby Lashley or any other recognised superstars from the regular TNA roster, but for six young Brits.

The two Scots Noam Dar and Kay Lee Ray looked like they were having the time of their lives as they posed for photos and signed autographs, soaking up the attention of being Impact Wrestling stars. Even burly Rampage Brown and the stern-faced Dave Mastiff looked like they were having a ball. Mark Andrews was the only one afforded the luxury of TV cameras, no doubt documenting the Boot Camp 2 winner's every move for a future TNA broadcast.

But the longest queue of fans, quite easily, was for Grado. He looked like he was having a whale of a time, basking in the love of his public. I shook his hand and hugged him, and wished him the best of luck.

Later, Grado told a backstage interviewer that he couldn't have been in better shape for his duel with Al Snow. He had been tanning religiously "because fat looks better when it's broon", showed discipline by avoiding the never-ending supplies of chicken, steak and croissants in TNA catering, and been getting into shape by walking his new dog twice a week. Then he proceeded to tell the reporter about his love of cheese.

"I could eat that Brie stuff all day, man!"

Yes, it's fair to say Grado was relaxed ahead of the biggest match of his life.

When Like A Prayer hit that night in the Hydro, the cheer could be heard everywhere from John O'Groats to Hadrian's Wall. As Grado came prancing to the ring, cheered on by his parents in the front row, not to mention Mark Dallas and Jack Jester who were sitting just across from me in a nearby section, and then climbed the turnbuckles to rip off his bumbag and sniff the air in trademark fashion, he looked like he belonged. He looked like a star.

Earlier, his proud and fiery mum had almost got into a ringside confrontation with Al Snow, as she'd hinted earlier in the day. So Grado was fired up and his people were with him every step of the way. And when the pride of Stevenston jacked The Snowman's jaw with a fierce Wee Boot and covered him for the three count, the crowd reaction was out of this world.

As the Hydro rose to its feet, cheering and applauding, and Snow finally showed respect for Grado by raising his arm in the air, the heel stable The Beatdown Clan hit the ring and brutally assaulted the pair as the fans once again began chanting "I-C-DUB! I-C-DUB!" in the hope that maybe Jack Jester would race to the rescue.

And indeed, a hooded figure did vault the barrier and storm the six-sided squared circle to make the save.

But it wasn't Jester.

It was Drew Galloway!

In an angle that echoed his return to ICW some months earlier, The Chosen One made his TNA debut by sending MVP, Low Ki,

Kenny King and Samoa Joe packing, then helped Grado to his feet. The two Ayrshire natives stood side by side, soaking up the adulation of their countrymen, then hugged.

It was quite something to be there. It felt like a historic happening, a watershed moment, and that's because it was. Two homegrown superstars - yes, *superstars* - closing a TV taping in Scotland for the second biggest wrestling company in the world, in an angle that would be shown across the globe on a TV show, on a live event in front of a crowd of thousands where a total of nine (yes, *nine*) British wrestlers appeared on the card.

This had never happened before. And it might never happen again.

I was also bursting with happiness for Grado, whose match with Al Snow was just the beginning of his TNA career. It was also the start of an unlikely rivalry which saw Grado's fearlessly opportunistic attitude towards self-publicity gain mainstream attention for both himself and British wrestling. Well, for a few days at least.

The Grado v Al Snow match was due to air on Impact Wrestling in America some three weeks after the Hydro taping, on February 20 2015. But then a few days before, Grado revealed on social media that Madonna, the Queen of Pop, had refused TNA permission to use Like A Prayer on television.

Grado's infectiously joyful ring entrance was such a major part of his act and the anthemic Like A Prayer had become synonymous with him. You just knew it wouldn't be the same if he came out to some generic 'basketball highlights' style TNA theme. But Madonna owned the rights to the song, a worldwide number one hit for her in 1989, and the multi-billionaire pop star wasn't about to give them up for some nobody pro wrestler from over the border.

So Grado did what Grado does best. He made a video. And he asked Madonna, very nicely, if she would reconsider.

"Madonna? It's yersel! This is Grado, a professional wrestler from Stevenston in Scotland. For the past two years, I've used Like A Prayer as entrance music. It's the best entrance music ever. It gets everybody going, singing, clapping and dancing. A couple of weeks ago I wrestled at the Hydro in Glasgow, Scotland. The match is going to be broadcast and I was going to use Like A Prayer. Everything was agreed between networks and publishers. Until today, when I received an email saying Like A Prayer has been denied on behalf of Madonna. Obviously I was absolutely gutted because I don't ever want to use any other music. I'm a fan, my sister and my mum are fans, and I'm asking if you could find it in yourself...if you could allow the version of Like A Prayer that I use to be used on American TV and on worldwide TV so everyone can enjoy the entrance and celebrate your wonderful song."

After releasing the clip, Graeme tweeted "This might fall on its arse but it's worth a go."

The next thing, the national and international media was all over the story. BBC Radio 1 Newsbeat, The Daily Record, ITV Loose Women, even Time Magazine...they all wanted to talk to Grado, share his video and get behind his internet campaign, which had been titled #SayYesMadonna. Within hours, so many people were retweeting and sharing the video that #SayYesMadonna was a trending topic nationwide alongside EastEnders' 30th anniversary Lucy Beale murder storyline and the Chinese New Year.

Even more unbelievably, on February 19 2015, the day before Grado's match with Snow was due to air, a Scottish MP lodged a motion in Parliament supporting the #SayYesMadonna appeal, as follows.

"Motion S4M-12369: Kenneth Gibson, Cunninghame North, Scottish National Party, Date Lodged: 19/02/2015

Say Yes, Madonna

That the Parliament supports the campaign launched by the North Ayrshire-based professional wrestler, Graeme Stevely, AKA Grado, to allow him to continue using his signature entrance theme, Like a Prayer, by Madonna; recognises that the current Pro Wrestling Elite Heavyweight Champion, Grado, is due to compete in the SSE Hydro against the veteran American wrestler, Al Snow, later in 2015; understands that this match was due to be shown live on US television, complete with Grado's now famous crowd-pleasing entrance, but that shortly before this deal was concluded, the management team for Madonna denied use of the song; understands that the campaign mounted by Grado is gaining momentum and is now top of the trending list on UK Twitter, and considers that, due to the strength of public feeling, Madonna and her management team should indeed say Yes, grant use of the song and let a new US audience witness the celebrated Grado entrance."

You couldn't make it up.

Sadly, despite 82,000 views of Grado's video and all the newspaper, TV, radio and even Parliamentary support and clamour, the #SayYesMadonna movement turned out to be the first real failure of Grado's career. Madonna just blanked the whole thing. The billionaire pop star just didn't respond. And the campaign fizzled out. With TNA execs unable to use Like A Prayer, Grado's replacement TV theme tune did indeed turn out to be tepid, watered down and totally uninspiring.

The #SayYesMadonna campaign proved Grado had the force of personality and the fan base to rally the masses behind him and gain mainstream attention. The fact that I'm even mentioning Grado and Madonna in the same sentence speaks volumes for the sensational progress he has made to minor celebrity status.

But it didn't matter at the end of the day because British wrestling is still an amoeba when compared to a mountain lion like the Queen of Pop, and Grado just didn't have the influence or name value to actually achieve his aim. It was kind of sad. Had Grado triumphed, had he managed to convince The Material Girl to take pity and change her mind, it would have been a significant victory for British wrestling's position in popular culture. As it was, defeat was a sobering reminder that in the grand scheme of things, we were still small fry.

But at least cheeky Grado got the last laugh when Madonna fell off stage during a live TV performance at the Brit Awards later that week.

"Karma," he tweeted.

Despite the lukewarm theme song, Grado's bout with Snow was a TV hit and the charismatic Scotsman was invited back to TNA later in the year, making the 4,000 mile trip from Stevenston to the States to continue what has become an almost unbelievable rags to riches tale. On June 24 2015 at Destination X, Grado actually competed in a TNA X Division Title match on worldwide television, and while he came out on the losing end against the masked Mexican champion Tigre Uno and Low Ki, the crowd at the Universal Studios in Orlando, Florida took the loveable buffoon and his rib-tickling comedy routine to their hearts. Although the athletic X Division wasn't the ideal showcase for Grado's unique talents, our boy has proved his act connects with wrestling fans not just in Scotland and England, but on the other side of the world too. So Grado continued to make appearances on Impact throughout 2015 and 2016.

The timing really couldn't have been better for Grado to get this shot at the big-time, for an ironic reason. In 2015, TNA was a promotion in decline, at least in America. In the States, Impact's viewership dropped to 1.06m viewers from 1.29m in the final three months of 2014 compared to the same period in 2013. Then on January 23 2015, Impact drew only 517,000 viewers on a new TV channel, Destination America. When you consider that WWE Raw pulled 4.09m viewers just four days earlier, it was clear to see that TNA was languishing behind Vince McMahon's federation in a one-sided battle for supremacy in the States.

By May 2015, TNA lost its short-lived contract with Destination America and already found itself searching for a new TV station. Meanwhile rivals Ring of Honor gained a slot on the same channel, leading some wrestling journalists to question for the first time in 13 years just who was the real 'number two' promotion in the US. There were also reports TNA had cut its production budget way back and some wrestlers weren't getting paid on time. In the summer, top stars left TNA such as MVP, Low Ki and the man who had been the first ever British World Heavyweight Champion when he won the TNA Title in December 2013, Nick 'Magnus' Aldis. To outsiders, it seemed that they were deserting a rapidly sinking ship. In early 2016, Kurt Angle, Bobby Roode and Eric Young left TNA too. The company was in dire financial straits.

But with the TNA roster depleted, the company gave TV opportunities to new talent who may never have had the chance otherwise. Such as Grado.

So with around 150,000 British eyes on him whenever he competed on Impact, Grado was slowly becoming a star to the UK wrestling fan base.

My main worry for him now is overexposure. Grado has been absolutely everywhere in recent years, particularly in 2014 and 2015. The time may come in future when he will have to freshen up his act.

The answer might well lie in a conversation we had during Grado's first appearance for Preston City Wrestling in February 2014.

Following his bout with Dave Rayne that night, Graeme and I were chatting backstage about nothing in particular when he suddenly turned serious.

"Greg, can I ask your advice on something? Do you think I should turn heel?"

When Graeme saw the bemused look on my face, he broke into a big smile, his eyes twinkling with his usual childlike innocence, and said "Nah, I'm just being a daftie!"

I told him he wasn't being a 'daftie', but it wasn't the right time for Grado to become a bad guy. Not yet. You have to reach the peak before you can come down the other side and this was before even the first Insane Fight Club had aired on TV and he had gone stratospheric. So instead, I said he should continue to be what has brought him so much success to date.

I told him "For now, you should carry on just being yourself."

And that's what he has done. But when the time is right, and it won't be for a few years yet, I am confident Grado will be an awesome villain. That's because he is adaptable. People say "Ahh, he's just comic relief" but he is much more than that. Grado can brawl, he can cut promos with fiery intent, he's proved that he can be taken seriously as a promotion's heavyweight champion, and he is a master at 'fighting from underneath'. In other words, he can sell a beating, get the crowd right behind him, and come back to win.

"I first met Graeme at a Triple X show in Coventry (in 2012) before I moved over to America and before I got there, I'd watched the YouTube documentary of him and his videos with ICW and I thought, he's f__king brilliant," said Rockstar Spud.

"When I met him, he said to me 'I'm crap, I'm sh_te man'. And I said to him 'Listen to me, don't you dare change for anybody.' And he said 'I can't wrestle'. I replied 'It ain't about that'.

"Graeme is a wonderful guy. I'm so glad for everything he's

achieved. I'd like to think I'm a part of his story and he knows he's part of mine. He's a brilliant lad and a good friend."

I have no doubt that Graeme 'Grado' Stevely will continue to tackle life head-on with that inspiring enthusiasm of his. From ICW to TNA, I have thoroughly enjoyed watching, and at times experiencing first-hand, his unprecedented and rapid rise to prominence. In three short years he went from an unknown struggler barely treading water on the Scottish grapple circuit to the most famous British-based professional wrestler of modern times. That is quite an achievement and one hell of a story.

And mark my words, it's not over yet.

CHAPTER 18

LUCKY MAN

On the night of Saturday, November 29 2014, Dann Read suffered a stroke.
He collapsed while ring announcing at a small show in Chelmsford, Essex and only prompt medical attention saved his life.
Dann, who had recently become the new promoter of the XWA, was 32 years old.
I owe my career in British wrestling to Dann. It was Dann who gave me my start. He booked me as a commentator for his first ever show as a promoter at Ipswich Corn Exchange on July 13 2002. He put in a good word for me with Dino Scarlo which led to the most high-profile run of my career as a manager with the FWA. For the past 14 years he has been a close confidant and my best friend in the wrestling business.
Like myself, Dann is incredibly passionate about wrestling. But that all-consuming passion has often come at the expense of his own health.
When Dann collapsed, he was in the process of announcing Rhia O'Reilly as the new Pro-Wrestling:EVE Champion. Rhia had just defeated Nikki Storm in the main event of a show where the vast majority of performers were men.
The fact that Rhia and Nikki were taken seriously as main eventers, that they could credibly headline in a male-dominated world, is testimony to how far women's wrestling in Britain has come in recent years. And a lot of the credit for that must go to Dann Read.
The first women's match Dann ever watched was Rockin' Robin v Leilani Kai on a WWF home video in 1989. Dann was only seven years old but was captivated as Robin, the sister of Jake 'The Snake' Roberts, pulled off a DDT and the kind of high-risk flying moves

normally only associated with men. Dann took notice because women's wrestling was barely featured on WWF television in those days. Sensational Sherri Martel and Miss Elizabeth were big stars in 1989 at the centre of the Hulk Hogan v Randy Savage main event feud at WrestleMania V, but they were used as managers, not wrestlers. Over in WCW, Madusa and Nancy 'Woman' Sullivan were prominent female performers but were also presented as valets accompanying the male superstars, rather than taking centre stage themselves.

So when it came to actual female grappling on TV, there was a real dearth.

It was much the same in Britain in the 80s and 90s. There were only a handful of female UK wrestling stars at the time, Mitzi Mueller and Klondyke Kate being the most heralded. Miss Linda and Princess Paula made names for themselves as the valets of Adrian Street and Dave 'Fit' Finlay respectively. Sweet Saraya and Nikita would come along later. But for the most part, female performers were marginalised. It was tough for them to get noticed.

Back in America, the WWF made an attempt to create a new female star in 1993 when the company resurrected its long dormant women's title, signed Deborah 'Madusa' Miceli from WCW, changed her name to Alundra Blayze and built a mini women's division around her as the champion. Dann loved her feud with Japanese star Bull Nakano because both girls could wrestle and were allowed to show it. Their matches had plenty of action, big moves and drama. There were a number of exceptionally talented female Japanese stars at the time who made their names in the exciting All-Japan Women's division in the early 1990s. For a short time in 1994/5, the WWF capitalised, bringing in not just the impressive Nakano, but the fearsome Aja Kong, Lioness Asuka, Kyoko Inoue and others.

But then Vince McMahon lost interest, Miceli was fired, the link with Japan was abandoned, and WWF women's wrestling was back to square one.

In a desperate attempt to win the Monday night ratings war with WCW in the late 1990s, Vince McMahon's product became more edgy, violent and sexy. During this Attitude Era, a number of women became big stars. But the likes of Sable, Terri Runnels, Debra and

Tammy 'Sunny' Sytch were eye candy, shameless sex objects for the young adult male demographic watching Monday Night Raw to drool over. Skimpy outfits, silicone-enhanced bosoms, and bra and panties matches became the norm for the WWF/E women's division at the turn of the century. Even the female grapplers on the roster who could actually wrestle a little bit, like Miss Jacqueline, Ivory and Molly Holly, were rarely given the opportunity to exchange holds on television for any discernible length of time.

Three of the biggest stars in North America during the noughties were Stacy Keibler, a glamorous girl-next-door type with extraordinarily long legs who would later earn tabloid fame for her brief relationship with Hollywood A-lister George Clooney, the late Joanie 'Chyna' Laurer, a powerhouse bodyguard-turned wrestler whose stoic look and muscularity made her a rarity in that she could believably compete against the men, and Stephanie McMahon-Helmsley, the boss's daughter turned manipulative superbitch wife of the company's top heel Triple H. All three were more renowned as personalities than for actual in-ring talent.

Then along came Trish Stratus and Lita. Their mid-noughties feud broke the mould because these girls were personalities who could also wrestle hard inside the squared circle, and management took notice. Stratus and Lita even main evented Raw in 2004. Dann sees their rivalry as a turning point for women's wrestling and feels the duo influenced an entire generation of girls who were coming up behind them.

"Trish and Lita was a great story that every single teenage girl could relate to," said Dann when reflecting on their feud many years later.

"Lita represented the community that were into wrestling and metal. She was perfect as a role model for that demographic, with the tattoos and the red hair. Then there was Trish, the girl in school who'd developed early who the boys all fancied. It was the perfect rivalry and great storytelling."

As Trish and Lita were breaking new ground in the States, Dann was cutting his teeth as a wrestling promoter thousands of miles away in lowly Sudbury, Suffolk. But he was struggling to make a success of it. His debut show lost money and a follow-up event in his home town under the FWA banner in 2003 was also a commercial failure.

Then in January 2006, he was hit by a car while crossing the road. His leg got trapped under the vehicle and he suffered knee and back injuries. He would require nine minor operations on his back and was told he needed knee surgery too. But fed up of the amount of time he was spending in hospital to fix his back, he eschewed the much-needed knee operation. He still hasn't had the corrective surgery to this day. As a result of overcompensating for his dodgy knee, both of his patellas are now completely knackered and he is in constant pain.

But despite his physical problems, Dann was determined not to give up on his dream of being a wrestling promoter. So he ran further FWA shows in 2006, including an event at Colchester Hippodrome nightclub called NOAH Limits featuring an appearance by Bret 'The Hitman' Hart, Japanese stars Takeshi Morishima and Mohammed Yone, and a main event of Jody Fleisch v Jonny Storm v former WWE superstar Billy Kidman.

Nightclub wrestling shows were a rarity back then. After seeing how the dark and dingy surroundings created an edgy atmosphere ideal for pro wrestling, Dann felt he could corner the market. So he set up his own promotion called X-Sports Wrestling and put on a series of events for adults only.

The first X-SW show, on December 3 2006 at Liquid nightclub in Gloucester, was main evented by a great Death Match between two of Britain's best hardcore wrestlers at the time, Iceman and Paul Travell. It also included a pulsating three-way between Storm, Fleisch and current WWE superstar Neville.

"I called the show 'Cursed'," said Dann.

"That's because there was a string of bad luck relating to the show being repeatedly cancelled and rearranged, and people pulling out. But to this day it's my favourite show I've ever done, although I have no footage of it whatsoever. It was just a fun show. Everyone left that show saying I was onto something special."

Dann always had problems with shows being cancelled. He was forever having run-ins with venue management, especially when said venues were run by health and safety-conscious local councils. A prime example came one week after Cursed when he ran virtually an entire show full of bloody and sadistic anything-goes action for over 18s called, appropriately, Gorefest.

"At Gorefest, we had a man v woman match between Ian Rotten v Mickie Knuckles, and the BBC and local newspapers campaigned to try to cancel it because it was encouraging violence towards women," said Dann.

"I didn't even know if that show was going ahead, the day before. It was touch and go. The manager of the nightclub was getting so much heat.

"We did eventually get the show going, although it started two hours late. Cesaro was on that show. He accidentally flashed my girlfriend Emily backstage. She wasn't feeling well and was laying across one of the benches. Cesaro didn't see her, and took off his towel. When he saw her he quickly covered himself up and apologised, and went so red in the face it was unbelievable."

Emily, the girl who'd caught a glimpse of The Swiss Superman's meat-and-two-veg, had started seeing Dann earlier that year. I met her for the first time at Ring of Honor's debut show in the UK in August 2006, when she and Dann sat with me at the Liverpool Olympia as we watched Nigel McGuinness and Bryan Danielson beat the living hell out of each other in the main event. I could see why Dann was smitten. Emily is a good looking girl with a great personality. And she loves wrestling too. I was delighted for him.

Dann ran two more adult wrestling events in 2007 but it soon became clear that ultra-violent shows only had a limited appeal. His last X-SW event, named after the Sophie Ellis-Bextor pop tune Murder on the Dancefloor, drew a paltry crowd of 60 to Liquid in Gloucester. It was also the night that the term 'death match' could have become literal. London-based hardcore wrestler Jimmy Havoc was lucky to walk away alive after he was choke slammed through an ironing board, one of the legs spiked up and missed impaling him by a couple of inches.

By then, Dann had begun another project. This one would allow him to pursue his lifelong interest in women's wrestling.

He read an article in Total Wrestling magazine about an independent wrestling company in America called Chickfight. This was an all-female promotion, where the girls competed in a much more hard-hitting and fast-paced style of wrestling to what many casual fans would have been used to seeing from the WWE.

Intrigued, Dann contacted the writer, Phil Austin, and asked to be put in contact with the Chickfight promoters Jason Deadrich and Melissa Anderson, better known as female grappler Cheerleader Melissa. They got talking and eventually struck a deal for Dann to run Chickfight shows in the UK.

"There was a niche market for girls wrestling at the time and I liked the idea of going against what the WWE was doing with women," said Dann.

"I thought I'd attract a market of people who wanted to rebel against the WWE and a market of girls who were fed up of not being given something that represents them. The quality of female role models on TV was, and is, terrible ever since we had Buffy the Vampire Slayer. Buffy was massive and had both female and male fans. She was a big inspiration to me from a marketing standpoint.

"Emily was very passionate about it too and her views with regards to how females are portrayed in media and TV were the same as my own.

"Business to me has always been about adapting and seeing where things were going to go. And I'd spotted what was going to happen with women's wrestling in the future. Even before Chickfight, I would always insist I had a girls match on my shows."

Dann hoped to run his first Chickfight show in 2006. But once again, the venue cancelled on him.

"It was because it was all women," he said.

"There was a lot of sexism. It's not as bad now. Back then I had so many problems with venues because I was doing all-women wrestling shows."

Instead, the first UK Chickfight show was held on January 14 2007 at The Marina Centre in Great Yarmouth, a WAW venue. Dann's Norfolk neighbours the Knight family, who run WAW, have also been tremendous champions of UK women's wrestling, particularly Saraya who has mentored numerous girls over the years, most famously her own daughter Paige, and run her own all-female promotion called WAWW (World Association of Women's Wrestling) later renamed Bellatrix.

For the first Chickfight event, Dann and the Knights worked together. So my pal set to work on trying to get bums on seats for a wrestling event made up entirely of the fairer sex.

"On the first show, I focussed the promotion online because the smart fans were the people who knew they were going to see a different style of women's wrestling and they would see women's wrestlers they wouldn't normally see in this country.

"I knew a lot of casual fans would look at Chickfight and think it was porn. And a lot of mums surely wouldn't be happy with their husbands taking kids to women's wrestling. But we did OK. A decent turnout. I remember being surprised. People travelled. There were a few locals. Some were WAW fans."

Saraya main evented that first show, losing to Cheerleader Melissa. But as far as Dann was concerned, his biggest star was his top babyface, a youngster called 'The Jezebel' Eden Black.

"She was our Lita," said Dann.

"She was smaller, her style was MMA based, and it made her an underdog you could really believe in because she could apply submissions and weird innovative moves out of nowhere. Melissa was a babyface in America but over here, she was so much bigger than the other girls. I called her The Female Terminator. She was deadpan, which came across as vicious and sadistic. There was a physical size difference between her and Jez, but because Jez had that believability the fans thought if anyone can beat Melissa, it's her.

"Jez and Lacey had a great match on the first show and I remember Ricky Knight saying these girls were showing up the guys.

"I still think Jez could have been a hell of a player on the UK scene. But she finished up after she got hurt. Her body couldn't take the constant beatings."

As for Melissa, she went on to work in TNA as Raisha Saeed, the associate of Awesome Kong.

Speaking of the 272lb female mastodon, whose real name is Kia Stevens, the future TNA Knockouts Champion and WWE superstar came over to the UK in June 2007 to work for Dann on a Chickfight show held on the afternoon of an IPW:UK event.

"That show drew well, about 200.

"I thought it was a good idea to run an afternoon show on a 'smart mark' promotion, so the smart fans would make a day of it, and they'd get to see two different distinct promotions in the same day in the same venue, and the main promotion would be happy because I split the cost of the venue and ring hire with them, so it was a win-win for everyone. That was how to expose new fans to my product.

"It was supposed to be Kong v Saraya in the first round of a tournament that day in Orpington, but Saraya had hurt her knee wrestling Melissa in a Chickfight match before an RQW show in Colchester the night before."

The Saraya-Melissa fight in Colchester was described by one observer as "the most brutal off the wall female wrestling match I've ever seen". This vicious arena-wide brawl ended when the American flung her Norfolk foe into a row of ringside chairs, Saraya landed awkwardly and severed a tendon in her knee. An ambulance was called and Saraya was rushed to hospital for emergency surgery to repair her ripped-apart kneecap. The incident fuelled a furious Saraya comeback and she eventually resumed her bitter feud with Melissa five years later in another American all-female company called SHIMMER.

Meanwhile, Dann ran further Chickfight shows in 2008 but nothing ever seemed to run smoothly for him.

"Back in those days, a lot of the girls were unreliable. A lot of it was nerves. The smart marks were watching them and reviewing them, and a lot of the girls found that criticism really hard. They couldn't handle it so they didn't want to come.

"I'd get all sorts of excuses on the day. It got to the point where I wouldn't fully book the Chickfight shows until the day of the show, until I saw who'd turned up."

Soon Dann became disillusioned with Chickfight. His growing feelings of discontentment coincided with a happy event in his life. In 2007 Emily gave birth to a baby girl, who they named Winifred.

"I stopped doing Chickfight because of Winnie. There were a lot of other issues at the time too. We'd been made homeless and needed to move away to find a new place to live.

"And I didn't like the Chickfight name. It was a strong brand name but not a family-friendly wrestling name. I couldn't get behind something that when you search for it on the internet, you get porn before you get wrestling. I put a lot of hours into Chickfight and I wasn't making any money from it. And I needed to, because now I had a kid.

"It became the female version of the original FWA too. The wrestling fans weren't getting into the Brit girls as much as the overseas girls. All they cared about was who I was bringing over from abroad. They just wanted to see Cheerleader Melissa and Awesome Kong."

Dann ran a couple of XWA shows, in conjunction with myself and Mark Kay, at his hometown venue The Delphi Club in Sudbury in 2009. But women's wrestling was on the backburner until he and Emily came up with the idea for their own all-female promotion, Pro-Wrestling:EVE.

"I didn't like what had happened to the women's scene after I stopped doing Chickfight," said Dann.

"A lot of the Chickfight girls had retired, gone, disappeared. There was a new breed coming through but nobody knew who they were."

So Dann and Emily launched their new venture in May 2010 and marketed it cleverly. The EVE name itself and the company's distinctive apple logo played off The Bible story of Eve, the first woman on Earth. They also divided their roster into groups, or stables, something no other UK promotion was doing at the time and years before WWE's Divas Revolution created all-female units Team PCB, Team BAD and whatever the other Team was called. Image-obsessed Scottish duo Carmel Jacob and Sara Marie Taylor were The Glamour Gym, the self-absorbed Nikki Storm and Becky James were Team Storm, while 'Lancashire Terrier' April Davids and Swedish submission expert Jenny Sjodin were The Northern Shooters. Davids and Sjodin were also stars of EVE's Catch division - a hybrid of the old British rounds system and MMA-style grappling.

The unique branding of EVE captured the imagination of many smart wrestling fans and the UK grapple media. Dann and Emily's debut show on May 8 2010 at The Delphi drew around 170 fans and The Sun newspaper was in the house too. Judging by his review, reporter Lee Burton was suitably impressed.

"Pro Wrestling: EVE has been a year in the making — its goal being to showcase the great grappling talent of women across the continent," he wrote.

"That meant EVE had wrestlers from England, Wales, Scotland, the Republic of Ireland, Sweden, Greece and Germany for its debut show.

"I strongly recommend that you pay a visit and see what will hopefully become the start of a new generation of girls grappling in Europe."

With the debuting 'Fighting Irish' Rhia O'Reilly, Sweet Saraya, the German duo of 'Hardcore Daredevil' Blue Nikita and the imposing 'Alpha Female' Jazzy Gabert, 'The It Girl' Melanie Price, Jetta, Britani 'Paige' Knight and Jemma Palmer, a former star of TV show Gladiators, all appearing on the first EVE event, Dann and Emily certainly had plenty of talent at their disposal. And there wasn't an American in sight.

"I said with EVE, right from the get-go, no imports," explained Dann.

"It's a European promotion. The second you bring over an import, all the attention is off the Brits and onto the Americans. I wanted to make stars of the Europeans first so the fans would want to see them wrestle the imports. And that's what I did."

Dann and Emily's second show on October 16 2010 saw the debut of a talented young woman who developed into arguably EVE's biggest star. At the time the real-life Nicola Glencross had only been wrestling for two years. But while still a rough diamond at the time, Nikki Storm was clearly a 5ft 1in ball of charisma and confidence who had the attitude, personality and work ethic to be a somebody in the wrestling business

"I saw something in Nikki," said Dann.

"She was raw as hell but the way she did little things, I knew she was going to be a star. I wanted to work with her."

Nikki wrestled Saraya on her debut show and then reached the final of the tournament to crown the first ever Pro-Wrestling:EVE Champion in April 2011, won by Paige.

That weekend, Nikki Storm's fellow Glaswegian Kay Lee Ray made her EVE debut.

"She was superb," said Dann.

"I knew she was going to be good because Doug Williams contacted me, he'd been in Scotland doing a seminar, and he told me I had to take a look at Kay Lee Ray. She's going to be a star. So I did."

By this time, Dann and I were having regular telephone conversations about EVE and he enthusiastically kept me updated about the project. Now, I have to admit, back then I wasn't all that bothered about Pro-Wrestling:EVE or women's wrestling in general. I just didn't think there were many British girls who were any good. Perhaps my views were blinkered by years of watching WWE and how they presented their women. Or maybe it was because I booked one or two female bouts on Morecambe shows over the years and the results were underwhelming. So whenever Dann waxed lyrical about Nikki Storm, Kay Lee Ray and the rest, I pretended to sound interested when really, I was just humouring him.

This all changed at XWA War on the Shore on July 4 2011.

Dann convinced me to book an EVE Title match in Morecambe. Being honest, I only did it as a favour to him. I wouldn't have had a girls match on the show otherwise, but he needed Britani to lose the EVE title to 'The Female Fight Machine' Jenny Sjodin because the Knight girl was about to leave the UK to sign for WWE. I just wasn't that taken with women's wrestling. And I wasn't the only one.

"Most UK promoters at the time weren't interested in the girls," said Dann.

"I wanted to do EVE matches on other promoters' shows because I needed more footage but also because I wanted the promoters to see them."

Britani, or Raya to use her nickname, was an absolute sweetheart to have around, full of chatter, smiles and hugs for me and everybody else backstage. It was a big deal personally to have her there, as the fifth member of the Knight family to wrestle for me in Morecambe.

Sjodin v Knight was also the best women's match we've ever had in my hometown. The stoic Scandinavian shooter and the effervescent Norfolk Doll hit each other with a plethora of eye-catching, athletic and daredevil moves, keeping the fans on the edges of their seats with their exuberant aggression and a series of dynamic near falls, until Jenny won the title with a cross armbreaker submission. I commentated on the bout alongside Jesse Ellis and could not contain my astonishment as the two fiery females tore into each other for 10 breathtaking minutes.

A WWE-style lingerie pillow fight, this most certainly was not.

Dann had been spot-on with his faith in the skills of his girls. When it came to the women's wrestling scene, he was a visionary.

Soon afterwards, Raya went to WWE and as Paige, became the first ever NXT Women's Champion and a two-time Divas Champion, as well as star of the hit WWE Network reality show Total Divas, and the first ever female guest on the Stone Cold Steve Austin podcast. At the WWE Hall of Fame ceremony in April 2016 she and Saraya (who has also appeared on Total Divas) sat in the second row, just behind the legendary Texas Rattlesnake. A few weeks later, Paige appeared as a guest on ITV This Morning. As a superstar, the Norfolk Doll had truly arrived.

EVE continued to turn heads and push boundaries. In October 2011 Dann and Emily ran a show in Nottingham in conjunction with Southside Wrestling and brought over some of Japan's best girls from the Ice Ribbon promotion. In January 2012, EVE was covered in The Sun magazine with a full-colour feature. Then in February 2012, we did another EVE match in Morecambe - a quality three-way between April Davids, Jenny Sjodin and the sexily arrogant Shanna, who billed herself as Portugal's Perfect Athlete.

Things were going well for Dann and Emily outside of wrestling too. In 2010, they had a little boy, Emerson. They also opened a health food store in Sudbury and for a time, had a steady stream of income to complement the volatile wrestling business.

Then on February 18 2012, came Dann's most ambitious project to date, as he broadcast a show from little old Sudbury live on the internet and charged fans to watch. Headlined by Sjodin v Alpha Female for the title and Nikki Storm's victory in the Queen of the Ring tournament, No Man's Land was the first ever iPay-Per-View wrestling show in Europe.

"The iPPV was a lot of stress and hassles," said Dann.

"The venue told me they had internet, which we needed, and then a week before the show when I went up to do a run-through, they told me they didn't have it in the venue after all. So I had to pay for a satellite truck. It cost me £500 plus 20% of the revenue.

"And then there were technical issues for the first third of the broadcast. It was laggy and we had to make the screen smaller for it to work. Once the show finished we uploaded it so you could watch it again without any issues."

There was another memorable EVE show on July 14 2012. Not only did it feature an all-twins battle between the sugar-sweet Blossoms and the sultry Owens sisters from Northern Ireland, but it featured Pro-Wrestling:EVE's first ever Battle of the Sexes, as Rockstar Spud came swaggering into Sudbury determined to put women's wrestling in its place once and for all.

"A women-only promotion?" sneered the Baby Jesus over the Delphi house mic.

"I find that kind of sexist!

"To be honest, what Pro Wrestling EVE should be is a promotion that does not have *any* women. Women are the second best sex. Women are no good for anything but cleaning and making babies and half the time they are lying on their backs doing that!

"I haven't seen any female wrestler or female promotion that's better than any male wrestler or male promotion. So I'm going to challenge any woman in the back who thinks she can beat any male wrestler. It will be a no disqualification match and the easiest payday of my life...and I'm going to prove once and for all that men are better than women!"

So this brought out the 6ft 1in, 220lb Alpha Female, who battered the terrified Spud all over the venue as the crowd clapped and cheered. This massacre ended when the towering Jazzy power bombed her tormentor through a table at ringside then rolled him back in, pinning Spud in less than five minutes! The whole angle and match was done brilliantly, with Spud showing no ego by strongly putting over a woman, something many male wrestlers would surely have refused to do.

Now I am no fan of inter-gender matches, as a rule. I believe physical confrontations between men and women on a wrestling show should be used sparingly, because when done properly a male attacking a female is a highly effective way of building heat for a heel. It lessens the effectiveness if you make it the norm. But this match was the exception. It sent out a positive message by putting the sleazy sexist Spud in his place and was really entertaining.

But while I am a traditionalist when it comes to the idea of a man fighting a woman in a wrestling ring, UK companies like PCW, Southside and ICW *have* promoted competitive matchups between the two sexes. And Dann too, believes there is a place for inter-gender bouts on the British circuit.

"I think it's all about how you present them," said Dann.

"Is there any reason why a really good girl wrestler can't do well against a guy wrestler if it's a legit technical fight? Jenny Sjodin competed against men in grappling competitions and won. I presented her as a legitimate mixed martial artist who has won gold medals, she could suddenly grab an arm and break it because that's how good she was with her knowledge and technique. So people bought into her and believed she could beat the majority of men in wrestling too.

"(UFC star) Ronda Rousey has never fought a man, but people wanted her to, because they believed she could do it. UFC would never have been able to do it but it didn't stop the speculation.

"I did a match between Jimmy Havoc and Kay Lee Ray. What a great match. But presented the right way, because Kay Lee is known for hardcore risk-taking, sacrificing herself. You know she knows what she's getting into and what she's capable of. So if any girl can do it, against this sadistic psychopath, maybe Kay Lee is crazy enough that she can beat him. We did a spot where Havoc force fed thumb tacks into her mouth and she spat them out into his face. It was the presentation of her mindset that made the difference."

But isn't this promoting violence against women?

"That match was an over 18s show," said Dann, when I asked him that question.

"You wouldn't do that kind of match on a family show. It depends on your audience. But there are two ways to look at it. If you've got an aggressive guy towards a woman, can you also be saying that we're telling a story that she shouldn't just accept this and it's OK to fight back? I think there's always going to be an argument for both sides.

"Personally, I would rather my daughter learned that she can kick someone's arse, male or female. That's what drives me in my decisions towards women, and Emily is involved in this process as well. What would we want Winnie to do or think in that situation? If she is taught properly, Winnie can defend herself and the guy will never try it again."

Spud, having had that match with Alpha Female, is a big fan of women's wrestling in Britain but believes intergender matches should be done sparingly and only promoted with a story in mind.

"You can do it with a f__king pipsqueak like me who comes out and says women shouldn't be anywhere near a wrestling ring, they should be cooking and cleaning, and any man can beat a woman, and I'll challenge any woman that comes out, and out comes Alpha Female and I die," said Jay, speaking in 2016.

"That puts women's wrestling over and that champion over, when promoted right with the right character. I can lose to anybody and I'll come back and still be Rockstar Spud.

"Nikki Storm is fantastic, Jetta I think is one of the best woman wrestlers for her mind, there is a girl called Jinny at PROGRESS who is fantastic, an absolute bitch on the mic and ahead of herself considering how long she's been working and a sweetheart as a human being. Kay Lee Ray is good as well and I love Viper.

"But I think women should stop wrestling dudes because they're never going to wrestle a man in WWE. Brock Lesnar is never going to fight Ronda Rousey. There is suspension of disbelief and eventually it gets really stupid. I think you can do it in a Tomb Raider style, because Lara Croft beat up dudes, but any punch from a woman to a man is going to be totally different to a man punching a woman.

"A lot of it is down to the lads who are letting the girls do what they want, being really nice, but f__k that. Do it properly."

As for my own personal opinion, I can't see a scenario where I would support an intergender match in Morecambe. Most of our fans have simple tastes and I don't believe they would buy into a competitive matchup between a man and a woman. Either that, or we would get complaints from mums, dads and grandparents. Kieran Engelke, the current Morecambe promoter, feels the same way.

But as Dann and Spud said, it is all about the presentation. So never say never.

On November 10 2012, Dann dipped his toes into the iPPV waters once again. This time, everything went like clockwork. The quality of the broadcast was flawless and the show itself, Wrestle-Fever, was a belter. With his roster of Europeans now established, Dann finally brought in an American star in TNA's 'Beautiful People' bad girl Angelina Love. The show ended memorably too, with Nikki Storm winning the title from Alpha but then losing it to Japan's Emi Sakura straight away.

"It was a sell-out," said Dann.

"We were carrying chairs in from the factory next door. We even brought in a sofa so there were some more seats. It was absolutely rammed. The interval took 45 minutes for people to get their photos with Angelina Love."

Dann had really built Pro-Wrestling:EVE into something special.

But then 11 days later, the Read family hit rock bottom.

Emily was hospitalised with a mental health condition.

Dann was heartbroken. To make matters worse, Emily's illness meant he was forced to close the health food shop to look after the two kids and this led to him going bankrupt. He was left struggling to make ends meet, missing his soulmate terribly as she got the help she needed, looking after two young children on his own for three long months. It was a dark time for him.

"I'm getting teary remembering it," said Dann several years later.

"I don't know how we got through that. You just carry on. They're my family. What else can you do?

"I remember just going from one day to the next. I had debt collectors at the door. I wasn't able to open windows of the house in case they got in. It sucked. It *sucked*."

Emily slowly got better and was allowed to return home. Meanwhile Dann struck a deal with Steven Fludder to run an EVE afternoon show at Preston City Wrestling in February 2013. This gave me the chance to catch up with my old mate in person and see his product first-hand for the first time.

I was really impressed.

Nikki Storm stood out to me. She was bubbly and we got along instantly backstage, but also had an aura of professionalism and oozed star quality once she burst through the curtain. Nikki stood there in the entranceway, arms outstretched for what seemed like an eternity, soaking in the spotlight as she was announced as 'The Best in the Galaxy'. Then she had the best bout of the show, regaining the EVE championship from Sakura. Such was her charisma, the pint-sized Scot was like a female Spud.

I also enjoyed the work of the towering 'Amazon' Ayesha Ray, who like Rhia O'Reilly was trained by my old FWA colleague Justin Richards, as well as cute fun-loving tag team The Lovely Peppers (Kirsty Love and Pollyanna) and the blonde-haired Viper. Real name Kim Benson, The Queen of Scots was friendly and huggable backstage, but a fearsome competitor inside the ring.

But what I liked most about the EVE event was that every girl had rounded personalities and images which were easily distinguishable. No one wrestler was exactly the same as the other and it was impossible for the fans to get any of the characters mixed up. You couldn't always say that about young male British wrestlers, many of whom are interchangeable. There are a lot of clean-cut, do-a-lot-of-moves, tights-and-boots men on the UK circuit whio are so similar none of them stand out from the pack.

"Having such a diverse roster is a major plus because it helps to create a distinctive brand identity for a promotion and means the fans will never get bored from match to match, because everything and everyone on the show is always going to be fresh and different from what's gone before," I later wrote in my column for the WrestleTalk TV website.

There was also a great atmosphere in the EVE dressing room. I have managed large groups of women before in an office environment, and there can often be a level of bitchiness, especially towards other women. There was no evidence of this in Preston that day. Everybody got along well and there was a great deal of respect for Dann and his booking abilities.

"My biggest problem running an all-girls show is people think you're only there because you're trying to get with the girls," said Dann.

"There's nothing you can do about that. If people are going to believe it, they'll believe it no matter what. You either let it get to you or you don't."

Dann *was* letting his personal situation get to him though. He was clearly fretting about leaving Emily on her own, so much so that he actually turned up late for his own show, and seemed to be in a mess organisationally. I know Steven Fludder was frustrated with him. Then came an incident during one of the EVE matches where a fan claimed to have been struck. Dann would soon have a threatened lawsuit hanging over his head too. This dragged on for months until finally, footage proved the spectator hadn't been hit at all. But Dann could have done without this added stress.

Then Emily had a bad reaction to her medication and suffered a brain seizure. With his wife back in hospital, Dann was forced to cancel his next EVE show and this sparked the problems with Sanjay Bagga who was supposed to supply the ring and still wanted payment. My old pal was badly hurt by the LDN promoter's attitude.

"Any time you lose someone that you thought was a mate, you feel gutted," he said.

"When someone is going to jump to such an extreme, you find out what you're really worth to them. And I'd always defended Bagga. I was always on the phone to him a lot when he needed advice. It's just a shame.

"It makes you realise that for the most part, people in the wrestling business don't give a s__t. They're only interested in a booking. Not everyone though. Rhia, Nikki and Kay Lee were really understanding."

The show eventually went ahead on April 27 2013 but Bagga's own event at the Delphi, organised for two weeks before Dann's and then cancelled last-minute, badly affected his ticket sales.

"We found out a lot of people had heard about a wrestling show being cancelled so a lot of people hadn't turned up to the EVE show," said Dann.

"It was hard to go from the sold-out Wrestle-Fever to the 2013 shows after the Bagga thing, because he killed the venue and nobody had faith in the venue any more. This was after I'd built EVE up into a wrestling promotion local people could trust.

"Not only that, but people were travelling. Tickets were going out all over the fricking world, to America, to Japan. People were coming from all over the world to the Delphi Club in Sudbury of all f__king places. But it stopped."

Dann ran his next EVE show in Nottingham on May 25 2013. He couldn't be there in person. Emily was hospitalised again.

He now realised he had to take some time away from promoting wrestling to look after his family and help his wife recover. He was also frustrated that attendances had plummeted and felt the novelty of all-women shows was starting to wear off because other promotions were starting to run them too.

"By 2013, I felt there was so much female content it wasn't special enough to make people come into Sudbury to see all-female shows. I stopped, and NXT started going, so there was more women's wrestling out there, the bubble had burst.

"There was enough product out there so people wouldn't go out of their way to come to see EVE in Sudbury. So I said I wouldn't do another EVE show until I could either get us into London or build EVE back up so enough people wanted to see an all-girls show again."

Certainly by 2014, the excellent women's matches on NXT, usually involving our own ex-pat Paige, Ric Flair's daughter Charlotte and the prodigious Sasha Banks, were starting to change the international audience's perception of what girl grapplers were capable of.

Meanwhile, Dann and Emily got married on May 2 2014. They made a striking couple, Emily with her gorgeous pink hair and Dann in a Dr Who-themed red checked suit, with the cute Winnie and Emerson at their side. It was a gloriously unconventional ceremony and I was really sad to have to miss their big day due to another commitment.

By this time, Dann wanted to start promoting again. Emily was doing well. The wrestling business was in his blood. And for the best part of two years, he had been asking me if he could use the XWA name. Dann always had a soft spot for XWA and felt it was an established brand that he could resurrect down south.

So in August 2014, I sold him Big Orange for £100 and with this transaction, gave him permission to bring back the XWA.

At first, Dann ran the re-born XWA alongside his friend Sam 'Slam' Nayler. This was ironic. Sam had been the co-owner of XWA in a storyline in Morecambe in 2011. Now he was co-owner in reality. Art sometimes tends to imitate life in professional wrestling. But this was a case of life imitating art.

Dann had problems in the run-up to XWA's comeback. There were issues with Bagga again, because he was running a show near to one of Dann's venues. But my old pal persevered and XWA rose from the ashes at the Delphi on October 31 2014 in front of a small but enthusiastic crowd. On a show featuring both male and female bouts, the main event saw 'The Beast of Belfast' Big Damo, Damian O'Connor, capture the XWA Championship in a four-way against Doug Williams, Martin Stone and Jimmy Havoc.

The draw wasn't great either for XWA's second of three comeback shows, at Liquid in Colchester the following night. Please Don't Die - an XWA adults-only show starring Paul London and Brian Kendrick - was the show where Kay Lee Ray spat drawing pins at Jimmy Havoc, so it was a far cry from the family-friendly fayre we used to do under the XWA name in Morecambe. Nevertheless, reviews were good.

But then came Chelmsford. The night Dann had a stroke.

"I had so much stress leading up to that night," said Dann.

"The Sudbury show lost money. Please Don't Die lost money. But I thought we needed to do a couple of shows to get us attention so people knew about us again, sell DVDs and get people to keep following us.

"For Chelmsford we did everything we could. I was there every night flyering and it was hard, with several hours' travelling every day.

"On the night, the attendance was horrible. 70 people. It was very stressful."

At the end of the show, Rhia O'Reilly beat Nikki Storm to win the EVE championship and Dann was announcing the Irish star as the winner and new champion.

"I'd fallen down earlier in the night. I thought I'd broken my arm or something. I couldn't move it. I was in a lot of pain and I was ring announcing so there was nothing I could do, I had to carry on.

"It turns out I'd actually had a mini stroke. That's what I was told later on.

"Then as I was announcing Rhia as the new champion, my voice went. And I went down.

"I remember this feeling, a wave, from the top of my head right through my body. I fell down and tried to grab onto something, tried to finish what I was saying. And it's going through my mind, you have to finish what you're saying, because I didn't want people to look at me, I wanted the attention on Rhia.

"That's what you're taught. You've got to finish.

"Then I get up, I'm wandering all over, holding onto things and I remember looking at a security guy asking him to get me to the back. The next thing I knew, the paramedics were around me.

"Kay Lee was there too. I believe she's a lot to do with why I'm alive.

"I was lucky because that night the private medical team I use were short-staffed, and one of the guys who runs the firm is an expert on strokes, and he came out and acted as one of the paramedics. I was lucky that he was there and he recognised it straight away and got an ambulance there straight away."

On the night Dann had the stroke, I was commentating on the first PCW/ROH Supershow in Preston. The next day, after getting home, Dann phoned me from hospital to tell me what had happened. Later, he had absolutely no recollection whatsoever of our conversation. The stroke affected his memory.

Dann made a remarkable physical recovery. Even so, his next hare-brained idea was one of the stupidest things he could possibly have done.

Just nine weeks after suffering the stroke, Dann decided to enter himself into the XWA Gold Rush rumble.

Yes, you read that right. Stroke victim Dann Read decided to wrestle a match.

"The reason why I did it was to get press," said Dann, sheepishly.

"Tickets weren't selling and it was the only thing I could come up with. It was Sam's idea to begin with. I was originally against it though, because of the stroke, but it got desperate."

Emily was outraged that non-wrestler Dann would even consider putting his long-term health at risk, just for the sake of getting an article in the Sudbury press to put a few extra bums on seats. She wasn't the only one. I thought he was a blithering idiot. I even recorded a YouTube message in a last-ditch attempt to get through to him. This was a wrestling promo, for sure, because if Dann was hell-bent on doing this then I wanted to help him sell a few last-minute tickets. But it was also a genuine effort from a concerned friend to get the stubborn pillock to change his mind.

"Dann, you do not come back from a stroke, and then two-and-a-half months later, put yourself in a match with 14 wrestlers," I pleaded into the camera.

"How many times have you told me over the years that your knees are knackered, your back's a mess? You're a physical wreck, Dann, and you're in your early 30s. You've got a wife and two young children, Winnie and Emerson. Do you think they look up to you? Are you doing this because you think it makes you some sort of superhero father? Just reconsider, OK?"

Of course, my speech fell completely on deaf ears.

"It's the wrestling mindset," explained Dann.

"It's just this business, I suppose. I was trying to make a living. I look at my life and my Emily's life and I can't do a 9 to 5 job. I've tried, but with Emily's ill-health, there are times when I can't leave her because she's not in a good place and needs somebody around and the kids need to be cared for. So I need to make this work. I need to be self-employed. It's the only way.

"There's a lot of passion for wrestling. But also, it's all I know. So I did it. And make no bones about it, everything I do is with the idea that I'm trying to forge a way for my family to live. And while the show didn't draw great, it trebled the tickets."

Jonny Storm, former XWA Champion and a cocky heel in the revived promotion, drew number one in the Gold Rush rumble that night at The Delphi. Dann drew number two, coming out to a huge hometown boy reaction. The Wonderkid got in Dann's face and slapped him dismissively, before turning around to mock the crowd.

But when Jonny span back around to face Dann, he was knocked to the floor by a spear that was incredibly and improbably delivered with perfect timing. Any professional, let alone a paunchy non-wrestler with two bad knees, a dodgy back and an iffy neck who was recovering from a stroke, would have been proud of that spear, which of course, Storm bumped for beautifully to make it look even more impressive.

"What we did looked great," said Dann.

"Look, it had been in the paper so I had to do *something*. I said if I'm doing it, I'm doing it with Jonny because I could trust him. And so I was able to do next to nothing, but the fans really disliked him and they were seeing him get his arse handed to him by the local boy, so I was able to maximise what I was comfortable doing."

Stunned by the spear, Storm staggered to his feet and took a swing at Dann, who ducked and executed a showy atomic drop, followed by a forceful body slam. Selling to perfection, Jonny reeled into the ropes, seemingly ready for a decisive blow. But when Dann came at him, The Wonderkid ducked and Dann went over the top rope to be eliminated, with far more grace than I managed in my two rumble outings.

More importantly, he avoided injury.

"I threw *myself* over, I was in complete control the whole time," said Dann.

"It was as safe and minimal as possible, while giving the people what they wanted to see."

Dann survived. But the bad luck and ill-health that has dogged his life just would not leave him alone.

In March 2015, he went to the dentist to have a tooth extracted. An infection went into his blood and he contracted septicemia.

Back in his second home of hospital, this time Dann was in a really bad way. A devastated Emily was told that this time, he was seriously ill and might even die.

"They told her they'd done everything they can, they'd just make me as comfortable as possible," said Dann.

"But I improved, then I discharged myself again a week later because I had a show coming up and I was waiting on a delivery of posters. Emily was really angry again."

And little wonder. Dann really can be his own worst enemy.

But he was determined to make XWA a success, even though it meant going his separate ways with Sam. Sometimes when you have a close friend in the wrestling business, it is difficult to work together. I found this at times with Mark, Alex, Dave Rayne, even Dann himself. And I think this is what Dann and Sam discovered too. So in the summer of 2015 they agreed to go their separate ways. And since then, Dann has found it easier to run the company on his own without a partner to answer to.

"Sam and I had different ideas about what we wanted to do," he said.

"And they didn't mesh. He wanted XWA to be a massive success straight from the get-go. I didn't believe we could do that, it was going to take time."

On June 5 2015, an XWA show drew 155 fans. In September, the next event drew 260. Then, after Dann was forced to move his shows away from The Delphi after more issues with the council, a December show at the Charter Hall in Colchester pulled in a record XWA crowd of 440. On February 28 2016, the attendance topped 700 for a show headlined by Nick 'Magnus' Aldis and Doug Williams reuniting as The British Invasion. Then on November 27 2016, 900 fans watched an XWA afternoon show in Colchester. This was a tremendous result.

Fighting through the pain, overcoming every obstacle, battling back from adversity after adversity, Dann has worked his socks off to rebuild the XWA and create a thriving, critically and commercially successful wrestling promotion, and one that I am delighted to say is a credit to my own legacy.

Then on March 20 2016, he achieved a long-term aim of running the first ever all-women's wrestling show in London, a city where female wrestlers were actually banned from competing at all for years until the late 1980s. His show at Cre8 in Hackney Wick, appropriately titled Let's Make History, went ahead to critical acclaim after, naturally, the original venue in Shoreditch cancelled on him due to a licensing cock-up.

By the way, Emily Read was the ring announcer that night. And she was superb in the role.

With Charlotte and Sasha Banks having broken new ground by main eventing a WWE pay-per-view in 2016, and with Pro-Wrestling EVE alumni like Paige, Nikki Storm, Kay Lee Ray and

Viper establishing themselves as genuine British stars in their own right, and with female wrestlers in general doing a magnificent job of proving themselves to be equal to, if not superior to the men, the timing has never been better for Dann to return to his pioneering women's wrestling roots. Because he has always known the girls had it in them to shine brightly on the world stage.

"I'm in a good place right now, I think," said Dann in 2016.

"The hardest part right now is I need more venues because I'm now trying to make a living out of this."

I wish nothing but the best for Dann, Emily, Winnie and Emerson. They have been through enough heartache to last several lifetimes. I really hope their run of good fortune lasts.

But Dann Read being Dann Read, I worry that bad luck won't ever be too far away.

"I guess I am unlucky, I don't know," he said.

"Maybe it's because I've always pushed boundaries. When you're creative and doing the same thing over and over, you get bored, you lose your passion, and you don't work as hard, and it shows in so many ways, with attendances and the like. So I've always pushed to do different things.

"Who was doing over 18s nightclub shows before me? And I was the first person to really go for it with women's wrestling and really push it. So I was upsetting the applecart and councils didn't know what to do with all-female wrestling and intergender wrestling. All the stresses with iPPVs. Nobody did it before me so who was there to learn from?

"So a lot of the stuff that's happened to me over the years, happened because I wasn't doing the same things as everyone else.

"I have no other way of explaining it."

My friend Dann Read is one of the most remarkable people I have ever met. He is a survivor, with a wonderful family. And he's doing what he loves most in life by running not one, but two wrestling promotions. After so many pitfalls over the years, he's finally making a real success of them. His place in British wrestling is secure as a visionary and pioneer.

Unlucky? Nah. Dann Read is actually a really *lucky* man.

CHAPTER 19

REVOLUTION AND PROGRESS

British wrestling was on fire in 2016, with the Big Four leading the way.

As PCW expanded into new markets, ICW explored new territories too, running debut shows in Cardiff, Wales and Belfast, Northern Ireland, even signing a TV deal in Italy. Then in May 2016, it was announced that ICW's weekly one-hour TV show ICW Fight Club would air on The Fight Network across the US, Canada and in over 30 countries in Europe, Africa and the Middle East. What a coup for Mark Dallas and his crew.

Meanwhile in the south of England, two other promotions continued their stunning rise to prominence.

Revolution Pro Wrestling had launched in August 2012 after promoter Andy Quildan parted company with IPW:UK. Former FWA referee Quildan had been IPW's booker since shortly after its launch in September 2004. From 2005, the Portsmouth-based Andy started promoting some of the IPW shows. Then in 2009 he upped his schedule of shows considerably, starting with a five-day tour headlined by Al Snow, then an event main evented by a tremendous Pac (Neville) v Bryan Danielson (Daniel Bryan) bout in May 2009 in Sittingbourne, Kent.

But the company was still owned by its founder, Daniel Edler. With both men having different visions for the future of IPW:UK, Edler and Quildan decided to go their separate ways.

"In the early years, when I was booking with somebody else's money, I was always saying 'I want this guy and that guy' but Dan was taking the financial risk, so it was a constant struggle," explained Andy in 2016.

"The Pac and Danielson show had given me a new identity in terms of what I was promoting. With IPW we were always about making the most of the talent we had. We had some of the absolute best talent but we also had talent with strengths, but also weaknesses which we hid as best we could. But after Pac v Danielson, we coined the phrase 'Pro wrestling at its best' because we started using the best of the best from that point forward. That's when things started to pick up. In those days, the IPW shows were a highlight for a lot of the UK wrestlers.

"There was a difference in philosophies between myself and Dan. We reached a crossroads where something had to give. I'd built a following in Sittingbourne, so I continued running my venues, Dan continued running his venues, and we managed to split without saying much nasty stuff about each other. It was as clean a split as you can get. We are now able to work together on stuff, share international talent. We're not best friends but we respect one another."

The split came a few months after IPW:UK ran its most ambitious event to date at the famous Troxy theatre in London's East End. Held on April 28 2012, Andy believes that IPW:UK Revolution saw him come of age as a promoter.

"I'd worked as a referee with NWE, a promotion from Spain, Italy and Canary Islands, who approached me about running shows in England.

"They were 100% financially backing them, my only financial commitment was to the UK guys and the cost of the ring hire. They were footing the bill for the international talent and we'd have a (financial) split at the end of it."

Nu-Wrestling Evolution had a big reputation at the time. The European company gained a lot of attention by promoting WWE Hall of Famer The Ultimate Warrior's last ever match in front of a huge crowd in Barcelona in June 2008.

"At this point, all I'd ever seen from NWE were massive shows in sell-out arenas," said Andy.

"Kevin Nash was going to be on the Revolution show, and Goldberg. He was going to do an angle where he speared someone, said 'You're next' and then set up a match for the next show.

"But as things went along, I could see it wasn't going to work out, because they were making mistakes. Then I got an email on my birthday, April 8 2012, telling me they'd decided to pull out. I was left in a position with no Nash or Goldberg, and where I'd put my name to this show, pushed that it was happening, and invested in newspaper adverts in The Daily Mirror and a promotional campaign around London. I'd invested so much time, money and effort into it, and the IPW brand was attached to it."

So the show went ahead regardless, with appearances instead by American stars Chris Masters and Carlito. They were a step down in terms of star power from Nash and Goldberg, but still helped IPW draw a respectable crowd considering the show could have easily been a complete flop.

"We managed 600 people in the building on the night," said Andy.

"It was far from a success but given the position I was in, it was kind of my crowning moment because I was able to achieve that from adversity, with everything against me. From that point on, I had the balls to take it to the next level. I thought, I can do this."

So Andy set up Rev Pro, running his first show under that name, Summer Sizzler at Wyvern Hall, Sittingbourne, Kent, on August 26 2012. IPW:UK Champion Sha Samuels became the Revolution Pro Champion and defeated Marty Scurll to retain the belt in the main event of a tremendous show.

Quildan built up the Rev Pro name cleverly as many of his early shows had an eye-catching promotional hook to get attention. On the weekend of October 13 and 14 2012, he brought over former WWE, TNA and ECW star Jerry Lynn for his final UK appearances before retirement. The veteran American put over young Noam Dar in his last ever match on British soil. Andy called the show Uprising and it was 10 years to the very weekend since Lynn appeared at FWA's groundbreaking British Uprising event at the York Hall, Bethnal Green.

"We did deliberately tip the hat to FWA because of the way they revolutionised British wrestling," said Andy.

"You can say whatever you want about them but I believe their fingerprints are all over British wrestling in the same way that I believe the fingerprints of my IPW shows in Sittingbourne are all over British wrestling at the moment. So I wanted to say that if it wasn't for FWA, this wouldn't be possible."

The following month, Andy brought over former WWE superstar Tajiri for a rare UK appearance in the unlikely venue of Burgess Hall, St Ives. Then in February 2013, at the height of the first TNA British Boot Camp, he ran a show headlined by a Marty Scurll v Rockstar Spud No Holds Barred grudge match.

"The Spud and Marty stuff had already started with us on the Troxy show in April 2012 and it escalated from there," said Andy.

"We *were* able to capitalise on British Boot Camp, although that nearly messed everything up for us as well because we were supposed to have Spud and Marty on the Jerry Lynn shows, but TNA pulled them at a week's notice, and it was our integral storyline of the whole weekend.

"That weekend was underwhelming to me. It could have been so much more and we didn't capitalise on the momentum from Summer Sizzler which we knocked out of the park. Also there were still some fans who were loyal to the IPW name and we had to gain their trust. Even though we were still the same stuff with a new coat of paint, they saw us as a new promotion. So I don't think it was until that No Holds Barred show that we were really able to start rocking and rolling again."

The month after the Spud-Scurll bout, Quildan created a buzz by booking a title match between Colt Cabana and Sha Samuels where if Colt lost, he would never wrestle in the UK again. Cabana won.

Then on June 15 2013, Andy ambitiously brought British wrestling back to the York Hall for the first time in many years. The main event saw Jushin Liger battle Prince Devitt. Both men were regulars for New Japan Pro Wrestling and it was the start of a flourishing relationship between Japan's number one company and the fledgling, Portsmouth-based group.

Andy had some experience of working for Japanese wrestling promotions, having been a referee and ring announcer on the Pro Wrestling NOAH and Dragon Gate tours of the UK since 2008.

"I'm a fan of all wrestling and I study the New Japan product; I study *any* successful product and I'm always looking for who the next big thing could be," he said.

"In 2013, New Japan were at the beginning of their big upturn. I remember a Hiroshi Tanahashi v Kazuchika Okada match at the

Tokyo Dome that year, with the big production, was a big turning point for them. I'd also never seen anybody like Shinsuke Nakamura before and I thought, I've got to have him on my shows. But I don't think I was an avid viewer of New Japan then but now I am. I'm very on point with the product.

"I originally brokered the deal with New Japan through Prince Devitt. The first show Devitt was on with me was the first Revolution Pro show and I used him regularly from that point. I ended up asking Fergal about it because he was a New Japan regular at the time. It took a long time to sort out, but Liger did come over and was treated well, and it went from there.

"At that time, in my mind the New Japan product wasn't strong enough to be able to fill York Hall on its own. But I felt if I could get some excitement going with Liger, whose wrestling is more distinguishable than some of the other New Japan guys, and we were able to tie in that it was 25 years since he'd been to the UK, and we were able to get Mark Rocco too, the guy who had looked after Liger in the 80s - Liger actually used to live with him - I knew we could make it special.

"Then the relationship with New Japan strengthened and that's when we started bringing over more guys."

Word was getting around. Revolution Pro was a company worth watching. And on October 19 2013, a sell-out crowd of 1200 turned up to watch. It was like the peak years of the FWA at the York Hall, only the quality of wrestling was higher. Uprising 2013 was headlined by New Japan's top star Tanahashi defeating Scurll, a technical classic between Davey Richards and Zack Sabre Jnr, and a storming bout between Prince Devitt and US indie star Ricochet. After the main event, Bret Hart, who was there for a personal appearance, slapped Marty in the Sharpshooter for a feel-good ending.

And so it continued. High Stakes on March 15 2014 was supposed to include an appearance by Ric Flair, but after The Nature Boy was unable to make it, Quildan arguably came up with an even better replacement in the WWE-bound Sting. The main event saw Scurll, after a visually spectacular Star Wars-themed ring entrance flanked by Stormtroopers, defeat Cabana to capture the Rev Pro championship.

Summer Sizzler on June 15 2014 sold out as well, fans lured by a match between the charismatic Nakamura and Zack Sabre Jnr, as did Uprising on October 18 2014, thanks to the UK debut of Okada and a breathtaking encounter between Will Ospreay and Matt Sydal. The York Hall shows were becoming a highly-anticipated attraction on the UK calendar, featuring some of the best matches anywhere in the country. They were putting Revolution Pro on the map.

A series of bouts involving AJ Styles brought the house down at Rev Pro in 2015/16, as the WWE-bound leader of The Bullet Club won the title from Scurll at Summer Sizzler 2015 before dropping it, just days before his WWE debut in the Royal Rumble, to Sabre Jnr at High Stakes 2016. Quildan even took his product to FWA's spiritual home of Broxbourne Civic Hall in September 2015. And the Uprising/Global Wars weekend of October 2 and 3 that year, saw a whole host of New Japan's finest mixing it with Britain's best. Liger, Tanahashi, Okada, Gedo, Nakamura, Satoshi Kojima, Hiroyoshi Tenzan, Tetsuya Naito and KUSHIDA were all there alongside Styles, ROH stars Kyle O'Reilly and ACH, and Brits Big Damo, Samuels, Ospreay, Jimmy Havoc, Martin Kirby, Scurll and Mark Haskins. No other UK company could boast such a talent depth of world class operators from the UK, America *and* Japan.

Then Andy announced a Rev Pro show for June 12 2016, with a main event of Zack Sabre Jnr v Kurt Angle. In just over a month, all the tickets had been sold. Rev Pro sold out the York Hall based on just that single dream match between Britain's slickest technical wrestler and the legendary Olympic Hero.

Not bad for what is essentially, a one-man operation.

"I think the growth of Revolution Pro Wrestling has been a case of me learning on the job," said Andy.

"The job I do is all-encompassing. I design the posters, the match graphics, I edit the DVDs, I book the talent and security, every aspect is run by myself. It's been a case of perfecting the craft and really starting to understand what I'm doing. I cringe at some of the earlier stuff even going back to my first York Hall show, even though there's some great stuff on it.

"I think over the past 12 to 18 months we're no longer an

afterthought when people mention the very top UK promotions. I think we've got there now."

While a British wrestling revolution was happening in East London, in North London there was also, erm, *progress* being made thanks to the appropriately named PROGRESS Wrestling. PROGRESS was founded by stand-up comedian and die-hard Leicester City fan Jim Smallman and his former agent Jon Briley. They were both huge fans of the American indies and especially companies like Ring of Honor and Pro Wrestling Guerilla who practiced the hard-hitting, high-flying, technical, progressive 'Strong Style' of wrestling. So they decided to set up a UK version. PROGRESS debuted with Chapter One - In The Beginning at The Garage nightclub in Islington on March 25 2012 and Nathan Cruz became the company's first champion after beating El Ligero, Marty Scurll and 'Loco' Mike Mason in a four-way elimination match.

"When they first contacted me to book me, I remember reading the email, and I receive a lot of emails from different promotions," recalls El Ligero, who would go on to himself hold the PROGRESS Title from November 2012 to July 2013.

"Some are horribly written and look like they've been done by a child and you immediately think this isn't going to be a particularly good show because the person in charge doesn't appear to have much of a brain. But the PROGRESS email was very well worded and written.

"The first thing they asked was how much I would charge (to work) two matches on one show, because they were doing a tournament to crown the first champion, and I thought, that's a bit overambitious for the first show. For all I knew, it could bomb and they might never run again. I've seen that happen. There are a lot of false dawns in British wrestling.

"So I had a 'wait and see' outlook. As it is, the first show they did sold out."

The second PROGRESS show sold out the 350-capacity club too. By the time 2013 rolled around, there was already a real buzz surrounding PROGRESS. So I contacted Jon Briley and he kindly allowed me to sell copies of *Holy Grail* at Chapter 5 - For Those About to Fight, We Salute You, a sold-out Sunday afternoon show on January 27 2013. This was the day after Rockstar Spud, Marty Scurll and The Blossoms' big night for TNA at Wembley Arena. By then PROGRESS had added a third member to their management team, actor Glen Joseph, whose main claim to fame is that he toured UK theatres playing the legendary Buddy Holly in a musical stage show.

Chapter 5 had some strong matches like El Ligero v Dave Mastiff, RJ Singh v Darrell Allen and The Leaders of the New School v The London Riots, but it wasn't the action that particularly grabbed me, because lots of UK promotions were showcasing great wrestling by this point. It was the branding. Even in its infancy, PROGRESS had a strong individual identity. The company logo, with its black and white imagery and phoenix emblem, was striking. The fact they named each show after numbered chapters was unusual. And they didn't have a title belt like all other promotions. Oh no. The PROGRESS champion proudly carried a black and silver ornamental staff instead.

The atmosphere was different to anything else on the scene, too. As master of ceremonies, the baseball cap-wearing, heavily tattooed Jim Smallman combined his adult-friendly stand-up comedy wisecracks with standard wrestler introductions to create a unique ring announcing style. The tightly packed-in PROGRESS audience lapped it up and responded with their own light-hearted heckling, quips and funny chants. At times it felt more like a comedy club than a wrestling show.

So being at PROGRESS was great fun, and I'm very thankful to Jon, Jim and Glen for inviting me along. It was interesting to see how the trio worked together, each bringing different skills to the table. Jon struck me as the calculating business brain, Jim was the energetic front man, and Glen was a personable presence with a lot of knowledge and passion for the PROGRESS vision.

I also bumped into quite a few people I hadn't seen in years, like my old sparring partners former FWA manager Dean Ayass and IPW:UK boss Daniel Edler, ex-FWA wrestler and Lucha Britannia trainer Greg Burridge, London Riot Rob Lynch and former FWA merch girl Georgy Bloomfield, and met others for the first time like WrestleTalk TV panellist and super-fan Justine Cager, the other

London Riot James Davis, and wrestling internet reporters Callum Leslie (who later became the PROGRESS commentator alongside RJ Singh), Stu Rodgers and Charman Morris. With representatives of IPW:UK, Future Pro Wrestling and Lucha Britannia all in attendance, it really felt like the London wrestling scene was evolving into a close-knit community once again, which it really hadn't been for years. The capital was once again leading the revival of British wrestling from the front, just like when the FWA was at its peak 10 years earlier. I also got some nice comments from the London fans who remembered me from those FWA glory days.

Meanwhile my travelling companion Stallion enjoyed himself too, in typical fashion. The butch lothario, a great admirer of the fairer sex, romanced a female fan while the show was in full swing, with an unusual flirting technique. He grabbed her for a flamenco dance at the bar to the sound of El Ligero's entrance music. Then they copped off outside The Garage.

PROGRESS continued to go from strength to strength, marketing itself as 'Punk Rock Pro Wrestling'. But for all the intense Strong Style grappling and impactful matches involving the likes of Prince Devitt, Samoa Joe and the best of the UK scene, it was a storyline - and one character, in particular - that I believe really shot the company to national and international prominence.

Along with the Get Grado Booked campaign in ICW, I would say that The Self-Destruction of Jimmy Havoc was the best storyline in British wrestling of the past five years. It was creatively different, pitch-dark, chillingly violent and full of emotional twists and turns, and Havoc's role as a warped mastermind with serial killer tendencies was one of the most compelling character portrayals I have ever seen in any form of entertainment, let alone pro wrestling.

Jimmy, who trained at the Hammerlock school in Kent that spawned Prince Devitt, Zack Sabre Jnr, Doug Williams, Alex Shane and Jonny Storm, has been a mainstay of the UK scene for years as a death match specialist. He was the UK's answer to Mick Foley who made up for athletic limitations with a flair for drama and an ability to absorb the most brutal of punishment. Like Foley, he put his body through hell to entertain the fans. The X-SW ironing board incident of 2007 was case in point.

In the formative months of PROGRESS, Havoc was the same willing crash test dummy he had always been. But no matter how much he bled, or was driven through barbed wire tables or smacked repeatedly with steel chair shots, he hardly won a match at The Garage. That is, until Jim Smallman awarded him a contract entitling him to a title match, any time, any place. It appeared to be a fitting reward to the cult hero for his selfless efforts.

Instead, it created a monster.

At Chapter 9 - Hold Me, Thrill Me, Kick Me, Kill Me on September 29 2013, Smallman was praising Havoc over the microphone for being the heart and soul of PROGRESS, when Jimmy did the unthinkable. He attacked the non-wrestler co-owner and beat him down with chair shots over and over and over again. The PROGRESS fans were shocked. And as Havoc slapped the likeable Smallman across the face, the crowd heat was off the scale for this unexpected heel turn.

At the next show on November 24 2013, Mark Andrews beat Paul Robinson to earn a title match and then, against all the odds, immediately defeated Rampage Brown to become PROGRESS Champion. But then Jimmy Havoc emerged with The London Riots, smashed the already-spent Andrews with a chair, poured lighter fluid over him, demanded his rightful title match there and then, forced Smallman to be referee, and pinned White Lightning to win the championship. The fans were disgusted. Even though PROGRESS has mainly a 'smart' audience, Havoc's performance as a villain was so thoroughly contemptible and unsettling, the regulars were able to suspend disbelief and absolutely *despise* him...maybe even be a little scared of him.

For the next 609 days, Jimmy Havoc was PROGRESS Champion and took the company to new heights. Coming out to the eerie Bring Me The Horizon track Hospital for Souls, clutching the PROGRESS staff with a detached grin, with his jet black jagged fringe, stubble and a middle finger for the fans, Havoc made it clear his days of risking his life for the paying public were over. Instead, the 31-year-old had no respect for anyone but himself. He transformed himself into the UK's most hated wrestler. 'DIE HAVOC DIE' signs became the norm at PROGRESS events, as Havoc entered the venue to a sea of middle fingers from the fans who loathed him.

On May 18 2014 at Chapter 13 - Unbelievable Jeff, came the most compelling angle of the Havoc reign of terror. Clad in a white collared shirt and skinny black tie, Havoc stormed the ring with his lackeys Lynch and Davis, taped Will Ospreay's hands behind his back as he sat on a chair, gagged the struggling fan favourite, and told the nervous audience that he was going to hurt people until PROGRESS management took him seriously.

"I'm sorry Will, this isn't your fault, it's Jim's fault," said the evil champion.

"I'm going to torture you and really f__king enjoy it."

Havoc then produced a pen knife. And as Ospreay gave a convincing display of a terrified young man in fear of his life, Jimmy and The Riots battered him while the iconic opening bars of Stuck in the Middle by Stealer's Wheel played over the house PA. Horrendously, Havoc even used the blade to nick at Ospreay's ear, in what was UK wrestling's answer to the scene in Quentin Tarantino's Reservoir Dogs where Mr Blond taunts and tortures a policeman. Thankfully the babyface crew of Mark Andrews, Pete Dunne and Eddie Dennis ran out to save Ospreay, who was on the verge of tears. It was an extremely macabre situation for those in attendance. But it was also utterly compelling, and made into a memorable piece of business not only by Havoc's calm and sinister demeanour, but by the awesome sell-job from a squealing Ospreay. Will proved he was much more than just a high-spot wonder boy that day. His facial expressions and ability to convey emotion are first class too.

In January 2015, horror film fan Havoc went to even more extreme lengths to get attention. He released arguably the most controversial YouTube promo video in the history of British wrestling.

There was a shadow of Havoc sharpening a meat cleaver behind a white curtain. And then, the leering champion was revealed, wearing a blood-spattered Hannibal Lecter mask and white smock, standing above a struggling body, an un-named male, lying in front of him, the new PROGRESS Championship belt (Havoc had burned the staff to mark the first anniversary of winning it) covering the victim's face and identity. And as the creepy Hospital for Souls echoed in the background, Havoc then addressed his upcoming opponent, Will Ospreay.

"There is nothing that I won't do to myself, or to you, to win that match," said Jimmy, in earnest.

"You wrestle for fun? *This* is what I do for fun. And if I'm doing this for fun, what the f__k do you think I'm going to do to some little prick that I f__king hate?"

And then he plunged the knife into his helpless victim, over and over and over again, grinned, and tasted the spurting blood. It was a sickening sight.

Jimmy Havoc had just murdered someone, supposedly, on YouTube. What an incredible vignette this was. You need to watch it, if you haven't done so already. But be warned, it's not for the faint-hearted.

The segment was shown to an enthralled but uneasy PROGRESS crowd at Chapter 17 on January 25 2015 before Havoc - who for some reason, hadn't been arrested and jailed for life - retained the title against Ospreay. The overall story was that the Essex daredevil was psyched out by the homicidal Havoc, and wary of hitting his spectacular 630 splash finisher because he almost broke his neck delivering that same move the previous year. It was such a simple storyline, but so effective. The fans were desperate to see Ospreay overcome his fears and rip the title away from the bloodthirsty champion.

By this time, PROGRESS had outgrown The Garage and moved to the 700 capacity Electric Ballroom in Camden. Such was the demand for tickets, Chapter 18 sold out in less than an hour. In November 2015, Briley, Smallman and Joseph put 2016 season tickets on sale so fans could attend all 11 Electric Ballroom events that year if they so wished. They sold over 200 of them with the front row (priced at £264) selling out in under a minute. In February 2016 PROGRESS even came up north, to the Ritz nightclub in Manchester city centre. They sold that out too, with a Marty Scurll vs Mark Haskins main event.

"It just kept getting bigger and bigger," said Simon Musk in February 2016.

"The way they have escalated and evolved is fantastic. Even when you watch the first shows, the production values and camera work aren't very good. You can see the sound desk at the bottom of the shot. But now, they have high quality filming, an On-Demand service, a fantastic range of merchandise all the time.

"At Christmas they released a Jimmy Havoc box set and the production was fantastic. It's just stepped up so much. Even little things, like at PCW, where they have the canvas with the name of the promotion on it. These separate you from an All-Star or a company of that ilk, who have a generic ring in the middle of a hall where there are no personal touches. We always prided ourselves on that at NGW too. It's a brand.

"Every single time they've run the Electric Ballroom they've sold it out. Now they're running Brixton Academy and it's a 2,000 seater arena, and I've no doubt they'll sell it out."

And on September 25 2016, they did exactly that.

Back in the previous year, as PROGRESS continued to grow, Havoc continued to retain his title by nefarious means. He even featured in the Fighting Spirit Magazine centrefold, his blood-soaked, black fingernailed hands giving the camera the double finger. British females like Lana Austin and Natalie Wild have been the FSM centre spread, but it was a rarity for a British male wrestler. It was evidence that Jimmy Havoc had become a star.

Finally, the downfall of Jimmy Havoc came in a climactic final battle with Ospreay on July 26 2015. In a lengthy, dramatic, anything goes fight, the Essex adrenaline junkie overcame his blind spot, hit the 630 off the top rope, and pinned his sadistic tormentor to capture the championship. The crowd went wild with delight. What a perfect blow-off to an amazing storyline.

Such was the excitement surrounding PROGRESS and also Revolution Pro, that in February 2016, when announcing plans for a Cruiserweight Classic tournament featuring the world's best indie wrestlers and promotions, Triple H, no less, mentioned both PROGRESS and Rev Pro as companies he would like to work with. It would have been utterly unthinkable five, 10, 15, 20 years ago for two tiny British wrestling organisations to be hailed in such exalted terms by the Chief Operating Officer of the WWE. But that is exactly what happened.

Then two months later, the deal between WWE and PROGRESS became official, as two matches on the April 24 Camden Town show - Zack Sabre Jnr v Flash Morgan Webster and Jack Gallagher v a super-talented young lad from Birmingham called 'The Bruiserweight' Pete Dunne - were confirmed as qualifiers for the tournament.

"The world is certainly starting to take notice and it's a fact that we've all known for years," said Andy.

"I don't know if it was PCW having all the WWE guys, or our work with New Japan, or PROGRESS having such a cult following, or the ICW Grado documentary, or a combination of all these things.

"It doesn't do us any harm having HHH name-drop us. I don't know what's going to happen. In a few months' time it will become a lot clearer. But I'm excited. To be mentioned in the same breath as WWE is a big compliment.

"I firmly believe British wrestling is now one WWE 'boom period' away from being set for life."

PROGRESS and Revolution Pro took their places beside ICW and PCW as the Big Four independent wrestling promotions leading a revival of British wrestling that by 2016, was gaining more and more momentum by the day, with PROGRESS as our version of Ring of Honor, Rev Pro our New Japan and ICW our ECW.

And Morecambe is still our Memphis.

CHAPTER 20

ALPHA OMEGA

In 2014, wrestling in Morecambe entered another golden era. Shows began to draw sizeable crowds again. Storylines clicked. The characters got over. The atmosphere at the breathtaking Winter Gardens was akin to the glory days of The Dome. It was Real in Morecambe once again.

I carried on working as a heel manager and had a ball. While once I was compared to Harry Potter, as I've grown older and my hair has thinned on top, the fans now called me Mr Burns after the tyrannical Simpsons nuclear plant boss. I played up to it on the microphone, bellowing "I'M MR MORECAMBE!" which usually led to a back-and-forth of the crowd shouting "MR BURNS!" in reply to my insistent cry of "MR MORECAMBE!"

I really enjoyed managing Chris Ridgeway in 2015 and 2016. Chris is an incredible in-ring talent and he will go far in the business. His stellar three-match series with El Ligero, culminating in Ridgeway beating the masked man in a 'Loser Leaves Morecambe' match in July 2015, really put him on the map. The Priority then really began to make his name and broke out into several of the country's top promotions.

These days managers are no longer as high profile as they were during the glory days of Bobby Heenan, Jimmy Hart and Jim Cornette. But I still believe the ringside antagonist has a role to play in 2017. In WWE and NXT, the verbal dexterity of Paul Heyman and the stoic presence of Paul Ellering contribute hugely to the overall aura of Brock Lesnar and The Authors of Pain respectively. Meanwhile my old friend and storyline arch-rival 'The Twisted Genius' Dean Ayass, as well as Gilligan Gordon, James R Kennedy, Charles Boddington, Richie West (Rich Dunn), 'The Man With The

Golden Tongue' Harvey Dale, Alan Alan Alan Tasker, Melanie Price, 'The Director' Tebraiz Shahzad and Chris Egan to name just a few, keep the underrated skills of the wrestling manager alive on these shores. I often think we should form a Managers Union just to say hey look, we managers deserve a bit more credit!

As Riddy's manager, my role was to add something to his matches and his overall act. I did this by cutting promos, telling everybody how exceptionally good he is, while adding an extra dimension to his performances as a villain with my ringside cheerleading and quite often, cheating. In 2015 and 2016, we drew some serious heat with our heel antics. One of my favourite incidents came in March 2016 when Ridgeway made Craig Kollins pass out to his submission hold the Bear Tooth Clutch, then destroyed The One Man Riot's shoulder with a chair. I celebrated by doing the classic Eric Morecambe 'Bring Me Sunshine' dance, skipping around my former charge Kollins as he lay in agony in the Winter Gardens ring. Half the crowd wanted to lynch us that night. And half the front row was actually in tears. Because it's...well, you know the rest.

I always enjoyed my off-screen roles with the company too. Up until late 2016 when things changed (and you'll have to wait for a third book for a full explanation of what happened) I had several responsibilities which included co-ordinating everything backstage on show days, keeping the wrestlers informed, 'live tweeting' match results and ensuring all the necessary YouTube videos were filmed.

I was also still heavily involved in the creative process. Kieran Engelke booked all the wrestlers and has the main vision for storyline direction, but I pitched a lot of ideas, came up with many of the main angles and questioned everything from a logic and continuity standpoint, which usually meant the show was rewritten many times before the actual performance. I have always been meticulous and a perfectionist when it comes to writing pro wrestling. So Kieran and I did a lot of long-term planning, had regular meetings, messaged each other and spoke constantly in our never-ending quest to make sure the Morecambe shows were as good as they could possibly be. I appreciated the fact that he always respected my ideas, shared my passion for the product and absorbed a huge amount of knowledge in the two-and-a-half years we worked together. I think we made a formidable writing team.

Our biggest long-term storyline came about when Kieran informed me, right at the start of his tenure, that he wanted to change the name of the company from PAID Promotions to Alpha Omega Wrestling. It made sense for a new start. Johnny Phere was having time off and Kieran wanted to completely rebrand the promotion. I felt that the Morecambe fans had seen so many name changes over the years, from FWA to XWA to PAID and now AOW, that it would be a mistake to become Alpha Omega overnight without explanation. So, taking a leaf from the FWA v IPW:UK Losing Promotion Must Fold book from 2007, I suggested that we create a scenario where the company name changed organically through an on-screen power struggle.

In order for this to work, I continued where I had left off with Phere The Truth as a mega-heel and cranked up the megalomania to record levels. So with Johnny nowhere to be seen, I became the sole authority figure of PAID Promotions.

Throughout the back end of 2014, I abused my power, forming an elite group called The Riot Club made up of my champion, 'One Man Riot' Craig Kollins, myself and 'Mr Big' Shaun Vasey, who we repackaged as an impassive suit-and-tie wearing corporate lackey. With his 6ft 5in frame and distinctive ginger beard, Shaun looked the business in a suit and he excelled in the role as my bodyguard. The three of us ran, well, *riot* over the Morecambe shows, cheating at every turn to make sure Kollins kept the belt. The Winter Gardens has a number of gorgeous overhanging balconies. So we decided to sit in one during shows, our own private Royal Box, where we observed the action with disdain and acted superior by lording it over the Morecambe peasants. I even cut promos from our box, high above the Winter Gardens ring, and made decrees to make life a misery for the fan favourites. The people *hated* us.

At the end of the September 28 2014 show, Kollins retained the PAID Championship against Joey Hayes with a little help from Serenity. Sadly this was Helen's final appearance for a couple of years; she soon split with Jamie and drifted away from wrestling for a time (she returned in 2016). But after the victory, as my heel stable were celebrating in the ring, we were stopped in our tracks when a mysterious white-on-black logo appeared on the big screen. It said: ALPHA OMEGA - WE'RE COMING.

I sold this with a mixture of bewilderment and anger. How dare somebody interrupt our celebration? And who the hell was Alpha Omega? The fans were intrigued too.

For the next show, Remember Remember on November 4 2014, Kieran got a load of Alpha Omega T-Shirts produced bearing the AOW logo, and piled them on the merchandise table. A few of them sold and he asked some of his friends and family to wear them too, so there was an Alpha Omega presence in the audience. During the interval, myself and Mr Big came storming out and created a huge scene as we confiscated the shirts, while I yelled at the merch team demanding to know who had authorised their sale. The whole idea was to make it look like this Alpha Omega was infiltrating PAID Promotions and I was furious about it.

Then at the end of the show, The Riot Club, which by this time had swelled to include CJ Banks and Chris Ridgeway, was destroying Ricky J McKenzie and Joey Hayes with a vicious beatdown in the ring. Suddenly, the Alpha Omega logo appeared on screen again, and out onto stage came first El Ligero, and then Dave Mastiff, both wearing AOW shirts. Finally, Stixx's music hit! The Heavyweight House of Pain hadn't been seen in Morecambe for months. Also sporting an Alpha Omega shirt, Stixx led a charge of his allies down to the ring and The Riot Club fled. To the fans' delight, he then explained that he was sick of my tyrannical leadership of Morecambe wrestling, so he formed a movement to remove me as figurehead. He also explained that Alpha Omega was so-named, because they were the first and last letters of the Greek alphabet.

"Alpha and Omega, the beginning and the end, and they signify a new beginning in Morecambe wrestling and the end for you, Greg Lambert!" he explained with serious intent. The fans were ecstatic.

This set the stage for an Alpha Omega v Riot Club four-on-four elimination match in the main event of the next show, Fightmare Before Christmas on December 7 2014. This ended with Stixx's team victorious and with me being physically ejected out of the front door of the theatre by a gang of fan favourites including The Heavyweight

House of Pain, Dave Mastiff, El Ligero, RJM and Stallion. This chaotic scene was memorable because first I was accidentally dropped on the hard wooden theatre floor when they tried to pick me up (I had a sore leg and elbow for a few days afterwards!) then when the Alpha Omega squad finally managed to drag me from the building into the icy December air of Morecambe seafront, they dumped me in a large plant pot like a piece of rubbish, much to The Truth's fury and disgust. Some fans had followed us out and were jeering at my demise, so I pulled myself out of the soil, brushed down my expensive shiny suit and silk scarf, ranted and raved at the baying spectators, vowed to return and get revenge, then stormed off down the promenade in a rage...before returning to the theatre through the back door once the public were out of sight.

I was then kept off the next three shows to sell my fury at being mistreated, which allowed Stixx to embark on a quest to win the PAID Championship in the second step of a three-point plan to oust me from power and put Alpha Omega Wrestling in charge.

It also enabled Johnny Phere to return.

Refreshed after his break and in a newly-relaxed backstage state of mind without the chains of responsibility, The Psychotic Warrior gatecrashed the closing moments of our next Winter Gardens show, Love and War on February 15 2015, to wreck the title match main event between Stixx and Kollins by delivering a Ram Slam to both men. This led to an epic rivalry between Phere and his pupil Kollins for the rest of the year as, from my self-imposed exile, I tried to keep my two former proteges from tearing each other apart.

Stixx eventually captured the PAID Title on June 20 2015 in a dramatic all-out war with The One Man Riot despite interference from the man I handpicked to hold the fort in my absence, Joe Hendry. The Morecambe fans were delighted as the man who had now been undefeated in Morecambe for seven-and-a-half years finally claimed gold in the seaside town. But Stixx wasn't done. He revealed the final part of his three-point plan and challenged Hendry to make a tag team match for the next show, Vendetta on August 16 2015 where everything would be on the line. Stixx and Joey Hayes versus a duo of Hendry's choosing, Alpha Omega v PAID Promotions, winner takes control of the company. Much to the fans' shock, The Local Hero picked the warring Phere and Kollins, the two men I claimed were "like sons to me", as the PAID team.

The tag team match at Vendetta 2015 saw us channel the WWF Over the Edge 1998 main event between Steve Austin and Mick Foley, where Vince McMahon stacked the odds against his hated enemy The Texas Rattlesnake by making himself special referee, his lackey Pat Patterson guest ring announcer and fellow stooge Gerald Brisco was made timekeeper. I did exactly the same in a power-abusing effort to ensure PAID Promotions stayed alive, appointing Hendry as ring announcer, Ridgeway as timekeeper and, in my big return, I donned the referee's stripes in an attempt to ensure Stixx and Joey went down to defeat. Of course, my evil plan failed. After a stupendously heated main event, the anger between Phere and Kollins spilled over. Craig accidentally nailed me with a roaring elbow (or ASBO, as I'd named his finisher) aimed at Johnny, knocking me spark out flat on my face. Then Phere actually threw Kollins to Stixx so he could deliver the match-winning power bomb. And in a poetic twist, the man who had once run PAID Promotions with an iron fist grabbed my hand and, as I lay 'unconscious', used it to count the winning pinfall.

Johnny Phere killed his own creation. And by doing so, I think he exorcised a few real-life demons in his mind.

The final scene of Vendetta saw Johnny rip down a PAID Promotions banner and, symbolically, hand it to Stixx, Joey and Stallion so they could rip it in half. The babyfaces then paraded the Alpha Omega colours to a standing ovation from the Morecambe faithful, while my cohorts Joe and Chris helped me, rubber-legged, back down the aisle, my face twisted in despair and defeat. It was great storytelling.

Alpha Omega Wrestling was established in a way that ensured the Morecambe fans were immediately behind the brand. The shows went from strength to strength afterwards.

Phere and Kollins had two all-time classic Morecambe bouts at the end of 2015. The last one was fought under 'Three Phases of Phere' rules - an idea for a stipulation I had in mind for years but never got chance to use until Fightmare Before Christmas 2015. Similar to the Steve Austin-Triple H Three Stages of Hell war from

2001 in WWE, this was a three-falls battle with added brutality where the first fall could only be won by submission, the second was Falls Count Anywhere in the Winter Gardens, and the decider was Last Man Standing. Johnny and his pupil created a 25-minute masterpiece of drama and violence ending when Phere Ram Slammed Kollins on the ring steps at the exact same time as The One Man Riot blasted his teacher in the forehead with his crowbar. Both men collapsed but Kollins managed to beat the count of 10 by a split-second, the student defeating the master by two falls to one. Afterwards the two men shook hands in a sign of respect after such an incredible fight.

Another success story in AOW was top heel group, The Referendum. Again this was my idea. The concept was for a super-stable where the members changed every single show but their ethos remained the same. The Referendum was led by Ryan Grayson, a staunch supporter of Scottish independence who brought different wrestlers from north of the border to each event to aid his cause. This enabled us to tap into the deep reserves of Scottish wrestling talent, keep the shows fresh by using new people all the time, and create a top faction unique to British wrestling which was hated by the English fans in Morecambe.

The concept worked a treat. Ever since The Referendum debuted in September 2014 just after the real-life Scottish independence vote, Grayson brought in some of Scotland's top grapplers to fight on behalf of 'The 45%'. Now billing himself as *Laird* Grayson with a shaggy beard, kilt and superior demeanour of a Scottish lord, the power-crazed Edinburgh Elite recruited Wolfgang, Stevie Xavier, BT Gunn, Liam Thomson, Lewis Girvan, Scott Renwick, Davey Blaze, Nikki Storm, Carmel Jacob, Kay Lee Ray, Bete Noire, Viper and his regular enforcer Bobby Roberts, among others, to help him leave a trail of English bodies in his wake, usually by burying them under the Saltire Scottish flag after a brutal beatdown. Grayson grew into the role, which was perfect for him, and The Referendum had inferno-like heat with the AOW crowd. Playing off the long-time rivalry of England v Scotland may be a little dated and xenophobic for some, but the simple 80s-style concepts always work best in Morecambe.

In another successful storyline, we also turned Cyanide face. The Toxic Terror has been a career heel in most UK promotions because of his monstrous size and look of a younger, much more agile Giant Haystacks. But in real life, Alex Walmsley is a softly-spoken pussycat. So we encouraged him to show his likeable and sympathetic personality by creating a scenario where the big man was forced do the dirty work of the spiteful Bubblegum and CJ Banks. For show after show in 2014 and 2015, Cyanide's shoulders slumped as he was on the receiving end of verbal abuse from the bullying pair. Eventually, the Morecambe fans were desperate to see Cyanide turn on Banks and Bubblegum. When he eventually did, the roof blew off the Winter Gardens.

Alpha Omega Wrestling continued to build momentum into 2016. Stixx remained the AOW champion, still on his undefeated Stixx Streak. As 2016 neared its end, this incredible undefeated run had now lasted almost nine years. Behind-the-scenes, Kieran and I talked constantly about how the streak should end. I always wanted the man who finally beat Stixx to be a rising star, somebody who would benefit from 'the rub' of beating the unbeatable. From October 2015 to September 2016, the storyline set the scene for Stixx's eventual demise as I made it my obsession to find a man to finally end the streak. Chris Ridgeway, Joe Hendry, Johnny Phere and Nathan Cruz all challenged the champion during that period, with myself in their corner, and all came incredibly close to beating Stixx in Morecambe. With every show the AOW fans rallied behind their hero with ever-growing fervour as these increasingly dangerous opponents put the Streak in jeopardy. Eventually after just about surviving a gruelling defence against Cruz in September 2016, an exhausted Heavyweight House of Pain announced that he would retire from wrestling, make his final appearance in Morecambe in November 2016 and vacate the championship in order to spend more time with his family. So it looked like the Stixx Streak would never be broken.

Elsewhere on the AOW shows, the Referendum consistently incited near-riots with their incendiary antics, with Laird Grayson developing nuclear heat as the promotion's top heel. The likes of Danny Hope, Sexy Kev and Cyanide were carrying on Morecambe's tradition of larger-than-life characters like Rockstar Spud, Stevie

Knight and Sam Slam from the past. We established a new Hall of Fame paying tribute to Morecambe's wrestling history, with Doug Williams and Marty Jones becoming the first inductees in 2015 and 2016 respectively. Young talent like Craig Kollins, Ricky J McKenzie and Ryan Hunter were ensuring the future was in good hands. And unlike in the early XWA days, women's wrestling was now an established and important part of the show. This was thanks mainly to Morecambe's first ever women's champion Viper, the fantastic Nikki Storm (now Nikki Cross in NXT) who wrestled for us regularly from 2014 to 2016, and our top female babyface Lana Austin.

By late 2016 Johnny Phere was on sabbatical again. I wasn't quite sure why because at time of writing, we hadn't talked for months. But as you know, this is what happens with Jamie. In the past he had frequently taken time off from wrestling, disillusioned, struggling with physical injuries and his own sense of belonging, then always came back. But this time, I understand he's saying his absence from the ring is permanent. His retirement has surprised me, timing-wise, because it came soon after one of his greatest ever wins.

At AOW Morecambe Mayhem on March 19 2016, JP scored a huge victory when he defeated Big Damo and Mikey Whiplash, two of Britain's best, in a triple threat main event at the Winter Gardens. As Damo's manager for the night, it was an honour for me to work with both him and 'Whippy', two top pros. Afterwards, Jamie was delighted with how the match had gone. I'd rarely seen him so happy.

I was proud of him for his performance and even prouder when, a few months later in May 2016, just days before JP unsuccessfully challenged Stixx for the AOW Championship, The Psychotic Warrior's name was etched on the wall of a Morecambe building as part of a permanent street art display paying tribute to the great grapplers who have graced our town over the years.

The names included Big Daddy, Giant Haystacks, The British Bulldog Davey Boy Smith, Rollerball Rocco and *Johnny Phere.*

As wrestling consultant on the project, I may have had a teeny tiny bit of influence on JP's name being included. But that's testimony to the respect I have for him and my gratitude for what he's done for wrestling in Morecambe.

"When the time comes to call it a day as a wrestler, I really want there to be something to show for it."

Now Johnny Phere has got his wish. His name is immortalised in print with the greats. So whatever his future may hold, he will always be a wrestling legend in Morecambe. I hope he realises his legacy and that it brings him some peace to his restless mind.

With AOW now firmly established on the North West scene, our longtime friends at FutureShock Wrestling also continued to grow from their humble origins.

"In the early days there was a lot of scraping by and saving, and making do," said Dave Rayne in February 2016.

"But then in 2011 we finally put some money into production. We got a new entranceway, got good cameras in and started filming for DVD. At the first show of 2011 we had about 95-100 people. By the sixth show we had 210 people. The guys were being received like stars when they came through the curtain.

"We have now increased our online content. We have an on demand service and a weekly YouTube TV show, a magazine show like WWE Superstars with highlights, interviews, direct to camera stuff. I love stories and not everyone can get to every venue. This is a story-driven product so we make sure people can stay up to date with what's going on. We're getting thousands of hits, the On-Demand service does really well, so people are watching and listening.

"I think On-Demand is the next step in programming. The traditional schedule of 'this show airs at this time' has gone. Now you can watch whenever you want, for example, 'the next episode is released on Netflix at a certain time'. People don't want to pay £40 a month for Sky any more. They would rather pay 50p or £1 for one thing. These micro transactions are the way forward. We're trying to get on that and it's a learning process. But it's on a shoestring budget with enthusiastic amateurs, like with many things in British wrestling."

The improved quality enabled FutureShock to expand to new venues in the Manchester area. They ran an event in August 2012 at the city's Royal Northern College of Music, headlined by Dave v Zack Gibson inside a steel cage and a match between Davey Richards and Jack Gallagher where 'The Grappler' Gallagher's classical music-style theme tune was played by a live string quartet. Then in 2013 they began to run regular events at the Longfield Suite in Prestwich, a step up from their longtime Stockport Guildhall venue which remains the company's main home. And they sold it out regularly with 500 people.

In 2016 FutureShock had built to the point where Dave could step away and let somebody else take charge of his baby. After losing a retirement match to Xander Cooper in 2015, Pownall decided to stop performing on FutureShock events and at time of writing in 2016, he had just handed the company over to a new owner, Chris Brooker.

"The roster is so talented they don't need me anymore and there hasn't been a Dave Rayne-shaped hole," he said.

"I would never try to put a flag on someone and say 'he's a Dave Rayne guy'. But FutureShock has definitely had a hand in Jack Gallagher, Zack Gibson, Cyanide, Lana Austin, (former XWA trainee) Dannii Hunter who has turned the corner this year, Mark Massa who is doing really well down south, Josh Bodom, Sam Bailey...there are a lot of people I'm very proud of.

"The teaching is now run by Xander because Monday to Friday I'm at college doing my access course. I've got homework and research to do, and I'm very much focussed on that and excited to be doing it. I wouldn't want to be half-arsed in the wrestling so I gave it to someone like Xander who was like me, who wants it, enjoys it, and gets something out of it and enjoys seeing what others achieve.

"There are a lot of guys helping out now. I feel like I've taken FutureShock as far as my energy has taken it. I've fuelled the jet. I took it from 50 people in the crowd to 500. The next guy could take it from 500 to 5,000."

Elsewhere in the North West, by 2016 GPW hadn't really kicked on since the high point of the feud with the XWA in 2012. Even Johnnie Brannigan, who like Dave Rayne had been making arrangements to pass the torch, worried they were being left behind.

"Recently I was supposed to be moving to Florida with my real-life job with a recruitment company but it's all been put on hold," he said in summer 2016.

"I passed on the running of our training school to The Island Brothers and the running of the shows to Bin Mann, but then I found out that I'm not going after all and it might now be next year. So I'm still doing the creative like I was before. But I don't have much time. I'm doing 60 hour weeks with my job. So next year I think we'll cut down from eight shows to six. If I wasn't in a stressful job working so many hours, which I do enjoy, then perhaps I would be branching out more and doing more shows.

"Other promotions seem to have come along and thrown themselves full-time into wrestling, devoting more time than I can, and have done really well. I don't begrudge them their success. But it has left us a little bit behind. And I'm OK with that. If we can continue delivering a quality wrestling product to the local community, I'm happy. We still develop talent, it gives me a real buzz seeing the trainees coming through, and we have an On-Demand service now which opens more doors for us. Hopefully people who understand what professional wrestling is will give us the credit in the long-run for the stories we've told and the characters we've developed, which is still going on today.

"We have T-Bone and Bubblegum who have been embroiled in a storyline all year. Dylan Roberts is chomping at the bit for a title shot, he's brilliant and now has 10 years under his belt and is doing his best work at the minute. Ricky J McKenzie, I'm shocked he's not with WWE yet. I know he's on the radar and is making the adjustments he needs to. We've got this opera singer called Magnificent Matthew Brooks, not the best wrestler but he's got a fantastic physique and a wonderful gimmick. He's classically trained as an opera singer and can entertain on different levels. The Island Brothers are a really good tag team. We've got a guy called Isiah Quinn who has the crowd in the palm of his hand with his delivery on the mic and his composure, and he's athletic in the ring. He's one to keep an eye on. Jumping Jimmy Jackson is someone I rate quite highly. He can do some eye-catching aerial manoeuvers. I really rate Ashton Smith. He's fantastic. So is Travis Banks. And we've got some trainees who are set to debut who are really exciting.

"And the ethos of GPW is still the same. We're still progressive, family-friendly, story-based wrestling with exciting characters. I don't expect people to go out there and have five-star wrestling matches. I tell people to go out there and tell five-star stories."

As this is precisely my ethos too, I respect immensely what Johnnie has achieved with GPW. The promotion may have been overtaken in many eyes but Grand Pro is still doing a lot of things right and in 2017 entered its 15th year in business. That's no mean feat.

Many UK promotions were in the midst of a profitable run of shows in 2016. And nobody knew this better than El Ligero, who that year worked for most of them. Simon Musk, who has been able to make a full-time living out of the British circuit since 2010, said he'd never had it so good.

"Financially, when you take into account both wrestling and holding training classes, it's definitely, 100% the strongest position I've ever been in," he said in February 2016.

"British wrestling in general is in such a massively healthy state compared to what it was, as far as the draws go.

"Take Southside. The very first show I ever did for them there was about 100 people there. Now they sell out pretty much all the venues. They run Stevenage Leisure Centre and sell that out with 800 people."

Meanwhile, Brian Dixon's All-Star Wrestling still ticked along. The product rarely varied from basic holiday camp-style goodie vs baddie panto fun for kids. But the family-friendly formula always seemed to work financially.

"Brian did a show in New Brighton (in January 2016) and drew 800, then he did Telford the next night and sold it out with 600," said Ligero, a full-timer for All-Star.

"It's been the same all these years. But what he's doing still works for him and it has its place in British wrestling. The All-Star team still has some fantastic workers. And Brian is so set in his ways, I don't think he will change until he either retires or passes it down to the next person in the family.

"As a worker, I'm pretty much doing the same thing every single show, but I'm in a different town in front of different audiences every night, and I'm not wrestling for myself, I'm wrestling for the crowd. So it works absolutely fine."

Nathan Cruz, like Ligero a full-timer, was also an All-Star regular. The Showstealer, known as 'The Prima Donna' in ASW, spoke to me with the utmost respect for how Brian Dixon's set-up had polished him as a performer.

"Brian's target audience isn't wrestling fans, it's families. Because of that, wrestling fans in general think All-Star isn't something they will enjoy. But I have a friend called Sam who used to edit the NGW TV show. He came to an All-Star show to catch up with me and he said afterwards that he really enjoyed it, more than other shows he'd seen across the country.

"I think a lot of other independent shows can be exhausting for an audience. A perfect example of this is earlier this year, PROGRESS held a tournament called Super Strong Style. Myself and El Ligero were in the main event of day one in a tag team title match against The London Riots. Rob Lynch came up to us, worried, because the fans had seen everything, every match had hit on all cylinders. But we told him not to worry, because we were the only match with a storyline going into it. And we proved it, because we stole the show, no pun intended. But I think generally, wrestling audiences are getting exhausted because you can only see so much and on that show, everyone had set out to have a five-star match.

"It's knackering for the wrestlers as well. It gets to the point where there is a risk-reward factor. You need to risk to get yourself noticed, but then you learn the job properly and the storytelling aspect helps you avoid getting hurt. I think the best place to learn that is with All-Star, because you're on the road, wrestling every single night, and your mind becomes so sharp. I can't say enough good things about the education you get working for Brian.

"This year (2016) I've been busier than I've ever been, British wrestling has exploded. Brian gives me 170 dates a year. There isn't a weekend in the year when I'm not wrestling and in summer I'm doing two or three shows a day. This summer I did a fortnight straight with no days off, with a horrendous travel schedule. All the Butlins shows are in the evening so this means travelling through the night to the next town and that's brutal. You get something to eat after the show, get to the next town at 4am and then wake up, go to the gym and then wrestle. But why I love working for All-Star is it's enabled me to meet so many friends who share the same mindset as me, who know how to have fun but are dedicated too.

"As long as you keep busy, it doesn't seem like work, as exhausting as it is. Sometimes it can be tough on my fiancee if I'm away for six or seven weeks at a time. She has a normal job at Specsavers and comes home and manages the house, while I'm living my dream. I'm a homeowner now, I've got a car, real life has caught up with me now I'm 26. And I do miss her. But this is all I've ever wanted to do.

"Some of the really bad experiences wrestling kids' parties in front of 10 people are worth it when you've wrestled at the Liverpool Echo Arena against The Uso Brothers in front of 12,000 people on a SmackDown TV taping. Sometimes I pinch myself."

In 2016 All-Star had some competition for the title of most prolific UK wrestling company. MegaSlam, run by pro wrestler Brad 'Flash' Taylor, had a busy calendar of 283 dates up and down the British Isles, running everywhere from Doncaster to Dover. It should come as no surprise that Ligero worked for them too!

Other promotions doing well included Ricky Knight's WAW, which reached its 24th year in 2016. The family-run company put on several TV tapings at Epic Studios in Norwich that year, headlined by the likes of WWE legend Scott Hall and former WWE World Champion Alberto Del Rio, which they distributed to 70 stations in an effort to get British wrestling noticed. This led to WAW inking a deal with Freeview and Sky channel Mustard TV for a 21-week series starting in September 2016, reaching half a million homes in the promotion's home county of Norfolk. The company also still toured East Anglia running regular, camp and trainee events and boasted one of the largest training schools in the country, with 150 students all eager to learn the ropes from Ricky, Saraya, Roy and Zak. And watch out for Roy's teenage son Ricky Bevis. He is the next generation of the remarkable Knight family who might well become a star.

As for IPW:UK, they celebrated their 10th anniversary in 2014 and continued to run well-attended regular events in their long time strongholds. I bumped into Dan Edler recently at a PCW show and he was waxing lyrical about how well the company was doing. It was heartening to hear.

NGW was still going great guns too. The promotion's success is a source of pride for Hull's own Nathan Cruz.

"When I regained the NGW Title from Rampage Brown (on July 5 2015) at Hull City Hall, there were over 1,000 fans in that building," he said.

"And we did that with no imports, just with British talent and a story of a local lad chasing redemption. Having that match with Rampage in Hull City Hall, where I used to go as a kid and watch Brian Dixon's shows, and have it shown on TV, and have my parents and my best friend Matt Myers there, that was an incredible moment. It's humongous to see the hard word that Rich Dunn has put in, and that Alex Shane is now putting in as well. To see how it's developed from struggling to draw 40 people in a community centre to see it now draw 1,000 people regularly at Hull City Hall for TV, and travelling to places like Liverpool, Hartlepool and Stoke-on-Trent, the sky's the limit for them."

A new company called 5 Star Wrestling also made a big splash in 2016, running huge venues The Metro Arena in Newcastle, Sheffield Arena and the Liverpool Echo Arena with cards headlined by international superstars AJ Styles and Rey Mysterio, and the British breakout generation of Will Ospreay, Marty Scurll and Jimmy Havoc.

More Brits started to gain employment abroad too. The Pro Wrestling Guerilla Battle of Los Angeles in August 2015, a standout showcase for indie grapplers from all around the world, saw frequent Japan and US traveller Zack Sabre Jnr win the tournament, while fellow Brits Marty Scurll, Drew Galloway and Will Ospreay joined him in creating some of the best matches of the weekend. The following year, Scurll won the tournament, beating Ospreay and TNA star Trevor Lee in the final. With such a buzz surrounding Ospreay, it wasn't long before New Japan recruited him for its prestigious Best of the Super Juniors Tournament in 2016. That year, Will and Marty also appeared for US indie fed EVOLVE on the WrestleMania 32 weekend and also signed for Ring of Honor, cementing their status as this decade's version of Jody Fleisch and Jonny Storm as two Brits who are joined at the hip and constantly have great matches against each other. Meanwhile in TNA, Ospreay, Big Damo and Jimmy Havoc wrestled on the promotion's 2016 UK tour, joining fellow Brits Spud, Galloway, Bram and Grado on the roster. Then in March 2016, the deserving Drew Galloway became TNA World Heavyweight Champion, finally proving Vince McMahon right.

Nathan Cruz was one of many bright young British talents chomping at the bit to join them.

"I think I'm in with a good chance of getting to WWE," he said.

"I've had a few try-outs and a dark match for them. I saw Regal at ICW and asked him, what am I doing wrong? He said it was just a case of waiting, just keep doing what you're doing, just raise your profile and make a bigger name for myself on the independent scene so if they hire me, I can bring more viewers to the WWE Network. I completely understand the logic behind that. So it's just a case of travelling more. I feel like I've done all there is to do in Britain, which sounds big-headed, but there isn't a place in the UK that I've wanted to work for, that I haven't worked for. It's time for me to move on.

"I'm a trained actor and I've got panto at the end of the year, which I'm excited about. This is something else within the entertainment industry which raises my profile. I've got a second tour of America in March 2017. So I'm hoping in the next two or three years something is going to happen. They have dangled the carrot in front of me. I worked a dark match at the Liverpool Echo Arena (in November 2014). Then I got asked to go to NXT where me and Rampage were supposed to be in a pre-show dark match at Wembley. We arrived there for a four corners tag, but they pulled us out and changed it to a three corners tag, and we sat in the back during the match and heard the crowd chanting 'This is PROGRESS!' We looked at each other and said 'F__k!'

"On the way back, Rampage said that if we'd gone out there, Triple H would have heard the crowd and thought 's__t, these guys have got themselves over on the indies'. Rampage said to me 'That could have been it for you, you could have been signed'. I said to him, jokingly, 'I'll get you home to see your daughter but when you've gone, I'm going to drive this car off a bridge!' It was emotionally tough. At times it does get to me, it really does. I think, am I going to achieve it? I've always believed I'm going to get to the

WWE. I firmly believed that. But now I wonder, are they interested or are they just giving me lip service? And if I don't go there, what else am I going to do with my life? I need to go there. Even if I went there for a while and it didn't work out, at least I could say I'd given it my best shot.

"Sometimes I feel like giving up on my dream. But I was talking to Fabian Aichner about it the other day. Fabian was in the WWE Cruiserweight Classic and he feels the same. He said to me 'Think about the man who is digging in a cave, and he digs for 18 miles, and right at the other side they are digging through to save him. But because he's been digging for so long, he gives up and turns back'. So maybe I am closer than I think. It's just patience, I guess.

"I don't think I could lie on my death bed, having not been to WWE, and genuinely be happy. No matter what else happened in my life, I would die an unhappy man."

With so many top British wrestlers like Nathan gaining worldwide acclaim, media coverage of British wrestling has risen markedly over the past couple of years. As a journalist, I always look upon this as a major indicator of UK wrestling's popularity. The websites of some of Britain's most popular national newspapers - like The Sun, The Mirror and The Guardian - cover British wrestling much more frequently than they did five years ago. And you only have to look at any edition of Fighting Spirit Magazine these days to see the change compared to eight or nine years ago.

I have a copy of FSM from 2008 which has a two-page British news section, a four-page feature on none other than Johnny Phere and a column by Alex Shane. And that's it for UK coverage. Fast forward to 2016, and there was a five-page UK news and reviews section, a two-page 'One to Watch' section featuring a different up-and-coming Brit every month, a full page devoted to a UK events diary, a five-page feature all about the British wrestling scene, a monthly four-page nostalgia piece about a UK grapple legend from days of yore, a column by Nick 'Magnus' Aldis, and Joanna Rose was the centrefold. Such was FSM's reliance on British wrestling in 2016 that the mag had a UK arm to its annual reader awards, which in 2015 saw Will Ospreay crowned UK Wrestler of the Year, The London Riots the Tag Team of the Year, Zack Gibson Most

Underrated, PROGRESS won Promotion of the Year and Show of the Year, and Ospreay's PROGRESS Title win over Jimmy Havoc took Match of the Year.

I wish Power Slam had thrown its weight behind British wrestling in a similar way. I always tried to push the growing strengths of British wrestling with a sceptical Findlay Martin over my 12 years working for him, as did Alex Shane, and towards the end, we were starting to make some headway. I was allowed a half-page semi-regular UK news column and the odd single-page interview with a Brit. But that was the extent of it. Incidentally, in Findlay's excellent 2015 e-book Pro Wrestling Through the Power Slam Years, he wrote that one of his biggest regrets as editor of Power Slam was that he hadn't increased his coverage of British wrestling during the magazine's final editions.

The US-based Wrestling Observer has also started to take notice of us. Reports from some of the bigger UK indie companies who use recognisable international names, like PCW and Revolution Pro, started to regularly appear in the industry-leading newsletter in 2015. Then in 2016 its website also began to feature a weekly UK round-up column penned by Alan Boon, who longtime FWA fans may remember as the Revival commentator Mark Priest. This is all very welcome and puts extra eyes on what we do. Zack Sabre Jnr even twice won the Observer's Best Technical Wrestler of the Year, the first Brit to win one of the industry-leading newsletter's awards since the mid-80s glory days of The British Bulldogs.

America is sitting up and taking notice. British wrestling is starting to conquer the world.

After years of hope, it finally feels like we are heading for glory.

"British wrestling is no longer second fiddle to other overseas indies - the British wrestling scene has now got the attention fans globally," said Alex Shane in April 2016.

"We've got the world's hottest indie talent right here in Britain. Will Ospreay, Zack Sabre Jnr and Marty Scurll are comparable to Low Ki, Bryan Danielson and AJ Styles in 2002, 2003. Zack watches the old World of Sport stuff and understands how to modernise it, he takes the principles and makes it work in a modern-day scenario.

"Grado is a f__king great worker. He knows how to totally work that character. He's gone from someone doing small shows to getting all this exposure and his in-ring work has caught up with his profile. I really rate him. Rampage Brown is just fantastic, so are Nathan Cruz and Zack Gibson. Bubblegum and (his NGW valet) Chardonnay are the perfect package, the Posh and Becks of British wrestling. Chardonnay is one of my favourite people to work with and Bubblegum is the Jim Breaks of today, only with a valet. Sha Samuels is fantastic. So are Joe Hendry and Joseph Connors. Mark Haskins is an on-the-edge character now in NGW. He'd go full Heath Ledger if we let him, so we won't for his mental sanity! I hope Grado inspires a few people, like Spud did, to take a punt on being a character, who can talk. We need more of that.

"Some fans actually think I get pissed off when other companies do well. What they don't realise is that this is my life's work and has been for nearly 25 years. Since I was 13 in fact. If somebody is doing good stuff in British wrestling then of course I'm happy about it.

"I was telling people who great this new British wrestling scene was in the national press when most of today's UK wrestlers were wearing Austin 3:16 T-Shirts and its fans were still at primary school. The TalkSPORT show was 15 bloody years ago and British wrestling was dead then. Yet there I was pushing it on national radio every week. Hell, my media GSCE course work was a documentary about getting British wrestling back on TV. The overall success of British wrestling is my actual life story. Never forget that..."

Spud himself, although now living thousands of miles away in Nashville Tennessee, is equally delighted for the success of the Brits. He also picked out a few names he rates highly.

"Sid Scala is the best, he's a Barry Charalambous guy, his (Del Boy from Only Fools and Horses) character is so English, he's great. Joseph Conners is fantastic, Alex Gracie is so good, absolutely love him, The Hunter Brothers are the best babyface tag team England has had in a long time, Rampage Brown is absolutely brilliant, Nathan Cruz is excellent, Ligero is working everywhere, Dave Mastiff is killing it, I love Jimmy Havoc, Martin Kirby is great too and should be a match agent too because his ideas are the best.

"I just wish the boys got paid more. The wrestlers aren't on guaranteed deals and the wrestlers are their own business. What they charge is up to them. But if you want your business to respect you, you've got to let everyone know that to have the best, you've got to pay the best. But a lot of the guys charge less just to get on shows to sell their merch. It happens all over the world.

"I think the only other weaknesses with a lot of British wrestlers are a lot of them need to learn to cut promos, to talk for three minutes and engage people, and also have better psychology. I wish there were agents (helping to lay out matches) in Britain. You can name the number one bad guy in Britain and I bet he still gets cheered.

"Except in Morecambe, where it's still f__king real!"

Amen to that.

"British wrestling is the best place to be right now," said Rampage Brown.

"It's frustrating though to see all the Americans coming over here, while there are so many other talented guys like Zack Gibson, Mastiff, Joe Conners, Nathan Cruz, Kirby, Ligs, so many other guys, who may go to Italy and places like that, but for some reason are not making it in the States and Japan, even though their wrestlers are coming to London to work. I'm not talking about myself. I've had my opportunities. And there are British guys like Zack Sabre Jnr, Jack Gallagher and Marty Scurll getting opportunities in the States and Will Ospreay going over to Japan. But there are so many others who could benefit from tours of Japan or six months in the States. Hopefully that will change soon because the UK is going from strength to strength. It is already starting to change."

Rampage is right. One of those he mentioned, Nathan Cruz, finally bagged himself a US tour in 2016. The Showstealer credits help from his friend, former WWE star Sami Callihan, and the mass exposure he's received from working TV tapings for NGW and ICW.

"It's crazy, the reach these promotions now have," he said.

"Because of The Fight Network deal I'm getting broadcast to 34 countries. That's bringing an entirely different audience and one of those countries is the United States of America. Now I'm going out to America at the end of September. Sami has got me booked all over the place. I often get tweets from Ohio, people asking when I'm coming over. This is because the channel we're on out there is quite popular. I'm really excited about it."

"I think the eyes are on the UK more than ever, now," said RJ Singh.

"These announced partnerships between WWE and PROGRESS and Rev Pro, means UK companies are getting mentioned on WWE and their footage has appeared on WWE, linked to the NXT brand. That's great because it will open up opportunities for UK guys to go to WWE but also it's turning American fans onto British wrestling.

"Glen Joseph from PROGRESS went out to WrestleMania this year and saw loads of PROGRESS T-Shirts, and had people coming up to him high-fiving him to say 'You're the PROGRESS guy'. There's an international reach now. And we have Will Ospreay, Marty Scurll, Zack Sabre Jnr, I say Tommy End too because although he's from the Netherlands he's practically a Brit, they are all going over to the States to work for companies like PWG and EVOLVE.

"We had a down period, around 2008, when a crowd of 150 used to be good. Now we're getting thousands. Since 2012, we've been on a rise. ICW are doing a show at the Hydro! That's insane! That's the building where WWE and TNA have run! PROGRESS Wrestling ran the Brixton Academy. Southside in Stevenage do 800 per show. These are the numbers back in 2008 we were only dreaming of. Where once we were talking hundreds, we're now talking thousands. We're not stupid, we're not talking tens of thousands yet. But could we be? It doesn't seem so impossible now, now our On-Demand services have such a global reach. And overseas wrestlers have always loved coming to Britain.

"The four main countries for wrestling in the world were always America, Japan, Mexico and Great Britain. But we always felt like the runt of the litter. I don't feel like that anymore. I think people are looking at the UK and thinking wow, look at the talent coming from the UK. Look at the shows coming from the UK. The British wrestling scene has gone from good to really good. It's such an exciting time to be a young hungry wrestler in Great Britain.

"I firmly believe the world is our oyster."

And never was this more apparent, than one night in Glasgow in November 2015.

CHAPTER 21

GLASGOW GLORY

On the afternoon of Sunday, November 15 2015, it was wet. Sodden, in fact. The kind of rain that stings your eyes and stiffens the spirit. Glasgow rain.

Hood up and shoulders hunched, I walked along the endless Sauchiehall Street. This one-and-a-half mile path through central Glasgow runs the full gamut of the city centre's cultural life. It's a shopping precinct flanked by your Primarks and Marks and Spencers, then as you walk further it transforms into a student-land stretch of bars and restaurants, before finishing with a section crammed with guesthouses and hotels.

As I made my way down Sauchiehall Street, I smiled at the familiar sight of The Garage nightclub, with its trademark yellow truck sculpture bursting out from above the front door. I stopped outside The Box, a bar directly opposite The Garage, my gaze ensnared by a poster. A giant photo of Grado dominated the window, advertising cocktails with names like The Grado Bomb, the Jack Jester Gut Fester and the Renfrew Rocket Fuel.

Because in Glasgow, ICW is so popular that alcoholic drinks are named after its stars.

A little further down the street there was an empty shop. Its curved glass frontage displayed a large banner advertising the nightlife of Glasgow.

It said: "IN THE STREET: THEATRE, CINEMA, COMEDY, RESTAURANTS, NIGHTCLUBS, PUBS, **WRESTLING**."

Yes. Wrestling.

Because in Glasgow, professional wrestling is not the b__tard child of entertainment. Glaswegians don't turn their noses up at ICW and look down on it as 'that fake wrestling crap'. Instead, it stands side by side in the city's cultural life with plays, films, concerts and gigs.

490

I snapped a quick photo of the banner on my smartphone. November 15 2015 was Alex Shane's 36th birthday. He would love to see this. This is what he wanted and worked towards for years. This is mainstream respect, in one of the biggest cities in Britain, for UK wrestling. And it's a respect, finally, that places it as an equal to more fashionable forms of entertainment.

A left turn under a flyover and down the main road towards Clydebank, stands the Scottish Exhibition and Conference Centre. For 30 years, the SECC has been there on the bonny banks of the River Clyde, hosting concerts by everyone from Luciano Pavarotti to The Who, Vivienne Westwood fashion shows, The Bolshoi Ballet and world championship boxing. The two-year-old, brand spanking new Hydro venue is next door. I smiled once again as I passed by, dwarfed by its spaceship-like exterior, as I recalled being there 10 months earlier on the night when Grado's incredible story led him to the TNA main event and a public embrace inside the six-sided ring with his countryman Drew Galloway.

On this night, those same two men would embrace again. Not in front of a crowd of wrestling fans. But backstage, after they made history.

The SECC is similar to the NEC Birmingham, home of FWA European Uprising five years ago almost to the day. It's a 64-acre site of numerous sprawling, self-contained indoor spaces where events, exhibitions and conferences are held. ICW Fear and Loathing VIII would take place in Concert Hall 3, a cavernous black-curtained hangar, with a 4,000 standing room capacity.

Less than a month before November 15 2015, every single one of those 4,000 tickets had been sold.

This made ICW Fear and Loathing VIII the biggest crowd for a British-based wrestling company since a sold out show at the Royal Albert Hall in February 1982, and the highest grossing gate at the box office since the famous Big Daddy v Giant Haystacks bout at Wembley Arena in June 1981.

History, indeed.

I had arranged to meet Mark Dallas at 4pm, but it took a further 20 minutes to get in. Security was tight outside Concert Hall 3 and it was certainly unusual to see suited and booted heavies with walkie-talkies manning the doors at a British wrestling event. Then again, maybe I shouldn't have been surprised. November 15 2015 was two days after terror attacks on Paris. It was 48 hours after 129 people were killed by suicide bombers and gunmen in a series of despicable murders at locations in the French capital including a rock concert and an international football match. On November 15 2015, the world was in mourning, full of trepidation for what the future might hold, and venues were being extra cautious.

If ever there was a day for an uplifting tale of joy and triumph, this was it.

Dallas eventually came striding to the door, dressed in a smart-casual black suit with open-necked crimson shirt and looking tense. The evil genius leader of ICW beckoned me in and we strode across the gaping hulk of Concert Hall 3 where I saw the familiar sight of crew members buzzing around building a ring.

There was also the less familiar sight of a WWE-style steel cage on overhanging pulleys, a 4D video screen and enormous lighting rig suspended above it, and stacks and stacks of speakers and technical equipment on an imposing stage.

Mark barked angrily at staff that they were behind schedule, with a distracted dancing look in his eyes. I hoped against hope that the pressure wouldn't get to Mark Dallas on this, the biggest of days.

That was the last time on November 15 2015 that any doubts would cross my mind.

Mark rounded up Jack Jester, Chris Renfrew and Davey Blaze, and ushered us into a private dressing room so I could interview the trio. I asked the three ICW mainstays how they were feeling. All three looked emotional, as if not quite believing what they were about to do.

"It still hasn't hit me I'm going to perform in front of 4,000 people," said Blaze. "I'm nervous but confident."

"I first came here as a fan to see the WWF," said Jester. "I cannae believe how many stars were here, Stone Cold, Undertaker, The Rock.

"The Hydro and the Braehead Arena weren't here when we were growing up. For people our age, the SECC is the Glaswegian institution."

Then I asked them - why ICW? Why has ICW managed to do what other UK promotions tried and failed to do?

"What we do is real," said assistant booker Renfrew.

"We build characters with individual stories people can get behind. A diverse range of characters, all completely different flavours.

"Only in Glasgow could this have been made, like ECW could only have happened in Philadelphia and New York, with the crowd's rabid passion. In Glasgow they either love you or f__king hate you, man. It's organic, the right product, the right fans in the right city. It's all come together.

"And ICW is a way of life for some people."

"Yeah, it feels like we belong to the fans,"chipped in Jester.

"It's personal. You don't get folk here who would watch Raw. They like ICW.

"I thought it was just Glasgow because we were here for years and ICW was *so* Scottish. But when we go to Liverpool, Nottingham or Sheffield, it's the same."

Then Jester and Blaze both told stories of how they've met ICW fans who have tattoos of the company logo on their bodies. Now that's devotion.

"I took my mum out for lunch nearly a year ago," said Davey.

"I was in a restaurant and a guy came in. He was gobsmacked and wanted a photo with me. A big fan of ICW, so overwhelmed that I was there.

"I don't understand. I'm not technically famous. It's confusing."

"And we did a promotional tour for our second tour," said Jester.

"We pulled up in Liverpool, 10 o'clock at night, people were beeping their horns. They knew who they were. They must have watched Insane Fight Club or ICW On Demand."

Renfrew and Jester then explained how ICW has allowed both of them to make a full-time living out of wrestling; Renfrew by working in the company office during the week, and Jack by coaching hopefuls at the ICW Asylum training school.

"This is a way of life," smiled Renfrew, proudly.

"You don't have to go to America.

"We're getting booked for midweek things. Appearances. Things you'd never expect. What, you want to pay me for a night out to appear in your club? Really? It's amazing."

And they all have a brotherly bond with Mark Dallas, a tangible feeling of warm affection and respect for their friend, the boss, his vision and his work ethic.

"He'll say we're going to do stuff," said Jester. "And it always happens.

"It's mental that we've sold out. Everything felt so untouchable when I used to come to the wrestling here as a kid. My main goal is to get through this night without bursting into tears.

"Everyone is always going to say Daddy and Haystacks are the two biggest stars in British wrestling. It's about time that changes. And it's always, what's next. This won't be our peak."

"No," said the husky-voiced Renfrew with a quiet determination. "Let's not rest on our laurels."

I then asked them why the talent pool in Scottish wrestling has suddenly become so deep in recent years.

"When we started years ago, the quality of training was awful," said Jester.

"We didn't really get trained, we were just getting facilities to train in. Then I started doing the holiday camps with All-Star; good workers like James Mason, Frankie Sloan, Robbie Brookside. And you learn while you're away, then come back and you apply it.

"And I think everybody has pushed themselves a bit more. When I started, everybody wanted to work in England. FWA was the big thing. Nobody really cared about up here and rightfully so. There was nothing happening.

"But over time, it's changed. Everybody wants to come up here now. And the fans really became a force up here. They showed up every time, giving us a place to work, learn our craft and apply a character."

Renfrew then started talking about how the Scottish wrestling scene was divided around a decade ago, which stifled its growth.

"Before ICW, Scottish wrestling was segmented into BCW guys and SWA guys," he said.

"I trained with BCW, our rivals were SWA, and we were almost taught this tribal mentality, that each other was the enemy. They kind of grabbed a stranglehold and taught us a hatred that wasn't even there."

Jester agreed.

"We were never in a situation where we could mingle and talk to each other. We'd avoid each other at shows. We were walking past each other on the street and I thought, why?

"Now I work for all the Scottish companies and it's good. There are no territories, Scotland isn't big enough for that. It's a big team and everybody is trying really hard to make the quality of the shows better so folk keep coming back."

At this point we'd been chatting for 20 minutes. Blaze and Renfrew had to leave, to prepare for the show. But Jester carried on, first of all praising Graham McKay for the fine job he had done since taking over BCW.

Then I asked him about his longtime friendship with Drew Galloway and their 2014 feud.

"It's been great. We've been mates since I was 15, my first day of training.

"The feud came about through time and place. It wasn't planned. Drew was under contract to WWE. When he got released, we thought, let's jump on this.

"It was so difficult because it was the first time in eight years I'd had time to hang out with him, but I couldn't because we were building the match at the Barrowlands. We wanted people to think it was real. And we wanted to make ourselves believe it too. So we said to each other, let's say things that touch a nerve. It started getting a bit close to the bone. I was picking up on things that I knew would hurt him and he was doing the same to me.

"When it came to the match, it was the biggest thing I've ever done, and Drew said it was the biggest thing he'd ever done, which considering he'd been in WWE, means a lot. And it was in the Barrowlands, where my grandparents met, so it was personal to me."

And then his thoughts turned back to the night ahead, and the barely believable achievements of ICW. The likeable Jester, this scary walking cartoon character with the jet black beard and the piercing eyes, but in real life a sensitive soul and self-confessed crier like myself, started getting choked up once again. It was touching to witness.

"I've been here since the start, I've been through all the crap, and it's so overwhelming what's happened. I'm so proud of everybody.

"It's real to me. It's everything. It's unbelievable. It's a dream come true."

I walked back with Jack into the main auditorium. The ring was almost fully assembled by then. And there were moving vehicles everywhere. Never in my 25 years of watching British wrestling shows have I had to dodge cherry pickers and forklift trucks zipping about. It was like being stuck in a giant game of Robot Wars.

In another sign of how big-time this show was going to be, Lionheart, Kid Fite and Joe Hendry were all dressed in smart shirts and trousers, as if adhering to a WWE or TNA dress code. Scruffier but no less sartorially splendid was Billy Kirkwood, in a T-shirt and kilt, a wild-haired fireball of tension as he stomped about hyping himself up with his teeth clenched, and he was just the commentator. I also said hello to Nikki Storm and Big Damo, both fresh from recent try-outs with WWE. Both would later end up signing and become part of NXT, the latest Brits to make their name overseas and deservedly so.

As for Mark Dallas, he was still striding around Concert Hall 3, eyes dancing, waving his arms. But minute by minute, as the technical side of this mega-event began to come together, he was starting to look more relaxed.

I ducked backstage and bumped straight into Spud. I had no idea my old mate was going to be there. We hugged, and the Rockstar explained that although he'd appeared on a few dates for ICW recently, he wasn't booked on this particular show. He went along, like myself, just to be there, just to experience the night because he realised its significance. He was mainly there to support Grado, with whom he shared a close bond after working together in TNA.

Spud and I spent a few minutes chatting. He told me how much he'd enjoyed his debut as a stand-up comedian in Wolverhampton the week before, an impromptu gig arranged by Chris Brooker. "Stand-up is just like cutting a wrestling promo," he said, which meant he was bound to be good at it. Then Jay revealed that, at the age of 32, he was already preparing for life after wrestling. He wanted to get more involved in training, agenting matches, editing and producing, to learn as much about the business as he could.

Then, who should pop his head around the curtain but Doug Williams. Doug *was* booked on the show to wrestle, but again his presence was a pleasant surprise to me as I didn't realise he'd be there. Myself, Spud and Doug, the FWA survivors, all together again, at a major UK wrestling event. I couldn't help but feel nostalgic.

Then I had a good chinwag with one of the new generation. It was my first meeting with Tom Irvin, one half of an upstart tag team who were making waves on the UK circuit. With his partner Sebastian, Irvin had formed The Geezers. Both had little experience, but through social media and clever marketing, the endearingly funny duo had earned themselves a cult following with their catchphrase "I am Geeze" and bookings with PROGRESS, PCW and ICW into the bargain.

"I thought to myself, there's a massive gap in the market now Mad Man Manson has retired and Grado's doing main events," explained Tom.

"So I thought that even though I'm not the best wrestler in the world, I'll tell everybody that I'm the greatest, and I'll get attention."

Smart lad, I thought.

Then, after the entire ICW roster posed for a team photo in the ring, I grabbed a hot dog from a fast food trailer. And who should be there in the queue beside me ordering a pre-match burger?

Who do you think.

"All right ma man, how are ye Greg, great to see ye!"

Of course. It was Grado. The biggest star in British wrestling today. The main event attraction of the biggest UK wrestling show in 33 years. The man whose poster is in The Box bar window advertising cocktails.

Still as down to earth, warm, welcoming and...erm...*hungry* as ever.

His opponent Drew Galloway was also hyped up ahead of the big match. Backstage, Drew beckoned me over and proudly showed me a video on his smartphone of the queuing crowd outside Concert Hall 3. The former WWE Intercontinental Champion doubled over with laughter as he watched his own video of himself filming the fans, which included him giving the middle finger to one supporter who had thrust a handmade "F__K YOU GALLOWAY!" sign in his direction.

I asked the first ever ICW Champion to think back to those early days in the Maryhill Community Centre in front of 30-odd people. Could he ever have envisaged this?

"You can't possibly compare how it was back then to how it is now," replied Galloway, in his intense Ayr-American drawl.

"Mark Dallas had a vision and a dream. He is a very driven and intelligent individual. It's like he was born with part of his brain specifically for wrestling.

"He never gave up on his dream and through chance, himself and Jack Jester saw an opportunity to promote, put it in a nightclub for the over 18s crowd, and slowly things began to steamroller from there.

"By then I'd gone to America, I was hearing about these things happening, how it was beginning to build up a Glasgow fan base, and I thought oh, that's cool, but I didn't quite process it until I started watching clips of Fergal Devitt coming over wrestling Jack Jester and I saw the crowds and how they were responding to the matches, and I thought wow, this is really happening, this vision Dallas told me about back in the day, when we were sitting drunk in Maryhill with big dreams.

"The reality is that most of us thought, well, that would be cool, but probably not possible. Coming from me, a guy who said I'm going to WWE, nobody from Scotland ever did, and I refused to give up on it...even I was unsure. I'm the guy who always says go for his dreams. And just like I went to America, Dallas kept pushing and pushing, and people believed in him like they believed in me. And it got going, and you can't process ICW until you see it with your own eyes, and when I returned last year and saw it with my own eyes, I was blown away. The video clips don't do it justice. The crowd is unbelievable.

"Then we ran the Barrowlands, I was fortunate enough to main event, we did it twice. Now the SECC. The first gig I ever went to was Oasis when I was 10 or 11 in the SECC. Now I'm main eventing in the SECC as champion. It's absolutely ridiculous.

"When he said SECC, Barrowlands, even in Maryhill keeping ICW alive, people said he was crazy. Now if he said 'I'm going to run Hampden' I wouldn't doubt it. He's got such a dedicated team backstage, who run the production side and leave him to the wrestling side, and magic just happens. An amazing crew. Nobody is selfish here. Everyone works together. We're all working for the show. That's the reason why ICW is so successful."

Then I asked Drew how he'd compare the British wrestling scene he returned to in 2014, to the one he'd left to go to the US in 2007.

"It's just night and day.

"Back in the day there were just few of us trying to get better. Myself and Sheamus were in a feud, working each other, watching videotapes, trying to get better, and there weren't that many guys you could do that with at the time.

"But now, there's lots of guys to work with in Britain. So much talent right now. The UK scene is on fire. PROGRESS, Southside, PCW, Rev Pro, and as far as I'm concerned ICW is leading the charge.

"The biggest gate since 1981. It's just absolutely obscene and I'm so fortunate to be part of it.

"And now it looks like Dallas is going to do one of his pep-talks."

So Drew joined his fellow ICW wrestlers and crew, as Dallas gathered them in tight in the backstage area to dispense some final words of wisdom. I observed from a respectful distance.

"You know I think you guys are s__t-hot, and that's why you all deserve to be here," Dallas told his stars and staff.

"But it's *just another show*."

I was really impressed by this one line. For those who were feeling the nerves, it took the pressure off immediately. Exceptional management.

Mark Dallas' eyes were dancing no longer. By now, he looked firmly in control.

After Chris 'Run Through' Renfrew ran through the card for the evening's show in double-quick time, the team dispersed with a pumped-up roar of solidarity, motivated beyond belief to "knock this mother f__ker out of the park", to use a Mark Dallas expression. Spud, meanwhile, was pulling up chairs in front of a luscious looking plasma screen, which would air crystal-clear high definition 'hard-cam' footage of the show to the backstage area. Yes, the international star of TNA was running menial behind-the-scenes errands, which should tell you all you need to know about the guy.

As the doors opened and 4,000 fans swarmed into Concert Hall 3, and thunderous "I-C-W!" chants began to echo all around, some roster members could barely contain their delight. Adam 'Coach Trip' Alexander and David 'DCT' Thomson were both wandering around backstage in an ecstatic daze, beaming like they had won the Lottery. Adam, a 12-year veteran who remembered the fractured Scottish scene of the mid-noughties and DCT, who three years earlier was a wrestling internet radio show host before he trained at the Source Wrestling School then was plucked from obscurity by ICW to become moustachioed lothario The International Sex Hero, were now members of Polo Promotions, alongside ICW Tag Team Champions Mark Coffey and Jackie Polo. And they were itching to get out in front of that raucous sea of people for the biggest match of their careers.

There were also a group of uniformed police backstage. Woah, security is even tighter than expected, I thought to myself. Until I realised these weren't real officers - they were actors from the BBC Scotland sitcom Scot Squad. The crafty Dallas! He'd recruited Scotland's funniest force to take part in an angle on the show.

Just after 7pm, ICW Fear and Loathing VIII began, with a trailer for the new ICW video game on the screens. Available for Steam, X-Box and PlayStation.

ICW. A British wrestling promotion. With its own video game. Who would have thought it?

Ring announcer Simon Cassidy, clad in a magnificent tuxedo and beaming the same ecstatic beam I had seen from DCT and Coach Trip just minutes before, climbed through the ropes. The fans serenaded him with a rumbling rendition of "WE LOVE YOU SIMON, WE DO! OH SIMON WE LOVE YOU!" Simon beamed some more.

Backstage, dozens of wrestlers and staff, some standing and others sitting on the row of chairs laid out lovingly by Spud, watched the entire show on the crystal-clear plasma screen. I was one of those who barely moved from my spot for the next three hours, utterly transfixed by what unfolded. It was like being part of a second audience of fans, only backstage. We watched, gripped by the action, popping at the big moves, laughed at the funny promo lines, cheered the victories, basically did everything we could to encourage and support our colleagues on the biggest night in modern-day British wrestling history.

And it is worth pointing out, this was unusual. Rarely at British wrestling shows, will more than just a handful of grapplers show much interest in observing the other matches.

But this was different. This was ICW.

Just as Simon Cassidy made his first announcement, a familiar towering bushy-bearded figure in a red-and-black checked flannel shirt arrived in the backstage area. Hobbling with discomfort from years of hurling himself off 15 foot high cages and through burning tables for the business he loves, this Hardcore Legend flashed a toothless smile of gracious acknowledgement as we broke into a spontaneous round of warm and respectful applause. Then he carefully manouvered his ample frame into a seat right in front of the TV screen and remained there virtually for the entire evening.

It was Mick Foley.

It was 10 years, almost to the very day since I managed the team of Alex Shane, Stixx, Martin Stone and Iceman against Foley and his team-mates The Sandman, Steve Corino and Paul Travell at Universal Uproar in front of 2,400 fans at Coventry Skydome. It was the first time I had met the former three-time WWE Champion and Hall of Famer since that auspicious moment in my personal and professional life.

I re-introduced myself to Mick, who eyed me for a split-second as if trying to recall where he had seen me before. Then the light bulb went on.

"I remember...Alex Shane's show, right?"

Foley was the guest ICW Commissioner on November 15 2015. He and Rhyno were the only former WWE superstars booked on the show and as ECW alumni, they were a perfect fit for the world of Insane Championship Wrestling. But while some of the 4,000 strong would have undoubtedly bought tickets to see the former Cactus Jack and the War Machine, the vast majority were there either on the strength of the ICW brand, or to see Grado, Drew Galloway and the rest of the homegrown talent. This was a very different situation to Universal Uproar a decade earlier, where the Brits were marginalised and everyone was there to see Foley, the Japanese legend Kenta Kobashi, and other overseas names.

The times, they are a changing. As Bob Dylan once said.

After Billy Kirkwood warmed up the crowd with some typically energetic, profanity-laced one-liners, Mark Dallas emerged into the arena to a mighty roar, carrying a golf club in one hand, a bottle of Jack Daniels in the other, and sporting a beam even bigger than DCT's, Coach Trip's and Simon Cassidy's combined. The ICW promoter has to be the most beloved authority figure in wrestling, well, ever.

Later that evening, after the show, I saw once again the love for Dallas in his home city when he arrived at the after-party to backslaps and handshakes from every single person in the queue up the stairs to the Cathouse rock club.

In Glasgow, Mark Dallas is God.

Mark was flanked by his entourage; the burly bodyguard Sweeney, the long-haired and sallow Scott Reid (who was the spitz of Findlay Martin circa 1993) and the diminutive cult figure of Chris Toal. Chris, a popular figure both on screen and off, was clad in a miniature smart grey suit as he seized the microphone and challenged Dallas to tell the crowd "the whole f__king story!" Later, Toal returned backstage and proudly declared: "How many wrestling promotions do you know where the midget isn't used as the comedy act?"

After this prompting from his tiny human conscience, the Machievalian Mark then dropped a bombshell on the fans. He announced that next year, ICW Fear and Loathing IX would come not from the SECC, but the "mother f__king HYDRO!"

The Hydro. The arena run by WWE and TNA when they visit Glasgow. 11,000 tickets. And Dallas was aiming for another sell-out. My God.

The words of Jack Jester and Drew Galloway echoed in my sceptical head. When Mark Dallas says it will happen, you'd better believe it will happen.

I believed.

There always has to be a party pooper in wrestling, and on this night that role was given to Red Lightning. No longer The People's W__ker, Andy Wason had reverted to his heelish ways as the company's General Manager and ally of Galloway and Jester - now reunited - in a trio called The Black Label. Lightning was furious with Dallas for stealing his glory, claiming that as GM, he'd been solely responsible for selling out the SECC. This brought out Mick Foley to a messianic response from the ICW faithful and Glaswegian chants of "FOLEY! FOLEY!"

As Red Lightning scowled, Foley promised to do an exceptional job as ICW Commissioner. Then, the Hardcore Legend said: "When I heard ICW had sold out Fear and Loathing VIII, I swear to you I thought it would be an 800-1200 seat theatre.

"Now I don't do this very often, but I'm going to drop a Foley F-bomb on you. Because when I heard it was the SECC, I thought WHAT THE F__K IS GOING ON?"

The crowd erupted as Mick, who hardly ever swears, used the F-word to express his complete awe at ICW's achievement. The camera panned to Billy Kirkwood, who has been known to drop the odd F-bomb here and there (well, in every single sentence). The crowd laughed at the sight of Billy, who has worked alongside Foley on the stand-up circuit, bouncing up and down in his seat in manic delight at Mick's coarse language. Although I have to say, the Foley F-Bomb still somehow sounded cuddly coming from the mouth of the former Dude Love.

Then after a brief verbal back-and-forth between Red Lightning and Mick Foley, the matches got under way.

The last time I'd been to an ICW show, The Bucky Boys were still one of the company's most popular acts. But Mark Dallas is a master of freshening up his show without making wholesale changes to his personnel. By November 15 2015, Stevie Boy had turned on his cousin Davey and The Wee Man, and joined forces with the New Age Kliq. Xavier was also the Zero-G Champion and defended the belt against his estranged relative in a supercharged opener. After blasting The Wee Man with a flush super kick, Stevie nailed Blaze with a Canadian Destroyer, but Davey kicked out and obliterated his ex-partner with a Destroyer of his own to win the title. A great start.

Next up, a six-man tag. Joe Hendry, Kenny Williams and Noam Dar v Lionheart, Doug Williams and Liam Thomson. The highlight of this match came before the wrestling even started.

Joe Hendry was by now gaining a reputation for creatively entertaining entrances; changing his theme music every match to parody a popular song. For one ICW entrance not long before, The Local Hero sang his own version of Phil Collins' In The Air Tonight ("I can hear Joe Hendry in the air tonight, oh Lord...") complete with Bobby Roberts playing the drums on stage in a gorilla mask a la the famous Cadbury's TV advert.

For Fear and Loathing, Joe turned Miley Cyrus' number one hit Wrecking Ball on its head, rewrote the lyrics, and then became the first professional wrestler, at least to my knowledge, to enter an arena wearing a giant inflatable ball, singing...

"I made my entrance in a Hendryball!
"I sincerely hope that I don't fall
"And I won't do drugs or alcohol
"The Local Hero, Joe He-e-e-ndry!"

Utterly surreal. But as the ball-wearing Hendry used his spherical PVC suit to propel himself down the aisle like a giant somersaulting Weeble, the fans absolutely lapped it up.

This incident-packed affair ended with the babyface team of Hendry, Williams and Dar scoring the pinfall after Jimmy Havoc interfered and destroyed the heels with his Rainmaker clothesline. Then The Scot Squad arrived and dragged the heel Lionheart away in handcuffs, and Carmel Jacob ran in to blast her real-life fiance Liam Thomson with a wicked steel chair shot to the head before informing him: "You would have made a sh_te f__king husband anyway!"

Arena setting or not, ICW was as crazily anarchic and politically incorrect as ever.

But it could also still present flawless wrestling matches. And the three-way for the vacant ICW Women's Title certainly fit that description. Viper, Nikki Storm and Kay Lee Ray proved why they are three of the best in the world right now with a gripping bout of perfectly executed moves, ever-increasing drama and a popular finish, as Viper pinned both Nikki and Kay Lee at the same time to win the championship.

Five, four, three, maybe even two years ago, it would have been unthinkable for a women's match to steal the show on the biggest British wrestling event in more than three decades. Dann Read would have been proud. And Mick Foley was certainly impressed, as he pulled all three ladies to one side to congratulate them when they returned backstage.

Somebody then asked Foley if ICW reminded him of ECW.

"Yes," he replied.

"But it's more disciplined. If this was the ECW Arena, three matches in and the main event guys would be worried."

What Mick meant was, while the early bouts at Fear and Loathing had been thrilling for sure, the ICW stars hadn't burned out the crowd too early by going too far too soon. Instead of throwing in tables, ladders, barbed wire baseball bats and kicking out of finishers left, right and centre, the British wrestlers laid out their matches with intelligent restraint, so not to detract from the marquee bouts later in the show. Not that this unstoppable ICW crowd ever showed any signs of burning out.

Then Viper, bless her, had her photo taken with both the ICW and the Alpha Omega championship belts, before bounding over to gleefully show me the picture on her phone. What a lovely gesture from the fearsome female warrior with the heart of gold. This was the first of two occasions that night when the tears almost came.

Joe Coffey v Rhyno was another tremendous match. The sturdy Coffey's Iron Man gimmick was super-over, and he literally fought his way to the ring through a stand-off of his Iron Man-mask wearing followers and security staff, fists flying, as the fans sang along with gusto to his theme tune Iron Man by Black Sabbath. Then the super-tough Scotsman engaged the first ever ECW Champion in a compelling bout where every single move was delivered with thought, precision and believable force. When Coffey kicked out of a Gore through a table, Rhyno's bewildered face was a picture. Joe eventually scored the clean pin with a Discus clothesline and continued what is surely a rise towards even greater things.

After Polo Promotions retained the ICW Title over James R

Kennedy's duo of Kid Fite and Sha Samuels, the steel cage lowered over the ring. The ensuing six-man war between The Legion (Mikey Whiplash and The Sumerian Death Squad) and the NAK (Chris Renfrew, Wolfgang and BT Gunn) was one hell of a spectacle. I particularly loved the dark gothic-religious look and presentation of The Legion, and the fact they had Minions, worshipped dark forces and threw up a triangle as their trademark hand signal made me nostalgic for a certain gimmick from FWA and XWA five years before.

Dangerous moves dominated this relentless brawl, as the 300lb Wolfgang pulled off a bonkers Swanton dive off the top of the bars, Gunn creamed Whiplash with a double foot stomp off the top, then BT and Mikey both fell off the side of the cage to crash through a jigsaw of ringside tables in a risky stunt that made even the watching Mick Foley wince. As the fans applauded in appreciation of such sado-masochism, and the NAK retreated bleeding down the aisleway, Whiplash somehow summoned the strength to pull his battered body in the direction of a microphone. The Potteries technical marvel, who made his name in the safe haven of All-Star holiday camp shows before he moved to Glasgow and transformed himself into a master of the macabre, dared Gunn to return to the ring to finish the sadistic job.

"I don't fear death," breathed Whippy.

"I just need to find a man worthy enough to kill me."

Gunn obliged, climbed back into the cage, and scored the winning fall. Thankfully, Whiplash didn't die in the process.

By this point, Jeremy Borash had arrived backstage to soak in the ICW experience too. Two days earlier, Borash had been in Paris, holed up in a hotel just a few miles away from where the terrorists attacked. This must have been a terrifying experience for JB, but you would never have known. The TNA ring announcer greeted everyone with his usual cheery enthusiasm.

Meanwhile, Mark Dallas was everywhere backstage, co-ordinating vignettes, passing on last-minute instructions, putting a reverent arm around the seated Foley and whispering in his one good ear to explain ideas for segments, and like most promoters, was so busy he had little time to watch what was unfolding in the arena.

At one point he asked me: "How's the show?"
When I replied positively, Dallas bowed his head, with a grin of humble pride at hearing praise for his product.

After Big Damo pinned Jack Jester with a chair-assisted senton bomb in another worthy contest, it was time for the main event.

"WE LOVE YOU GRADO, WE DO! OH, GRADO, WE LOVE YOU!"

"F__K HIM UP GRADO! F__K HIM UP!"

And, to the tune of 1980s hit 'D-I-S-C-O' by Ottowan...

"G-R-A-D-O...IT'S YERSEL!"

Even before the protagonists came through the curtain, the crowd chants built up a special *special* atmosphere for Grado v Drew Galloway.

Backstage, both Grado and Drew had the gamest of game faces on. Although they had wrestled each other on TNA Impact just a few weeks earlier in front of an international television audience - a short TV-style bout won by Galloway - they were treating this like the biggest moment of their professional lives. As wrestling writer Allan Blackstock later tweeted "TNA is now something Grado and Drew Galloway do when they're not booked for ICW."

I shook hands with both men and wished them luck.

Soon, 4,000 people were singing along to Like A Prayer as the underdog challenger emerged with his familiar dance down the ramp. I ducked out of the backstage area to sample the almost evangelical atmosphere in person. This was the second time my eyes felt misty. The place was going absolutely berserk for the wee fat lad from Stevenston.

Drew Galloway's heel turn and alliance with The Black Label a few months earlier ensured his response would be exactly what was desired for this ultimate battle of good guy versus bad. The Sinister Scotsman was greeted with passionate boos.

With the tension in Concert Hall 3 palpable, Simon Cassidy then announced both men, raising a laugh when he introduced Grado as "weighing in tonight at *who gives a f__k?*"

The match saw Grado complete his transformation from comic cult hero to fully-fledged main event superstar. And no little credit must go to Galloway, whose departure from WWE and overwhelming desire to prove himself transformed him from 3MB jobber to one of the very best in-ring professionals in the world.

With the fans, both in the arena and backstage, behind him every step of the way, Grado pulled off moves we'd never seen from him before. An RKO on the ring apron. A huracanrana, for heaven's sake. The sight of the man who had been scoffing a burger just hours before leaping high in the air to scissor Galloway's head, then roll backwards to flip him down with perfect athletic timing, was a superlative sight.

Eventually, the ferocious Drew caught Grado in mid-air attempting one further ill-advised aerial move, and began a methodical beatdown. Grado's typical Dusty Rhodes-style comeback was met with fervent expectation by the crowd, and when he hit a Brock Lesnar F5, it was the first of a series of heart-stopping near falls. Grado then landed his Roll and Slice in the corner, but Galloway saw the follow-up Wee Boot coming, countering it into a smooth power bomb for his own close two count.

A piledriver, a phenomenal sit-up suplex from out of a Tree of Woe position, then his finishers the Claymore kick and even a FutureShock DDT. Nothing Galloway tried could quell the heart and spirit of his challenger on this night, as Grado survived it all. In desperation, the champion decked the referee and out came his allies Red Lightning and Jack Jester. But they reckoned without our valiant Commissioner! Mick Foley rolled back the years to sock Red in the forehead with a mighty punch, then brought out an actual sock, Mr Socko, to be exact, which he stuffed down Jester's gullet to rapturous acclaim from the fans.

The furious Galloway watched Foley ruin his best-laid plans and didn't see Grado stagger to his feet behind him. When Drew turned around, he did so just as the hero of the hour Wee Booted a steel chair full into his face. Galloway collapsed. Grado followed him down and hooked the leg.

Out of nowhere, the omnipresent Mark Dallas slid into the ring and made the count as 4,000 mighty ICW fans counted along in joyous unison.

One! Two! THREE!

The roof came off the SECC. And probably the Hydro too.

What a celebration then ensued as Mick Foley entered the ring and raised the new ICW Champion's arm aloft. Despite his creaking bones, Mick even did a bit of dancing, while Grado pulled off the famous Cactus Jack 'Bang Bang' sign. Then the ultimate superfan could barely disguise his glee as Foley offered him his famous red and black checks to wear.

Mark Dallas, his face a mixture of sheer delight for Grado's moment and relieved ecstasy that everything had gone to plan, now embraced the man who symbolises his company. And as I joined in with the loud and sustained applause backstage, the ICW babyfaces disappeared down the aisle to join in the in-ring party too as 4,000 people serenaded Grado with "YOU DESERVE IT!" It was an emotional scene.

ICW had done it. They had indeed knocked the motherfucker out of the park. Excuse my French.

As Simon Cassidy, referee Thomas Kearins, Red Lightning, Jester, then Foley, Drew Galloway and finally Grado, clutching his newly-won belt, returned to the dressing room area, the entire ICW crew who had been hanging on every move and every word displayed on the backstage TV for the entire night, greeted them all with a standing ovation. And I have never seen that happen before at a British wrestling show either.

I managed to grab the first interview with the new ICW Champion backstage just moments after his inspiring triumph. Graeme was still sweating, beaming and hyped up as he told me he would be DJing and hosting an after-show party at the Walkabout bar in Glasgow city centre. Meanwhile photographer Robbie Boyd strived manfully to manoeuver him in front of a green screen and stay still long enough to snap some pictures of the new champ with his belt. The problem was, Grado was being interrupted every five seconds by the well-wishes of ICW wrestlers, or staff members, or even friends who'd managed to get backstage to hug and congratulate him. "You're the only person who can make Madonna sound cool!" laughed one of them.

When he finally finished his duties as a one-man welcome committee, the grinning Grado said: "Greg, fire some questions at me, ma man, while I'm still in the zone!"

So I asked him the obvious question. How do you feel?

"I feel amazing.

"The first time I ever saw a wrestling match in this arena was Sting v Lex Luger, December 6 2002, it was the very first day I ever met Jeremy Borash. I was ringside and TNA had only been started for six months. And I went up to Jeremy Borash, he was covered in make up, and he f__king strawbed me off! I went up to him and said 'When's TNA coming?' and he said (Borash impression) 'ahh, probably next summer'. I also saw Stone Cold vThe Big Show here, May 4 2002.

"But it's f__king funny to think that Borash...(interrupted by well-wisher) how's it going ma man!...so now Borash is here! He got me into TNA and he's been a big f__king help, so it's great that he's here for my match."

Then I asked Grado to think back four years ago, when he was still Grant Dunbar, when he was still a no-name on the UK circuit. How the hell did this happen?

Grado replied excitedly, barely pausing for breath.

"ICW got a TV deal on a s__tty Sky channel, and I used to wake up every morning and think you know what? I'm going to put steroids in my arse, I'm going to get tanned, I'm going to do my best to look like a wrestler and impress Mark Dallas. But I didn't f__king do that, did I? There was a show two miles from my hoose, so I did a promo that blew Dallas away, and he said would you think about coming to do an advert for ICW? Might lead to a match...*might* lead to a match. Then the Get Grado Booked campaign started and it all went from there.

"Now my Gradoberg (Goldberg parody) entrance at Shug's Hoose Party has half a million views on YouTube. It got press in Australia two days ago. Now we're going to the Hydro next year. I'm the biggest f__king British wrestling fan you'll ever meet. Trust me. I had every FWA video. I nearly made it to Uprising 1. I was called The Lost Scot on the UKFF. And who would think I'm the champion of the number one British wrestling company right now? It's mental, you know what I mean?"

So do you get recognised everywhere now? Even in England?

"People stop me in England and say (Grado puts on London

accent) 'Are you the wrestler Grado?' The documentaries have given me press. Everywhere I go I get a great reception. It's the best feeling in the world.

"The first time tonight I did a huracanrana. Never even practiced it. Did that RKO on the ring apron look all right, aye? Did it look all right?"

It looked more than all right, Graeme.

"That's good to hear. I love your first book Greg. I wish Alex Shane was here. The amount of times I've tried to bring Alex Shane out of retirement. He won't do it. Foley is amazing as well. I wrestled on a show with him 10 years ago, the night Eddie Guerrero died, I was f__king rotten. I done a run-in, it was crap. I've got a good picture of it."

And then Grado was finally able to stand in front of the green screen and pose for Robbie's pictures, still clutching Mick Foley's flannel shirt.

"You need to read Greg's book, Robbie," Grado grinned as the photographer snapped away. "It's a really good read.

"But I never got to wrestle for FWA, did I Greg? Ha ha!"

It warmed my heart to hear the biggest star in British wrestling today, the successor to Daddy and Haystacks, still being a mega wrestling fan at heart. Still being true to himself.

Then I asked my final question. Why you, Grado? Why do you think you've become *the man* in British wrestling?

"I think it's being able to not take myself serious and have a good time.

"People said to me tonight, you're s__tting yourself, you're scared. I said no I'm f__king not. What's the f__king point? Drew's telling me to do a huracanrana. Never f__king attempted one in a wrestling ring. And I said f__k it. If it goes tits up, it goes tits up.

"It's all about having a bit of belief in yourself, a bit of heart and f__king going for it.

"I'm just like everybody else. I'm the fan who managed to jump the guard rail and get in the ring and wrestle with his heroes."

He is the fan who became the biggest draw in British wrestling for 33 years and led us one step closer to the Holy Grail.

Within 24 hours, the entire show was up online on ICW On-

Demand so the world could watch it too. And within 24 hours, ICW had sold more than 1,000 tickets towards the 11,000 they would need to sell out the Hydro for Fear and Loathing IX on November 20 2016.

I still believed.

Then I got a taxi to the Cathouse with Mark Dallas and joined him and the ICW roster as we drank in celebration until the early hours. In the VIP area. Being treated like stars.

It was an incredible night. A night when British wrestling well and truly regained its place on the world stage. A night when British wrestling rebounded from years of being on the ropes. A night when British wrestling experienced ultimate glory.

All we needed now was a TV deal with one of the 'Big Five' UK channels. Then the revival of British wrestling would truly be complete.

EPILOGUE

THE HOLY GRAIL?

June 2016 was an unsettling month to be a Brit. The chaotic political aftermath of the EU Referendum and England's abject defeat to rank outsiders Iceland in the European football championship made many question their pride in being from this broken country.

But there was still much to be proud of in British wrestling.

On June 7, Will Ospreay made history by defeating Ryusuke Taguchi to become the youngest ever and the first British winner of the most prestigious junior heavyweight tournament in the world, the New Japan Best of the Super Juniors. When Will returned to Revolution Pro Wrestling just days later, he was given a standing ovation by a proud and emotional London crowd. The response to the conquering hero, this amazing home grown talent, eclipsed even the mouthwatering main event between Kurt Angle and Zack Sabre Jnr that night.

Two weeks after Ospreay's triumph, Sabre Jnr joined fellow Brits, Noam Dar and Jack Gallagher as part of a 32-strong field from all over the world in the inaugural WWE Cruiserweight Classic tournament at Full Sail University in Orlando, aired on international TV on the WWE Network. All three emerged victorious in their first round matches in a clean sweep for Britain, Sabre Jnr going on to reach the semi-finals. It was yet another proud moment for the UK scene.

Also in June 2016, a new company, What Culture Pro Wrestling, ran its debut shows in Newcastle. Spawned out of the popular What Culture website, this new promotion for the YouTube generation quickly made a huge impact to the point that within months, WCPW dipped its toes in the iPPV waters and was challenging The Big Four for popularity and notoriety.

Meanwhile on June 18 2016, I joined fans and wrestlers at the

Hillsborough Arena in Sheffield, a community football pitch close to the stadium where 96 of my fellow Liverpool fans lost their lives in the infamous 1989 Hillsborough disaster. We gathered at a charity football day named Soccer and Spandex where I coached one of the sides in a match between two teams of wrestlers - sadly with little success as we lost! Not that this mattered a jot because the day wasn't about winning or losing, it was about our friend and colleague Kris Travis.

Organised by a local wrestle fan called Dean Mitchell, who himself had battled cancer, Soccer and Spandex raised more than £3,700 to split between Trav's favourite charity Cavendish Cancer Care and Kris' family. It was an emotional day but also tremendously rewarding and great fun to socialise with some of my wrestling colleagues like Mad Man Manson, Ashton Smith, Sam Bailey, Roy Knight, Joe Conners, Danny Hope, Mark Adams, Steve Evans, Keith 'Ruffneck' Colwill, Dan Evans, Bobby Cash, Rob Maltman, Harvey Dale, T-Bone, Alex Gracie, Paul Winstanley and many others.

Once again British wrestling rallied together for a great cause and showed what an amazing community it is to be part of. And once again, we united because of Trav.

One week later on June 25 2016, PCW put on its biggest ever show in front of 2,500 fans at Preston Guild Hall. With the help of the fabulous PCW production team, I commentated live with Stallion as viewers paid £3 to watch PCW's first ever internet pay-per-view available all over the globe.

The conclusion of Tribute to the Troops 3 saw Noam Dar capture the PCW Title from Sha Samuels, and as the iPPV went off the air, Stallion, myself and the rest of the production crew were absolutely jubilant. We felt we had nailed it. We knew we'd made history as a British wrestling company to put on an iPPV event watched live by thousands.

Shortly afterwards, Steven Fludder asked if I would help him book storylines for PCW in 2017. I accepted his offer. Ten years after the first demise of the FWA, I had once again been given creative input into one of Britain's top wrestling promotions. But things are very different now. I'm not the naive newcomer I was back then. I have proven myself over time and I know I can make a positive impact on the future of Preston City Wrestling. With Steven's business brain and my mind for wrestling, I think we'll make a great team. At time of writing I've just scripted my first PCW shows for the 2017 Road to Glory weekend, now renamed the Kris Travis Memorial Tournament.

I won't let you down, Trav.

Then in November 2016, as the entire world faced the uncertainty brought on by Donald Trump's election as President of the United States, there were yet more exciting happenings in British wrestling.

The Stixx Streak finally ended. In his last match in Morecambe before retiring, Stixx was pinned by Alpha Omega Wrestling's hottest heel Ryan Grayson in front of a Winter Gardens crowd whose stunned and angry reaction proved that wrestling is as Real in Morecambe as ever.

Noam Dar became the latest British star to hit the big time in the States, debuting on WWE Monday Night Raw in front of a joyous partisan crowd in Glasgow. Jack Gallagher's Raw debut wasn't all that far behind. And after the biggest ever group of Brits were called to WWE try-outs in Glasgow, Sam Gradwell, James Drake, T-Bone, Trent Seven, Pete Dunne, Tyler Bate, Wolfgang and Joseph Conners were among a group of 16 British grapplers to ink deals to appear in WWE's first ever UK Championship Tournament, which would take place at the Empress Ballroom in Blackpool in January 2017 and air on the WWE Network.

As for Nathan Cruz, he hopefully took one step closer to his dream that month too, when he appeared on NXT.

It seemed WWE was pushing harder than ever into its share of the UK wrestling market, ironically just as TNA was losing control of theirs. November 2016 would see the flagging Nashville promotion lose its Challenge TV deal after UK ratings regularly dipped below 100,000, and there would be no 2017 Maximum Impact tour either. But there was a light at the end of the tunnel for my old pal Spud and his TNA colleagues. A new owner, Anthem Sports and Entertainment, took over and in early 2017, TNA founder Jeff Jarrett returned to the promotion in a consultant role.

Meanwhile Ring of Honor *did* return to the UK in November 2016, as two other Brits took turns to win one of American independent wrestling's biggest titles. First Will Ospreay then his arch-rival Marty Scurll became Ring of Honor Television Champion.

As for Mark Dallas, well he and ICW did indeed run The Hydro that month. It wasn't quite a sell-out, but then again WWE did appear there two weeks before. But still, a paid audience of 6,193 broke their own record from one year earlier for the biggest attendance at a British wrestling event since Daddy faced Haystacks.

And last, but certainly by no means least, in November 2016 ITV filmed a pilot British wrestling show in front of a studio audience at Media City in Manchester. The wrestlers included the cream of the UK's golden generation; the likes of Dave Mastiff, El Ligero, Johnny Moss, Viper, Sha Samuels, Danny Hope, Ashton Smith and Rampage Brown. And of course, the entire programme was built around the star of the show, Grado. British wrestling's very own Medium Daddy. Who after filming the pilot, immediately began preparing for a stint at Glasgow's Pavilion Theatre...in panto. A sign of mainstream culture stardom for a British wrestler if ever there was one.

The lead commentator for ITV World of Sport Wrestling was Jim Ross, arguably the greatest wrestling announcer of all-time.

As for his commentary partner?

None other than Alex Shane.

Alex Shane, who it was also revealed that month, had led NGW to take over the running of the lucrative Butlins holiday camp shows from Brian Dixon – the 'Ark of the Covenant' he'd mentioned to me eight months before.

Alex Shane, whose entire life's work has been geared towards getting British wrestling back on mainstream TV was about to present its glorious return to the entire nation.

There is something rather appropriate about that.

As I finished writing this book, the pre-recorded taping of ITV1's 'World of Sport Wrestling' was screened at 5pm on free to air, terrestrial British television on New Year's Eve 2016. It was watched by more than 1.25 million people and talk of a series soon followed.

The ITV special was quickly followed by the incredible WWE UK Championship tournament of January 14 and 15 2017 on the WWE Network. It was fantastic to see my friends and colleagues taking centre stage, tearing the house down on a national and international platform. It makes me feel emotional just thinking about this, and all the other amazing opportunities happening in British wrestling right now.

Then a few days later, after recommendations by Drew Galloway and Billy Kirkwood, I was recruited by 5 Star Wrestling to commentate on their live TV special on the Channel 5-owned Spike channel on January 28 2017, appropriately alongside one of my favourite British wrestlers, Joe Hendry. The kid who used to commentate in his bedroom as escapism from the bullies who made his life hell, finally proved them all wrong and became the voice of the first live show aired by a British wrestling company on prime time British television for 50 years. I can't thank Drew, Billy and Dan Hinkles from 5 Star Wrestling enough for their faith in me.

It's the perfect end to the book, isn't it?

British wrestling has risen again. It's been one hell of an emotional ride. But maybe, just maybe, this is it. This is what we've worked for, for so many years.

We are on the verge of a return for weekly British wrestling to a main TV channel. British wrestlers are close to making some real money without having to go across the Pond. And my brothers and sisters in British wrestling now have the opportunity to become the household names they deserve to be.

The Holy Grail, people. The Holy Grail.

We might have done it. Finally, deservedly, *we might just well have done it.*

My only regret is that Kris Travis isn't here to share in it.

Interviews for this book were conducted by the author in 2015 and 2016 with: Noam Dar, Rampage Brown, Andy Quildan, Simon 'El Ligero' Musk, Dave Rayne, Drew Galloway, Grado, Davey Blaze, Chris Renfrew, Jack Jester, Des Robinson, Dann Read, Johnnie Brannigan, Alex Shane, Rockstar Spud, RJ Singh, Nathan Cruz, Tony Simpson.

Photo Credits: Robbie Boyd from Warrior Fight Photography (including front cover), Tony Knox and Gordon Harris.

Cover text design: Owen Lambert

Thank you to everyone who has helped make this book a reality.

British wrestling is the best. And we're proving it.

ABOUT THE AUTHOR

Greg Lambert has been active on the British wrestling scene since 2002. He has worked as a manager, commentator, promoter or Master of Ceremonies for many of the top UK wrestling promotions. Companies he has worked for include FWA, XWA, Preston City Wrestling, Southside, IPW:UK, WAW, FutureShock, GPW, RQW, NGW, LDN, PAID Promotions and Alpha Omega Wrestling.

He is also a fully qualified journalist who wrote for Power Slam magazine from 2002-2014 and has also written articles for Fighting Spirit Magazine.

His first book Holy Grail: The True Story of British Wrestling's Revival was released in 2012. He lives in Morecambe, Lancashire with his wife and two sons.

Printed in Poland
by Amazon Fulfillment
Poland Sp. z o.o., Wrocław